NZ
zines

NZ Zines

Punk to Present

Bryce Galloway

MASSEY UNIVERSITY PRESS

1

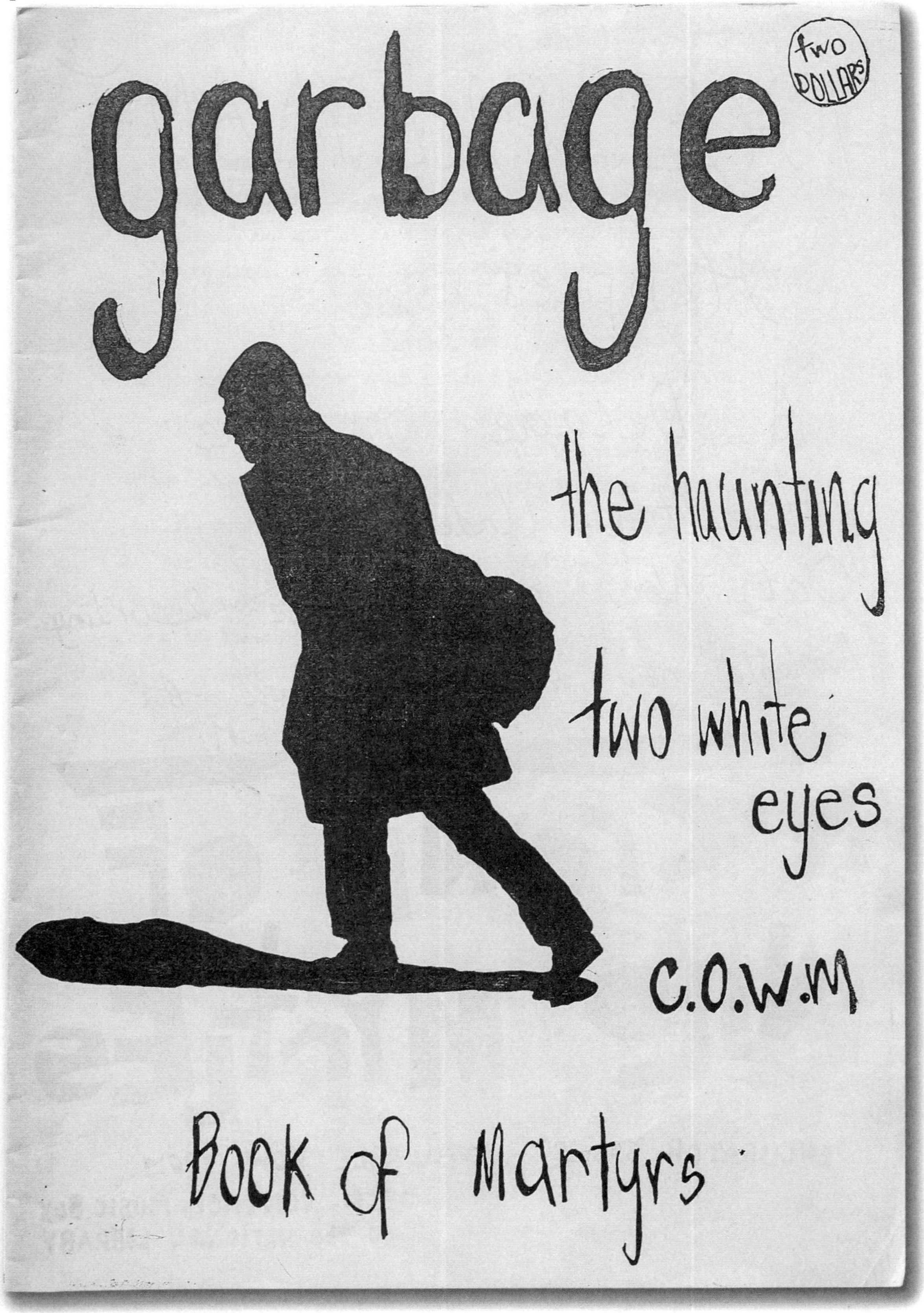

1. *Garbage*, edited by Adam Hyde, A4, 1990s. Kirikiriroa Hamilton.

Contents

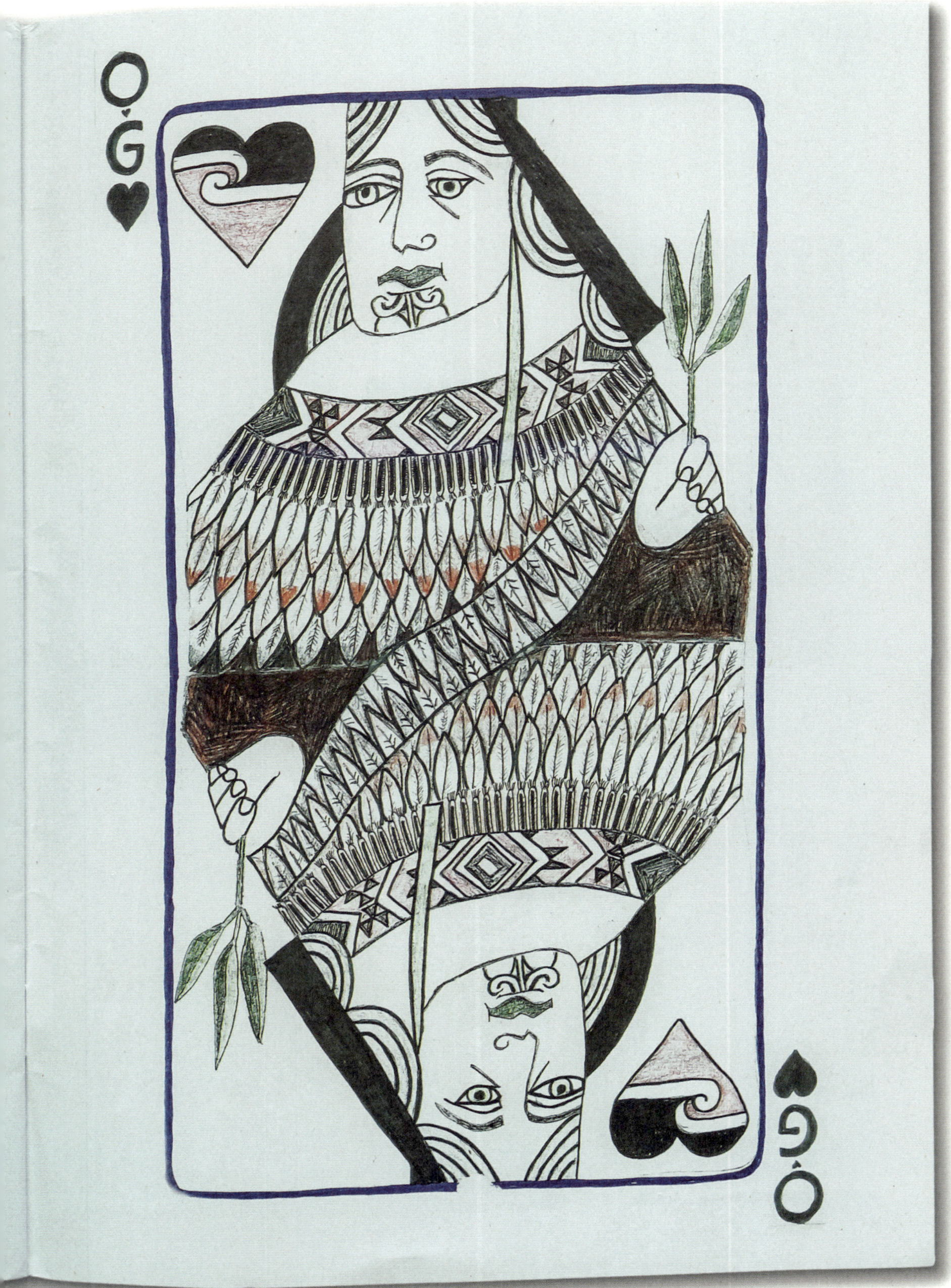

2. *Philosoflygirl #1*, Coco Solid aka Jessica Hansell, 170 x 230mm, 2011. Tāmaki Makaurau Auckland.

Intro

Almost every mainstream media article you're likely to read about zines in Aotearoa asks, and then attempts to answer, the question 'What's a zine?', as if every article is the very first to be written on the subject. This despite there being 12 zine festivals (or zinefests) in Aotearoa at the time of writing, despite numerous library collections, despite the many zine projects now in primary through to tertiary-level classrooms, despite the thousands of titles and millions of artefacts. This book hopes to go well beyond 'What's a zine?' to investigate the contexts, motivations, processes, tools, distribution strategies and highs and lows of zine-making in Aotearoa since punk rock.

The first Aotearoa punk zines popped up in the 1980s, made by zinesters using professional printers, Gestetners[1] and the new xerographic (photocopy) technology that was becoming more common. The word 'fanzine' was coined in the United States in 1940 to describe the amateurishly produced fan magazines being shared among science fiction fans. Like sci-fi fans, punk-rock zinesters were obsessives, but beyond that there may not be too many similarities in their creative output apart from the whiff of amateurism and their use of accessible printing technologies.

Why start with punk? The politics of punk still informs the Aotearoa zine scene to a greater or lesser degree, depending on the region, and — full disclosure — it's this author's bias. The subculture not only promoted a do-it-yourself ethos across music, fashion and zines, it also married this with a challenging love of the abject. Audiences were invited to become creators; you didn't even need to work through the bum notes, poor construction and spelling mistakes before going public. Non-musicians and amateurs picked up guitars, playing original songs at parties, pubs and community halls. Attitude and ideas prevailed over musicianship. The idea of wooing the public by seamlessly playing covers in a pub before wowing them with a couple of originals suddenly seemed stupid and safe. It took a little longer for zines to follow the music, but there would have been little in the way of inspiration from overseas zine ephemera compared to the number of punk records finding their way to these shores.

When zines did arrive, attitude and ideas prevailed there as well. A zine-maker might play writer, illustrator, photographer and designer, without training or prior experience in any of those things. Zinesters learned on the job, a job that no one was paying them to do. With punk music being actively ignored by the mainstream media, punk zines attempted to fill the void as zinesters reviewed gigs, record or cassette releases by a favourite new band, or conducted interviews. The politics in the music then became the politics outside it, as zinesters took it upon themselves to editorialise on matters of government and society, taking a right of reply that had never been offered to them. A grassroots national network in punk zines became the only way to find out about local punk music and culture. Zines helped young punks build an identity that ran counter to the conservatism of their parents, their government and society at large.

Those early sci-fi self-publishers were fans of a literary genre, just as punk-rock zinesters were fans of a type of music (genre or attitude?). But the 'fan' tag was never going to weather punk rock, with its manifesto of bands and audience existing on an equal footing — sometimes quite literally, with there being no stage. 'Anti-fanzine' was even stamped across the cover of the mid-eighties Ōtepoti Dunedin zine *PMT* in acknowledgement of these etymological tensions. And so it was that the fanzine became a 'zine', opening up to accommodate all forms of amateur publishing: comics, collage, poetry, fiction . . . you name it.

Fast-forward, and a visit to your local zinefest will impress upon you not just a diversity of content, but also the diversity of gender, sexuality, class, age and neurodiversity of the zine-makers and zine-readers. (Ethnic diversity is improving but has been the harder battle.) Punk's 'death to disco' mantra inadvertently raised a barrier along ethnic lines, when all it really wanted was to fight the corporatisation of music. Ever since, anything deemed 'indie' has had to actively try to shake off this historical baggage. In addition, the skinhead thing looked to many outsiders like evidence of punk's racism, when inside the scene anarcho-punks and skins were at war over that very issue.[2]

* * *

The drugs took their toll, that and other aspects of the rock 'n' roll life. The time is right for an oral history of this kind before anyone else expires. Each of the ageing punks I interviewed asked who else I'd spoken to, and on several occasions a surprised 'They're still alive!?' bounced back. But that was not the catalyst for this history being an *oral* history. That decision points to the motivations of punks and zinesters, for at heart both are amateurs suspicious of any so-called experts. The all-comers community that amateurism invites hates the idea of the distant expert canonising a singular story. The zine voice is subjective and plural, so my job has been to gather together some of these voices and offer them up to you (after extracting several thousand 'ums' and 'ahs', 'y'knows' and 'kind-ofs').

* * *

Even though we're a quarter-century into internet ubiquity, we're talking print media here, or at least I am. I know there are things called e-zines but this book is more interested in the limited print run of the physical artefact, the tactility, the craft, the embodied trade, the proximity of audience — things that have become all the more cherished as we otherwise fade into our online avatars.

This is *a* history, and these are *some* voices. Without any disrespect to the 50 zinesters interviewed, another history might have picked a different 50 interviewees. Many of the zinesters interviewed were selected for the longevity of their zine practice, their starting of a zine distro (distribution outlet) or zinefest, but it would be impossible to try to map out zine activity in Aotearoa in its entirety over the past 45 years, and that's not the point of this book. Instead, it's an attempt to catch some sense of time and place, contextual considerations, shifting technologies and shifting scenes. Many zinesters reading this might be thinking 'I should have been interviewed'. You're probably right. Sorry about that. But in reading this book I hope all zinesters out there recognise something akin to their own experiences.

It's a narrative to be experienced rather than an encyclopedia of zines in Aotearoa. There is an index at the back and I know some zinespotters will go straight to it to check whether certain zinesters or titles have been mentioned. Get ready for disappointment, the zine scene has a cast of thousands, well beyond the scope of this book. All power to the unnamed.

Every attempt has been made to select zinesters operating between 1980 and the 2020s. And while I'm no doubt guilty of giving less coverage to small-town Aotearoa, many provincial titles are mentioned by those interviewed. There are voices from each region and decade, although the spread is less even than I would have liked. Sometimes social media and email enquiries were ignored or disappeared into the dead-letter offices of the world wide web. Sometimes interview requests were declined. Thankfully, not often.

Men, women and non-binary individuals have been interviewed. As many women have been interviewed as men, not that you'd guess it from a glance at the opening eighties chapter. One feminist historian tried to impress upon me that it was my obligation to uncover the hidden female zinesters of the eighties. I've not. The evolution of the zine scene is its own revision. Nineties Riot Grrrl[3] balked at the machismo of eighties punk. When I entered the world of zines in the early 2000s there were three zine distros from which to get local zines, one run by a non-binary individual, one run by a woman and one run by a feminist collective.

I travelled the length of the country twice to conduct face-to-face interviews, and when the travel budget ran out I conducted the last few interviews via Zoom. I talked too much. Apologies to Richard Langston, who suffered my very first interview. Listening to the recording afterwards I realised I'd need to dial it back a bit, but not all the way back. You have to give a certain amount away to gain the trust of your interviewees. You have to let them know that you can identify by sharing some of your own experiences, especially if you're hoping that they'll offer chatty and revealing answers rather than anything stiff and perfunctory. Being a middle-aged post-punker and a zinester for the past 20-something years definitely helped me bridge the gap between curmudgeonly old zinesters beaten by drugs and politics and fresh-faced young zinesters enthusiastically wondering, 'What's next?' Of course, it wasn't that binary, but you get my point.

Is there a through-line from 1980s punk zines to contemporary zines? I often asked the eighties zinesters if they'd been to a modern-day zinefest, and, if so, whether they recognised the artefacts on offer there *as* zines. They generally acknowledged the radical shift away from the rough-and-ready media of punk and its politics, and were wowed by the greater investment in the object and its artistic and artisanal qualities. The urgent political text or attempt to promote your band is something that now largely happens online. This has left zines with a more acute sense of their own tactility and object presence.

Many contemporary zinesters consider paper stock, spot-colour Risograph printing, hand-stitched binding, and all manner of bespoke qualities with real acuity. Yet the collage aesthetic has endured, and represents not just a literal cut-and-paste of materials, but also a copyleft plundering of source material and an absurdist celebration of the non sequitur. Sometimes it's the meme-like mixing of a disparate image and phrase, sometimes it's the non-linear narrative of a simple family of drawings. In some ways, such qualities are not unlike the aesthetics of punk as it kicked against cultural conservatism with an iconoclastic DIY attitude and sense of fun.

The zinefest has taken over from postal networks, gigs and shops as the place to get zines. Barriers to participation are incredibly low. No zinefest turns stallholders away because their zines aren't of a 'quality', and booking a stall is often cheaper than buying a cup of coffee. This has made zinefests an incredibly valuable first outlet for many creatives. Other zinesters keep coming back year after year, long after their zines have moved on from those beautifully awkward first steps to becoming what you'd call an established practice, in poetry, illustration, writing, and so on. The energy at your local zinefest is always the most welcoming and participatory, with the sharing of artwork and ideas outweighing any commercial imperatives or competition.

This oral history is itself a collage of 50 interviews. The reader will need to relax the usual narrative expectations and be prepared to flit from voice to voice. Let each chapter paint an impression of a certain time and set of experiences.

The book is divided into sections determined by decade, with an introduction to each of them. In a demonstration of both how long and how briefly some zine-makers stay/ed in the scene, some of them pop up throughout the book, others we meet only once. We start with biographical notes on each of the zine-makers interviewed, in order of appearance.

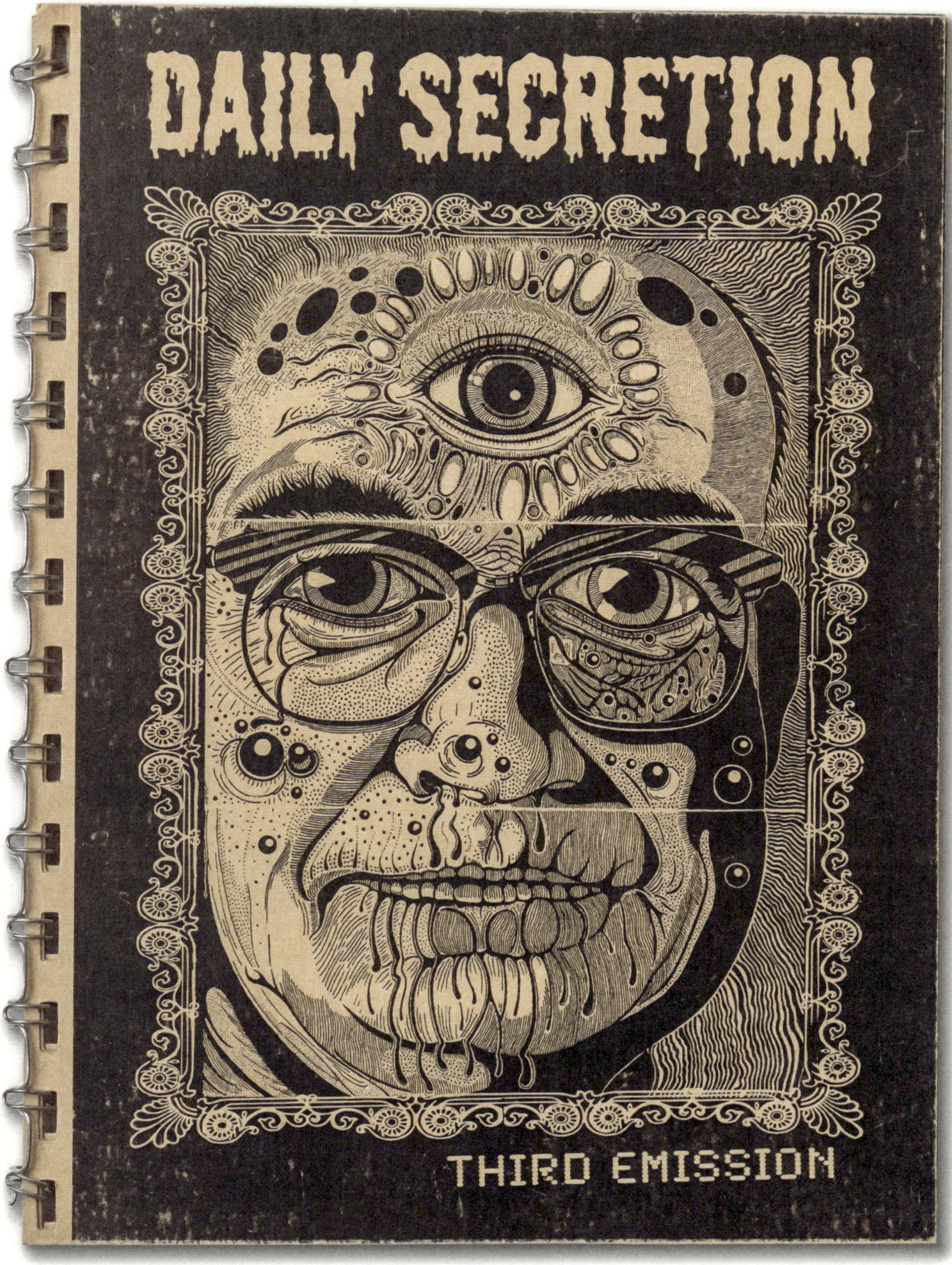

3. *Daily Secretion* #3, Hannah Salmon and Ben Knight, A5, 2012. Te Whanganui-a-Tara Wellington.

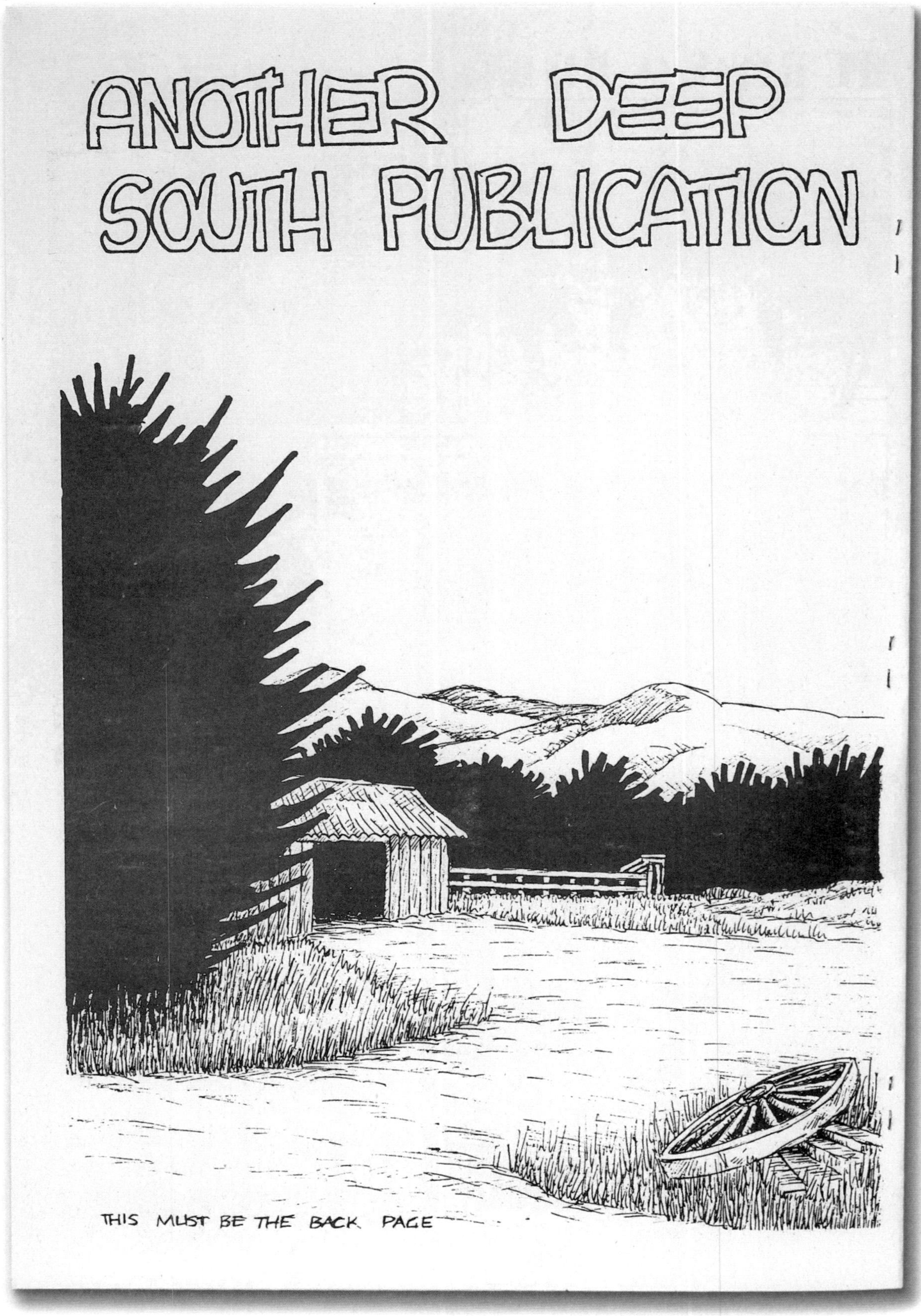

4. *Every Secret Thing* #10 back cover, Robert Scott, A4, 1985. Ōtautahi Christchurch.

Bios

in order of appearance ...

Dave White

Dave White has long been singer/guitarist in the band Lung. White was instrumental in setting up both The Stomach and Yellow Bike Records in Te Papaioea Palmerston North. He picked up *Valve* zine after it was dropped by Massey University student radio, producing several additional issues until his move to Whakatū Nelson in the late 1990s. The first so named 'zinefest' in Aotearoa was the International Zinefest (1997), which White organised in his role as director of the Nelson Community Arts Centre. It opened with a performance by Fugazi.

Paul Luker

As a then printer's apprentice, Paul Luker is credited with starting New Zealand's first punk zine, *Empty Heads*, in Tāmaki Makaurau Auckland in 1980. Luker had already self-published chapbooks of his own work and that of fellow poet John Pule. *Empty Heads* ran for two issues before Luker shifted his energies to running his Industrial Tapes label, starting the Flying Nun band Phantom Forth, and eventually moving on to create bespoke one-off artist's books.

Ania Glowacz

Ania Glowacz is the creator of mid-eighties Te Whanganui-a-Tara Wellington zine *Submission*, which mixed socio-political commentary and collage with Glowacz's fandom for the band Flesh D-Vice. *Submission* ran for several issues before Glowacz moved on to other forms of music journalism, magazine production, radio work and audio engineering.

Robert Scott

Robert Scott might be best known as the singer-songwriter-guitarist for The Bats. Scott has been in numerous other bands including The Clean. While on hiatus from The Clean in Ōtautahi Christchurch during the early eighties, Scott started throwing together *Every Secret Thing*, an idiosyncratic mixture of music reportage, comics and pranksterism. He had long been an avid drawer, and *Every Secret Thing* enabled him to combine his various interests.

Andrew Schmidt

In 1983 Andrew Schmidt started the music zine *Ha Ha Ha* with his brothers and a bunch of friends, drifting between university life in Kirikiriroa Hamilton and his hometown of Paeroa. Schmidt has had the longest self-publishing career of any of those interviewed for this book. His titles include *Ha Ha Ha*, *Social End Product* and *Mysterex*. Schmidt has qualifications in history and journalism, and has made a staggering contribution to the AudioCulture website – 'the noisy library of New Zealand music'.

Richard Davies

Richard Davies (Tainui) followed his best friend Brett Taylor into self-publishing and the 'shroom paddocks of Taranaki. Originally from Tāmaki Makaurau Auckland, Davies produced many anarcho-punk political zines under an array of different titles as Taranaki became something of a punk-rock and magic mushrooms mecca in the late eighties. Davies has also performed with punk bands Red Cross, Dioxin OD, Toxic Avengers and Evilis.

John Farrow

In the mid-eighties, John Farrow collaborated on Ōtepoti Dunedin zine *PMT* with Tracey Wedge. After Wedge left Ōtepoti, Farrow pulled together issues two and three himself. *PMT* included contributions by many others and was part of a nationwide network of punk zines offering mutual support and promotion. Farrow was heavily involved in the scene in and around the squatted venue the Nerve Centre. He was lyricist-vocalist in the band Gorse.

Tony Renouf

Tony Renouf grew up in the rural settlement of Hukanui Gordonton, just north of Kirikiriroa Hamilton. After moving to Ōtepoti Dunedin in the mid-eighties, he started self-publishing mini-comics, drawing regular strips for *Critic* and contributing strips and cartoons to zines and comic anthologies like Chris Knox's *Jesus on a Stick* and Cornelius Stone's *Razor*. By the early nineties, the network of Ōtepoti-based comics artists had grown and Renouf started his own local comics anthology, *Treacle*.

Simon Cottle

Most zines come and go after one or two issues, but Simon Cottle's anarcho-punk zines ran for more than 10 years under the titles *Anarcho-Pacifist*, *Anti-System* and *Social Dis-Ease*. Cottle started producing zines in mid-eighties Te Whanganui-a-Tara. Like other punk zinesters, Cottle was important to a national anarcho-punk network that largely operated outside of the mainstream media and music press, promoting gigs, records, cassettes and other zines from across Aotearoa.

Matthew Campbell Downes

Matthew Campbell Downes joined his good friend Mark Rastrick (aka Mark Morte) in the Ōtautahi band Ballon D'Essai at the dawn of the eighties. The band members were still at Christchurch Boys' High School. Several members of Ballon D'Essai were as enamoured with comics as they were music. Their Flying Nun record releases came with comics, or did the comics come with records? Downes, Morte and others were inspired by the self-published comics of fellow Boys' High student Lorenzo van der Lingen.

Ross Gardiner

In the mid-eighties, Ross Gardiner released his first zine, *Positive Approach*, while still at high school in Tāmaki Makaurau. Gardiner opened the anarchist outlet Books from the Black Lagoon with his partner Lyn Spencer in the early nineties. Remaining Black Lagoon stock helped the couple start The Freedom Shop when they moved south to Te Whanganui-a-Tara in the mid-nineties. Gardiner also made several anarchist publications with the help of printer Bruce Grenville, including the quarterly anarchist zine *The State Adversary*. Gardiner is interviewed here alongside his partner Lyn Spencer, which is why their responses run together at times.

Tracey Wedge

Issue 1 of *PMT* was submitted as course-work for Tracey Wedge's Home Science qualification at the University of Otago, but the zine had a vigorous life beyond any course requirements. Wedge and collaborator John Farrow were interested in contributing to Ōtepoti's growing anarcho-punk community of the mid-eighties. Wedge started work on issue two of *PMT* before returning to her hometown of Whangārei. Later Wedge would apply her zine-making skills to the newsletter of the Costume and Textile Association of New Zealand.

Lyn Spencer

Lyn Spencer was one of many who moved to Taranaki in the late eighties to plug into the local punk scene. A little later, Spencer and her partner Ross Gardiner opened anarcho-punk outlets Books from the Black Lagoon (Tāmaki Makaurau) and The Freedom Shop (Te Whanganui-a-Tara). Between the opening of those outlets, Spencer and Gardiner experienced punk networks in Europe and the USA, bringing new ideas home. Spencer was also involved with the anarcho-feminist zine *Sekhmet* and anarchist quarterly *The State Adversary*. Spencer is interviewed here alongside her partner Ross Gardiner.

David Merritt

David Merritt is Aotearoa's only zine busker. You might stumble across him armed with scissors, glue sticks, repurposed book covers and banana-box linings, constructing bespoke fold-out poetry publications on the street. Merritt has embraced an alternative DIY production and distribution model for his works of poetry. He's also the zinester most likely to get from Ōtepoti Zinefest to Auckland Zinefest and everywhere in between. In another life David Merritt has been an IT expert, tour manager, magazine editor and a bunch of other things.

Richard Langston

Richard Langston took a step outside of his day job, writing conventional print media journalism, to produce six issues of *Garage*. The fanzine started in 1984 after Langston returned from London to find an unrivalled local music scene in Ōtepoti. He was eventually joined by others, interviewing and reviewing local and then international musicians of interest. Langston and co. had a real affection for bands of the Flying Nun ilk, and his zines became a valuable resource for Matthew Goody's encyclopaedic 2022 book – *Needles and Plastic* – about the Flying Nun record label.

Dave Hegan

Dave Hegan is another who made the pilgrimage to the Taranaki punk and 'shrooms scene in the late eighties. Hegan was forced to return to Ōtautahi and clean up before entering rehab. Inspired by Simon Cottle's *Anti-System* and other punk zines, Hegan used the time to start posting interview questions to favourite international bands (and a few locals), garnering enough responses to release the zine *Alien-Nation* in 1990, followed by *Soap Up!* in 1991.

Andrew Stephens

Andrew Stephens already had teenage children when he started releasing issues of his *Severed Head* zine. Stephens had enrolled in media studies courses at Massey University in Te Papaioea. Deconstructing media agendas collided with local post-punk energies, encouraging Stephens to turn his essays into zines. He added economical collages and contributions by friends to produce three issues of *Severed Head*. Andrew Stephens is interviewed here alongside his wife, Trish Stephens, and son Sam Stephens, which is why Andrew's and Trish's responses run together at times.

Bruce Grenville

Bruce Grenville (aka Bruce Ronald Henderson) is a commercial print-maker, printing 'proselytiser', rogue philatelist, Egyptologist and former member of Bondi's Carnival Anarchists. In the 1980s Grenville was gifted a large Heidelberg Platen printing press, which he convinced the University of Auckland to house. There followed a prolific 10-year period during which Grenville produced untold books, magazines, zines and posters, introducing various waifs and strays to the wonders of letterpress printing, including Ross Gardiner and Max Reeves. Grenville is a former editor of quarterly anarchist zine *The State Adversary*.

Kerry Ann Lee

Kerry Ann Lee is based in Te Whanganui-a-Tara and has been an active zinester and DIY champion since the late nineties. Lee's influences were more hybrid, crossing the anarchist punk, indie music and comics fraternities, even adding formal design training to the mix. In 2001 Lee started Red Letter Distro, a mail-order service for favourite titles from Aotearoa, the USA and elsewhere. Its zine catalogues could be found among the café flyers. Lee's interest in independent publishing, its aesthetics and communities, has endured, and she is still active in these spaces.

David Tulloch

David Tulloch was instrumental in producing 12 issues of the comic-book anthology *Pistake* between 1992 and 1994 alongside others from Te Whanganui-a-Tara: Simon Morse, Martin Emond and Rufus Dayglo. Tulloch worked at the comics shop VMS (still in Cuba Street as Graphic) and had already published the anthology comic *Desperate Ink*. After *Pistake* burnt out, Tulloch took a 10-year break from comics before returning to publish online, eventually returning to print and tabling at various zinefests.

Tim Danko

Tim Danko started making comics in Melbourne in the late eighties. In the early nineties he started Dead Xerox Press, distributing selected local and international titles. In the mid-nineties he started working with the comics imprint Silent Army. In 2005, Danko and Silent Army's Michael Fikaris headed over to Aotearoa to attend the Armageddon Expo, and Danko relocated to Aotearoa thereafter. Danko is an art tutor at Māpura Studios, which supports artists from the disability community. Since 2016, he has facilitated Māpura's comics collective TV Competition FutureFutureFuture.

Liz Mathews

Liz Mathews is a zine-maker and musician from Tāmaki Makaurau. She grew up in Kerikeri, where she produced nineties zine *Flying Fox*. Her later titles include *The Wishbone Your Majesty*, *Robo-Theory*, *Golden Opportunity* and *Stink Lines*. Mathews organised the girl-rock Get Set Go Festival in the late nineties and has played in a total of 13 bands. She is still involved in self-publishing through the annual production of the beautiful, witchy, hand-drawn calendar *Stay Trashy*. She is interviewed here alongside Beth Dawson, which is why their responses run together at times.

Indira Neville

Indira Neville was part of Kirikiriroa's Oats Comics collective, established in 1993. She contributed to the collective's anthology comics and produced her own serial, *Nice Gravy*. She's since made a lot of other comics, both self-published and through publishing houses. In 2014 she joined Rae Joyce and Sarah Laing to produce *Three Words: An anthology of Aotearoa/ NZ women's comics*, a reaction to the exclusion of comics by women from the national canon. Neville is also a musician, mother and teacher.

Beth Dawson

Beth Dawson produces zines, art and music under the moniker Ducklingmonster. Her first zines were shared with friends in nineties Tāmaki Makaurau, and this grew to sharing zines alongside wider musical releases from her new base in Ōtepoti. Dawson has been a member of the band The Futurians since 2001, and regards music and zines as part of the same creative expression. This understanding prompted her to join Indira Neville and Chris Cudby for *Sonic Comic* (2017), a survey of artist-musicians producing similarly hybrid works. She is interviewed here alongside Liz Mathews.

Tui Gordon

Tui Gordon ran Tāmaki Makaurau's Cherry Bomb Comics with her friend Melissa Steiner from 2004 to 2007 before moving the shop online for another four years. Cherry Bomb Comics drew inspiration from earlier punk hub Misfit Theatre, even inheriting Misfit's zine library. The shop platformed comics by women, minorities and allies. In the early 2000s, Gordon self-published the *Revolutionary Women Stencil-Book*. Gordon is a librarian and recent essayist for *Life on Volcanoes: Contemporary essays*, published by Beatnik in 2019.

Moira Clunie

Moira Clunie (Te Rarawa) is that rare thing: somebody who in the late nineties saw emerging internet technologies and zines as offering equal but different self-publishing opportunities. Clunie ran Aotearoa New Zealand's first online zine distro, Moon Rocket, from 2000 to 2006. In 2003, they were one of the crew that brought Aotearoa its first dedicated zine market, Small Print, which ran at the Grey Lynn Library hall. The event ran again in 2005 and provided the inspiration and template for the Wellington and Auckland zinefests.

Kenneth Merrick

Based in Tāmaki Makaurau, Kenneth Merrick has an exhibition practice, and also tables at various zinefests around the country. He has tertiary qualifications in painting, audio engineering and music. Merrick taught English, drawing and comics in Japan in the late 2000s. He enjoys the economy of scale offered by zines after wrestling with the real estate required to support large studio paintings. He also enjoys the low-stakes, all-comers atmosphere of zinefests after the pressures of gallery shows. Merrick has taken out Best of Fest awards at both Auckland and Kirikiriroa zinefests.

Pritika Lal

Pritika Lal is a graduate of the Elam School of Fine Arts and AUT in Tāmaki Makaurau. She and Coco Solid self-published the freebee *This Is Not a Comic* from 2005 to 2008, contributing to the cultural community in and around Karangahape Road. The pair also posted the zine for distribution in other towns around Aotearoa and Australia. Lal has contributed to the zine *Foxy Moron* and performed in the all-girl band The Pussies. She now lectures at the Media Design School in Tāmaki Makaurau.

Tessa Stubbing

Tessa Stubbing (Tainui, Ngāti Awa) was designing future branding for Tāmaki Makaurau Auckland's Small Print zinefest while still at high school in the mid-2000s. When Small Print folded, Stubbing took the baton from Moira Clunie and launched Auckland Zinefest in 2009 with her mates from Cross Street Studios. In 2013, Stubbing and Wellington Zinefest instigator Kylie Buck started the annual *New Zealand Zine Review*, which they then took online. Stubbing also contributed to the launch of Auckland Libraries' zine collection alongside Hamish Noonan and Angeline Chirnside.

Kylie Buck

Kylie Buck started making zines as an art student at WelTec. Then, as a librarian at Wellington City Libraries, Buck found a zine ally in collections librarian Stephanie Poulopoulos. The pair put out the call for zine donations and Wellington City Libraries became the first public library in Aotearoa to have a zine collection the public could borrow. Buck and Poulopoulos convinced the library to fund the first Wellington Zinefest in 2007, joined in organising the fest by zinester Kim Gruschow. Buck would later co-produce the *New Zealand Zine Review* annuals and website with Tessa Stubbing.

Sam Orchard

Sam Orchard has employed the accessibility of comics to educate on queer and trans issues for young people. The confidence of Orchard's later comics belies a nervous start when he used comics to come out to friends, a way of saying what Sam was (at that stage) too scared to speak. His *Family Portraits* (2014) series of comics was funded by a successful Kickstarter campaign which also allowed him to tour them through the USA. Orchard is now the curator of the New Zealand Cartoon and Comics Archive at the National Library of New Zealand Te Puna Mātauranga o Aotearoa.

Spencer Hall

Spencer Hall's love of comics saw him step in and help produce *DUD: The Dunedin Comic Revue* when instigators of the project found themselves floundering. Hall ended up being instrumental in the release of *DUD* #1 and #2. He briefly ran his own comics shop in Koputai Port Chalmers under the same name – DUD. When organisers of the inaugural Dunedin Zinefest (now Ōtepoti Zinefest) moved on, Hall took up the challenge of keeping the event going, sometimes single-handedly, and often from another part of the country. Zines have started to inform Hall's own publications as much as comics, with his recent series *Scraps* including notebook doodles, diary entries, essays and reviews alongside the comics.

Mieke Montagne

Mieke Montagne is an artist, zinester and tattooist who lives in Ōtautahi Christchurch. Her introduction to the world of zines came through her sister and Ōtautahi Zinefest, which she would later go on to run alongside local zinesters Jane Maloney, Alice Bush, Sarah Lund, Nate Tamblyn, Maya Templer and others. Montagne also joined the collective running a local mecca of weird records, comics and zines – Ride On Super Sound. Making a space for the 'weird shit' is one of her prime motivators.

Liam Goulter

Liam Goulter joined the Wellington Zinefest committee of Rachel Lynch, Milly Hampton and Caitlin Lynch in 2017. In 2020 the old committee moved on, and Goulter ran the show alongside zinester Lucy Black. When Black left, Wellington Zinefest incorporated and established a board (since lapsed) so that decision-making was not left to Goulter alone. During Goulter's time doing the heavy lifting for Wellington Zinefest, additional funding avenues were identified and various marginalised communities had zines sponsored and facilitated, with Goulter also taking on design and production duties at times.

Murtle Chickpea

Murtle Chickpea (aka Sam Dew) was part of the artist collective at 91 Aro Street in 2004, but it wasn't until she attended Wellington Zinefest's winter market that the penny dropped as to the potential of zines. In 2016 Murtle Chickpea toured provincial libraries on the North Island's east coast, running zine-making workshops for kids. Her travelling Zine Museum was a vast collection of international zine titles that travelled the North Island, popping up at zinefests, libraries and book fairs before being retired to the Massey University library in Te Whanganui-a-Tara Wellington with support from librarian Lauren Deacon. Murtle Chickpea remains a prolific collage artist and zinester, largely selling works online.

Catalina Paz Nuñez Elevancini

Catalina Paz Nuñez Elevancini studied communication design at Auckland University of Technology before joining her sister Camila (involved since 2016) in a lead role with Auckland Zinefest. The sisters work alongside a committee of volunteers. During their term, Auckland Zinefest has established a home at Auckland Art Gallery and grown to offer zine-making workshops, pop-ups and markets throughout the year. Catalina is a zinester herself, largely working in the perzine genre (diaristic personal zines).

Hannah Wynn

Hannah Wynn came to zines as the co-organiser of the inaugural Tauranga Zinefest years before turning her own hand to the medium. In 2016 Wynn joined fellow creative industries student Lynette Fisher in running Tauranga Zinefest out of Tauranga Art Gallery with the support of the gallery director Karl Chitham. Wynn ran Tauranga Zinefest solo from 2019, and in 2024 handed over the running of the fest to Tauranga Arts Festival. Wynn's own zines have explored obscure phobias, introduced favourite kupu Māori in tiny concertina form and collaged the faces of odious dictators onto pickles.

essa may ranapiri

Before essa may ranapiri (Ngaati Raukawa, Ngaati Puukeko) was a celebrated poet published by Victoria University Press they were a zine-maker, hawking their wares at the Kirikiriroa Hamilton and Tauranga zinefests. Despite the publishing deals, ranapiri still makes zines, sometimes as a way to share poems that fall outside of the scope of themed collections, sometimes as a way of responding to the experience of the book. ranapiri is the recipient of the inaugural Keri Hulme Award 2023 and the 2023 Janet Frame Literary Trust Award for Poetry.

Marijke van Schaardenburg

Marijke van Schaardenburg is a fine arts graduate of the Ilam School of Fine Arts in Ōtautahi. After graduating, van Schaardenburg moved to Tāmaki Makaurau, where the zine scene proved more accessible and zine-making more sustainable than film. Van Schaardenburg joined the Auckland Zinefest committee in 2022. In 2021 they were awarded Best Art Zine for *Hero to One*, and in 2022 and 2024 Runner Up Narrative Zine for *Bundle of Sticks* and *We Make the Space Work*. Van Schaardenburg's zines examine or celebrate queer culture and selfhood.

Regan Kupu Stokes

In 2013, Regan Kupu Stokes (Ngāi Te Rangi, English) helped resurrect Christchurch Zinefest (now Ōtautahi Zinefest) after the devastating 2011 earthquake and the exodus of some of the original 2011 Zinefest organisers. Stokes worked alongside Jed Crowther, Rosa Hughes-Currie and Rose Lu. Stokes' first zine was an explainer for Occupy Christchurch, out of their encampment in Hagley Park. From there, he increasingly used te reo Māori in his zines, undertaking postgraduate study in Māori language and translation, and since 2020 has been guitarist-vocalist in the band HOIHOI, which sings in English and te reo Māori.

Gini Jory

Gini Jory works in the Published and Special Collections at the Hocken Library, University of Otago, where processing zines donated by Ōtepoti Zinefest sparked the decision to start making them herself. Jory's work often pulls from historical material found in the online Papers Past archive, with zines themed around knights, sirens and witches through a queer feminist lens. Archival material meets Jory's own writing and collage across a staggering number of titles for someone so new to the medium. Jory's interest has started to inform her work at the Hocken, with an eye to collecting zines and facilitating zine-making workshops.

Arwen Miriama Sommer

Arwen Miriama Sommer (Te Āti Haunui-a-Pāpārangi, Uenuku) gatecrashed the first Christchurch Zinefest (now Ōtautahi Zinefest) with poetry zines they'd constructed the night before, having just heard about the event from friend Isla Martin. Sommer has tabled at every Ōtautahi Zinefest since. Sommer is a librarian for Christchurch Libraries Ngā Kete Wānanga o Ōtautahi, where they champion zines and often run zine-making workshops for kids and adults. Sommer took out Best Lit Zine at Ōtautahi Zinefest 2019. They have a Bachelor of Broadcasting Communications (Journalism) from Ara Institute.

Nina Harper

Nina Harper exited art school once she realised it was all about the conceptual and not the narrative illustration she so loved. Harper has since developed her practice by regularly tabling at her hometown Kirikiriroa Hamilton Zinefest as well as zinefests in Auckland and Wellington. Harper's work selling art materials has given her access to a range of new tools, with her recent discovery of watercolour enabling a style reminiscent of classic children's book illustrations, but with a dark twist. Harper has won and placed at the Kirikiriroa Hamilton Zinefest Best of Fest awards for titles *Itsy Bitsy* and *Fun and Games for Bright Young Girls*.

Maya Templer

Maya Templer had an intuitive love of comics and animation from an early age. Her father, Stephen Templer, is an illustrator, also providing context for these fascinations to flourish into making. Templer gained a diploma in animation from Yoobee, has worked as an animator in children's television, and furthered her animation studies at Griffith University in Brisbane. Templer was instrumental in helping Ōtautahi Zinefest double in size, taking the fest from community halls to Christchurch Art Gallery Te Puna o Waiwhetū with support from other local zinesters (see Mieke Montagne's bio). Templer produces her own small full-colour comics in a range of formats, and has also produced political card game – *Meet the Candidates*.

Helen Yeung

Helen Yeung moved to Tāmaki Makaurau Auckland's North Shore from Hong Kong with her family when she was a child. She discovered zines online, and started the Migrant Zine Collective (2017), working with other migrants to share their stories, sometimes through workshops fostering participant community. *Gen M* was the collective's first title, followed by others including *Musubi*, *Radicalised Memes 4 the Disoriented Teen*, *Goodbye Turmeric Latte*, *Recipes for Resistance* and *Anti-Racist Soup*. In 2023 Yeung moved to Guåhan (Guam), where she lectures in communications and media. She still facilitates zine-making and workshops exploring feminism, marginalisation and the migrant experience. She is completing a PhD in communication studies at AUT.

Jewelia Howard

Jewelia Howard grew up in Kaikōura before moving to Tāmaki Makaurau then settling in Te Whanganui-a-Tara. Howard is that rarest of zinesters: one who manages to make a living out of the attendant stickers, badges and merch while still celebrating the accessible price point of zines. Howard can be found tabling not only at zinefests around the country but also at the touring Armageddon Expo, Overload, Big Gay Out, Out in the City, Ratbag Market and many more. Howard discovered zines online — an extension of the emo music they engaged with during their teenage years. Howard is a member of the Wellington Zinefest committee.

Victoria Armstrong

Victoria Armstrong undertook an online Diploma in Creativity with The Learning Connexion in 2022. Upon graduating, she found the iconoclastic humour and accessibility of zines too inviting to resist. Armstrong helped out with the organisation of her hometown Palmy Zine Fest and has tabled there and at zinefests in Tauranga, Whanganui and Kapiti. Collage is Armstrong's media of choice, sometimes silly, sometimes dark and risqué. Armstrong has been trying to work out whether the naughtier elements of her zine collage will translate to the gallery walls. Armstrong collaborates on some zines with her partner, Billy Douglas (bio below). The pair have three children.

Billy Douglas

Billy Douglas was a high school tearaway who loved winding up his teachers by penning disturbing stories. The school did its best to extinguish Douglas's penchant for the unsettling, and it wasn't until his partner Victoria Armstrong asked him to collaborate that he found his way back to writing. The pair has collaborated on multiple issues of the zine *Screaming Monkeys* (Whanganui Best of Fest); Douglas supplies original writing when time allows and works with ChatGPT when due to parenting and a full-time plumbing apprenticeship it doesn't. Douglas has found the zinefest communities incredibly inviting and full of modest brilliance.

Maia-Jeanne Woolkirk

Maia-Jeanne Woolkirk grew up in Ōtautahi, before moving on to Te Whanganui-a-Tara, then Whanganui, and now Te Papaioea. Woolkirk ran Whanganui Zinefest along with Abby Stewart and Anique Jayasinghe in the early 2020s. In its first year (2021), Whanganui Zinefest squeezed into Article Café before finding bigger premises at the Whanganui Musicians Club on Drews Avenue. While Woolkirk has made several zines herself (including a deep dive into the magic of the band Soul Coughing), she admits being distracted by the craft, merch and bunting that was required to bring Whanganui Zinefest to the public. Woolkirk hates cat zines.

Panty Baggers

Panty Baggers is an Ōtepoti Dunedin collage collective made up of the artists Prudence Edge, Sapph Prentice, Sarah Sharma and Anna Ward. The collective has flirted with the Pussy Riot stylings of balaclava-adorned anonymity and, while this has been relaxed, the collective is still very much a holistic entity, hence the interview answers in this book have not been individually attributed. Panty Baggers are active in international paste-up and zine communities. The collective's collage work is process heavy, sometimes silly and salacious, sometimes politically feminist. The collective regularly tables at the Ōtepoti and Ōtautahi zinefests. When not 'panty bagging', the various members work in the creative sector and education.

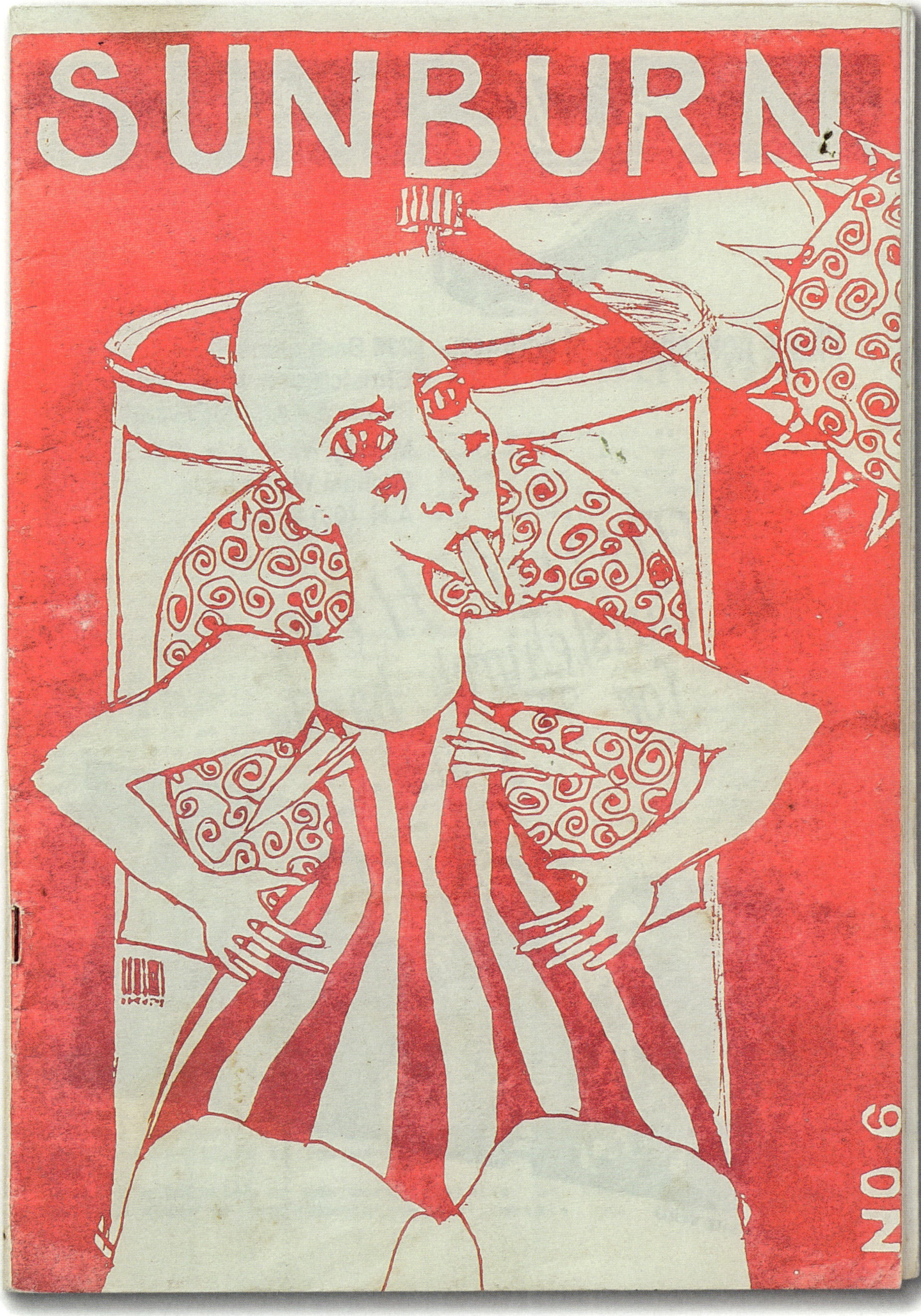

5. *Sunburn* #6, Grant McDonagh, Jools Sorrell, Brian Wafer, Scott Miller and others, A5, 1990. Ōtautahi Christchurch.

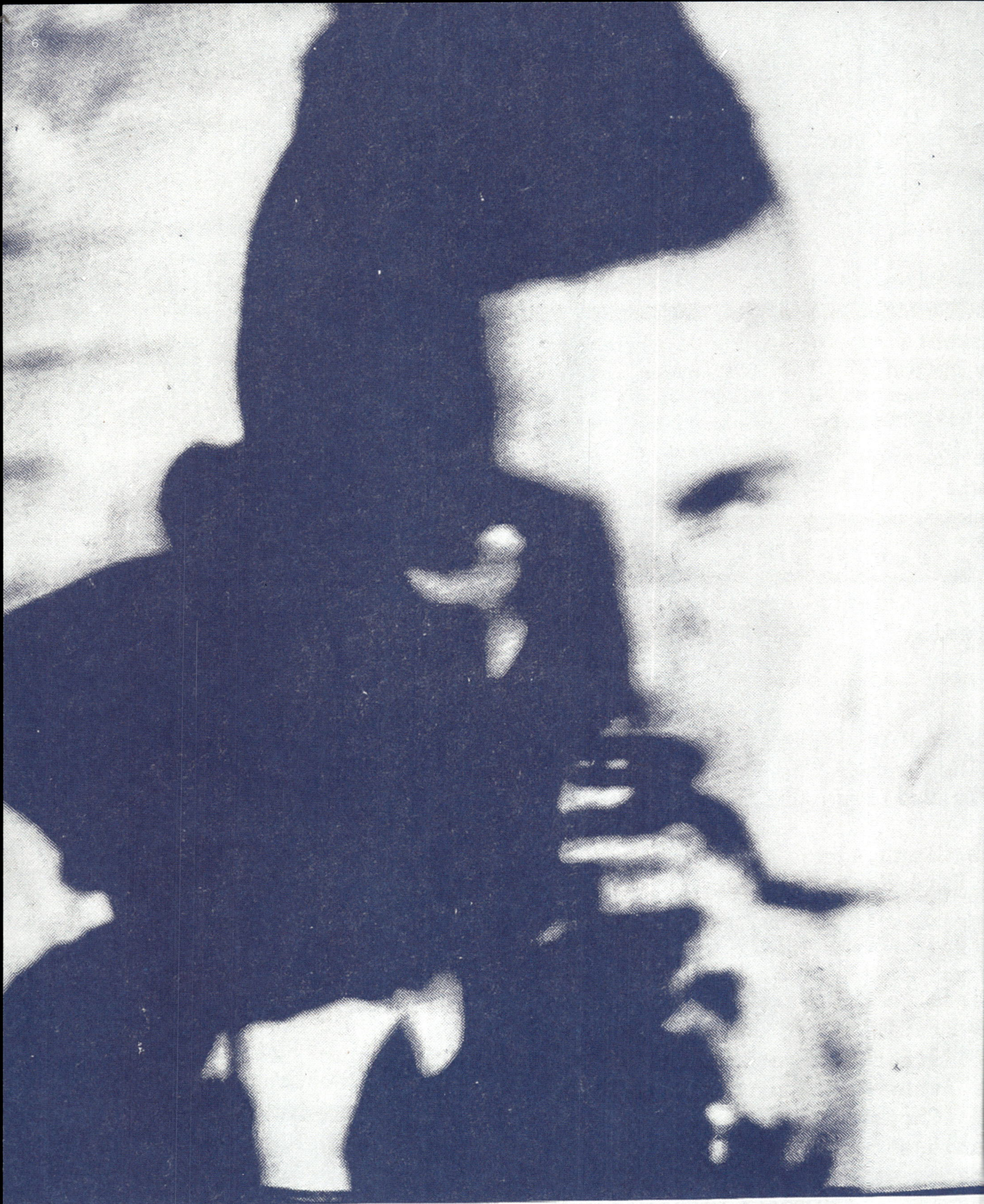

MY-TOY LOVE-T.DW

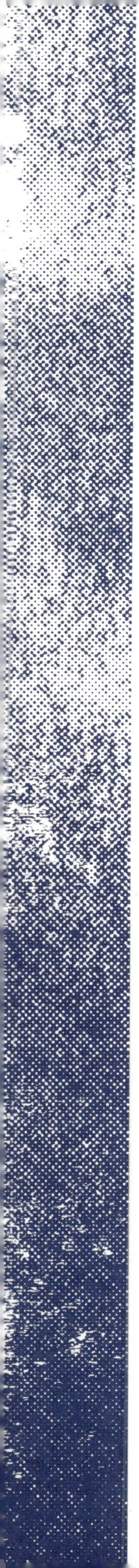

Eighties Aotearoa

1980s Aotearoa is a world away! Here are some of the contextual considerations that will, I'm sure, confound the younger reader and make those who can remember the eighties feel as though they've been alive for a very long time.

6. *Garage #5* cover detail, edited by Richard Langston, A4, 1986. Ōtepoti Dunedin.

In January 1980, Aotearoa New Zealand had enjoyed a second television channel for fewer than five years. With TV2 came the late-night music videos of *Radio with Pictures*, videos deemed inappropriate for daytime broadcast. You were less likely to see anything exciting on the daytime top 20 rundown *Ready to Roll*. Some top 20 songs didn't even have music videos, in which case TV1 might roll out the Oomph Dance Troupe for some synchronised leotard action.

Import tariffs and licensing controls meant that any records, clothes or books beyond mainstream interests might be hard to get hold of. Conversely, Aotearoa was flooded with weekly music tabloids from the UK that reported on the post-punk revolution in music. In response, bands were formed, street fashions changed, and fanzines and independent record labels were launched.

In June 1981, Joy Division's 'Love Will Tear Us Apart' was the top-charting song in the country, despite receiving no commercial airplay. A month later it was the New Zealand population that was torn apart as every adult was compelled to decide whether they did or did not support a tour by the visiting Springboks rugby team from apartheid South Africa. Every test match invited a violent pitched battle between police and anti-tour protestors.

Former Napier mayor Peter Tait and businessman and former mayor of Mount Maunganui Keith Hay carrying boxes into Parliament containing the petition against homosexual law reform, 24 September 1985. *Alexander Turnbull Library, EP/1985/4285/25-F*

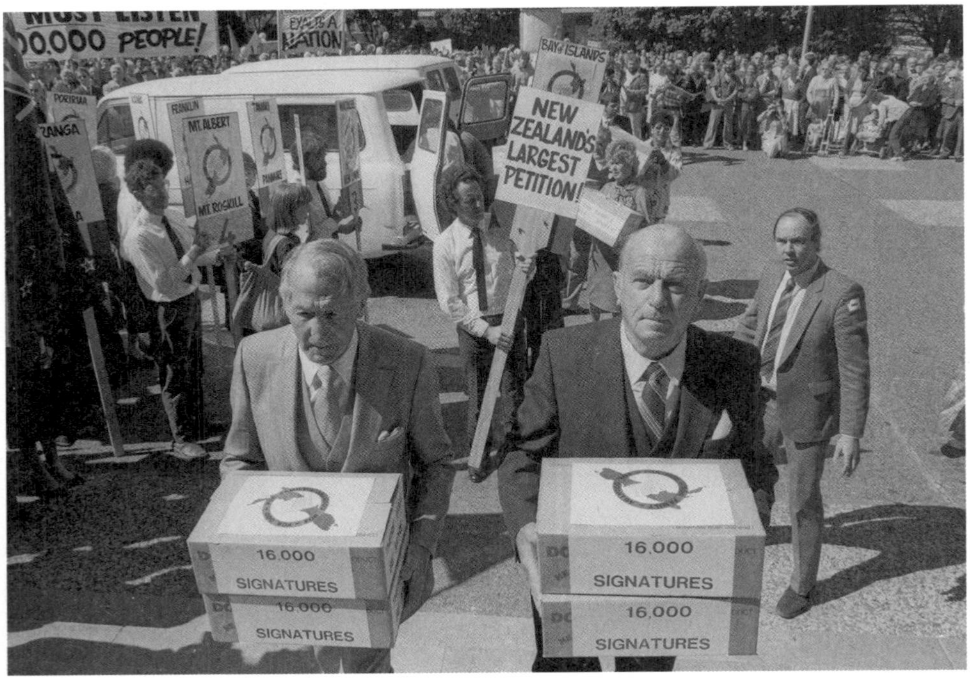

In November 1982 a young Auckland punk and Springbok protest veteran named Neil Roberts attempted to blow up the centre of state surveillance, the Wanganui Computer Centre. Roberts died in the blast, damaging the building's foyer but failing to disrupt the centre's operations.

A heated social divide of a different kind arrived a few years later when MP Fran Wilde introduced a parliamentary Bill designed to decriminalise gay sex. The Homosexual Law Reform Act was voted in by a narrow majority and signed into legislation in July 1986.

Anti-Springbok tour demonstrators overturning a car on Onslow Road, Kingsland, Auckland, 12 September 1981. *Alexander Turnbull Library, EP-Ethics-Demonstrations-1981 Springbok tour-0*

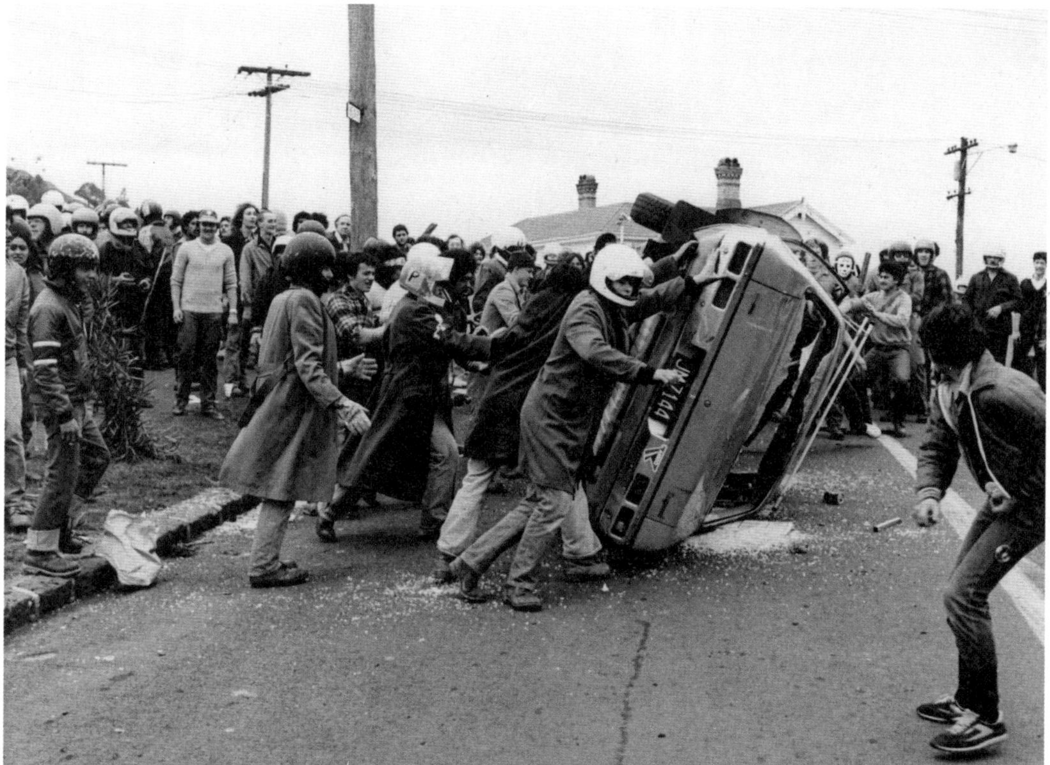

The National Party had been in power since 1975, winning a third term in 1981. National Party prime minister Robert Muldoon pushed protectionist policies and used heavy overseas borrowing to realise his government's 'think big' industrial projects. The party-political actions of eighties Aotearoa defy our current understandings of left–right politics. It was the newly elected Labour government of 1984 that pushed through neoliberal free-market policies in a brand of economics that came to be known as Rogernomics, named for then Minister of Finance Roger Douglas.

Meanwhile, a 'David [Lange] and Goliath' battle ensued between Aotearoa and its old ally the United States when a ban on US nuclear ship visits was enacted. The Cold War was still in full swing, and citizens of the world were living under the nightmare scenario of a global nuclear apocalypse fuelled by the mutual suspicions of the United States and the Soviet Union.

In 1985, the nuclear debate came to our shores when state-backed French terrorists bombed and sank Greenpeace's ship the *Rainbow Warrior* — the lead protest vessel monitoring French nuclear tests in the South Pacific — while it was berthed in Auckland, killing crew photographer Fernando Pereira.

Prime Minister David Lange (left) and Minister of Finance Roger Douglas announcing the economic reforms that would become known as Rogernomics, 1984. *New Zealand Herald*

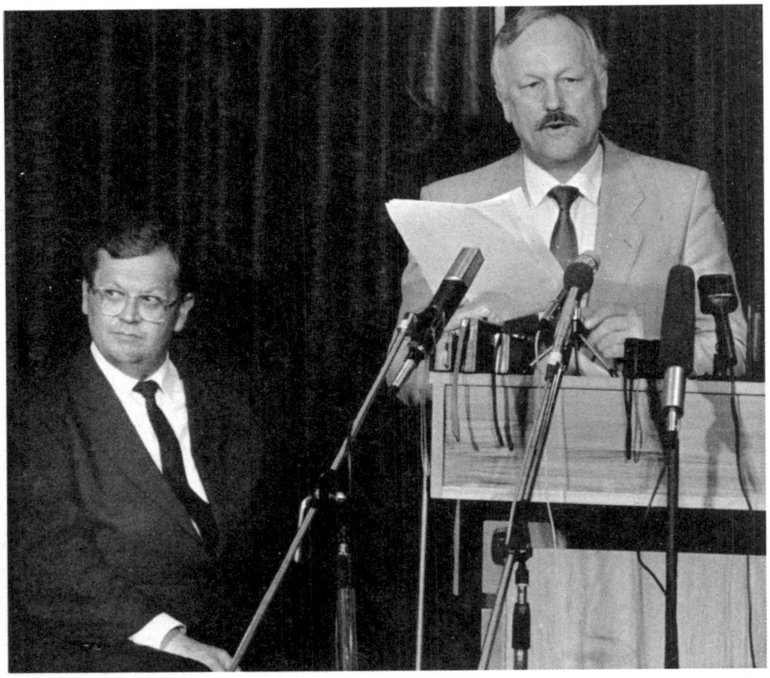

Musical responses to the Cold War and Aotearoa New Zealand's place in it had already emerged, with Herbs' 'French Letter' (which spent 11 weeks in the charts in 1982) and Birmingham ska band The Beat's 'Dream Home in New Zealand'. The Beat's 1981 song macabrely imagined the extra seven minutes it would take the nuclear missiles to arrive downunder.

The Commodore 64 computer, so named because its memory capacity was 64 kilobytes of RAM, was launched in 1982. The user had to learn BASIC computer coding to make it do anything.

There's no mention of computers among the eighties zinesters of this chapter, but there is a passing mention of a word-processor. All are acutely aware of how alien 1980s politics, markets and technologies might sound to younger generations, and this colours their dialogue at times.

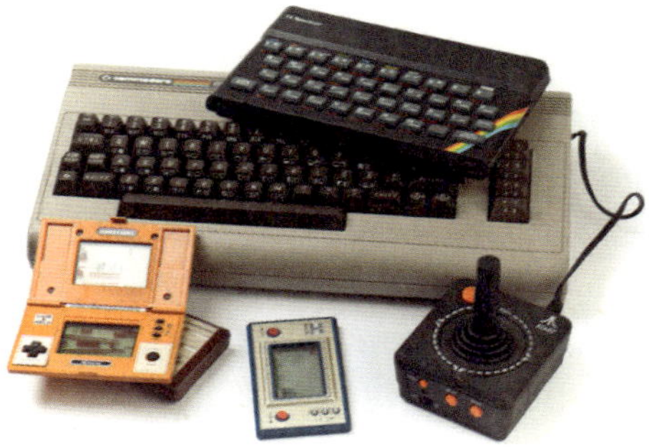

Eighties tech: a Commodore 64, Sinclair ZX Spectrum, Nintendo Game & Watch and Atari joystick. *iStock*

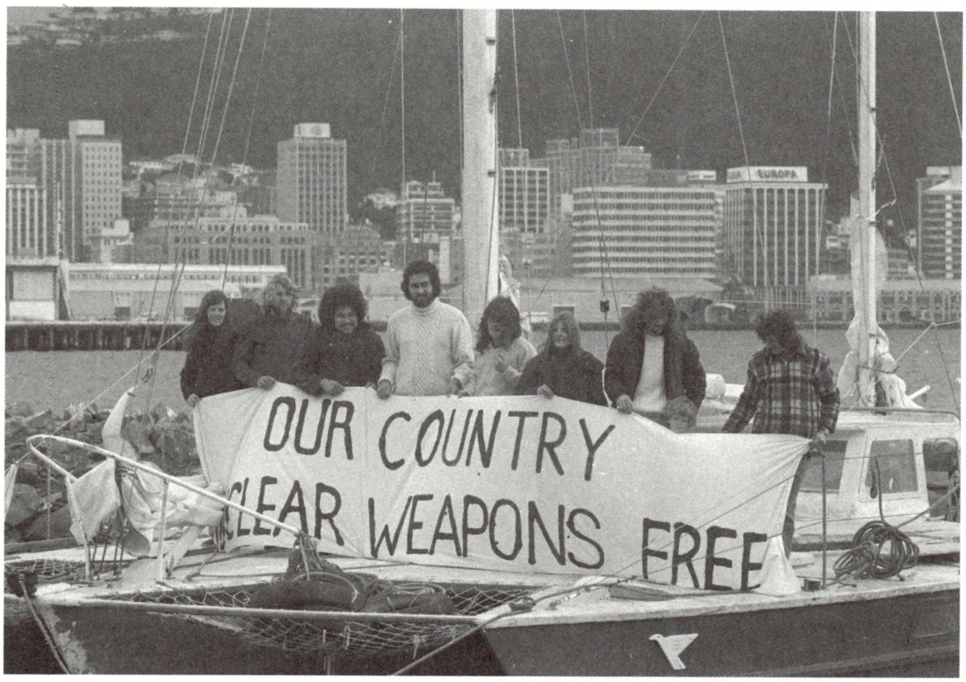

Members of CANWAR (Campaign Against Nuclear Warships) on board the yacht *Phoenix* inside the breakwater in Wellington Harbour during protests at the arrival of the USS *Longbeach*, 13 August 1976. *Alexander Turnbull Library, EP/1976/2841/26a-F*

Even within the decade itself there were very different experiences. Several eighties punk-rockers talked about being politicised by the 1981 Springbok tour and Cold War dread, but these issues were of less concern to those who got started in zines at the decade's close. There's also quite a stretch between the experience of printer's apprentice Paul Luker in 1980 Tāmaki Makaurau Auckland and the late-eighties zinesters who flocked to the 'shroom paddocks of Taranaki.

Most of those interviewed for the eighties chapter were punk-rockers. Others represent the localised hybrid that bubbled up in the South Island. I wondered whether the 'pyjama people' — the Dunedin punk term for Flying Nun types — were distinctly apolitical compared to punks, but then I considered The Clean changing their name to The Great Unwashed to distance the taint of their own chart success. That's pretty punk.

Initially I treated comics and zines as distinct, but I revised that view after considering the number of comic strips that adorned punk-rock music zines, the cartoonists commissioned to draw zine covers, the collaging of pilfered images from *Oink!* comic and others, and the zine *Taranaki Underground*, whose creator, Brett Taylor, was just as prolific with his *Ritchie Rat* comics.

There were also zinesters whose first encounter with self-publishing came via comics. Printers also give voice in this eighties chapter, as at the start of the decade photocopying was not quite the ubiquitous zine technology that it later became.

The Clean, 1981. From left: Hamish Kilgour, Robert Scott and David Kilgour. *Carol Tippet*

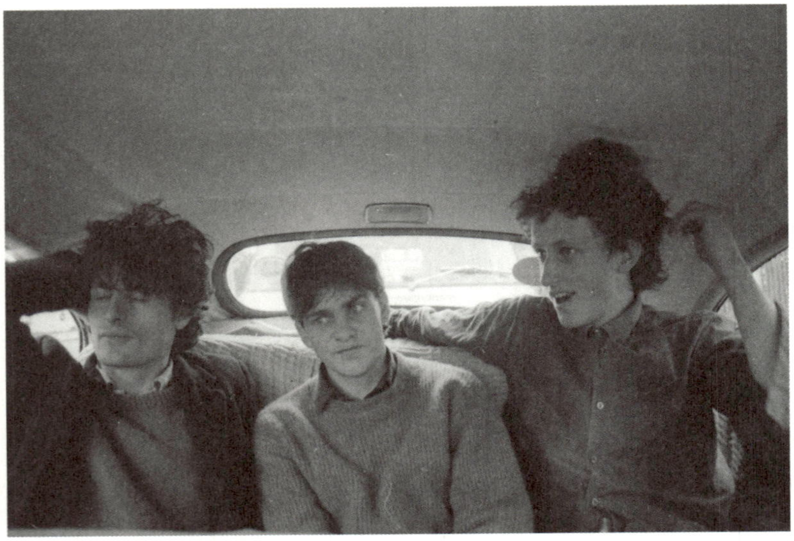

7

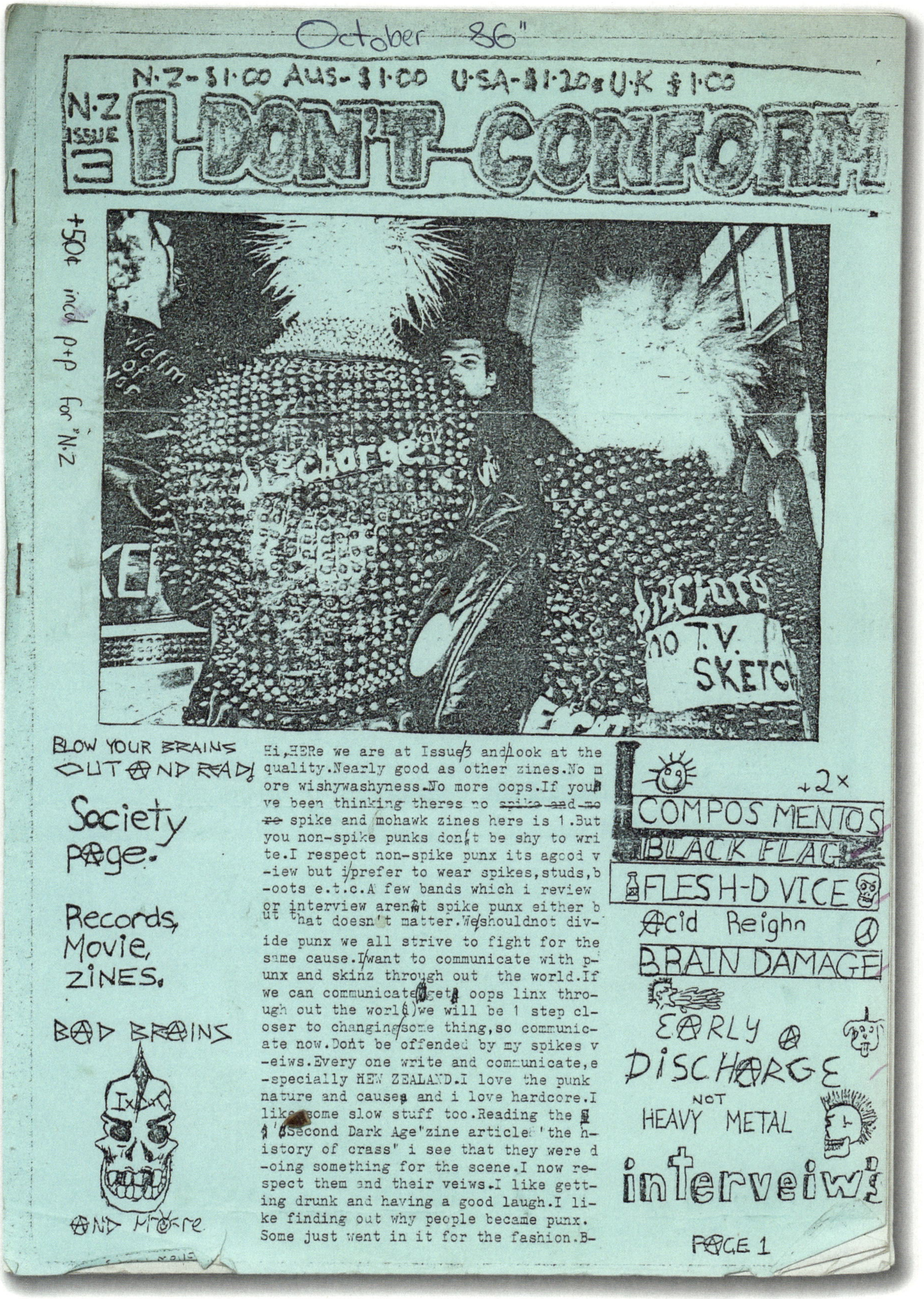
October 86"

N·Z-$1·00 AUS-$1·00 U·SA-$1·20 U·K $1·00

N·Z ISSUE 3

I-DON'T-CONFORM

+50¢ incl p+p for N·Z

BLOW YOUR BRAINS OUT AND READ!

Society page.

Records, Movie, ZINES.

BAD BRAINS

AND MORE

Hi,HERe we are at Issue 3 and look at the
quality.Nearly good as other zines.No m
ore wishywashyness.No more oops.If you'
ve been thinking theres no ~~spike and mo
re~~ spike and mohawk zines here is 1.But
you non-spike punks don't be shy to wri
te.I respect non-spike punx its agood v
-iew but i prefer to wear spikes,studs,b
-oots e.t.c.A few bands which i review
or interview aren't spike punx either b
ut that doesn't matter.We shouldnot div-
ide punx we all strive to fight for the
same cause.I want to communicate with p-
unx and skinz through out the world.If
we can communicate(get oops linx thro-
ugh out the world)we will be 1 step cl-
oser to changing some thing,so communic-
ate now.Don't be offended by my spikes v
-eiws.Every one write and communicate,e
-specially NEW ZEALAND.I love the punk
nature and causes and i love hardcore.I
like some slow stuff too.Reading the
'Second Dark Age"zine article 'the h-
istory of crass" i see that they were d
-oing something for the scene.I now re-
spect them and their veiws.I like gett-
ing drunk and having a good laugh.I li-
ke finding out why people became punx.
Some just went in it for the fashion.B-

+2×

COMPOS MENTOS

BLACK FLAG

FLESH-D VICE

Acid Reighn

BRAIN DAMAGE

EARLY DISCHARGE NOT HEAVY METAL

interveiw's

PAGE 1

7. *I Don't Conform*, created by Robert (no surname), A4, 1986. Te Whanganui-a-Tara Wellington.

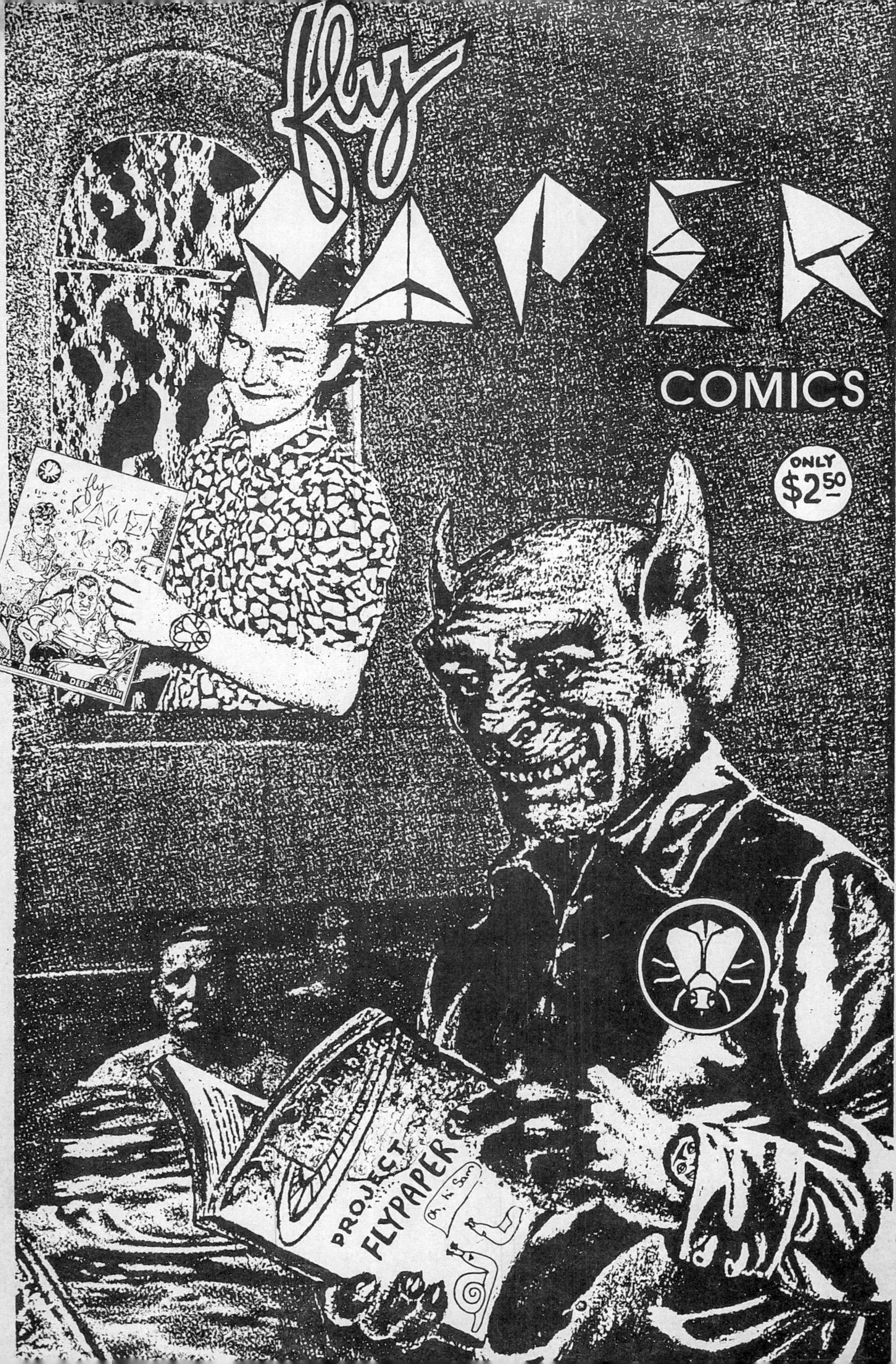
fly PAPER
COMICS
ONLY $2.50
COMICS FROM THE DEEP SOUTH
PROJECT FLYPAPER

Eighties Zines

Dave White I'm getting all inspired to start writing again, eh. All this zine shit. It's like, fuck, I've still got heaps of stories I want to tell.

Paul Luker I think I was quite comfortable going back to school, because in my last year I'd been a shocker. I was a second-year sixth. I repeated — yeah, I failed University Entrance. I was not focused at all. I can remember coming back for that second year from Nambassa,[1] rocking into school thinking 'Shit, enrolment's today!' Being dropped off by mates and going straight into school to meet the form teacher and being sent home for a shave, which I thought was a really good start. [Laughs.]

Dave White The first punk bands were at Nambassa. A band called The Plague played completely nude: a little guy painted blue, women painted yellow. So, there was definitely punk at Nambassa, and there was a feeling that anything went, like you could do anything you wanted, and it didn't matter. You could always make money by playing crappy old hippie music, but if you wanted to do something different . . . I don't know whether we realised that it was a revolution or if it just seemed like the music scene was evolving.

Paul Luker I think *Rip It Up*[2] was probably doing a fine job at the time, but anyone *really* into punk rock would've been left thinking 'More Warners ads', 'Hello Sailor again', 'Oh, for fuck's sake, Dragon — just let Australia keep them'. That was *Rip It Up*'s bread and butter; it would have made some think 'Is it worth reading all this just to get to a one-inch column on The Steroids?'

Ania Glowacz I'm just the black sheep of the family. When I was burning candles and incense and listening to records in my bedroom and my little brother's going 'Urgh, the incense is giving me a headache', and my dad thinks I'm devil-worshipping. It's like, 'Man, I've gotta get out of here.'

8. *Fly Paper*, edited and cover by Gregory Edwards, A4, 1984. Ōtepoti Dunedin.

Robert Scott There was the searching for music, trying to get it as quickly as possible, the same with the publications. There was a cassette label in America called ROIR, and they released Television, Suicide and The Raincoats very early on, start of the eighties. I remember writing away and sending an international money order and getting those. It was that kind of thing . . . the thrill of the chase, finding stuff. No computer obviously. Finding stuff that you liked: 'That leads to that.' The actual chase and purchase and getting that stuff was half the fun in some ways.

Then you've got it and someone else hasn't got it, so they're like, 'Right, let's go and see him, he's got such-and-such.' There was a lot of that; people would be constantly borrowing LPs and taping them. I ended up bootlegging Swell Maps. I got their album, no one else had it, no one really knew who Swell Maps were. I didn't know that it was illegal, I didn't know what bootlegging was, so I just made *My Greatest Hits with Swell Maps* on cassette and sold some of those.

Maybe I thought that they were so obscure that nothing would happen and no one would come after me. Just, 'Oh, what the heck, it's better to spread the word about this band.' Years later I ended up meeting the Swell Maps bass player, Jowe Head. He's a friend now. I forgot to tell him about my bootlegging, he would've laughed. I'll message him later today, now that I've been reminded. I'm sure I only sold about 10 copies.

Andrew Schmidt We definitely saw the Muldoon era as being very conservative, which it was. It wasn't just Muldoon; it had been a politically conservative era across the board. Labour were still quite a conservative grouping back then as far as social things went, though politically a little bit more radical. So we were reacting to what we viewed as fifties and conservative sixties values in the seventies and the early eighties, and things felt very constricted. When neoliberalism came along, the takeaway for us was just, 'Cool, now we can get more records from overseas.' [Laughs.]

Richard Davies The political dimensions of punk music and zines were no surprise to me. My best mate at high school — at Auckland Grammar — was really into Che Guevara. His mum was a university lecturer who was into James K. Baxter. We were learning all this stuff. Che Guevara was my idol for a long time — now I know that he did a lot of bad things too. We were also getting this political awareness through bands like The Clash and stuff at a very early age. I think I was 13 when I started learning about Che Guevara, about revolutions; that 20 guys could jump on a boat and take over Cuba.

John Farrow I had pretty strict parents, so I rebelled against them. That certainly set me up for punk, and so did hearing the Sex Pistols for the first time. This guy from England came and played me the song 'Bodies'. I think you either get it or you don't. You actually feel it in the gut.

I wasn't really dressing punk 'til I got to varsity. My parents and I didn't talk for quite a long time. I can remember one time I'd come home for the holidays, the washing got hung on the line and my mother walked along it going 'That's banned, that's banned, that's banned, that's banned', as in: If you want to stay here you've got to wear what we want you to wear. So I ended up not going home for the holidays and staying down here and not talking to them for about three or four years.

Tony Renouf I was at Fairfield High School right on the cusp of the disco-versus-punk thing. You couldn't walk down the concourse without getting shouldered. We had mufti, so you'd have a suit jacket and a couple of badges on and maybe a skinny tie, so you'd get pushed around a bit.

Simon Cottle White Bata Bullets and fluoro rattle cans, one fluoro yellow, one fluoro green, right? Well, then you step out and people are freaking out, and it's just 'Made them myself', make a statement. People are crossing the street because you've got fluoro sneakers on. Excellent.

Matthew Campbell Downes Oh, it was terrible. Absolutely. If you've read Shayne Carter's book, he describes a hall gig where the car boys — or bodgies as you called them — were basically lined up at the door to give people the bash as they came out of the gig. That was what it was like. There was a very rugby-head, bodgie kind of crowd whose passion in life was beating the shit out of anybody who appeared to be slightly different. The most common catch cry was 'Queer cunt . . . Oh, you fucking queer cunt.' You'd hear that shouted at you from a car as you walked down the street. If you were lucky, that's all they would do. If you were unlucky, they'd just fucking stop the car in the middle of the road and jump out and chase you. It was like that.

Ross Gardiner I remember the 1981 Springbok tour, that's the first time I remember really feeling any kind of political engagement for a cause of some kind. I mean it was vaguely understood what apartheid was about, that it was a bad thing, and my mother in particular hated Robert Muldoon with a passion, so there was a little bit of political sentiment there, and then the anti-nuclear issue started coming through. When I first started listening to punk I was 12, and the politics of it weren't so obvious to me. Like, Sex Pistols, sure; they had songs like 'God Save the Queen' or whatever, but mostly I was just into the music because it was something weird and new. But then I heard more bands and I began realising they weren't just singing songs about driving round in cars or, y'know, cheesy love songs. The politics of it started to come through a bit. Once I came across zines, well, you could put a lot more ideas in a zine than you could on a record . . . Certainly, zines helped develop my political ideas.

Tracey Wedge There was certainly a sense of the nuclear threat and the Cold War in the material that we were listening to. The British anarcho-punk scene was quite strong on that. Certainly, the anti-nuclear stance was quite important to me — going to the rallies and wearing my 'France Out of the Pacific' t-shirt when I visited France in '89.

Richard Davies 1981, the Springboks want to play the All Blacks. My best mate — Steven Belson — his mum was a university lecturer teaching us about Che Guevara and all this stuff. It was unreal. She was a marshal for the protestors, and we had to go with her. It was a year before the Springboks arrived. We were going on practice marches and the police were there, and we were seeing the police attacking people! It was ruthless. I went to all these practices, for a whole year I was marching. That really politicised me. I was thinking, 'I'm Che Guevara. Revolution. Change the world.'

Tracey Wedge I sent my parents to the anarchist bookshop in Redfern, Sydney, to buy records for us to review. So they obviously accepted what I was doing, they were more supportive than judgmental.

Lyn Spencer Punk introduced me to a lot of ideas that I otherwise wouldn't have known about. I got into punk after working on sheep farms and mustering. I arrived home having decided I didn't like killing sheep — the farm always used to get me to kill sheep to feed the dogs — I hated it. I got home and my sister had got into punk, and she'd gone vegetarian, and I go 'Oh! Vegetarian? I didn't know that was a thing. Oh, yes, I want to go vegetarian.' I didn't like what I was doing on the farm.

David Merritt As soon as I heard Mark E. Smith, that was it. I thought, 'Fuck, this is amazing. It's not even good but I like it.' I don't like polished music. I don't like music that's clearly been through the hands of 16 professional engineers to get to that sparkly FM sound.

Robert Scott We'd get the *NME*[3] and *Melody Maker*[4] three months after they'd come out, coming over on the boat from England, that would be us keeping up with the music scene. There wasn't an equivalent American magazine, maybe *Creem*,[5] but I don't think the American publications came over as much, it was definitely the English ones. Then there was Barry Jenkins on ZM. He would play a lot of new music. He'd have excerpts from the John Peel show, and he'd got the English records somehow and played a lot of new stuff that shaped a lot of people's musical tastes, whether it was Buzzcocks or Wire, stuff like that or slightly more left-of-field stuff like Vic Godard and John Cooper Clarke.

Andrew Schmidt The journey began back in London on the boat, and then we got it. The three-month thing is something that always comes up and it interests me in a way, as a historian. I don't think the time lag was, in a historical sense, that long, but because it's popular culture it seemed quite long back then. Nobody ever stopped reacting to it just because three months had passed. We were still going to do something once we got that information.

David Merritt God, CAN were a big thing for me. I loved CAN when I discovered them. It's funny, eh, we would have to listen to Barry Jenkins on the one radio station — this is pre-student radio — or Radio Hauraki, just to try and get interesting music from overseas, otherwise it was just bullshit, bullshit, bullshit, y'know, crooners and middle-of-the-road America, 'A Horse with No Name'. If I fucking hear that song again! 'Welcome to the Hotel California', ad nauseam.

Paul Luker I'd walk through the railway station to catch the bus to my Comprint job. The railway station had the best newsagent in town. It had the airfreighted *NME* and *Melody Maker*. If I had the money I'd buy the airfreighted issues. I'd rather not eat because, honestly, there were some amazing writers in there. It was fucking weekly, what luxury. 'Oh, Joy Division, well, if you think that's good . . .' I would order the records I was reading about. It was easy to send to the UK for them: Swell Maps, Joy Division.

9. *Strips #16*, *The Rock Issue*, guest editor Chris Knox, 165 × 243mm, 1981. Tāmaki Makaurau Auckland.

Andrew Schmidt It was really a combination of growing up with magazines like the *NME*, which we would get in Paeroa every week, and a lot of people had that experience — it would go all around the country. There were four music magazines coming in from Great Britain. That's a hell of a lot of information and that's a hell of a lot of influence. *Sounds*,[6] *Melody Maker, NME* and *Record Mirror*,[7] which was a bit more mainstream, but it was the one that Peter Jefferies and Graeme Jefferies[8] read in Stratford. *Record Mirror* had a lot more disco and stuff, which I would love now but back then I probably would've preferred the *NME*.

Tony Renouf Love onomatopoeia, love *MAD* magazine. Don Martin, Sergio Aragonés are my big loves. It was all really cool, and I kind of liked *Spy vs Spy*, but that got a bit same-y. Don Martin and Sergio Aragonés, what those guys could say with one picture, or one silly word was just fabulous.

Matthew Campbell Downes The other thing to mention is of course *Strips*, which was Joe Wylie and all that lot. That would've been Lorenzo van der Lingen's guiding light. I believe *Strips* started in '77. We were sort of like '79 to '81. *Strips* was the shining light. We were all like: 'Wow, these comics are as good as *Heavy Metal* magazine, and they're made here!?' It showed that it was possible. We used to pore over *Strips*. There probably wasn't a drawing session where *Strips* comics weren't on the table next to us and if you look at Mark Morte's comics and mine, and maybe to a lesser extent, Lorenzo's, you'll see direct influences from the likes of Joe Wylie. He was our clear favourite. To us Joe was up here [holds hand aloft] and everybody else was a big chunk below, still quite good, but Joe was up here.

No, you wouldn't find *Strips* in the Four Square, you'd go to Scorpio Books. They also had *Heavy Metal* magazine, which was probably the only really alternative comic you could get in New Zealand. The other big influence of course was *MAD* magazine. We were big fans of *MAD*, and being big fans of *MAD* we hated *Cracked* and all the other *MAD* copyists. But Sergio Aragonés and Al Jaffee, we loved all that stuff. You *could* get *MAD* at the local book shop. That *was* available.

9

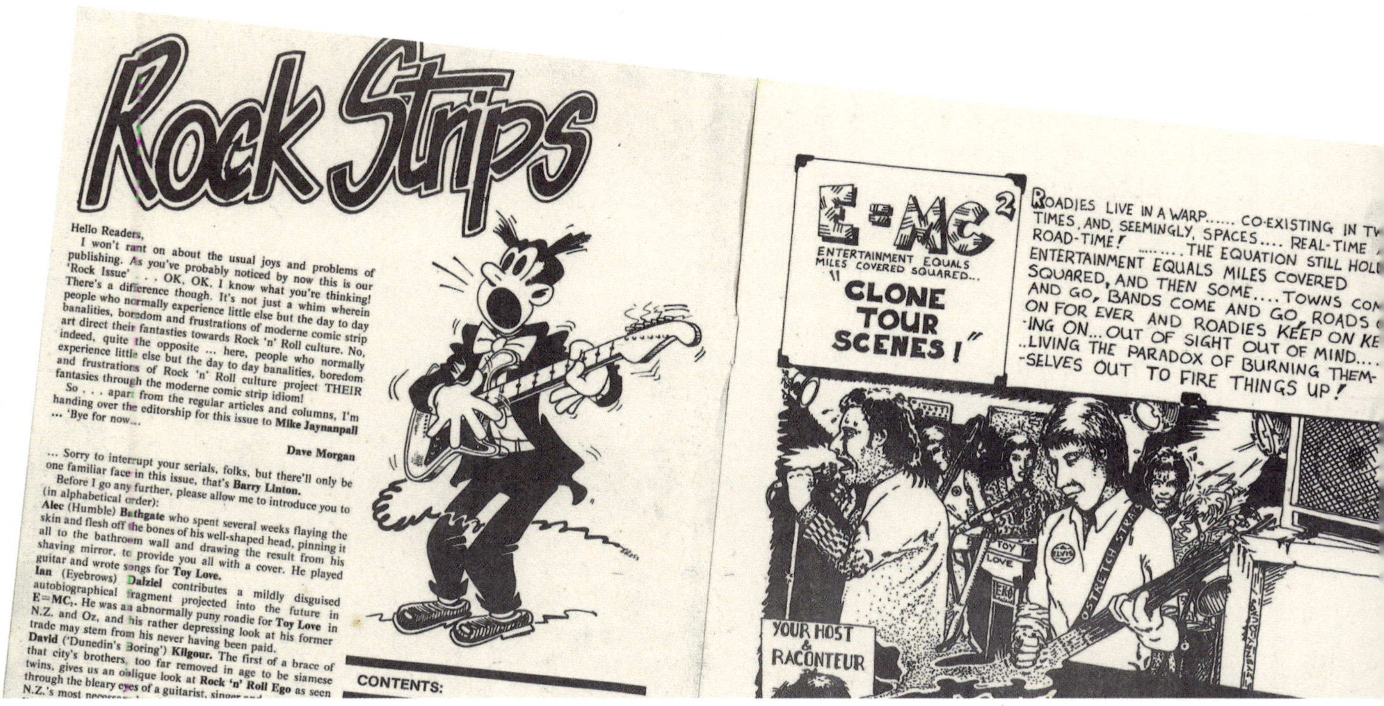

Tony Renouf When I was at school I was really interested in art. I was copying other people's comics and reading comics and cartoons voraciously, anything I could get my hands on. Mum had introduced us to second-hand bookshops, because that's where she got her Mills & Boon. We'd go along with her, and the second-hand shops let you swap comics. I collected so many different comics as a kid. My brother started on *Bobo Bunny*, I started on *Beano* and when my brother — who hates to be reminded about his *Bobo Bunny* phase — graduated to *Beano* I moved onto *Cor!!* Then from there I went to *Commando* comics, *War Picture Library*, *Battle Picture Weekly*, *Action*, which later became *Battle Action* . . . My brother by this time had started buying *2000 AD*. I also discovered *Cracked* magazine and *MAD* magazine, so, y'know, every genre.

Robert Scott I don't think I'd seen any equivalent fanzines or magazines. I mean, I got the *NME* and *Melody Maker* and stuff, but that was straight music journalism. I didn't really collect comics as such. Like some people are really into *The Fabulous Furry Freak Brothers* or whatever, but I never got into that stuff. I'd glance at them and go, 'Oh, I quite like the look of that', but I never obsessed about collecting those comics at all. It was more about having fun doing it myself as a project. I just taught myself how to draw. I was an obsessive drawer; I'd draw for two hours before going to school each day, and then for another three hours when I got home. We didn't have television at home, so it was either playing outside, making music with Electric Blood or drawing. At the time I thought not having a telly was the worst thing in the world. Everyone else had a telly, but we didn't. Now I think it's great that I had to find other things to do. At the time I felt like I was deprived, though we would go up to friends' houses and watch telly. On a Sunday night we'd go to a friend's place and watch Jacques Cousteau. That was pretty exciting. Also, *Wacky Races*, cartoons and stuff.

Paul Luker If it wasn't by a publisher it was 'vanity published'. It didn't matter who might've written it. I'd bought a little Gestetner. I printed my poetry books in my room. I'd seen other people make poetry books, but they'd got a printer to do it. I didn't have the money and I thought, 'I'm in the printing trade, I can cobble this together.' I'm sure I was influenced by the things I was reading in the *NME* about the independence that was developing over in the UK for doing your own thing. It didn't bother me that it was vanity published, I thought that distinction was just stupid.

But things must've been changing, because John Pule and I got an Arts Council grant to tour, and all we had to show them were the poetry books I'd printed, one for John and one for me.

David Merritt We had Red Mole. We had Blerta. They were role models in a funny way, because they were operating outside the established art and culture industry.

Paul Luker I started to find music more interesting because poetry was a very small world. The art world was bigger but it was equally as closed, particularly as it leaned towards the academic. The writers could be quite academic as well, and you really had to be in boots-and-all and play it socially, and it just wasn't very comfortable.

10. *Strips #16*, *The Rock Issue*, cover by Alec Bathgate, guest editor Chris Knox, 165 × 243mm, 1981. Tāmaki Makaurau Auckland.

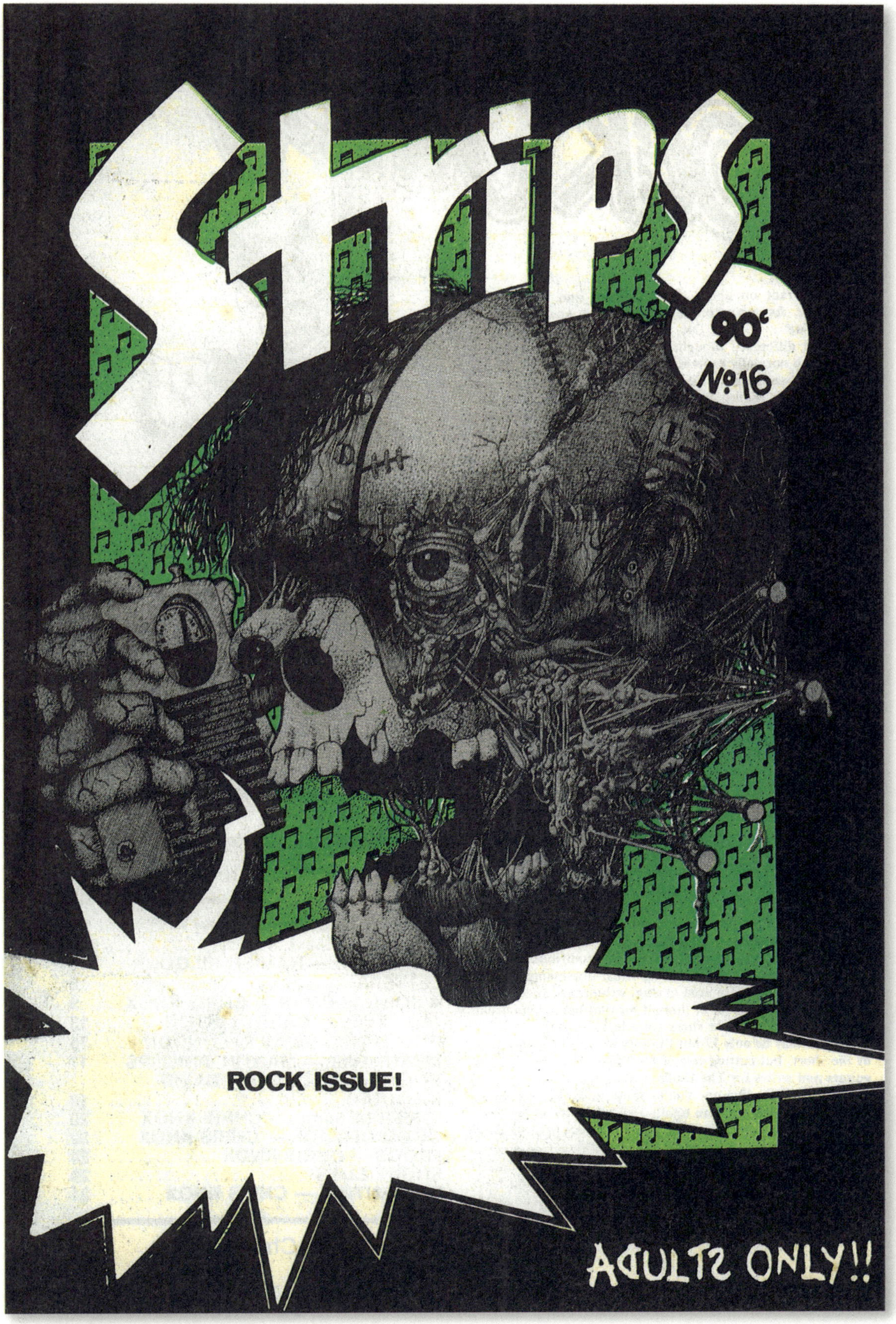
Strips
90c
No16
ROCK ISSUE!
ADULTS ONLY!!

Richard Langston The fanzines at Rough Trade [store in London] were a real mixture. There was one called *Snipe*, I remember that, then there was also *Bucketfull of Brains*, now that was kinda what we modelled *Garage* on, loosely. It was a lot fancier than we ever had intentions of being . . . their lines were very straight. But what you would see at Rough Trade was reasonably crude, stapled together, and you thought 'I could do that. Y'know, if I lower my standards, I could do that.' I was used to having stuff published in magazines or newspapers, very conventional journalism.

Paul Luker I don't know how much it registered at the time, but there were definitely some ads for fanzines in the *NME*. And there would've been something written about fanzines and it was a perfect name for this medium. I must've read about *Sniffin' Glue*. I can't remember, but I know that the first time I saw a *Sniffin' Glue* t-shirt — when I finally got to the UK — I thought 'I'm fucking having that'. It's just in your fabric. I can remember thinking with the music of The Smith Brothers and The Criminals . . . 'C'mon, Auckland City, let's do something ourselves.' I was a fan and there were these things in the UK called fanzines, 'Well, fuck, let's do one.'

David Merritt By the late eighties I'd come to think of chapbooks as zines. I was exposed to a thing called *Factsheet Five*, which was a compendium of all of the indie zine publishing around the world. That's when I first read the word 'zine'; I thought, here's a term I didn't know. That was about '83 or '84.

Richard Davies From age 14 I didn't go to school. I was living with 21 to 25-year-old skins that wanted me in this band called Red Cross. They weren't real skins, they were just short-haired, boot-boy rock 'n' rollers. Real good guys, man. They helped me learn about zines and stuff. I'm not sure if I did one up in Auckland; I know Brett Taylor did. He was already making zines before he moved to Taranaki.

Tracey Wedge I've still got all of my Crass albums and the compilation albums. They came with booklets about politics and world peace. Punk definitely informed my politics.

Dave Hegan Crass were almost mythical to me in the eighties because their records were so hard to get, and I'd see their name spray-painted around the place and it had this mythical presence. You knew they were super political, but you could never get their records. When I did eventually track them down it was like gold. You read their song lyrics, you read every single word that came with their releases, they included essays and stuff. Because it was so hard to get that stuff, there was more value to it when you did get it. Whereas now everything's so easy to get. Back then you treasured it. You had your Crass records, I used to carry them around with me. One time this skinhead guy threatened to throw my Crass records in the fire, so I grabbed a brick and I threatened to brick him in the head, then we were like 'Let's be mates.'

Why did he want to burn my Crass records? He was just being a dick. Skinheads didn't like Crass. Now if you want a Crass record you just go online, you buy it, but back then you'd hunt through record shops or find someone who had it. The first Crass I got was someone taping it for me, and then that cassette became like treasure. I had this Crass *Christ — The Album* on tape, and it was like, 'Wow, I've finally got Crass.' It took years to get it.

I was reading that in my journals from the time. I'd go down to the record store and I'd order the latest Conflict album or something. Back then we had such a different concept of time, like it was quite alright to wait months for it to turn up, *if* it turned up. Now everyone wants everything straight away. I used to go up to Auckland to Real Groovy, because Real Groovy was like a goldmine in the eighties for punk records. It was the first place we'd go when we got into town.

Ross Gardiner The first zine I ever came across was *One World*. Some friends from high school saw it promoted on *Radio with Pictures* one Sunday night, just like, 'Here's a punk magazine that costs $1 from record shops.' We were like 'Holy shit!' So we all jumped on the bus into town the following Saturday and bought copies. It was quite exciting. I mean, I'd come across a UK magazine — not really a fanzine — called *Punk Lives*. I think the first one was 1982 or something, but it was a glossy magazine, not a fanzine. So when we saw *One World*, a local punk zine, we were just like 'Wow! It's a magazine made by people, with no adverts', or its adverts were cheap or free or whatever. How the hell do these things make a living? It was a new concept to us; just making a magazine as a passion project, or for a cause. *One World* on *Radio with Pictures* sparked a whole lot of people around the country, who thought, 'Wow, we can do this too. We can interview friends' bands or whatever . . . and photocopy it and sell it for a dollar or two.'

Simon Cottle I was involved with the New Zealand Anti-Vivisection Society, and they got all sorts of stuff from all over the world, newsletters and stuff. I would've tapped into that and just gone, 'Oh, so magazines don't have to be professionally printed and be about making money.'

What's the difference between a newsletter and a fanzine? That's a tricky question but I think of fanzines as a lot more celebratory, it's for the love of the medium, whereas a newsletter can often be quite practical. For all the political statements and cop cars on fire in those zines they were still joyous, even lots of the hard political content was still kind of joyous in its countercultural rebellion: 'Hey, there are alternative narratives out there.' The other big distinction would be the concept of a movement. When you're thinking pre-internet, it's like you are actually creating a web, like you can trace something via something else, y'know? You get a zine or a record because you read about it in something else that directed you to something else that directed you to something else. You've got to place yourself back in the eighties when your access to those alternatives wasn't a Google search away. It was more like, 'Hey, wake up, there are different narratives out there!'

Andrew Schmidt Masterton, Whangārei, Napier . . . I mean, it's just like you have a newsletter for every society or organisation in New Zealand. Fanzines were effectively the newsletter for punk communities, but because we understood punk as not just local, that we were part of this wider community, they were also a conduit and a connective to all the other scenes in New Zealand. Most of those towns had punk bands. Morrinsville did. Paeroa — where I was from — produced at least half a dozen punk-related bands.

Simon Cottle Now you start getting down to the whole essence of fanzines, right? It's your local band, your mates from high school or whatever. Are they getting any publicity or coverage? No, well I can, DIY.

David Merritt I left the Auckland music scene specifically because I didn't like how established and traditional it was at the time. It was ruled by about four large booking agencies, and all they wanted to do was book Dave Dobbyn and Coup D'État through the big pub circuit, that ilk . . . The Pink Flamingos . . . That was the established music industry that, at the time, punk rock was banging its head against.

Andrew Stephens I thought punk was great. I was really impressed with the whole thing from go to whoa. Punks started a lot of good magazines, they opened shops, they formed bands and they're all self-starters. They didn't come through the industry, they did it themselves and that's what I liked about it.

John Farrow I don't remember the first zines I ever saw, but I knew what they were and that they were called zines. The most significant ones were the American ones like *Maximum Rocknroll* and *Flipside*. In New Zealand, *Rip It Up* was sort of running alongside contemporaneously with zines, so you would see that as well.

11

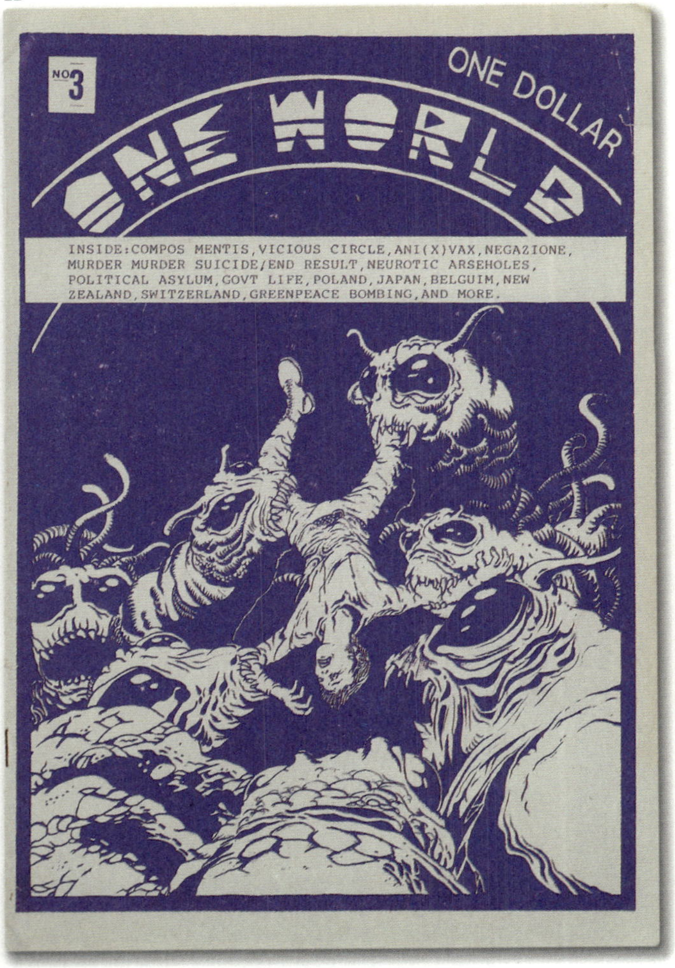

12

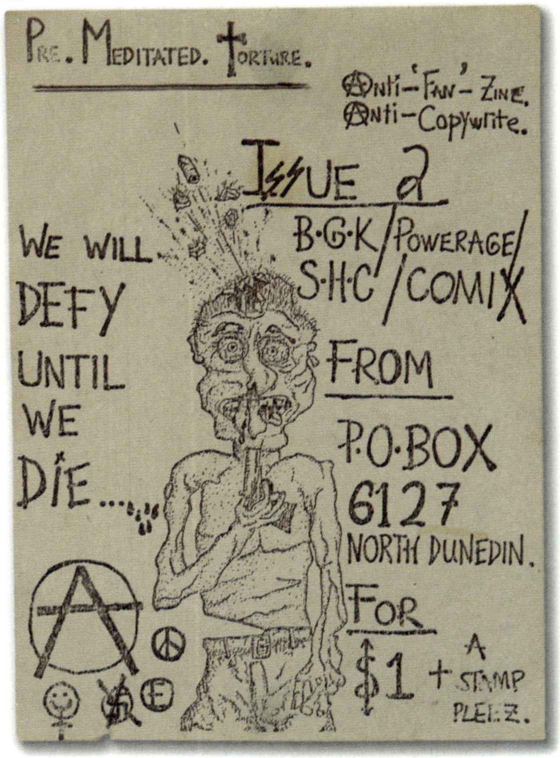

11. *One World* #3, cover by Mark Daniel, edited by Neil Cartwright, 230 × 223mm, mid-1980s. Tāmaki Makaurau Auckland.

12. Flyer for *PMT* #2, Malcolm Campbell, 1986. Ōtepoti Dunedin.

13

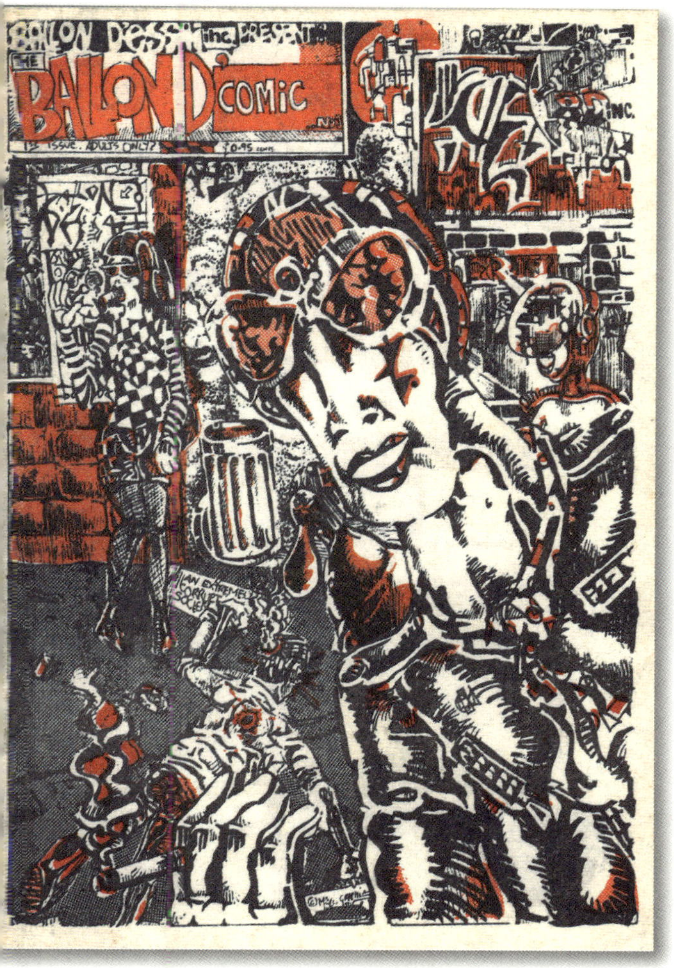

14

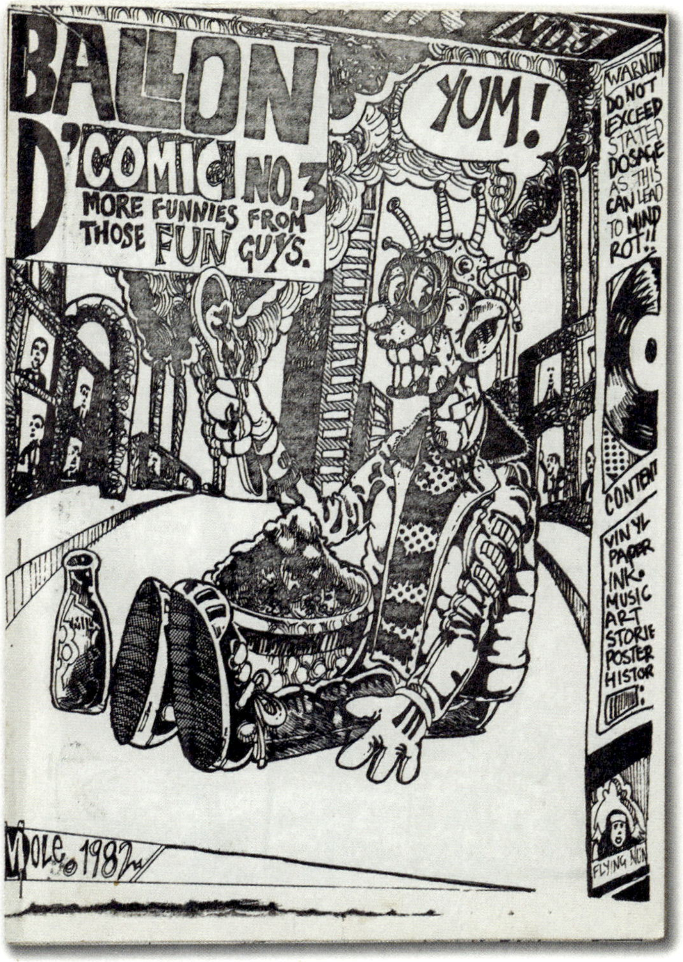

Matthew Campbell Downes To understand *Ballon D'Comic*, you have to go back to Lorenzo van der Lingen's *Visions*. We were all very influenced by *Visions*. Lorenzo was already making comics before Ballon D'Essai. He was at Christchurch Boys' High, and he was a year older than most of the band, and two years older than me. Lorenzo is important because he really blazed the trail, he was the one who was right there at Boys' High making a comics publication all by himself. *That* was amazing. We were literally incredulous. I guess what was important about it is that it made us all realise 'Oh, that's a thing you can do'. He was there, literally right in front of us at lunchtime, going 'Do you want to buy my comic?' And we'd buy it and go 'Wow, this is fucking great.' It wasn't even photocopied, it was printed. That was one of the major incentives: here's a guy making comics right at our school, they're really good, we love comics, we could do that.

13. *Ballon D'Comic* #1, edited by Mark Rastrick, A4, 1981. Ōtautahi Christchurch.

14. *Ballon D'Comic* #3, edited by Mark Rastrick, A4, 1984. Ōtautahi Christchurch.

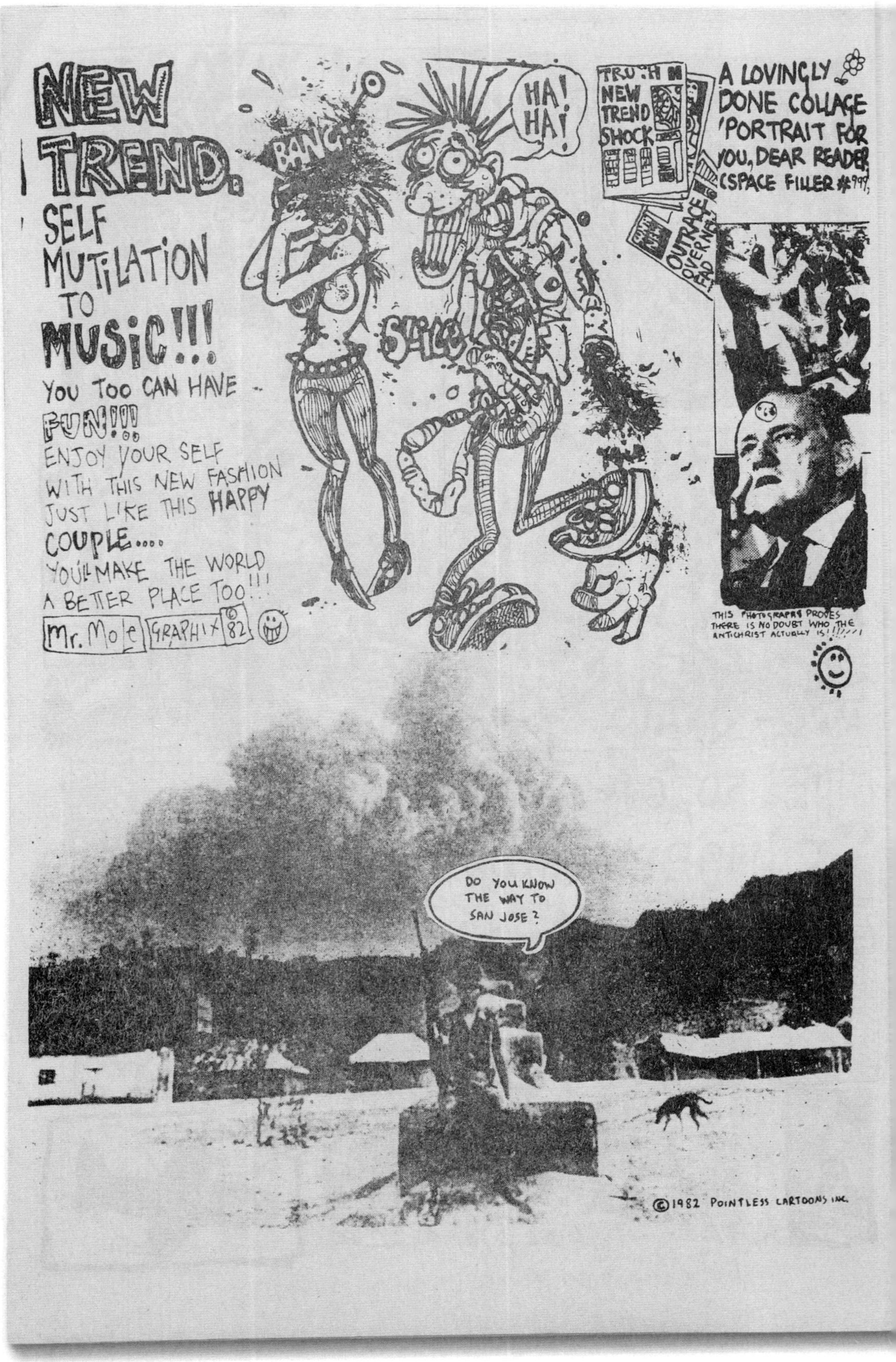
NEW TREND.
SELF MUTILATION TO MUSIC!!!
YOU TOO CAN HAVE FUN!!!
ENJOY YOUR SELF WITH THIS NEW FASHION JUST LIKE THIS HAPPY COUPLE....
YOU'LL MAKE THE WORLD A BETTER PLACE TOO!!!
Mr. Mole GRAPHIX © 82
BANG
HA! HA!
TRUTH
NEW TREND SHOCK
OUTRAGE
A LOVINGLY DONE COLLAGE 'PORTRAIT FOR YOU, DEAR READER (SPACE FILLER #999)
THIS PHOTOGRAPH PROVES THERE IS NO DOUBT WHO THE ANTICHRIST ACTUALLY IS!!!
DO YOU KNOW THE WAY TO SAN JOSE?
©1982 POINTLESS CARTOONS INC.

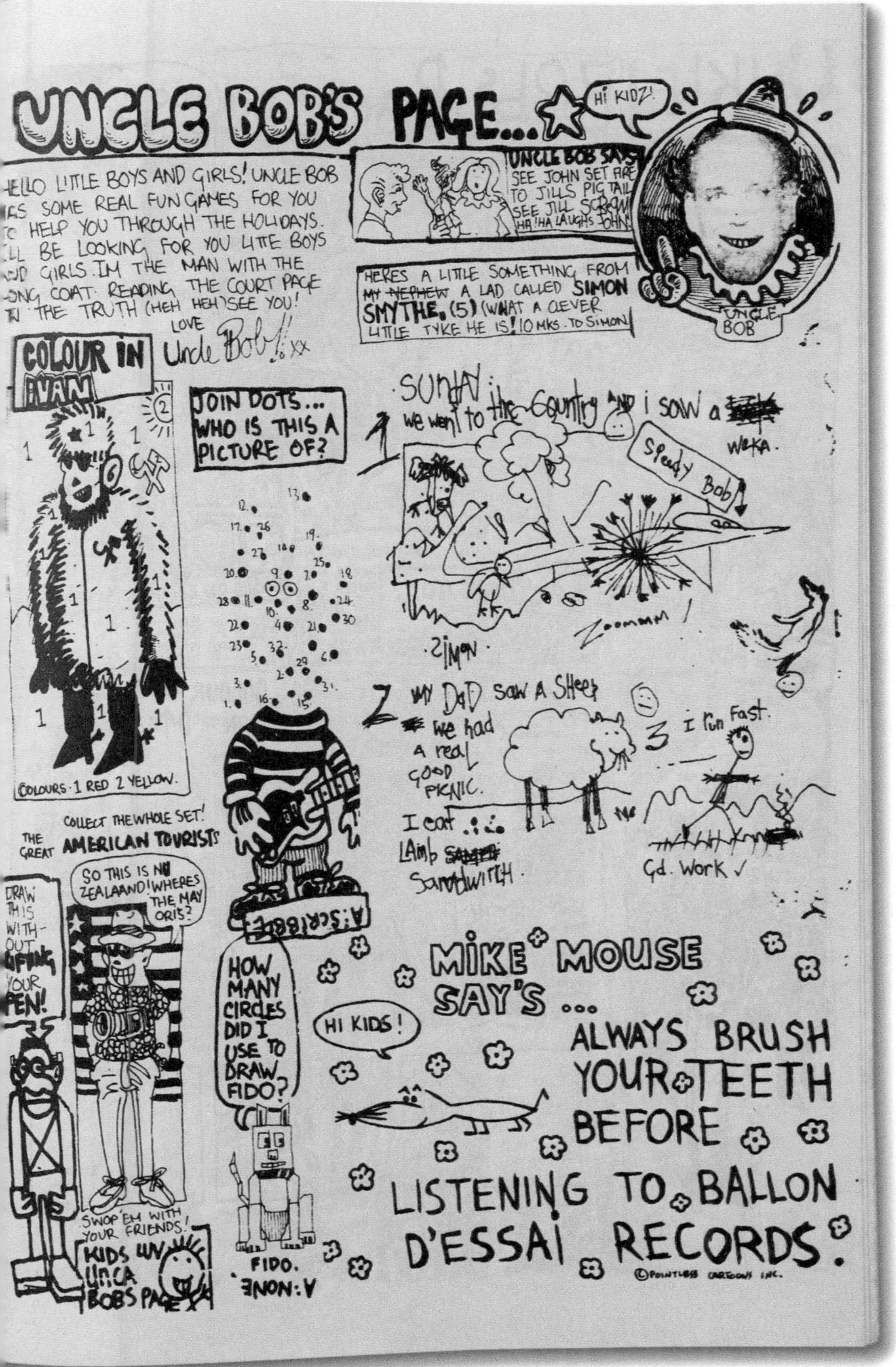

15. *Ballon D'Comic* #3, edited by Mark Rastrick, A4, 1984. Ōtautahi Christchurch.

John Farrow The popularity of comics among the punks surprised me because I hadn't grown up with comics. A lot of the punks were fans of different comics, especially *Judge Dredd*, but not me so much.

Richard Langston I was a city council reporter for the *Otago Daily Times*, and Jesus, it wasn't gripping and exciting. I mean local politics has its moments, but I wasn't enthusiastic about it the way I was about music. So that's another reason *Garage* started.

Robert Scott It's all about the 'do it yourself' ethos really. Record yourself on cassette if that's all you've got access to, like those early Electric Blood recordings were. And in terms of fanzines, that's as basic as you get: photocopying images out of magazines or books, writing freehand, sticking it together.

Ross Gardiner Obsessive science fiction fans and nerds or whatever . . . Over in the UK, football zines are a thing too, made by obsessive football fans. So it's an idea that came from people who are quite obsessive or enthusiastic about a thing. Football zines by people who support crappy clubs that go nowhere.

John Farrow The cover of that first *PMT* says 'anti-fanzine' on the front. They weren't called 'zines' back then, they were called 'fanzines'. I don't know where the word came from. I guess they were made by fans, but we were anti-fanzine because no punk-rocker should idolise any other punk-rocker. So while you supported other bands, you weren't a 'fan' in the sense of a 'Swiftie' or something like that.

Robert Scott I was stuck in Christchurch with too much time on my hands. I always draw and I always write. I didn't have a starting point as such, I just started compiling this thing, and then that dictated the direction of the subsequent ones. Looking back at *Every Secret Thing*, it's not a fanzine, it's not a comic, it's pretty free-form. I definitely wasn't trying to copy or ape anything, that's for sure.

Matthew Campbell Downes I might have The Fall's *Live at the Witch Trials*. Mark might have their album *Totale's Turn*. It's not like I could just go and buy *Totale's Turn* — there were only five imported, and he bought one of them and I didn't. So there was a big trade in cassette recordings of each other's stuff. But there was limited access to the material that we were inspired by, so it felt like you kind of had to make stuff yourself. If I couldn't get a copy of *Strips* #3 when it came out it was like 'Well, I'll draw my own comic.' I think that was part of it.

Richard Langston I thought, 'I wanna write about these bands in a way that's not necessarily conventional journalism.' I mean, it just started off as a very amateur enthusiasm, but because the music was so good and it had an audience . . . So, for issue one, I did 50 xeroxed copies.

Paul Luker In the first year or so in Auckland I did spend most of my social time at the Globe [pub] where they had poetry readings, and in between the poets we'd hang out. I met John Pule through the Globe, and then we got a grant and we toured the country, so we gave it a good crack, but honestly, how could you resist the music? So I thought that writing about the music would be the best thing.

16. *Positive Approach* #2 spread and cover, by various authors including Ross Gardiner, A5, mid-1980s. Tāmaki Makaurau Auckland.

Matthew Campbell Downes The first *Ballon D'Comic* came out as a teaser for the first Ballon D'Essai record, and the second comic was *in* the sleeve of the first record. I only recently figured that out. It wasn't: 'We're a band, let's make a comic.' It was: 'We make comics *and* we're in a band, so let's put a comic in the record.' The comics came first in a way.

Ross Gardiner When I was at high school I made a zine called *Positive Approach* with some guys I was in a band with. It lasted for, I think, four issues. I was involved with at least two of them, possibly three. The drummer of our band came up with the name because he'd got into the posi-hardcore thing: Minor Threat and 7Seconds and all that wayward stuff. There was a punk band in the States called Negative Approach. He thought 'That sounds bad, they should be called Positive Approach', and that became the name of the zine. It was kind of a bit corny, but I couldn't be bothered arguing against it, so we went with that.

Ania Glowacz I wasn't in a band because I had no one to be in a band with, and if I was in a band I would've wanted it to be with chicks. I wasn't actually sure what part I would play in the music scene, I just knew I wanted to do something. That's probably why I made a fanzine instead of not doing anything.

Ross Gardiner There weren't many people at my school who were particularly interested in *Positive Approach*, we probably only ever made 50 . . . maybe 100 copies. **Lyn Spencer** I think there were only about five punks at his school. [Laughs.]

16

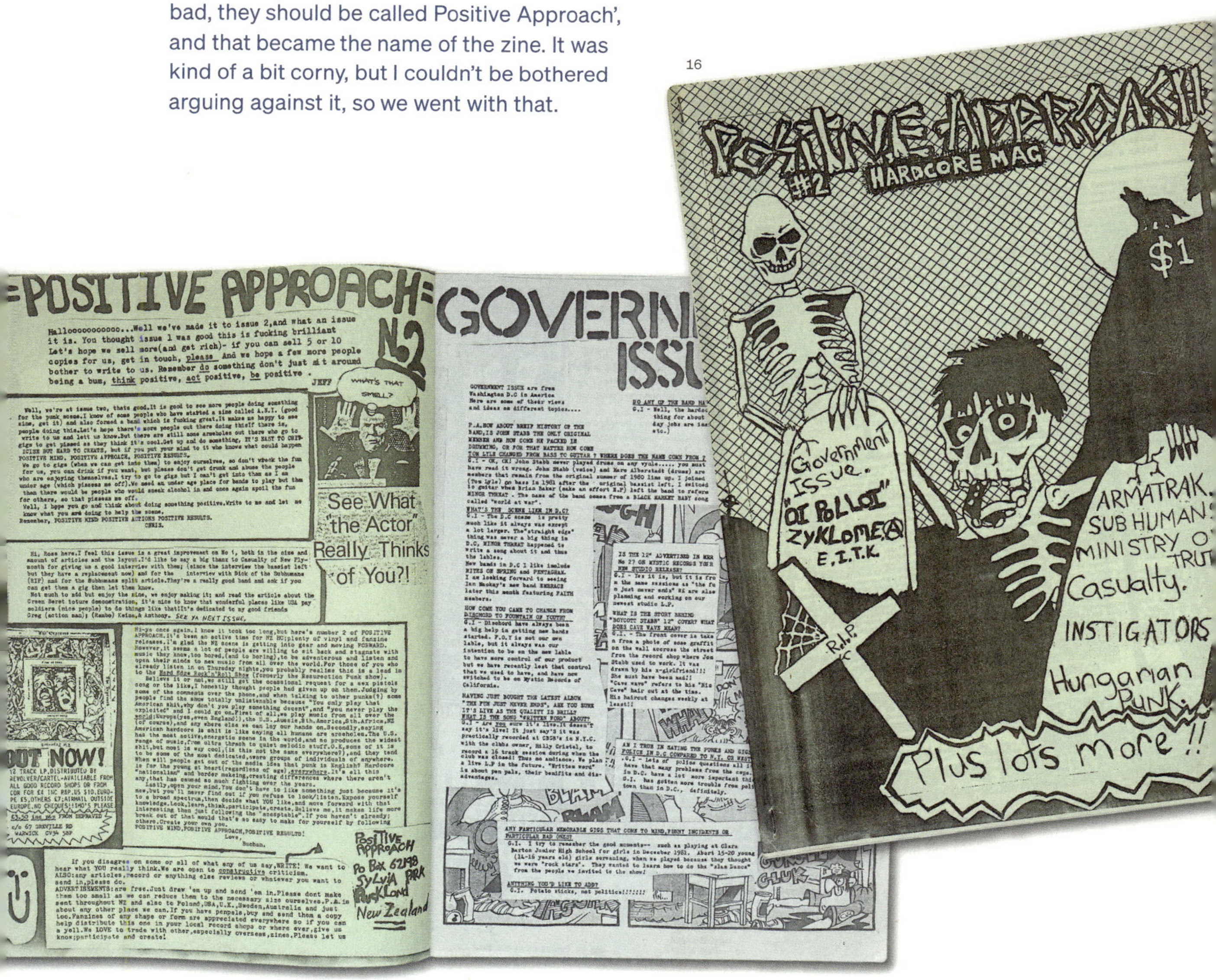

Simon Cottle I was always good at technical drawing at college, and that really appealed to me because I couldn't paint, I couldn't sketch, I couldn't sing, I couldn't play a musical instrument . . . So that was my real artistic outlet. With fanzine design there was lots of technical drawing, lots of angles, lots of measuring, lots of mechanical dividers to work out spacing, things like that. And then the idea of presenting something that didn't look like *The Listener*; if you've got quite radical content, you need quite a radical presentation to match it, coupled with the whole DIY punk ethic . . . So you've got muso friends practising in bedrooms, pressing their own records, gluing together the covers, etc. You're making your own clothes, you've got mates screen-printing patches for you. These days everything's available, but back then you had to be in the know.

> 'Hey, Bryce, man, where did you get that patch on your arm?!'
>
> 'That's one of Ross's' – that kind of thing.

Ania Glowacz There were two reasons for me starting *Submission*. One was obviously the punk-zine scene, but it was also about Flesh D-Vice. I think I had something about Flesh D-Vice in every issue. I went to every single gig at the Clarendon Tavern, and even though they used to take hours to finally get on stage, it was worth it. There was one great gig where there were pigs' heads hanging above the stage dripping blood. That was Flesh D-Vice, they were horror-punk or whatever you want to call it.

17

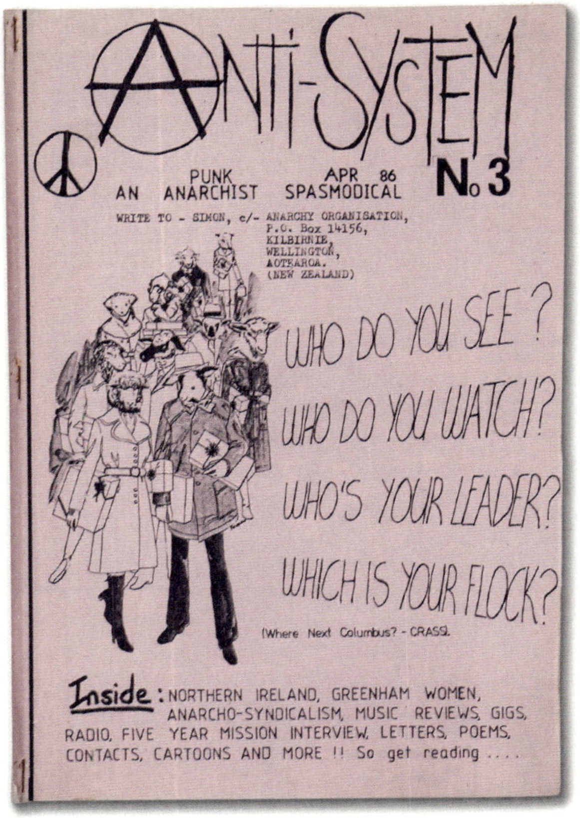

18

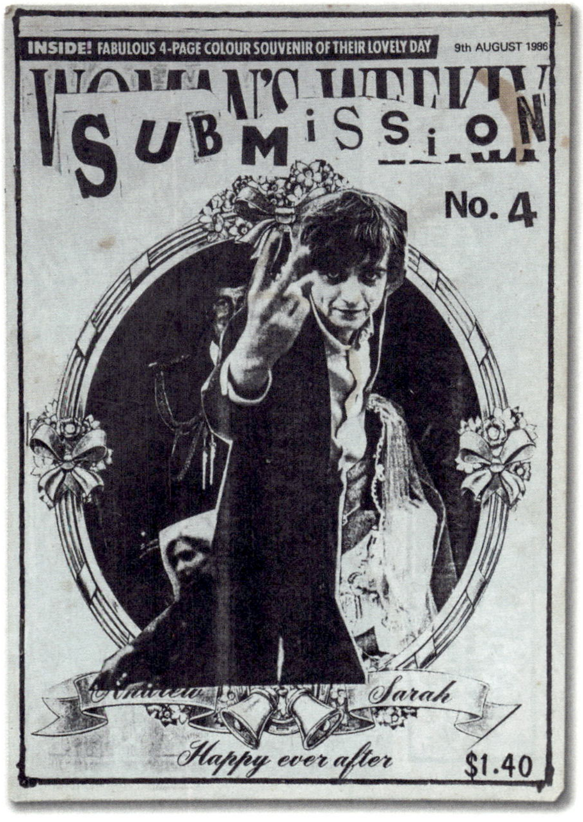

17. *Anti-System #11* cover and spread, edited by Simon Cottle, A4, 1988. Te Whanganui-a-Tara Wellington.
18. *Submission #4* cover and spread, Ania Glowacz, A4, 1986. Te Whanganui-a-Tara Wellington.

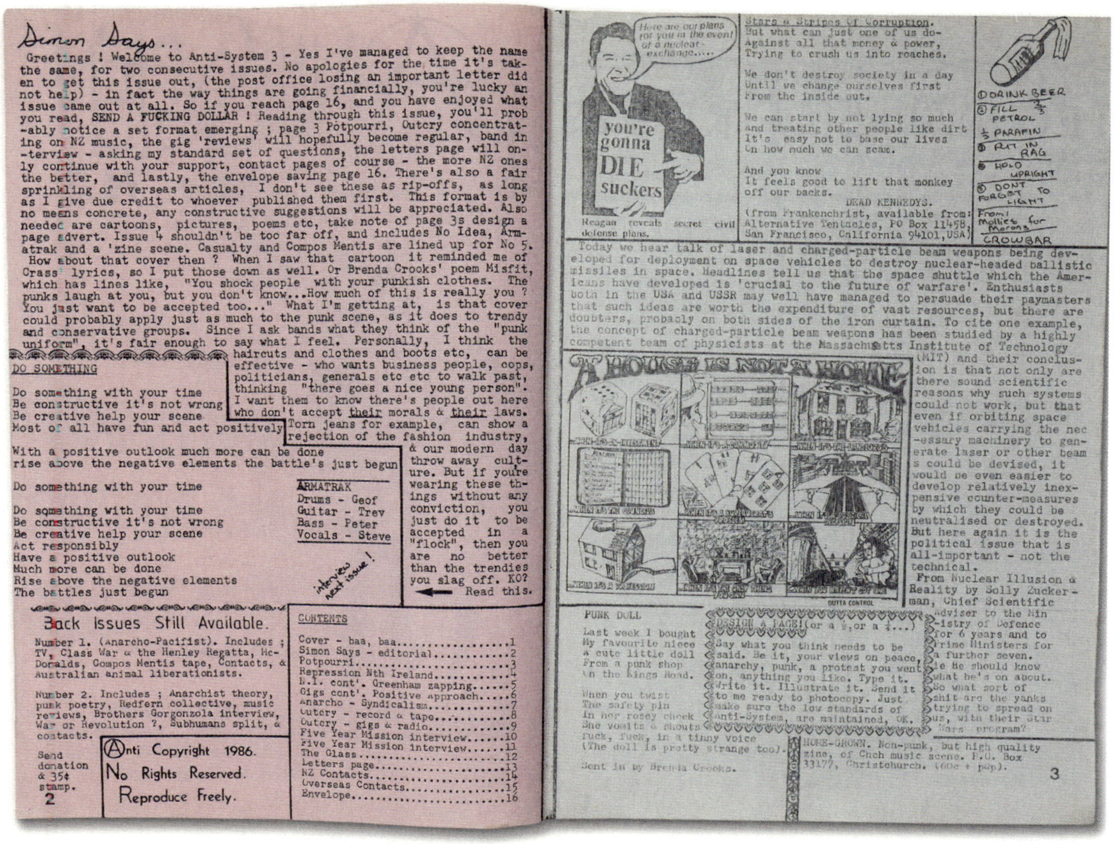

Simon Says...

Greetings ! Welcome to Anti-System 3 - Yes I've managed to keep the name the same, for two consecutive issues. No apologies for the time it's taken to get this issue out, (the post office losing an important letter did not help) - in fact the way things are going financially, you're lucky an issue came out at all. So if you reach page 16, and you have enjoyed what you read, **SEND A FUCKING DOLLAR** ! Reading through this issue, you'll probably notice a set format emerging ; page 3 Potpourri, Outcry concentrating on NZ music, the gig 'reviews' will hopefully become regular, band interview - asking my standard set of questions, the letters page will only continue with your support, contact pages of course - the more NZ ones the better, and lastly, the envelope saving page 16. There's also a fair sprinkling of overseas articles, I don't see these as rip-offs, as long as I give due credit to whoever published them first. This format is by no means concrete, any constructive suggestions will be appreciated. Also needed are cartoons, pictures, poems etc, take note of page 3s design a page advert. Issue 4 shouldn't be too far off, and includes No Idea, Armatrak and a 'zine scene. Casualty and Compos Mentis are lined up for No 5.

How about that cover then ? When I saw that cartoon it reminded me of Crass' lyrics, so I put those down as well. Or Brenda Crooks' poem Misfit, which has lines like, "You shock people with your punkish clothes. The punks laugh at you, but you don't know...How much of this is really you ? You just want to be accepted too..." What I'm getting at, is that cover could probably apply just as much to the punk scene, as it does to trendy and conservative groups. Since I ask bands what they think of the "punk uniform", it's fair enough to say what I feel. Personally, I think the haircuts and clothes and boots etc, can be effective - who wants business people, cops, politicians, generals etc etc to walk past, thinking "there goes a nice young person". I want them to know there's people out here who don't accept their morals & their laws. Torn jeans for example, can show a rejection of the fashion industry, & our modern day throw away culture. But if you're wearing these things without any conviction, you just do it to be accepted in a "flock", then you are no better than the trendies you slag off. KO? ← Read this.

DO SOMETHING

Do something with your time
Be constructive it's not wrong
Be creative help your scene
Most of all have fun and act positively

With a positive outlook much more can be done
rise above the negative elements the battle's just begun

Do something with your time

Do something with your time
Be constructive it's not wrong
Be creative help your scene
Act responsibly
Have a positive outlook
Much more can be done
Rise above the negative elements
The battles just begun

ARMATRAK
Drums - Geof
Guitar - Trev
Bass - Peter
Vocals - Steve

Back Issues Still Available.

Number 1. (Anarcho-Pacifist). Includes ; TV, Class War & the Henley Regatta, McDonalds, Compos Mentis tape, Contacts, & Australian animal liberationists.

Number 2. Includes ; Anarchist theory, punk poetry, Redfern collective, music reviews, Brothers Gorgonzola interview, War or Revolution ?, Subhumans split, & contacts.

Send donation & 35¢ stamp.

Ⓐnti Copyright 1986.
No Rights Reserved.
Reproduce Freely.

CONTENTS

2

Reagan reveals secret civil defense plans.

Stars & Stripes Of Corruption.
But what can just one of us do-
Against all that money & power,
Trying to crush us into roaches.

We don't destroy society in a day
Until we change ourselves first
From the inside out.

We can start by not lying so much
And treating other people like dirt
It's easy not to base our lives
On how much we can scam.

And you know
It feels good to lift that monkey
off our backs.
DEAD KENNEDYS.
(from Frankenchrist, available from: Alternative Tentacles, PO Box 11458, San Francisco, California 94101,USA)

Today we hear talk of laser and charged-particle beam weapons being developed for deployment on space vehicles to destroy nuclear-headed ballistic missiles in space. Headlines tell us that the space shuttle which the Americans have developed is 'crucial to the future of warfare'. Enthusiasts both in the USA and USSR may well have managed to persuade their paymasters that such ideas are worth the expenditure of vast resources, but there are doubters, probably on both sides of the iron curtain. To cite one example, the concept of charged-particle beam weapons has been studied by a highly competent team of physicists at the Massachusetts Institute of Technology (MIT) and their conclusion is that not only are there sound scientific reasons why such systems could not work, but that even if orbiting space vehicles carrying the necessary machinery to generate laser or other beams could be devised, it would be even easier to develop relatively inexpensive counter-measures by which they could be neutralised or destroyed. But here again it is the political issue that is all-important - not the technical.

From Nuclear Illusion & Reality by Solly Zuckerman, Chief Scientific Adviser to the Ministry of Defence for 6 years and to Prime Ministers for a further seven. He should know what he's on about. So what sort of shit are the yanks trying to spread on us, with their Star Wars program?

PUNK DOLL

Last week I bought
My favourite niece
A cute little doll
From a punk shop
On the Kings Road.

When you twist
The safety pin
In her rosey cheek
She vomits & shouts
Fuck, fuck, in a tinny voice
(The doll is pretty strange too).

Sent in by Brenda Crooks.

DESIGN A PAGE!(or a ½,or a ¼...)
Say what you think needs to be said. Be it, your views on peace, anarchy, punk, a protest you went on, anything you like. Type it. Write it. Illustrate it. Send it to me ready to photocopy. Just make sure the low standards of Anti-System, are maintained, OK.

HOME-GROWN. Non-punk, but high quality zine, of Chch music scene. P.O. Box 33177, Christchurch. (60c + p&p).

3

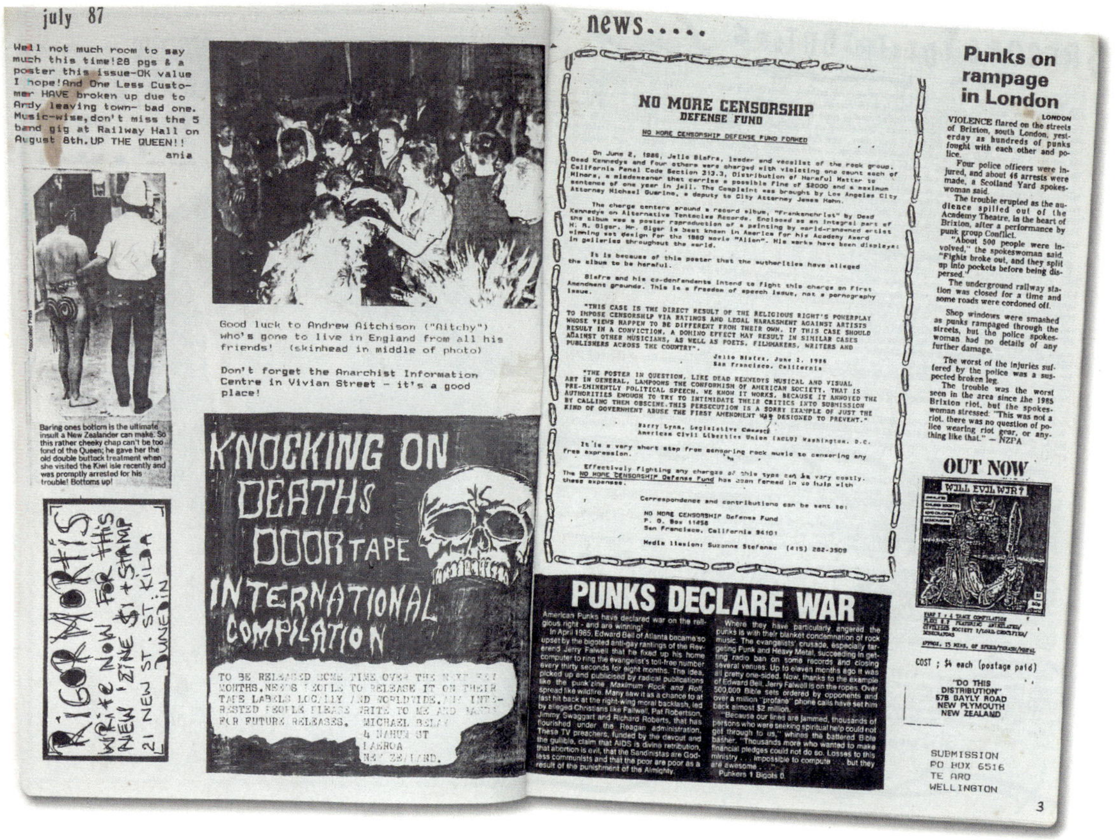

july 87

Well not much room to say much this time!28 pgs & a poster this issue-OK value I hope!And One Less Customer HAVE broken up due to Andy leaving town- bad one. Music-wise,don't miss the 5 band gig at Railway Hall on August 8th.UP THE QUEEN!!
ania

Associated Press

Baring ones bottom is the ultimate insult a New Zealander can make. So this rather cheeky chap can't be too fond of the Queen; he gave her the old double buttock treatment when she visited the Kiwi isle recently and was promptly arrested for his trouble! Bottoms up!

Good luck to Andrew Aitchison ("Aitchy") who's gone to live in England from all his friends! (skinhead in middle of photo)

Don't forget the Anarchist Information Centre in Vivian Street - it's a good place!

TO BE RELEASED SOME TIME OVER THE NEXT FEW MONTHS.NEEDS PEOPLE TO RELEASE IT ON THEIR TAPE LABELS LOCALLY AND WORLDWIDE.ANY INTERESTED PEOPLE PLEASE WRITE TO ME AND BANDS FOR FUTURE RELEASES. MICHAEL BELAY
4 NAHUM ST
TAEROA
NEW ZEALAND.

news.....

NO MORE CENSORSHIP
DEFENSE FUND

NO MORE CENSORSHIP DEFENSE FUND FORMED

On June 2, 1986, Jello Biafra, leader and vocalist of the rock group, Dead Kennedys and four others were charged with violating one count each of California Penal Code Section 313.3, Distribution of Harmful Matter to Minors, a misdemeanor that carries a possible fine of $2000 and a maximum sentence of one year in jail. The Complaint was brought by Los Angeles City Attorney Michael Guarino, a deputy to City Attorney James Hahn.

The charge centers around a record album, "Frankenchrist" by Dead Kennedys on Alternative Tentacles Records. Enclosed as an integral part of the album was a poster reproduction of a painting by world-renowned artist H. R. Giger. Mr. Giger is best known in America for his Academy Award winning set design for the 1980 movie "Alien". His works have been displayed in galleries throughout the world.

It is because of this poster that the authorities have alleged the album to be harmful.

Biafra and his co-denfendents intend to fight this charge on First Amendment grounds. This is a freedom of speech issue, not a pornography issue.

"THIS CASE IS THE DIRECT RESULT OF THE RELIGIOUS RIGHT'S POWERPLAY TO IMPOSE CENSORSHIP VIA RATINGS AND LEGAL HARASSMENT AGAINST ARTISTS WHOSE VIEWS HAPPEN TO BE DIFFERENT FROM THEIR OWN. IF THIS CASE SHOULD RESULT IN A CONVICTION, A DOMINO EFFECT MAY RESULT IN SIMILAR CASES AGAINST OTHER MUSICIANS, AS WELL AS POETS, FILMMAKERS, WRITERS AND PUBLISHERS ACROSS THE COUNTRY".

Jello Biafra, June 2, 1986
San Francisco, California

"THE POSTER IN QUESTION, LIKE DEAD KENNEDYS MUSICAL AND VISUAL ART IN GENERAL, LAMPOONS THE CONFORMISM OF AMERICAN SOCIETY. THAT IS PRE-EMINENTLY POLITICAL SPEECH. WE KNOW IT WORKS, BECAUSE IT ANNOYED THE AUTHORITIES ENOUGH TO TRY TO INTIMIDATE THEIR CRITICS INTO SUBMISSION BY CALLING THEM OBSCENE.THIS PERSECUTION IS A SORRY EXAMPLE OF JUST THE KIND OF GOVERNMENT ABUSE THE FIRST AMENDMENT WAS DESIGNED TO PREVENT."

Barry Lynn, Legislative Counsel
American Civil Liberties Union (ACLU) Washington, D.C.

It is a very short step from censoring rock music to censoring any free expression.

Effectively fighting any charges of this type can be very costly. The NO MORE CENSORSHIP Defense Fund has been formed to help with these expenses.

Correspondence and contributions can be sent to:

NO MORE CENSORSHIP Defense Fund
P. O. Box 11458
San Francisco, California 94101

Media liasion: Suzanne Stefanac (415) 282-3509

PUNKS DECLARE WAR

American Punks have declared war on the religious right - and are winning!

In April 1985, Edward Bell of Atlanta became so upset by the bigoted anti-gay rantings of the Reverend Jerry Falwell that he fixed up his home computer to ring the evangelist's toll-free number every thirty seconds for eight months. The idea, picked up and publicised by radical publications like the punk zine *Maximum Rock and Roll*, spread like wildfire. Many saw it as a chance to at last hit back at the right-wing moral backlash, led by alleged Christians like Falwell, Pat Robertson, Jimmy Swaggart and Richard Roberts, that has flourished under the Reagan administration. These TV preachers, funded by the devout and the gullible, claim that AIDS is divine retribution, that abortion is evil, that the Sandinistas are Godless communists and that the poor are poor as a result of the punishment of the Almighty.

Where they have particularly angered the punks is with their blanket condemnation of rock music. The evangelists' crusade, especially targeting Punk and Heavy Metal, succeeding in getting radio ban on some records and closing several venues. Up to eleven months ago it was all pretty one-sided. Now, thanks to the example of Edward Bell, Jerry Falwell is on the ropes. Over 500,000 Bible sets ordered by opponents and over a million "profane" phone calls have set him back almost $2 million.

"Because our lines are jammed, thousands of persons who were seeking spiritual help could not get through to us," whines the battered Bible basher. "Thousands more who wanted to make financial pledges could not do so. Losses to this ministry . . . impossible to compute . . . but they are awesome . . ."

Punkers 1 Bigots 0.

Punks on rampage in London

LONDON

VIOLENCE flared on the streets of Brixton, south London, yesterday as hundreds of punks fought with each other and police.

Four police officers were injured, and about 46 arrests were made, a Scotland Yard spokeswoman said.

The trouble erupted as the audience spilled out of the Academy Theatre, in the heart of Brixton, after a performance by punk group Conflict.

"About 500 people were involved," the spokeswoman said. "Fights broke out, and they split up into pockets before being dispersed."

The underground railway station was closed for a time and some roads were cordoned off.

Shop windows were smashed as punks rampaged through the streets, but the police spokeswoman had no details of any further damage.

The worst of the injuries suffered by the police was a suspected broken leg.

The trouble was the worst seen in the area since the 1985 Brixton riot, but the spokeswoman stressed: "This was not a riot. there was no question of police wearing riot gear, or anything like that." — NZPA

OUT NOW

COST ; $4 each (postage paid)

"DO THIS DISTRIBUTION"
57B BAYLY ROAD
NEW PLYMOUTH
NEW ZEALAND

SUBMISSION
PO BOX 6516
TE ARO
WELLINGTON

3

19

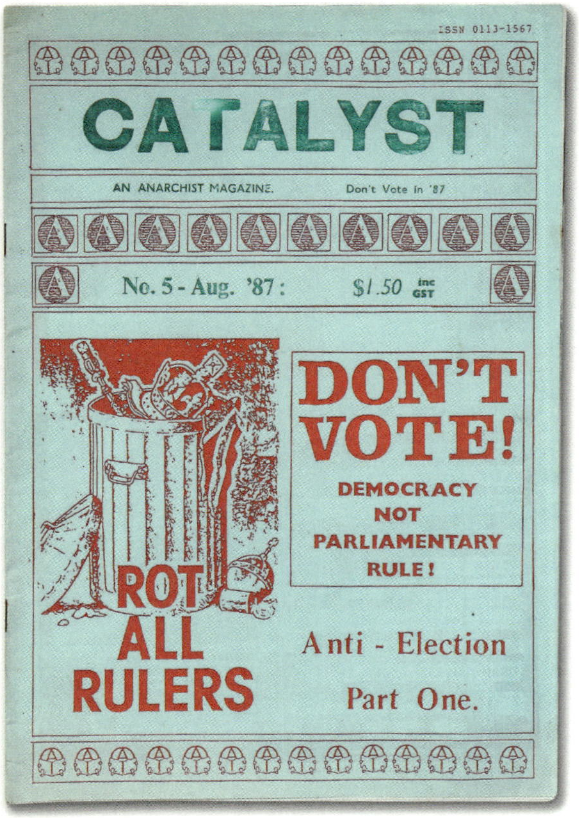

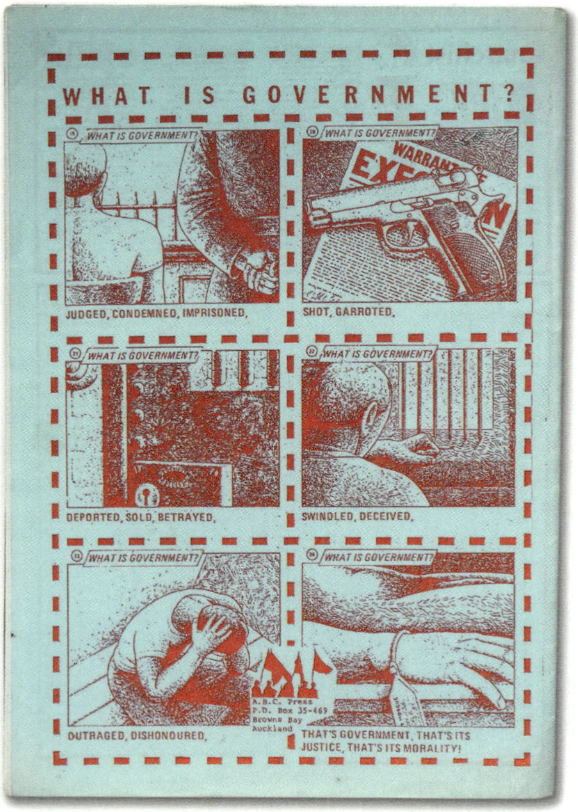

Richard Langston My obsession with The Clean and The Great Unwashed was kind of a backbone to the whole thing. We got a few letters by about issue three saying 'Oh, Jesus, mate, can you get over your Clean thing!?' I want to write back to them now and say 'Mate, it's 40 years later and I'm still not over it. How are you going?'

Ania Glowacz Simon Cottle set the standard for Wellington zines really. So partly I was inspired by Flesh D-Vice but also his zine, and I thought 'Well, I can do a fucking zine as well', y'know?

Bruce Grenville I have been a letterpress printer for many years. Earlier in my life I had the good fortune to be given what is commonly considered the Rolls-Royce of printing machines, a Heidelberg Platen letterpress. When I was a teenager down in the South Island, I asked my tutor: 'What's the ultimate thing in printing? Are these things the ultimate?' He said, 'No, the ultimate is a thing called the Heidelberg, which is the Rolls-Royce of printing machines', and then later on, many years later, my little brother who was a demolition contractor at the time called me up: 'Hey, I'm demolishing this building that's got a printing press in it, do you want it?' I said, 'Oh, what sort of printing press is it?' He said 'Oh, hang on, I'll have a look', and then he goes 'Oh, it's called a Heidelberg.' I said, 'YES! YES! YES! I DO!' But it didn't have a motor, the motor was fucked, that's why the previous people had just walked out and left it.

When you're living in a small flat it's very hard to accommodate a big machine like that. It weighed several tons. Through various circumstances I met a guy from the English Department at Auckland University who asked if he could buy the press off me. I said, 'No, no, no, I'm not gonna sell this. This is the Rolls-Royce. My dream forever was to have a big press like this.' One thing led to another. The final upshot was I was having to move flats and he was trying to buy my press, so we did a deal. The press would go and live at Auckland University, and we each had access 50 per cent of the week. So I was Monday, Wednesday, and he was . . . Anyway, they moved the press at their expense, got carriers and stuff, and they also provided a motor for it.

19. *Catalyst*, edited by Simon Coffey, A4, 1987. Tāmaki Makaurau Auckland.

20

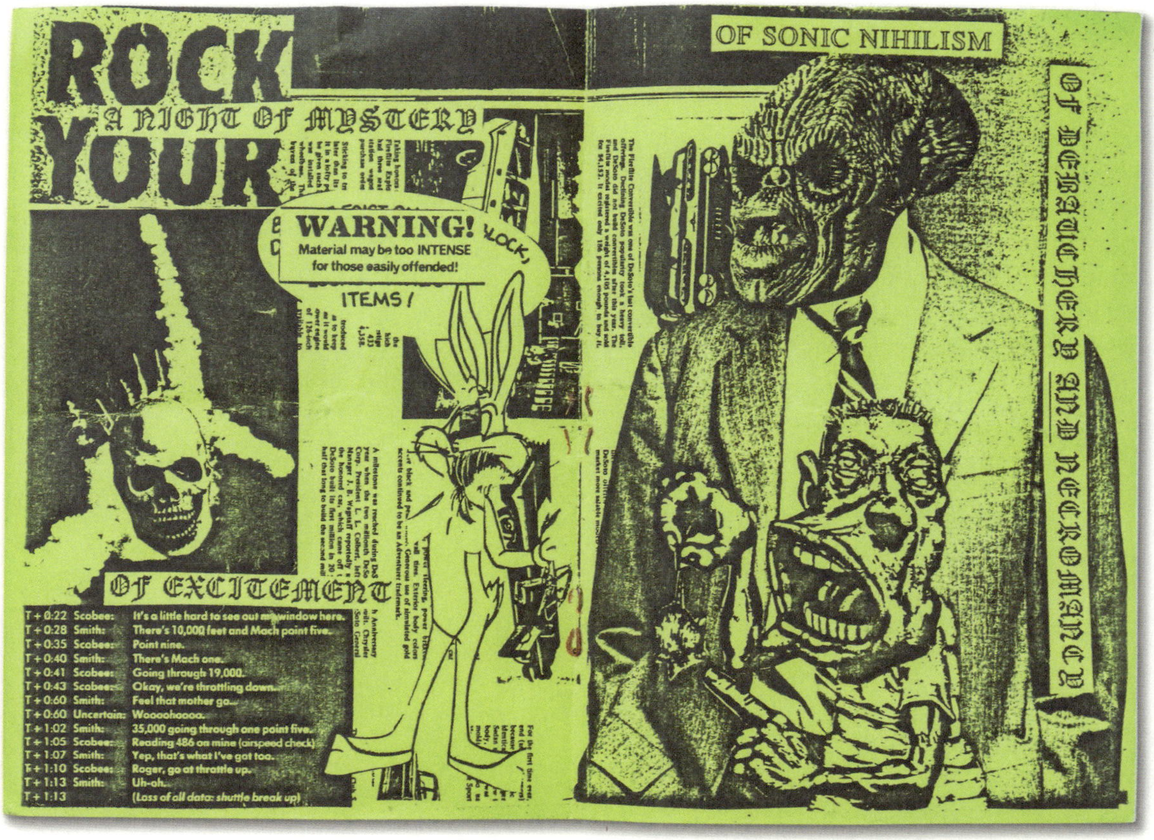

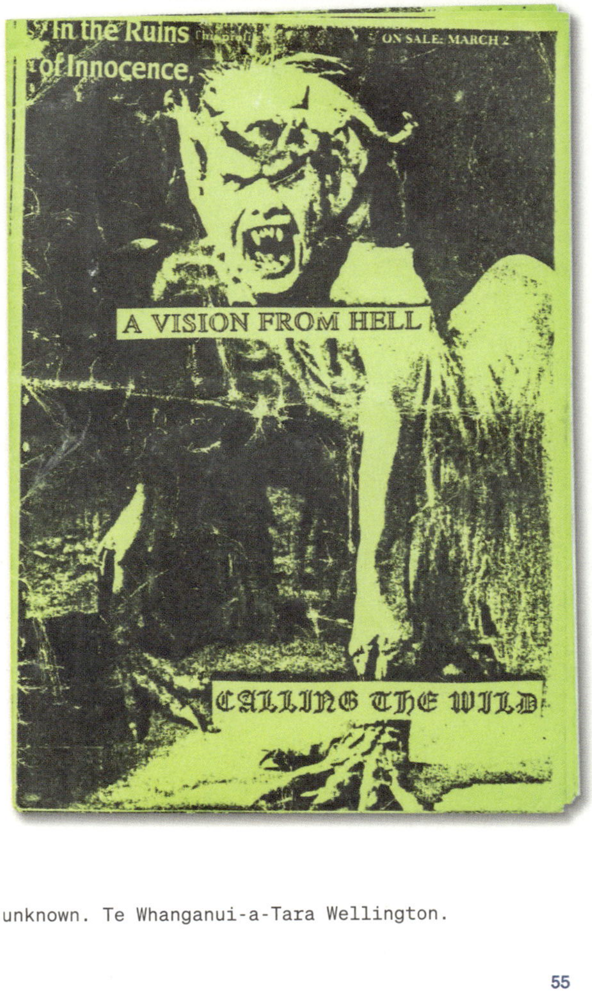

The other funny thing about the Auckland University connection was that a couple of weeks after we signed the contract, moved in, got the press operating etc., etc., the university had serious budget cuts and the English Department cut the bibliographic course, so instead of me only having access to the press half a week I suddenly had access 100 per cent of the time. So I'm going 'Gosh, I've got a five-year free print studio, free electricity, free hot water, free toilet, free motor for the press, everything!'

20. Untitled zine/flyer for a Flesh D-Vice gig, A6, date unknown. Te Whanganui-a-Tara Wellington.

Ania Glowacz *Submission* was a labour of love. It wasn't to get people to like me or to be cool or anything like that. It was just 'Here you go, take it or leave it. This is what I feel like saying.'
Tracey Wedge We were trying to offer an alternative way of looking at things. We wanted to lift up the voices of women and disadvantaged communities. Veganism was important. Anti-vivisection was important. We weren't so into government institutions. We attended lots of the protests happening in Dunedin, we were quite politically active in that way.
Tony Renouf I didn't know how to make a comic book, so for my first attempt at self-publishing I decided just to photocopy a cartoon and stick it up around the city like a band poster. This would be early '85. We photocopied this thing and we were walking around — we even had one of those snail Sellotape dispensers — and we were sellotaping this cartoon over band posters. We're down by Frank's Chicken Bar and this cop car pulls up, and the window's wound down, squeak, squeak, squeak — this is before electric windows — and this cop goes 'What are you boys doing putting those band posters up? You know that's illegal?' I said 'It's not a band poster, officer, it's a cartoon. Here.' and I handed it through the window to him. He looked at it and he went [stilted] 'Ha-ha ha-ha', and handed it to his mate who pretty much did the same standard cop laugh. And then they went 'You mind if we hang onto this?', and 'You better stop doing that. Away you go!', and they drove off. Years later, through my partner Deirdre, I'm at this professor's house with all the library staff, and I relay this same story. This cop who was there goes 'Y'know what? That cartoon was on the noticeboard at the police station until it faded to nothing.'

21

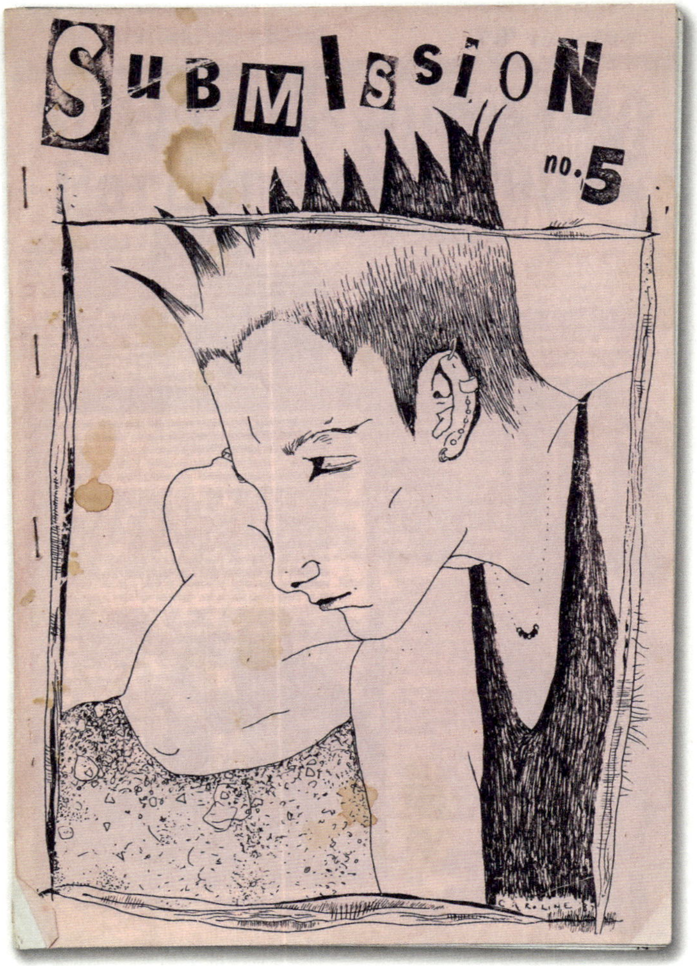

21. *Submission* #5 cover and spread, Ania Glowacz, A4, 1987. Te Whanganui-a-Tara Wellington.

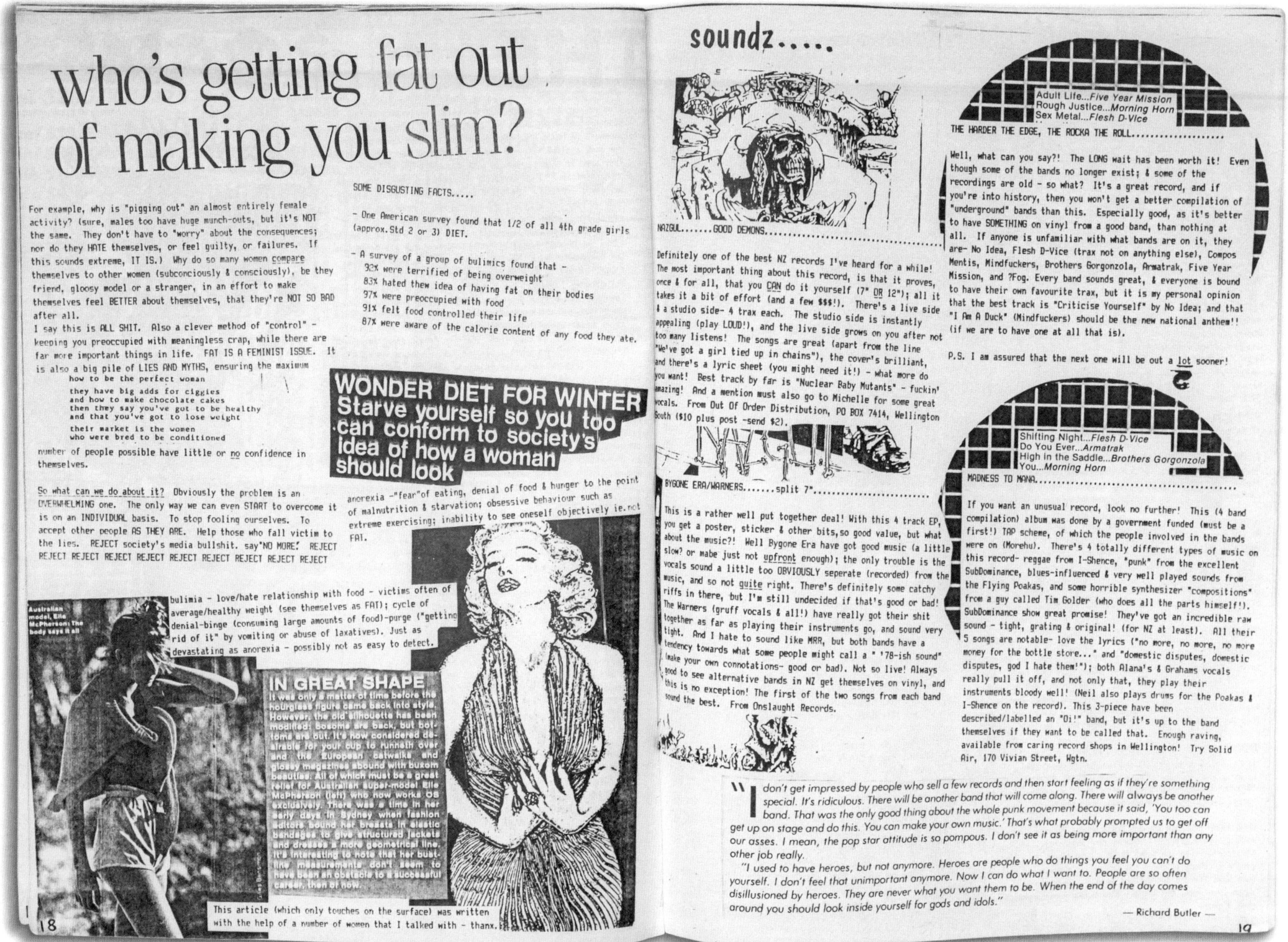

who's getting fat out of making you slim?

For example, why is "pigging out" an almost entirely female activity? (sure, males too have huge munch-outs, but it's NOT the same. They don't have to "worry" about the consequences; nor do they HATE themselves, or feel guilty, or failures. If this sounds extreme, IT IS.) Why do so many women compare themselves to other women (subconciously & consciously), be they friend, gloosy model or a stranger, in an effort to make themselves feel BETTER about themselves, that they're NOT SO BAD after all.

I say this is ALL SHIT. Also a clever method of "control" - keeping you preoccupied with meaningless crap, while there are far more important things in life. FAT IS A FEMINIST ISSUE. It is also a big pile of LIES AND MYTHS, ensuring the maximum number of people possible have little or no confidence in themselves.

how to be the perfect woman

they have big adds for ciggies
and how to make chocolate cakes
then they say you've got to be healthy
and that you've got to lose weight

their market is the women
who were bred to be conditioned

SOME DISGUSTING FACTS.....

- One American survey found that 1/2 of all 4th grade girls (approx. Std 2 or 3) DIET.

- A survey of a group of bulimics found that -
  - 32% were terrified of being overweight
  - 83% hated them idea of having fat on their bodies
  - 97% were preoccupied with food
  - 91% felt food controlled their life
  - 87% were aware of the calorie content of any food they ate.

WONDER DIET FOR WINTER
Starve yourself so you too can conform to society's idea of how a woman should look

So what can we do about it? Obviously the problem is an OVERWHELMING one. The only way we can even START to overcome it is on an INDIVIDUAL basis. To stop fooling ourselves. To accept other people AS THEY ARE. Help those who fall victim to the lies. REJECT society's media bullshit. say "NO MORE." REJECT REJECT REJECT REJECT REJECT REJECT REJECT REJECT REJECT REJECT

anorexia -"fear" of eating, denial of food & hunger to the point of malnutrition & starvation; obsessive behaviour such as extreme exercising; inability to see oneself objectively ie. not FAT.

bulimia - love/hate relationship with food - victims often of average/healthy weight (see themselves as FAT); cycle of denial-binge (consuming large amounts of food)-purge ("getting rid of it" by vomiting or abuse of laxatives). Just as devastating as anorexia - possibly not as easy to detect.

Australian model, Elle McPherson: The body says it all

IN GREAT SHAPE

It was only a matter of time before the hourglass figure came back into style. However, the old silhouette has been modified: Bosoms are back, but bottoms are out. It's now considered desirable for your cup to runneth over and the European catwalks and glossy magazines abound with buxom beauties. All of which must be a great relief for Australian super-model Elle McPherson (left) who now works OS exclusively. There was a time in her early days in Sydney when fashion editors bound her breasts in elastic bandages to give structured jackets and dresses a more geometrical line. It's interesting to note that her bustline measurements don't seem to have been an obstacle to a successful career, then or now.

This article (which only touches on the surface) was written with the help of a number of women that I talked with - thanx.

18

soundz.....

NAZGUL.......GOOD DEMONS..............................

Definitely one of the best NZ records I've heard for a while! The most important thing about this record, is that it proves, once & for all, that you CAN do it yourself (7" OR 12"); all it takes it a bit of effort (and a few $$$!). There's a live side & a studio side- 4 trax each. The studio side is instantly appealing (play LOUD!), and the live side grows on you after not too many listens! The songs are great (apart from the line "We've got a girl tied up in chains"), the cover's brilliant, and there's a lyric sheet (you might need it!) - what more do you want! Best track by far is "Nuclear Baby Mutants" - fuckin' amazing! And a mention must also go to Michelle for some great vocals. From Out Of Order Distribution, PO BOX 7414, Wellington South ($10 plus post -send $2).

BYGONE ERA/WARNERS.......split 7"..........................

This is a rather well put together deal! With this 4 track EP, you get a poster, sticker & other bits, so good value, but what about the music?! Well Bygone Era have got good music (a little slow? or mabe just not upfront enough); the only trouble is the vocals sound a little too OBVIOUSLY seperate (recorded) from the music, and so not quite right. There's definitely some catchy riffs in there, but I'm still undecided if that's good or bad! The Warners (gruff vocals & all!) have really got their shit together as far as playing their instruments go, and sound very tight. And I hate to sound like MRR, but both bands have a tendency towards what some people might call a " '78-ish sound" (make your own connotations- good or bad). Not so live! Always good to see alternative bands in NZ get themselves on vinyl, and this is no exception! The first of the two songs from each band sound the best. From Onslaught Records.

Adult Life...*Five Year Mission*
Rough Justice...*Morning Horn*
Sex Metal...*Flesh D-Vice*

THE HARDER THE EDGE, THE ROCKA THE ROLL..................

Well, what can you say?! The LONG wait has been worth it! Even though some of the bands no longer exist; & some of the recordings are old - so what? It's a great record, and if you're into history, then you won't get a better compilation of "underground" bands than this. Especially good, as it's better to have SOMETHING on vinyl from a good band, than nothing at all. If anyone is unfamiliar with what bands are on it, they are- No Idea, Flesh D-Vice (trax not on anything else), Compos Mentis, Mindfuckers, Brothers Gorgonzola, Armatrak, Five Year Mission, and ?Fog. Every band sounds great, & everyone is bound to have their own favourite trax, but it is my personal opinion that the best track is "Criticise Yourself" by No Idea; and that "I Am A Duck" (Mindfuckers) should be the new national anthem!! (if we are to have one at all that is).

P.S. I am assured that the next one will be out a lot sooner!

Shifting Night...*Flesh D-Vice*
Do You Ever...*Armatrak*
High in the Saddle...*Brothers Gorgonzola*
You...*Morning Horn*

MADNESS TO MANA..

If you want an unusual record, look no further! This (4 band compilation) album was done by a government funded (must be a first!) TAP scheme, of which the people involved in the bands were on (Morehu). There's 4 totally different types of music on this record- reggae from I-Shence, "punk" from the excellent SubDominance, blues-influenced & very well played sounds from the Flying Poakas, and some horrible synthesizer "compositions" from a guy called Tim Golder (who does all the parts himself!). SubDominance show great promise! They've got an incredible raw sound - tight, grating & original! (for NZ at least). All their 5 songs are notable- love the lyrics ("no more, no more, no more money for the bottle store..." and "domestic disputes, domestic disputes, god I hate them!"); both Alana's & Grahams vocals really pull it off, and not only that, they play their instruments bloody well! (Neil also plays drums for the Poakas & I-Shence on the record). This 3-piece have been described/labelled an "Oi!" band, but it's up to the band themselves if they want to be called that. Enough raving, available from caring record shops in Wellington! Try Solid Air, 170 Vivian Street, Wgtn.

"I don't get impressed by people who sell a few records and then start feeling as if they're something special. It's ridiculous. There will be another band that will come along. There will always be another band. That was the only good thing about the whole punk movement because it said, 'You too can get up on stage and do this. You can make your own music.' That's what probably prompted us to get off our asses. I mean, the pop star attitude is so pompous. I don't see it as being more important than any other job really.

"I used to have heroes, but not anymore. Heroes are people who do things you feel you can't do yourself. I don't feel that unimportant anymore. Now I can do what I want to. People are so often disillusioned by heroes. They are never what you want them to be. When the end of the day comes around you should look inside yourself for gods and idols."

— Richard Butler —

19

Richard Davies The interesting thing about all this cutting up the media is that Brett's dad was Ross Taylor from Television New Zealand, and my dad was John Davies from Television New Zealand. Both our fathers were journalists. His dad was an investigative journalist, and my dad was a sports journalist. So we had that connection from the day we met, our dads both knew each other. They didn't like what *we* were doing. [Laughs.] Well, my dad didn't see what I made down in Taranaki. I'm pretty sure he knew I was up to no good. Sorry, it wasn't 'no good', I shouldn't say that, but when you put out a zine called *Dead Cops* one month, you're gonna attract the heat of the police.

I wasn't really looking to make zines. Brett made zines. I'm living with him, and this is before smartphones, and we didn't watch TV. So we were always playing music and mucking around. I'm like 'Shit, can I do one?' He goes 'Yeah, that box of paper is for you. You use that box' — and then there's another 20 boxes for him. The cops took the boxes of paper, the Gestetner and everything when they raided the place over the zines. But Brett got a lawyer and won the case.

Bruce Grenville My view has always been that it's better to have a good time and make it an interesting adventure, take the piss, and generally you can do that remarkably well with a printing press. I mean in this day and age everybody's got a printing press, because everyone can push 'Control+P' on their computer and make a print, but back in those days we didn't have computers and we didn't have 'Control+P', and basically we printers always joked 'Freedom of the press belongs to those who own one', because if you've got your own press you can print what you like, but if you work for a boss you print what the boss likes. Like you can't imagine the *New Zealand Herald* is going to put anything in the *New Zealand Herald* that the boss does not approve of, and the boss is only going to approve of things that don't offend the advertisers.

Richard Davies Brett's fanzines were very different to mine. His were much more professional. Mine were all crooked, but I liked that, I wanted mine to be organic. Brett was trying to grow his into something bigger.

See that [pointing]: 'City Punks Blamed for Mall Strife'. We were pulling these things out of the newspaper and highlighting the fact they were picking on us.

Simon Cottle I'd collect bits and pieces to use in future zines, like a bit of wrapping paper: 'Oh, that will make a cool background or a bit of a border.' I'd keep an eye out for anything and everything, a few comics — *Oink!* comic was a really exceptional comic that got right into the vegetarian animal rights stuff.

My other interest is motorbike racing, and it's kind of the same as zine collage in some ways. A jug breaks and you think 'Actually, that aluminium shell might come in useful' or 'that tea-strainer could actually make a filter down the line'. So I've kind of still got the mechanical equivalent of seeing something and thinking 'That could be worth holding onto, that could be useful.' There's a punk-rock string singlet I photocopied to make a background, lots of little things like that.

Ania Glowacz There was no team, it was just me. I'd collage stuff from *Oink!* comic. I just put lots of stuff together: photocopies of newspaper reports that were obviously full of BS, y'know what I mean? Like 'Read this: is this what you're supposed to swallow?' It was sarcastic, see if your brain works. 'Read this: are you gonna do something about it?'

[Reading from *Submission*] '24 packed A4 pages for fourth issue of Wellington fanzine with Nazgûl and Oi Polloi interviews'. I can't remember who they are, um, 'Tom Thug cartoon strip, punk and thrash discussions, stacks of witty anti-royalty stuff, interview and review of Flesh D-Vice, Jack the Ripper story and a piece on connections between feminism and anarchy. $2.00 including P&P from . . .'

John Farrow There was definitely a shared aesthetic between the music and the zines. The ones that we liked had a mix of political articles and viewpoints and music reviews . . . everything. That's where we picked up that the English scene was really anti-vivisection and pro-vegetarian, anti the hunt, which was unique to England, but those sorts of things really interested us, the bands as well.

Because the lyrics were political there'd be this osmosis into politics. I suppose a criticism of punk is that it actually wasn't that unique, that everyone followed everyone else. If so-and-so was a vegetarian everyone else was a vegetarian, but then there was genuine individualism as well.

People either loved or hated [the band] Crass. People who hated them said they were just a bunch of old hippies and university students and not real punk. Then there were a lot of us who really liked them and their politics.

Tracey Wedge It's hard to describe the aesthetic. Anti-establishment, I suppose; the choice of graphics reflects that. It was very much of its time. It's a cut-and-paste aesthetic, it isn't trying to be aesthetically pleasing, it's that Crass kind of aesthetic I suppose. It's pared-back to the basics, 20 pages of A5 black-and-white.

Bruce Grenville I didn't go for the deconstructed collage aesthetic of punk. I was trying to be bold and make a point. If you've made a small sticker to slap up somewhere you've only got five seconds for someone to read it. If they've got to go 'Well, here's something here, and here's something else down here . . .' it's just too busy. It's a second-year Elam class assignment. I didn't go for the collage thing at all. It just wasn't me.

Tracey Wedge Figuring out the layout was quite an organic process. We relied quite heavily on some great local artists to supply us with wonderful illustrations.

22

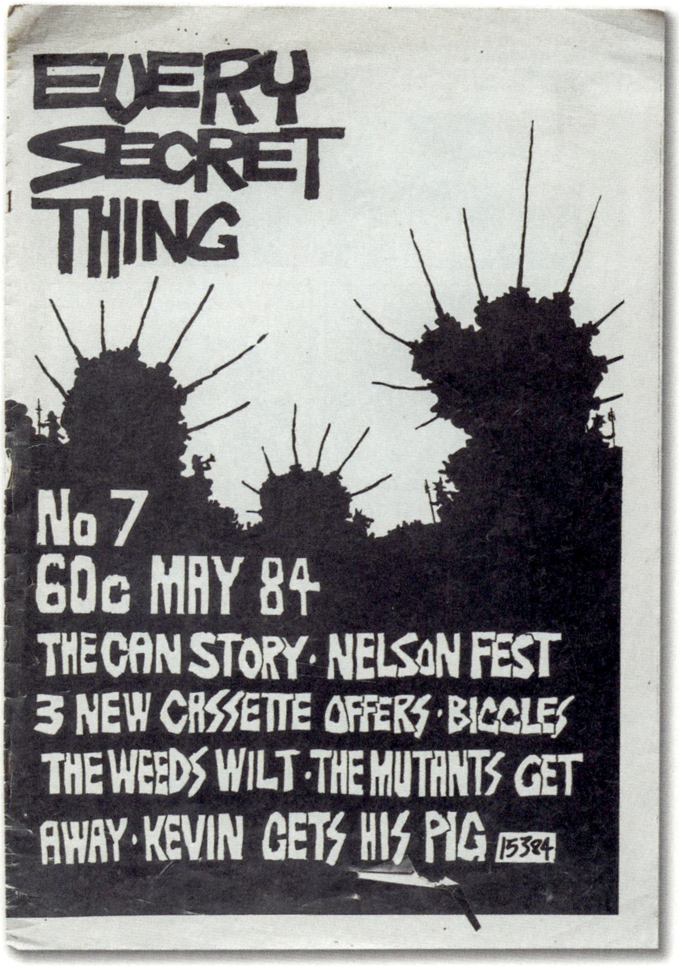

Robert Scott There wasn't much thought about production. I mean, look at this one, the quality of photos is absolutely terrible. They were prints from an old camera and then those have been photocopied, you can't even see what's going on in them.

Paul Luker I took photographs for my *Empty Heads* zine. In those days it was very expensive getting an SLR [single-lens reflex] camera, but you could buy a Russian one called a Zenit. I bought one of their enlargers as well and had a wee darkroom in the bathroom. That Zenit was great. It was really heavy, but it was great.

22. *Every Secret Thing #7*, Robert Scott, A4, 1984. Ōtautahi Christchurch.

23

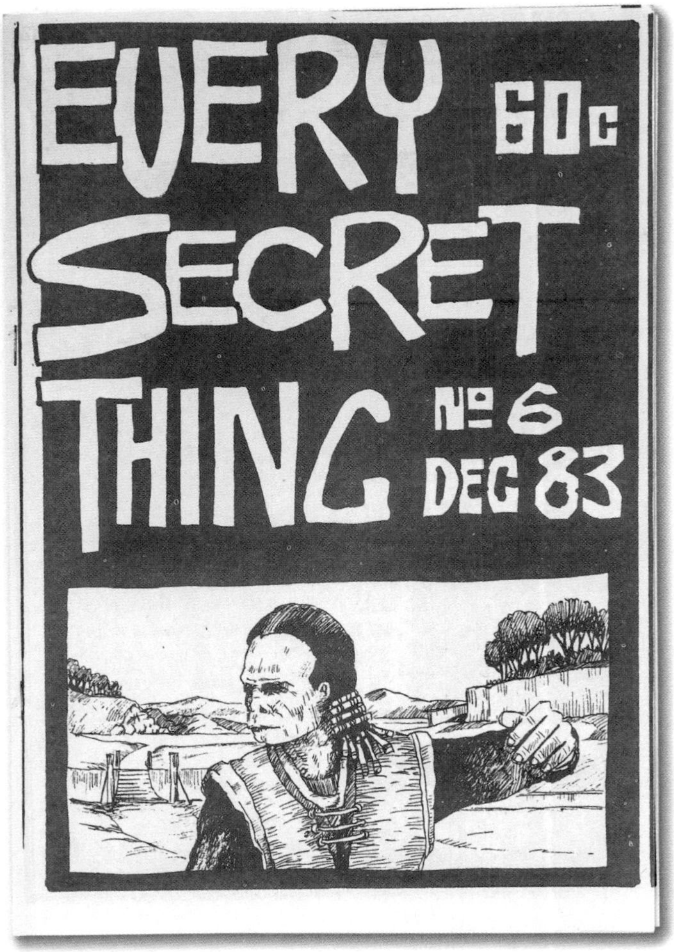

Robert Scott Then there's really oblique nonsensical stuff, [reading] 'Your day, starts in bed', so very downplayed, British humour almost. 'Dashing into the kitchen, breakfast, off to work, sitting in front of a TV.' That's also a reflection of being on the dole at the time. I was doing some music and art, but I didn't have much going on that was pressing.

There's the science-fiction-y strips, *The Terror of the Inner City*. Then there's random images of bands where I made up stuff about them, maybe taking the mickey a wee bit. Then I've got a picture of Peter Gabriel and I'm not even a fan of him or Genesis, so I don't know why that's in there. I think maybe in some issues, it was like 'I've gotta get this out quickly, I've gotta fill it up with any kind of shit.'

Then there's stupid things like 'Here are the answers from four news agents in town when asked if any issues of *Every Secret Thing* had been returned.' I've obviously found some typed answers that pertain to something else, [reading] 'Only a very low percentage are brought back, and all the complaints we've had have been minor ones.' So I've obviously found some random answers and made up some random questions to fit those.

Ah, letters . . . they're just made up by me. [reading] 'Dear Ed, I'm writing in because I know you won't have many letters to print as this is your first issue, so, I'm helping you out.' Any slightly humorous angles like that that I could put in to fill it up. I think the sense of humour came from my dad. He was very keen on practical jokes and he was always playing tricks on us. I think that would've also come from listening to things like The Goons. There was a real love of that style of British comedy.

Matthew Campbell Downes The comics that Hugh and Stephen did in *Ballon D'Comic* were very silly. They're very sort of non-stories. *Story of the Mouse*, the mouse comes out of the hole and goes 'Oh, I feel a bit lazy today, I was going to get some cheese, but I don't think I will. I think I'll go back in the hole and have a lie down.' That was their idea of a comic, like nothing happens. They were really into that.

So anyway, two guys who were already in this imaginary band called The Berts joined the real band — Ballon D'Essai. Then Mark got them all organised and was like 'We're gonna make this comic, it's gonna come out with our record', because Mark had this sense of 'We're an entertainment company, we're gonna have comics and art and music videos.' He had big visions, which of course were very hard to achieve in Christchurch, especially when you were 16. Warhol was a precedent, and the punk ethic. We loved The Fall, we loved the Sex Pistols and that whole Malcolm McLaren blah blah of 'You don't need to be able to play your instruments, just have fun.'

23. *Every Secret Thing* #6, Robert Scott, A4, 1983. Ōtautahi Christchurch.
24. *Every Secret Thing* #7 back cover, Robert Scott, A4, 1984. Ōtautahi Christchurch.

24

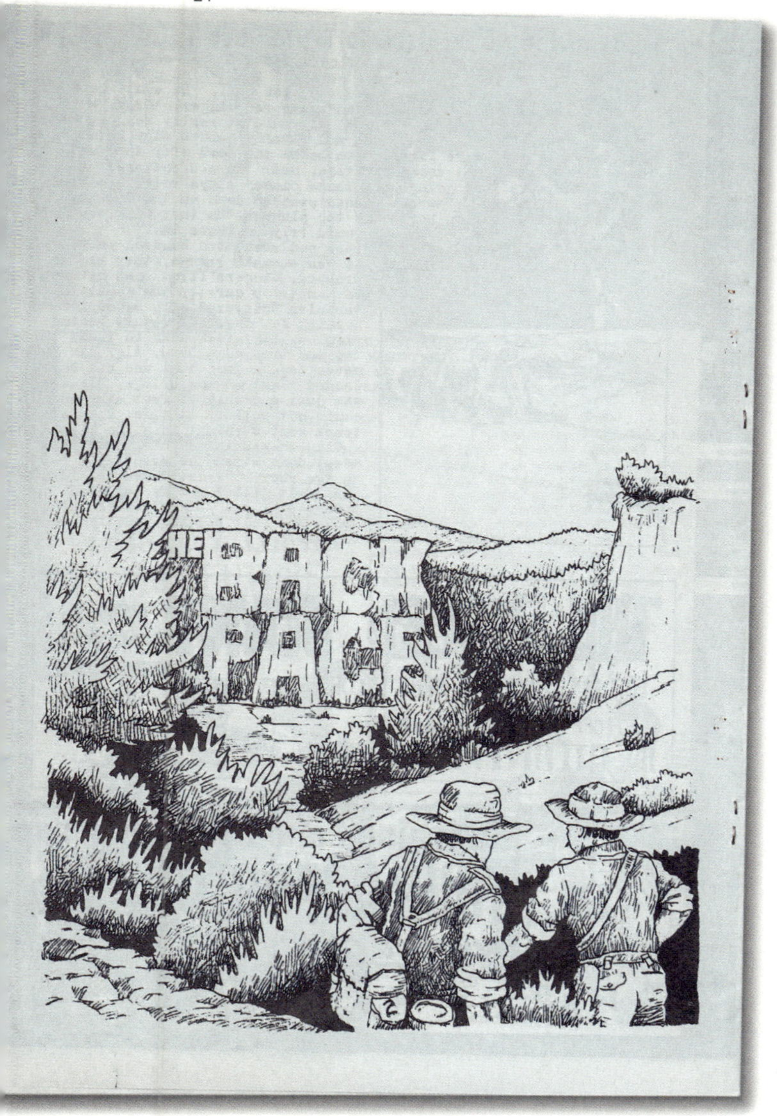

25

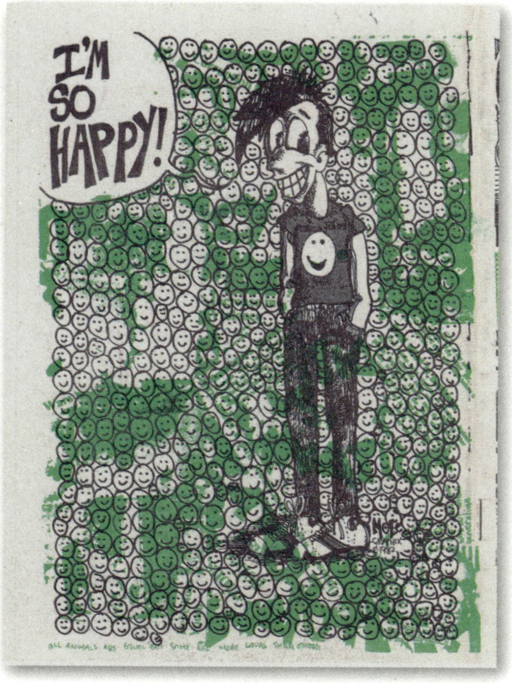

Robert Scott The disregard for fame was a punk-rock thing, but it's also part of the way Kiwis downplay stuff, not quite 'tall poppy', more of the humble as opposed to 'Hey, look at me, I'm amazing, I'm fantastic and here's some big bold statements of intent or ambition or . . .', stuff like that. But that's probably also my upbringing, even though there was a lot of fun stuff and creativity, there was also a bit of Scottishness: keep in your place, don't get above your station, behave yourself. There was quite a bit of that, but that's part of that humour as well, self-deprecating.

Matthew Campbell Downes The covers, the labels, the text, the posters were all a huge mismatch with that first Ballon D'Essai record. It wasn't a conscious belief in radical autonomy or anything. It was just like: you do that, you do that, you do that, alright, put it all together. I don't think there was much intent apart from everyone liking irreverent stuff. Everyone was a bit sort of 'Make it a bit fucked-up. Make it a bit silly' — the Monty Python thing. Like the fact that in Monty Python the guy gets both legs chopped off but he's still trying to fight, or the fact that the monster is a bunny, that stupidness informed a lot of what we did. Like here's a comic where nothing happens, or there's a bum note in every second bar of this song. It came from that school of 'make it up as you go along, there are no rules'.

Simon Cottle I didn't go about delegating reviews and articles and that. Something would just arrive in the mail. I'd have a blank page, I might have even done the background patterns for that page, just needed some copy for it. Sweet as. Pack it in. Collage was my creative outlet. There's some quite hilarious letters in there as well.

25. *Ballon D'Comic* #2 back cover, cartoon and edited by Mark Rastrick, A4, 1983. Ōtautahi Christchurch.

Richard Langston I was enthusiastic about everyone and when I interviewed Sneaky Feelings, David [Pine] and Matthew [Bannister] didn't even want to do an interview, they sent their drummer. *Garage* was very much aligned with the aesthetic of Chris Knox, The Velvet Underground — rough 'n' ready, you can make mistakes, mistakes don't matter, that's just harmonics — whereas Sneaky Feelings wanted to make lush adult pop records . . . and good on them, occasionally they achieved that. Matthew could be a bit whiney. He's a really good writer, he just doesn't need to whine. He had a chip shop on his shoulder. I was enthusiastic. I think people were slightly taken aback by my enthusiasm. I think Graeme Downes [The Verlaines] was a bit.

The bands weren't suspicious, they just thought 'Oh, you can be a little more understated in your enthusiasm.' I thought, 'Nah. I have to be cool and considered and fair and balanced in my work as a daily journalist, not when I'm doing my zine. You are going to get a raver.'

26

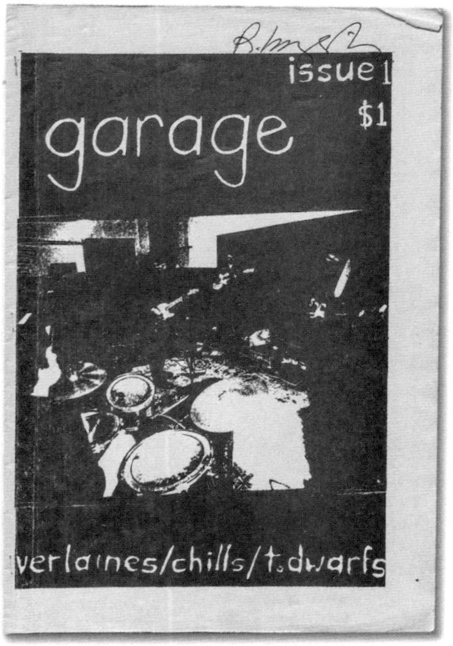

27

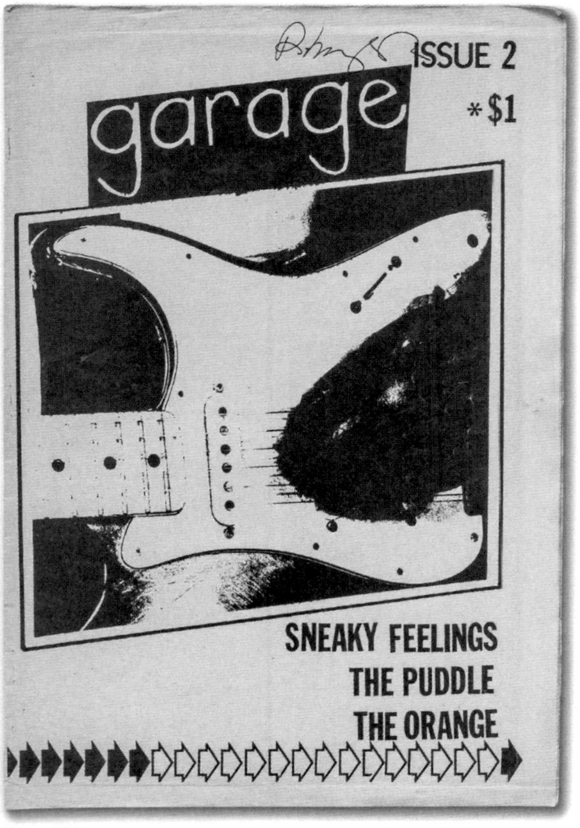

28

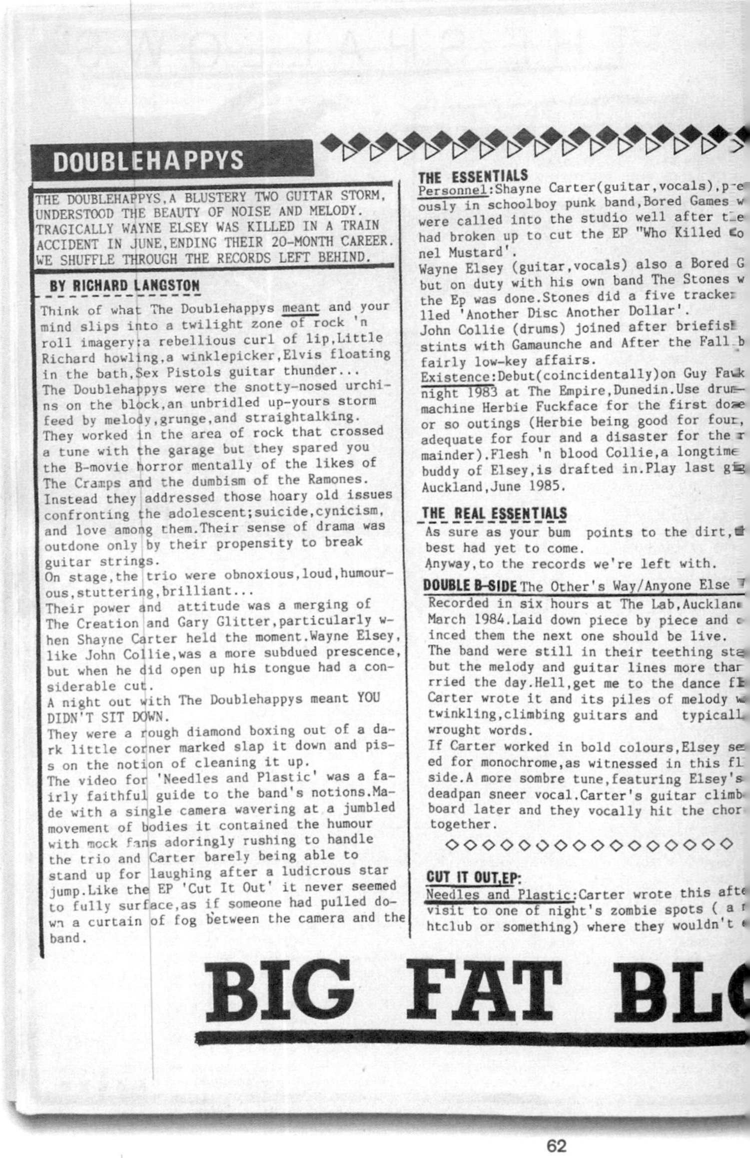

DOUBLEHAPPYS

THE DOUBLEHAPPYS,A BLUSTERY TWO GUITAR STORM, UNDERSTOOD THE BEAUTY OF NOISE AND MELODY. TRAGICALLY WAYNE ELSEY WAS KILLED IN A TRAIN ACCIDENT IN JUNE,ENDING THEIR 20-MONTH CAREER. WE SHUFFLE THROUGH THE RECORDS LEFT BEHIND.

BY RICHARD LANGSTON

Think of what The Doublehappys meant and your mind slips into a twilight zone of rock 'n roll imagery:a rebellious curl of lip,Little Richard howling,a winklepicker,Elvis floating in the bath,Sex Pistols guitar thunder...
The Doublehappys were the snotty-nosed urchins on the block,an unbridled up-yours storm feed by melody,grunge,and straightalking.
They worked in the area of rock that crossed a tune with the garage but they spared you the B-movie horror mentally of the likes of The Cramps and the dumbism of the Ramones.
Instead they addressed those hoary old issues confronting the adolescent;suicide,cynicism, and love among them.Their sense of drama was outdone only by their propensity to break guitar strings.
On stage,the trio were obnoxious,loud,humourous,stuttering,brilliant...
Their power and attitude was a merging of The Creation and Gary Glitter,particularly when Shayne Carter held the moment.Wayne Elsey, like John Collie,was a more subdued prescence, but when he did open up his tongue had a considerable cut.
A night out with The Doublehappys meant YOU DIDN'T SIT DOWN.
They were a rough diamond boxing out of a dark little corner marked slap it down and piss on the notion of cleaning it up.
The video for 'Needles and Plastic' was a fairly faithful guide to the band's notions.Made with a single camera wavering at a jumbled movement of bodies it contained the humour with mock fans adoringly rushing to handle the trio and Carter barely being able to stand up for laughing after a ludicrous star jump.Like the EP 'Cut It Out' it never seemed to fully surface,as if someone had pulled down a curtain of fog between the camera and the band.

THE ESSENTIALS

Personnel:Shayne Carter(guitar,vocals),p-e ously in schoolboy punk band,Bored Games w were called into the studio well after the had broken up to cut the EP "Who Killed Co nel Mustard'.
Wayne Elsey (guitar,vocals) also a Bored G but on duty with his own band The Stones w the Ep was done.Stones did a five tracker lled 'Another Disc Another Dollar'.
John Collie (drums) joined after briefis stints with Gamaunche and After the Fall b fairly low-key affairs.
Existence:Debut(coincidentally)on Guy Fawk night 1983 at The Empire,Dunedin.Use drum-machine Herbie Fuckface for the first doze or so outings (Herbie being good for four, adequate for four and a disaster for the r mainder).Flesh 'n blood Collie,a longtime buddy of Elsey,is drafted in.Play last gig Auckland,June 1985.

THE REAL ESSENTIALS

As sure as your bum points to the dirt, best had yet to come.
Anyway,to the records we're left with.

DOUBLE B-SIDE The Other's Way/Anyone Else
Recorded in six hours at The Lab,Auckland March 1984.Laid down piece by piece and c inced them the next one should be live.
The band were still in their teething st but the melody and guitar lines more thar rried the day.Hell,get me to the dance fl Carter wrote it and its piles of melody w twinkling,climbing guitars and typicall wrought words.
If Carter worked in bold colours,Elsey se ed for monochrome,as witnessed in this fl side.A more sombre tune,featuring Elsey's deadpan sneer vocal.Carter's guitar climb board later and they vocally hit the chor together.

CUT IT OUT,EP:

Needles and Plastic:Carter wrote this afte visit to one of night's zombie spots (a n htclub or something) where they wouldn't

BIG FAT BL

26. *Garage #1*, edited by Richard Langston, A4, 1984. Ōtepoti Dunedin.
27. *Garage #2*, edited by Richard Langston, A4, 1985. Ōtepoti Dunedin.
28. *Garage #4* spread, edited by Richard Langston, A4, 1985. Ōtepoti Dunedin.

Andrew Schmidt A lot of journalists were music fans, and even though they were writing mainstream objective reportage, they were also music fans. This was something they weren't really allowed to do in their main jobs. So in some ways it was another outlet for their different types of writing.

Richard Langston Bruce Russell was on board really early. We attracted good people and, y'know, they were all good conventional journalists. I mean, David Swift worked for the *NME* as a sub.

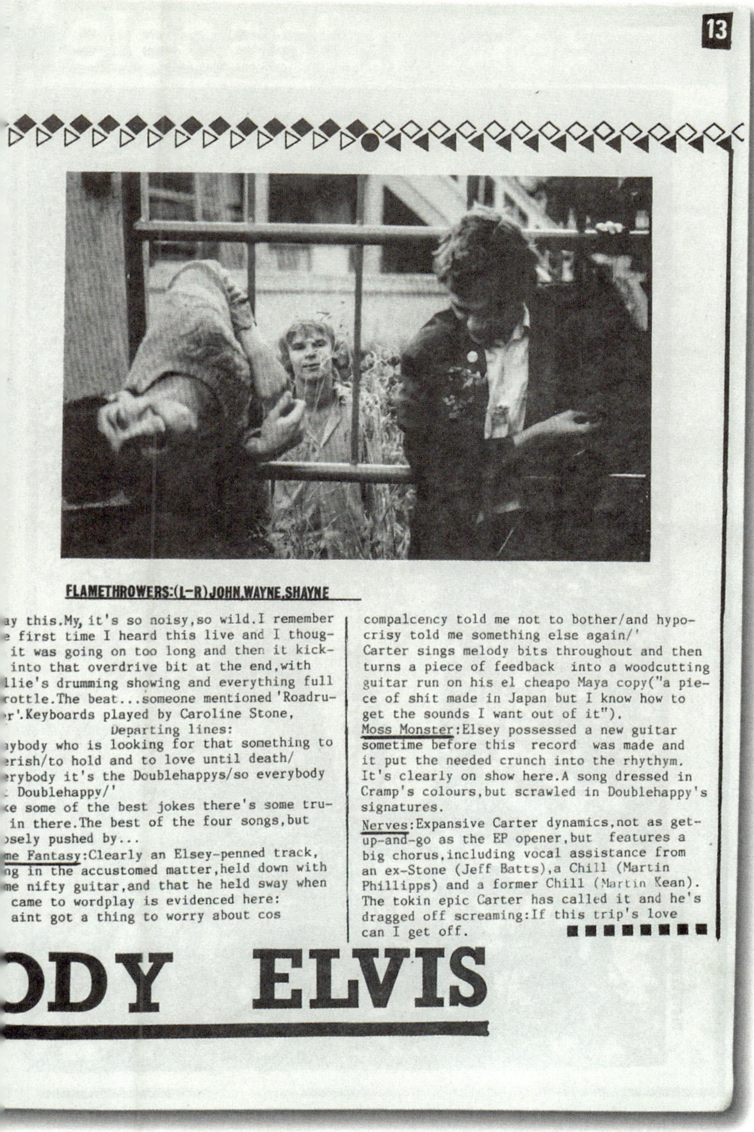
13

FLAMETHROWERS:(L-R)JOHN,WAYNE,SHAYNE

ay this.My, it's so noisy,so wild.I remember
e first time I heard this live and I thoug-
it was going on too long and then it kick-
into that overdrive bit at the end,with
llie's drumming showing and everything full
rottle.The beat...someone mentioned 'Roadru-
r'.Keyboards played by Caroline Stone,
Departing lines:
ybody who is looking for that something to
rish/to hold and to love until death/
rybody it's the Doublehappys/so everybody
Doublehappy/'
ke some of the best jokes there's some tru-
in there.The best of the four songs,but
osely pushed by...
me Fantasy:Clearly an Elsey-penned track,
ng in the accustomed matter,held down with
me nifty guitar,and that he held sway when
came to wordplay is evidenced here:
aint got a thing to worry about cos
compalcency told me not to bother/and hypocrisy told me something else again/'
Carter sings melody bits throughout and then turns a piece of feedback into a woodcutting guitar run on his el cheapo Maya copy("a piece of shit made in Japan but I know how to get the sounds I want out of it").
Moss Monster:Elsey possessed a new guitar sometime before this record was made and it put the needed crunch into the rhythym. It's clearly on show here.A song dressed in Cramp's colours,but scrawled in Doublehappy's signatures.
Nerves:Expansive Carter dynamics,not as get-up-and-go as the EP opener,but features a big chorus,including vocal assistance from an ex-Stone (Jeff Batts),a Chill (Martin Phillipps) and a former Chill (Martin Kean). The tokin epic Carter has called it and he's dragged off screaming:If this trip's love can I get off.

ODY ELVIS

Richard Davies For me, making zines happened organically. Brett [Taylor] was very focused. He'd be chopping stuff and leaving stuff and not using it, and I'm grabbing what he's not using and turning it into something else.

I didn't need any additional encouragement to publish. I just watched what he did and followed his lead. Sometimes I might ask him 'How d'ya fit this in here?' or 'Where do I go to get a bromide for this?' I actually really wanted to do one on American punk bands, like Black Flag and that sort of early American punk, like *Flipside* magazine. That's where I wanted to head with it, but I ended up in Toxic Avengers, and that was all-consuming.

Richard Langston We had to measure, cut, type . . . And with every typing error we'd have to glue a letter over the mistake. The whole thing was so hands-on. There *was* Wite-Out [correcting fluid or tape], but it was always more effective to actually type the letter again, cut it out, and glue it over the mistake. It was like twelfth-century monk behaviour. It was, honestly. Wearing gloves, too, because I used to produce the zine in a room without a wall — sort of just sarking on the side — and in the southerly with a balaclava on I'd be cutting out these things and then gluing them individually and putting them on . . . I mean, they were bloody works of art in their own rough way. I should have kept the originals. They were things to behold. The glue was one of those paste bottles with a red top. You'd end up with glue on your hands and the fucking thing would be blowing away in the wind.

Ania Glowacz I'd photocopied as many as I could afford to do. I don't even know how many I did. It was definitely a collector's item, especially the spraypainted one with the different DayGlo colours on the cover: lime green, hot pink.

Richard Davies We were reprinting articles from other zines, right? So, that's why there's a *PMT* ad in there, because they're helping us and we're helping them. It was really a lot of letter-writing and helping each other. We didn't have a telephone. We didn't *want* a telephone. It was done by mail, and it would take you two weeks to get your answer. It was a slow process. That's why it was only once a month that we could dump a zine. But Brett was very consistent.

Brett had a self-imposed monthly deadline for *Taranaki Underground*. His dad was an investigative journalist, and he grew up watching him and basically operated in a very similar way. His dad wouldn't have ever seen his stuff. They were working stiffs up in Auckland.

29

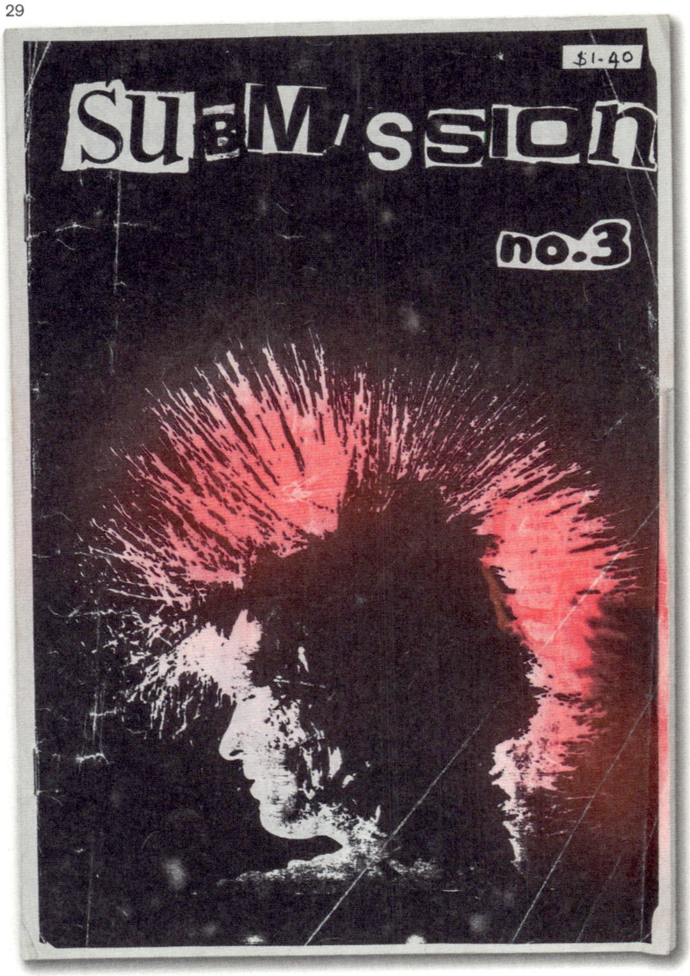

30

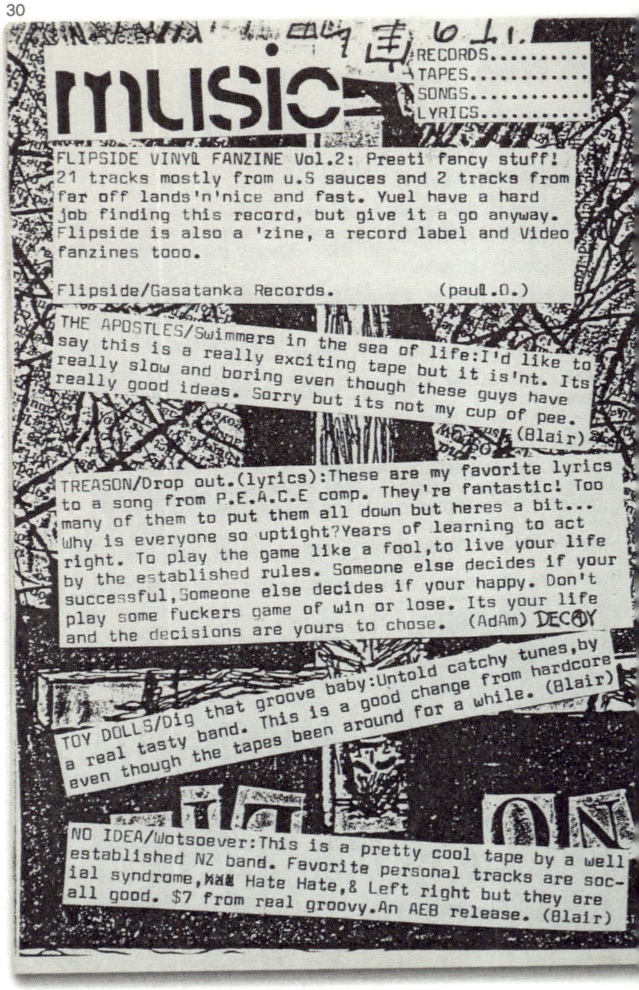

music
RECORDS..........
TAPES............
SONGS............
LYRICS...........

FLIPSIDE VINYL FANZINE Vol.2: Preeti fancy stuff! 21 tracks mostly from u.S sauces and 2 tracks from far off lands'n'nice and fast. Yuel have a hard job finding this record, but give it a go anyway. Flipside is also a 'zine, a record label and Video fanzines tooo.

Flipside/Gasatanka Records. (paul.O.)

THE APOSTLES/Swimmers in the sea of life:I'd like to say this is a really exciting tape but it is'nt. Its really slow and boring even though these guys have really good ideas. Sorry but its not my cup of pee. (Blair)

TREASON/Drop out.(lyrics):These are my favorite lyrics to a song from P.E.A.C.E comp. They're fantastic! Too many of them to put them all down but heres a bit... Why is everyone so uptight?Years of learning to act right. To play the game like a fool,to live your life by the established rules. Someone else decides if your successful,Someone else decides if your happy. Don't play some fuckers game of win or lose. Its your life and the decisions are yours to chose. (AdAm) DECAY

TOY DOLLS/Dig that groove baby:Untold catchy tunes,by a real tasty band. This is a good change from hardcore even though the tapes been around for a while. (Blair)

NO IDEA/Wotsoever:This is a pretty cool tape by a well established NZ band. Favorite personal tracks are social syndrome, Hate Hate,& Left right but they are all good. $7 from real groovy.An AEB release. (Blair)

29. *Submission* #3, Ania Glowacz, A4, 1987. Te Whanganui-a-Tara Wellington.

30. *A.N.I.* #1 spread and cover, credited to Adam W. Decay, Blair and Paul, A5, date unknown. Tāmaki Makaurau Auckland.

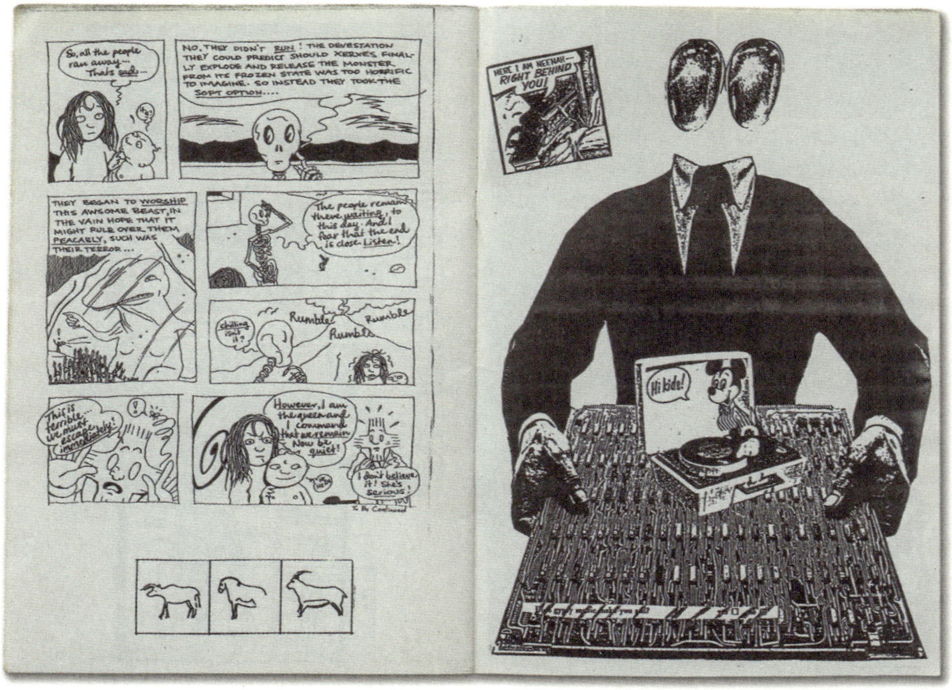

31. *Fly Paper* spread, Tim Bollinger (left), Gregrory Edwards (right), edited by Dave Hall, Tim Bollinger and Gregory Edwards, A4, 1985. Ōtepoti Dunedin.

YOU CAN HELP END THIS CRUEL SLAUGHTER

Last year 30,000 young Harp seals were killed -the majority of them between two weeks and twelve months old. They don't kill so many whitecoats now (1 day to 12 days old) because Europe and the USA banned imports of the white furs but they still kill those a few days older when their fur changes colour because they use the skins for leather and the fat for margarine Haven't they heard of vegetable oil ??? Europe and USA have banned them - WHY NOT AUSTRALIA ?? Even though Australia may not be your country 180,000 Harp seals willdie this year. The more people who support this murder the more they will kill. HERE'S HOW YOU CAN FINALLY END THE SLAUGHTER:

Write to R.J. Hawke,
Prime Minister,
Parliament House,
Canberra ACT 2600
AUSTRALIA

And ask him to keep his promise to ban imports of Harp seal products.

There is a Royal Commision into Sealing taking place in Canada. You can make a submission to it with a letter stating what you would like done about the seal slaughter. Write to:
Mr Denny Stimpson/Consul/Canadian
Consulate General / 50 Bridge Street
/ Sydney 2000 / AUSTRALIA.
Ask him to forward your letter to the Royal Commision. Be polite. Don't forget most Canadians don't like the seal slaughter either.

25

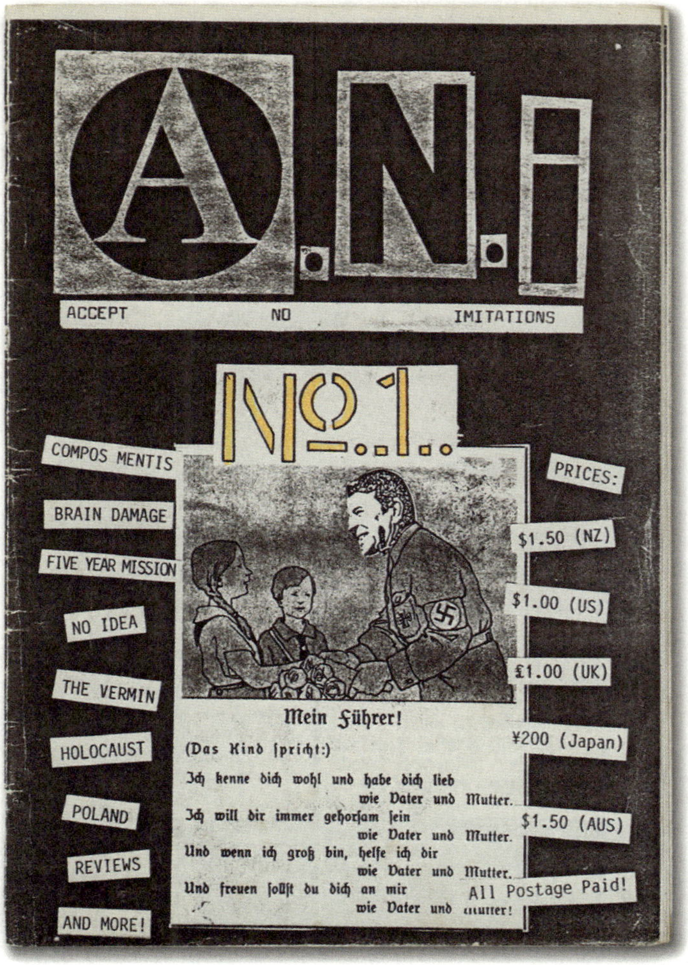

Andrew Schmidt We'd go directly to the bands and send them questions. We were quite historically minded, even in the *Ha Ha Ha* days, because there wasn't a lot of information available. I mean, gosh, yep, letters, and they would write back letters, some of which I still have. I've definitely got one from Hamish Kilgour[9] where he sends us all the addresses of the different band members. They were really into the idea of having a fanzine. There wasn't a Flying Nun fanzine at that point. *Garage* hadn't started.

Paul Luker In Parnell it was Taste Records. It was long and narrow. It was only this wide [stretches arms out], and there was a counter by the door and a row of records against the wall. It was tiny and it had everything. Fuck, the amount of records I bought there . . . And Simon Grigg, really nice. You know that this is the guy who's worked with the Suburban Reptiles and he's just up the road and so you could meet people. You could meet *the* people. I walked out of Taste Records' High Street store one day and there's Chris Knox walking in. I didn't know the guy.

'I thought Toy Love were in Australia?'

'Oh, we were, mate. Yeah, we've broken up.'

'Excuse me, what!?' *Hang on a minute Scoop!* Just chatted on the footpath. Didn't know me, didn't know him. Wrote it up.

And The Gordons moving in with Shoes This High around the corner in Parnell on Bath Street. Saw them in the pub. Saw Brent [Hayward] from Shoes This High in the Windsor [Castle pub]. How the fuck we ever got to know each other I do not know, but clearly there's me standing at the back and then over on the other side's probably him straight from Wellington. There was something about him that was very anarchic, but at the same time he was another outsider. So I talked to Shoes This High, and then he says, 'Oh, The Gordons are coming up next week, their van broke down, took a little bit longer.' When I interviewed The Gordons, Alister Parker didn't say much at all. I think he just stared at me the whole time. It was quite uncomfortable.

Simon Cottle As it developed, there were definitely photos of bands. Like, you're not gonna see Wazzo Ghoti at the Clarendon, because really the only thing out there was *Rip It Up*, which wasn't always favourable to punk. The zine ended up with a pretty clear format. There'd be a band interview, promotion of gigs, gig reviews, promotion of other fanzines that were out there, and letters coming in. So you pretty much had some bare bones right there, and inevitably I'd be up to something with the Anti-Vivisection Society, plus whatever I happened to come across in *The Evening Post* that sounded a bit naughty. I also had people sending in poetry or comic strips and things like that. So that was always the basis of the content. There were already lots of ideas for graphic backgrounds, bits that had been snipped and flogged from other sources.

John Farrow There was a mix of zines at the time. You had *Black Flag* anarchist news [UK] at one end, which was pure politics, and then you had some that were pure art. A lot of the New Zealand ones in the eighties were a mix of politics, music, reviews, art and poetry.

32

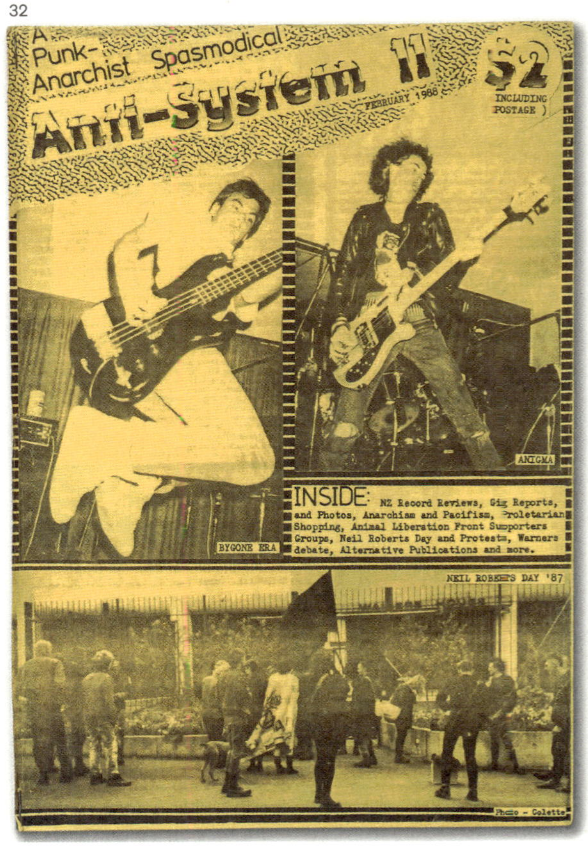

32. *Anti-System* #11 cover and spread, edited by Simon Cottle, A4, 1988. Te Whanganui-a-Tara Wellington.

OUTCRY Music Pages:

The "it rips, it shreds, it cuts waves through the carpet" award, goes to this one. NAZGÜL have achieved what they set out to do, that is, "play a style no other band in NZ is playing". They've done it more in the hardcore/thrash style (DISORDER influence) than metal, although 'demon hardcore' does incorporate very gruff vocals from both Wayne & Michelle and dominant guitar. Four studio songs on one side, with a raw dis-torted guitar, at a speed perfect for insane slamming! Lyrics are a strong point to, although some may take exception to 'Good Demons' (alot of bullshit eg STORMTROOPERS OF DEATH, is passed off as 'piss-takes' these days). Live recordings of 'Farce' (about the SEX PISTOLS swindle) and 'Masters' from the Breakout gig, are a bit too chaotic. 'Practice What You Preach' (when you talk of unity) really boils, but is close to the studio version on side 1, as is the live 'Private War' close to the NZ 7" comp. version. Overall this is an outstanding record, made better with its splendid cover artwork, lyric sheet and the fact it is on NAZGÜL's drummer & vocalists own label. An essential purchase!

I'd describe it as a fusion of '60s (STOOGES, HENDRIX, drugs, wah-wah pedal) and punk (RUTS, HUSKER DU, alcohol, AFTERSHOCK - Kevin and Dean's earlier band). But then that doesn't cover the full on Ska-ish 'Back Beat', or my favourite of the twelve songs 'Certain Death', which is more metal-ish (in the traditional sense). I'm surprised (but glad) Jayrem released this, as they wouldn't do anything with Kevins earlier band THE GLASS, as 'it couldn't be easily pigeon-holed' and the same applies for NUMBER NINE. Seeing them live will give you a greater appreciation of how powerful these songs are, but a lot of the power (not to be confused with speed) is here on the album. This is so good, while listening to the line 'There is a point, everything must explode', my toaster exploded! Looking forward to more NUMBER NINE vinyl - how about live favourite 'Getting Too Quiet'? P.S. Gary Steele (Evening Post) fuck off.

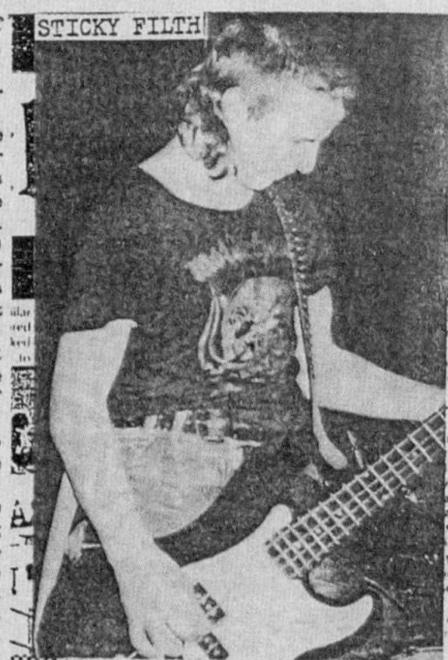

STICKY FILTH

STICKY FILTH: 'At Least Rock n Roll Doesn't Give You AIDS', 7" on Ima Hitt Rec. Available for $5 to Ima Hitt, 143 Devon st East, New Plymouth. 3 live songs (from Nov '86) of a sort of saltatorial rock n roll, that some days I like, & other days I find it boring. My view is tainted by the bullshit packaging which incorporates religion, pornography & blames 'homos' for AIDS. - Is this pub rock, or punk rock?

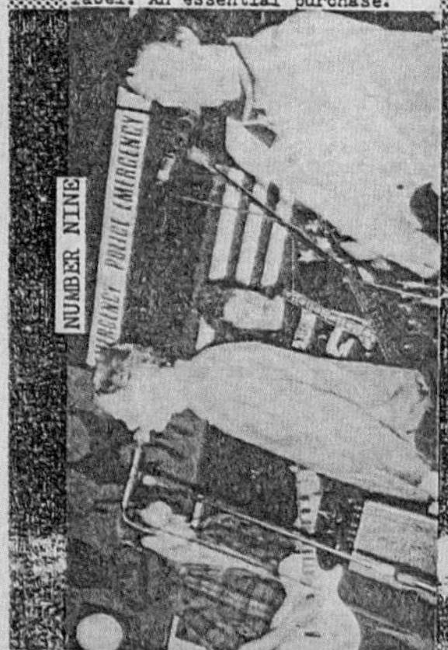

NUMBER NINE

NUMBER NINE: 'Nowhere Fast', LP on Jayrem Records (Jay 329). Available for $14.99 from shops, or $12 from Ania at Submission 'zine, PO Box 6516, Te Aro, Wellington. No doubt a lot of punks trapped in their pathetically narrow musical dogma, will call this album boring, but I'm sure that won't worry NUMBER NINE too much - they appeal to a wider audience, one that can appreciate powerful, non-commercial, NZ garage music. (Submission/ What would you say if someone called you a punk band? Kevin/ I'd just laugh at them). Labelling NUMBER NINE is a no no, they might go as far as saying 'rock n roll' -

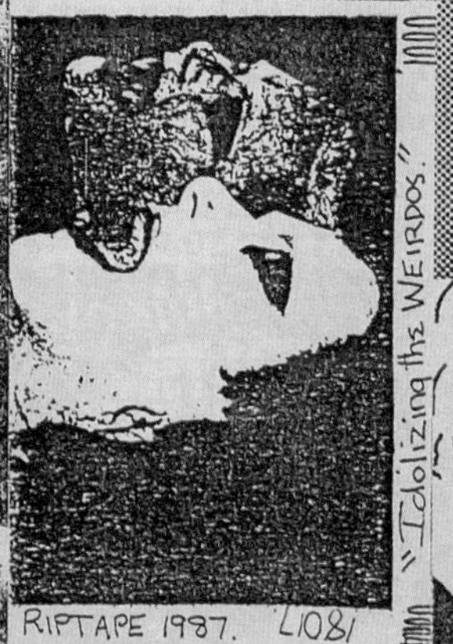

SURVIVORS OF THE PLAGUE: 'Idolizing the Weirdos', Cassette, on Riptape. Available for $5, to PO. Box 2181, South Dunedin. "Worlds flare and die... plague extinguishes the last light of the universe... but out of the darkness a dim light shines... SURVIVORS OF THE PLAGUE". A C-60 with 8 Radio One & 6 live recordings, + some other Dunedinites. SOTP are a 5-piece (2 drummers) that play slow songs, some of which grind, others are bouncy, & some thump! They have mid-paced songs, and 'Farewell O England' reminds me of DISORDER. There's also a couple of fast thrashers, eg the awesomely rad 'Aggresive Suicide' !

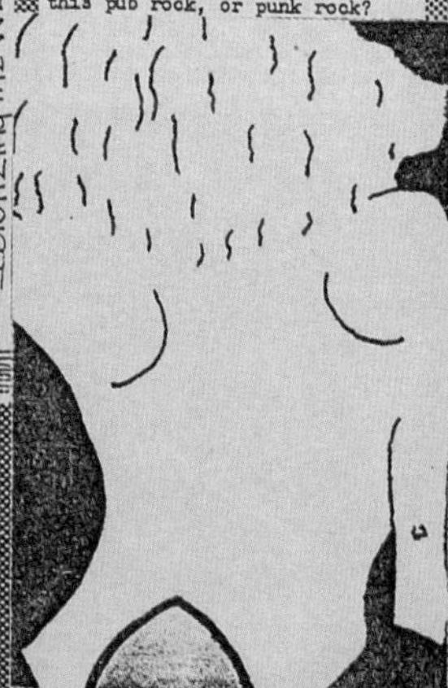

ONAWETA: 'Dance Little Children' 7" on Weta. Available for $3.50 from shops. The mind-blowing video on RWP reminded me of this release. I love the funky bass on this dance (hardedge?) numben

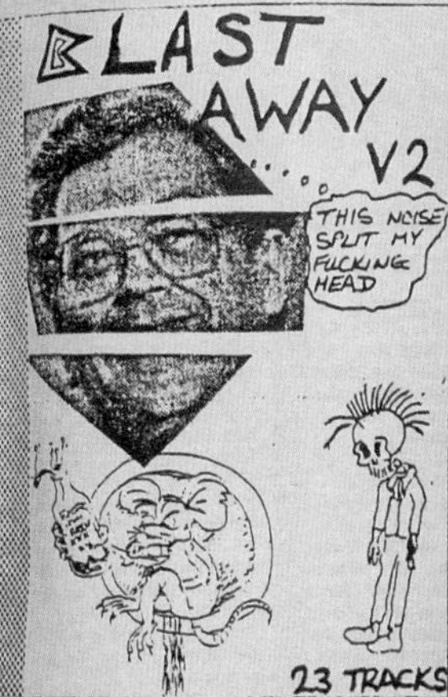

VARIOUS ARTISTS: 'Blast Away V2' Cassette, on Out Of Order tapes. Available for $6 to 000 Distrib, P.O. Box 7414, Wellington South. Good quality recordings of NZ & Australian bands. DIOXIN O.D. grind out two versions of their 'Psycho Ward 13', COMPOS MENTIS have the best song of their last studio session, with 'Divide and Rule' great lyrics and an excellent mix - this should definately be on vinyl! Also from NZ are DEAD IMAGE, a defunct Auckland band, both their songs are on their 'Orswell In '84' EP, ACID REIGN have their best recordings so far on here, including 'Carnivore' live, sounding better than the version on the NZ 7" Compilation - Off which NAZGÜL'S 'Private War' is taken, a thrash classic, with hot lyrics and intro. Another defunct NZ band on 'Blast Away' is FALSE EXISTENCE, with the speedy 'Fucking Bullshit' off V1 and SUBHUMAN'S 'No' sounding similar to ACID REIGN doing 'Not Me'. END RESULT have 1 song, sounding like early (ie great) INSTIGATORS. The Aussie stuff is more metal based, with the mid-paced EXTREMES, RENEGADE go the whole way with silly wail-ing vocals, lead breaks and talk of 'Black Rituals' and speaking of silly vocals, NON COMPOS MENTIS have Beaker from the Muppets singing for them over a fast metal fuzz. There's a couple of DEPRESSION tracks of-f V1, which suits me, 'Soldiers Never Cry' is a favourite, plus the weak 'Du Press Shun'. GREENHOUSE EFFECT are slow and heavy, while REJECTED are more British hardcore with a good drum sound. That leaves GASH'S two fast song-s, which of course 'wail and scream, loud and mean'!

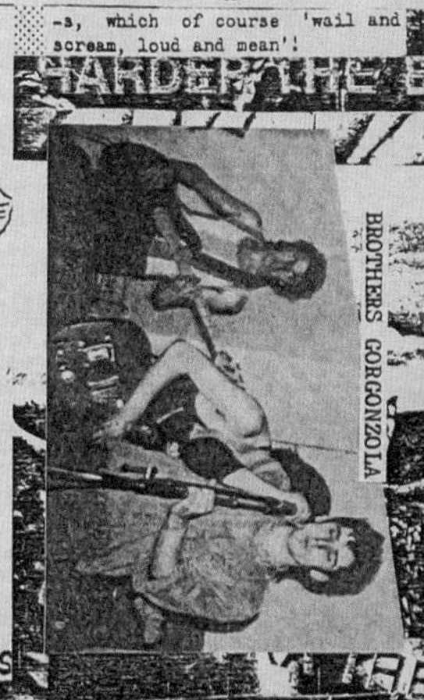

BROTHERS GORGONZOLA

VARIOUS: 'The Harder The Edge The Rocka The Roll', LP on Hardedge Records (cat. no. WILD XXX) distributed by Jayrem. Available from shops for $14.99, or $12 to Ania at Submission 'zine, PO Box 6516, Te Aro, Wellington. This has been in the pipeline quite awhile, so has the wait been worth it? It surpasses other notable NZ compilations like AK 79, and Capitol Kaos, so the answer is an overwhelming yes! 'Features 9 of this countries hottest bands': NO IDEA have 2 songs sounding similar to their Class War EP material - yep, that excellent. FLESH D-VICE suffer from a weak mix, their frenzied guitar is there, but they're not very inspiring overall. MORNING HORNS play two ragey songs, love the intro to 'You'. FIVE YEAR MISSION provide one of the stand out tracks with 'I, Myself', their other song is also super-catchy. COMPOS MENTIS reconfirm that they were one of punks greatest, with Heather's striking vocals on 'Confused' and the anti-nazi 'Run For Shelter' (a crowd favourite). ARMATRAK's 2 songs are of their older stuff ie faster hardcore, and they're real lively buggers. ?FOG have only 1 song, cool lyrics over a backward music backing. The talentless (pure attitude man) MINDFUCKERS produce music for mutants, including bizzare classic 'I'm A Duck'. BROTHERS GORGONZOLA are the least 'punk', but produce good alternative sounds. Originally "the whole idea of the thing was to give bands the encouragement to keep on going", well the last 5 bands mentioned appear to have split, but this album is still a sucess. A high quality record - buy before that next import!

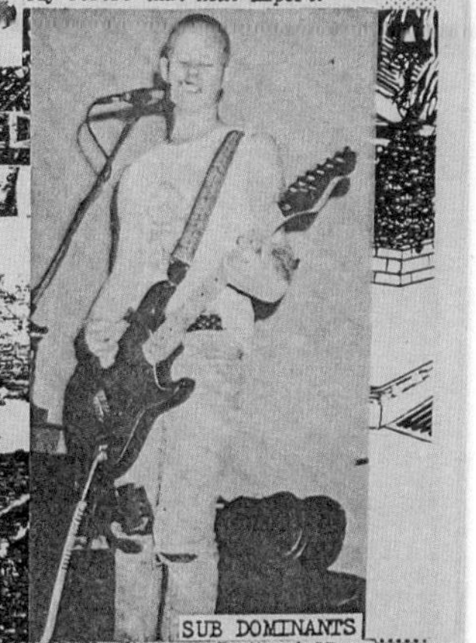

SUB DOMINANTS

VARIOUS: 'Madness To Mana' LP, a product of a govt. funded T.A.P. scheme. Available for $14 from shops. 2 tracks each from blue's FLYING POAKAS, reggae's I-SHENCE & synthesizer from TIM GOLDER - + of more interest, 5 songs from SUB-DOMINANTS (up to you to decide if that's $14 worth). 'Help Me Please' gets 14 'OI's in, but I'd describe this as slow sing-a-long punk. Catchy tunes which stick in your head! Fun lyrics & I especially like Allana's vocals on 'Insanity'.

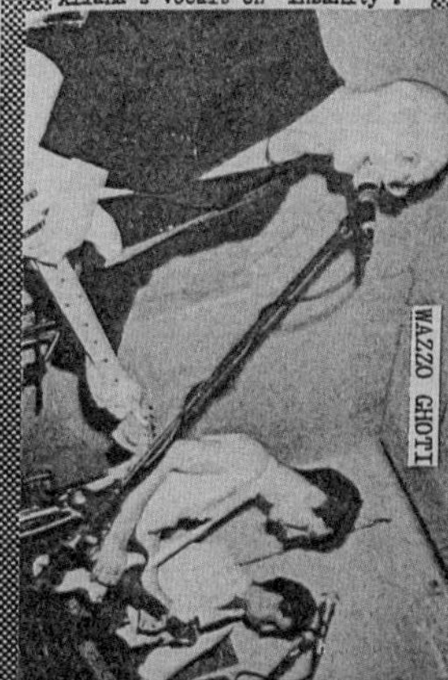

WAZZO GHOTI

WAZZO GHOTI: 'Stuff What We Did You're a Beautiful Audience'. Available for $4 + 70¢ stamped SAE, to WAZZO GHOTI, c/- PO Box 14156, Kilbirnie, Wellington. 12 live song tape now available.

Richard Davies No, my zines weren't riddled with spelling mistakes. My mum was a schoolteacher, and my main subject was English. I did a lot of the editing. I used to go over everything. The ADD [attention deficit disorder] didn't adversely affect that; it actually made me really good at spotting spelling mistakes. I'd read things and I could spot a spelling mistake like that [snaps fingers]. At school, if I didn't get 100 per cent in spelling I'd kick my own ass.

Simon Cottle It's hard to say exactly how much my academic training was spilling over into my zine writing at the time, but — coupled with my anti-vivisection work — there was definitely training in a kind of conciseness, getting thoughts onto paper in a non-rambling way. So lots of influence there in terms of writing style. Also taking pride in spelling and grammar — which was kind of my mum's thing — and again, remember, you're whacking it out on the old Imperial 66 typewriter, there's no spell-check or whatever.

Andrew Schmidt When I got to Waikato University, there was this fantastic library there full of new journalism, Hunter S. Thompson, but also more conservative stuff like Tom Wolfe, Joe Eszterhas, and that was really vibrant, alive, where the writer was very much present and sometimes actually part of the story, but generally in a more fictional sense as well. So we were describing environments, and all that sort of descriptive active writing was very much current back then. For me having a fanzine was just an opportunity to be able to do that type of writing and get it out there, and also to learn as I went along, because it's a big step from a small town to a media environment. I don't come from an academic or a creative background. I come, like most of my music friends, out of the rugby clubs in Paeroa. We had no background to draw on. There were more immediate influences that were motivating us. I'd get these books, and I would give them to my friends to read. I was very much a book person as well. Words were always important. It came before music, but once music kicked in it was an opportunity to combine the two things.

I didn't have a lot of confidence as a kid. I was a really anxious, shy kid, and writing was a way to express what I was feeling. Music was another stimulant. Together it was a way to get some sort of identity going.

Richard Langston All the people had some kind of journalist training or were big readers or writers, so it was incredibly lucky that it attracted other people who knew their stuff and could write. David Swift, Ian Henderson — who was writing for *The Southland Times* — reviewed the first *Garage*, and so I immediately got him to start writing for us because obviously he was interested. That's how that kind of networking worked really. And that networking worked for getting in touch with *B Side* in Australia and *Forced Exposure*. That snail mail worked as a way to contact people and build a network. It was just slower, and probably more hit-and-miss. People sent records from places like the Midwest of the United States. How the hell did they find out about *Garage*? Well, we got reviewed in a few mags, I guess.

Tony Renouf We put the poster up, and at about the same time I'd started doing page-y stuff and strip stuff for *Critic*, the Otago University student magazine. This happened through Bruce Mahalski, who had a strip cartoon in *Critic* at around the same time. *Critic* ran 25 issues a year, so I had to produce a strip a week during semester time. At the same time, I'd found *Razor* — Cornelius Stone's monstrosity — and written to him, and also written to Chris Knox about *Jesus on a Stick*. Both Cornelius and Chris were quite welcoming, saying 'Yeah, sure, draw some stuff and send it on up', which I did. I got published in both.

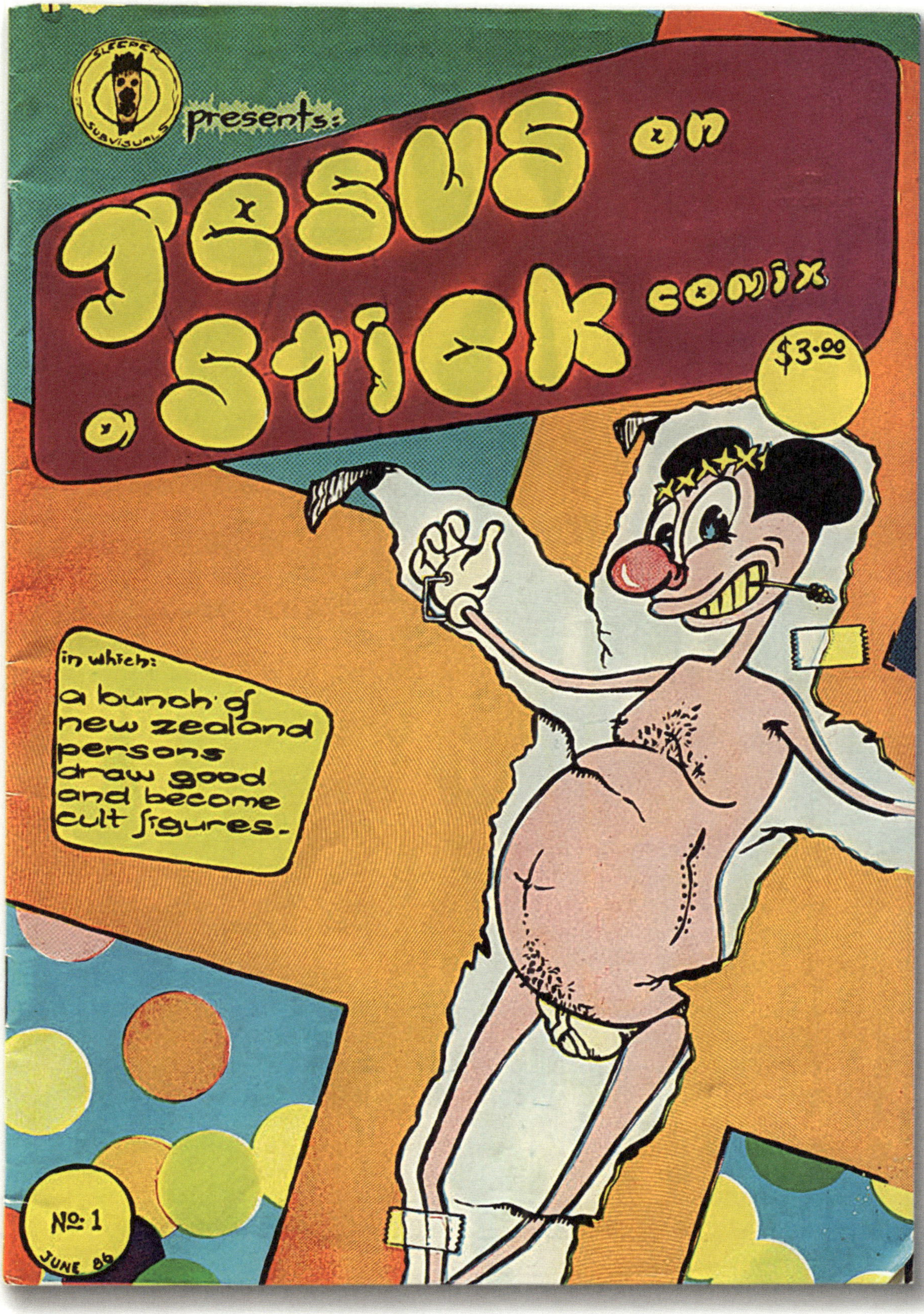

33. *Jesus on a Stick #1*, edited and cover design by Chris Knox, A4, 1986. Tāmaki Makaurau Auckland.

34

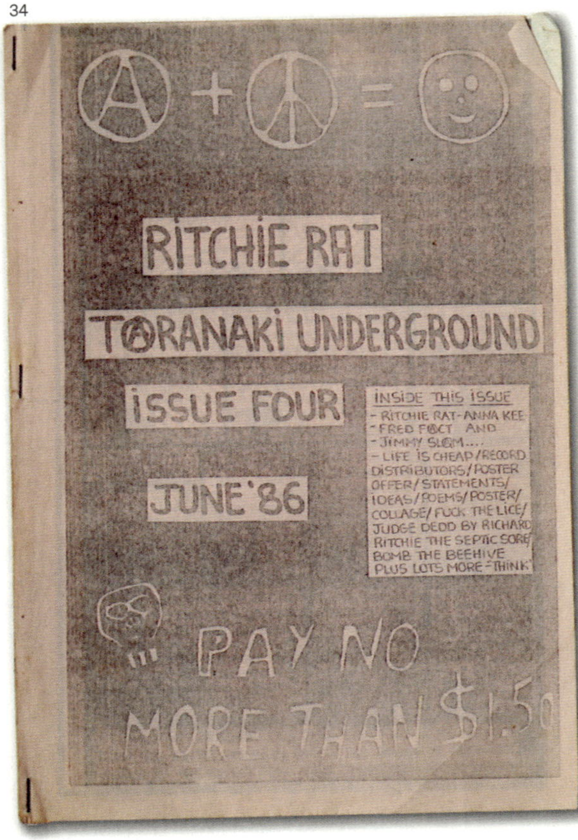

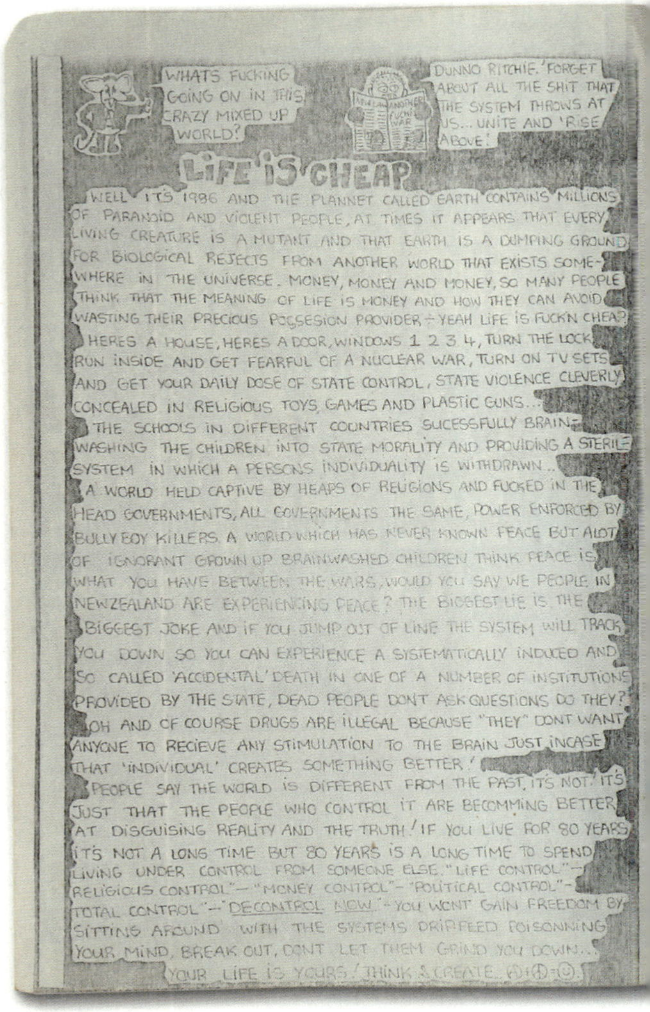
WHATS FUCKING GOING ON IN THIS CRAZY MIXED UP WORLD?

DUNNO RITCHIE. 'FORGET ABOUT ALL THE SHIT THAT THE SYSTEM THROWS AT US... UNITE AND 'RISE ABOVE'.

LIFE IS CHEAP

WELL ITS 1986 AND THE PLANNET CALLED EARTH CONTAINS MILLIONS OF PARANOID AND VIOLENT PEOPLE, AT TIMES IT APPEARS THAT EVERY LIVING CREATURE IS A MUTANT AND THAT EARTH IS A DUMPING GROUND FOR BIOLOGICAL REJECTS FROM ANOTHER WORLD THAT EXISTS SOMEWHERE IN THE UNIVERSE. MONEY, MONEY AND MONEY, SO MANY PEOPLE THINK THAT THE MEANING OF LIFE IS MONEY AND HOW THEY CAN AVOID WASTING THEIR PRECIOUS POSSESION PROVIDER - YEAH LIFE IS FUCK'N CHEAP.

HERES A HOUSE, HERES A DOOR, WINDOWS 1 2 3 4, TURN THE LOCK RUN INSIDE AND GET FEARFUL OF A NUCLEAR WAR, TURN ON TV SETS AND GET YOUR DAILY DOSE OF STATE CONTROL, STATE VIOLENCE CLEVERLY CONCEALED IN RELIGIOUS TOYS, GAMES AND PLASTIC GUNS...

THE SCHOOLS IN DIFFERENT COUNTRIES SUCESSFULLY BRAIN-WASHING THE CHILDREN INTO STATE MORALITY AND PROVIDING A STERILE SYSTEM IN WHICH A PERSONS INDIVIDUALITY IS WITHDRAWN..

A WORLD HELD CAPTIVE BY HEAPS OF RELIGIONS AND FUCKED IN THE HEAD GOVERNMENTS, ALL GOVERNMENTS THE SAME, POWER ENFORCED BY BULLY BOY KILLERS. A WORLD WHICH HAS NEVER KNOWN PEACE BUT ALOT OF IGNORANT GROWN UP BRAINWASHED CHILDREN THINK PEACE IS WHAT YOU HAVE BETWEEN THE WARS, WOULD YOU SAY WE PEOPLE IN NEWZEALAND ARE EXPERIENCING PEACE? THE BIGGEST LIE IS THE BIGGEST JOKE AND IF YOU JUMP OUT OF LINE THE SYSTEM WILL TRACK YOU DOWN SO YOU CAN EXPERIENCE A SYSTEMATICALLY INDUCED AND SO CALLED 'ACCIDENTAL' DEATH IN ONE OF A NUMBER OF INSTITUTIONS PROVIDED BY THE STATE, DEAD PEOPLE DONT ASK QUESTIONS DO THEY?

OH AND OF COURSE DRUGS ARE ILLEGAL BECAUSE "THEY" DONT WANT ANYONE TO RECIEVE ANY STIMULATION TO THE BRAIN JUST INCASE THAT 'INDIVIDUAL' CREATES SOMETHING BETTER!

PEOPLE SAY THE WORLD IS DIFFERENT FROM THE PAST, IT'S NOT! IT'S JUST THAT THE PEOPLE WHO CONTROL IT ARE BECOMMING BETTER AT DISGUISING REALITY AND THE TRUTH! IF YOU LIVE FOR 80 YEARS IT'S NOT A LONG TIME BUT 80 YEARS IS A LONG TIME TO SPEND LIVING UNDER CONTROL FROM SOMEONE ELSE. "LIFE CONTROL" - RELIGIOUS CONTROL" - "MONEY CONTROL" - "POLITICAL CONTROL" - TOTAL CONTROL" - "DECONTROL NOW" - YOU WONT GAIN FREEDOM BY SITTING AROUND WITH THE SYSTEMS DRIPFEED POISONNING YOUR MIND, BREAK OUT, DONT LET THEM GRIND YOU DOWN...

YOUR LIFE IS YOURS! THINK & CREATE. Ⓐ+☮=☺.

Richard Davies Brett actually got an office in town. He lived out on the coast but spent all day in his office. He literally dedicated an office to producing *Taranaki Underground*, *Ritchie Rat* and his other titles. I think he wanted a headquarters where people could come and hang and have a coffee and talk about this stuff and get zines and contribute, more so contribute, hang out, give him an idea. But also, after the house had been raided . . .

Brett stole Ritchie Rat off the cover of this cassette tape that we got from America called *New York Thrash*. There's a rat with boots and a leather jacket. It's got Bad Brains on it, Beastie Boys when they were punk, heaps of wicked bands on it. And then he used my first name for the rat. [Laughs.] He always denied that's where he got the name, but I don't know, seemed a bit weird to me that it was Ritchie Rat and I'm sitting right next to him when he decided. He kept a lot to himself. He didn't tell you all of his plans.

Ania Glowacz People did say nice things about the covers, which is cool. I've been a magazine junkie my whole life. The cover is what sells it.

Richard Davies You'd get a zine-maker to do your album cover back then because they knew how to do bromides, get stuff done, they knew the process. I've done a couple of album covers, nothing worth mentioning, but I have. Oh, and my own stuff as well.

Robert Scott I remember having big sheets of Letraset.[10] How the hell did I line it up so well? Then it's like 'Oh, I can't be bothered doing the rest like that, so I'll do the rest by hand.'

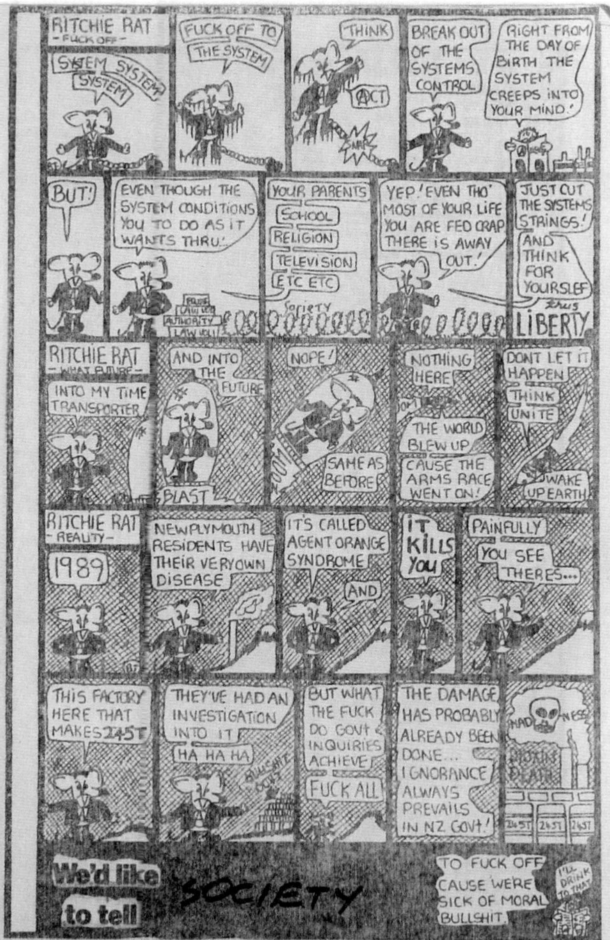

Robert Scott The drawing style was my own self-taught thing, not really part of my art-school training. I dropped out of art school in 1980, once the music took over. Fantastic tutors, though — people like Peter Nicholls and Derek Ball. That zine cover's definitely from the local landscape: macrocarpas, hedging, local buildings, a phone box . . . I wasn't trying to pretend that it was anything else, like anything overseas, that's for sure. There was no question of trying to make it something it wasn't; it was very much grounded in what was around me, what was close to me and what was part of my upbringing. When I was 15 or 16, I used to make a bit of extra money by cycling around the Taieri Plains doing pen-and-ink drawings of people's houses and then selling them to them. Do the drawing first, and then knock on the door and say, 'Would you like to buy this?' Sometimes I'd ask them first. Sometimes it'd be a building in public view, but other times they'd be up a big leafy driveway, so I'd need to go up and get proper access.

Simon Cottle The headings are all rendered in Sharpie [pen] and a ruler, typewriter, stencil, and then — lah-dee-dah — got a bit of Letraset going. Letraset, man, it was so fun! I'd go to the big art supplies shop on Victoria Street, where you'd pull out multiple trays, each with about 10 sheets of Letraset inside. A pretty different age to desktop publishing for sure. I wasn't particularly artistic, but I was good at technical drawing. I've got a logic brain more than an art brain, so the layout and pasting up columns and everything was totally my cup of tea. And then I did quite a lot of photographing of bands as well.

Richard Davies I moved in with Brett, and he starts doing all this stuff and gets this Gestetner, and is basically sponsored by Collier's bookshop. Not just the machine, the ink and paper as well. It wasn't costing anyone anything. So, he was happy to let me in on it. Brett comes home and I'm like 'What?! A bookshop gave you — the dirty punk-rocker from out the coast — like thousands of dollars of free stuff?!' I think they thought that what he was doing was positive, even though they might not have politically agreed. I don't know if they even read it. I just think they thought this guy's doing something creative and positive and so they supported him. I wish Brett hadn't disappeared. He's the one you should be interviewing.

34. *Ritchie Rat / Taranaki Underground #4* cover and spread, Brett Taylor, A4, 1986. Taranaki.

Paul Luker Eventually I did a photo-engraving apprenticeship as a camera operator. That whole industry was a chemical flood plain. The apprentice initiation was to be dumped in the ferricyanide bath, which was as big as this table. It was a good metre square and it was maybe 8 to 10 inches deep, and that's where the ferricyanide was used to deep-etch negatives, [in the days] before scanners. The joke was that it was yellow and it stained you yellow, so everyone knew you'd been dumped, initiated. Photocopies were obviously around, but in 1980 the photocopy machine was a rarity and it was seen as something inferior to printing. If you wanted anything — vanity-published poetry, anything — you just had to stump up to a printer, but there were so many of them, those little back suburban printers with a GTO[11] and probably a little letterpress for wedding cards . . . Making a plate was easy enough, and if you weren't making the plates there were plenty of platemakers around. That's what most of the people in my apprenticeship ended up doing, working in a platemaker's.

35

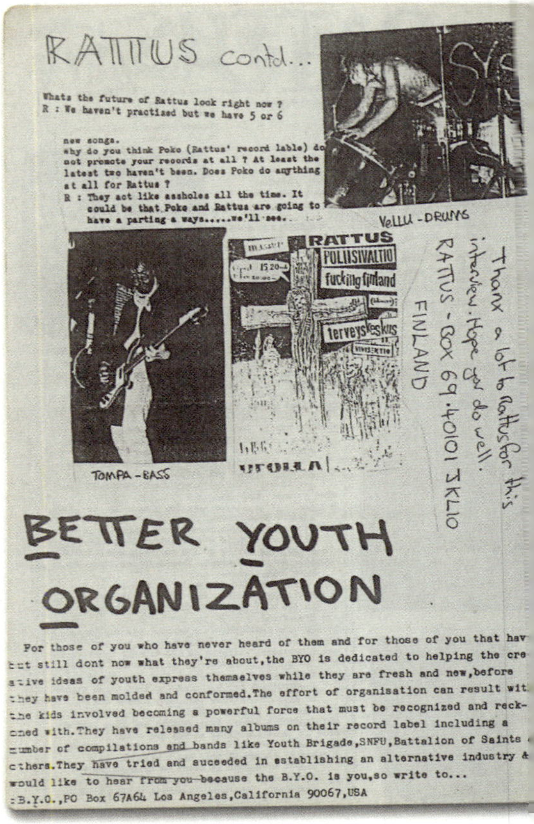

RATTUS contd...

Whats the future of Rattus look right now ?
R : We haven't practised but we have 5 or 6 new songs.
why do you think Poko (Rattus' record lable) do not promote your records at all ? At least the latest two haven't been. Does Poko do anything at all for Rattus ?
R : They act like assholes all the time. It could be that Poko and Rattus are going to have a parting a ways.....we'll see.

BETTER YOUTH ORGANIZATION

For those of you who have never heard of them and for those of you that hav but still dont now what they're about, the BYO is dedicated to helping the cre ative ideas of youth express themselves while they are fresh and new, before they have been molded and conformed. The effort of organisation can result wit the kids involved becoming a powerful force that must be recognized and reck oned with. They have released many albums on their record label including a number of compilations and bands like Youth Brigade, SNFU, Battalion of Saints others. They have tried and suceeded in establishing an alternative industry & would like to hear from you because the B.Y.O. is you, so write to...
:B.Y.O., PO Box 67A64 Los Angeles, California 90067, USA

36

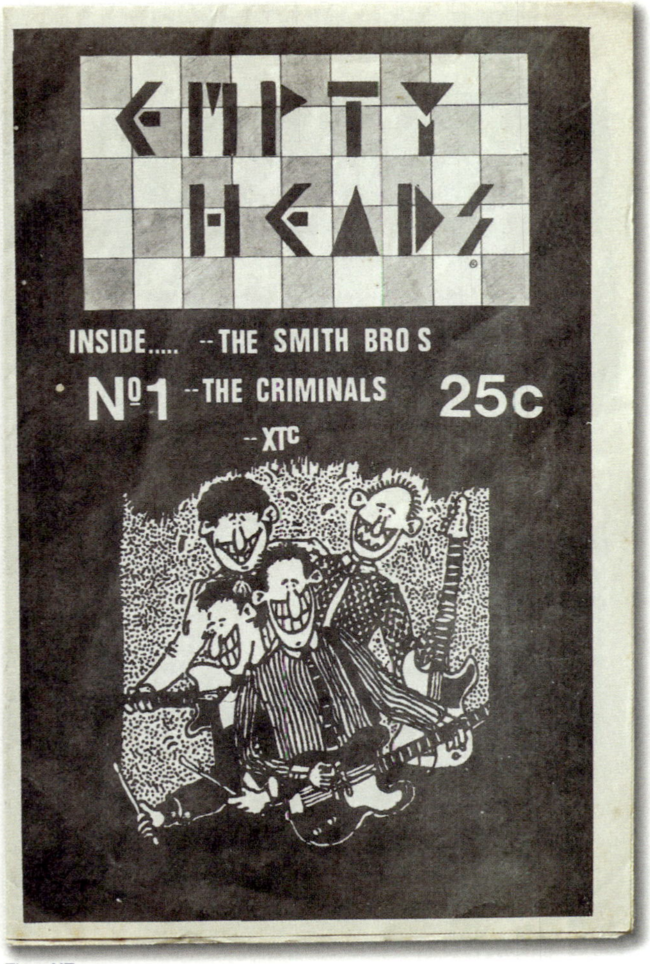

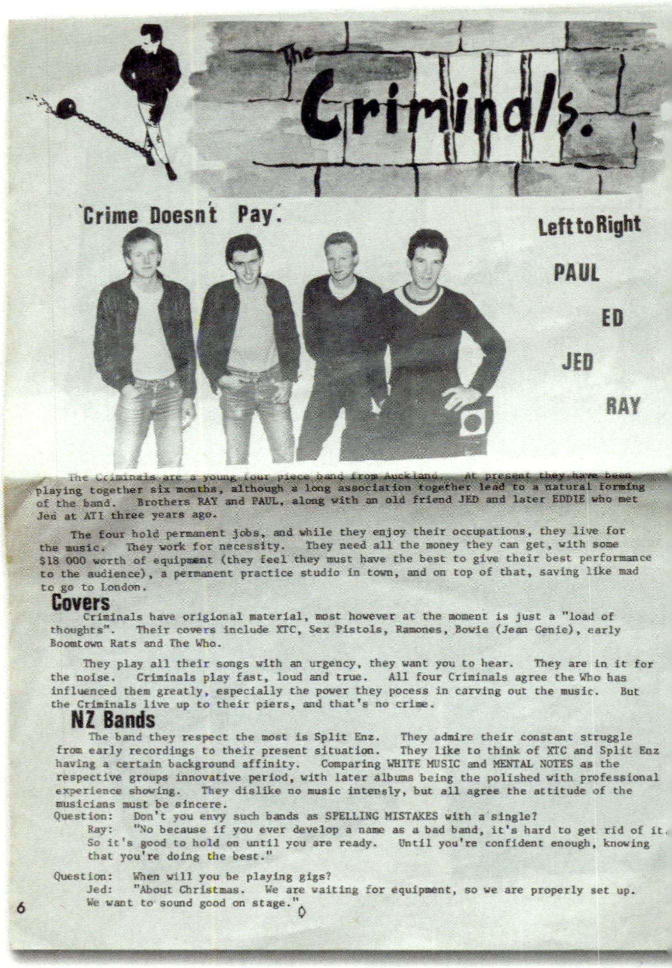

The Criminals are a young four piece band from Auckland. At present they have been playing together six months, although a long association together lead to a natural forming of the band. Brothers RAY and PAUL, along with an old friend JED and later EDDIE who met Jed at ATI three years ago.

The four hold permanent jobs, and while they enjoy their occupations, they live for the music. They work for necessity. They need all the money they can get, with some $18 000 worth of equipment (they feel they must have the best to give their best performance to the audience), a permanent practice studio in town, and on top of that, saving like mad to go to London.

Covers

Criminals have origional material, most however at the moment is just a "load of thoughts". Their covers include XTC, Sex Pistols, Ramones, Bowie (Jean Genie), early Boomtown Rats and The Who.

They play all their songs with an urgency, they want you to hear. They are in it for the noise. Criminals play fast, loud and true. All four Criminals agree the Who has influenced them greatly, especially the power they pocess in carving out the music. But the Criminals live up to their piers, and that's no crime.

NZ Bands

The band they respect the most is Split Enz. They admire their constant struggle from early recordings to their present situation. They like to think of XTC and Split Enz having a certain background affinity. Comparing WHITE MUSIC and MENTAL NOTES as the respective groups innovative period, with later albums being the polished with professional experience showing. They dislike no music intensly, but all agree the attitude of the musicians must be sincere.

Question: Don't you envy such bands as SPELLING MISTAKES with a single?
Ray: "No because if you ever develop a name as a bad band, it's hard to get rid of it. So it's good to hold on until you are ready. Until you're confident enough, knowing that you're doing the best."

Question: When will you be playing gigs?
Jed: "About Christmas. We are waiting for equipment, so we are properly set up. We want to sound good on stage."

6

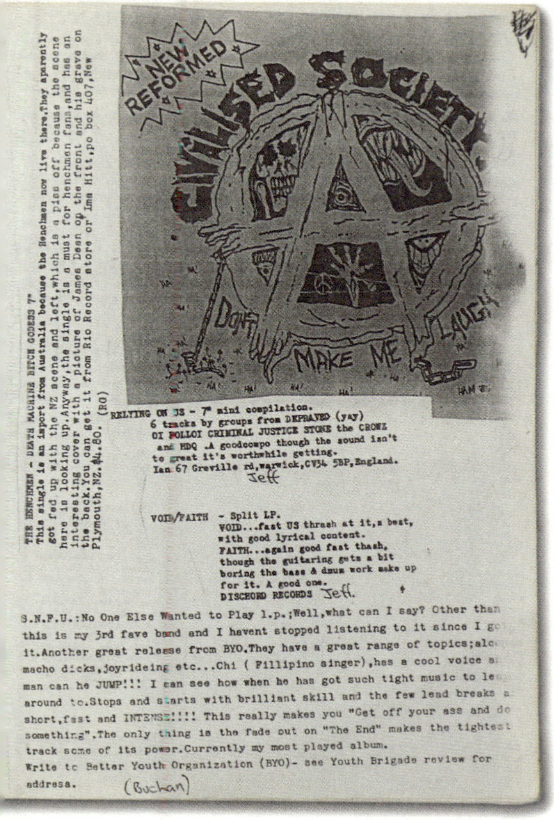
NEW REFORMED
CIVILISED SOCIETY?
DON'T MAKE ME LAUGH

THE HENCHMEN - DEATH MACHINE BITCH GODESS 7"
This single is an import from Australia because the Henchmen now live there.They aparently got fed up with the NZ scene and left,which is a piss off because the scene here is looking up.Anyway,the single is a must for henchmen fans,and has an interesting cover with a picture of James Dean on the front and his grave on the back.You can get it from Rio Record store or Ima Hitt,po box 407,New Plymouth,NZ.$4.80. (RO)

RELYING ON US - 7" mini compilation.
6 tracks by groups from DEPRAVED (yay)
OI POLLOI CRIMINAL JUSTICE STONE the CROWZ
and HDQ .A goodcompo though the sound isn't
to great it's worthwhile getting.
Ian 67 Greville rd,warwick,CV34 5BP,England.
Jeff

VOID/FAITH - Split LP.
VOID...fast US thrash at it,s best,
with good lyrical content.
FAITH...again good fast thash,
though the guitaring gets a bit
boring the bass & drum work make up
for it. A good one.
DISCHORD RECORDS Jeff.

S.N.F.U.:No One Else Wanted to Play l.p.;Well,what can I say? Other than this is my 3rd fave band and I havent stopped listening to it since I go[t] it.Another great release from BYO.They have a great range of topics;alc[ohol], macho dicks,joyrideing etc...Chi (Fillipino singer),has a cool voice a[nd] man can he JUMP!!! I can see how when he has got such tight music to le[ap] around to.Stops and starts with brilliant skill and the few lead breaks a[re] short,fast and INTENSE!!!! This really makes you "Get off your ass and do something".The only thing is the fade out on "The End" makes the tightest track some of its power.Currently my most played album.
Write to Better Youth Organization (BYO)- see Youth Brigade review for address. (Buchan)

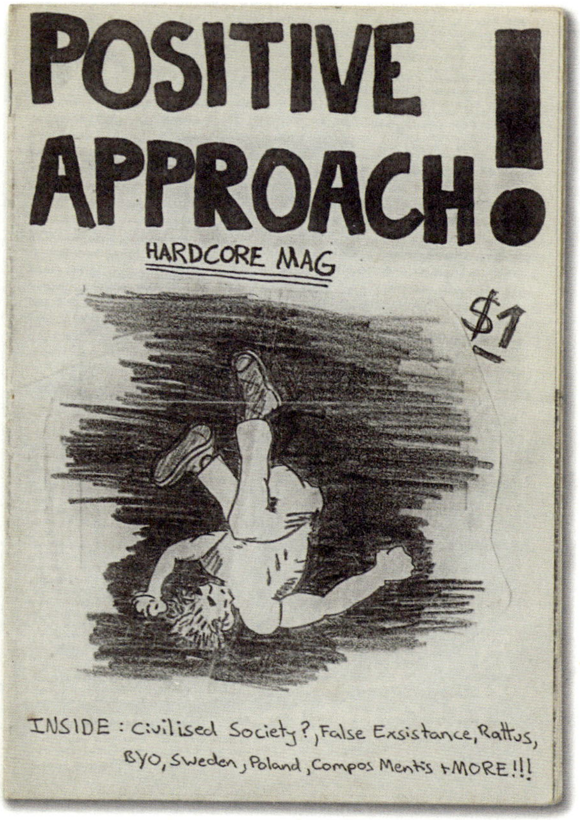
POSITIVE APPROACH!
HARDCORE MAG
$1
INSIDE: Civilised Society?, False Exsistance, Rattus, BYO, Sweden, Poland, Compos Mentis +MORE!!!

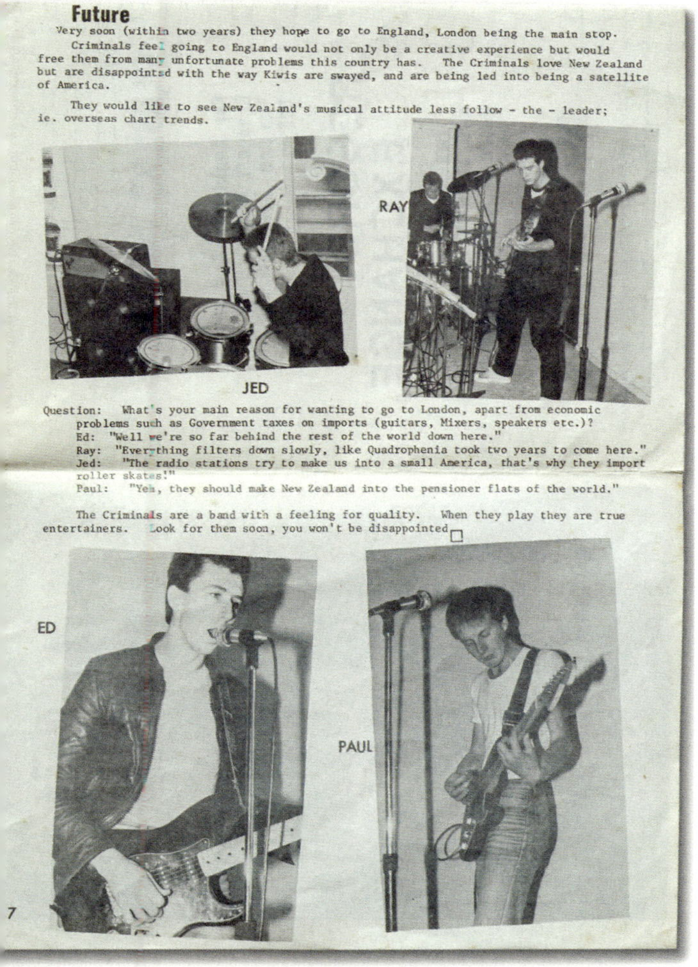
Future

Very soon (within two years) they hope to go to England, London being the main stop.

Criminals feel going to England would not only be a creative experience but would free them from many unfortunate problems this country has. The Criminals love New Zealand but are disappointed with the way Kiwis are swayed, and are being led into being a satellite of America.

They would like to see New Zealand's musical attitude less follow - the - leader; ie. overseas chart trends.

RAY

JED

Question: What's your main reason for wanting to go to London, apart from economic problems such as Government taxes on imports (guitars, Mixers, speakers etc.)?
Ed: "Well we're so far behind the rest of the world down here."
Ray: "Everything filters down slowly, like Quadrophenia took two years to come here."
Jed: "The radio stations try to make us into a small America, that's why they import roller skates!"
Paul: "Yeh, they should make New Zealand into the pensioner flats of the world."

The Criminals are a band with a feeling for quality. When they play they are true entertainers. Look for them soon, you won't be disappointed

ED

PAUL

7

35. *Positive Approach* spread and cover, cover drawing by Buchan Love, A5, 1985. Tāmaki Makaurau Auckland.

36. *Empty Heads* #1 cover and spread, Paul Luker, A5, 1980. Tāmaki Makaurau Auckland.

Bruce Grenville Before the Heidelberg Platen, I already had a small letterpress called an Adana, made in the UK. I trained up Ross Gardiner and lots of other people on how to use it. I'm a bit of a proselytiser for letterpress, so my enthusiasm was getting it more widely used. I didn't try to seek out people who would necessarily be as enthusiastic as me. I'd just be introducing people to it, and if they felt interested, go for it. In [print enthusiast] Max Reeves's case, I didn't know he'd also get into the Ancient Egyptian Church of the Infinite, he just heard me raving on about it while we were printing.

Paul Luker I was working as a photolitho apprentice.[12] Everything was on one sheet; it was literally all paste-up. My mother typed up the text on her typewriter. The photographs were ones I'd taken. I took the whole paste-up to a printer around the corner and he made two pieces of A2 film, and the plates. (I would've asked for production advice down in the platemaking department at work.)

It was easier to find a printer than trying to do it at work; there were lots of jobbing printers around town at that time that just had a GTO, a little German press, and they could take an A3 or A2 [page size]. The GTO is only small. They were beautiful little machines, one colour at a time. All of the [music label] Industrial Tapes covers were printed on a single-colour GTO. Doing full-colour registration [i.e. getting the colours lined up] was not a problem, just a bit laborious.

Tony Renouf In 1987 I bought Matt Feazell's [*The Amazing*] *Cynicalman* from The Comics Shop, and it included instructions on how to make your own mini-comic. When I found that, I went 'Oh, shit, you can just fold a piece of paper in four, slice the top off and staple it together.' So, I recycled a lot of my earlier comics and started making these eight-page mini-comics. I made four: *Teenage Irradiated Jazzercize Sheep* (having never picked up a *Teenage Mutant Ninja* . . . um, comic), then it was *Everything Off the Sides But Don't Touch the Middle*, which is all of the punk-rock cartoons, then *Sedgewick* #1 and #2.

At that stage I was doing my artwork on A2 sheets. I was doing it huge because I wasn't that skilled. I thought that if I did 'em big and then reduced them down . . .

Bruce Grenville I was printing this one-off publication on glossy paper at huge expense [for a client], and as I was helping this guy set it up I suddenly realised that something else could be printed for free in the margins. The customer wanted a square-format publication, and as all the paper stock is A scale — A3, A4, etc. — there was going to be a lot of wasted space. I suddenly realised here's this thing that's going to be printed tomorrow, why don't I rush home, grab Albert Meltzer's[13] book [*Anarchism: Arguments for and against*] and splice it into the edge of the print job, then we'd print this job and I'd get all these nice offcuts and we could make a book.

So, here's the book, which as you can see is quite small and all done on nice glossy paper. I got several thousand copies of this book printed for free, because it was all done on the edge of this magazine job, so that's probably where Ross got the idea that I'd printed *One World* zine on the margins. I've always been a bit of an anarchist propagandist. And I'm a bookbinder as well, so, I just sew them all together and there's a nice book.

Richard Langston You can hardly read issue two of *Garage*. I was so stupid, I didn't replace the typewriter ribbon. It's like 'Urgh'. You can see technology was not my strong point.

John Farrow We'd just shuffle bits and pieces around on the page until we were happy with it and then we'd paste it all down. Then we would take them to a local printer and get them photocopied. Every so often we'd cheat a little bit. I was just remembering that I had a cleaning job at night, and one time when we were hard-up I photocopied a few issues at the business I was supposed to be cleaning. The next week I came in and there was a copy of *PMT* sitting on this guy's desk and I thought 'Oh, far out, cool, this guy's tracked down our zine.' So, I left him a note saying, 'Are you into *PMT*?', and he said 'No, you left it in the photocopier.' I later got fired from that job, but yeah.

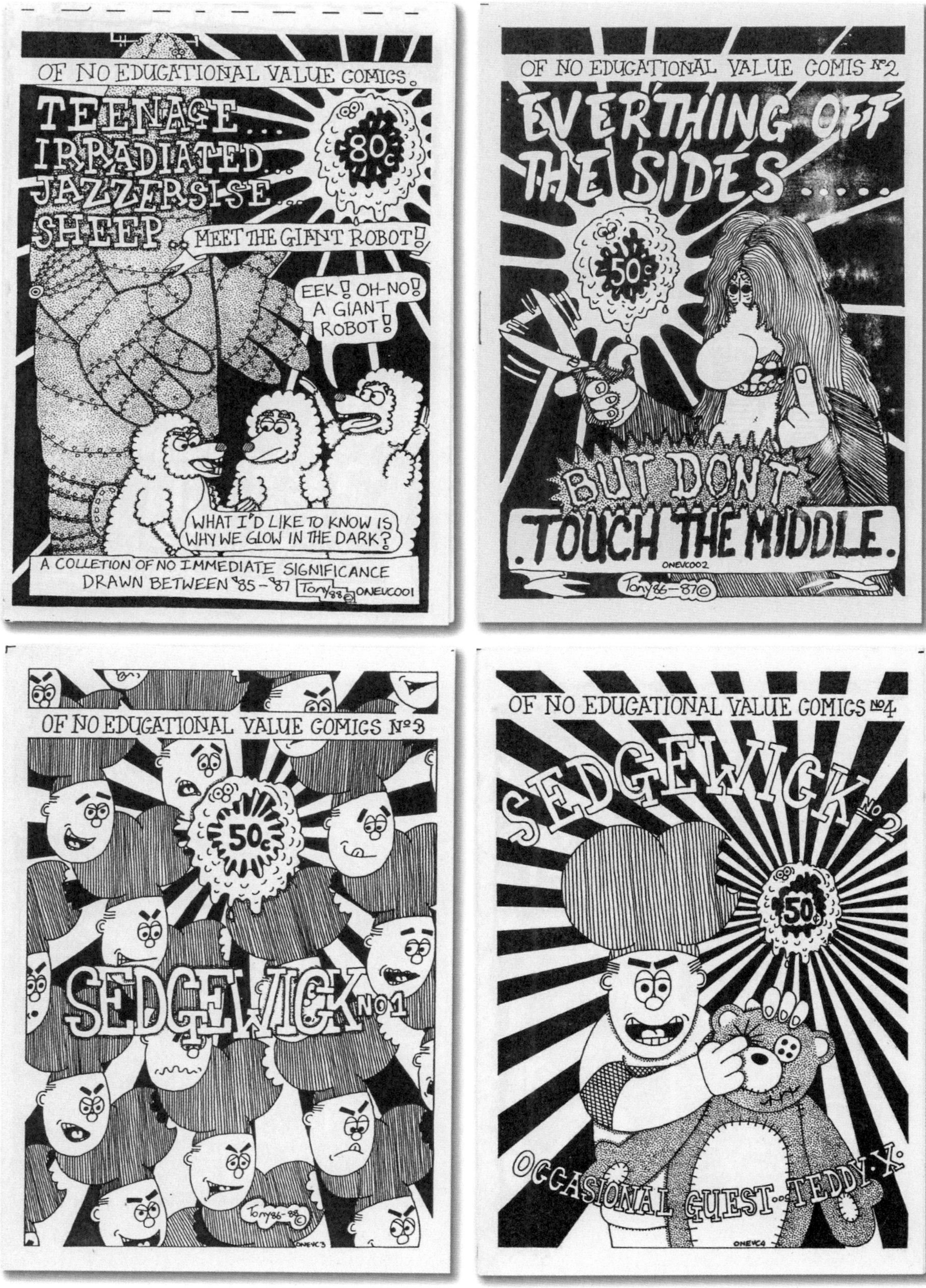

37. *Teenage Irradiated Jazzersise Sheep*, *Everything Off the Sides But Don't Touch the Middle*, *Sedgewick #1* and *Sedgewick #2*, Tony Renouf, all A6, 1987-88. Ōtepoti Dunedin.

Richard Langston The printer was down by the university in Dunedin, and he was so keen, just enthusiastic. I took in this thing. I wasn't sure if you could actually print it. I mean I'd worked in newspapers and I knew about setting type, but I didn't know if or how he would print this thing which was already constructed and wasn't set in type. It must've been offset printing or whatever it is that you do.

He was enthusiastic because, I don't know, printers love printing things. He was just a neat guy, and all these things matter when you're trying to do something and you don't really know what you're doing, like a band walking into a recording studio not knowing . . . *How does this thing work?* I just came in with my demo, and he printed it.

Simon Cottle It was all hardcopy. Things photocopied, then literally cut-and-paste using a proper scalpel. It always amuses me, some of the computer terms we use now: y'know, those 'files', those 'folders'? They were actually manila folders; now it's a picture of a manila folder. We were using manila 'folders', and we were 'cutting', and we were 'pasting', and we were 'copying' — all those terms. So anyway, that would get the guts of the zine out, and then length was kind of important, like 'What can I actually afford, given that recuperation of the money is never going to be there?' At one point — and they haven't lasted well — I got a very cheap second-hand photocopier and was doing lots of the photocopying myself. Then I moved onto getting bromides made of the photographs — that's where the image is broken down into little dots that'll reproduce in black-and-white. I can't remember where the bromide studio was, but there were often people who would be into printing and into publishing who'd do things at a discounted rate. They'd be like, 'Good on you.'

38

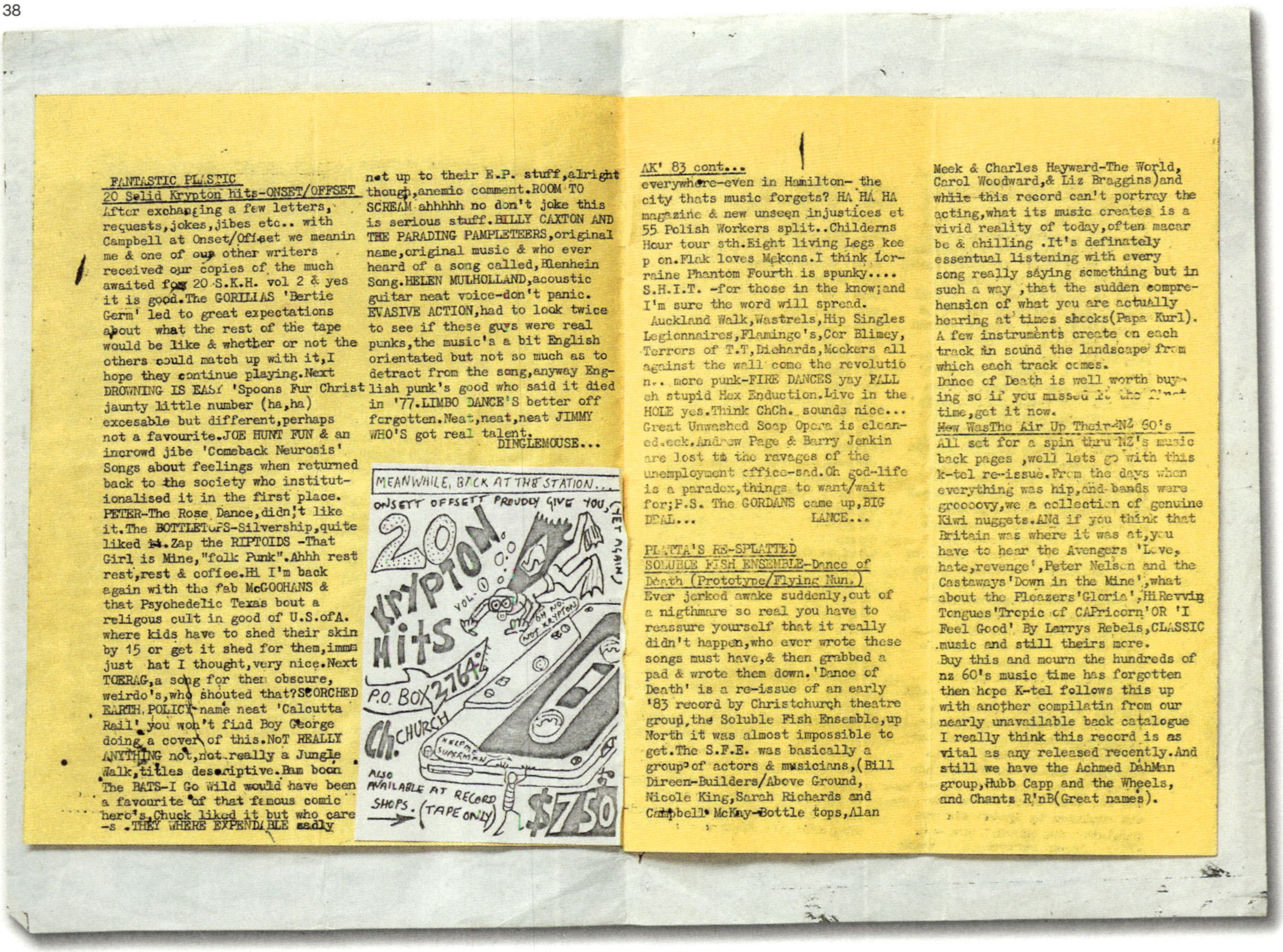

FANTASTIC PLASTIC
20 Solid Krypton hits-ONSET/OFFSET
After exchanging a few letters, requests,jokes,jibes etc.. with Campbell at Onset/Offset we meanin me & one of our other writers received our copies of the much awaited for 20 S.K.H. vol 2 & yes it is good.The GORILLAS 'Bertie Germ' led to great expectations about what the rest of the tape would be like & whether or not the others could match up with it,I hope they continue playing.Next DROWNING IS EASY 'Spoons Fur Christ jaunty little number (ha,ha) excesable but different,perhaps not a favourite.JOE HUNT FUN & an incrowd jibe 'Comeback Neurosis' Songs about feelings when returned back to the society who institutionalised it in the first place. PETER-The Rose Dance,didn't like it.The BOTTLETOPS-Silvership,quite liked it.Zap the RIPTOIDS -That Girl is Mine,"folk Punk".Ahhh rest rest,rest & coffee.Hi I'm back again with the fab McGOOHANS & that Psyohedelic Texas bout a religous cult in good of U.S.ofA. where kids have to shed their skin by 15 or get it shed for them,immm just hat I thought,very nice.Next TOERAG,a song for them obscure, weirdo's,who shouted that?SCORCHED EARTH POLICY-name neat 'Calcutta Rail' you won't find Boy George doing a cover of this.NoT REALLY ANYTHING not,not really a Jungle Walk,titles desoriptive.Bam boon The BATS-I Go Wild would have been a favourite of that famous comic hero's,Chuck liked it but who cares .THEY WHERE EXPENDABLE sadly not up to their E.P. stuff,alright though,anemic comment.ROOM TO SCREAM ahhhhh no don't joke this is serious stuff.BILLY CAXTON AND THE PARADING PAMPLETEERS,original name,original music & who ever heard of a song called,Blenhein Song.HELEN MULHOLLAND,acoustic guitar neat voice-don't panic. EVASIVE ACTION,had to look twice to see if these guys were real punks,the music's a bit English orientated but not so much as to detract from the song,anyway English punk's good who said it died in '77.LIMBO DANCE'S better off forgotten.Neat,neat,neat JIMMY WHO'S got real talent.
DINGLEMOUSE...

AK' 83 cont...
everywhere-even in Hamilton- the city thats music forgets? HA HA HA magazine & new unseen injustices et 55 Polish Workers split..Childerns Hour tour sth.Eight living Legs keep on.Flak loves Mekons.I think Lorraine Phantom Fourth is spunky.... S.H.I.T. -for those in the know;and I'm sure the word will spread.
Auckland Walk,Wastrels,Hip Singles Legionnaires,Flamingo's,Cor Blimey, Terrors of T.T,Diehards,Mockers all against the wall come the revolution.. more punk-FIRE DANCES yay FALL eh stupid Hex Enduction.Live in the HOLE yes.Think ChCh. sounds nice... Great Unwashed Soap Opera is cleaned.eck.Andrew Page & Barry Jenkin are lost to the ravages of the unemployment office-sad.Oh god-life is a paradox,things to want/wait for;P.S. The GORDANS came up,BIG DEAL... LANCE...

PLATTA'S RE-SPLATTED
SOLUBLE FISH ENSEMBLE-Dance of Death (Prototype/Flying Nun.)
Ever jerked awake suddenly,out of a nigthmare so real you have to reassure yourself that it really didn't happen,who ever wrote these songs must have,& then grabbed a pad & wrote them down.'Dance of Death' is a re-issue of an early '83 record by Christchurch theatre group,the Soluble Fish Ensemble,up North it was almost impossible to get.The S.F.E. was basically a group of actors & musicians,(Bill Direen-Builders/Above Ground, Nicole King,Sarah Richards and Campbell McKay-Bottle tops,Alan Meek & Charles Hayward-The World, Carol Woodward,& Liz Braggins)and while this record can't portray the acting,what its music creates is a vivid reality of today,often macarbe & chilling .It's definately essentual listening with every song really saying something but in such a way ,that the sudden comprehension of what you are actually hearing at times shocks(Papa Kurl). A few instruments create on each track in sound the landscape from which each track comes.
Dance of Death is well worth buying so if you missed it the first time,get it now.

How WasThe Air Up Their-NZ 60's
All set for a spin thru NZ's music back pages ,well lets go with this k-tel re-issue.From the days when everything was hip,and bands were groooovy,we a collection of genuine Kiwi nuggets.ANd if you think that Britain was where it was at,you have to hear the Avengers 'Love, hate,revenge',Peter Nelson and the Castaways'Down in the Mine',what about the Pleazers'Gloria',Hi Revvig Tongues'Tropic of CAPricorn'OR 'I Feel Good' By Larrys Rebels,CLASSIC music and still theirs more.
Buy this and mourn the hundreds of nz 60's music time has forgotten then hope K-tel follows this up with another compilatin from our nearly unavailable back catalogue I really think this record is as vital as any released recently.And still we have the Achmed DahMan group,Hubb Capp and the Wheels, and Chants R'nB(Great names).

Richard Langston An Olivetti [Lettera] 32 typewriter put in good service for the first two issues, and then we got a grant from Internal Affairs. Miraculously they gave us 1800 bucks with which I bought a very rudimentary Brother word-processor. It had a little screen, and you could type about five lines [which would display on the screen, allowing you to check and correct], and then hit the button to type to paper.

Andrew Schmidt We were flatting in Hamilton, but because we were either at university or studying we would spend a lot of the summer back in Paeroa and maybe give up the flat and go back there, as that was where our resources were. That was where my parents had their tax accountant's office. So, we would take all these different pieces of writing back to Paeroa, and my mum would type them up onto these stencils for the Gestetner machine. Yep, my mum . . . radical. Love her. And she would ink it up and then we would run them off on the barrel-roll Gestetner machine that they had in the office, which I think belonged to Paeroa Racing Club. That was the inners, which we would put onto different-coloured paper as well, but we couldn't do graphics on those. It was just text, but we also had access to the family photocopy machine, and Ross — who was our art guy — would design the cover. He also did the cartoon that was on the back, and whatever the graphic was on the front was always his idea.

By the second issue we were getting ads. So we had this dilemma: do we give up the cover and the cartoon and the stuff on the back and put the ads on there, or do we find another way of doing it? What we did eventually was just photocopy multiple versions of the same ad onto one sheet, then we would cut them out and paste them into the zine. As we had two ads, that was a labour-intensive thing. We'd get our mates around — few beers and we'd do that, we'd assemble it. That was the process until the third issue, when we were largely based solely in Hamilton and Ross decided he was gonna do a linocut cover. He did one of a jack-in-the-box that we had in the house, and we changed the name of the magazine — just for that issue — to *Nebulous Reasons*.

Ross Gardiner You got the hang of layout and pagination quite quickly, because you'd look at other zines and see what they did right and what they did wrong. The first thing to learn was not doing things too close to the edge of the page because the photocopier couldn't handle it. You'd get someone to do a zine, and the last five letters of each line weren't there because they'd worked too close to the edge of the page and the photocopier wouldn't pick it up . . .

My mum was a secretary for an athletics club in Auckland for a little while, and she had a photocopier that was kept in my bedroom because there was nowhere else in the house it could fit. She would photocopy the club's newsletters and send them out, and so every morning when she was on the phone to my grandmother I'd sneak in and photocopy more pages for *Positive Approach* without her knowing.

Richard Langston Bruce Russell from [record label] Xpressway, who was a writer for the fanzine, was always a hands-on grafter. He came out and helped me staple. He was great. We had what we called a 'stapling party', which probably gave us both temporary RSI. We used one of those really long staplers.

Tracey Wedge I doubt that the zines came back from the printer folded and stapled, because looking at my copy there's just one slightly skewed staple holding it together.

38. *Ha Ha Ha #2* spread, covers and cartoons by Ross Walmsley, writing by Andrew Schmidt, Phillip Gooch, Ross Walmsley, Lance Strickland and Grant 'Gonzo' Schmidt, typing and printing by Gweneth Schmidt, A4, 1983. Paeroa / Kirikiriroa Hamilton.

Richard Langston Issue one of *Garage* sold out really fast, then we got it professionally printed with the money that we'd generated, which was nothing, like, I don't know, 100 bucks? But it didn't cost much to get it printed.

We just increased the print run with each issue. I remember hitchhiking to Auckland to interview Chris Knox, and on the way distributing copies of *Garage*.

Paul Luker I was in Record Exchange all the time. I would be in there 'til they shut, because I'd get off the railways bus on Karangahape Road and then I just had to walk down the hill and there's the bus station, and that's where I lived. So I'd get off and I'd sit in there and I'd talk to Neville Lynch and Chris Hart — who still runs Real Groovy — chat, chat, chat,

`'Um, if I did this thing, would you sell some?'`

`'Yeah, just put 'em on the counter, man.'`

So a stack on the counter, and they were so sweet. I'd go back and then I'd count them and say, 'Thirty have been sold', and he'd go 'Oh, I think they were fucking *stolen*. Here's your 30 times 25c.' They still paid me. They knew they were being nicked.

Simon Cottle Remember Colin Morris Records? He's still a bit of a celeb; I hear him on Radio New Zealand every now and then. He was just like *the* total music guy, and he would have the zine in his shop. Half of them would get stolen, but he'd still pay me the money for them. He was kind of our go-to guy. He would import Crass records and stuff if we were struggling to do it ourselves, and he had a good punk collection in his store. The main way I'd promote the zine was take out an advert in *Rip It Up*: 'Hey, the latest issue is out.' I don't know if they put it in for free because we sent them a copy, or whether it was in the classifieds — but, y'know, classifieds, 50 cents a line or whatever. Then people would write to me for zines. That's why I got a post office box. They would put cash in envelopes, or swap something, or just plead for a free copy.

Andrew Schmidt We were lucky with the distribution of *Ha Ha Ha*. We would just send the bulk of them to Flying Nun, and they would drop it into their mail orders and they'd go all around the country. We'd send the other ones to Ima Hitt; Brian Wafer's record label in New Plymouth. Brian had a similar mail-order service, and he would do the same thing. We had a lot of trouble getting *Ha Ha Ha* into the Hamilton shops where we were based. We dropped the first issue into Chelsea Records in the Government Life mall. They read it and they just trashed them all. We went in and said, 'Where are they?', and they said, 'We threw them in the rubbish, because it was rubbish.'

Paul Luker I was still doing poetry. I can remember there was a good barter system with tapes early on, but it started with poetry. You'd swap a book with someone, and then someone else might see it and . . . What was his name from Hamilton? Hard Echo Press . . . Warwick Jordan. Warwick Jordan was writing. I swapped a number of books with him, just, y'know 'Hey, man. I'll swap you mine if you give me yours.'

Ross Gardiner We'd take them around to record shops. For a little while in Auckland there were quite a few shops that were really into selling zines. There was Rock'n'Roll Records on Fort Street and Kerry Buchanan, who was the drummer for the Terrorways, worked there. He was really supportive. He'd buy them off us for a dollar each and sell them for a dollar. Real Groovy Records was at the top of Queen Street. They would often take a lot of zines, and then there were a few other little record shops that would sell them. We'd go around the shops, put 5 or 10 copies in there, and then go around a month later and collect the money if they'd sold.

Andrew Schmidt We would always take an ad out in *Rip It Up*. *Rip It Up* was a good conduit for that. They would always review our zine as well. You had guys like Russell Brown in there who were writing well about the local music scene. They would be encouraging, and they would print your address and how much it cost. And that was a nationally distributed magazine — 30,000 copies I think at its peak. So, yeah, we had that, we were lucky. I sent the second issue of *Ha Ha Ha* into Frank Stark at *The Listener* (he later became the head of the New Zealand Film Archive). We didn't really expect anything, and next thing you know we're reading about *Ha Ha Ha* while we're in Woolworths; there's a full-page article on our fanzine in *The Listener*!

Ross Gardiner The record shops, especially the second-hand ones, were run by people who were really into music, so when a bunch of high-school kids came around with a music zine they'd made themselves, they were quite into the idea, quite supportive.

Tracey Wedge We distributed a lot of the zines through the post. We had a post office box for people to write to. We also had them in some stores, some of the smaller record shops. Other zine-makers helped distribute, word-of-mouth was really important. I had a show on Radio One, and so did John, so potentially we mentioned the zine there as well. It was priced at 'one lousy buck' — that's what it says on the cover.

Ross Gardiner We did *Positive Approach* at high school, and it was lots of fun, but it was also a lot of work, and I realised I'd rather just help distribute other people's zines. People from out of town would send me a pile, I'd take them into the record shops and sell them then and there, and send them the money.

Richard Davies I had a motorbike, a GS1000, and I rode down to Taranaki from Auckland. Brett's doing all this stuff, making these *Ritchie Rat* zines, and I'm like 'Heck, man, I'll go back to Auckland.' Because we'd only come down here for the magic mushrooms. Everybody came here for mushrooms because you couldn't get them anywhere else; now they're all over the country. The mushrooms made Taranaki a focal point for a whole lot of stuff, a whole lot of people came here. But I stayed on, and the zines became prolific. Every dole-day Thursday we'd be down-town with our stacks of zines, selling them for a buck, and all the punks and alternative folk would buy them off us. We'd just sit outside the post office and sell them, or walk around with them in a duffel bag. You'd have all your zines in there and you'd see someone who looked interested. Everyone wanted to support it.

39

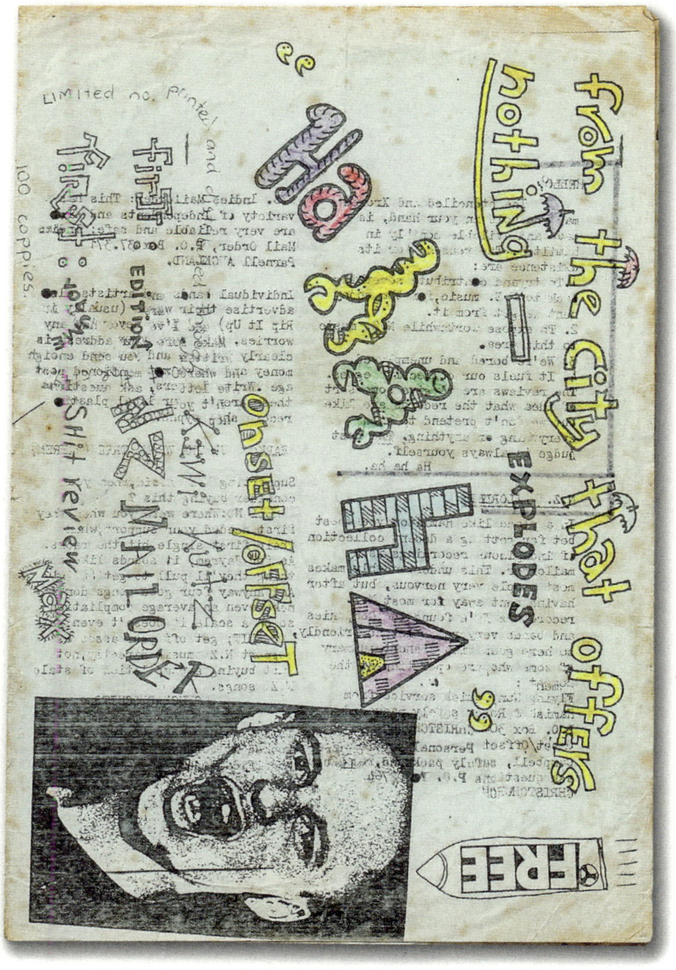

39. *Ha Ha Ha* #1, covers and cartoons by Ross Walmsley, writing by Andrew Schmidt, Phillip Gooch, Ross Walmsley, Lance Strickland and Grant 'Gonzo' Schmidt, typing and printing by Gweneth Schmidt, A4, 1983. Paeroa / Kirikiriroa Hamilton.

John Farrow The Comics Shop was part of the punk community. Malcolm Campbell, who was in Gorse with me, and his girlfriend at the time — Teresa Stevenson — were the mainstays of that, and then there was Dave Crowther and a bunch of volunteers. Malcom and Teresa were into the bands and into the fanzines, Dave was just a pure comics guy. They were happy to distribute our stuff and others. Outside of The Comics Shop you'd mainly just swap 10 of your zine for 10 of someone else's, and then distribute them direct. I'd swap and sell *Submission*, *Taranaki Underground* (I think the early version was called *Fuck It Up*), *Anti-System* from Simon Cottle, whatever zines Craig and his girlfriend [Michelle] from the band Nazgûl were making . . .

Richard Davies My zines were mainly anti-police, stuff about American punk bands, bits of collage that I made up.

It was scary, man. You make this thing, and then you've got to go into town and hawk them. Some dudes are scary-looking, y'know what I mean? You're like 'You want to buy a zine?', and you half expect them to crack you in the head, but they're like 'Yeah, man, I'll buy one.' Even the hardest-looking skins were buying them off me and not giving me a hard time. I was like 'What?!' They would give me a buck just because I'd made something. I don't even know if half of them gave a shit what was in my zine, or what was in *Taranaki Underground*. I think a lot of people thought Brett was just a conspiracy theorist.

Taranaki Underground had political statements through Ritchie Rat, and ads for local businesses that were our mates. Not Whitcoulls or McDonald's, that's for sure. We used to advertise Lighthouse Windows because Robert Clement, the father of [actor and comedian] Jemaine, rented Brett the office, so of course we're gonna advertise for him.

40

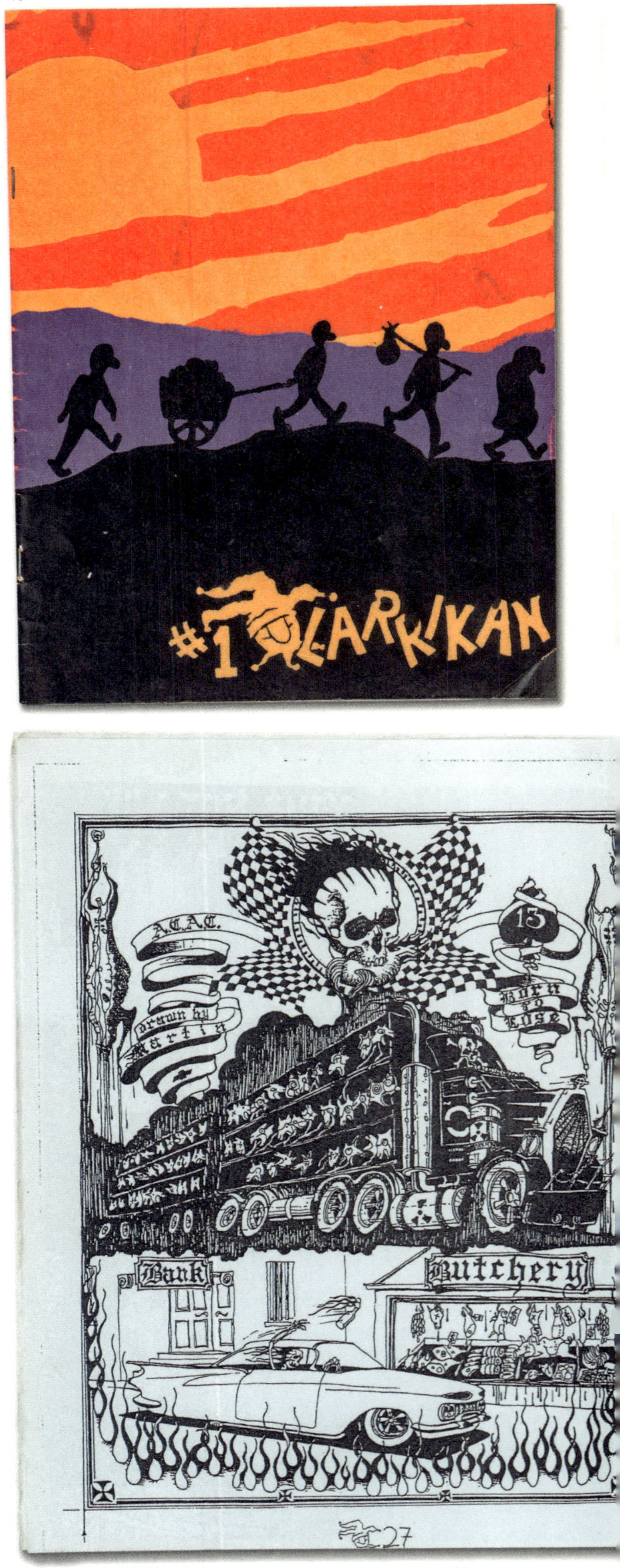

40. *Larrikan* #1 cover and spread, various artists, spread by Martin Sullivan, A4, 1980s. Ōtepoti Dunedin.

Richard Langston I'm not deluded about it. No one was ever gonna become, like, Crowded House. It's not that sort of music. It's always gonna be off to the left. It's gonna find an audience all over the world, but that audience will be in pockets and that's what happened with the *Garage* fanzine. It found an audience in pockets all around the world. We sold in Rough Trade [in London], and we sold in New York. People would send us their fanzines and make contact.

John Farrow The Flying Nun scene coexisted in Dunedin with the punk scene. We called them the 'pyjama people', as they sort of wore paisley like hippies. That was Straitjacket Fits and The Bats and fringe bands like Alpaca Brothers. They were always a little bit nervous about the punks because some of the punks were too violent for those guys, but the more pacifist punks that they got to know they were alright with. The Comics Shop here stocked comics, fanzines and records. The Flying Nun stuff would be in there as well, and also up at Records Records, Roy Colbert's shop.

41

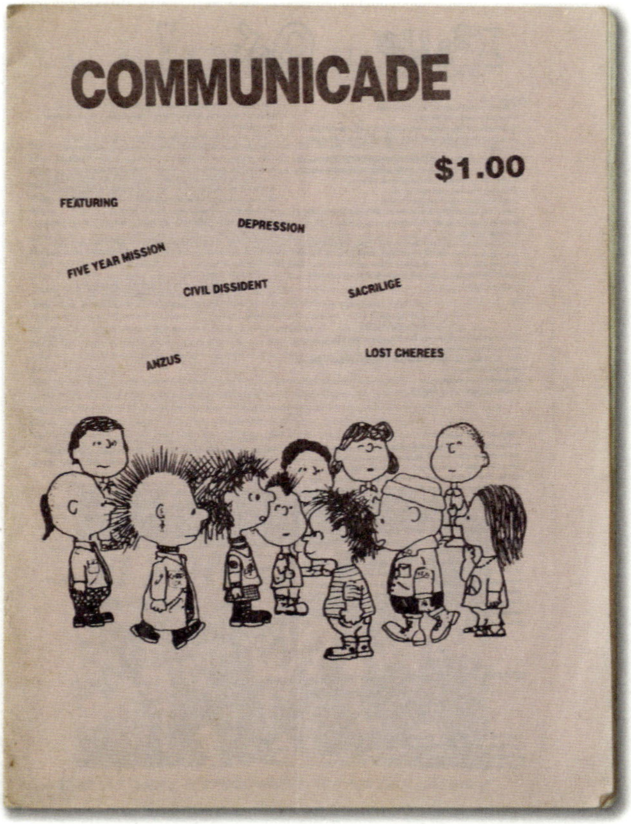

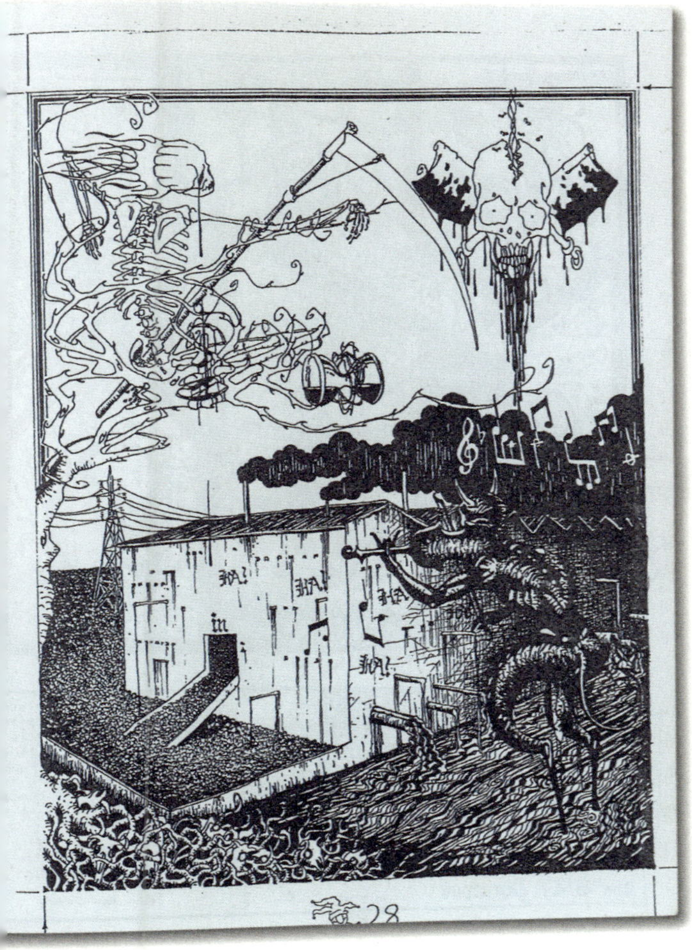

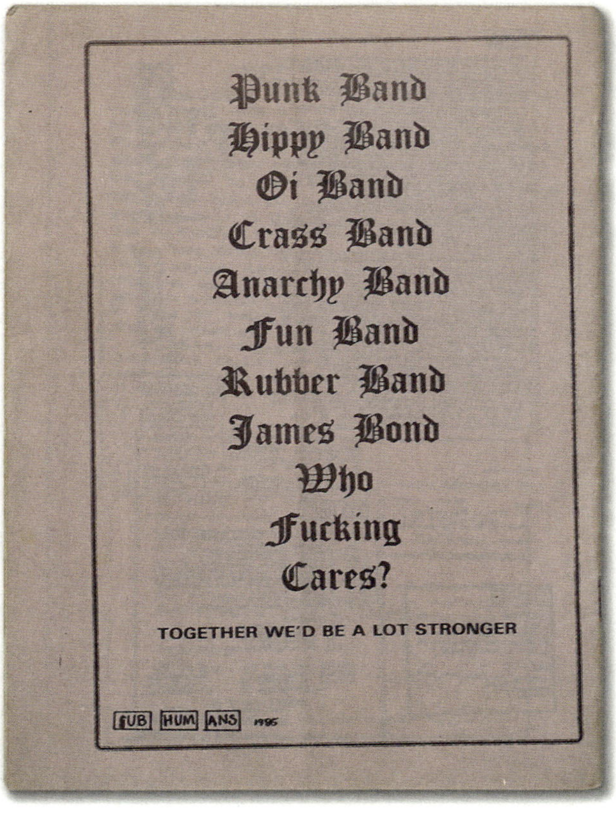

41. *Communicade* front and back covers, credited to Dave, Craig, Simon and Heather (no surnames), 216 × 165mm, 1985. Te Awa Kairangi ki Uta Upper Hutt.

42

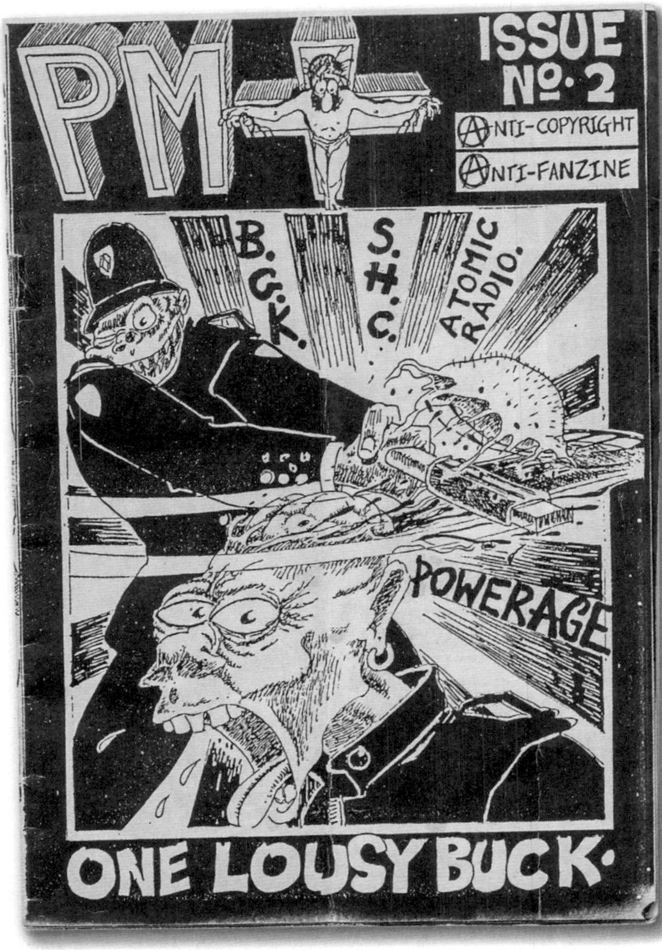

42. *PMT* #2, cover by Terry Perkins, edited by John Farrow and Tracey Wedge, A5, 1986. Ōtepoti Dunedin.

Richard Davies Brian Wafer was like our dad. He had this record shop and he just let us hang out there all day, every day. Even when Brett got the office for *Taranaki Underground*, we still hung out there with Brian at Ima Hitt all day, every day. If you watch the Sticky Filth 'Weep Woman Weep' video on YouTube you'll see a lot of posters me and Brett made. If you don't look at the people and you look at the walls, you'll see Toxic Avengers, and Sticky Filth posters in the background that Brett made, all done on the same gear that the zines were made on.

Andrew Schmidt Bruce Russell is a great performer. He makes it work. I remember seeing The Dead C for the first time. It was stunning. He's also a fantastic writer, and he's got a couple of different styles. He can actually do quite a good popular style, but can also do the art criticism end as well. He wrote for *Alley Oop* and *Garage*.

Richard Langston Bruce Russell was also heavily involved in Jeff Ruston's *Alley Oop* zine. Jeff worked in a print shop — that's why the production quality's so good.

Tony Renouf I drew comics for *PMT*, and for *Alley Oop*, which was Jeff Ruston's music zine. We made a comics insert for that. How the fuck did I meet Jeff? Jeff was running a print shop, and I think I'd been going in to get photocopies of mini-comics from Jeff. I worked with him later at Echo Records, that's how incestuous this town is. It's insane.

John Farrow *PMT* had a couple of pretty cool artists. Terry Perkins did all the covers — he went on to become a graphic designer for Taylormade Media — and we had Tony Renouf, who I think you knew. Didn't you buy his guitar?

Tony Renouf When I met John Farrow, he was trying to avoid clothing made of leather. I was giving him shit about his wool socks or something like that. Something along those lines. I was just winding him up. Lovely bloke. Really intelligent.

Lyn Spencer In the late eighties a whole lot of people moved to New Plymouth because of the local punk scene. It was cheaper living. There were a bunch of punks from Auckland living around Inglewood, and there were people there making zines. Then in New Plymouth you had that anarcho zine *Taranaki Underground.*

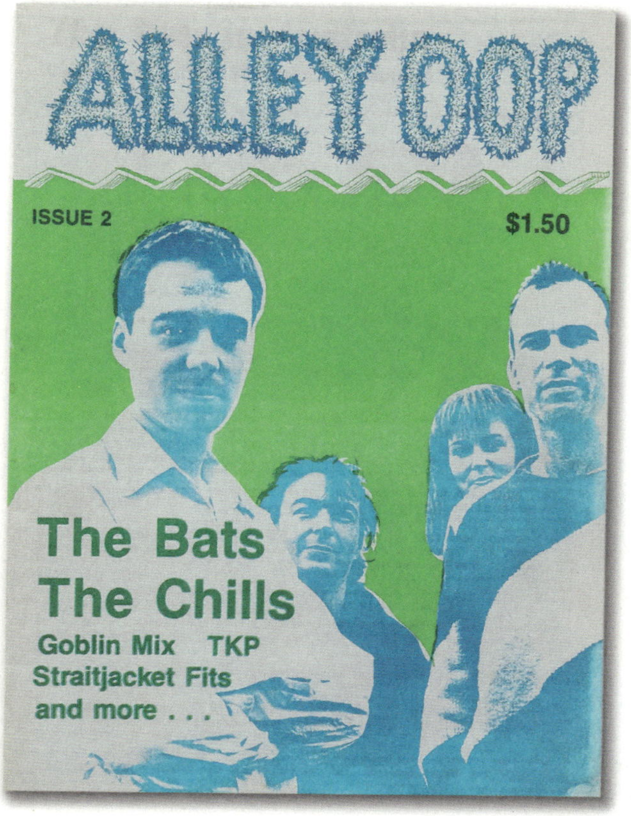

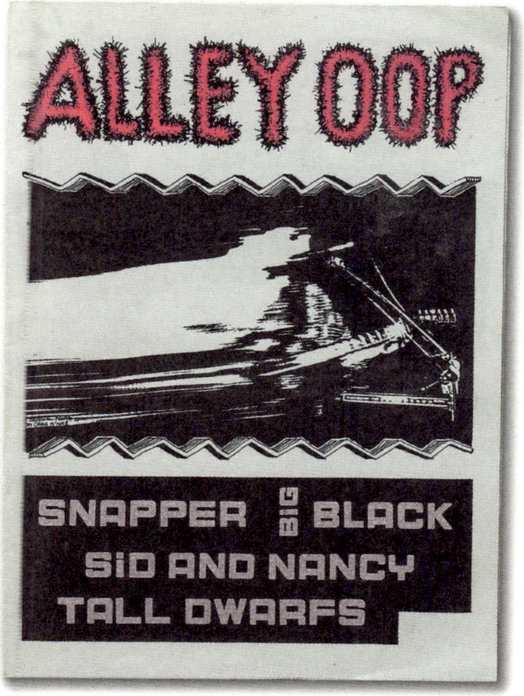

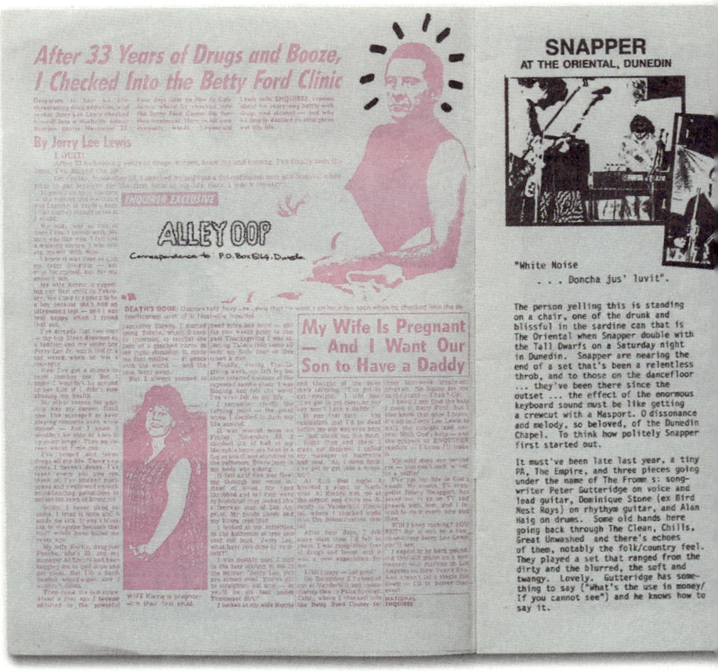

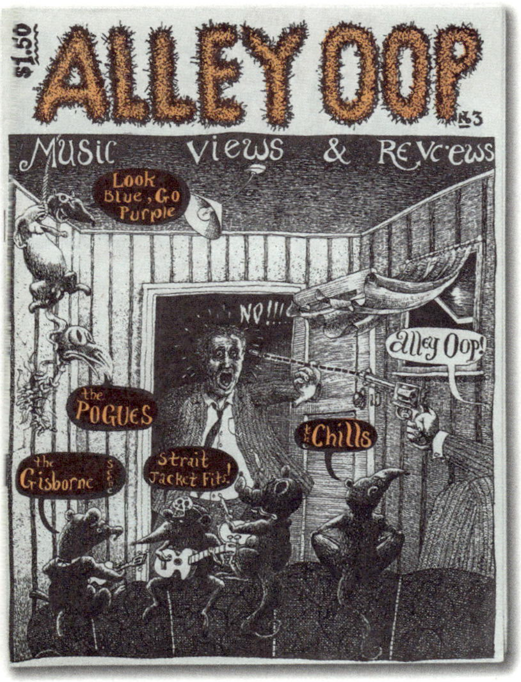

43. Various issues of *Alley Oop*, the music zine started by Jeff Ruston. David Saunders' signature drawing style can be seen on the cover of #3. Ōtepoti Dunedin.

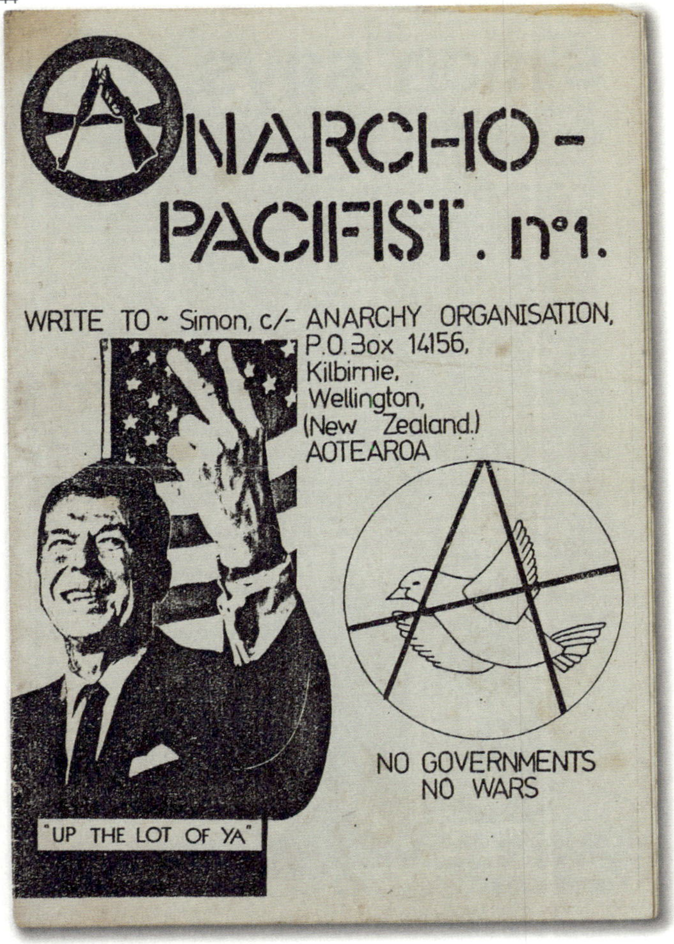

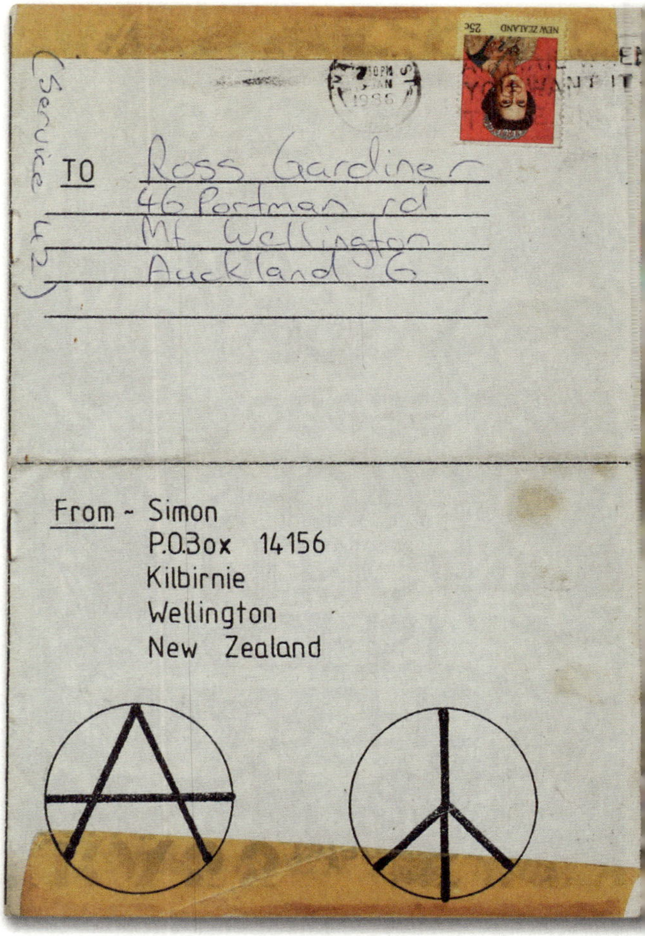

Tracey Wedge With *PMT* I was interested in developing community connections, music communities, connecting with people who were interested in anarchist thought.

John Farrow It was a community. People would say 'I've got an idea', and we'd say 'Well, that's cool — you do it.' We wouldn't ever censor the content or stuff like that. If people wanted to put stuff in, we'd let them, because we saw it as a community thing. I never had to turn someone away; never ever received contributions that were homophobic or fascist or anything like that.

Tracey Wedge We were trying to get people on board to supply gig reviews and record reviews. We were engaging our community in Dunedin as well as across the country. Looking back at the zines, it appears some contributors were anonymous, though I can see my flatmate Lucy Holmes contributed a little essay about incest and violence toward women. She was involved in the Women's Refuge, so she was invested in bringing those issues to the fore.

Simon Cottle Every zine I put out would promote all the other zines that were around; zines from the South Island, Auckland, Wellington, New Plymouth. And those zines would promote my zine in return. We were very anarchic about the exchange of zines. We'd put Sellotape or soap over the stamps so they could be used again.

The most rewarding thing about making the zines was knowing that it hooked people up with

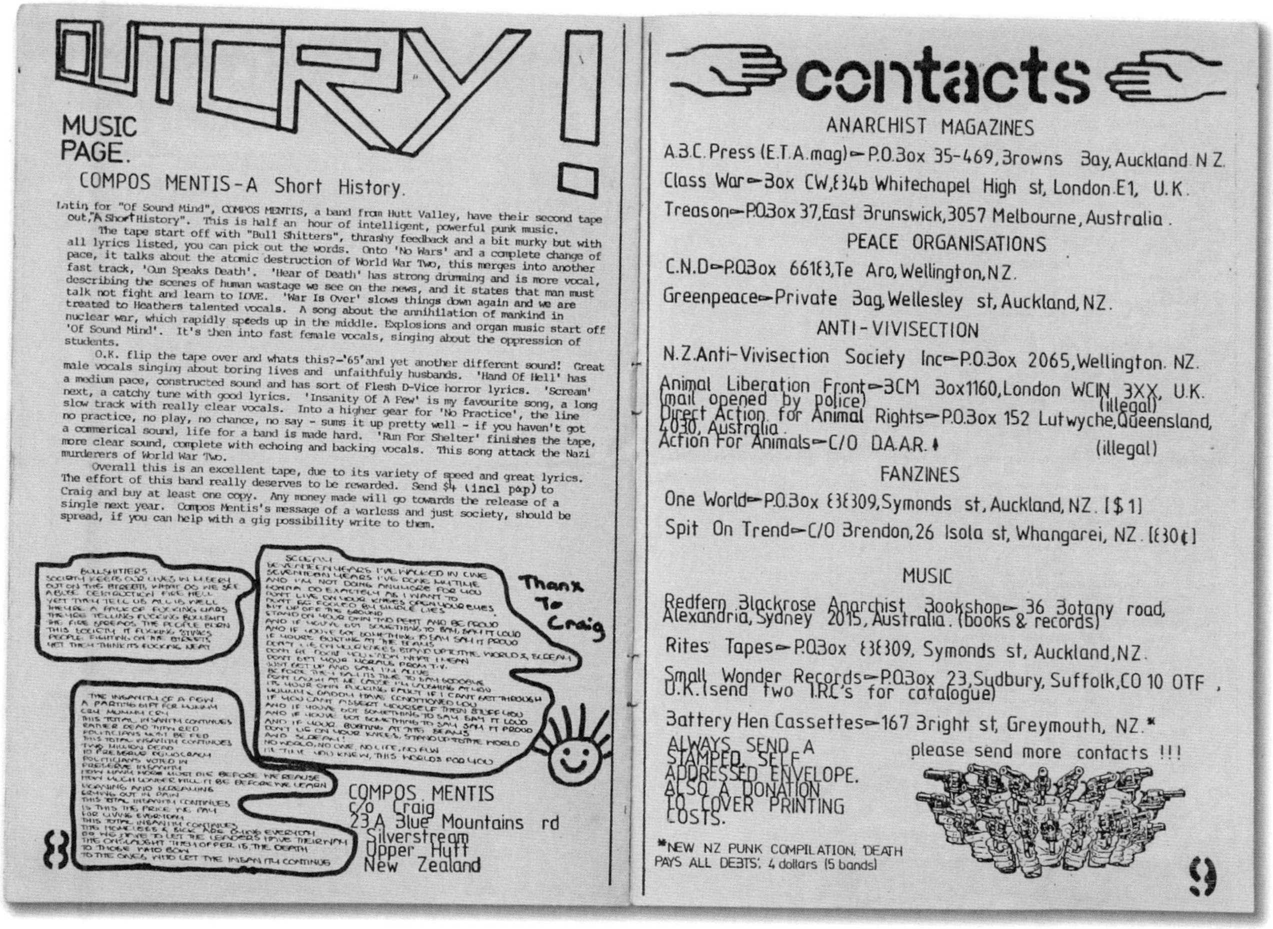
OUTCRY!

MUSIC PAGE.

COMPOS MENTIS-A Short History.

Latin for "Of Sound Mind", COMPOS MENTIS, a band from Hutt Valley, have their second tape out,"A Short History". This is half an hour of intelligent, powerful punk music.

The tape start off with "Bull Shitters", thrashy feedback and a bit murky but with all lyrics listed, you can pick out the words. Onto 'No Wars' and a complete change of pace, it talks about the atomic destruction of World War Two, this merges into another fast track, 'Gun Speaks Death'. 'Hear of Death' has strong drumming and is more vocal, describing the scenes of human wastage we see on the news, and it states that man must talk not fight and learn to LOVE. 'War Is Over' slows things down again and we are treated to Heathers talented vocals. A song about the annihilation of mankind in nuclear war, which rapidly speeds up in the middle. Explosions and organ music start off 'Of Sound Mind'. It's then into fast female vocals, singing about the oppression of students.

O.K. flip the tape over and whats this?-'65'and yet another different sound! Great male vocals singing about boring lives and unfaithfuly husbands. 'Hand Of Hell' has a medium pace, constructed sound and has sort of Flesh D-Vice horror lyrics. 'Scream' next, a catchy tune with good lyrics. 'Insanity Of A Few' is my favourite song, a long slow track with really clear vocals. Into a higher gear for 'No Practice', the line no practice, no play, no chance, no say - sums it up pretty well - if you haven't got a commerical sound, life for a band is made hard. 'Run For Shelter' finishes the tape, more clear sound, complete with echoing and backing vocals. This song attack the Nazi murderers of World War Two.

Overall this is an excellent tape, due to its variety of speed and great lyrics. The effort of this band really deserves to be rewarded. Send $4 (incl p&p) to Craig and buy at least one copy. Any money made will go towards the release of a single next year. Compos Mentis's message of a warless and just society, should be spread, if you can help with a gig possibility write to them.

COMPOS MENTIS
c/o Craig
23A Blue Mountains rd
Silverstream
Upper Hutt
New Zealand

8

contacts

ANARCHIST MAGAZINES

A.B.C. Press (E.T.A. mag) – P.O.Box 35-469, Browns Bay, Auckland N.Z.

Class War – Box CW, 84b Whitechapel High st, London E1, U.K.

Treason – P.O.Box 37, East Brunswick, 3057 Melbourne, Australia.

PEACE ORGANISATIONS

C.N.D – P.O.Box 6618, Te Aro, Wellington, N.Z.

Greenpeace – Private Bag, Wellesley st, Auckland, NZ.

ANTI-VIVISECTION

N.Z. Anti-Vivisection Society Inc – P.O.Box 2065, Wellington. NZ.

Animal Liberation Front – BCM Box 1160, London WCIN 3XX, U.K. (mail opened by police) (illegal)

Direct Action for Animal Rights – P.O.Box 152 Lutwyche, Queensland, 4030, Australia.

Action For Animals – C/O D.A.A.R. (illegal)

FANZINES

One World – P.O.Box 68309, Symonds st, Auckland, NZ. [$1]

Spit On Trend – C/O Brendon, 26 Isola st, Whangarei, NZ. [80¢]

MUSIC

Redfern Blackrose Anarchist Bookshop – 36 Botany road, Alexandria, Sydney 2015, Australia. (books & records)

Rites Tapes – P.O.Box 68309, Symonds st, Auckland, NZ.

Small Wonder Records – P.O.Box 23, Sudbury, Suffolk, CO 10 OTF, U.K. (send two I.R.C's for catalogue)

Battery Hen Cassettes – 167 Bright st, Greymouth, NZ.*

ALWAYS SEND A STAMPED SELF ADDRESSED ENVELOPE. ALSO A DONATION TO COVER PRINTING COSTS.

please send more contacts !!!

*NEW NZ PUNK COMPILATION, 'DEATH PAYS ALL DEBTS', 4 dollars (5 bands)

9

44. *Anarcho-Pacifist* #1 front and back covers and spread, Simon Cottle, A4, 1985. The back cover illustrates the popular fold-and-tape method that allowed zines to be posted without the need for an envelope. Te Whanganui-a-Tara Wellington.

others. People actually sold their records because of the zine; punters would be like 'We saw the review and . . .' That interconnectedness was the most rewarding, especially when people were living somewhere really remote and would say: 'We would make sure that we got your zine as soon as we saw it in *Rip It Up*. We'd get your zine and then we'd know to get the cassettes, get the records, get the other zines that you covered.' You gotta put it in its time [context], right? The Yellow Pages [phone directory] was your main way of connecting commercially, and when you've got a subculture you just haven't got a hope, so it was very dependent on promotion from within, connecting with people who know people.

Dave Hegan I remember it was a bit like a jigsaw. You'd find one piece — 'Cool, I can get this from this person here' — and then they'd introduce you to another bunch of people who had punk stuff coming out. The next minute you're getting stuff from Wellington, Dunedin, Auckland. But as to how it actually happened, it's so long ago, I'd be lying if I said I could remember exactly how it happened. It was really organic, one thing just leads to another. I remember getting this New Zealand punk seven-inch [record] in 1987, and it came with a list of addresses where I could find other stuff. It's funny, now you can get whatever you want [online] with the press of a button.

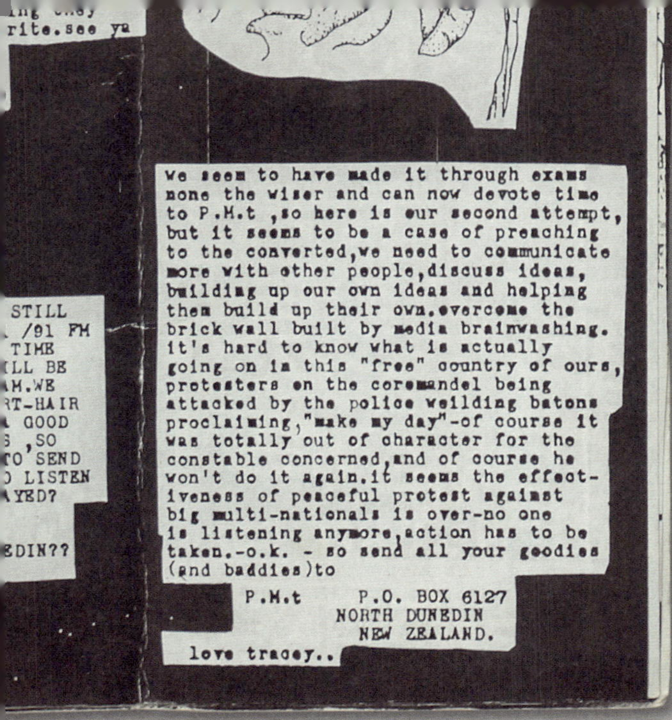

ing they
rite.see ya

STILL
/91 FM
TIME
LL BE
M.WE
T-HAIR
GOOD
,SO
O SEND
LISTEN
YED?

DIN??

we seem to have made it through exams none the wiser and can now devote time to P.M.t ,so here is our second attempt, but it seems to be a case of preaching to the converted,we need to communicate more with other people,discuss ideas, building up our own ideas and helping them build up their own.overcome the brick wall built by media brainwashing. it's hard to know what is actually going on in this "free" country of ours, protesters on the coremandel being attacked by the police weilding batons proclaiming,"make my day"-of course it was totally out of character for the constable concerned,and of course he won't do it again.it seems the effectiveness of peaceful protest against big multi-nationals is over-no one is listening anymore,action has to be taken.-o.k. - so send all your goodies (and baddies)to

P.M.t P.O. BOX 6127
NORTH DUNEDIN
NEW ZEALAND.

love tracey..

45

46

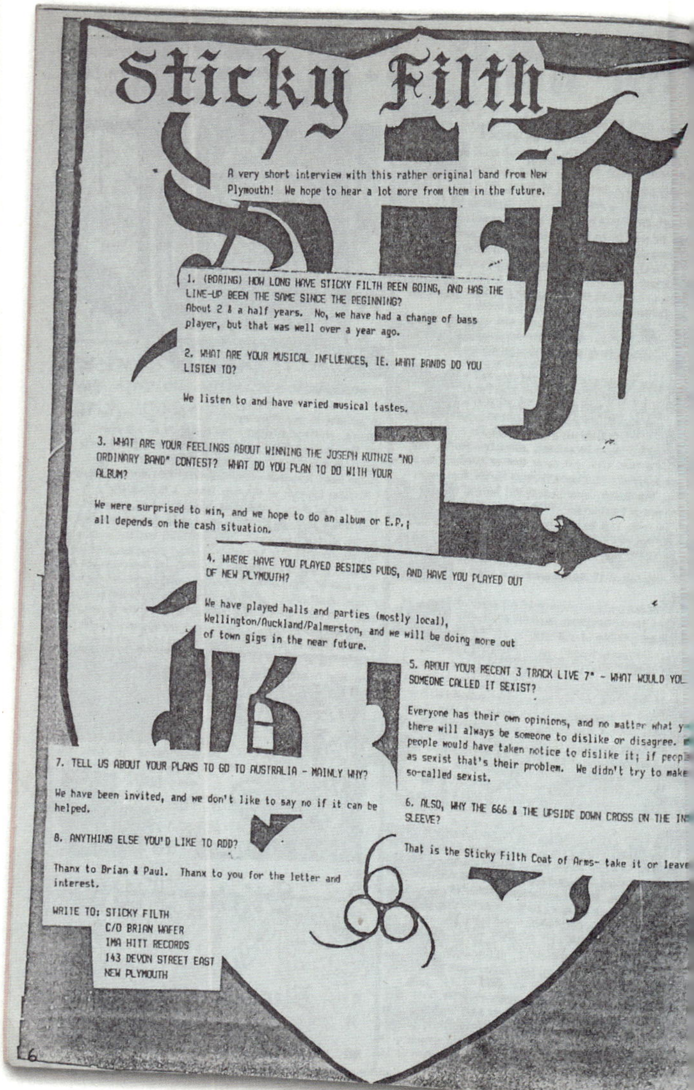

Sticky Filth

A very short interview with this rather original band from New Plymouth! We hope to hear a lot more from them in the future.

1. (BORING) HOW LONG HAVE STICKY FILTH BEEN GOING, AND HAS THE LINE-UP BEEN THE SAME SINCE THE BEGINNING?

About 2 & a half years. No, we have had a change of bass player, but that was well over a year ago.

2. WHAT ARE YOUR MUSICAL INFLUENCES, IE. WHAT BANDS DO YOU LISTEN TO?

We listen to and have varied musical tastes.

3. WHAT ARE YOUR FEELINGS ABOUT WINNING THE JOSEPH KUTHZE "NO ORDINARY BAND" CONTEST? WHAT DO YOU PLAN TO DO WITH YOUR ALBUM?

We were surprised to win, and we hope to do an album or E.P.; all depends on the cash situation.

4. WHERE HAVE YOU PLAYED BESIDES PUBS, AND HAVE YOU PLAYED OUT OF NEW PLYMOUTH?

We have played halls and parties (mostly local), Wellington/Auckland/Palmerston, and we will be doing more out of town gigs in the near future.

5. ABOUT YOUR RECENT 3 TRACK LIVE 7" - WHAT WOULD YOU SOMEONE CALLED IT SEXIST?

Everyone has their own opinions, and no matter what y there will always be someone to dislike or disagree. people would have taken notice to dislike it; if peop as sexist that's their problem. We didn't try to make so-called sexist.

6. ALSO, WHY THE 666 & THE UPSIDE DOWN CROSS ON THE IN SLEEVE?

That is the Sticky Filth Coat of Arms- take it or leave

7. TELL US ABOUT YOUR PLANS TO GO TO AUSTRALIA - MAINLY WHY?

We have been invited, and we don't like to say no if it can be helped.

8. ANYTHING ELSE YOU'D LIKE TO ADD?

Thanx to Brian & Paul. Thanx to you for the letter and interest.

WRITE TO: STICKY FILTH
C/O BRIAN WAFER
IMA HITT RECORDS
143 DEVON STREET EAST
NEW PLYMOUTH

6

45. *PMT #2*, editorial by Tracey Wedge, A5, 1986. Ōtepoti Dunedin.

46. *Submission #5* spread, Ania Glowacz, A4, 1987. Te Whanganui-a-Tara Wellington.

47. *Pow-Wow* cover and spread, uncredited, A4, late 1980s. Ōtepoti Dunedin.

47

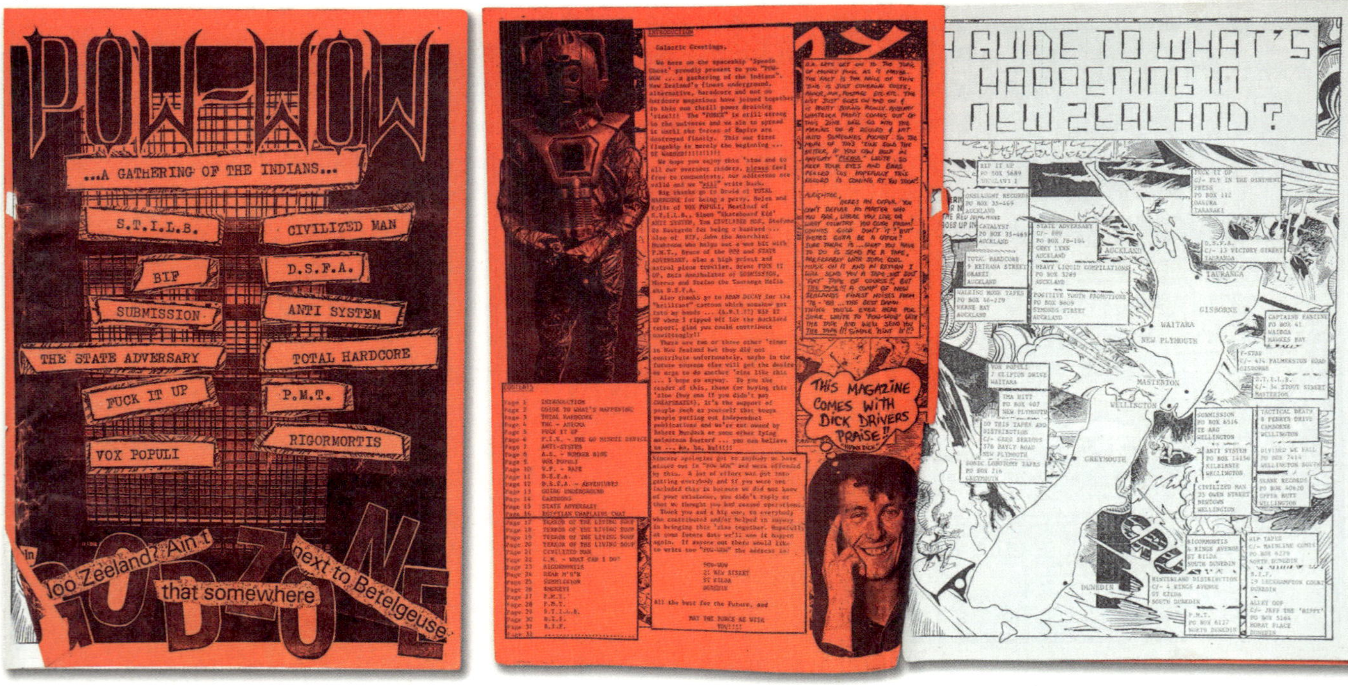

POW-WOW
...A GATHERING OF THE INDIANS...
S.T.I.L.S.
CIVILIZED MAN
BIF
D.S.F.A.
SUBMISSION
ANTI SYSTEM
THE STATE ADVERSARY
TOTAL HARDCORE
FUCK IT UP
P.M.T.
VOX POPULI
RIGORMORTIS
Noo Zeeland! Ain't that somewhere next to Betelgeuse

Galactic Greetings.

THIS MAGAZINE COMES WITH DICK DRIVERS PRAISE!

A GUIDE TO WHAT'S HAPPENING IN NEW ZEALAND?

AUCKLAND
TAURANGA
GISBORNE
WAITARA
NEW PLYMOUTH
MASTERTON
WELLINGTON
GREYMOUTH
DUNEDIN

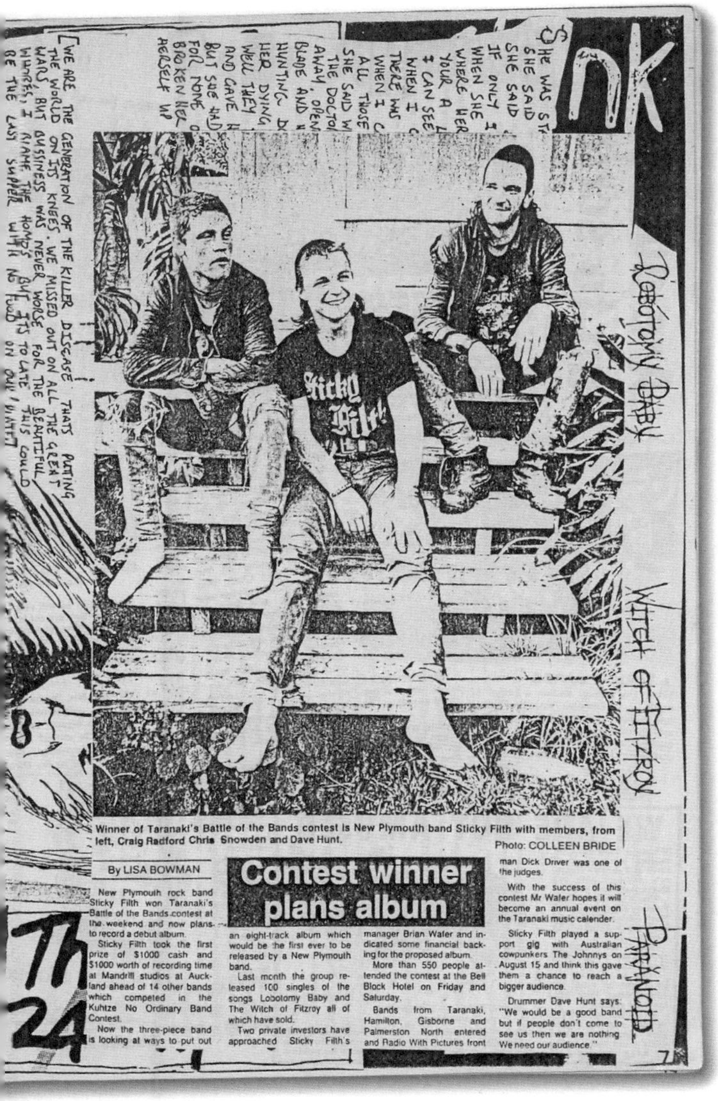

Winner of Taranaki's Battle of the Bands contest is New Plymouth band Sticky Filth with members, from left, Craig Radford Chris Snowden and Dave Hunt.

Photo: COLLEEN BRIDE

By LISA BOWMAN

Contest winner plans album

New Plymouth rock band Sticky Filth won Taranaki's Battle of the Bands contest at the weekend and now plans to record a debut album.

Sticky Filth took the first prize of $1000 cash and $1000 worth of recording time at Mandrill studios at Auckland ahead of 14 other bands which competed in the Kuhtze No Ordinary Band Contest.

Now the three-piece band is looking at ways to put out an eight-track album which would be the first ever to be released by a New Plymouth band.

Last month the group released 100 singles of the songs Lobotomy Baby and The Witch of Fitzroy all of which have sold.

Two private investors have approached Sticky Filth's manager Brian Waler and indicated some financial backing for the proposed album.

More than 550 people attended the contest at the Bell Block Hotel on Friday and Saturday.

Bands from Taranaki, Hamilton, Gisborne and Palmerston North entered and Radio With Pictures frontman Dick Driver was one of the judges.

With the success of this contest Mr Waler hopes it will become an annual event on the Taranaki music calender.

Sticky Filth played a support gig with Australian cowpunkers The Johnnys on August 15 and think this gave them a chance to reach a bigger audience.

Drummer Dave Hunt says: "We would be a good band but if people don't come to see us then we are nothing. We need our audience."

John Farrow We ran out of Dunedin content because there were a limited number of local bands. We started to include overseas stuff, but tried to be a bit obscure with it. We found this all-women band from Boulder, Colorado, called Anti-Scrunti Faction. I imported their record, and when the women down here heard that record they were just into it. There was a band down here called Spermicide — which you'll see in [video documentary] *The Other Dunedin Sound* — and they were all bolstered by this all-women band from over in Boulder. The world just started opening up, and suddenly you were finding punk-rock bands from Italy and Holland and stuff, and we would try to interview them, or at least the ones that had really cool politics or were a bit different. We interviewed a band from South Africa that was there in the middle of the apartheid regime. You'd read about them and there'd be a post office box and you'd write them an old-fashioned letter. We even got a letter back from Eve Libertine and Joy De Vivre from Crass telling us about what their flat was like in London. It took about three months for the letter to arrive, but that was pretty cool.

Richard Davies I didn't intend to move to Taranaki. We just came to pick mushrooms. I get off my motorbike, walk into the post office, get my money out, had an altercation with a gang. That was all good, I didn't back down to them, even ended up friends with a couple of them actually. Then I walked through town and I saw a punk-rocker. I was like 'Hey, bro, where's all the punks?' and he goes 'My name's Isaac, come with me', and he took me down to Young Street, here's this house, and it's full of punks and there's a band called Sticky Filth and they start playing gigs in the back garden and they were wicked. That's when I woke up to 'This is the centre of it.' So, I realised it was a mecca *once* I got here . . . A really constructive music scene, people helping each other, not just tall poppy syndrome, knocking each other down; the bands and the zines and the mushrooms was just all so intertwined back then. Taranaki's very different.

Later I was going down to the mushroom commune every day, hanging out with Colin Long and trying to get him to join my band because he was such a brilliant songwriter. He's the guy up on that poster. [Points.] He was killed during a punch-up outside the Texacana [Burger Bar] in 1990. That just shattered the scene. That killed it. He also did these amazing drawings for his *BENTEDGE* zine, sometimes drawings for mine and Brett's zines as well.

Bruce Grenville After the five-year contract with Auckland University ran out, they renewed it for another five years. So I had this wonderful situation of having a free studio, electricity, hot water, shower next door, all laid on, and no rent. So, that was really cool.

I was the printer at Auckland Uni, and I became known as the Mad Kiwi Printer. At that time there was an Auckland poet called David Eggleton, whose nickname was the Mad Kiwi Ranter. I was his publisher.

Matthew Campbell Downes My mother was very supportive of me pursuing art. She was working as an architectural draughtswoman designing houses and doing interiors. As a woman of that generation, it had been a struggle to get her art taken seriously by her parents, her father anyway, not her mother. So, she was defiantly supportive of my artistic pursuits. Some of the others weren't so lucky. My mother was very, very encouraging, and one of the ways that she actively supported me was allowing me to get art supplies on her account at the art supplies shop. There was no real limit on my spending, apart from 'Don't be a greedy jerk.' So if I went there and decided I needed another Rotring pen, she'd be 'Oh, that's fine.' So, I could go and buy a Rotring pen and a pad and some ink, no problem. She'd only look at my art portfolio and never look at my comics, never saw the band live, because she'd hear us jamming and was basically 'I think it's very nice that you do what you do, but it sounds bloody awful to me, so, no.'

John Farrow People got around the country. If we were in Auckland and wanted to meet Adam Decay we'd just bowl up to his house, or we'd stay with all the Compos Mentis guys in Wellington. They had this flat called the Hinau Hilton in Hataitai, and you'd meet them, you'd go to gigs and 'Oh, that's Craig from Nazgûl' or 'There's Ania from *Submission* zine.' Everyone would hitchhike around the country and meet people, so after that it'd just be 'Well, John in Dunedin, he'll be my distributor down there' and 'Simon Cottle in Wellington will be my distributor up there.' More through people than shops most of the time.

Dave Hegan Zines were really important because that's how you read record reviews, or you got addresses for contacting bands, or you were introduced to different political ideas. There was no internet. There were no other publications out there saying what we were saying, you had to do it yourself. Everyone was connected by that. I remember writing to John Farrow who did *PMT* down in Dunedin to get a zine, and then heading down there and staying with him. This would've been in '88 or '89. So, it was all real, y'know; real connections, not just superficial ones. You could go stay at another punk's house or whatever. I think it was really important, and every zine would lead on to something else, like an article or a record review or an interview with a band, there might be an address, you might send off for something. That's just how it worked. There was no other media out there doing that sort of thing.

48

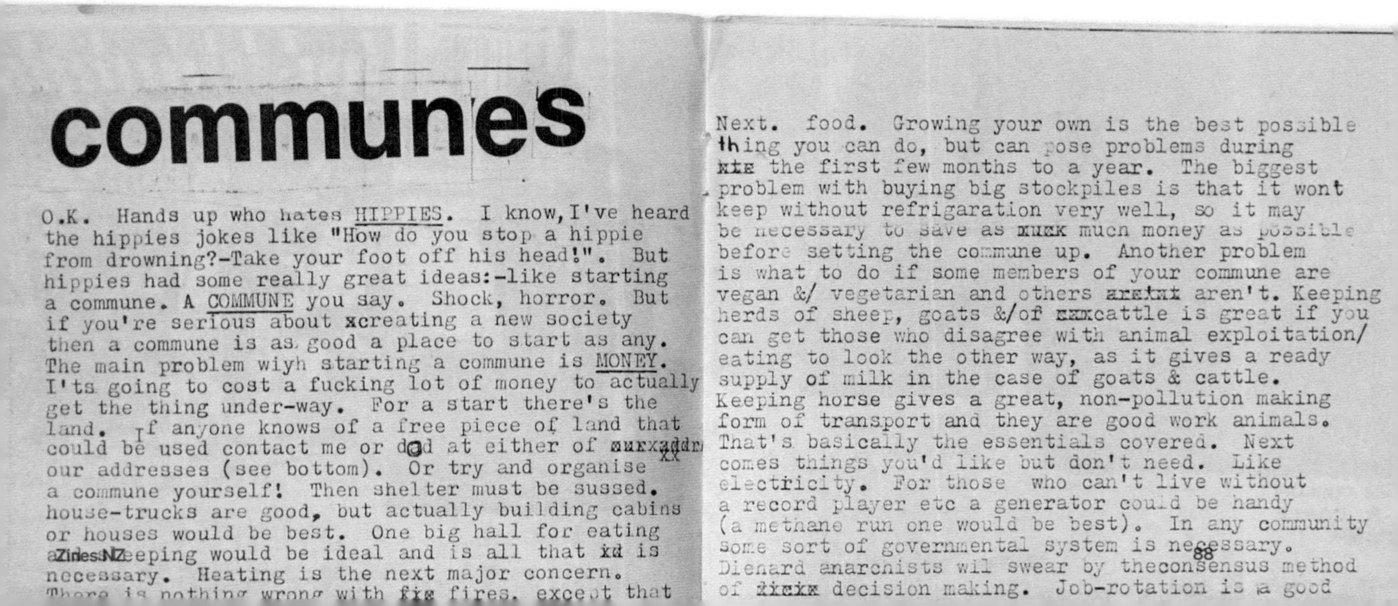
communes

O.K. Hands up who hates HIPPIES. I know, I've heard the hippies jokes like "How do you stop a hippie from drowning?-Take your foot off his head!". But hippies had some really great ideas:-like starting a commune. A COMMUNE you say. Shock, horror. But if you're serious about xcreating a new society then a commune is as good a place to start as any. The main problem wiyh starting a commune is MONEY. I'ts going to cost a fucking lot of money to actually get the thing under-way. For a start there's the land. If anyone knows of a free piece of land that could be used contact me or dad at either of ourxaddr our addresses (see bottom). Or try and organise a commune yourself! Then shelter must be sussed. house-trucks are good, but actually building cabins or houses would be best. One big hall for eating a[...]eeping would be ideal and is all that xd is necessary. Heating is the next major concern. There is nothing wrong with fix fires, except that

Next. food. Growing your own is the best possible thing you can do, but can pose problems during xtx the first few months to a year. The biggest problem with buying big stockpiles is that it wont keep without refrigaration very well, so it may be necessary to save as xuxk much money as possible before setting the commune up. Another problem is what to do if some members of your commune are vegan &/ vegetarian and others arxtxt aren't. Keeping herds of sheep, goats &/of xxxcattle is great if you can get those who disagree with animal exploitation/ eating to look the other way, as it gives a ready supply of milk in the case of goats & cattle. Keeping horse gives a great, non-pollution making form of transport and they are good work animals. That's basically the essentials covered. Next comes things you'd like but don't need. Like electricity. For those who can't live without a record player etc a generator could be handy (a methane run one would be best). In any community some sort of governmental system is necessary. Diehard anarchists wil swear by theconsensus method of xxxxx decision making. Job-rotation is a good

John Farrow We would have people stay with us. It was just the experience of meeting someone new in a different band or from a different scene. It was a good experience. But looking at it, the punk scene — as opposed to, say, the skinhead scene — wasn't actually that different from what the hippies were into. There was communality and punk ethics, which changed, but the ethics I was into in the eighties were pacifist, anti-homophobia, anti-sexism and pro-vegetarian, so they're pretty consistent with hippie politics.

There was a guy on the West Coast, from Greymouth, called Gonk. He was prolific, he would make up these compilation tapes of really obscure overseas bands, introduce you to all these obscure bands and fanzines. We were going 'What!? You bloody live in Greymouth — how do you know about all this stuff?' He just said, 'Well, there's nothing better to do in Greymouth.'

Paul Luker *Ha Ha Ha* rocked our world. It was one thing for non-Aucklanders to come here and do something, but for the regions to do something and send it here . . . It was a frustration among people I knew that we couldn't get a copy, and we didn't know when it was out. We might not know about it until *Rip It Up* said there was another copy and it was too late by then, and it frustrated us that we didn't have it. Yeah. We wanted it.

49

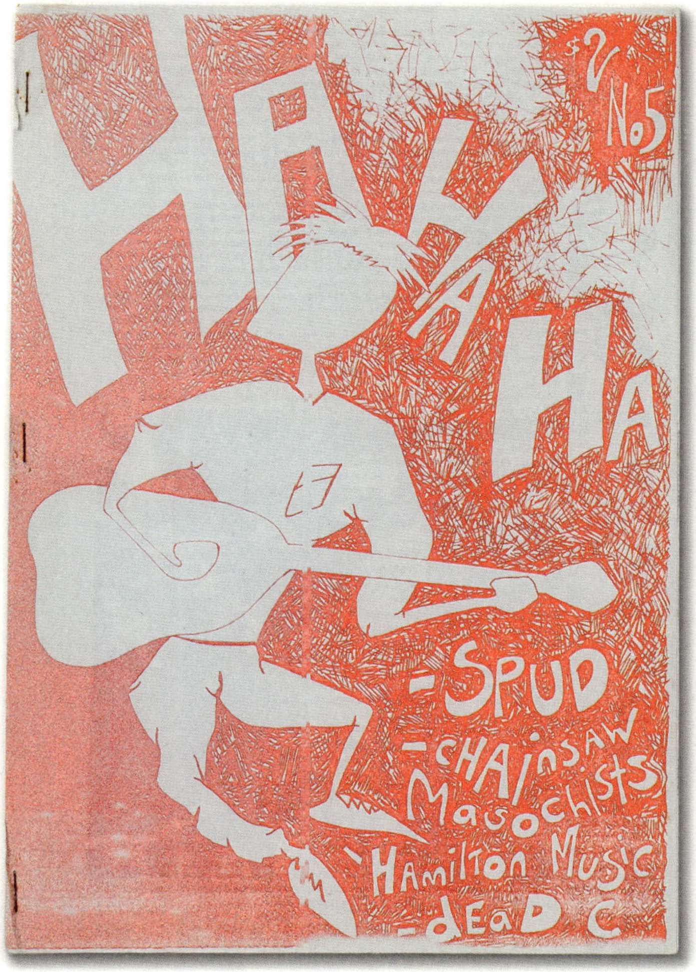

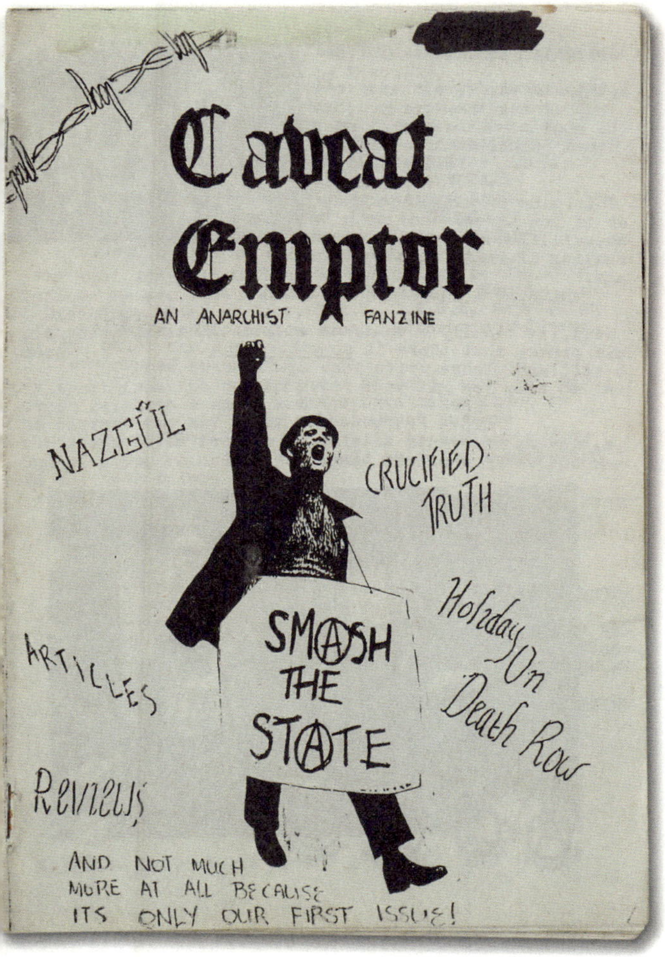

48. *Caveat Emptor* spread and cover, Steve Foetus, A5, date unknown. Whakaoriori Masterton.

49. *Ha Ha Ha* #5, cover and layout by Andrew Schmidt, writing by Andrew Schmidt and Stuart Schmidt, A4, 1988. Paeroa / Kirikiriroa Hamilton.

50

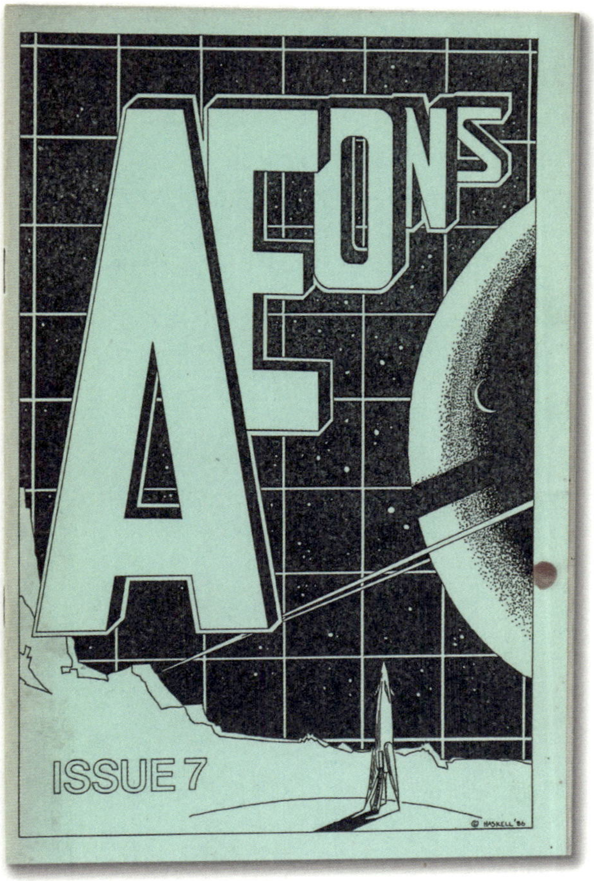

AEONS OF AEONS

Sometime in 1980, the Auckland University Science Fiction Society decided to produce a magazine, as an outlet for members' fiction and artwork. The name 'AEONS' was chosen.

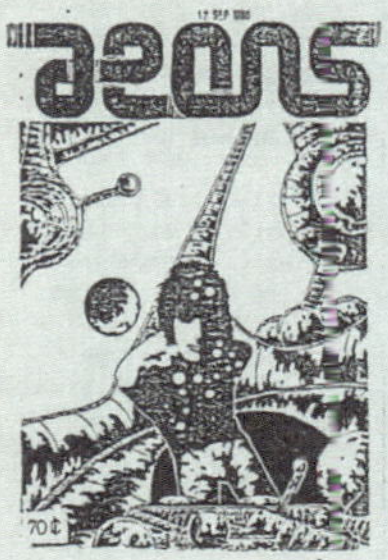

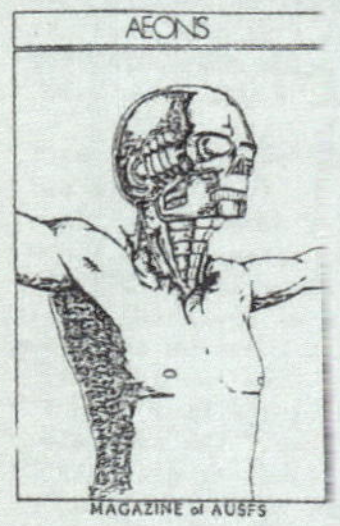

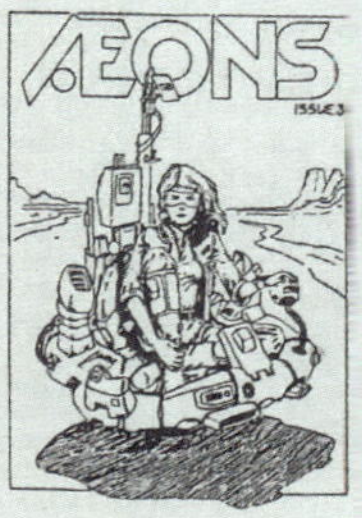

The first issue of AEONS was photo-copied on A4. Perhaps the kindest thing to say would be that it had a certain amateurish charm. Josef Hurtubise edited and co-conspired with Duncan Lucas on the first episode of the long-running serial 'Saga'. A "Story so far" has never been included with 'Saga' - it is assumed the reader can extrapolate backwards (or alternatively buy back issues).

Perhaps you might recall AEONS 2 more as a thin tissue of typos than anything else. This was not really the fault of anyone involved, as AEONS 2 was a hastily grown clone of the original, taken from a tissue sample with some chromosomal damage. The original copy went astray before reaching the printers, when Jeff Leddra's mini was stolen and the contents burned. So several month's work had to be repeated in a few weeks. The results included Anne McCaffrey using the word "satyrically" and 'Episode Zero' being untitled. The concluding part of 'Lightsk[y]' was lost to the flames (or something), so a cash prize was offered for the best ending to this story. Graham Collins managed to wrap it up in a later episode of his own serial but the editors felt his ending couldn't possibly be the best! AEONS 2 was offset in an A5 format and while this lead to a much more professional looking product, artwork other than line drawings still didn't fare too well. Andrew Stewart edited.

AEONS 3 rolled around the next year with Andrew still at the helm. The format remained the same, with another wonderful McIlhagga cover, but this time we dabbled in word-processing. This involve[d] typists being smuggled up into an unnamed Auckland computer firm in the dead of the night (more often than not to play computer games). The result was right-hand justified, but the typeface has more than once been described as "illegible". The typos were on the wane by now. Bruce Grenville wangled a free ad on the back cover, although no one can remember how.

The national SF convention was held in Wellington in 1983, and there was a frantic rush to complete AEONS 4 in time. As usual the artwork was the last to arrive and had to be patched in with the text somehow. Michael Kowalski edited. After an abortive attempt on the Studass photo-copier, AEONS 4 was offset on the day of departure.

Hicmael Skiwalko

50. *Aeons* #7 cover and spread, edited and cover by Dean Haskell for the Auckland University Science Fiction Society, A5, 1986. Tāmaki Makaurau Auckland.

51. *D.W.F.* #6 cover and spreads, edited by Michelle and Craig from punk band Nazgûl, A5, 1982. Te Whanganui-a-Tara Wellington.

51

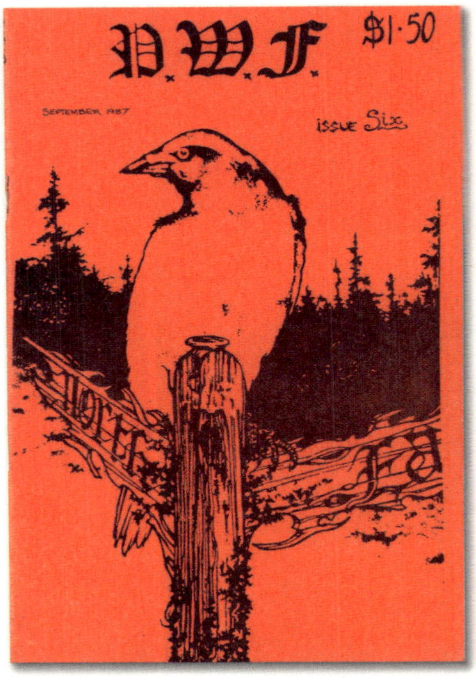

Greetings Folks,

* Here is issue 6 finally and I did it all by myself, well nearly all by myself, Craig did the record reviews and helped with some of the typing.
* Big apologies to "Holiday On Death Row", I kind of misplaced their interview which was supposed to be in this issue but I will do another one with them and it should be in the next issue.
* Here in Wellington there are no pubs that will let punk/alternative bands play, but the good news is that the Rock Theatre has re-opened for gigs and a few have been held at the Railway Hall. So support your local bands and have an excellent night out.
* Another big news item is that E.M.I, New Zealand's only record pressing plant is closing it's doors at the end of this month. It's bloody slack, their excuse is that compact disc's are in more demand and records are not making E.M.I enough money to keep their plant open. A year or two ago, E.M.I purchased the other record pressing plant(s) and dumped all the equipment at the bottom of the Cook Strait so that so that no one else can use it. What a was
* There is still time left to send an entry in to our Design a record cover competition for the next New Zealand compilation 7"E.P. Details are in issue 5 or just write for details.
* Well, the Labour Party is still government so I wonder what damage they are going to do this three years. Do you remember on telly at the beginning of the year when they showed the ACCESS ads all the time? ACCESS is a job training scheme introduced by the Labour government to replace STEPS, TAPS and PEP schemes but already things are going wrong. There are heaps of people on their waiting lists, so they have taken the ad off T.V. and to top it off, they are cutting out alot of the training modules here in Wellington with the excuse of not enough money for the rest of the year. So training such as horticulture, textiles, dress making, life skills and many more are ending on 31st October, but hospitality, catering and clerical training are staying because these skills are in more demand from the business community. Graphics might be staying also but it's not sure. What a big have it all is.
* Anyway thats enough moaning so I hope you enjoy this issue of D.W.F.
* Oh yeah, I would like people to send in photo's so I can use them on the poems page and I will send those kind people a free copy of the zine. The more photo's the better.
* Anyway take care and stay kool til after skool.

Michelle

Dear Michelle
Just writting to comment on the Miss Universe thing in issue 3. I went to school with Ursla Ryan who won, and I'm happy to tell you she's a fuckin horrible mole. She's skinny to the point of being laughable and the most ignorant bitch I've meet, no bullshit, I'm not just saying it. She sux. No one can believe she won it out of the people who know her. I didn't see her as I haven't watched T.V for a year and a half, but I bet she had make-up thick as on and she must have been doing more than fucking the judges. She never had one boyfriend once for the 5 to 6 years I knew her. She's YUCK.
From a 10 stone weakling who can't fight for shit and doesn't wanna.
Yours Shawn xxx (P.T.F)

(Shawn - Sorry I haven't written back to you cause I lost your letter and only found it again a few days ago.)

THE BROMIDE EXPRESS

Next Issue Craig will be back and we should have interviews with : Arm Th[e] Insane, Bovvett, Extremes and hopefully another New Zealand band interview maybe

This Zine is distributed in the follow[ing] countries : New Zealand, Australia, Engl[and], South Africa, Belgium, America.
Anyone wanting to help with distributi[on] get in contact, swaps with your zine ca[n] be arranged.
D.W.F : c/o Michelle and Craig
P.O. Box 7414
Wellington South
New Zealand

<u>THANKS TO</u>: Craig, Gregg & Casualty, Steve(666 1/2 zine), Colette(photo's), Darren, Sean, Edward and Carl, Ross(Bromide Express) and everyone who helps distributing this zine. Ta very much.

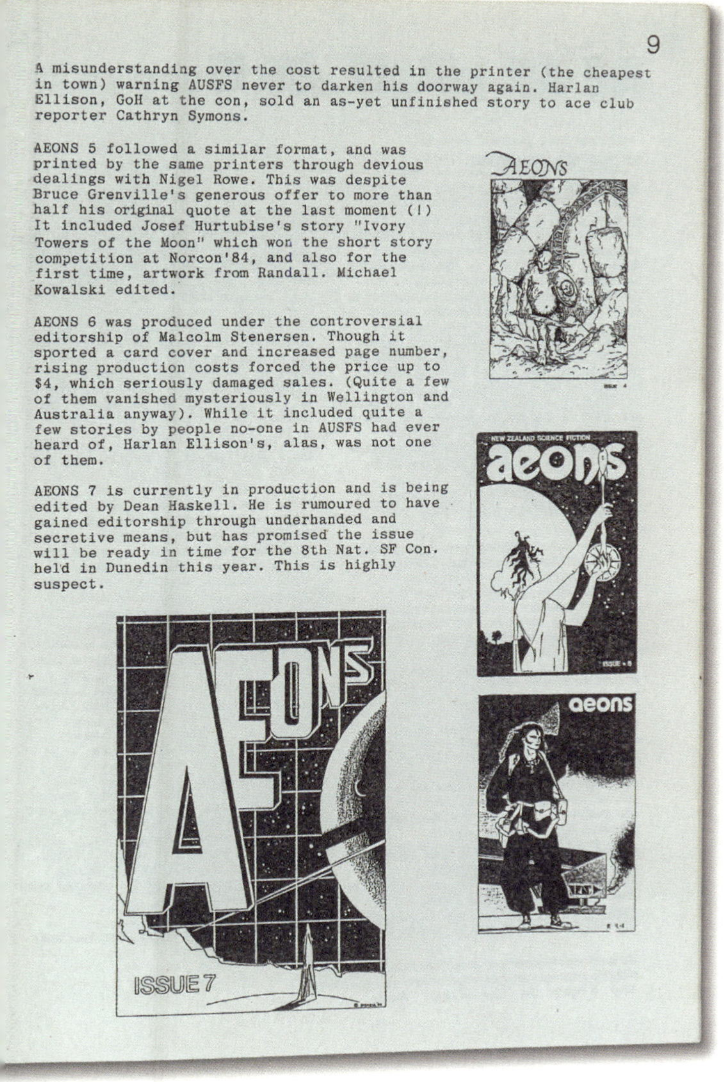

9

A misunderstanding over the cost resulted in the printer (the cheapest in town) warning AUSFS never to darken his doorway again. Harlan Ellison, GoH at the con, sold an as-yet unfinished story to ace club reporter Cathryn Symons.

AEONS 5 followed a similar format, and was printed by the same printers through devious dealings with Nigel Rowe. This was despite Bruce Grenville's generous offer to more than half his original quote at the last moment (!) It included Josef Hurtubise's story "Ivory Towers of the Moon" which won the short story competition at Norcon'84, and also for the first time, artwork from Randall. Michael Kowalski edited.

AEONS 6 was produced under the controversial editorship of Malcolm Stenersen. Though it sported a card cover and increased page number, rising production costs forced the price up to $4, which seriously damaged sales. (Quite a few of them vanished mysteriously in Wellington and Australia anyway). While it included quite a few stories by people no-one in AUSFS had ever heard of, Harlan Ellison's, alas, was not one of them.

AEONS 7 is currently in production and is being edited by Dean Haskell. He is rumoured to have gained editorship through underhanded and secretive means, but has promised the issue will be ready in time for the 8th Nat. SF Con. held in Dunedin this year. This is highly suspect.

52

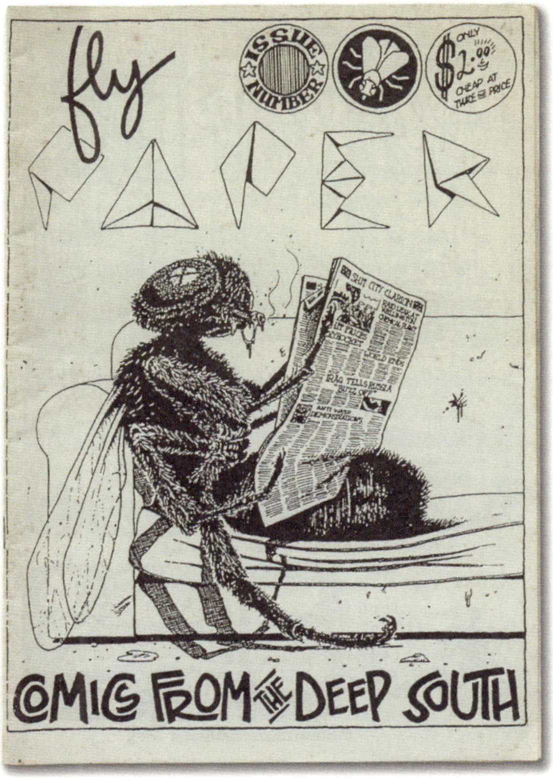

52. *Fly Paper* #3, edited by Dave Hall, Tim Bollinger and Gregory Edwards, A4, 1985. Ōtepoti Dunedin.

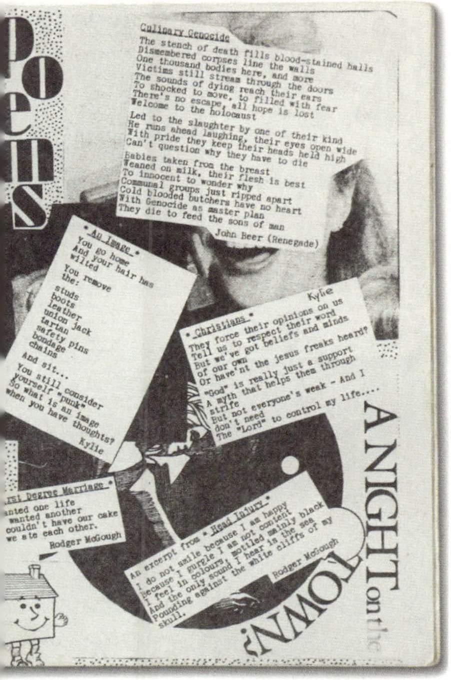

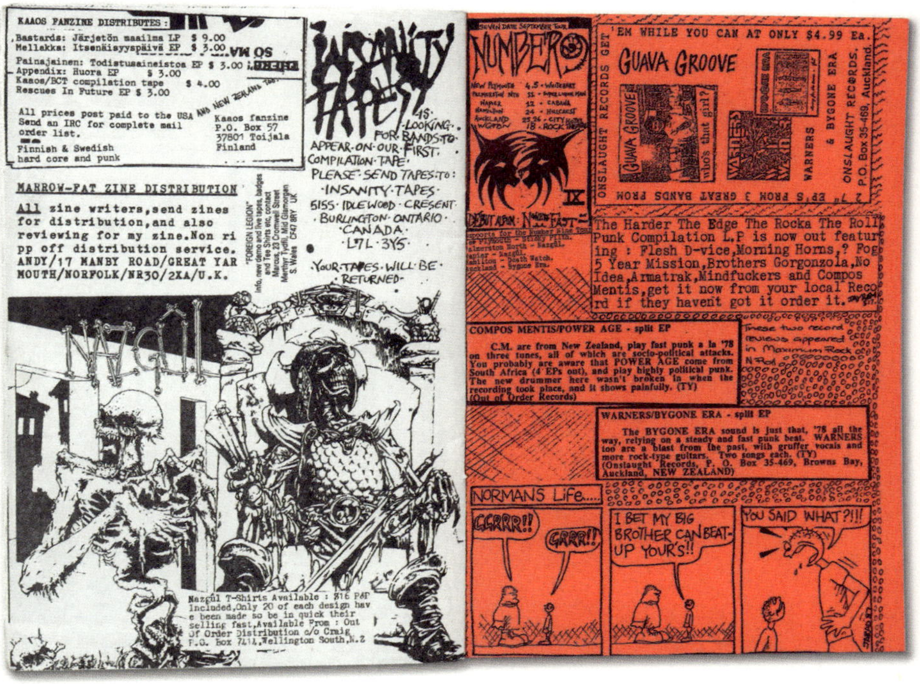

Simon Cottle There'd be a mix, my shitty old photocopier, some commercially reproduced bromides . . . Covers might be photocopied on a *good* machine, and then I'd just make up the content using my shitty copier. Always trying to juggle the costs.

Richard Langston I never gave anyone a bean, and we never asked for any money from Flying Nun for any of their ads, it wasn't about that. I was so naïve, but it would have changed the nature of the thing if we'd made it about the money. We broke even, which is pretty good, because things like *Jesus on a Stick*, Chris Knox's thing, it lost money hand over fist. Well, it was very flash. Chris would've been driven by the art not the commerce, but you come unstuck if you've got a high-grade colour publication.

Tracey Wedge I still have the quotes for printing. It looks like it cost us $75 to $80 to have it printed. So, if we printed 100 copies, sold them for a dollar each, that would cover postage and printing. I think that's possibly how we worked out the cost: selling *at* cost, there was no profit margin.

Paul Luker I didn't earn $100 a week in my apprenticeship until I was over 21, and I've got a feeling that it cost maybe $150 to print 1000 copies of *Empty Heads*. I have a notion it was $154 for some reason.

Bruce Grenville I was mostly printing for bands around Auckland because I was an offset guy as well. Nowadays everything's done online via social media, but back then if you were doing a gig you had to print a poster. Most people would go to a photocopy place and xerox it, but some would go and see a printer, which was usually me because I was doing it way below the commercial rates, like cost price plus a little bit. Zines as well, all sorts of stuff.

Paul Luker I do like making the books. I think, in the end, the books won out over music. I mean, that's why I ended up exhibiting these artist's books. I remember going to Peter McLeavey Gallery in Wellington, when I was taking some records and tapes and stuff to a store there during one of my road trips, and I can remember saying to him, 'Here's my new record. I'm also making a whole lot of books. They're big one-offs.'

'What's this?'

'Well, I'd like to sell them in an exhibition.' He's probably thinking 'Okay, what a weirdo.'

'What art school did you go to?'

'I didn't.'

'Oh, okay. And how old are you?'

'Oh, 26.'

'Mmm, might not be too late ...'

And that was it. He just tapped his chin and left it at that, and so I waited and waited and waited [for him to say more], but that was it: he just told me 'It might not be too late.' So I left.

When I got back to Auckland, I did see some-one who I thought would be a dead-setter. They'd had a gallery in Christchurch that occasionally put on bands like Playthings. I thought 'Okay, we'll go and see her.' She just sort of leaned back, got out her business card, which had the names of all the artists that she managed on the back, and threw it across the desk and said, [puts on supe-rior voice] '*These* are the people that I deal with.'

53. *Anti-System #14* cover and spread (following page), Simon Cottle, A4, 1989. Te Whanganui-a-Tara Wellington.

Simon Cottle I think the longevity of my zine activity just came from the joy of the Wellington punk scene. And I mean, what's a punk-rocker? [Laughs.] It just appeals to something inside of you, and you wanna share the experience, coupled with the political side to it as well, thinking about protest, thinking about actually making societal changes. But mostly the joy of going to a gig and being 'Woah, that was awesome! We had such a good time. Let's write about it and share a photo, and maybe someone else will be inspired to start a band and bring that joy, or to move to Wellington.' Yeah, I think there's a lot of celebratory aspects.

53

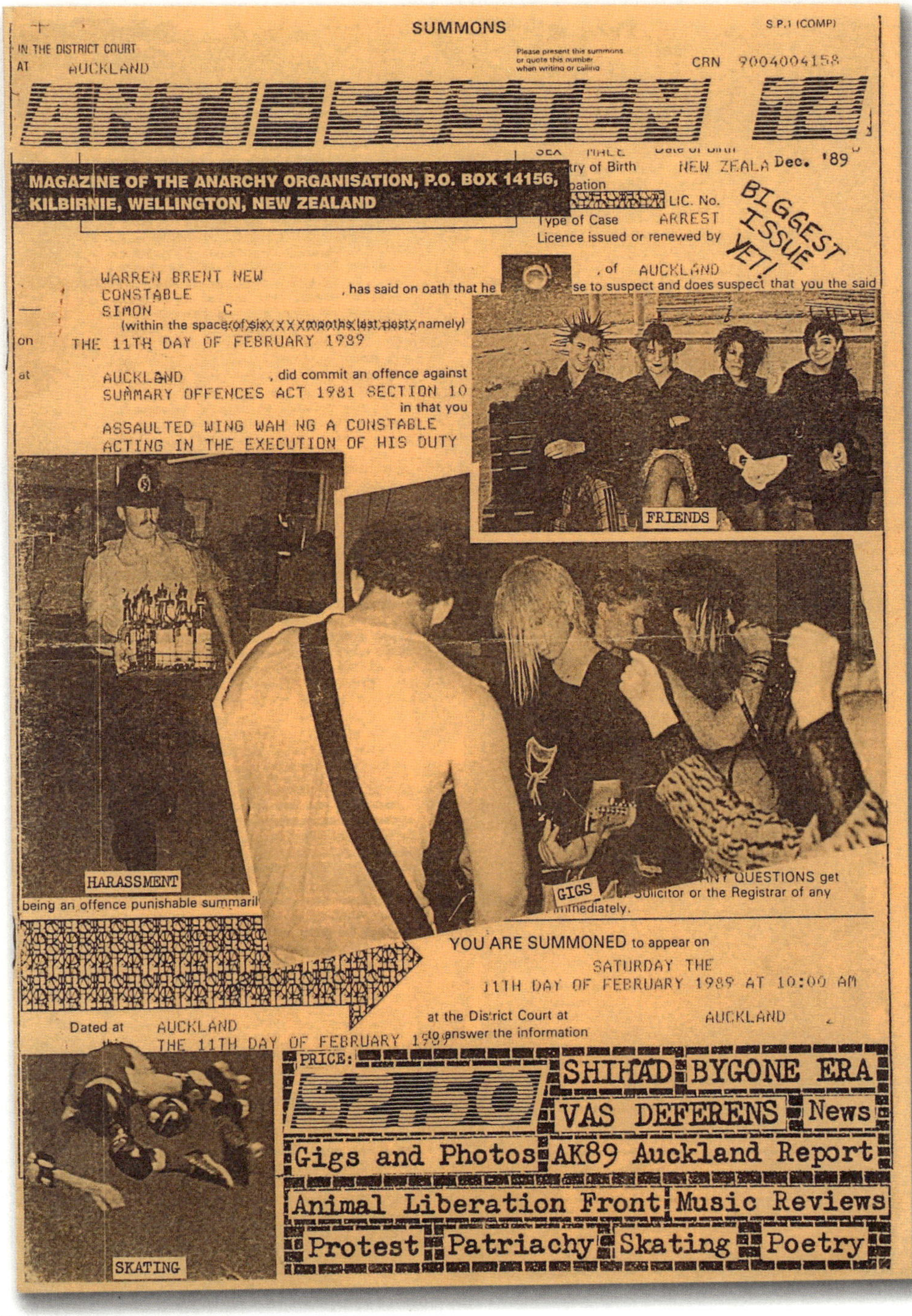

SIMON SAYS

All rightee! Another issue already and I've got out the birthday trimmings because Anti-System is now four years old (stick-ability does it).

Thought a charge sheet would make a good cover, it's meant to tie up with the Holidaze theme, since that is something that happened to me last holidays - Where I was unfortunate enough to be at a Rising Sun gig during a Team Policing Unit raid. Dancing there has been deemed illegal - the cops wade into the slamming, then do you for assaulting a police officer (my saga is covered in the Gigs section).

Then I see on the tele. that the Team Policing Unit are just riot squads and in Auckland they're well known for storming into pubs fond with Pacific Islanders (and punks!) and when they don't find aggro, they cause it. In a Wellington case the TPU batoned a guy unconscious and left him in the gutter, later a cop dragged him 10m by his feet while 25 cops watched. In court Robert Lithgow, a defence lawyer, said the TPU use excessive violence and it was time for the court to signal its disapproval - After which a senior police officer approached the Evening Post's reporter and said he did not think the comments should be reported! (How often does the media comply with these requests?).

Another comment of Lithgow's was that whenever TPU officers give evidence in court, they can't remember what other officers were doing at the time, nor were they doing anything themselves. This is what the women who were arrested at Waihopai came up against with their complaint against the police. The police investigated themselves, then wrote back saying they couldn't recall anything incorrect happening.

Laying the complaint was an ordeal too. My friend Terri, one of the three arrested women, was picked up from her flat and the cop gets on the car radio and says "I'm bringing in the suspect for interrogation." At Central Terri was asked questions such as "What were you doing at the Base?" and "What political groups are you involved in?", which she refused to answer because of their irrelevance. Being driven home (2 hours later) the cop started on the line of "Are you sure it happened that way?" and "Laying false complaints is a serious offence." Interestingly enough, he also said "Was it the TPU again? We are always getting complaints about them. It's the boys out trying to prove themselves."

Now then if you make it through these value-packed-reduced-type-pages to page 27, you can read about the latest Waihopai protest, but before that was the court case for the nine who were arrest-ed at the May protest. I went down to the Blenheim District Court for the hearing on the 16th of October, where all nine were up on the charge of "Found without reasonable excuse in a building, situated at Waihopai Defence Satellite Communications Unit."

First up was Don Allen from the Government Communications Security Bureau, he was the Officer in Charge of the Base on the night of the protest. He was out of his "commando style" (wanna be Action Man) pants and had some useful information about the damage to the Base: $432 for the window that was smashed to gain entry to the main build-ing, $464 to remove spraypainting, and $3487 to repair the compound fence! He presented photos of the damage, which the accused decided to take as momentos.

Sergeant Morris was the main prosecution witness and his credibility should of been questioned when he identified the wrong protestor on the 'phone contacting the media and when he talked to the group he said it was a woman that replied, when in fact it was a male. The other cops didn't add much, except to confirm that on the night of the protest they were so out-numbered that they were powerless. - Ha, ha!

On the Cover

It's that time of year again, so I thought I would give the cover a 'holidaze' theme.

FRIENDS. Even if they are throwing a can at me. Thanx to everyone who put me up, or more to the point, everyone who had to put up with me.

HARASSMENT. Seven cops in one photo! This is the poo-lice at last year's New Year's Eve gig, removing the alcohol from the venue, even though it was a licensed café.

GIGS. PHOBIA hurrying '88 on its way, with their aversion to slow, melodious music.

SKATING. Drier weather means more skating hours. Backside aerial from Richard Knott.

NB. All photos this issue by me, unless otherwise stated.

In defence, all nine explained the failure of legal channels to obtain information about the Base. It was obvious that they were in the Base's main building with reasonable excuse, to obtain both information about the Base and to get publicity and media attention - necessary to remove the secrecy and spark off public debate. It is also a defence to show that there was no intention to commit further offences once inside, but the defence lawyer was a typically useless legal aid job and didn't raise this point (nor of course did the judge).

In summing up, the judge went on and on about unlawful protest and the damage to the Base - irrelevant to all but one, who faced the further charge of wilful damage. He also said that the protestors were warned and had the opportunity to leave on 2 occasions - which was news to Terri, and bullshit anyway, 'cause one guy did try to leave, but still got charged. Besides this wasn't a trespass charge, so that's irrelevant. The key point of reasonable excuse wasn't addressed at all and all nine were found GUILTY AS CHARGED.

On the 29th of November everybody had to travel to Blenheim for the third time (not cheap for those who live far away, eg AK), for sentencing. Terri and the others got thirty hours community service each.

As for the Bust Fund run last issue, I should of expected 100 punx to be able to afford (what with the price of alcohol and drugs these days) a contribution of $5 each, but instead the Fund received $16! - boosted by non-punk donators to $86. The only conclusion I can draw is that punx are prepared to talk about peace & against the government (or even buy a record which expresses that), but we are not only unprepared to physically protest for peace, but won't even help out someone arrested for protesting on our behalf. NO THANX.

Thanx to the seven people that did contribute and Ross Gardiner who donated $204 gig proceeds (see page 20). Even then the Bust Fund fell short of covering mere travelling costs, so if Terri's sentence had been a fine...

Please note that due to the lack of response to Anti-System 13, that no A-S 15 is planned until I get some feedback (positive, or otherwise) over this issue.

CONTENTS

NEWS

Hey, if any of this News is wrong blame the source - don't sue me.

Armed with three songs recorded in June, Chris and Mike Fegan, of CASUALTY, along with manager Greg Serious, left in September for Sydney. The plan is for Waterfront, or another

continued over

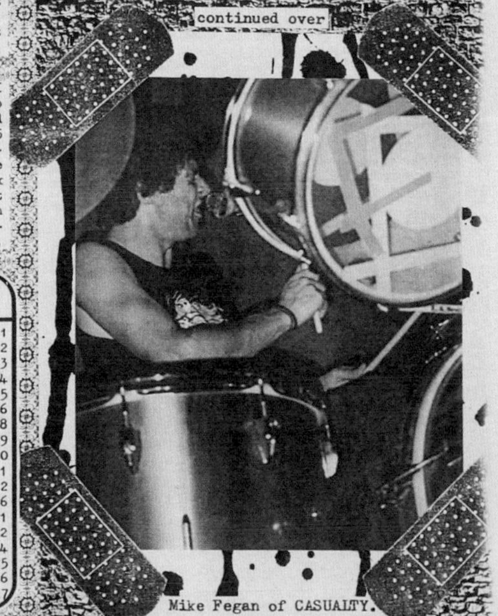

Mike Fegan of CASUALTY. No doubt it was bass player Sid De Torquemada's xenophobia which prevented him travelling to Australia.

Paul Luker But I didn't stop. I don't know why I was so determined for someone so shy, but I took my one-off artist's books to [gallerist] Rodney Kirk Smith. I hadn't initially gone to him, even though he was just down the road from *Rip It Up* and really near the Rumba Bar. I mean, everyone knew Rodney Kirk Smith. I'd gone in there many times just at lunchtime to look at the shows, and he always sat above the staircase so he got to turn around just as you were entering. *No turning back now.* And he said yes straight away, but he said something else really interesting; not exactly 'This will be a breath of fresh air', but something to that effect. I can remember thinking, 'Oh, fuck, that's different. He just said yes, but he thinks . . .' He said, 'You can have this side of the gallery', and I look back now and I realise that he liked a bit of disruption. He had big artists in his gallery, but he liked a bit of disruption, especially on opening nights. He was a lovely guy.

That's why I say the books took over in the end. I did feel legitimised, because Rodney then invited me to do other things: I was invited to make a book for [the exhibition] *ANZART*, and I was invited to make a book for [the exhibition] *Cross Currents*, overseas, and so on.

Richard Langston We got unsolicited poetry from Peter Olds and Cilla McQueen. I was taken aback by that. *Proper poets are sending their stuff . . . to us!?* Maybe that was a bit of a moment for me where I thought, 'Oh, okay, maybe we can do something mildly significant here.' Peter Olds wrote a poem about music and the impact it had on your body, which was really great, and it was going to be on the back page of issue four or five, but it got swamped under a Flying Nun ad. Chris Knox had a gift for getting a back-page ad to us just before we went to print. All those ads that are on the back of *Garage*, Chris drew all those.

John Farrow I think I've only got *PMT* #3. I don't know what's happened to two and one, I think they must've sold out. I'd have to look in the box that's under the stairs.

Tracey Wedge I know more people bought issue two than issue one, so *PMT* must've been received well.

54

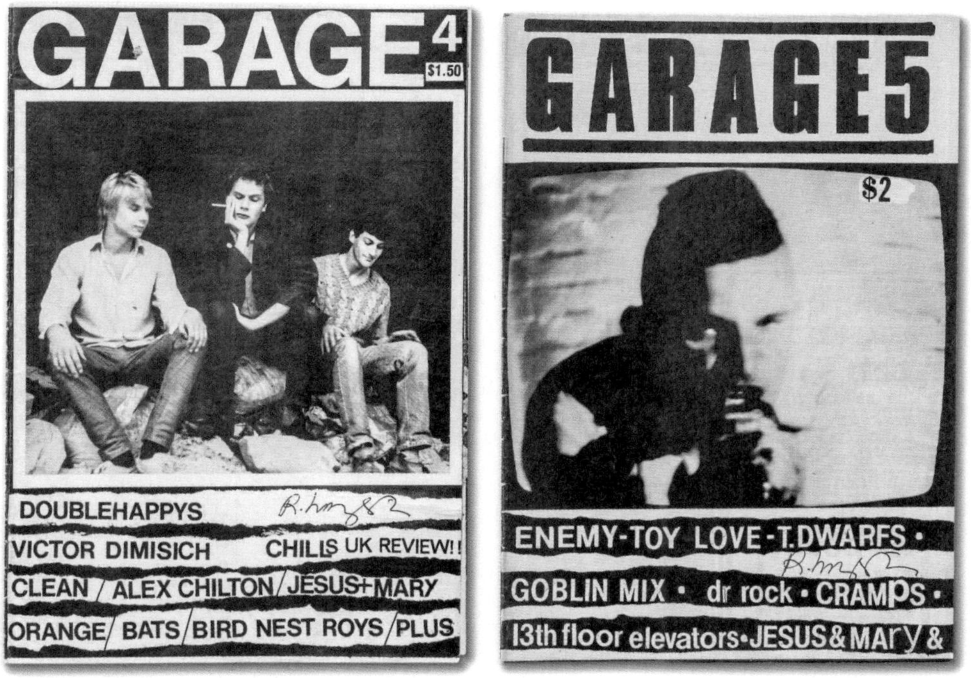

54. *Garage* #4 and *Garage* #5, edited by Richard Langston, A4, 1985/86. Ōtepoti Dunedin.

Richard Davies After years of *Taranaki Underground* people recognised Brett's commitment, the consistency, the quality always getting better. He was always working on it. You should see the first stuff he did, rough; but later, very well put together. At the time I think some people might've realised its importance. I don't think Brett and I realised how it would come to be understood, that it would be like a bit of gold. We were just doing it because we wanted to spread our message.

John Farrow I was stoked to read Lauren Deacon's essay about Gorse ending up on the Bruce LaBruce Queercore mix. I worked hard on those lyrics. Some of the punks thought that was too liberal, while others liked them. No one in the band ever read my lyrics, so it was quite cool to read that essay. Especially when you look back and see how far rainbow communities have come, to think that you're writing that in your twenties. But, to be fair, in that scene it wasn't that radical to be embracing of diversity.

Richard Langston David Swift saw The Jesus and Mary Chain in London, and Bruce Russell saw Sonic Youth. That was a pivotal moment for Bruce, and he wrote a review for *Garage*. We got international by about issue four . . . David or someone, a mate, wrote a piece about Alex Chilton, who we all loved, and in the eighties he was rediscovered by the indie music scene all around the world. I think I started using my real name. In the first issues I made up all these pseudonyms because I wrote the whole thing. Pseudonyms like 'Ralph E. Stanley', that was me. I thought it was kind of funny or stupid. It was childish in a way, but it kind of appealed to my sense of humour; we looked like we had lots of writers when in fact all of them were me.

Simon Cottle I started off doing a Bachelor of Science majoring in physics. Turning up to lectures with a purple mohawk and all the rest, it was kind of inevitable that I'd end up doing a BA in political science . . . No blowback from the university for looking like that, not in that sort of setting. I mean, avoidance yes, but not the hostility that you got everywhere else.

People were shocked, even though we were second-wave punks. It was a different world back then. Chelsea Records had a branch in James Smith [department store], and the owner went completely off her nut when I tried to order *Never Mind the Bollocks*. She was not gonna have that filth in her shop. People would gather up their children and run because you had blue hair, I mean that quite literally . . . The look has been around so long you kind of forget that it was ever confrontational. People refusing to serve you in stores, etc.

55

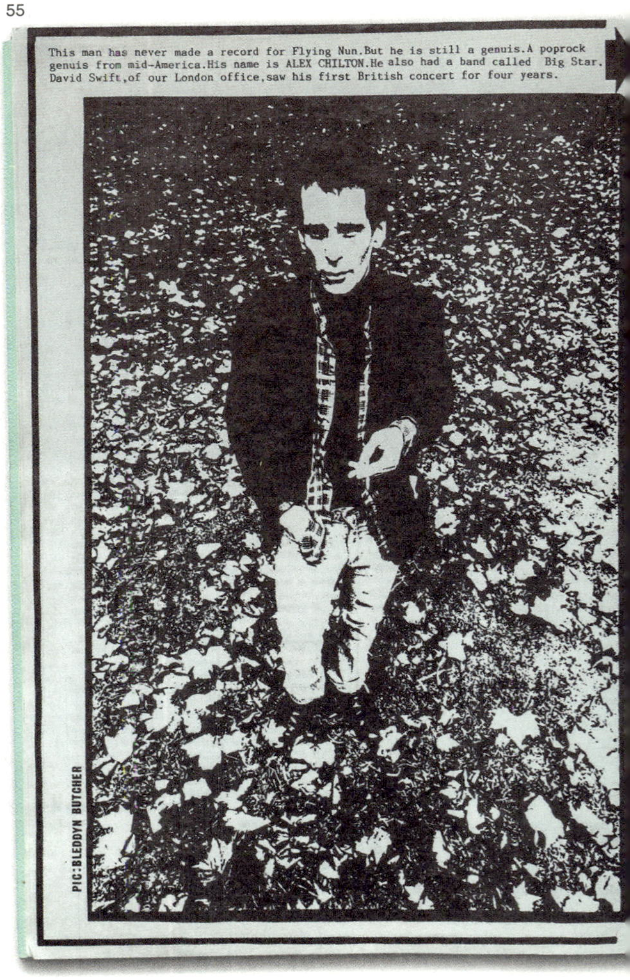

55. *Garage #4* spread, Alex Chilton, review by David Swift, A4, 1985. Ōtepoti Dunedin.

Ross Gardiner I think of zines as being normal, y'know? Normal people make zines, but I'd take them to school, and people would be like 'What the hell!? This thing cost $1? How do they keep publishing?' Zinesters don't care about the money. I guess people are used to magazines and newspapers, or the newsletter of a society of some kind, but the idea of self-published things certainly weirded people out a bit.

Simon Cottle I wrote a zine article about Neil Roberts' attempt to blow up the Wanganui Computer Centre. It was a fair time after the incident (I didn't start my zine until '85). I remember going to the public library and going through the microfiche of *The Evening Post*, *The Dominion*, *Truth* (terrible newspaper) and getting printouts to do the article, which seems weird in this day and age of Google, Google, Google.

A bit later, a friend had just done some work on his car and we decided to run the engine in by going on an all-night adventure. We stopped outside the police computer centre in Whanganui. Next thing you know, we're surrounded by about three police cars and we're getting dragged out. It was obviously still a sensitive topic. They asked to search the car, and I refused, saying 'You haven't cited the correct Act to search the car', and they said, 'We'll fucking search it under the Fish and Chip Act if we want to.' It's like, okay . . . looks like refusal isn't an option here.

That's total eighties punk stuff, cops driving past in cars calling out: 'Hey, Grant' — you'd be walking with some punk and the cops would know their name. And they'd be opening your mail, like the fanzines arriving at my post office box. Well, I mean, you're receiving zines about class war, 'no government', etc., etc. I could go to the post office box any day and there'd be mail from all around the world, but then you'd go and there'd be nothing for two weeks and then . . . *bang!* Suddenly it would be overflowing. It's like 'Mmm, okay, that's interesting.' My partner at the time got arrested at the Waihopai spy base, and that was even more blatant. She'd get letters in her letterbox just ripped open, sending the message: 'We're going through your mail.' Deliberately not hiding it. Definitely a different period of time.

John Farrow Punks who didn't like the Flying Nun stuff would just ignore it. But having said that, one of the first gigs I ever went to was Sneaky Feelings and The Verlaines, and this local skinhead came in and went 'Give us The Exploited! We want Exploited!', and I was standing there thinking 'How the fuck do you think you're going to hear The Verlaines play The Exploited?' It was just stupid.

Some of the skinheads would hassle 'the Dunedin sound'. It was only called that later. I had the privilege of being at two milestones in music: the Dunedin sound and hardcore punk. You look back at the eighties and it's like *Woah, that was a moment in time*, especially when decades later you see punks in Wellington wearing patches of bands that you'd been listening to.

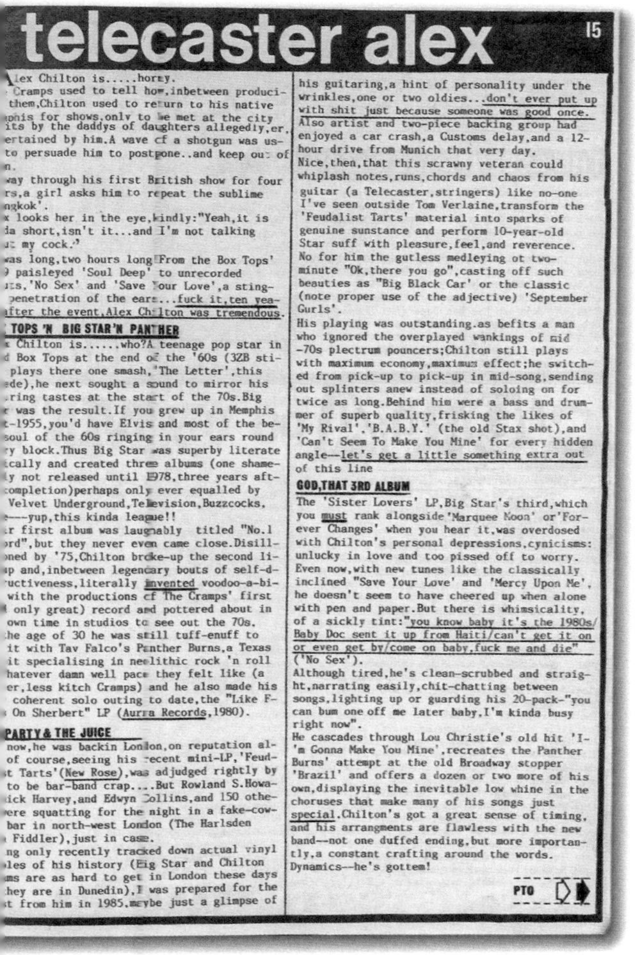

telecaster alex 15

Alex Chilton is.....horny.
Cramps used to tell how,inbetween produci-
them,Chilton used to return to his native
phis for shows,only to be met at the city
its by the daddys of daughters allegedly,er,
ertained by him.A wave of a shotgun was us-
to persuade him to postpone..and keep out of
n.
way through his first British show for four
rs,a girl asks him to repeat the sublime
ngkok'.
x looks her in the eye,kindly:"Yeah,it is
da short,isn't it...and I'm not talking
ut my cock."
was long,two hours long.From the Box Tops'
9 paisleyed 'Soul Deep' to unrecorded
its,'No Sex' and 'Save Your Love',a sting-
penetration of the ears...fuck it,ten yea-
after the event,Alex Chilton was tremendous.

TOPS 'N BIG STAR'N PANTHER

x Chilton is......who?A teenage pop star in
d Box Tops at the end of the '60s (3ZB sti-
plays there one smash,'The Letter',this
ade),he next sought a sound to mirror his
ring tastes at the start of the 70s.Big
r was the result.If you grew up in Memphis
t-1955,you'd have Elvis and most of the be-
soul of the 60s ringing in your ears round
ry block.Thus Big Star was superby literate
cally and created three albums (one shame-
ly not released until 1978,three years aft-
completion)perhaps only ever equalled by
Velvet Underground,Television,Buzzcocks,
e---yup,this kinda league!!
r first album was laughably titled "No.1
ord",but they never even came close.Disill-
oned by '75,Chilton broke-up the second li-
up and,inbetween legendary bouts of self-d-
uctiveness,literally invented voodoo-a-bi-
with the productions of The Cramps' first
only great) record and pottered about in
own time in studios to see out the 70s.
he age of 30 he was still tuff-enuff to
it with Tav Falco's Panther Burns,a Texas
it specialising in neolithic rock 'n roll
hatever damn well pace they felt like (a
er,less kitch Cramps) and he also made his
coherent solo outing to date,the "Like F-
On Sherbert" LP (Aurra Records,1980).

PARTY & THE JUICE

now,he was backin London,on reputation al-
of course,seeing his recent mini-LP,'Feud-
t Tarts'(New Rose),was adjudged rightly by
to be bar-band crap....But Rowland S.Howa-
ick Harvey,and Edwyn Collins,and 150 othe-
ere squatting for the night in a fake-cow-
bar in north-west London (The Harlsden
Fiddler),just in case.
ng only recently tracked down actual vinyl
les of his history (Big Star and Chilton
ms are as hard to get in London these days
hey are in Dunedin),I was prepared for the
t from him in 1985,maybe just a glimpse of

his guitaring,a hint of personality under the wrinkles,one or two oldies...don't ever put up with shit just because someone was good once.
Also artist and two-piece backing group had enjoyed a car crash,a Customs delay,and a 12-hour drive from Munich that very day.
Nice,then,that this scrawny veteran could whiplash notes,runs,chords and chaos from his guitar (a Telecaster,stringers) like no-one I've seen outside Tom Verlaine,transform the 'Feudalist Tarts' material into sparks of genuine sunstance and perform 10-year-old Star suff with pleasure,feel,and reverence.
No for him the gutless medleying ot two-minute "Ok,there you go",casting off such beauties as "Big Black Car' or the classic (note proper use of the adjective) 'September Gurls'.
His playing was outstanding.as befits a man who ignored the overplayed wankings of mid-70s plectrum pouncers;Chilton still plays with maximum economy,maximum effect;he switched from pick-up to pick-up in mid-song,sending out splinters anew instead of soloing on for twice as long.Behind him were a bass and drummer of superb quality,frisking the likes of 'My Rival','B.A.B.Y.' (the old Stax shot),and 'Can't Seem To Make You Mine' for every hidden angle--let's get a little something extra out of this line

GOD,THAT 3RD ALBUM

The 'Sister Lovers' LP,Big Star's third,which you must rank alongside 'Marquee Moon' or 'Forever Changes' when you hear it,was overdosed with Chilton's personal depressions,cynicisms: unlucky in love and too pissed off to worry.
Even now,with new tunes like the classically inclined "Save Your Love' and 'Mercy Upon Me', he doesn't seem to have cheered up when alone with pen and paper.But there is whimsicality, of a sickly tint:"you know baby it's the 1980s/Baby Doc sent it up from Haiti/can't get it on or even get by/come on baby,fuck me and die" ('No Sex').
Although tired,he's clean-scrubbed and straight,narrating easily,chit-chatting between songs,lighting up or guarding his 20-pack-"you can bum one off me later baby,I'm kinda busy right now".
He cascades through Lou Christie's old hit 'I-'m Gonna Make You Mine',recreates the Panther Burns' attempt at the old Broadway stopper 'Brazil' and offers a dozen or two more of his own,displaying the inevitable low whine in the choruses that make many of his songs just special.Chilton's got a great sense of timing, and his arrangments are flawless with the new band--not one duffed ending,but more importantly,a constant crafting around the words.
Dynamics--he's gottem!

PTO

Dave Hegan The New Plymouth scene was really heavy. There was a lot of drug use going on and a lot of magic mushrooms, too, which is the main reason people moved there. We were all taking mushrooms every day we could, which is just not good for you. We didn't know that at the time, we just saw it as free drugs. The New Plymouth scene went from being this very positive and vibrant scene to becoming really dark over a period of a few years. People were burning out from mushrooms, just going a bit mental, *actually* mental. So, the scene became really dark, and a lot of the punk-y dudes became skinheads. It just got really heavy.

When I got sent to rehab I was at death's door. I had a death wish. Y'know how there's that Sid Vicious stereotype? Getting wasted as much as possible, you're gonna screw everything up, that's what I was doing. I was doing it quite consciously. I was like 'I'm just gonna destroy', that's what punk became. It went from being really positive when I first got into it to total nihilism. But that was the drugs.

Richard Davies Brett *tried* to do it anonymously and he got raided, because in a little town like this, y'know? We were kids — 17, 18, 19 years old — and we were hardcore, trying to be as hardcore as we could, six foot tall and bulletproof as all youngsters are. So, we didn't expect anything. We weren't afraid. Next minute I come home and Brett's in the cells.

It didn't make Brett more cautious, it just upped the game for him to take on the state. The lawyer didn't want money, the lawyer wanted to do the case because it was such an awesome case. The lawyer'd never heard of anyone getting busted for making zines in their living room and then the police come round because you've said something they don't like.

We got it off the Yanks, the American punks. We'd seen US zines, that's where we got the idea. I used to write to SST Records like every week and ask, 'Can you send me Raymond Pettibon posters?' which are the hand-drawn Black Flag posters. I had stacks of his stuff, man. I lost them over the years. As a kid I used to write to Black Flag and hopefully Henry [Rollins] would talk to me [laughs] like, yeah nah, but they always sent me stuff. They would slip in little zines and posters. I'm like 13, 14, 15. I hadn't even hardly heard them. My mate went to America, then asked me, 'Heard of SST?' I don't know how I found out, because you didn't have Google — I think it was on the back of a record or somehing — and I started writing to them and it became this regular thing. I also liked Beastie Boys, Bad Brains, Fear, Fang . . . Fang were massive for us, they blew our minds. Brilliant band. Love Minor Threat . . . and Fugazi, they're one of my favourite bands. That song Nirvana covered 'The Money Will Roll Right In', that's Fang.

John Farrow The creator of this first *PMT* cover is Terry Perkins who works for Ian Taylor down here in animation graphics. The original picture had the Christ on the cross directly beneath the rocket, and the rocket was much more of a phallus, and for all our rebelliousness we worried about getting sued or getting busted by the cops for having something like that, so we changed the tip on the rocket to be less phallic and moved the Christ on the cross over. That could have been the law school in me being a bit paranoid, but Ritchie Rat [Brett Taylor] in New Plymouth got busted by the cops for some of the anarchist material in his zine, got his whole flat raided. The reason we had a post office box was so that we were anonymous so that our flats wouldn't get busted, because we were up to other stuff that we didn't want to get busted for.

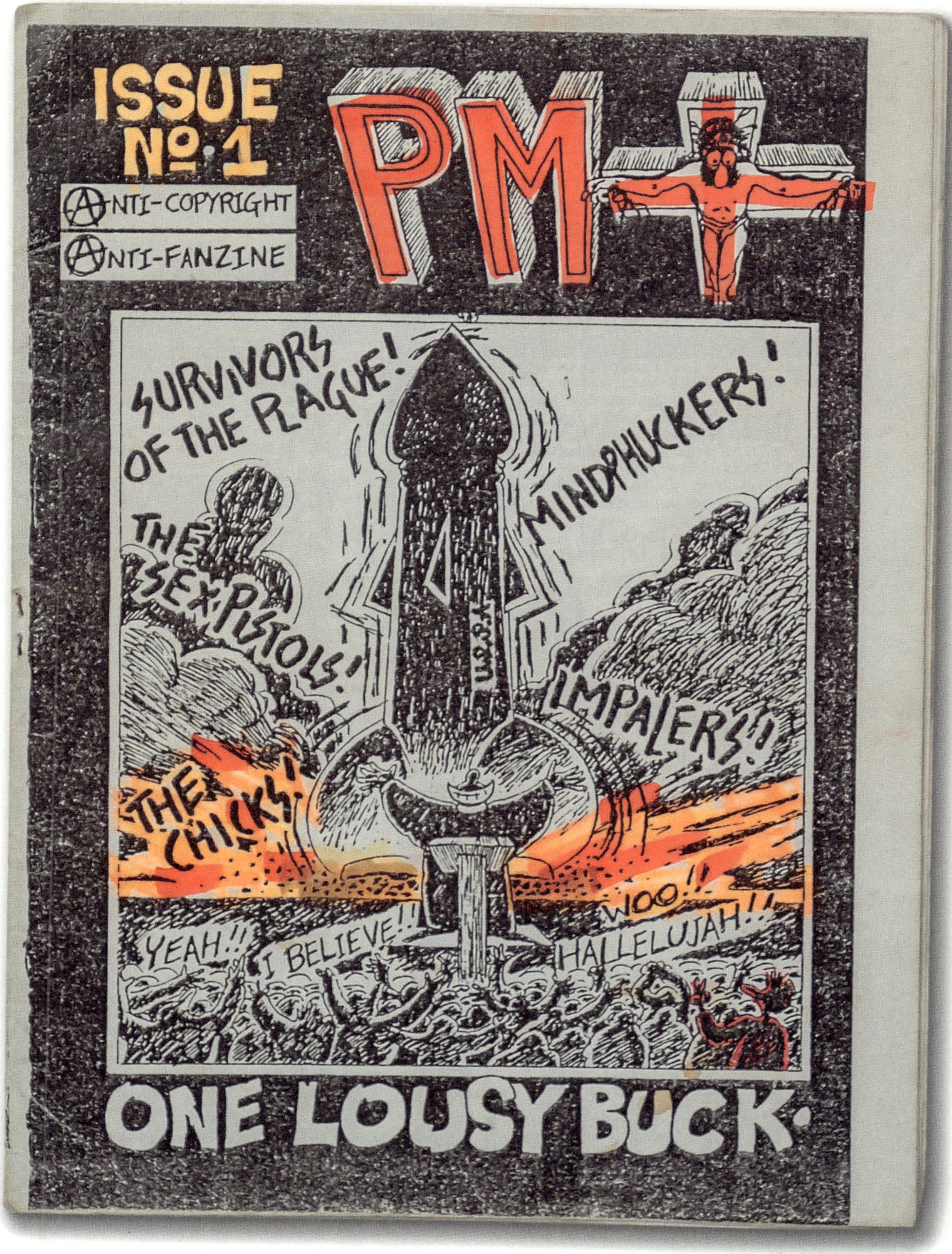

56. *PMT* #1, edited by John Farrow and Tracey Wedge ('Anti-Fanzine' posted top left), A5, 1985. Ōtepoti Dunedin.

Ross Gardiner In that mid-eighties period, *One World* spawned this idea of doing zines and lots of people outside of the main centres were putting out zines. One of the early ones I got was called *Spit on Trend*, which came from Whangārei. *Out Here*, that was from Rotorua.

Richard Davies Brett was mainly in touch with Greymouth, and we wanted to go there. Greymouth had its own punk scene — you wouldn't even think there'd be one punk there. [Laughs.]

Paul Luker I think the motivation for *Empty Heads* #1 was that I had met people through work who lived out in South Auckland and South Auckland became quite familiar to me. That's where these two bands came from, The Smith Brothers and The Criminals. I'd spend more time in South Auckland, weekends, and it was easy to hire a hall. At the time it was getting quite rough in town — boot boys were a real problem. The KCs [King Cobras] were a real problem. It was just a drag. It was very odd.

Richard Langston I'd say Dunedin people are more guilty of being parochial snobs about music than Auckland people. Well, I mean, they were definitely different cultures. Dunedin was an op-shop, don't-be-a-poser culture. Whereas Auckland was more looking towards London and a haircut. Well, I mean, Shayne Carter had a mullet. I mean, fuck, that was about as uncool as you could get back then. Dunedin was street clothes and no bullshit. Well . . . there was an element of bullshit, but it was a very understated bullshit. Whereas in Auckland . . .

There were always exceptions because This Kind of Punishment were from Auckland, Children's Hour, the bands that ended up on Flying Nun . . . And there were also bands that went from Auckland to Dunedin because they recognised that was the kind of music they liked and what they wanted to make: Bird Nest Roys, Goblin Mix . . . they all made a huge contribution.

See, that's classic of the scene, finding a similar scene in another town. You find your scene and you find your zine. And that's how it works, it's tribal. And the zine's tribal-as: it's saying we're important and here we are. It's probably not the case for a very *personal* zine, but a music one is like that because music's a tribal thing and it stakes out the ground for music obsessives.

57

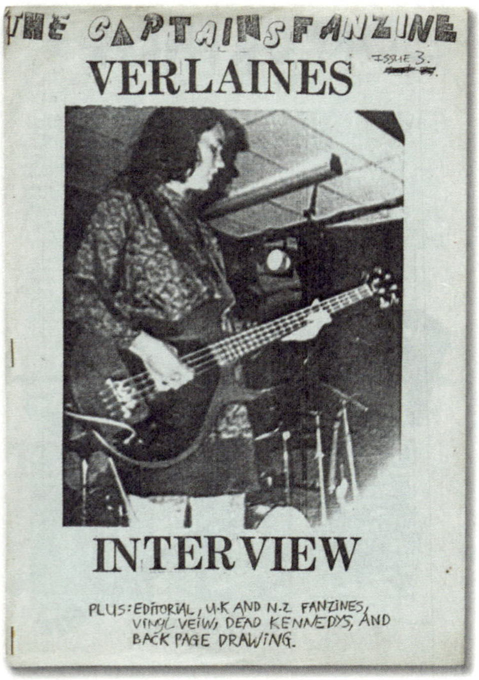

58

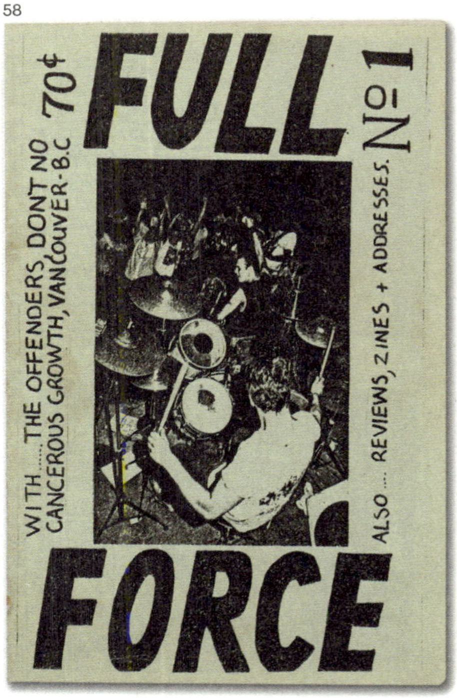

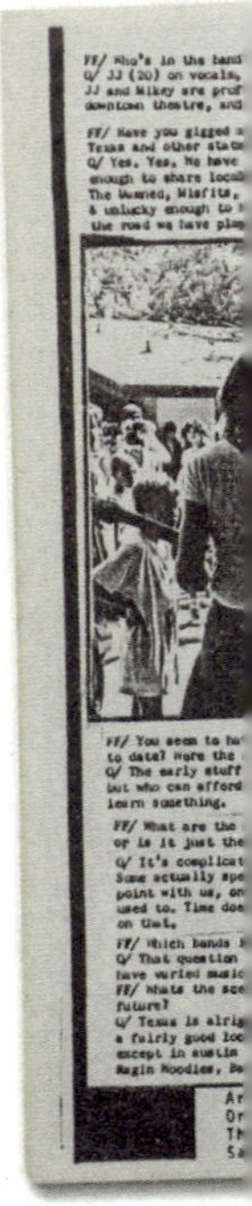

Matthew Campbell Downes We didn't think Auckland sucked. *AK79* we mostly loved. The Screaming Meemees we liked — some of us liked them more than others. We quite liked the Wellington scene, too; Beat Rhythm Fashion and all that. We knew about their music, we had their singles and we thought they were cool. We really loved The Features, we really liked The Swingers, we were massive Toy Love fans. Toy Love were just gods, y'know? My favourite comics artist was Joe Wylie and he did stuff for Toy Love, did their posters, did their music videos, and to us comics and music were part of the same world — that was probably set in place by Toy Love as far as we were concerned.

Christchurch was very brother–sister with Dunedin, but we didn't love all the bands, some of them were a bit twee for our liking. We loved The Clean, The Chills, Sneaky Feelings, DoubleHappys, The Rip, The Verlaines . . . We played with The Bats a lot. I guess we felt like we were part of that world, we were part of the Dunedin–Christchurch Flying Nun world, and we were too young to go to Wellington or Auckland. That was a long way away to us, and by the time we were old enough to consider it, the band had finished.

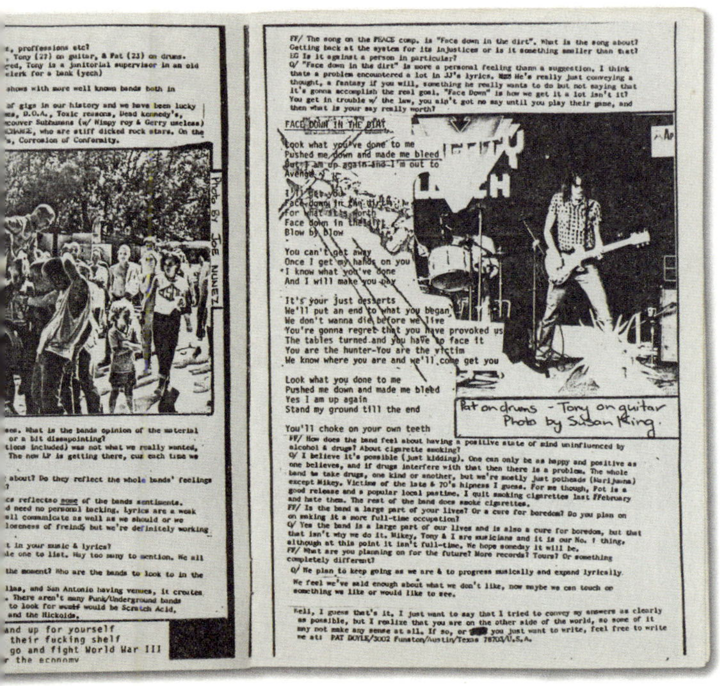

Simon Cottle There was a lot going on in Taranaki. Casualty were a *really* good hardcore band from Taranaki. Ima Hitt Records was in Taranaki; often the scene will revolve around a good independent record label. New Plymouth might not have been your usual cultural mecca, but often the more redneck the town the more you're gonna get punk-rockers rebelling against the norm.

John Farrow I really liked *Anti-System*, really liked *Fuck It Up* and then *Taranaki Underground*. I quite liked *One World*. I liked *One World* more before I met Neil Cartwright. He was just not my sort of person, but his radio show was good and his fanzine was good, but it became more and more slick and commercial, and we didn't like that. If I look back on it, the people who were the most political and had the scene that I most aligned with were in Wellington; bands like Compos Mentis and fanzines like Ania Glowacz's *Submission* and Simon Cottle's *Anti-System*. And overseas ones like *Maximum Rocknroll* and stuff like that.

Tracey Wedge *PMT* was quite important to me, and I enjoyed making it. Issue one was also submitted as a uni course project. I wouldn't have started working on issue two if I wasn't into it.

Coming from Whangārei, Dunedin was a really interesting place to go to university, a tight-knit community, the access to different thinking. It was a really fertile ground for young minds. I thought it was fantastic. There was always something to go to, lots of people pushing boundaries. You could have great bands playing in your living room and then they'd be down the pub the next weekend.

I've never liked Whangārei. I find it very angry. I needed to get out of there as soon as I could. After Dunedin, Australia was another explosion of access to new ideas and experiences. Really fantastic. I meant to travel further, but I spent all my money in Sydney.

57. *The Captains Fanzine* #3, Grant McDougall, A4, 1987. Tūranga Gisborne.

58. *Full Force* #1 cover and spread, Greg Jarman, Annette Gray and Geoff Wright, A5, date unknown. Tāmaki Makaurau Auckland.

Ania Glowacz I'm not sure why I stopped making *Submission*. I think I got tied up with the radio stuff and doing *RAD* magazine [*Radio Active Digest*], stuff like that. Or maybe the scene had changed a bit. It wasn't an intentional stop, just a natural stop.

Paul Luker It's very hard to maintain momentum with an object that you're putting out regularly, and a magazine or a fanzine requires some serious focus. But I never felt when I moved from one medium to another that I was giving up on something, I was just progressing.

John Farrow I was trying to rememer why *PMT* finished. I'd started focusing more on Gorse and writing lyrics for it, and I was trying to get better at that. We were also running an underground venue and we did a show on Radio One, and I was distributing other people's tapes and singles and zines as well. It got quite busy. I didn't have a distro name, just contact 'John PMT'. The venue was called the Nerve Centre: if you're interested, hop on YouTube and look for *The Other Dunedin Sound* and there's a whole documentary on Dunedin punks in the eighties and that venue.

If I'm really honest, there was a downwards slide in terms of drugs and you just lost motivation. Distributing was fine, but what would happen is people would come around and say, 'Can you tick me up?' And then suddenly I'd end up owing some other guy across the country for 10 swapped zines that I couldn't get the money back on. I'd end up running out of money because I never wanted to hold off on paying another zine-maker. The distribution and the making of the fanzine started to hurt financially. So it was just like 'Wah, it's too much effort, it's costing me.'

Andrew Schmidt All my friends went off to another life quite quickly after *Ha Ha Ha* finished. I was the one who carried on, and carried on writing about music. That zines are an ongoing culture? Yeah, I love that.

Ross Gardiner I definitely think the mid to late eighties was the high point for New Zealand punk zines, because once the idea caught on everyone did their own zine.

Richard Davies We grew older, people settled down, started to focus on getting jobs and buying houses. I suppose we were hoping that the next generation were gonna continue to do this, and from what I'm hearing from you they are . . . It doesn't have to be political. It can be whatever you want.

59

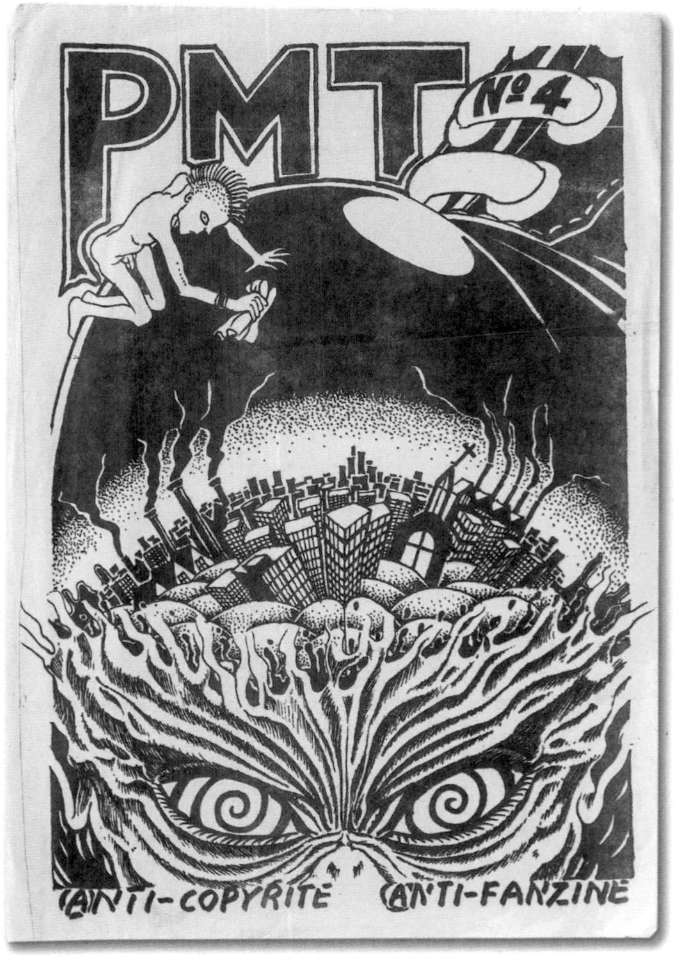

59. *PMT* #4 (which never made it to print), cover by Terry Perkins, A4, 1980s. Ōtepoti Dunedin.

60

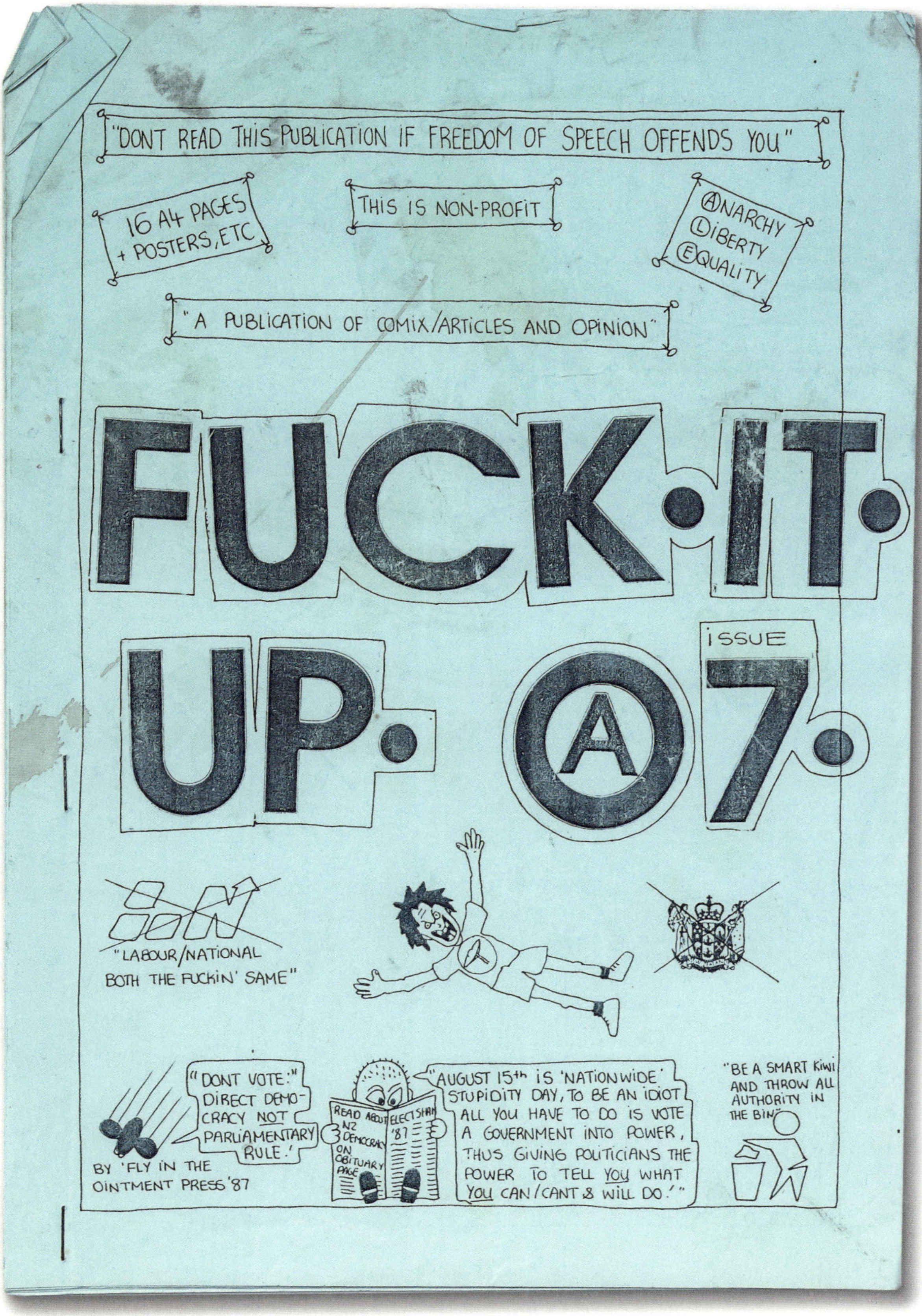

60. *Fuck It Up #7*, edited by Brett Taylor, 1987, A4. Taranaki.

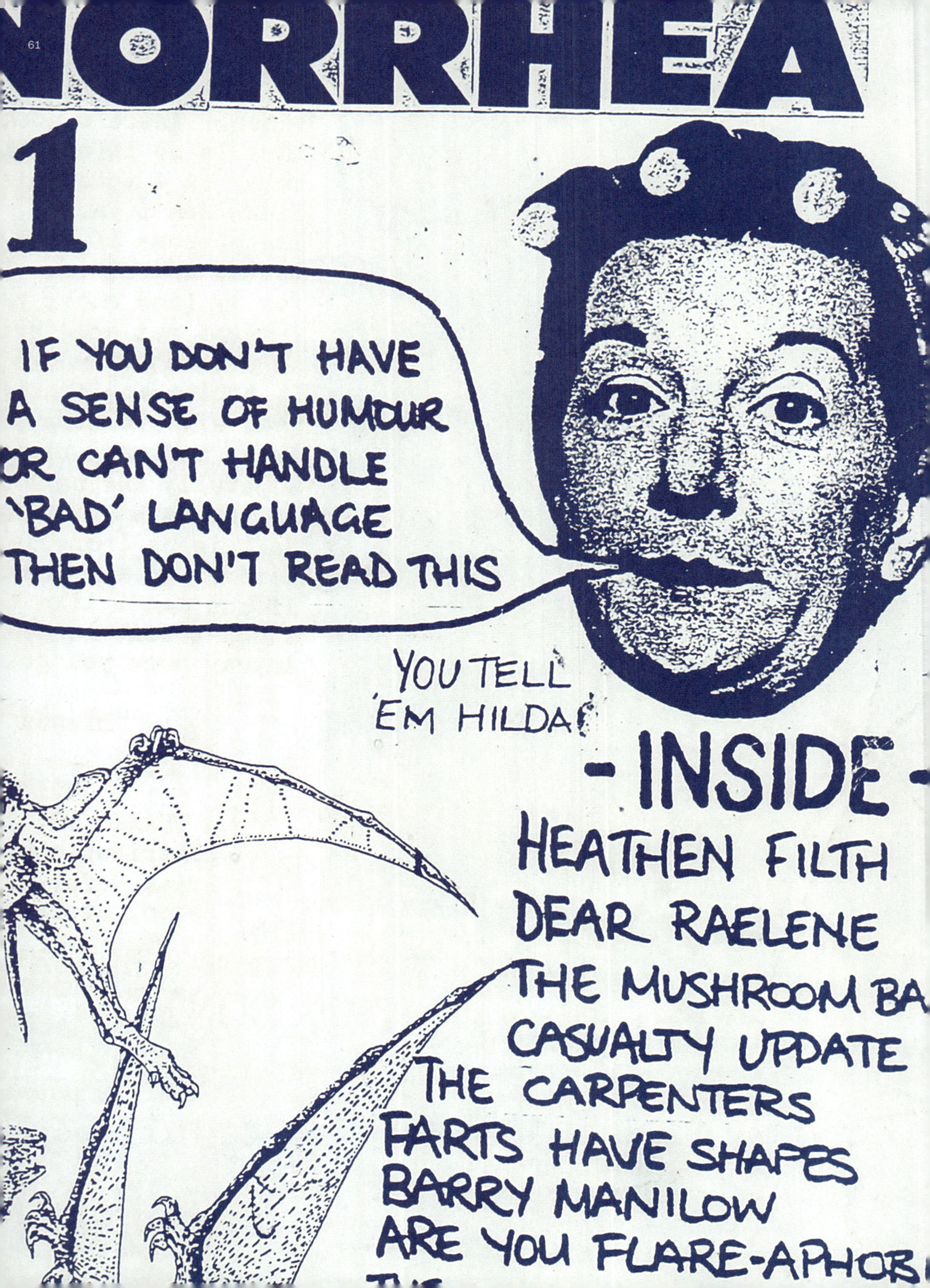
NORRHEA
1
IF YOU DON'T HAVE A SENSE OF HUMOUR OR CAN'T HANDLE 'BAD' LANGUAGE THEN DON'T READ THIS
YOU TELL 'EM HILDA!
-INSIDE-
HEATHEN FILTH
DEAR RAELENE
THE MUSHROOM BA
CASUALTY UPDATE
THE CARPENTERS
FARTS HAVE SHAPES
BARRY MANILOW
ARE YOU FLARE-APHOB

Nineties Aotearoa

The Cold War and South African apartheid were 'officially' over by the end of 1991. The world felt less conflicted and full of dread; the very idea of climate change had yet to take hold in the popular consciousness, but anarchist punk-rockers and their zines and networks endured, so there must have been something to rally against.

61. *Nasal Gonorrhoea #1* detail, Brenda Crooks, A4, 1990. Ngāmotu New Plymouth.

By the late eighties, the neoliberal economic policies of Labour's finance minister, Roger Douglas, had caused an identity crisis for the Labour Party, leading to in-fighting and contributing to the loss of the 1990 election to National by a landslide. National governed for most of the decade, and had no qualms about picking up on any neoliberal policies left behind by a conflicted Labour. National's finance minister, Ruth Richardson, slashed welfare payments in her so called 'mother of all budgets' in 1990. That may well have been a motivator for zinesters who'd seen the dole as something of an artists' subsidy.

Labour had already introduced a user-pays approach to tertiary education via student fees and loans, and National pushed the new business model into overdrive. New Zealand's many decades of free tertiary education were over, resulting in mass protests.

From left: National government ministers Ruth Richardson, Jim Bolger, Bill Birch and Simon Upton at a press conference, 20 December 1990. *Alexander Turnbull Library, EP/1990/4372/21-F*

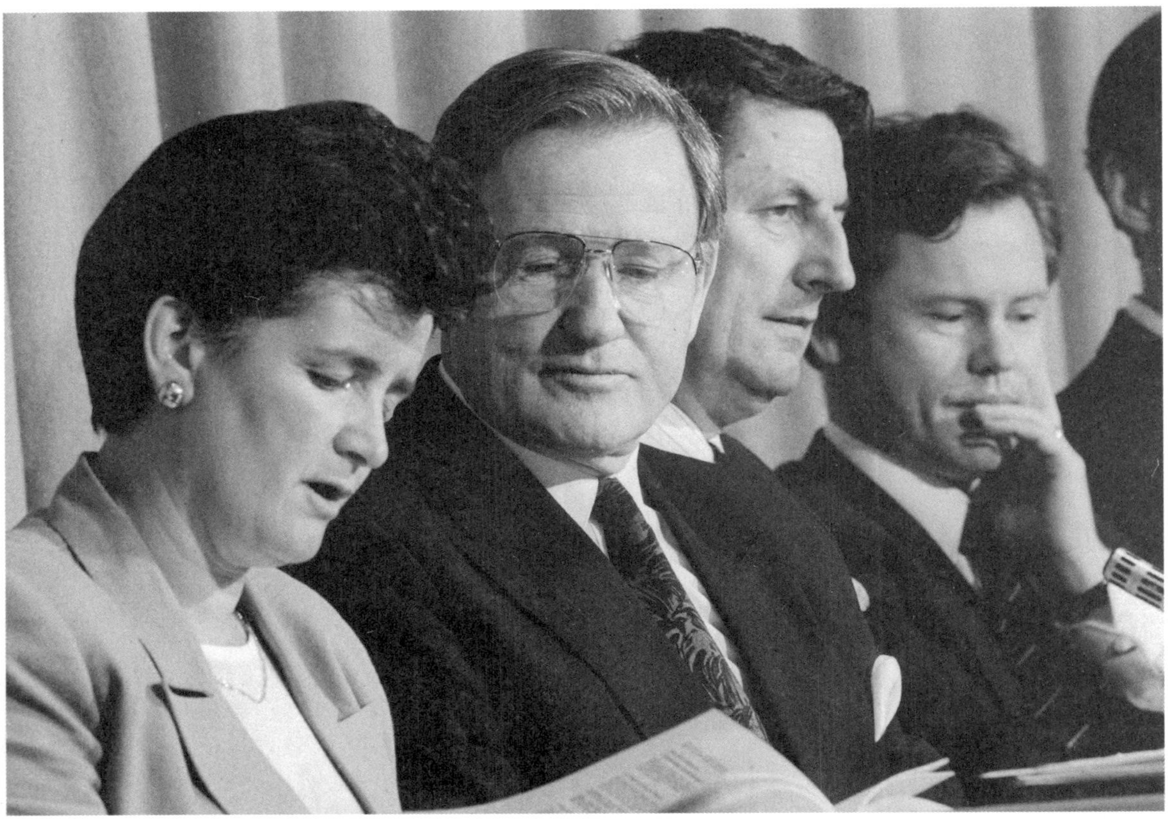

Of course, many nineties zinesters would have been less interested in the decade's political machinations and more enthralled by the pop culture of the time. As Andrew Schmidt observed in the eighties chapter, the arrival of free trade globalisation simply meant it was easier to get cool records.

Nirvana's 'Smells Like Teen Spirit' would become a touchstone for the new generation of punk rock known to many as 'grunge'. The third-wave feminism of Riot Grrrl emerged contemporaneously. (One for the pop quiz: the title of Nirvana's stellar song came after 'Kurt smells like Teen Spirit' was graffitied onto singer Kurt Cobain's bedroom wall by Riot Grrrl mover Kathleen Hanna of Bikini Kill, Teen Spirit being a budget deodorant brand available in the USA.)

University students demonstrating outside Parliament, calling for Minister of Education Lockwood Smith to abandon the student loan policy, 22 September 1993. *The Dominion*

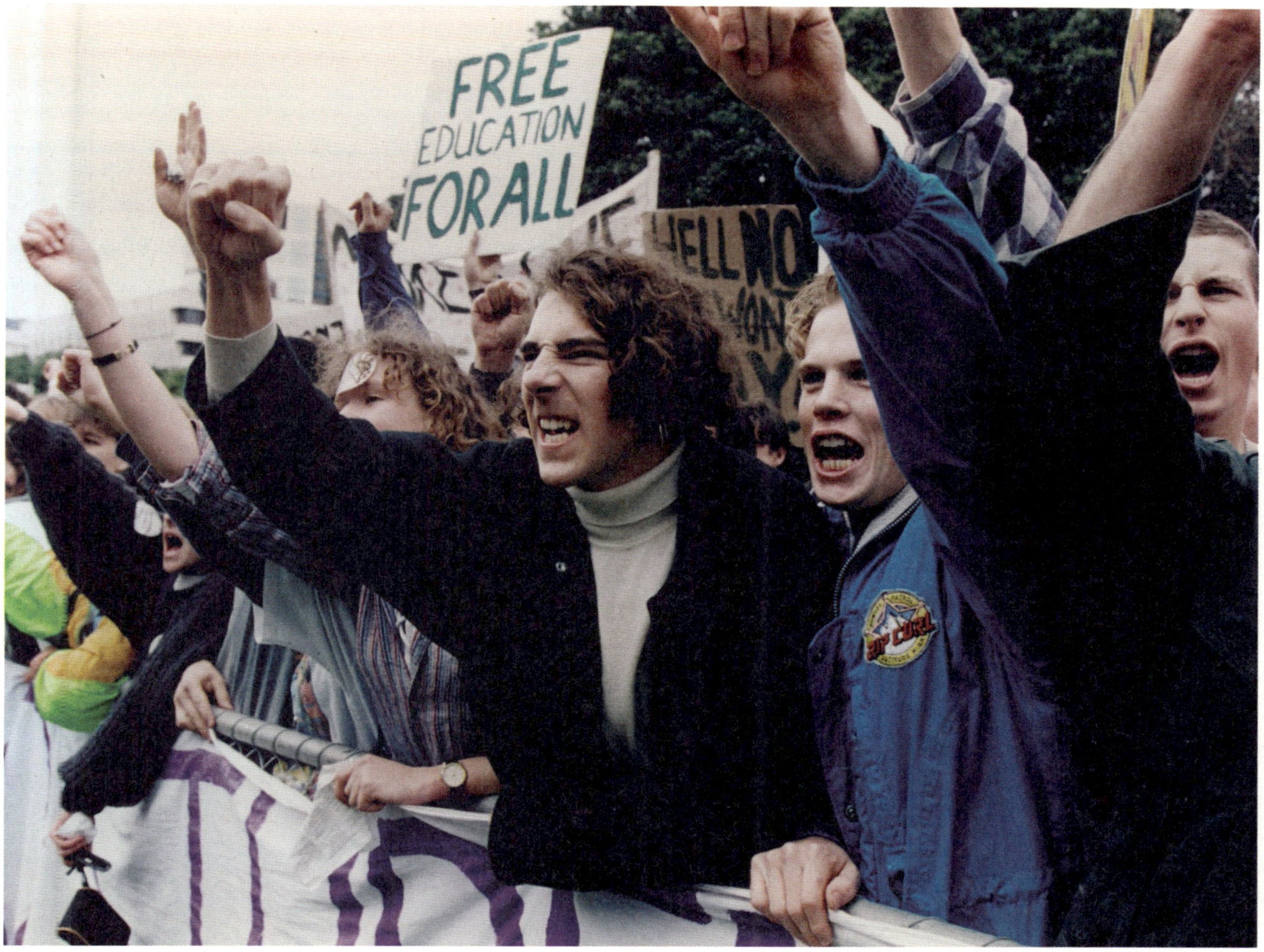

Riot Grrrl was a response to the machismo of US hardcore. Grrrl bands and zines attempted to wrestle punk away from the sweaty grip of the boys and make a space for women. Riot Grrrl zines often shared the personal politics of various feminist issues, while zine aesthetics skated somewhere between the abruptness of earlier punk graphics and a knowingly 'girly' scrapbook process-appearance. The arrival of Riot Grrrl here emboldened young New Zealand women, and many in this chapter namecheck the movement.

'Smells Like Teen Spirit' was number one in the New Zealand music charts for one week at the end of February 1992. In August 1996 the hip hop song 'Chains' by Aotearoa's DLT (featuring Che Fu) held the number one slot for five weeks. The rise of hip hop held increasing sway over popular music in Aotearoa and globally, with hip hop proving to be far more enduring than anything grunge.

Beth Heke (Rina Owen) confronting Bully (Cliff Curtis) in a still from the film *Once Were Warriors*, released in 1994. *Alexander Turnbull Library, PA1-q-1175-16-4-4*

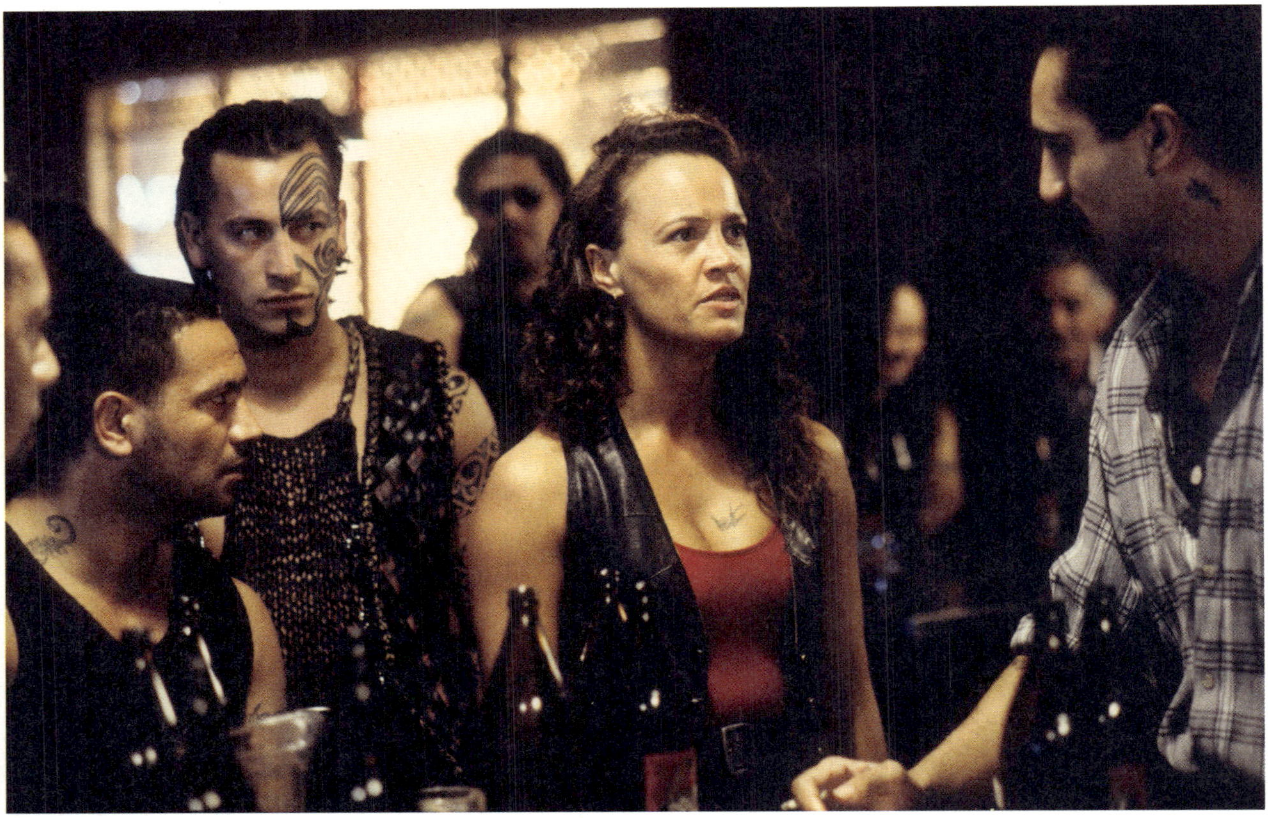

Shortland Street, which was to become one of the country's most popular television shows, was first broadcast in 1992. *The Piano*, Jane Campion's tale of broken colonial dreams, was the top-grossing local movie of the nineties. Alan Duff's novel *Once Were Warriors* was lauded by many critics, while others damned it for unhelpful cultural stereotyping of urban Māori. Either way, Aotearoa increasingly considered its place in the South Pacific, rattling the blinkered 'Little Britain' idea that many Pākehā had grown up with.

Generation Xers came of age in the nineties. The arrival of Generation X marked a steep decline in generational wealth after the Boomers, a trend that has tragically accelerated through subsequent generations, Millennials and Gen Z. Generation X are thought to be marked by a protective cynicism born of diminishing expectations. When fury bubbled up through the cynicism, it might take the form of 'culture jamming', a term that came to prominence in the nineties to describe the camouflaged defacing of advertising. The rise of Canadian magazine *Adbusters* signals the popularity of this strategy. Employing an energetic cut-and-paste, punks had been messing with the messages of advertisers and corporates for some time, but culture jamming offered an almost seamless manipulation of message, sometimes born of access to more sophisticated digital tools.

Photoshop 1.0 was released in February 1990 exclusively for Macintosh. The first Compact Apple Macintosh with a built-in colour monitor was the Macintosh Color Classic of 1993. Throughout the nineties, Macintosh and Microsoft continued a war over market share.

***

The first broadcast of Shortland Street was 25 May 1992. *Wikipedia*

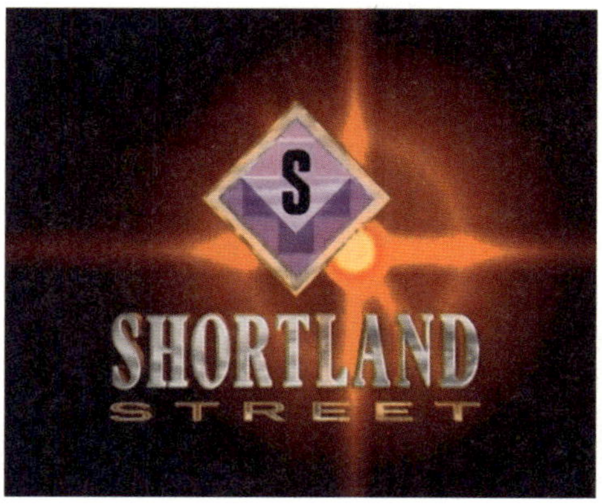

A Macintosh Color Classic II from 1993. *Shutterstock*

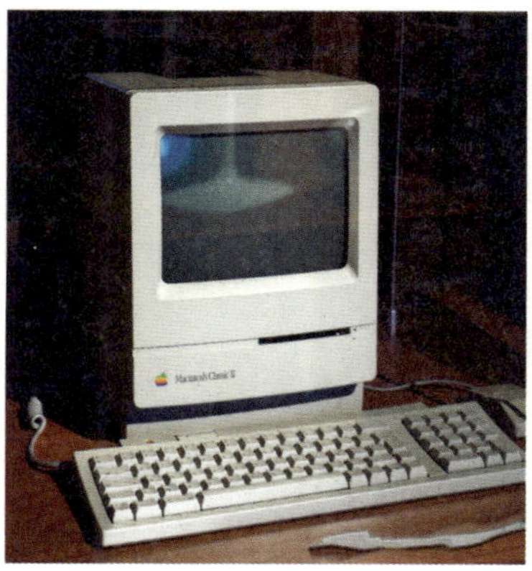

A couple of other fun facts on the tech front: the first mobile phone without an antenna was launched in 1997; Vodafone launched text messaging in New Zealand in 1999.

What technologies were zinesters in Aotearoa using? Those voicing the nineties chapter speak of both industrial-revolution letterpress technology and digital-revolution desktop publishing as the old side-eyed the new. Between these poles we have the humble photocopier, now ubiquitous and reliable enough to be the go-to tool for most zinesters. Meanwhile, the emerging internet whispered of an egalitarian future of free information. Zinesters like David Merritt and Moira Clunie recognised the inevitable rise of the internet and familiarised themselves with the necessary coding and software.

Back in the realm of the physical artefact, distribution opportunities for zines were still compartmentalised into those that headed to the record store, comics shop or anarchist info store. Zine distributors or zine markets were yet to collapse such boundaries, allowing zines to be their own enigmatic thing. Nevertheless, many eighties and nineties zinesters took it upon themselves to include the seeming disparities of politics, music, comics, collage, poetry, (vegan) recipes and plundered content.

The Record Exchange in St Kevins Arcade, Karangahape Road, Auckland, 1990. Note the poster for Sticky Filth and Spermbank Five at the University Café. *Auckland Libraries Heritage Collections, 273-MAT110-04, photographer Christopher Matthews*

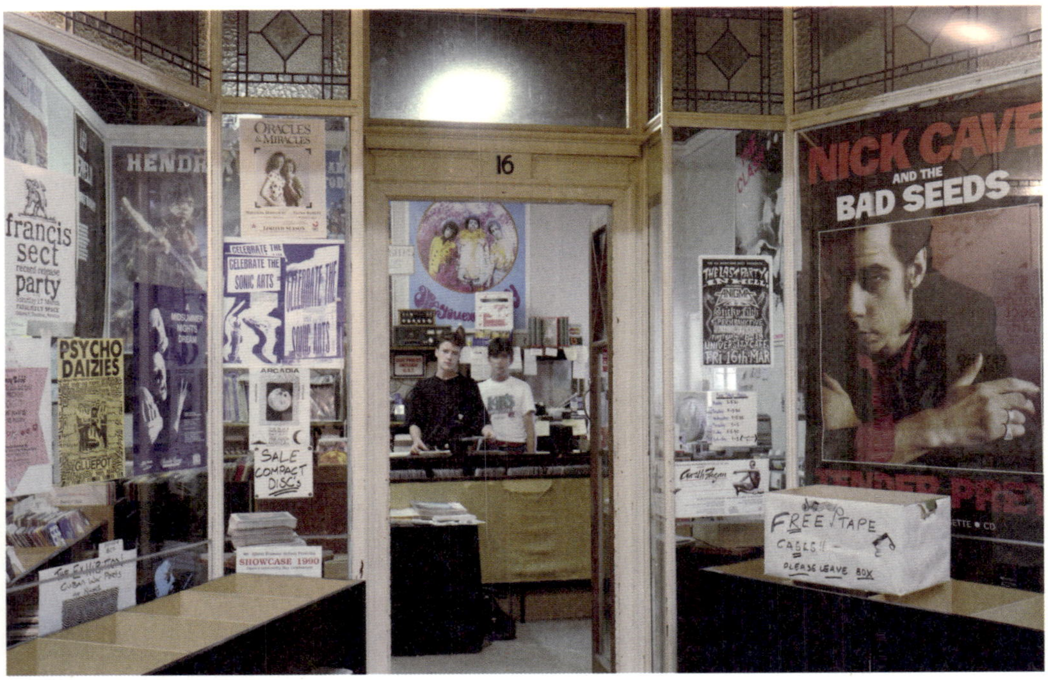

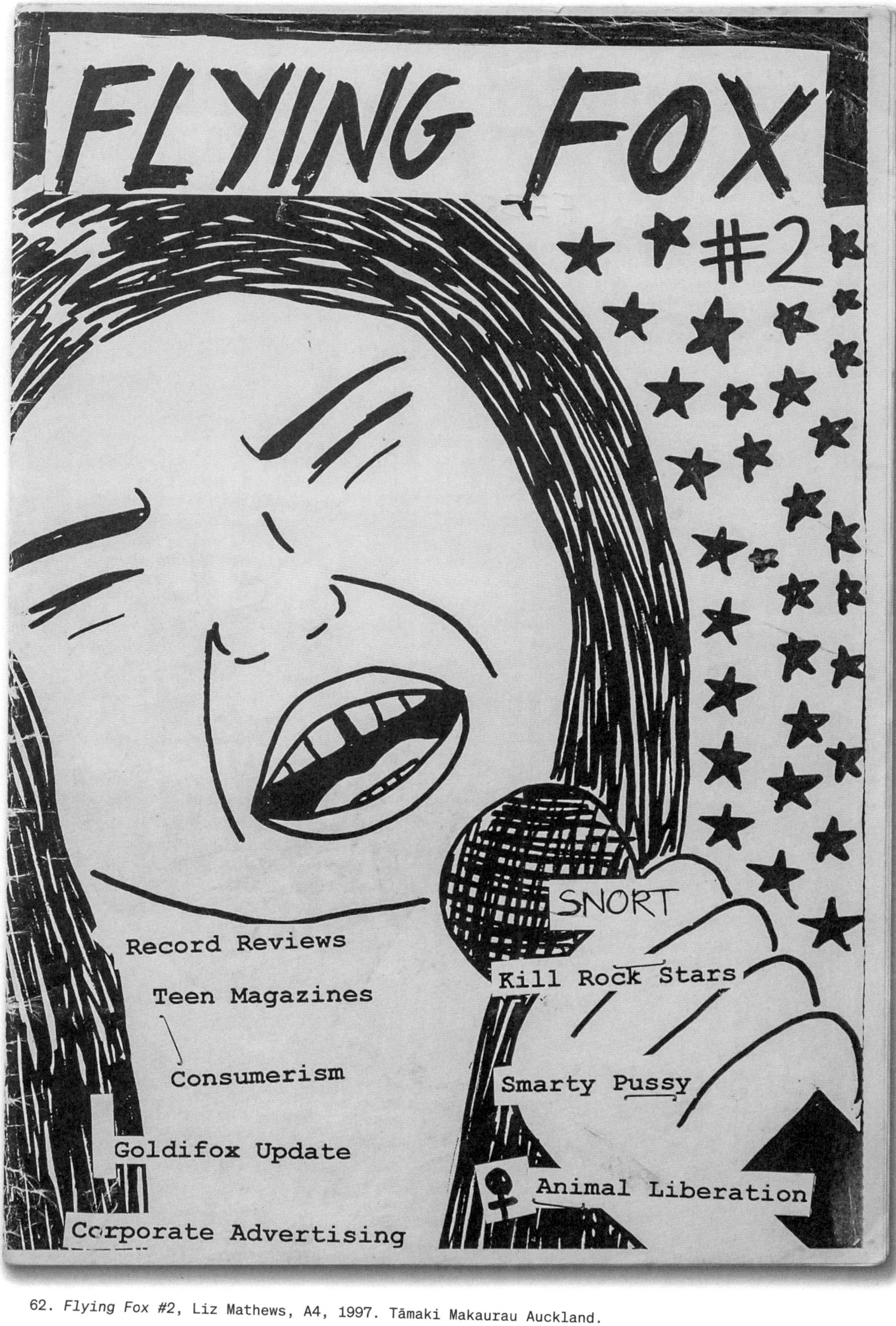

62. *Flying Fox #2*, Liz Mathews, A4, 1997. Tāmaki Makaurau Auckland.

THE BLACK SHEEP pt. 4

... an hour and a bit later...

ANT SANG '95

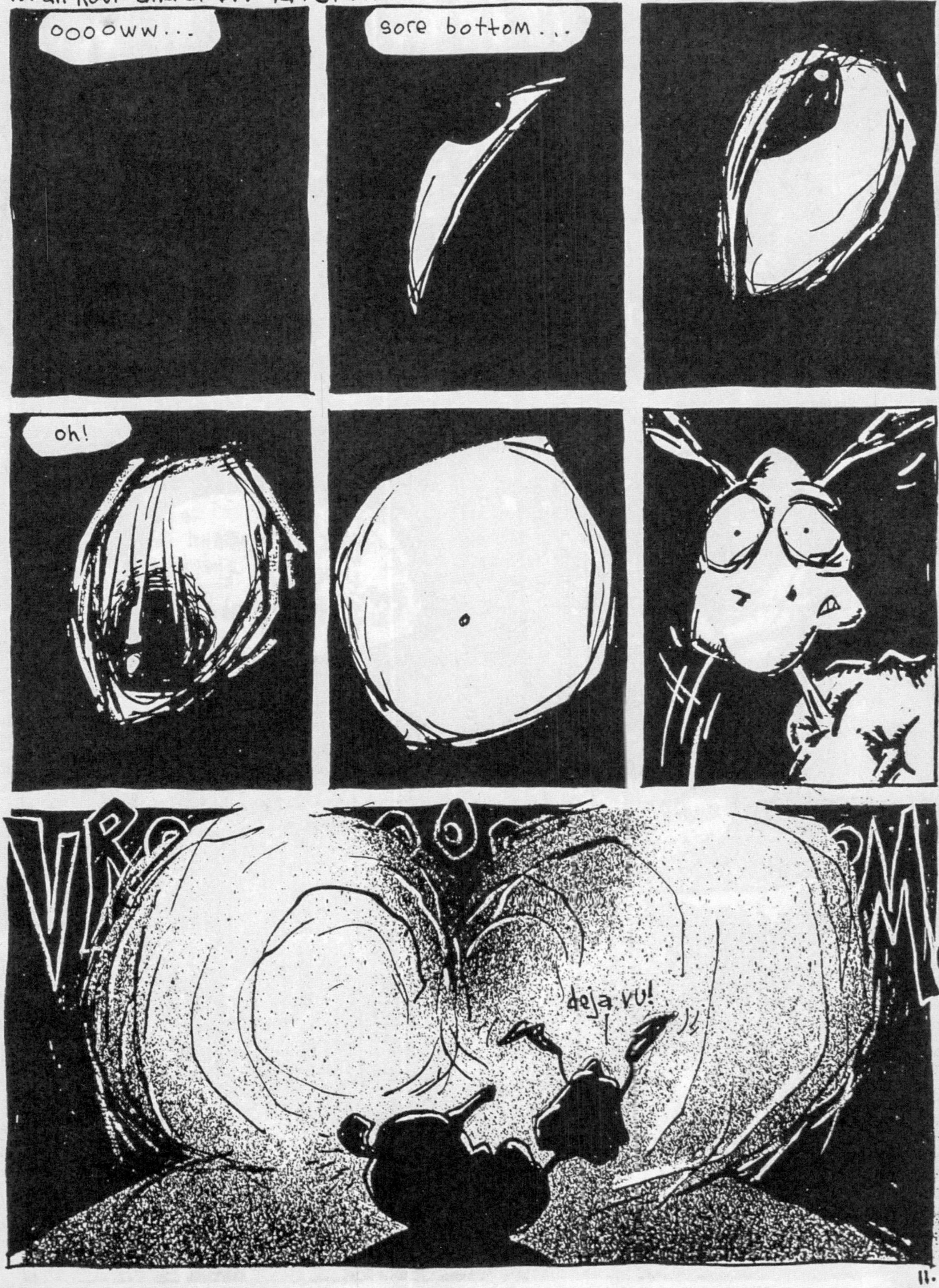

Ninetes Zines

Dave Hegan I left Christchurch in about May 1988 because I'd heard there was a good punk scene in New Plymouth.

I'd been flatting with some punks and skinheads. Back then, punks and skinheads all hung out. Now they hate each other. They hated each other then, but it was just more relaxed. They said, 'Oh, you should go to New Plymouth, there's heaps of drugs and lots of good bands', and I was like, that sounds good to me and so I just moved up. I moved to Hamilton first. My dad was living there, and I lied to him and said, 'I'm coming up to go to university', because I needed to get to Hamilton to get to New Plymouth, but when I got to Hamilton he figured out what was up and kicked me out. So I just caught a bus down to New Plymouth on a dole day, that's how I ended up in New Plymouth. I knew the punks drank at the White Hart pub, so I went there.

Long story short. I got into the whole punk scene, but everything got out of control, the drugs and stuff like that. I ended up getting done for burglary of a supermarket, which I didn't actually burgle. There was a whole bunch of us, and I crashed out at the scene because I was too wasted. I didn't even get inside the building. The police found me outside and said, 'What are you doing?', and I'm like 'Oh, I'm just having a sleep.' But anyhow, they said to me 'Look, we're sick of this. If you plead guilty to being unlawfully on the premises, we'll charge you for that and we won't charge you for burglary', and I'm like 'Great, let's do that', and then they chucked me in the cells for the night. The next morning, I'm up in front of the judge and he says 'Dave Hegan's pleaded guilty to burglary', and I'm like 'What!? This is news to me.'

Life changed really dramatically. I got a year's probation and I got sent to drug rehab, which was actually a good thing because I was doing a Sid Vicious — crash and burn, die young. I ended up coming back to Christchurch to live with my mum.

It's weird, you've got to sober up before you go to drug rehab. At least that's how it was back then. You had to have a few weeks clean before you could go to Queen Mary Hospital in Hanmer. It made sense for them. There was six months of drying out in Christchurch before rehab. All of a sudden I had all this time on my hands because all I'd been doing was getting wasted, hitchhiking around the North Island and going to gigs, so that's when I decided to do a zine. I was really into all the bands and the politics and stuff, so I just started posting interview questions off to bands and asking all my mates if they wanted to contribute. I had all this energy. I was also screen-printing and all sorts of other stuff. I got out of rehab in November '89 after six weeks, and then I published my first zine in early 1990.

63. *Filth* #5, Ant Sang, A5, 1995. Tāmaki Makaurau Auckland.

64

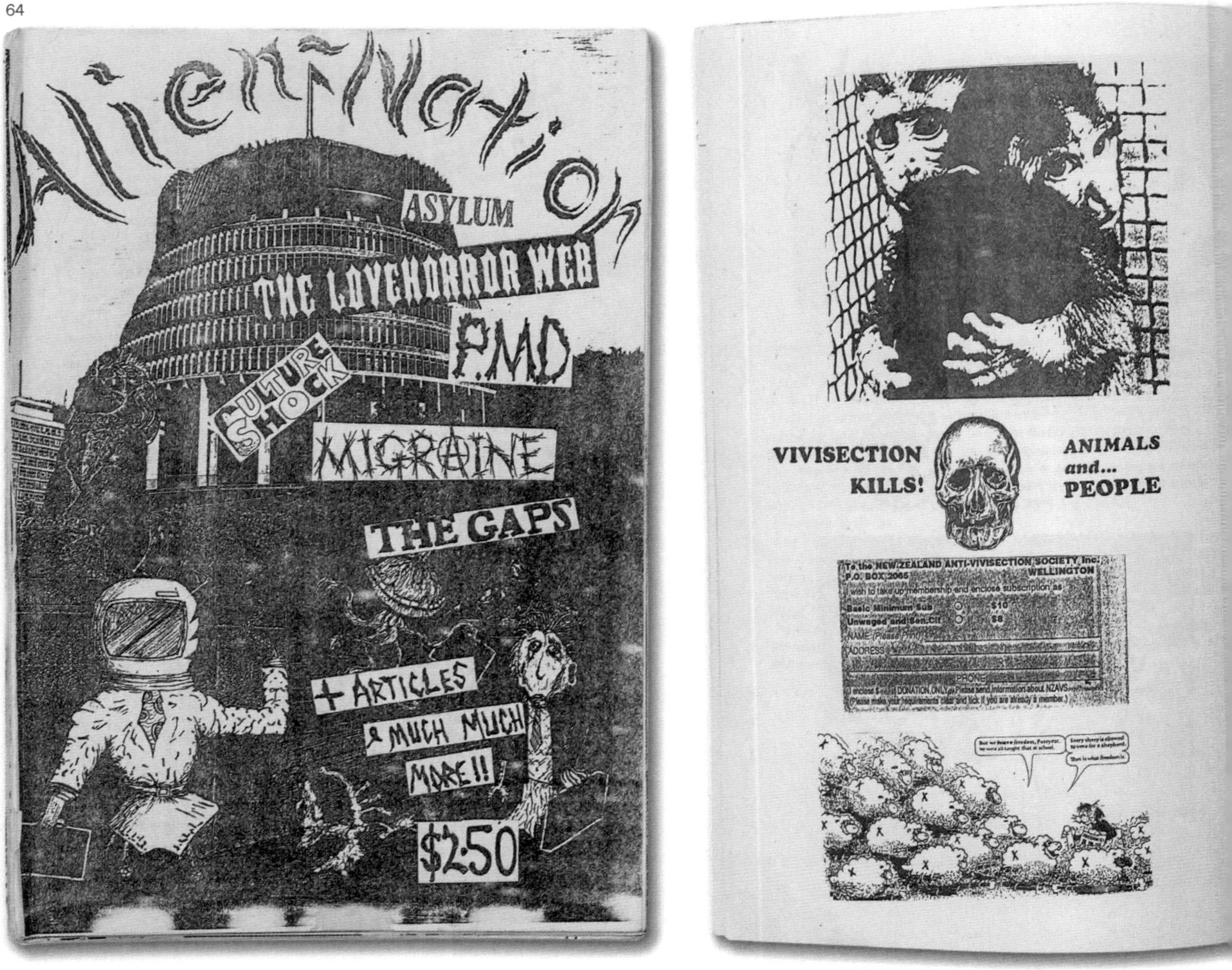

Simon Cottle A lot of the naughtiness of fanzines is just deliberately winding people up. We'd play with the media, like 'Okay, well if you can say stupid things about us, we'll say stupid things about you.' For example there's a photo in there of Ross Gardiner all spiked up at one of our anti-vivisection protests, and the newspaper leads with 'Protestors Make Pointed Point For Dumb Animals'. Okay, so they're definitely referring to his hairstyle and wanting readers to construe punk-rockers as dumb animals. Okay, so we'll just rip into you in *our* publication. We were also dealing with lots of things like the media underestimating protest numbers, and us not having the right of reply to misleading editorials.

Andrew Stephens I saw the nineties as monetarist, basically. The profit motive seemed to be above all else. Public morality seemed to have gone out the door. When Trish and I grew up, there was a feeling of public morality among the public service. My dad worked in advertising, but he was a moral man and the people he worked for were essentially moral people, but that seemed to change somewhere, ethics took a slide at some point. That's how it looked to me.

Trish Stephens And the other thing that we noticed was how everything on the TV news was suddenly evaluated in terms of how much money it generated: 'Oh, we're putting on this WOW event and it's gonna bring in millions of dollars.' Suddenly they were reading out the stock market reports on RNZ.

64. *Alien-Nation* cover and spread, Dave Hegan, A4, 1990. Ōtautahi Christchurch.

65

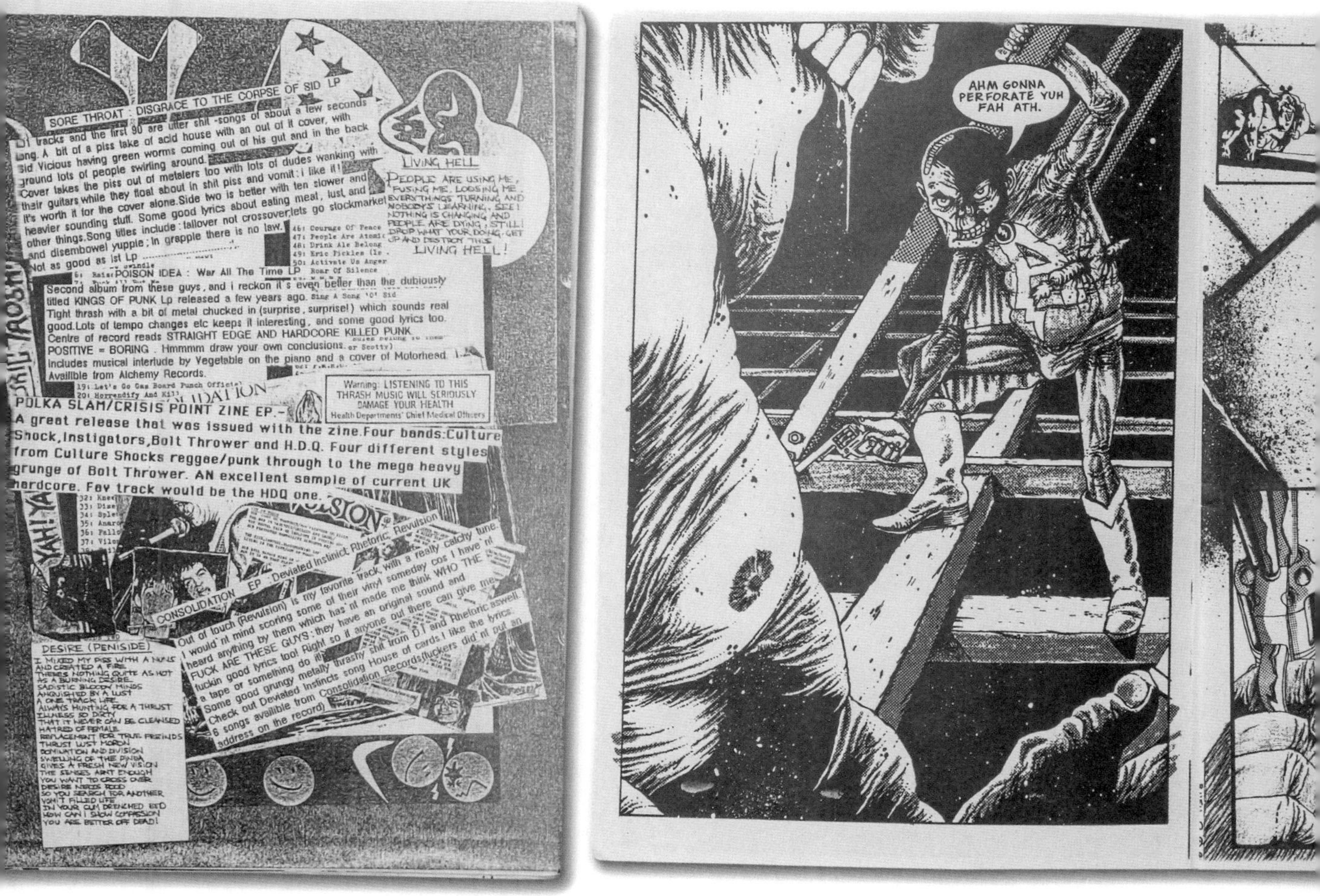

David Tulloch *Pistake* [comic] might've offended some people, particularly with some of the later stuff that we put out when Rufus [Dayglo] was really pushing the boat out. There was graphic violence in some, but I don't remember any specific incidence where we caused upset. It was a time when there was a lot of censorship going on, though. I ended up getting involved in an Indecent Publications Tribunal hearing. A comic called *Exquisite Corpse* which came out from the USA — I think it was published by Fantagraphics — had autoerotic asphyxiation in it, and they wanted to ban that on the grounds that people might look at this comic and then strangle themselves to death for sexual pleasure. The tribunal hearing was a really weird process.

They seized a whole bunch of comics, but in the end they let most of them through. *Heavy Metal* kept getting seized. Comics Compulsion[1] owner Rod Mill's theory was that the guy at Customs liked reading it; that he was just seizing it to read it, and when he was finished with it he'd let it go through. [Laughs.]

The writer Keri Hulme came up to us after the inquiry saying that she found the whole process completely awful, and asking us if there was an organisation she could join to oppose what the tribunal was doing.

65. *Pistake* #12, page by Rufus Dayglo, edited by David Tulloch, A5, 1994. Te Whanganui-a-Tara Wellington.

Tim Danko I did a printmaking major. At that point in time printmaking was possibly the most conservative department, at least at my art school. I don't know what other art schools in Melbourne were like; it might have changed dramatically since then. I was mixing fine art with comics stuff, like sampling really, collaging these things together. In the crits, I'd get [assumes disparaging tone] 'What is this stuff you're putting here? Why are you doing that? We come into the studio, Tim, and we see that you're reading, but you're reading comics.' [Laughs.] It was just kind of weird. I still get shocked by that attitude. I still got that later on in my master's, my supervisor saying, 'You can't just come here and expect to make comics', and I'm like 'But that's what I brought to my interview.'

Andrew Stephens Ever since zines turned up I had the idea that I should put something in print. I didn't think anyone would publish what I was writing, so I thought I'd have to publish it myself if I wanted to see it in print. My lecturers weren't interested in the zines, they really weren't. What they were used to from me was a clever A+ essay. I could do that sort of stuff standing on my head. But the zine was, I thought, actually worth doing. Their reaction didn't surprise me be honest. Academics are like that.

Kerry Ann Lee . . . just being very bored as a kid, as a teenager. That teenage boredom stuff's like super real, and that's the stuff that catapults people into doing fun stuff, as you know.

Simon Cottle The names *Anti-System* and *Social Dis-Ease* were a promotion of a kind of political activity, not just passively dancing to a band and rebellion through clothes. It was definitely a push for wider political action than that, but I included apolitical bands — for lack of a better term — if their style of music and dress was still some sort of rebellion in itself.

Andrew Stephens Most of the people who wrote zines in Palmy also went to The Stomach. That was the alternative venue that everyone went to, and then Harvesters [Bar] started doing gigs, too, but The Stomach was the centre of the counterculture in Palmy. **Trish Stephens** Palmy's quite centralised. No having to travel any great distance. You could almost walk everywhere, so all the freaks knew each other pretty much, right through the age groups as well.

Ross Gardiner There was a bit of a cross-over between the punks and McGillicuddys [McGillicuddy Serious Party]. The McGillicuddys had a thing called the Regressionist Society where they were gonna get rid of technology. They'd do street performances, smashing up TVs. We went to watch one of their performances in Aotea Square, and they did one in Cuba Mall as well.

Kerry Ann Lee We also had the birth of the anarchist info store, The Freedom Shop, which occurred in the mid-nineties, and that was a locus for us to learn more, get more politicised, contribute to that space, connect with the outside world, with international publishers and distros. That's where I started learning about DIY record distros like Flat Earth and Ebullition, learning about the 'pay no more than' stickers on things: pay no more than 50 cents, $2, or free. Free for prisoners. And for a teenager, it's like 'Okay, tell me more about the prisoners: why are they getting this for free?' And it's because they don't get access to literature, and part of the kaupapa with punk-hard-core-anarchist zines is that you want access.

You get to learn about international struggles, what people were tuning into, the Zapatistas, Leonard Peltier, the writings of Noam Chomsky, and drawing that back to older anarchist histories. It was really fascinating if you're interested in history, politics, culture and communities. A space like that was so vital as a teenager. There were a whole bunch of us in the anarchist and punk scenes.

There was a lot of crossover. I went to Wellington High, and if I had a free session or something in the afternoon I'd volunteer at the anarchist info store. I was 16, 17. I got as much

66

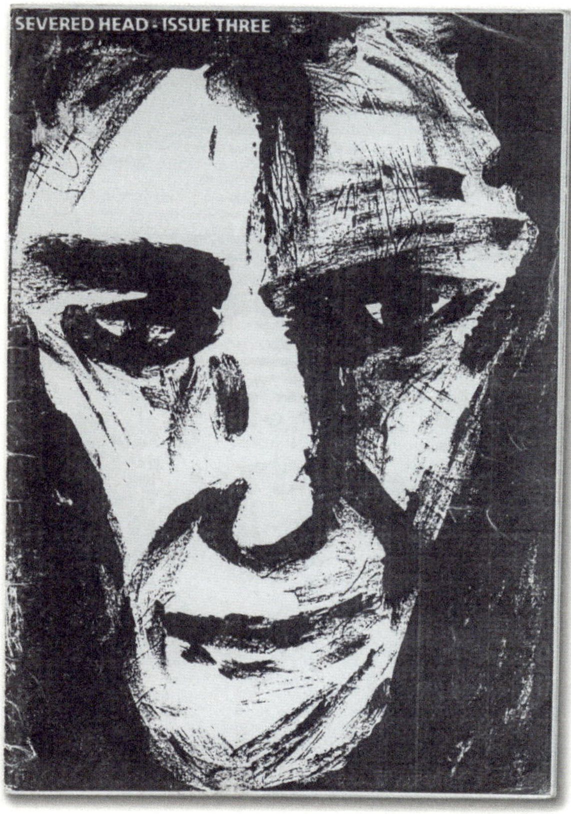

67

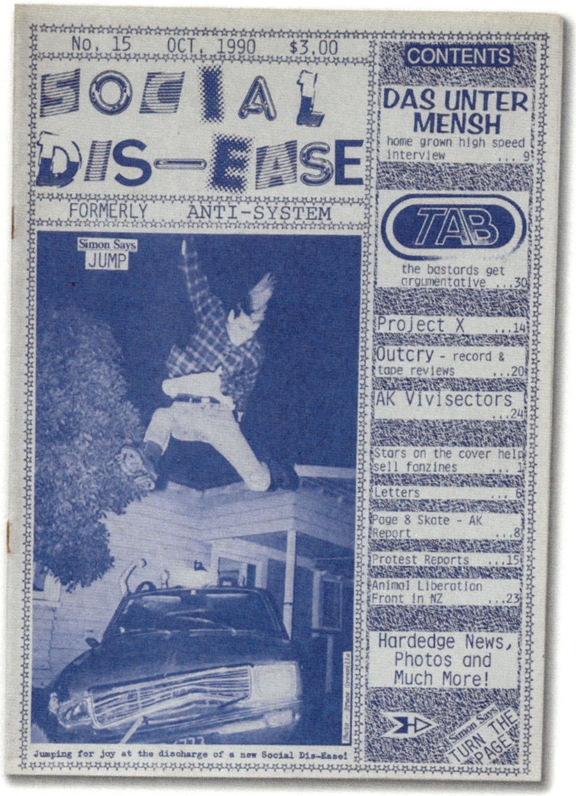

education there as I did in school — the drudgery of making high-school friends and dealing with the formal school set-up — it made life more interesting to make other friends and learn about the world in that kind of way.

Lyn Spencer The Freedom Shop felt like more of a hub than Books from the Black Lagoon ever did, because it was on Cuba Street.

Liz Mathews I grew up in Kerikeri. At the age of 15 I heard Nirvana. That started a trajectory, lots of different roads came off that. One of the things that it led me to was Crawlspace Records on Karangahape Road, that was the first place I sent my zine, *Flying Fox.* That was my Auckland connection. Crawlspace had Sonic Youth and Free Kitten, and they told me about Huggy Bear and all these Riot Grrrl bands. They also had zines in the shop, like *The Jewish Beatle* [Duane Zarakov]. **Beth Dawson** Yeah, and *Daughters of Slaughter*.

Indira Neville There were women's comics anthologies in the eighties–nineties here in New Zealand: *Twisted Sisters* and *Daughters of Slaughter.* They were really important. I keep saying that *Three Words* was not the first anthology of women's comics . . . but the misogyny thing is fascinating.

There's this world of 'competent boy comics', which is horribly sexist, even though they all deny it because 'We're comics and we're nerds.' The Oats Comics collective was the same in some ways. At the time I didn't think about it. Oats Comics was a big group of really great friends who lived in Hamilton in various flats. It was a really creative, big-drinking culture, just the joy of doing stuff together and making stuff. There were quite a few women in this group of friends. Anyone could do anything, and lots of women did. They'd be in a band or they'd contribute to Oats Comics anthologies, but the culture was real blokey in that punk-rock sort of way.

66. *Severed Head* #3, edited by Andrew Stephens, A5, 1999. Te Papaioea Palmerston North.
67. *Social Dis-Ease* #15 cover and spread (following pages), edited by Simon Cottle, A4, 1990. Te Whanganui-a-Tara Wellington.

from previous page

TE ROOPU RAWAKORE O AOTEAROA

ACTION
— AGAINST —
UNEMPLOYMENT
AND
BENEFIT CUTS

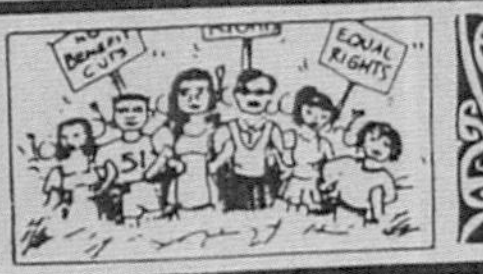

JULY 10-12 1990 WELLINGTON

MARCH ON PARLIAMENT
12.30 THURSDAY
12 JULY
FROM PIGEON PARK

Have you had enough of:

- attacks on beneficiaries by politicians and the media?
- redundancies - hundreds more announced every week?
- Government "schemes" which don't go anywhere or achieve anything and just raise false hopes for people?

Where are the the jobs which Labour keep promising and where is the economic recovery?

Neither Labour nor National has a policy which offers any hope for unemployed people or beneficiaries. Both parties accept high unemployment while attacking beneficiaries and benefit rates, and dreaming up schemes which don't create any new jobs.

Have you had **enough?**

Join us in collective action this July. Don't let unemployed and beneficiaries be forgotten this year. Only by joining together will our voice be heard.

We Demand:

1. **Government Commitment To Full Employment** - fulltime work at award wages and conditions. Job creation should meet social needs such as housing, health and education.

2. **No Further Sale Of State Assets.** Use our natural resources for job creation which benefits all our people, through projects such as environmental and wildlife protection, recycling, reafforestation, regeneration of kaimoana, research and development in horticulture and agriculture.

3 **State Support For Small Scale Cooperative And Business Initiatives By The Unemployed;** an enterprise allowance so that people can stay on the benefit while they get established.

4. **A living Wage For All, Whether In Or Out Of Work.** No cuts to Benefits, ACC or National Super. No forcing beneficiaries into part-time work. No work-testing for DPB or sickness beneficiaries.

5. **No Work Conscription - No Work For The Dole Schemes.** We totally oppose any work-for-the-benefit programmes, whether under the guise of 'training' or 'community work'. We want real jobs for real wages with the right to join a trade union.

6. **Equal Opportunities For All - An End To Discrimination In The Job Market.** There must be support programmes and legislation to combat widespread existing discrimination which leaves women, Maori, tangata Pasifika, disabled and older people disproportionately unemployed. Te Tiriti O Waitangi will not be honoured until nga tangata whenua have equal access to jobs, real training and resources.

Help us build the Unemployed Movement

Whether you are out of work, on a benefit, doing unwaged work, or in a job - we share a common cause. Mass unemployment is destroying our society, our families and our lives.

Labour and National see cutting benefit levels and introducing work for the dole schemes as the solution.

We don't. The only answer is to get our economy moving again with real jobs for real wages - that means a living wage for all.

Unite to build an Aotearoa which belongs to it's people. Join your local unemployed group or work with your own trade union to help us fight back.

Te Roopu Rawakore O Aotearoa - the National Unemployed and Beneficiaries' Movement -

can be contacted at:
Phone (09) 399-682;
Fax (09) 775-541;
PO Box 68-488, Newton, Auckland 1.

Your local Unemployed and Beneficiaries' Group can be contacted at:

WELLINGTON UNEMPLOYED WORKERS UNION
3 EVA ST., (OFF DIXON ST., BY PIGEON PARK)
PHONE 858596

PO BOX 11 503.
WELLINGTON

Weekly Campaign Organising Meetings - Every Tuesday 5.30 pm at WUWU.

The unemployed protest on the 12th of July, started with street theatre (including some AK punx) in the Manners Mall, followed by a march of over 500 people from Pigeon Park to parliament. The police had crowd control barriers up which the march organisers soon encouraged people to jump over. Politicians were not allowed to speak as "We hear them everyday, today the unemployed's voice will be heard". In much smaller number -s we then formed up again and marched back into the city. All four lanes of Lambton Quay were blocked to cries of "Stop the City"! Things were pretty tense, with numerous police, and paddy wagons pulling up, then some pushing, but we moved off through the traffic and blocked the street outside the Stock Exchange. After plenty of chanting there as well, the protest came to an end.

Listener 30/7/90!

DENIS WELCH

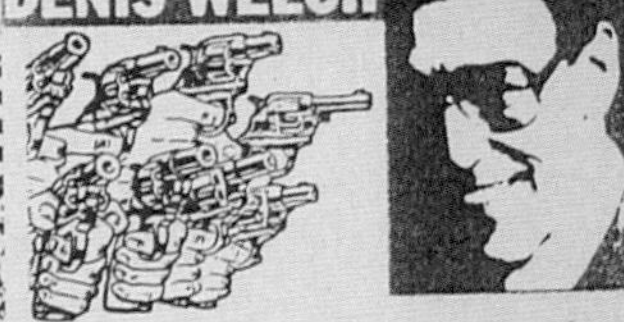

IT'S A WEIRD week in more ways than one, especially with a series of unemployment protests popping up not just at Parliament but all over downtown Wellington. These are not the protests of old, with thousands of workers getting agitated about wage cuts, but the province of a bunch of young activists whose general demeanour ranges from post-punk to sub-skinhead. They're almost indistinguishable, in fact, from the kind who turn out for anti-vivisection marches, right down to the Doc Martens and op-shop gear. They look beleaguered and marginalised, without serious political support, representing nobody but themselves. They put on a good show, though; should they find work, their best career prospects appear to be in street theatre.

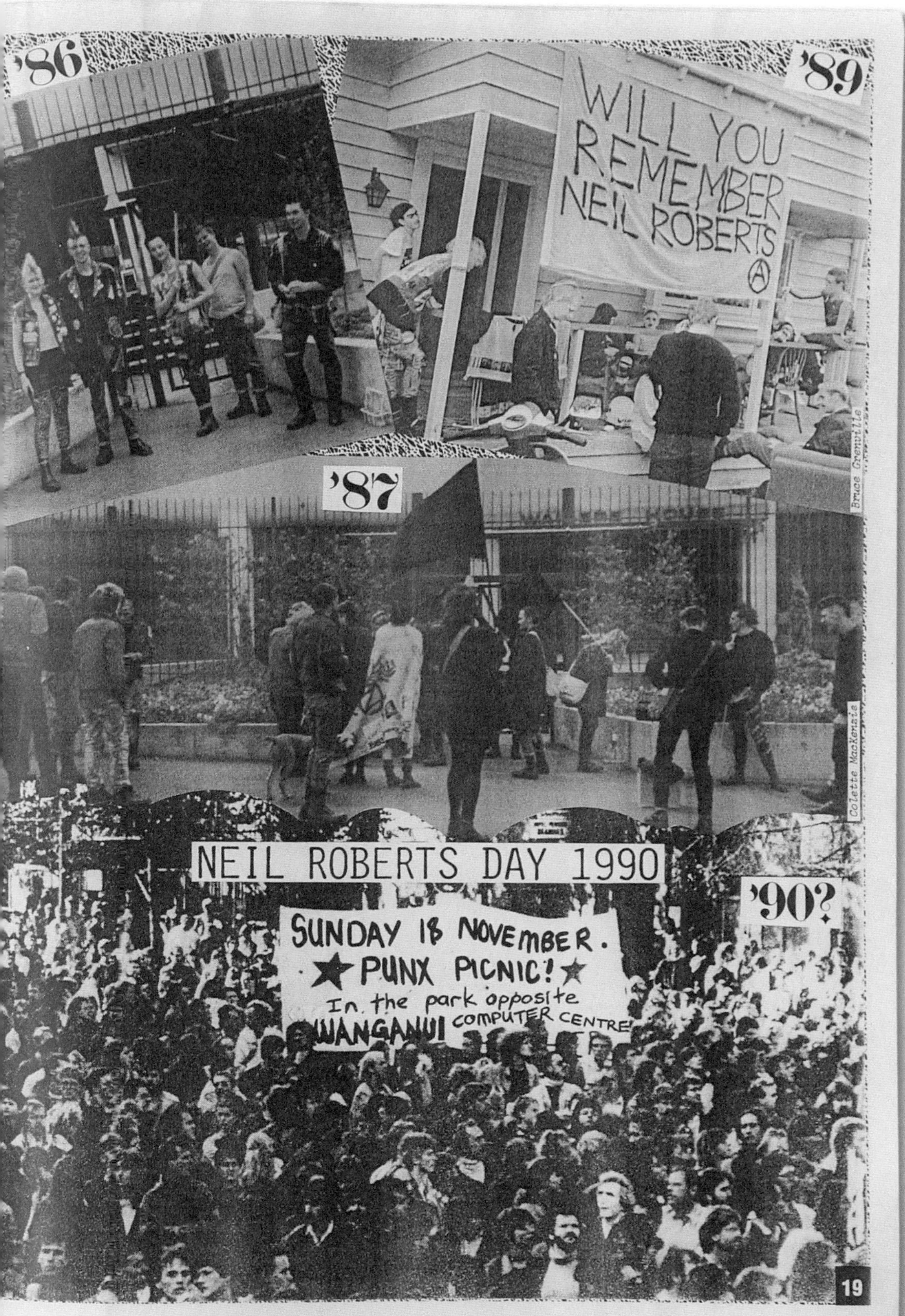
'86
'89
WILL YOU REMEMBER NEIL ROBERTS
Ⓐ
'87
Bruce Grenville
Colette MacKenzie
NEIL ROBERTS DAY 1990
'90?
SUNDAY 18 NOVEMBER.
★ PUNX PICNIC! ★
In the park opposite
WANGANUI COMPUTER CENTRE
19

68

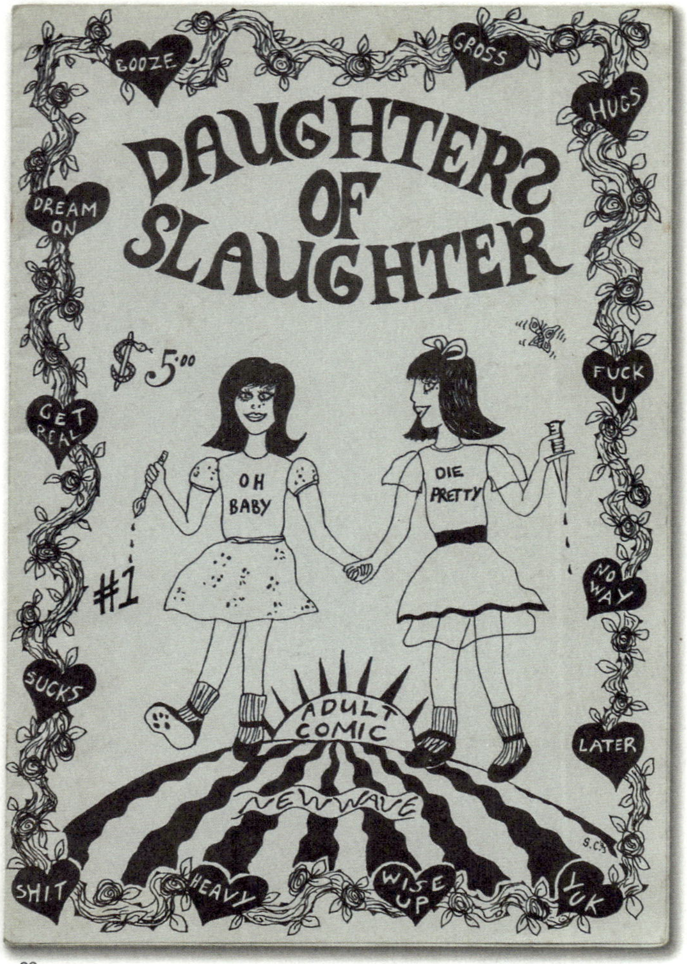
BOOZE
GROSS
HUGS
DAUGHTERS OF SLAUGHTER
DREAM ON
$5.00
FUCK U
GET REAL
OH BABY
DIE PRETTY
#1
NO WAY
SUCKS
ADULT COMIC
LATER
NEW WAVE
SHIT
HEAVY
WISE UP
YUK

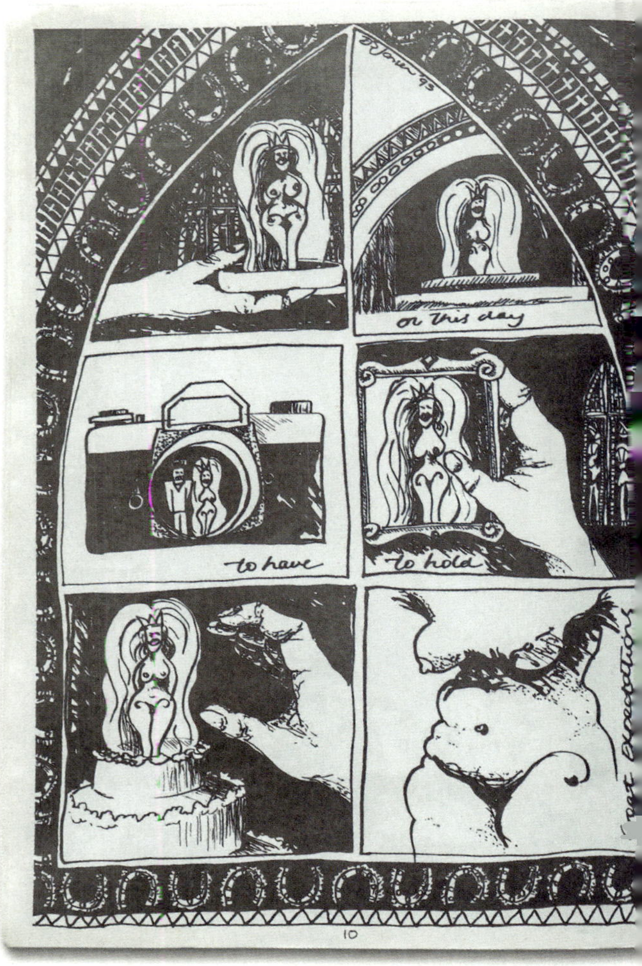
on this day
to have
to hold

69

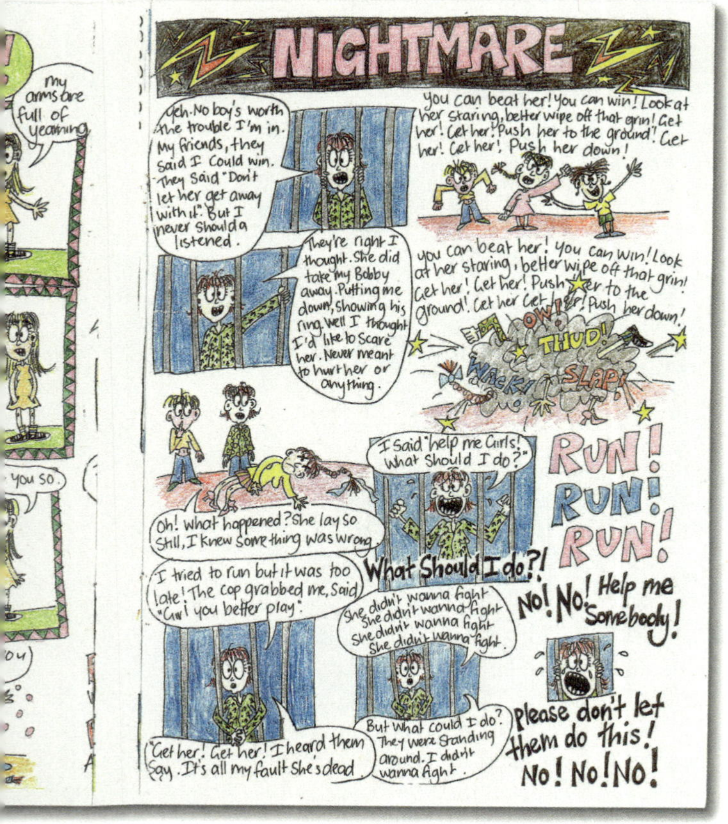
my arms are full of yearning
NIGHTMARE
Ooh. No boy's worth the trouble I'm in. My friends, they said I could win. They said "Don't let her get away with it." But I never shoulda listened.
You can beat her! You can win! Look at her staring, better wipe off that grin! Get her! Get her! Push her to the ground! Get her! Get her! Push her down!
They're right I thought. She did take my Bobby away. Putting me down, showing his ring. Well I thought I'd like to scare her. Never meant to hurt her or anything.
You can beat her! You can win! Look at her staring, better wipe off that grin! Get her! Get her! Push her to the ground! Get her Get her! Push her down!
OW! THUD!
WACK! SLAP!
I said "help me Girls! What should I do?"
RUN! RUN! RUN!
Oh! What happened? She lay so still, I knew something was wrong.
What should I do?!
I tried to run but it was too late! The cop grabbed me, said "Girl you better play".
She didn't wanna fight She didn't wanna fight She didn't wanna fight She didn't wanna fight.
No! No! Help me Somebody!
Get her! Get her! I heard them say. It's all my fault she's dead
But what could I do? They were standing around. I didn't wanna fight.
Please don't let them do this! No! No! No!

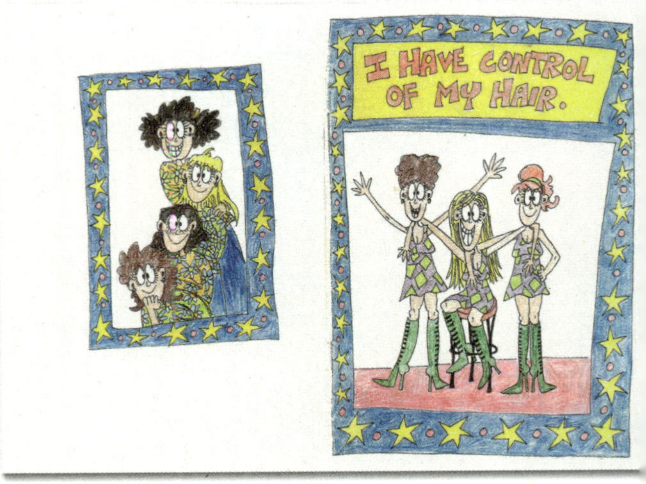
I HAVE CONTROL OF MY HAIR.

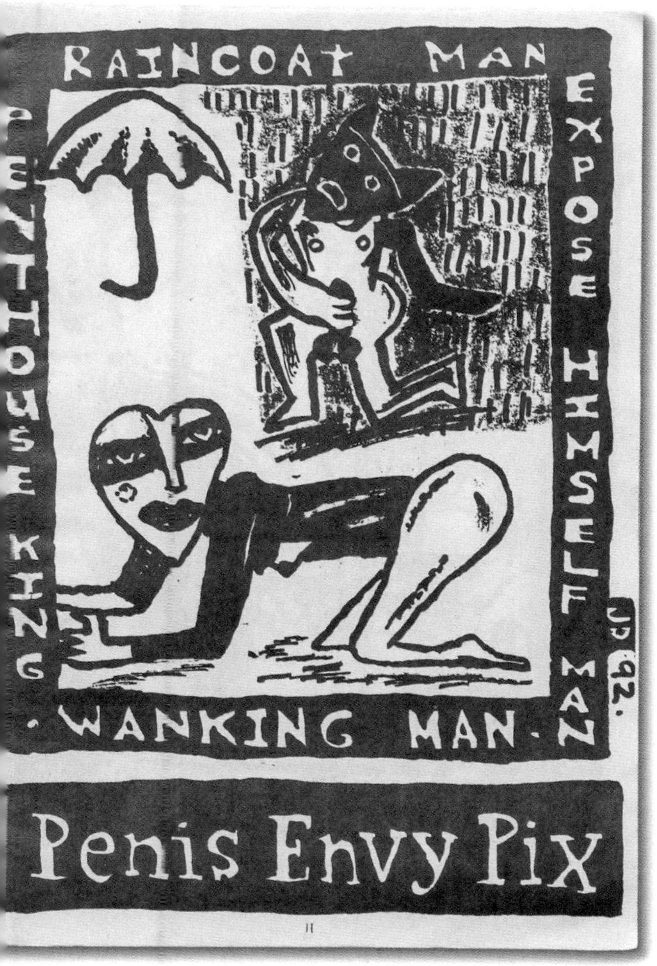

Beth Dawson My mum's a teacher, my dad was a potter, so I grew up in a household that really embraced making things and really valued people. My brother and I were always encouraged to draw. My first zines or comics were probably making stuff with my brother. When I was a teenager I was into grunge music. I started hanging out at Crawlspace Records. I don't think I was like 'There's the zines, there's the comics, there's the music', I was just like 'This is all the stuff that is cool to make, that I can make, and be part of'.

Indira Neville It was a bit like rugby blokes drinking and talking about their passion — it just happened to be punk music instead of sport. I was the first woman to regularly produce a comic within their world, and it really was a bit of a Smurfette situation, looking back. At the time I kind of thought of myself as one of the guys and that was kind of cool, but it was also weird. I was making these comics in this world, and this world just made comics about whatever the fuck we wanted and — looking back — some of them have horrific politics. We just didn't care. It didn't even occur to us. So we just made them about all kinds of things, and I was totally complicit in that, but it was also the Riot Grrrl time as well, so at the same time I very much considered myself part of *that* scene.

I was making my own comic *Nice Gravy* and they were all about body politics and the whole Riot Grrrl aesthetic. Because of this I wanted to be connected to that girl punk scene like Liz Mathews and bands like Fake Purr. I actually purposefully made a comic about girl groups to give to Fake Purr and try to make friends with them — and succeeded! So I was in this weird liminal space. I'm full of contradictions.

When people wrote about Oats they'd go 'Stefan Neville's sister Indira also makes comics' — *every* single time. And my comics would be described as having something of a singular style, which is a polite way of saying they're a bit off. The 'competent boy comics' — for all that they aspire to be published and flash — still have this desperate need to cling onto the rebellious history of comics, and so Oats was their touchstone. They would always hype up Glen Frenzy and Stefan because they're the flashest drawers, essentially. I mean, all this *Truck Guy* stuff. I doubt if any of those comics boys have even seen that zine, but it's kind of become a symbol of how cool you are if you know about it.

David Tulloch We would take comics from anyone. We weren't a boys' club, but comics was a bit of a boys' club. It was becoming less so. We featured comics by a few women.

68. *Daughters of Slaughter* cover and spread, cover by Stella Corkery, pages by Dieneke Jansen and Jane Dodd, A4, 1993. Tāmaki Makaurau Auckland.

69. *I Have Control of My Hair* spread and cover, Indira Neville, A5, 1990s. Tāmaki Makaurau Auckland.

Tui Gordon I actually quite liked that heavier aesthetic of Riot Grrrl. When it got poppy and people started talking about the Spice Girls bringing feminism to the masses I was like 'Nah!' Girl Power it was not.

David Tulloch There weren't a lot of New Zealand comics anthologies around at the time. Cornelius Stone was putting stuff out up in Auckland, including *UFO*, which had a *Straightjacket Ninja* story in it. $6.00, A4 black-and-white with glossy pages. *Pistake* was a more modest publication, priced at $1.95.

Tony Renouf The encouragement of being part of a community started to happen down here in Dunedin. I got introduced to Glen Ross. I think I met Paul Potiki through Jeff Ruston; no, I did some murals for the school where my father-out-law was the caretaker. The principal introduced me to Paul and then . . . Who else was there? I can't remember how I met Finn (Anthony Behrens). Colin Andrews sort of bumbled into the scene. He's a cock by the way. You can print that. [Laughs.] I said Colin Andrews is a cock and he still owes me money; in fact, I'm getting a t-shirt made. So, there was a core of comics people forming some sort of community.

I'd got back into *Critic*. I'd done a year with Bruce Mahalski, and then there was a gap of a few years before I returned. About 1993 I went down to *Critic* and said, 'Do you want a cartoon every week?' I did that for a year and then started the *Treacle* anthology. I was working at the university print shop — a run of 200 comics, could be 500 if the boss was away. Two-colour front cover, everything else black-and-white. I was pressing anybody I knew who I could get to draw.

70

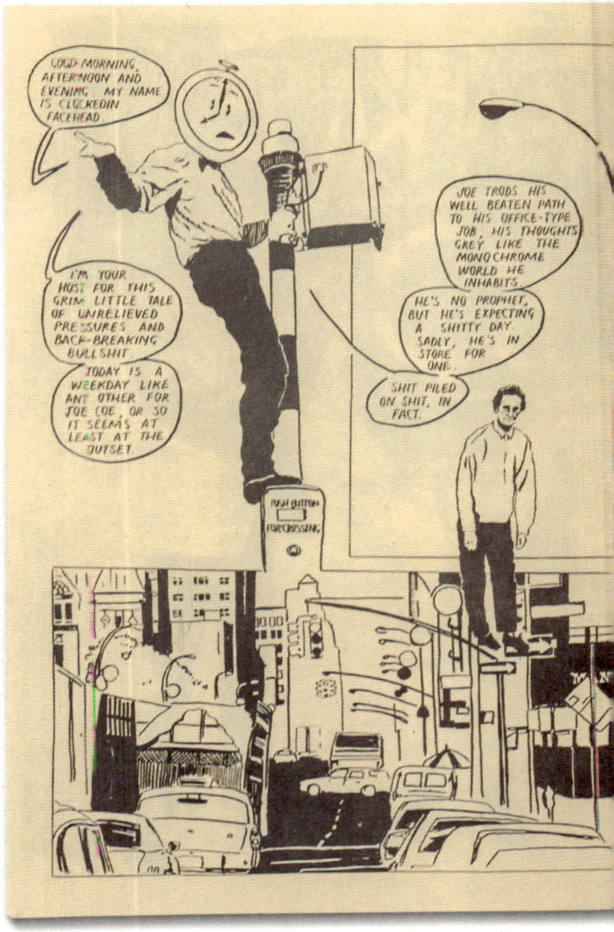

Lyn Spencer We stayed with the *Profane Existence* people when we first went overseas, but we just visited the *Maximum Rocknroll* guys. We had this zine called *Book Your Own Fuckin' Life* put out by *Maximum Rocknroll*; people would advertise, gig venues and promoters, crash pads and shops. **Ross Gardiner** It was a do-it-yourself travel network. **Lyn Spencer** We met so many people, and we stayed with people who'd advertised their crash pads, and it was so good. **Ross Gardiner** It wasn't like the internet, there was a filter. You had to ring people up or write to them, they wouldn't necessarily give their home address. *Maximum Rocknroll* was a monthly, so it was the best way to keep up-to-date with anything. They started running one page of each issue called 'Book Your Own Fuckin' Tour', where people listed: 'If you're in a band and you wanna come to my town, here's my details, I'll put on a show for you . . .'

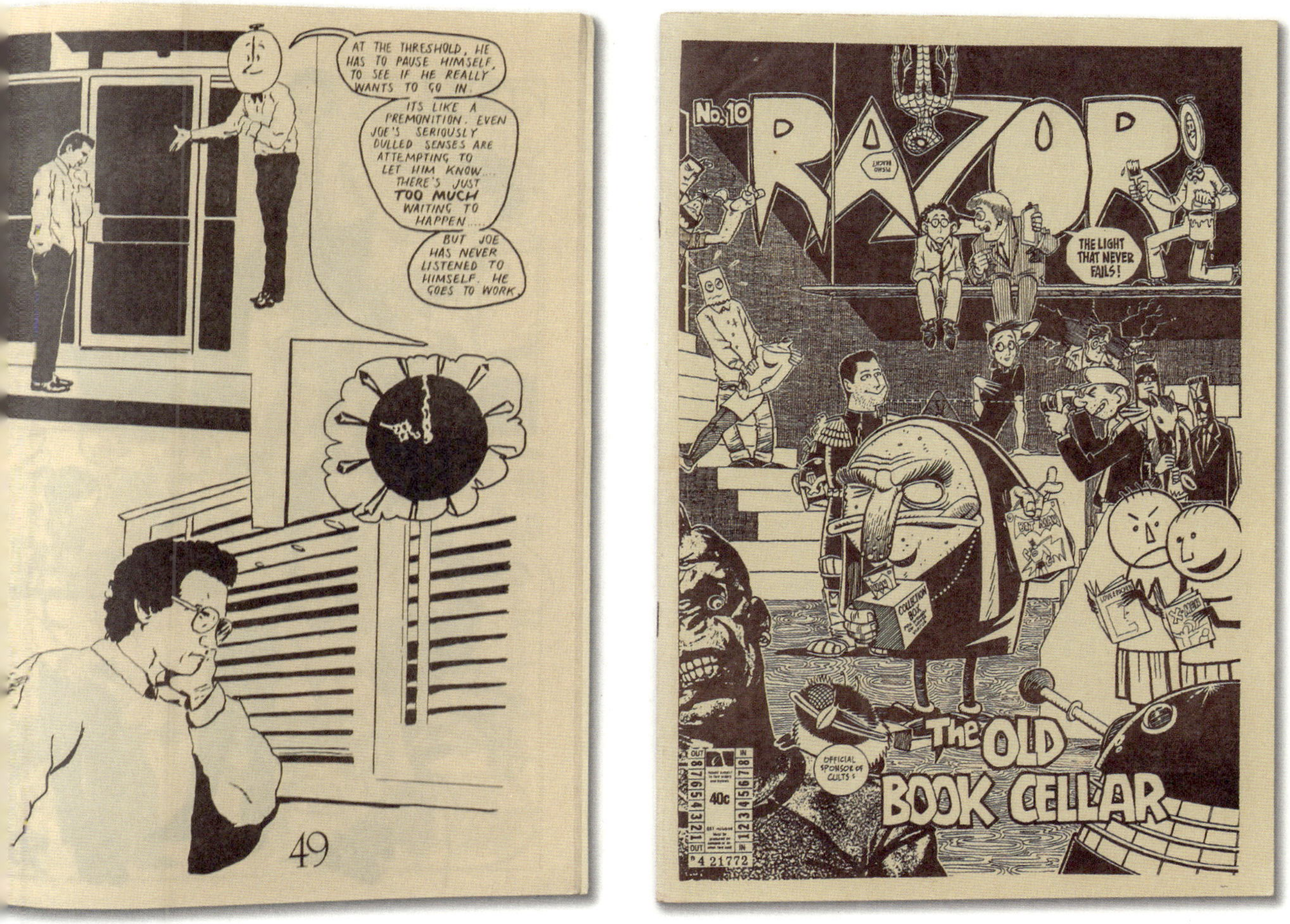

And then *Book Your Own Fuckin' Life* came out of that, because so many people were like 'Well, why should it just be about touring bands? Why not about record shops and all these other things in cities around the world? Where to get vegan food, crash pads . . . everything.' It became a punk network thing.

Moira Clunie I was always interested in pen pals. I remember having a few pen pals and being really interested in the mail, that sense of connecting with people outside of my immediate network was always a thing.

Liz Mathews I had always had pen pals, that was something that my mum always encouraged. You'd eventually meet some of these pen pals in real life. One of them became my girlfriend. She'd been to America with her parents and picked up some zines over there and brought them back. They were some of the first zines I ever saw. Then I got the Sonic Youth fan-club zine, which I absolutely loved. It was all cut-and-paste, bits and pieces from here and there. It included an interview with Yoshimi from the Boredoms. I remember writing out the entire interview by hand to send to another pen pal, who also became my girlfriend. Through her I met Beth Dawson. **Beth Dawson** It was also a thing that was happening in *Tearaway*, the print newspaper that went to all the high schools across Aotearoa. It had a pen-pal section. **Liz Mathews** I met Greta Welson through *Tearaway*. We were in [the band] HEX together. I was pen pals with Greta's bass player from an earlier all-girl band. I started organising the girl rock festival Get Set Go in 1998 and they came and played. Heaps of my pen pals were into the same Riot Grrrl kinda music.

70. *Razor* #10 spread and cover, edited by Cornelius Stone, A4, early 1990s. Tāmaki Makaurau Auckland.

71

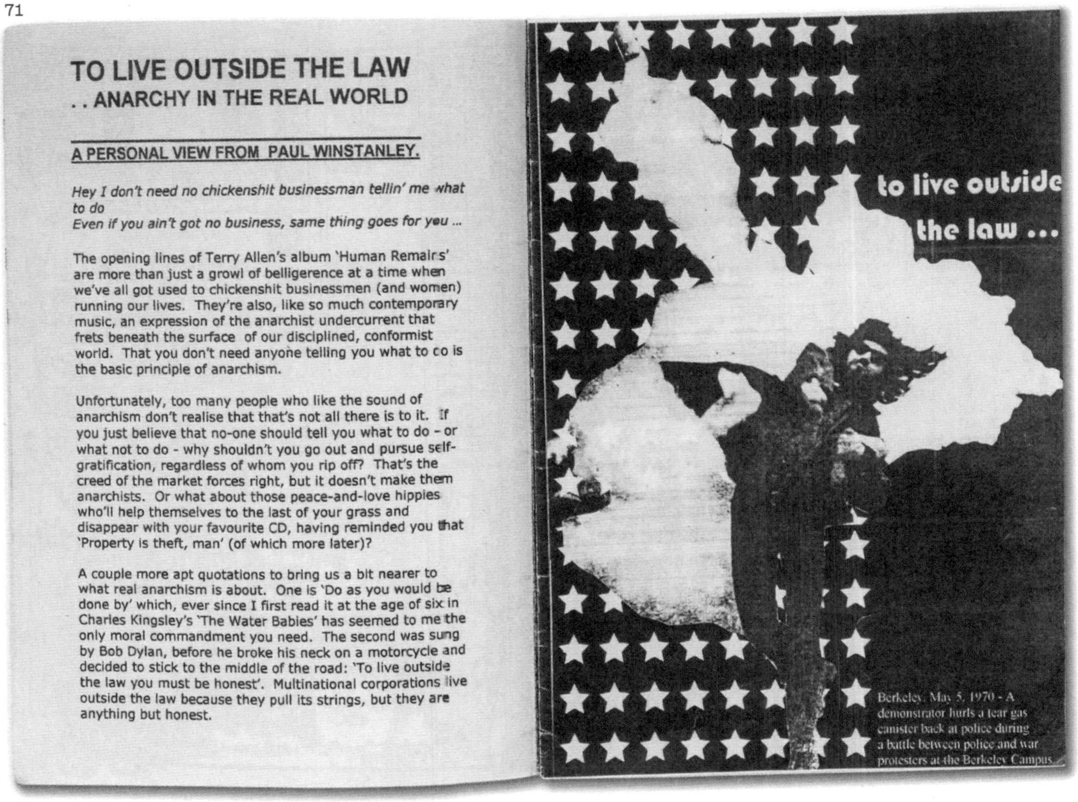

TO LIVE OUTSIDE THE LAW
. . ANARCHY IN THE REAL WORLD

A PERSONAL VIEW FROM PAUL WINSTANLEY.

Hey I don't need no chickenshit businessman tellin' me what to do
Even if you ain't got no business, same thing goes for you ...

The opening lines of Terry Allen's album 'Human Remains' are more than just a growl of belligerence at a time when we've all got used to chickenshit businessmen (and women) running our lives. They're also, like so much contemporary music, an expression of the anarchist undercurrent that frets beneath the surface of our disciplined, conformist world. That you don't need anyone telling you what to do is the basic principle of anarchism.

Unfortunately, too many people who like the sound of anarchism don't realise that that's not all there is to it. If you just believe that no-one should tell you what to do - or what not to do - why shouldn't you go out and pursue self-gratification, regardless of whom you rip off? That's the creed of the market forces right, but it doesn't make them anarchists. Or what about those peace-and-love hippies who'll help themselves to the last of your grass and disappear with your favourite CD, having reminded you that 'Property is theft, man' (of which more later)?

A couple more apt quotations to bring us a bit nearer to what real anarchism is about. One is 'Do as you would be done by' which, ever since I first read it at the age of six in Charles Kingsley's 'The Water Babies' has seemed to me the only moral commandment you need. The second was sung by Bob Dylan, before he broke his neck on a motorcycle and decided to stick to the middle of the road: 'To live outside the law you must be honest'. Multinational corporations live outside the law because they pull its strings, but they are anything but honest.

Kerry Ann Lee Simon Morse and Martin Emond had a studio upstairs above Comics Compulsion on Cuba Street, and they were so welcoming and inclusive. It was a really cool entry into seeing how print media works for people who want to have a life in the visual arts. I don't think anyone used the word 'career'. It's just what people did. It was survival and it was communication, and it was a way to make friends. That also stretches to music. The music scene was big, and it felt really integrated with the visual culture that came from that independent punk DIY scene.

Andrew Stephens Dave White and Yellow Bike Records in Palmy, I really liked that sort of philosophy — people who actually do it themselves, completely independent of the machine. I've always gone my own way, I suppose. I've never really had a steady job, I've just drifted here, there and everywhere. I've been a loose cannon. That's the best way I can describe it. I've never really been all that normal, y'know? I just drifted into this, if anything looked interesting, I'd have a crack at it. Whether it was working in forestry or writing a zine, if it looked interesting, I had to have a go at it. I was good at writing at school. I always could write a decent essay and I liked writing stories. **Trish Stephens** Your father was in advertising, and he painted. **Andrew Stephens** Yeah, creative family, definitely. When I was at Massey University I put a lot of time into getting that degree. It didn't give me much time for anything else. The only other serious writing I'd ever done was writing regular letters to my mother. She's an extremely well-read, literate woman, so we used to write quite interesting letters to each other. I had to be on my game writing to her. I couldn't just say 'Hope you're having a nice time. Love Andrew.' I really had to talk about books and music and stuff because she was always on her game. Her letters have always been an influence. She wrote a really good letter.

71. *Severed Head* #3 spread, edited by Andrew Stephens, A5, 1999. Te Papaioea Palmerston North.

Dave White I like writing and I like music, so I just thought I could combine the two. *Valve* was officially started by Radio Massey in the early eighties. They did two issues and then gave up on it. I'd been overseas touring, came back and I was no longer running The Stomach, so I was kind of at a loose end and was looking for a project, so I picked up *Valve* and kept it going. All our gigs in Europe were organised by zines. There was a really major one called *Hyacinth* in Paris which was the same size as *Valve*, over 100 pages. The punk scene in France was really underground. If they hadn't done their own zine, they'd get no press at all. There was nothing like *NME* or *Melody Maker* in France at the time. It was quite amazing actually. It was an incredibly sophisticated crowd. You'd play in Germany or England or whatever and it kinda looked like a punk crowd, but in Paris it was these *immaculately* dressed people.

Then we went to Bordeaux. There was a club in Bordeaux which was awesomely promoted. Three hundred people knew the words to all our songs, which was like *What the fuck?!* No one in France would speak English except in the music scene, where everyone seemed to speak English. *Hyacinth* was printed in English, which is really unusual for a French magazine.

72

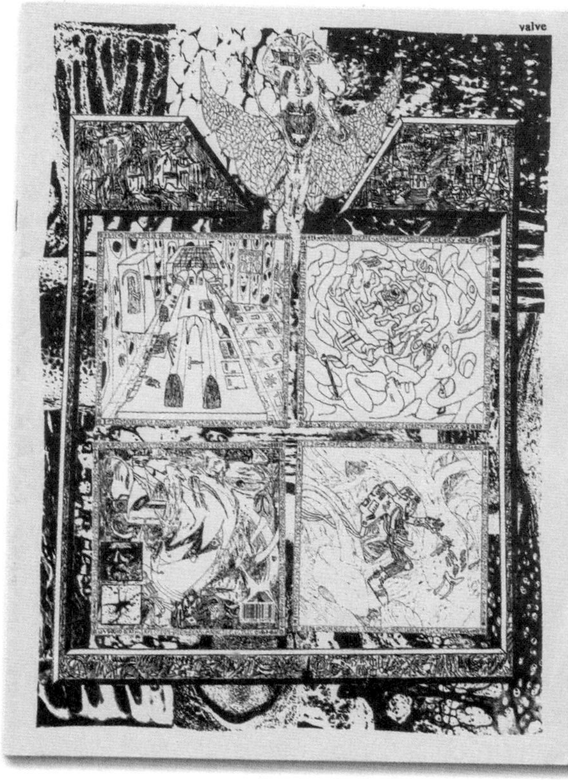

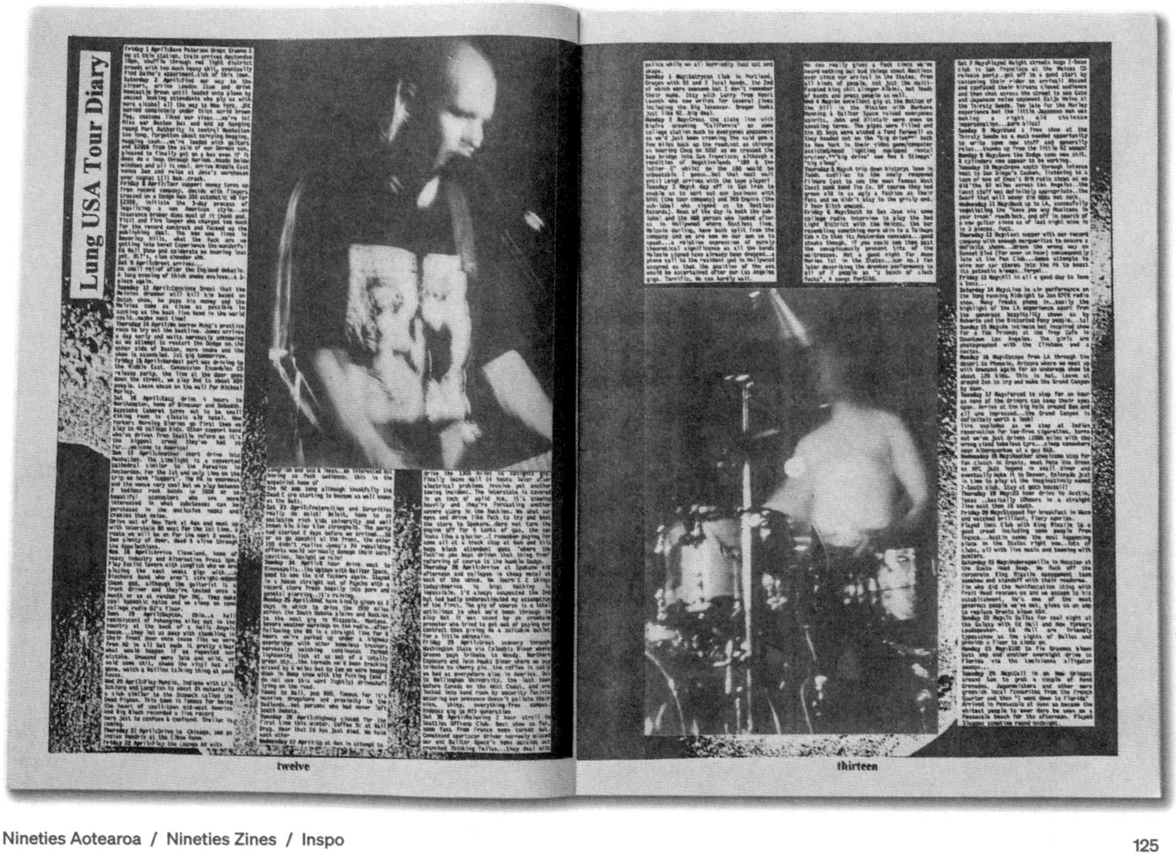

72. *Valve* Vol 3 #2 cover and spread, cover by Jack Black, edited by Dave White, 270 × 202mm, 1994. Te Papaioea Palmerston North.

73. *Hit This Up*, various contributors, A5, 1991. Waikouaiti.

Tony Renouf To me, 'fanzine' means something completely different to 'zine'. From what I've seen and what I've had come through my hands, a 'zine' is just whatever you want it to be, it's much less specific.

Moira Clunie I started making zines before I knew what zines were, I only knew about the comics. Learning that there was this other thing that was open-ended and could be whatever you wanted it to be was quite cool, quite creatively motivating.

Kerry Ann Lee I sometimes describe zines as a love letter out to the world.

Dave White When I started doing *Valve*, I don't even know whether I thought of it as a zine, I just thought this is a thing I'm doing. When we came up with the International Zinefest in Nelson, by that stage I kind of understood what was happening a bit more, but up until then it was just another tool for me to get my music out. *Valve*'s just a zine by default because it's a short-run photocopied magazine. The motivation for most of what I've done has been me just trying to get my music out there, and in the early days it was bits of paper and MySpace and now it's who knows what.

Ross Gardiner *The State Adversary*? Well, how do you define a zine? It was self-published, and came out whenever we could get enough stuff together and afford to get it done. The aim was to have it quarterly, but really it came out about three times a year. The print runs were usually a few hundred of each issue. A few of them we managed to get a thousand or so done, when we could scam some kind of printing deal with someone.

David Tulloch *Pistake* was a zine in many ways, rather than a professional comic. I had tried to do some bigger A4 things and they'd just cost me a lot of money. The zine format, the tiny format, black-and-white photocopy that meant we didn't lose money, or if we did it wasn't much. Maybe we'd lose 20 bucks putting out an issue rather than losing a couple of hundred, which was a lot of money for me at the time.

Pistake was smaller than my earlier effort, *Desperate Ink*, both in terms of the number of pages and the length of the stories. When you first start doing comics you're thinking about some epic story that's going to go on for pages and pages. I'd made that mistake. 'Get it into six pages or less, damn it.' Preferably one or two pages. *Pistake* was quicker, more ephemeral. I mean, we put out 12 issues between August '92 and late '94.

Rufus Dayglo wants me to tell this story. I was talking to him yesterday and he wants me to tell the story of him coming into VMS, Visual Media Services [later Comics Compulsion, then Graphic]. Rufus found a copy of *Desperate Ink*, issue one. He brought it up to the counter and said 'Wow, is this made in New Zealand?' And I went 'Yep.' He goes 'I've gotta have it. This is great.' I never told him I was the guy who had put it out because I was very unsure of myself and I had no idea who this guy was. So he comes back a little while later and says, 'Do you know who did this? I wanna try and contribute to it?' And I went 'Oh, it was me.' He goes 'Why didn't you tell me!?' And that's how we met.

Kerry Ann Lee Along with local comic zines like *Pistake* and Oats, feminist comics were an influence for me, as well as Riot Grrrl. One of the early interviews I did was with Roberta Gregory from *Bitchy Bitch* comic. I was just like 'Fuck, you're funny. This is great (totally unashamed feminist comics). I wanna talk to you.' Kathleen Hanna from Bikini Kill was saying one of the sweetest things at their gig. She talked about her friend Tobi Vail, the drummer. They made friends through fanzines, they were into the same stuff. Being kind of awkward and shy, writing a letter and going 'I think your project's really cool, and can I interview you?', that's how those two made friends. That's how I made a lot of my early friends, who I'm still in touch with today.

74

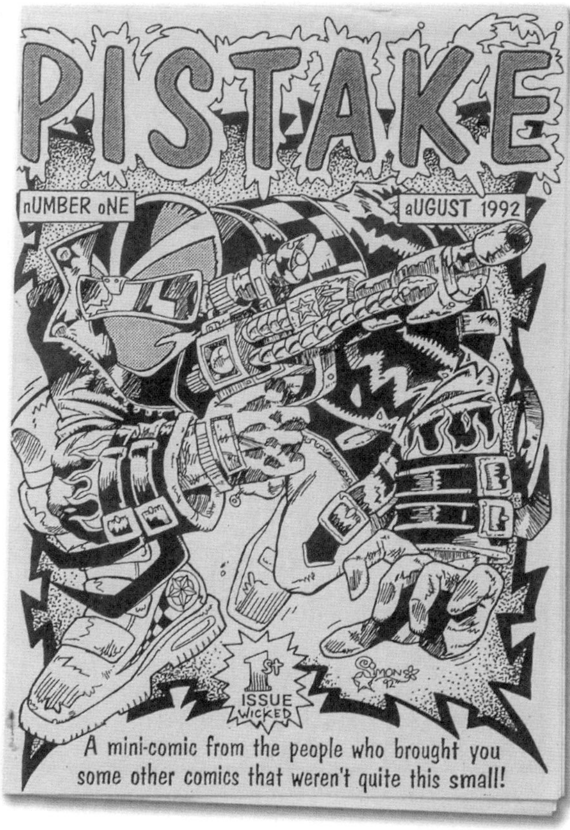

74. *Pistake* #1, cover by Simon Morse, edited by David Tulloch, A5, 1992. Te Whanganui-a-Tara Wellington.

75. *Pistake* #11, front cover by Rufus Dayglo, back cover by Lars Cawley, edited by David Tulloch, A5, 1994. Te Whanganui-a-Tara Wellington.

75

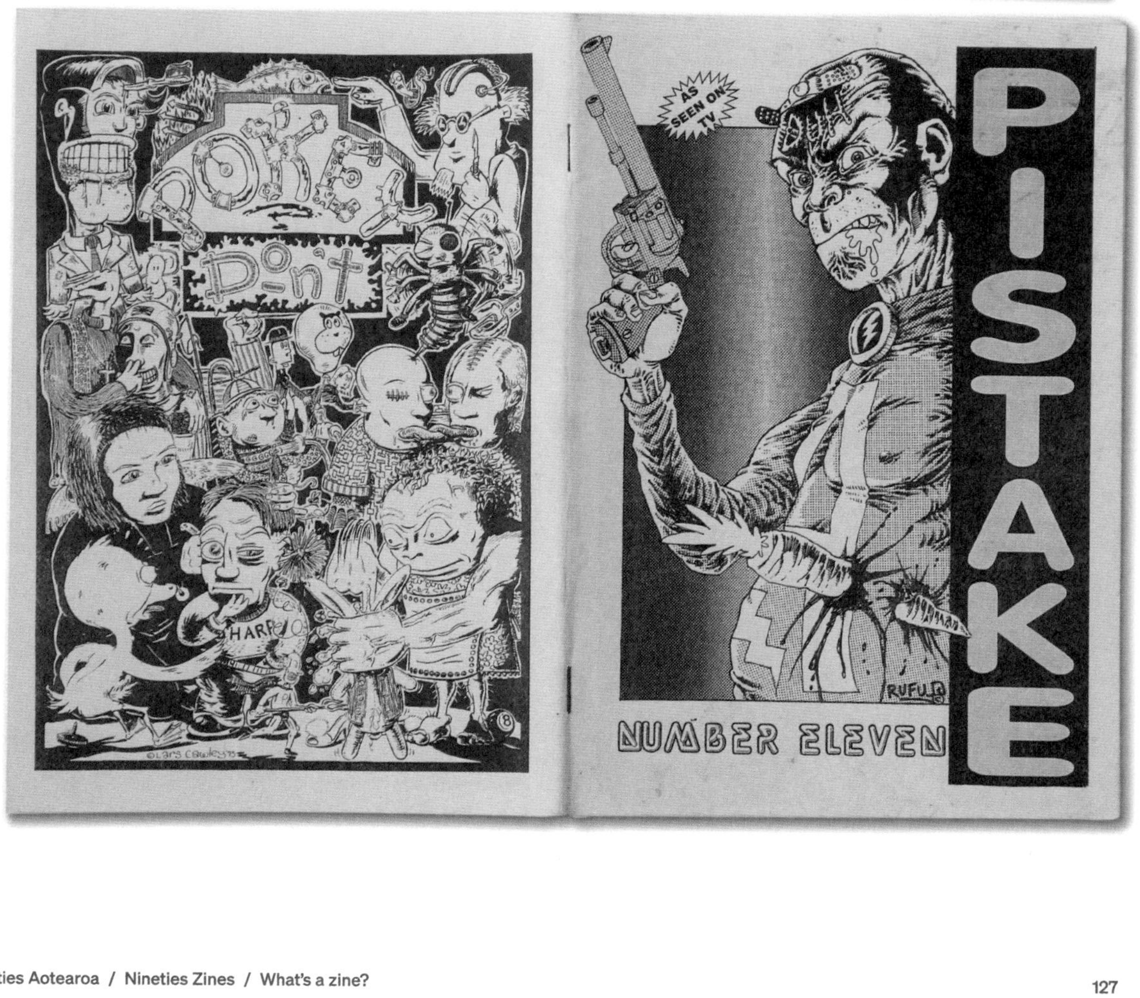

Liz Mathews Seeing zines made you think 'I could do that', because they were cut-and-paste, you could see exactly how they'd been constructed: they'd stapled it, they'd folded it, they'd stuck some pictures on here, they'd typed it up . . . I had a typewriter. Zines were like letters but with a different layout. When you're writing to all these different pen pals, you're sort of saying the same stuff over and over — 'I've been doing blah blah blah' — so it was like 'Oh, I can put it all in one place.'

Moira Clunie I discovered zines online, but the first zine-y *object* I ever came across was at a comic shop called Pop Culture in High Street, Auckland. There was this tiny little mini-zine/mini-comic on the shelf. I've still got it. It was obviously handmade by somebody who wasn't necessarily profit-motivated. It was really interesting and compelling, and I took it up to the counter and the shop assistant said 'What is that? I've never seen that before.' So they had no idea how much to charge me. It's called *A Comic Book* and it's credited to 'Danielle from Boulder Colorado, 1996.' Maybe Danielle was some backpacker who just snuck it onto the shelf at Pop Culture — who knows? The shop assistant didn't know what to do. I can't remember if I just took it or if they charged me $2 or something.

So one day I was at home at a loose end and thought 'Maybe I could make a little comic book as well?', and I made this even smaller comic called *Life Sucks* and photocopied it at work. The tiny scale just seemed more manageable, I guess. I wasn't a comics artist; *Life Sucks* was stick-figures meditating on the difficulties of life. I made the first one in 1999, then put out another four issues and a Christmas special. [Laughs.]

Kenneth Merrick As a kid I got to experience the comics of the eighties, and then into the nineties. I turned 15 in 1995. Me and my high-school friends realised 'Hey, we can make our own comics', and we started to photocopy them at school. We had a pretty cool art teacher, and he was like 'Yeah, just use the photocopier.' We'd make something infrequently, because it's quite a slow process pulling a comic together. It was never like 'Hey, let's sell this.' It was just casual and like 'Hey, oh, I made this little thing'; maybe it's an eight-page mini-comic or maybe something a little bigger. It was just a trade thing. It happened for a couple of years through that intense speculator boom of the nineties, that era of MTV, when everything was sort of popping off in the media, 'We've got four channels!' [Laughs.] It was an interesting time.

Andrew Stephens Self-publishing might not have been on my radar until Palmy, when I met Dave White and found people making zines. I started working at the library, too, so suddenly I had access to very cheap photocopying. That makes a big difference. If you're doing a zine and you have to pay commercial photocopying rates it's bloody crippling, I reckon, but because I worked at the library I could get a discount, especially when they knew what I was doing, that I was partly writing about the local music scene. They saw that as a good community thing to do, so I got a cut price on doing all the photocopying.

Dave White I didn't really think of *Valve* as a zine, it was more like a music release. I just gave every band two pages: a double-page spread to do anything they wanted, and they would just send me their two pages of content. It was all done cut-and-paste — glue stick, scissors, photocopy machine. And then I'd add interviews with people who I wanted to talk to. It was just an excuse for me to go and talk to people.

Andrew Stephens Then I sort of veered off music. I had a lot of beefs with the world that I wanted to get out there, and once I had a voice I thought, 'Right, now you're gonna hear what I've got to say, you buggers.' I just let rip basically. I'd done media studies papers at Massey University, and we had an American lecturer named Scott Eastham who had a radical political bent. I did some of his media courses, which covered a lot of critical theory.

It was cathartic to put those ideas into a zine [*Severed Head*]. I'd actually written the basis of the essay while at Massey, during a media studies course that focused on propaganda. I had all the material ready, and it really was just a matter of reshaping it for the zine. When I did that course I'd bore Trish stupid, I'd come home and talk and talk about it because I thought these were really important ideas: how manipulated we are in ways that we hadn't even realised. There's so much media that looks user-friendly but if you actually sit back and examine it, it's selling a message. It's selling a lifestyle and it's a consumer lifestyle, wasteful and greedy. Even the most innocent-looking magazine like the *Woman's Weekly*, that's what they're flogging basically, and that's what this lecturer woke me up to: how to read these things critically.

Indira Neville There was never a conscious plan to form an Oats Comics collective, it was just a bunch of mates. We liked drinking and making stuff. The name came from this terrible card game called Pit. It was such a bad card game. Someone got it from some op-shop. The card game had wheat, oats and barley. Someone would say 'The pit is open', and you'd go 'WHEAT WHEAT WHEAT BARLEY BARLEY BARLEY . . .' We just thought it was hilarious, and that's where the name Oats came from. There was nothing conscious about it, we were just a bunch of mates who liked drinking. We'd all sit around and draw together, get drunk, just the joy of hanging out and making stuff. It wasn't about product at all, that was almost incidental.

Everyone would say 'Fucking oats' all the time, a classic Kiwi saying that we just thought was hilarious, so Oats was just a joke name. The first few comics were those *Oats* anthologies where everyone drew. There was a phase of *Oats* anthologies and then it kind of turned into everyone's individual comics: Glen [Frenzy] started making *Choice Guy*, Clayton Noone started making *Scorch*, Stefan [Neville] and Sugar Jon Arcus started making *Dad & Tracy*, I started making *Nice Gravy*, Adrian Ganley (aka Biff Bangle) started making *Buffalo*. And then occasionally we'd come back together and do an anthology. There was also a horror anthology called *The Hood* which was Chris Lander's baby. Then there were heaps of people in the gang who would just contribute a page or two: Matthew 'Ugly Dog' Davies, my friend Sarah (aka Soft Keith), Rachel Lander, Tamara Howie . . .

David Merritt Michael O'Leary, he's a lovely man, he was the best poetical role model I had at the time. He's like me now, but I met him when I was 25. He was this big man. He had a huge beard, he was Irish, he drank like a fish and he ran this thing called the Earl of Seacliff Art Workshop, or ESAW. That was his press. He'd always run bookshops. When I got to Dunedin he had a bookshop in The Octagon called The Mother of All Potatoes, don't ask me why. Of course, I headed straight in there, couldn't resist, met him, liked the bookshop, volunteered to work there because, y'know, I'd arrived in Dunedin. I was working three dishwashing jobs trying to get by. I was flatting in View Street, which is in the middle of town, but my rent was like $12 a week. I was living on maybe 50 bucks a week or something, and I could earn that money as a dishwasher. I had time up my sleeve . . . I had PageMaker skills by then, and I was doing the *Spec* magazine with Caro McCaw for Radio One. I'd learnt a bit, so I started to help Michael O'Leary put out publications. We did about three or four books in the space of a year, and I got the bug after that. I thought, this is what I want to do. I think I already knew that anyway.

You pick up skills when you're young and they're useful to you all your life. Often the skills that you pick up are just a reincarnation of a skill that you've already picked up, just applied slightly differently or with a new form of media.

Indira Neville It didn't occur to any of us that you didn't have licence to just make whatever, it wasn't a choice or anything. The music's funny, too. Now it's weird that these fancy arty European labels are re-releasing all this early Plop stuff [Oats's music arm]. It is weird how what starts out as drunken mucking-around becomes art in a different context years later. I don't know, it's fascinating. Even *Funtime*, they didn't drink but it was still mates just doing shit over cups of tea. Back in the day, they were the only group with the same ethos as Oats.

Beth Dawson As a piece of journalism, zines are such a good capture of a particular time and place. They capture a scene and the voice of that scene, which is why it's so nice that my friends and I have those zines that Liz made in our teenager years and our early twenties. It's this little snapshot.

76

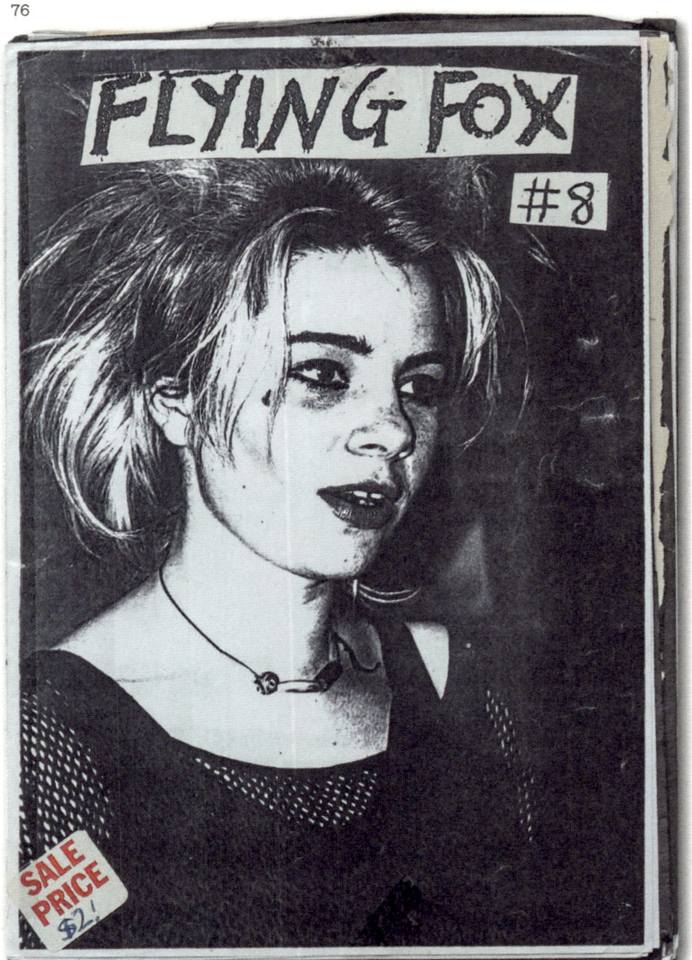

76. *Flying Fox* #8 cover and spread (analogue master for black-and-white photocopying), Liz Mathews, A4, 1998. Tāmaki Makaurau Auckland.

77

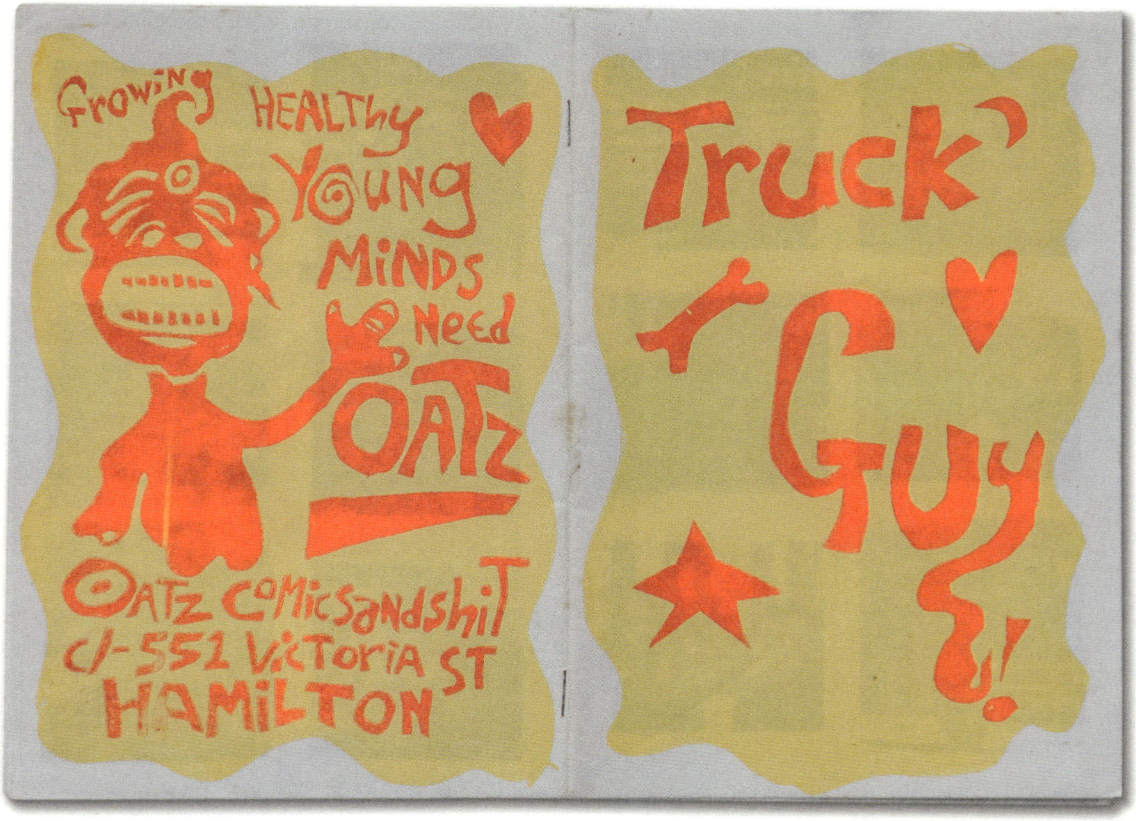

77. *Truck Guy* front and back covers, Glen Frenzy, A5, 1990s. Kirikiriroa Hamilton.

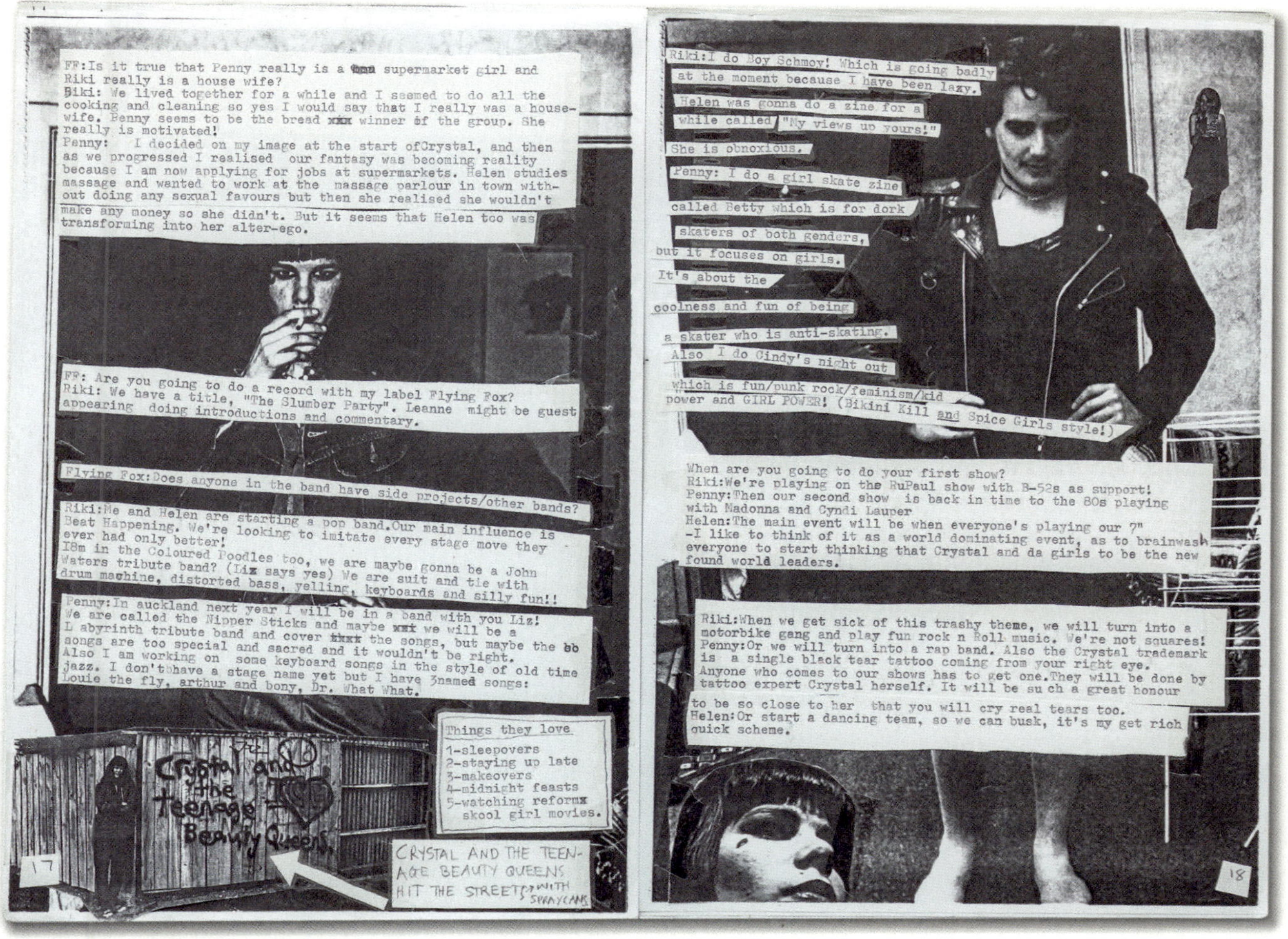

FF:Is it true that Penny really is a supermarket girl and Riki really is a house wife?
Riki: We lived together for a while and I seemed to do all the cooking and cleaning so yes I would say that I really was a house-wife. Penny seems to be the bread winner of the group. She really is motivated!
Penny: I decided on my image at the start ofCrystal, and then as we progressed I realised our fantasy was becoming reality because I am now applying for jobs at supermarkets. Helen studies massage and wanted to work at the massage parlour in town with-out doing any sexual favours but then she realised she wouldn't make any money so she didn't. But it seems that Helen too was transforming into her alter-ego.

FF: Are you going to do a record with my label Flying Fox?
Riki: We have a title, "The Slumber Party". Leanne might be guest appearing doing introductions and commentary.

Flying Fox:Does anyone in the band have side projects/other bands?

Riki:Me and Helen are starting a pop band.Our main influence is Beat Happening. We're looking to imitate every stage move they ever had only better!
I8m in the Coloured Poodles too, we are maybe gonna be a John Waters tribute band? (Liz says yes) We are suit and tie with drum machine, distorted bass, yelling, keyboards and silly fun!!

Penny:In auckland next year I will be in a band with you Liz! We are called the Nipper Sticks and maybe we will be a L abyrinth tribute band and cover the songs, but maybe the bb songs are too special and sacred and it wouldn't be right. Also I am working on some keyboard songs in the style of old time jazz. I don't have a stage name yet but I have 3named songs: Louie the fly, arthur and bony, Dr. What What.

Things they love
1-sleepovers
2-staying up late
3-makeovers
4-midnight feasts
5-watching reform skool girl movies.

Crystal and the Teenage Beauty Queens

CRYSTAL AND THE TEEN-AGE BEAUTY QUEENS HIT THE STREETS WITH SPRAYCANS

17

Riki:I do Boy Schmoy! Which is going badly at the moment because I have been lazy.
Helen was gonna do a zine for a while called "My views up yours!"
She is obnoxious.
Penny: I do a girl skate zine called Betty which is for dork skaters of both genders, but it focuses on girls. It's about the coolness and fun of being a skater who is anti-skating.
Also I do Cindy's night out which is fun/punk rock/feminism/kid power and GIRL POWER! (Bikini Kill and Spice Girls style!)

When are you going to do your first show?
Riki:We're playing on the RuPaul show with B-52s as support!
Penny:Then our second show is back in time to the 80s playing with Madonna and Cyndi Lauper
Helen:The main event will be when everyone's playing our 7"
-I like to think of it as a world dominating event, as to brainwash everyone to start thinking that Crystal and da girls to be the new found world leaders.

Riki:When we get sick of this trashy theme, we will turn into a motorbike gang and play fun rock n Roll music. We're not squares!
Penny:Or we will turn into a rap band. Also the Crystal trademark is a single black tear tattoo coming from your right eye. Anyone who comes to our shows has to get one.They will be done by tattoo expert Crystal herself. It will be su ch a great honour to be so close to her that you will cry real tears too.
Helen:Or start a dancing team, so we can busk, it's my get rich quick scheme.

18

Dave White 'Battery Acid' was originally a tour diary from the Lung tour. I came back from overseas broke as fuck, and there was a short story competition with Reed Publishing, 500 bucks. I thought I'll enter that, and just started writing. I sent it in and it got shortlisted, but they said I'd have to work with an editor and in those days I was in no mind to work with an editor. I'd just come back from being a rock star, there's no way I was working with an editor. Of course, now I know that's how it works; the editor's not there to steal your voice, they're there to make your voice better.

'Battery Acid' turned into *Bad Acid Soundtracks* and the feedback I got was, 'No one's gonna believe this shit', so I said 'Okay, well, I'll just call it a novel then, which means I can write anything I want.' Once I'd decided it was a novel, I thought 'Oh, I've gotta make up a whole story now' and I played with it for about three years. I'd rush home from work and just type, type, type all night. It went up to tens of thousands of words and then I'd come in drunk one day and just delete heaps of it. [Laughs.] The story went all over the place. It was my pet project. Then one day I suddenly went 'Nah, this has to stop: I'm gonna print it and then that'll be it.' The first version came out as a little A5 thing with a black cover, shiny so you could snort off it. [Laughs.] That sold out real fast, so a year later I decided to do it again and found this printer in the States.

Tony Renouf I don't think I cut anything from *Treacle*. When I put the first issue together I didn't read any of it because I wanted to experience it as a comic book when it was completed, experience it fresh. I'd seen all the artwork and it was all the right size and all the pages were in the right order . . . now I'll read it. I read it to discover that one guy — who'd done this science-fiction thing — had started every other frame with 'And then . . .' [Laughs.] But no, I didn't want to be the editor who cut stuff.

Simon Cottle Sometimes I did have to reject things I'd been sent because they were just not in the flavour of the thing. The politics might be off. I'd just say 'Knock yourself out. Make your own zine.' Lots of that's washed up in the letters column, people slagging me off. I'd acknowledge that my zines were pretty opinionated, reasonably singular in focus: 'This is kind of what I'm into, what I'm promoting, take it or leave it. I'm not offended if you leave it, just do your own zine.'

Andrew Stephens I wanted to get a lot of text into the first issue of *Severed Head*, that's why the layout's more straightforward. I had stuff I wanted to say. I mean, the whole point of my zines was to preach to people. I guess I just left the church and started my own, the church of Andrew; God help the rest of you, that's all I can say. There was more art and collage in issues two and three. I've always liked doing stuff like that. I've always painted and drawn, and I did art at teacher training college. Yeah, one year, and then it turned out to be a bit tedious so I moved on. I found that you might like your own kids but you don't necessarily like a class full of other people's.

78

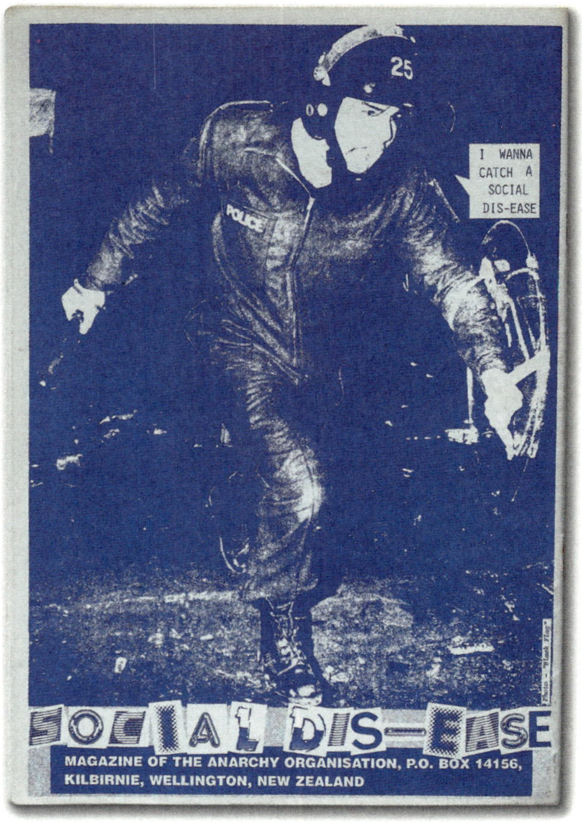

78. *Social Dis-Ease* #15 back cover, edited by Simon Cottle, A4, 1990. Te Whanganui-a-Tara Wellington.

Kerry Ann Lee As a teenager I just knew that learning and self-discovery were really important. I even kept scrapbooks; later I threw them all away, I sometimes regret that. If there was something really cool that I'd read I'd photocopy it or keep it or cut it out for later reference, that whole collaging of knowledge.

Andrew Stephens I was photocopying a lot of magazines rather than just cutting them up, so the collages started off with photocopied bits and pieces. I didn't want to destroy too many magazines. I'd mostly photocopy magazines rather than books because they lie flat in the photocopier. Books are much more awkward. At the library job I had access to a lot of good illustrated magazines, so there was no trouble finding pictures.

As I remember, I pasted things up a page at a time and just made sure everything looked okay, had balance. I was quite happy to have a page full of text, but then I'd want something to break it up on the next page, maybe an illustration or something.

If that way of working left me with a spare panel, I always had shorter bits and pieces of writing around. When you've got a zine, that's the perfect opportunity to use up all those little bits of egotism that nobody else is interested in, but you can publish yourself. It was stuff that I couldn't really hand in as Massey coursework because it was a bit scurrilous or it wasn't their speed, but I really felt the world should read it.

79

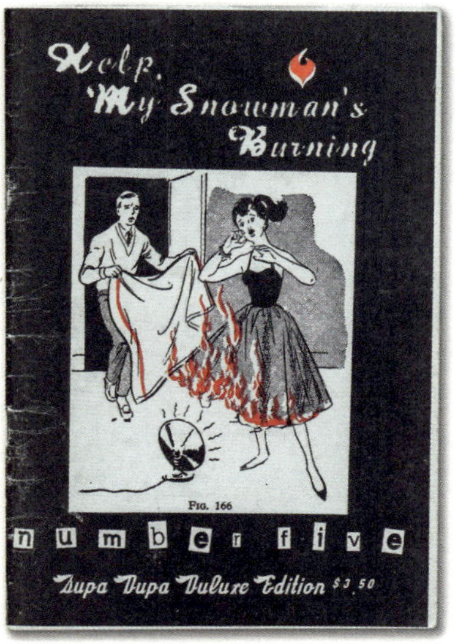

79. *Help, My Snowman's Burning* #5 cover and spread, Kerry Ann Lee, A5, 1999. Te Whanganui-a-Tara Wellington.

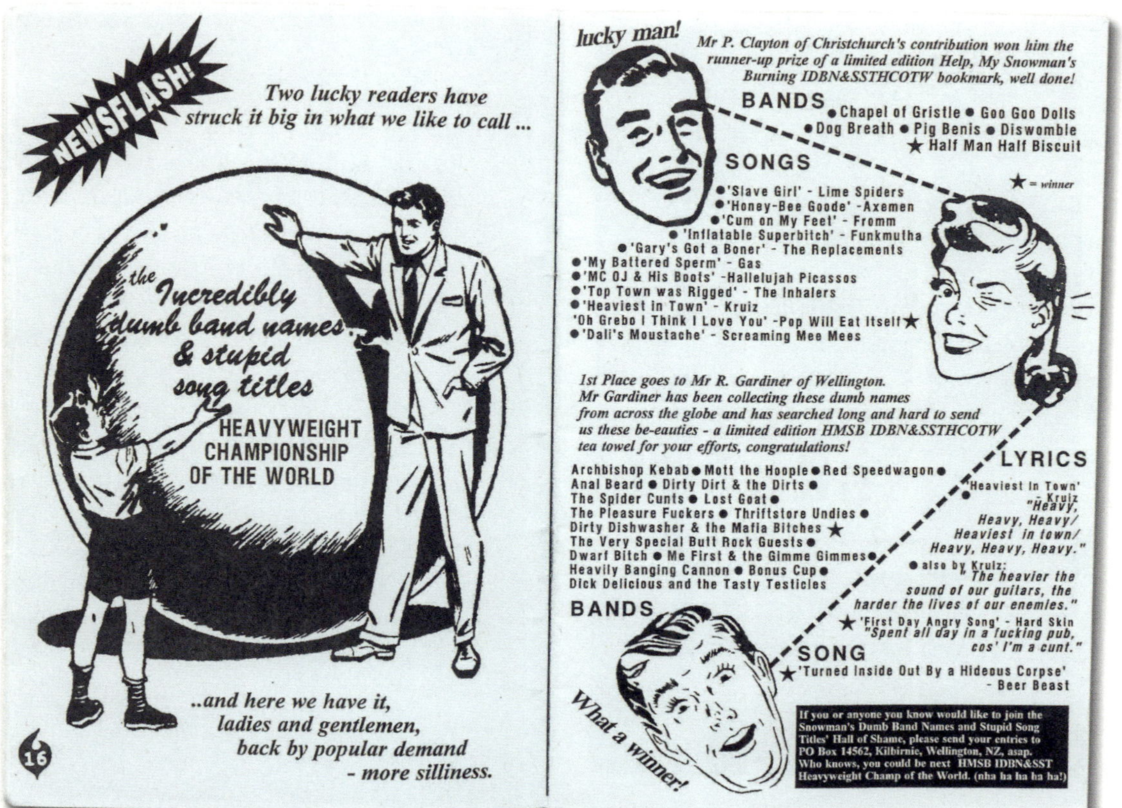

David Merritt David Carson did these two magazines, *Ray Gun* and *Beach Culture*. *Ray Gun* was famous because he'd take text and he'd do things like slice the first two letters down there so it was unreadable. He'd be interlacing lettering from this column into that. All sorts of tricks. He came to New Zealand in 1993. He went to the Whanganui Polytech Design School camp, and he talked and gave lectures. He went surfing mostly. We all travelled up and we all met him, and we all sat enthralled and listened to what he had to say because he was at the top of his game globally. Saatchi was employing him because he was cutting-edge. He was making it difficult, fuck yeah. That was the first time I learnt about text as a visual object, as something needing to be reinterpreted; not just a thing to be read but an object that you could view for its aesthetic, how it looked on the page.

It was very Dada. He was an enormous influence on the zine work we were doing. We went to big, ugly strange types and compressed them and stretched them and everything. Every trick we tried because you could — with the new software, you could.

Kerry Ann Lee We also had newspapers and things like *Rip It Up* magazine and *NME*, and the libraries would cancel out their mags, or dairies would throw out stuff, so there was like a glut of print culture that we could then synthesise and filter and make stuff with.

Ross Gardiner I still have an index of cool little pictures in a drawer somewhere; a pile of pictures I've cut of magazines or just found somewhere and thought 'That'd look really cool in a zine, or on a gig poster.'

80

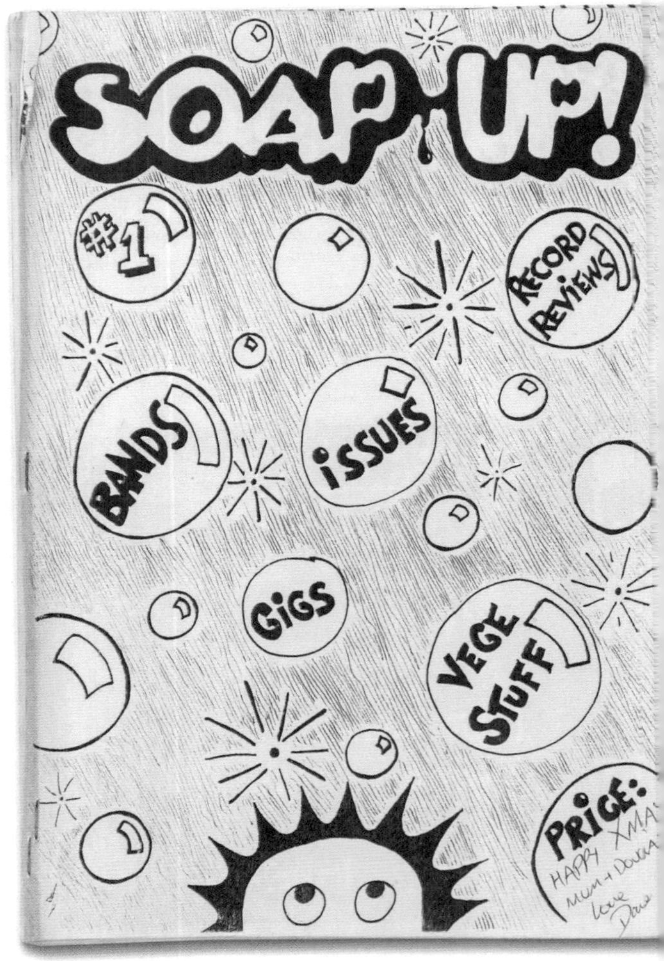

80. *Soap Up!* #1 cover and spread, Dave Hegan, A4, 1991. Ōtautahi Christchurch.

Kerry Ann Lee I indexed my collage bits and pieces across an array of shoeboxes and biscuit tins. Some things were arranged by size. Weird little seed packets go in here. And then, from the same pool of zine-making detritus would also be the decals and ephemera that would adorn mix-tapes, and remember the art of the mixtape cover was also an important form of communication. There'd be funny cartoons in this box. Sarcastic slogans cut out of newspapers in this biscuit tin. Quasi political stuff, like 'I could use this for a protest flyer, this could get under people's skin', would go in the agitprop biscuit tin. Because it was all about the juxtaposition, that's what good collage is about.

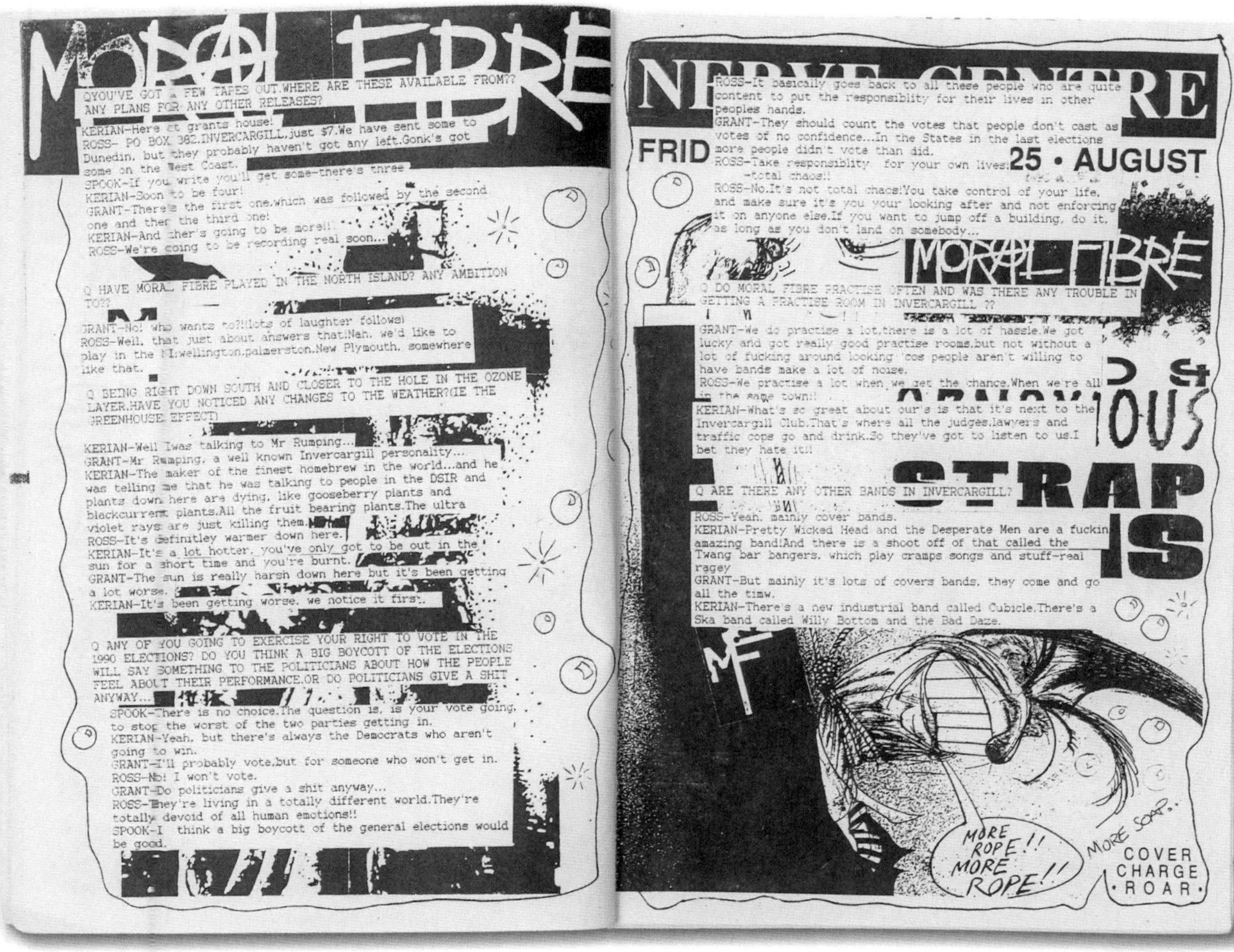

MORAL FIBRE

QYOU'VE GOT A FEW TAPES OUT.WHERE ARE THESE AVAILABLE FROM??
ANY PLANS FOR ANY OTHER RELEASES?

KERIAN-Here at grants house!
ROSS- PO BOX 382.INVERCARGILL.just $7.We have sent some to
Dunedin. but they probably haven't got any left.Gonk's got
some on the West Coast.
SPOOK-If you write you'll get some-there's three
KERIAN-Soon to be four!
GRANT-There's the first one.which was followed by the second
one and then the third one!
KERIAN-And ther's going to be more!!
ROSS-We're going to be recording real soon...

Q HAVE MORAL FIBRE PLAYED IN THE NORTH ISLAND? ANY AMBITION
TO??

GRANT-No! who wants to?!(lots of laughter follows)
ROSS-Well. that just about answers that!Nah. we'd like to
play in the NI:wellington.palmerston.New Plymouth. somewhere
like that.

Q BEING RIGHT DOWN SOUTH AND CLOSER TO THE HOLE IN THE OZONE
LAYER.HAVE YOU NOTICED ANY CHANGES TO THE WEATHER?(IE THE
GREENHOUSE EFFECT)

KERIAN-Well Iwas talking to Mr Rumping...
GRANT-Mr Rumping. a well known Invercargill personality...
KERIAN-The maker of the finest homebrew in the world...and he
was telling me that he was talking to people in the DSIR and
plants down here are dying. like gooseberry plants and
blackcurrent plants.All the fruit bearing plants.The ultra
violet rays are just killing them.
ROSS-It's definitley warmer down here.
KERIAN-It's a lot hotter. you've only got to be out in the
sun for a short time and you're burnt.
GRANT-The sun is really harsh down here but it's been getting
a lot worse.
KERIAN-It's been getting worse. we notice it first.

Q ANY OF YOU GOING TO EXERCISE YOUR RIGHT TO VOTE IN THE
1990 ELECTIONS? DO YOU THINK A BIG BOYCOTT OF THE ELECTIONS
WILL SAY SOMETHING TO THE POLITICIANS ABOUT HOW THE PEOPLE
FEEL ABOUT THEIR PERFORMANCE.OR DO POLITICIANS GIVE A SHIT
ANYWAY...
SPOOK-There is no choice.The question is. is your vote going
to stop the worst of the two parties getting in.
KERIAN-Yeah. but there's always the Democrats who aren't
going to win.
GRANT-I'll probably vote.but for someone who won't get in.
ROSS-No! I won't vote.
GRANT-Do politicians give a shit anyway...
ROSS-They're living in a totally different world.They're
totally devoid of all human emotions!!
SPOOK-I think a big boycott of the general elections would
be good.

FRID 25 • AUGUST

ROSS-It basically goes back to all these people who are quite
content to put the responsiblity for their lives in other
peoples hands.
GRANT-They should count the votes that people don't cast as
votes of no confidence...In the States in the last elections
more people didn't vote than did.
ROSS-Take responsiblity for your own lives!
-total chaos!!
ROSS-No.It's not total chaos!You take control of your life.
and make sure it's you your looking after and not enforcing
it on anyone else.If you want to jump off a building. do it.
as long as you don't land on somebody...

MORAL FIBRE

Q DO MORAL FIBRE PRACTISE OFTEN AND WAS THERE ANY TROUBLE IN
GETTING A PRACTISE ROOM IN INVERCARGILL ??

GRANT-We do practise a lot.there is a lot of hassle.We got
lucky and got really good practise rooms.but not without a
lot of fucking around looking 'cos people aren't willing to
have bands make a lot of noise.
ROSS-We practise a lot when we get the chance.When we're all
in the same town!!
KERIAN-What's so great about our's is that it's next to the
Invercargill Club.That's where all the judges.lawyers and
traffic cops go and drink.So they've got to listen to us.I
bet they hate it!!

Q ARE THERE ANY OTHER BANDS IN INVERCARGILL?

ROSS-Yeah. mainly cover bands.
KERIAN-Pretty Wicked Head and the Desperate Men are a fuckin
amazing band!And there is a shoot off of that called the
Twang bar bangers. which play cramps songs and stuff-real
ragey
GRANT-But mainly it's lots of covers bands. they come and go
all the timw.
KERIAN-There's a new industrial band called Cubicle.There's a
Ska band called Willy Bottom and the Bad Daze.

Indira Neville My old comics were much rougher, and I wasn't the central character, otherwise they were quite similar to more recent stuff. I am very influenced by the British newspaper comics with the big round eyes. I really want them to look cartoony. That's partly the influence of my dad's drawing. My brother Stefan went off on his own path, he's a real flash drawer and he's real unique. I stayed with a much more cartoony vibe.

Dave Hegan For me, one of the big things about punk was having spiky hair. I always had massive spikes or a big mohawk. You use Sunlight soap to stick it up. My graffiti name — because I used to do tagging and stuff — was Soap and Spikes, so I just called my second zine *Soap Up!* Not a lot of thought went into it. Back then, that was my logo — Soap and Spikes. I used to paint it on my leather jacket and spray-paint it around the place. I think I was trying to create my own little brand. I came up with the name in drug rehab actually. *Alien-Nation* was just a one-off. My friend Rob did the artwork for the cover. He came up with the cover image of the Beehive and the politicians and whatnot. I think it was his idea to call it *Alien-Nation*.

Indira Neville *Truck Guy* is great. It's a great comic. See, I'd call that a comic; the comics fraternity would never call it a comic. I personally believe that if the person who made it calls it a comic, it's a comic, regardless. Glen Frenzy says it's a comic, so it's a comic.

Andrew Stephens That 'Angry from Remuera' letter in my zine was a bit of a space-filler. I just thought I'd take the piss out of myself. Usually I tend to take myself a bit seriously, and every now and again I have to step back and go 'Christ, son, it's only a zine that four people read, get over yourself.' I have to take that step now and again, otherwise I can get quite carried away, like I'm gonna change the world with this.

81. *NADA*. #2 cover and spread, Rheet and Other, A4, 1990. Kemureti Cambridge.

81

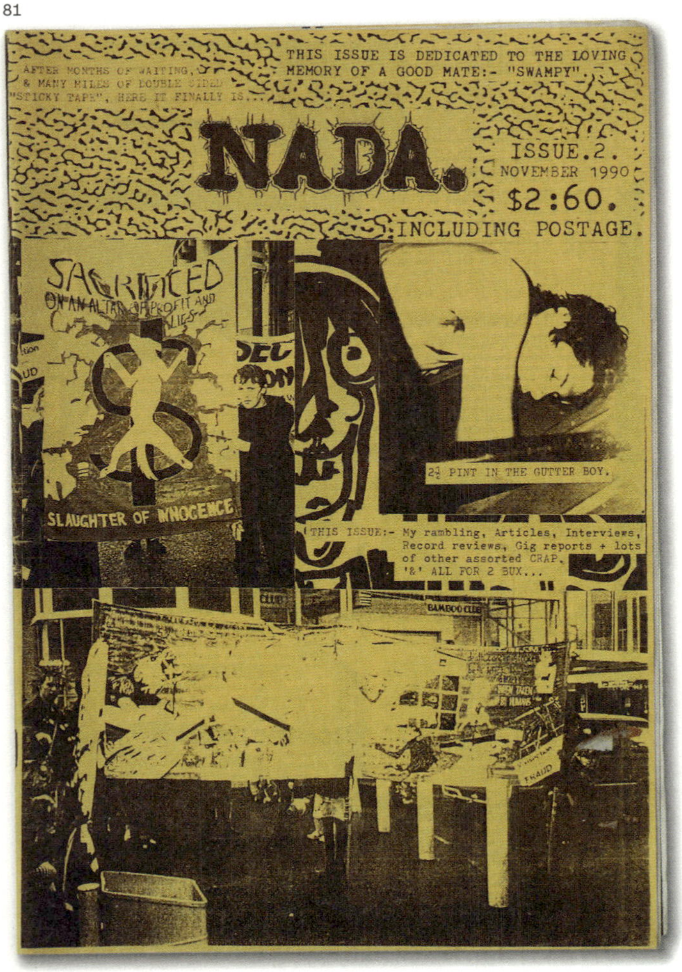

Dave Hegan I think the interview I was most thrilled about was when Poison Idea got back to me, because they were a big band in America. They were from Portland. They're still going. A lot of these bands are still going now, I don't know if they should or not. It's usually just one original member and a bunch of ring-ins. But I remember being pretty stoked about Poison Idea because they were a big name.

I think the interview I enjoyed most was with Dick Lucas of Subhumans. It just went on and on and on, and he also sent me a drawing to put in the zine and a list of stuff that he had for sale. He was just so happy to talk about everything, and it was all stuff that I was really interested in. There's the picture he did [pointing at zine page]. I think that and Poison Idea were probably the best ones. You're doing something that you're really interested in so it's not hard work. You want to do it and you enjoy doing it. But the transcribing was always a pain, having to listen to the tape and then write it all down. I can't say I enjoyed that too much.

I was really happy when Doom wrote back, because they were a really big band at the time. I used to have their logotype painted on my leather jacket. I was pretty stoked when these dudes wrote back to me. When I read the questions now, I still think they're pretty good. It feels like a lifetime ago. It's been interesting looking at it. I didn't really have any bad interviews. Most bands were pretty happy about being interviewed.

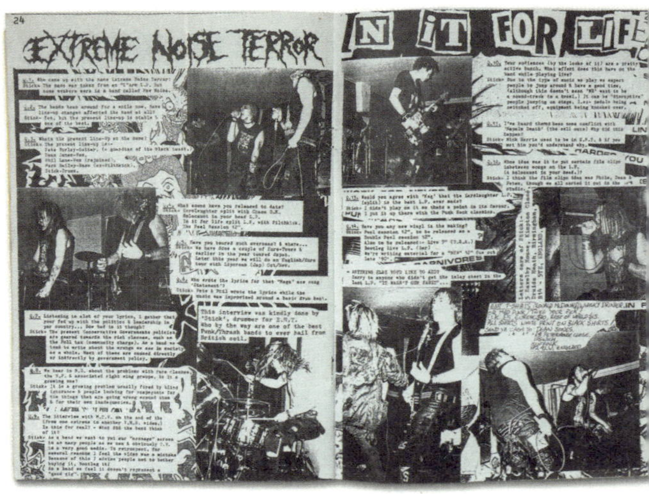

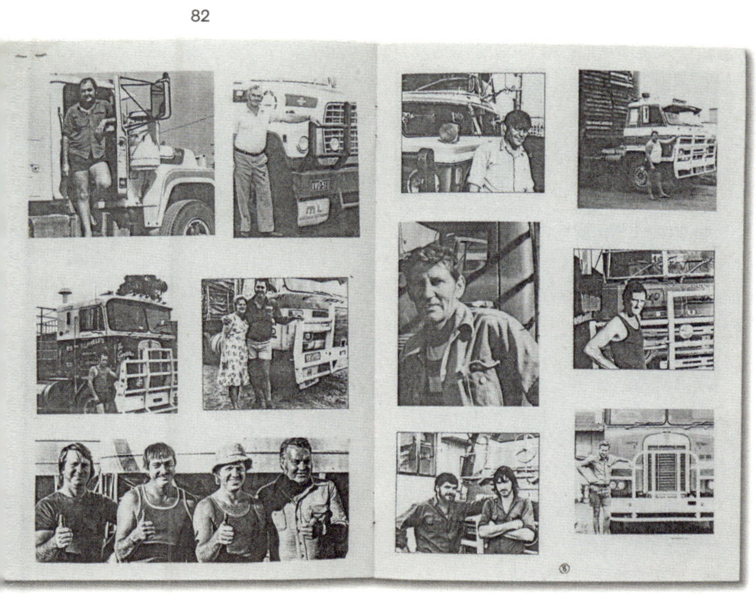

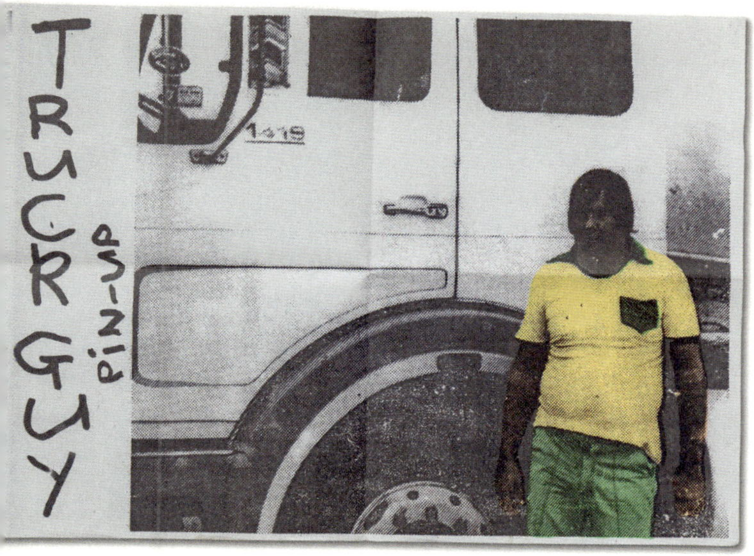

82. *Truck Guy* spread and poster, Glen Frenzy, A5, 1990s. Kirikiriroa Hamilton.

Andrew Stephens When you do something like a zine there's no editor, you're in charge, you can say what the hell you like and publish it. Because of that, I felt like I had to be careful that I didn't sound too earnest, balance that out with some self-deprecating humour at times.

Dave White Yellow Bike was me, so I put the *Valve* zines' discs under that production name as well. Each band in the zine got a double-page spread to do whatever they wanted. I liked it because there was absolutely no censorship. Whatever they gave me was what went into the zine. That method told you more about them and what they were like. Yellow Bike had been integral to The Stomach when I was running it, but once I was no longer employed by The Stomach I took Yellow Bike on as my own thing. I could've thought of another name, but I just liked it.

Dave Hegan I remember learning that you had to ask open-ended questions otherwise you're just gonna get yes/no answers. You've gotta have these prompts to get people to talk, and then just let them talk. Some of the bands I would interview by sending out questions and a tape, but other ones I would actually interview in person and tape the conversation myself. It was all pretty easy, because all of the bands I interviewed I was really, really interested in, and I wanted to ask these questions myself. I was like, great, now I've got the chance to find out, and it just took care of itself.

Andrew Schmidt John Baker, he's a fanatic. If some 'John Smith' was in a band he would go through the phone book and ring up all the John Smiths. He was a fantastic natural researcher but not a historian, more of a fan. So we combined our skills and did a zine called *Social End Product.* John also started to compile LPs of a lot the different bands and he would get me writing the sleeve notes for those, which was fun. I always wanted to do that. I loved that garage stuff, but he's intensely energetic and I'm an introvert and he burnt me out pretty quickly. It's something I sort of noticed after a while. I tend to partner up with people who balance me out, but after a while they burn me out.

Kerry Ann Lee There are some layouts that would've happened with early desktop publishing programs like PageMaker 5.0. My mum used to make these newsletters for her business and a lot of it was computer cut-and-paste using clip art, back in the day of clip art. She said, 'You'll have some fun with this. Do you wanna help me with this?' So I would help her create these newsletters.

Ross Gardiner It's a funny thing, when people started doing layout on computers, it kind of made them feel a bit sterile. There were two kids out in the Hutt who used to do a zine. I can't remember what it was called now, but it was one of the first I'd ever seen done on a computer and it just didn't feel quite right. At the same time computers were becoming the ubiquitous technology, it was the new thing. Prior to that we'd type things on a typewriter, then go into a photocopy shop and get the type shrunk down or enlarged up to make headlines or whatever. And then you'd cut-and-paste: literally, cut it all up and glue it onto a page and then photocopy it again.

Dave Hegan The first thing I'd do is type out the interviews and other text. I liked the idea of using an old-fashioned typewriter, but I also used a word-processor. You can tell when I've used the typewriter because I've had to cross out all the typos. I used to photocopy pictures that I liked, and that would be the background, and then I'd just cut out text and stick it on, just real cut-and-paste, and then I'd draw a border around it. Looking at it now, it's not too bad actually. It's probably not that fashionable to do that now, and people would probably find that a bit too cluttered. I think it's an easy way of doing it, and it allows you lots of creative freedom to do all sorts of things. People knock up stuff on computers now with all sorts of programs, but back then . . . What you could do with just was a sheet of paper, some glue, maybe a typewriter. If I was to make a zine now, I'd still do it that way actually.

Indira Neville We would all sit around a table drinking and drawing together, and then you'd cut out the originals and tape them however you wanted on the A4 page. They were all pretty much an A4 folded in half, except for the big group ones, which were A3 folded in half. You'd tape it all up, real ratty, and I could never quite figure out the pagination, and so then you'd take it into the copy shop to find that some pages were upside down. [Laughs.]

Ross Gardiner Sometimes with *The State Adversary* we would ring up a photocopier company and say, 'We're interested in buying or renting a machine for our print shop, can we have one on demo?' And then they'd bring it in and explain how it all worked. They'd leave it with us, and we'd print off 500 copies and then go 'Nah, we don't want it . . .' Quite naughty, but fucking funny.

Dave Hegan It was probably a bit chaotic, but I didn't have much of a process for producing the zine. Things just came in and then 'Oh, I've got enough now', and I'd put it out.

Simon Cottle Pretty much anything that anybody sent me would make it in. Lots of poetry, which I thought was cool, even though — if you look at it — some of it's pretty simple. I mean it's young people writing it. I kind of liked the concepts. Somewhere in here I'm simultaneously doing a BA in political science at Victoria University *and* studying American literature, so I was just like 'Good on ya, I think it's pretty gutsy', especially poetry. It's pretty personal. So I'd put that in, put some articles in, lots of articles were sourced from other magazines, UK *Class War* stuff . . . still oblivious to indigenous rebellion, history and culture, though.

83

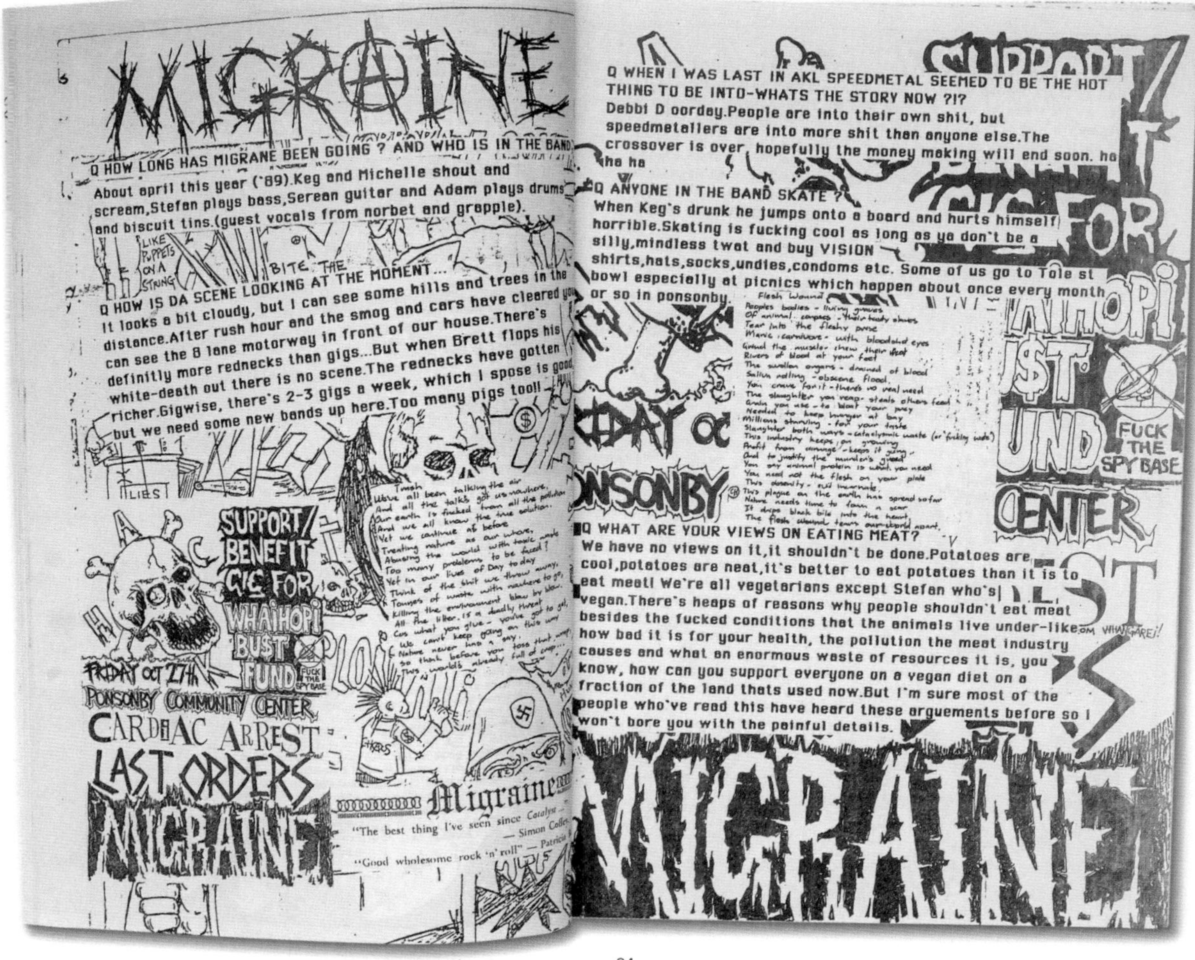
MIGRAINE

Q HOW LONG HAS MIGRANE BEEN GOING ? AND WHO IS IN THE BAND
About april this year ('89).Keg and Michelle shout and scream,Stefan plays bass,Serean guitar and Adam plays drums and biscuit tins.(guest vocals from norbet and grapple).

Q HOW IS DA SCENE LOOKING AT THE MOMENT...
It looks a bit cloudy, but I can see some hills and trees in the distance.After rush hour and the smog and cars have cleared you can see the 8 lane motorway in front of our house.There's definitly more rednecks than gigs...But when Brett flops his white-death out there is no scene.The rednecks have gotten richer.Gigwise, there's 2-3 gigs a week, which I spose is good but we need some new bands up here.Too many pigs too!!

SUPPORT/ BENEFIT GIG FOR WHAIHOPI BUST FUND
FRIDAY OCT 27th
PONSONBY COMMUNITY CENTER
CARDIAC ARREST
LAST ORDERS
MIGRAINE

Migraine
"The best thing I've seen since Catalyst" — Simon Collen
"Good wholesome rock 'n' roll" — Patricia

Q WHEN I WAS LAST IN AKL SPEEDMETAL SEEMED TO BE THE HOT THING TO BE INTO-WHATS THE STORY NOW ?!?
Debbi D oordey.People are into their own shit, but speedmetallers are into more shit than anyone else.The crossover is over, hopefully the money making will end soon. ha ha ha

Q ANYONE IN THE BAND SKATE ?
When Keg's drunk he jumps onto a board and hurts himself horrible.Skating is fucking cool as long as ya don't be a silly,mindless twat and buy VISION shirts,hats,socks,undies,condoms etc. Some of us go to Tole st bowl especially at picnics which happen about once every month or so in ponsonby.

Q WHAT ARE YOUR VIEWS ON EATING MEAT?
We have no views on it,it shouldn't be done.Potatoes are cool,potatoes are neat,it's better to eat potatoes than it is to eat meat! We're all vegetarians except Stefan who's vegan.There's heaps of reasons why people shouldn't eat meat besides the fucked conditions that the animals live under-like how bad it is for your health, the pollution the meat industry causes and what an enormous waste of resources it is, you know, how can you support everyone on a vegan diet on a fraction of the land thats used now.But I'm sure most of the people who've read this have heard these arguements before so I won't bore you with the painful details.

FUCK THE SPY BASE

MIGRAINE

84

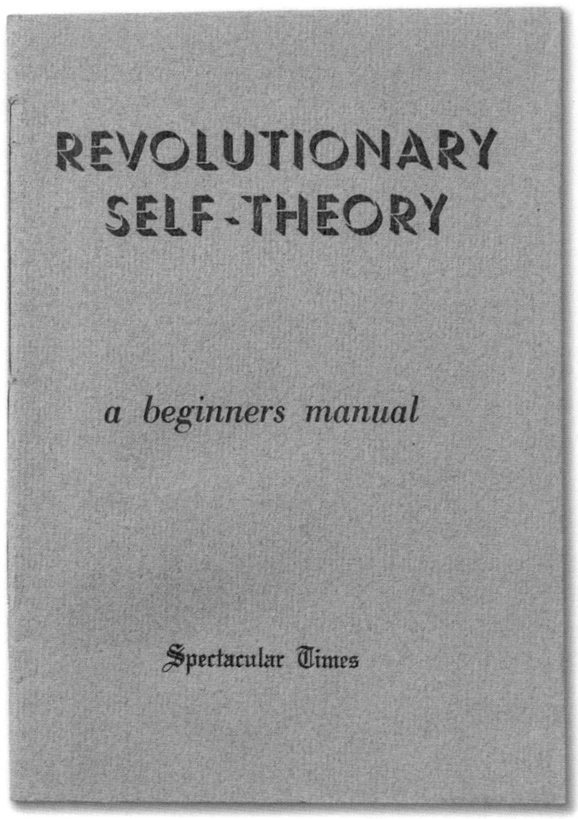

Ross Gardiner I used to do a lot of the printing for the Freedom Shop [in Wellington]. Earlier we'd started Books from the Black Lagoon in Auckland. We'd print little booklets: you'd get something interesting from another country and just do a photocopy run of 10 or 15. Mostly essays or short books, but still self-published. It was another way of getting ideas out there. A lot of it was political, but there were music things as well.

83. *Alien-Nation* spread, Dave Hegan, A4, 1990. Ōtautahi Christchurch.

84. *Revolutionary Self-Theory*, Larry Law, A5, first published in 1975. Reprinted by Bruce Grenville and the Anarchist Alliance of Aotearoa for New Zealand distribution in the 1990s.

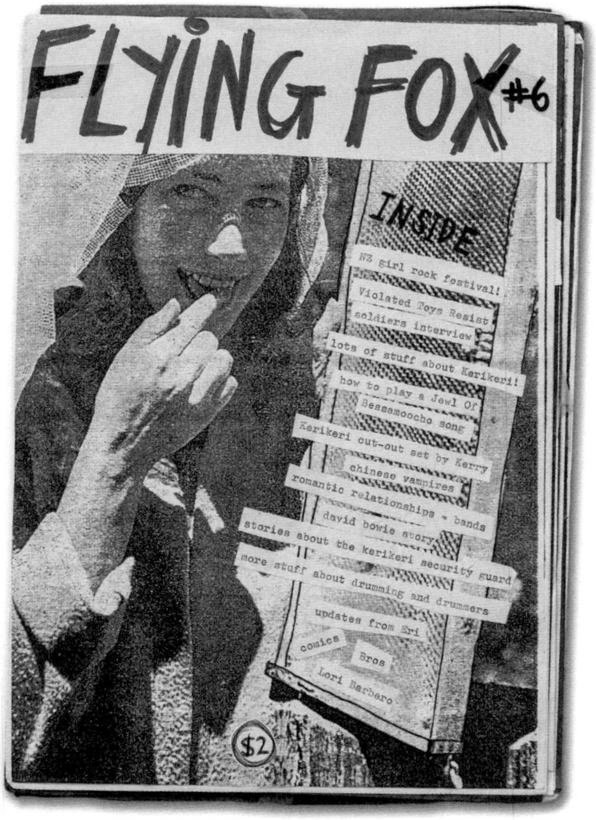

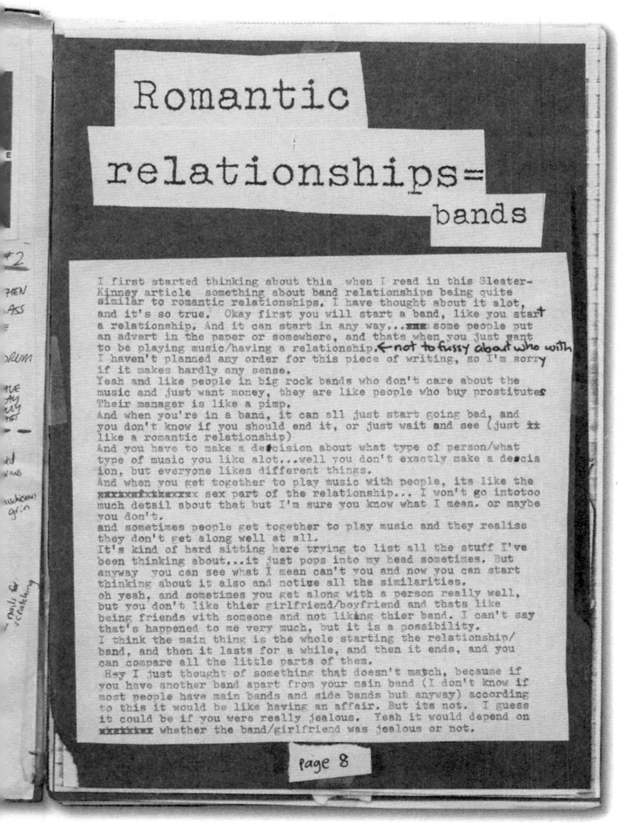

Romantic relationships= bands

I first started thinking about this when I read in this Sleater-Kinney article something about band relationships being quite similar to romantic relationships. I have thought about it alot, and it's so true. Okay first you will start a band, like you start a relationship. And it can start in any way... some people put an advert in the paper or somewhere, and thats when you just want to be playing music/having a relationship. ← not to fussy about who with
I haven't planned any order for this piece of writing, so I'm sorry if it makes hardly any sense.
Yeah and like people in big rock bands who don't care about the music and just want money, they are like people who buy prostitutes Their manager is like a pimp.
And when you're in a band, it can all just start going bad, and you don't know if you should end it, or just wait and see (just like a romantic relationship)
And you have to make a decision about what type of person/what type of music you like alot...well you don't exactly make a decision, but everyone likes different things.
And when you get together to play music with people, its like the sex part of the relationship... I won't go intotoo much detail about that but I'm sure you know what I mean. or maybe you don't.
and sometimes people get together to play music and they realise they don't get along well at all.
It's kind of hard sitting here trying to list all the stuff I've been thinking about...it just pops into my head sometimes. But anyway you can see what I mean can't you and now you can start thinking about it also and notice all the similarities.
oh yeah, and sometimes you get along with a person really well, but you don't like thier girlfriend/boyfriend and thats like being friends with someone and not liking thier band. I can't say that's happened to me very much, but it is a possibility.
I think the main thing is the whole starting the relationship/ band, and then it lasts for a while, and then it ends, and you can compare all the little parts of them.
Hey I just thought of something that doesn't match, because if you have another band apart from your main band (I don't know if most people have main bands and side bands but anyway) according to this it would be like having an affair. But its not. I guess it could be if you were really jealous. Yeah it would depend on whether the band/girlfriend was jealous or not.

page 8

Simon Cottle Copyright wasn't even on the radar. My zines say 'anti-copyright, take whatever bits you like, reproduce it as much as you like'. I'm not sure I still think the same way about plundering someone else's intellectual property. I think accreditation — at the very least — is really important, but I also think that in the arts, whether it's the Royal New Zealand Ballet or some garage band, that's unique labour and those people should be rewarded.

Ross Gardiner Anarcho-political content followed punk music pretty much straight away. Punk music was all about ideas, so whatever causes people were into they'd put that in their zines as well. Animal rights was quite an early one, and peace, anti-militarism, anti-apartheid, anti-nuclear, all those issues that were quite big in the mid-eighties that punks put in their zines. By the late-eighties/early-nineties you started getting zines that were published from outside punk or music. The idea of doing a zine was catching on. I guess partly because photocopying was becoming more common. That made it easier, and the idea of self-publishing was catching on a bit more. All to be ruined by the internet years later.

Indira Neville There was *Plop*, which was the music bit, and there was a zine *Plop It Up*, a take-off of *Rip It Up*. That was a music zine about the Oats people's own bands basically. *Plop* was the music bit and *Oats* was the comic bit, but it was very overlappy.

Beth Dawson Someone can make a fanzine about a thing that they're intensely into for just a few months. It doesn't have to be an interest that will sustain years producing a book. **Liz Mathews** *Flying Fox* included stuff about funny people that I thought were cool. There was one about this old man in Kerikeri who'd always be very beautifully dressed, and we'd do fashion updates on what he had worn each day, that sort of thing.

85. *Flying Fox #6* cover and page (analogue master for photocopying), Liz Mathews, A4, 1997. Tāmaki Makaurau Auckland.

Ross Gardiner That photograph we reprinted in *The State Adversary* is of the top of Cuba Street during the riots in 1932. I was in The Freedom Shop one day and this old guy came in and started talking about this riot that he'd watched from his house. He said, 'I was born in that house over the road'. He was a little kid looking out the window. The way he described it, the police charged and chased everyone, and they were jumping over fences to escape. He said: 'They jumped the fence into this guy's backyard, and he was a home-brewer and he had crates and crates of beer bottles. They all started throwing these beer bottles at the police.'

86

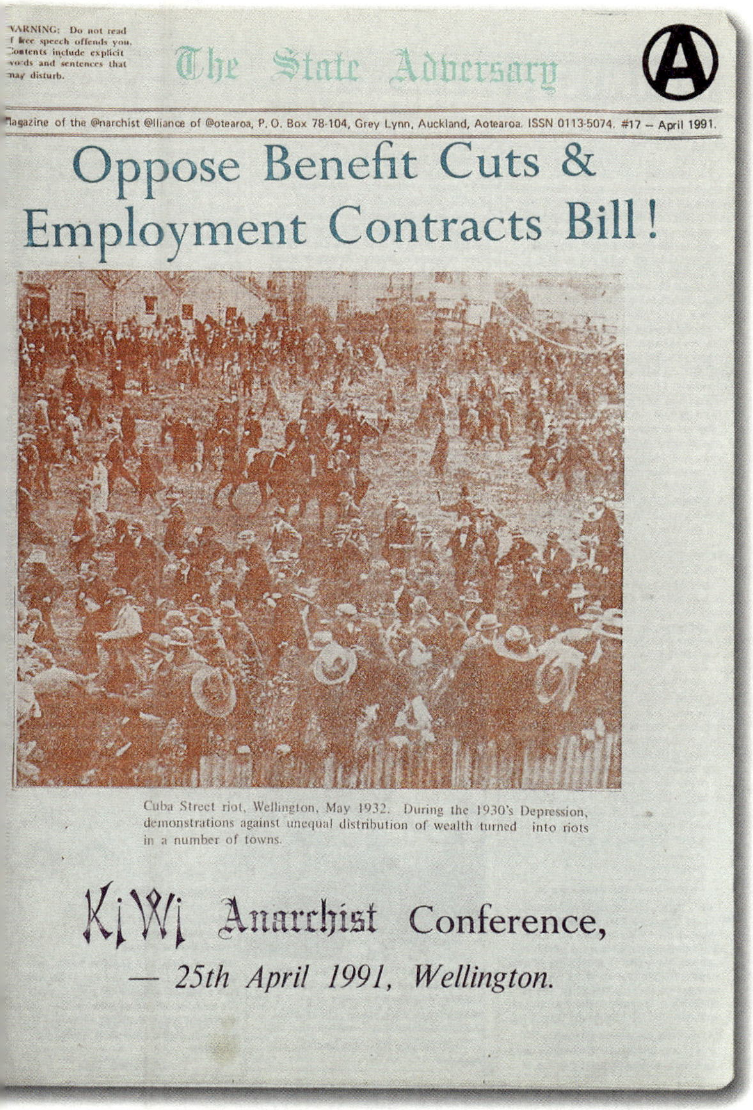

VARNING: Do not read f free speech offends you. Contents include explicit words and sentences that may disturb.

The State Adversary

Magazine of the @narchist @lliance of @otearoa, P. O. Box 78-104, Grey Lynn, Auckland, Aotearoa. ISSN 0113-5074. #17 – April 1991.

Oppose Benefit Cuts & Employment Contracts Bill!

Cuba Street riot, Wellington, May 1932. During the 1930's Depression, demonstrations against unequal distribution of wealth turned into riots in a number of towns.

KiWi Anarchist Conference,

— 25th April 1991, Wellington.

Indira Neville The early issues of *Nice Gravy* were quite full-on. The protagonist was drawn naked and cutting herself up. Mark One Comics sold them in a brown paper bag on the porn shelf. [Laughs.] Certain people thought the protagonist was me; I don't know, maybe she was. At the time I had raging undiagnosed bipolar, so . . . Then I stopped drawing her and I just started drawing me. 'Me' was a bit calmer, the actual me. But that was cool. I loved that it was in a brown paper bag on the porn shelf. None of the other Oats comics achieved that.

Dave White I remember Bruce Russell telling me about the Siltbreeze record label pushing his Dead C stuff in Chicago and saying how he got sent a copy of their zine. He was horrified because it was basically bad porn and record reviews, and he got fucking hassled by Customs for importing child-trafficking material. He had to tell Siltbreeze: 'Don't send me your zine, just cut out the review and send us that.' I guess if you're trying to shock people . . . Perhaps not these days.

Simon Cottle I mean, standing on a stage playing a gig? Frig, that's gutsy stuff. Making zines was a way *I* could contribute . . . Some of it was a bit of a catalogue for the gigs, and a lot of that was a bit of Wellington promotion, like we've got a happening scene here. Things were at their peak. We'd have two gigs on a Friday night. You had to pick between one of the two, and two on a Saturday night . . . So you had four gigs and you reluctantly had to pick two. There was definitely a bit of Wellington promotion going on in the zine, and in terms of the music and the interviews it was like 99 per cent Kiwi, which was part of *my* punk ethos, that it shouldn't be about celebrating overseas bands and seeing them as bigger and better and brighter. That's not the punk ethos. The punk ethos is your mates have picked up some instruments and are gonna give it a go.

86. *The State Adversary* #17, quarterly zine by the Anarchist Alliance of Aotearoa. Edited and typeset by Bruce Grenville and Ross Gardiner, A4, 1991.Tāmaki Makaurau Auckland.

Andrew Schmidt Nick Cain was a very dry and distant sort of chap, but *Opprobrium* and *de/ create* — the two fanzines he was involved with — were real high points, I thought. They set a real tone. I'm not gonna say I actually thought the tone was that good, I thought it was a little bit too exclusive and too passive-aggressive, but the quality of the writing and layout and the spread of coverage was impressive. He's an interesting part of the history. That really came out of that whole free-noise thing, where music was sort of moving a little bit away from the alternative punk movement and was trying to create a different identity. You've got guys like Bruce Russell, who's got a master's degree, and Mike Morley, who lectures in art at Otago Polytech. That's another different sort of slant; I'm more rugby club . . . mainstream sort of thing. I fall back on that anyway.

Dave White The very first *Valve* came out with a 7-inch record called *The Valve Thing* and then the next one had a 12-inch.

David Merritt Caroline McCaw and a guy called Danny Butt and a couple of other people went from Dunedin to Wellington for the summer. We were part of the Fringe Festival or the Arts Festival. They gave us a couple of grand and we were able to put out four weekly issues of *@Punnet*.

87

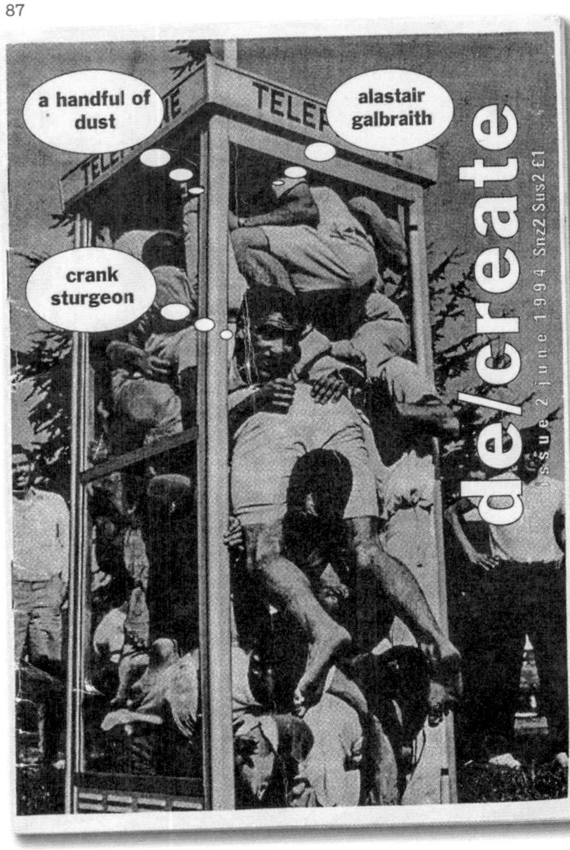

87. *de/create #2*, edited by Nick Cain, A5, 1994. Te Awa Kairangi ki Tai Lower Hutt.

88. Untitled cover and spread from zine attributed to Crushed Honey Press, edited by Giovanni Intra, A5, 1991. Tāmaki Makaurau Auckland.

88

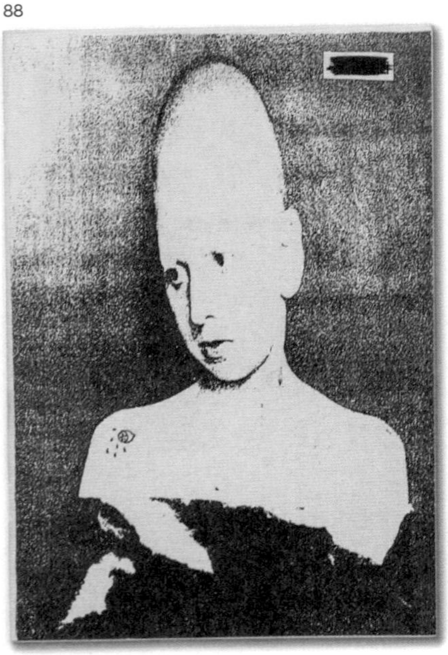

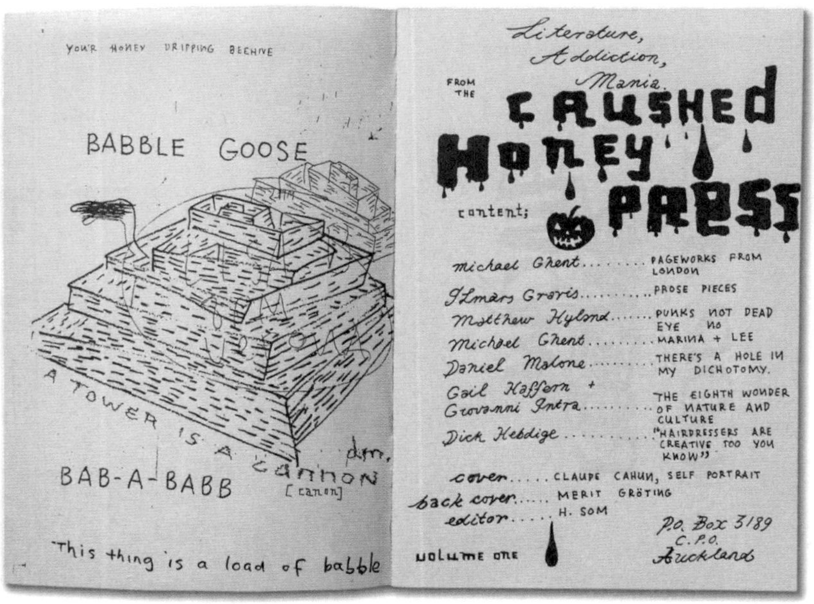

89

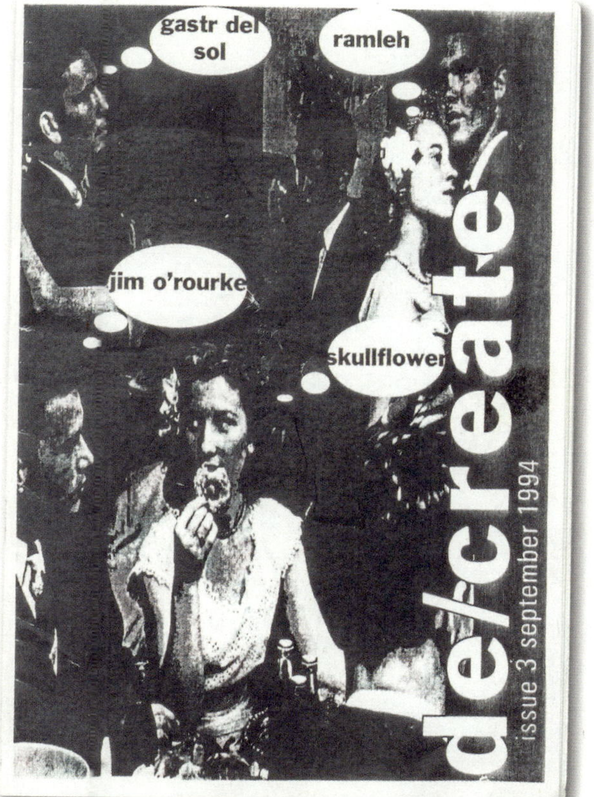

89. *de/create* #3, edited by Nick Cain, A5, 1994. Te Awa Kairangi ki Tai Lower Hutt.

90

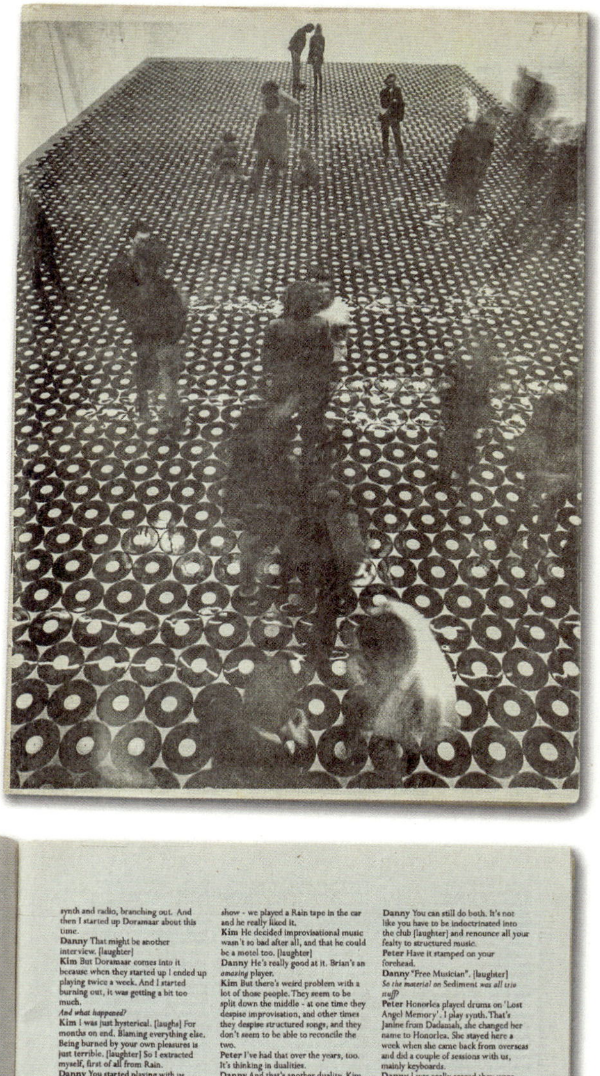

90. *Opprobrium* #3 cover and spread, edited by Nick Cain, 275 × 198mm, 1996. Ōtautahi Christchurch. A substantial zine of 135 pages.

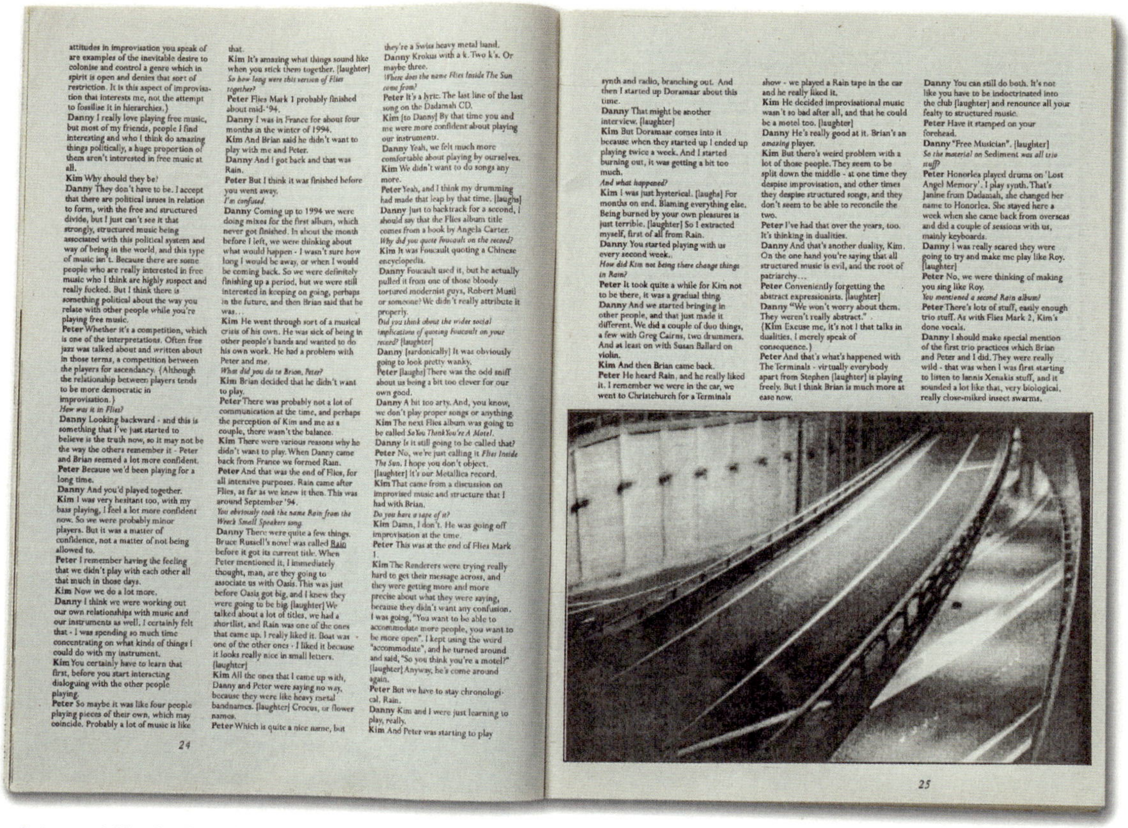

attitudes in improvisation you speak of are examples of the inevitable desire to colonise and control a genre which in spirit is open and denies that sort of restriction. It is this aspect of improvisation that interests me, not the attempt to fossilise it in hierarchies.)

Danny I really love playing free music, but most of my friends, people I find interesting and who I think do amazing things politically, a huge proportion of them aren't interested in free music at all.

Kim Why should they be?

Danny They don't have to be. I accept that there are political issues in relation to form, with the free and structured divide, but I just can't see it that strongly, structured music being associated with this political system and way of being in the world, and this type of music isn't. Because there are some people who are really interested in free music who I think are highly suspect and really fucked. But I think there is something political about the way you relate with other people while you're playing free music.

Peter Whether it's a competition, which is one of the interpretations. Often free jazz was talked about and written about in those terms, a competition between the players for ascendancy. (Although the relationship between players tends to be more democratic in improvisation.)

How was it in Flies?

Danny Looking backward - and this is something that I've just started to believe is the truth now, so it may not be the way the others remember it - Peter and Brian seemed a lot more confident.

Peter Because we'd been playing for a long time.

Danny And you'd played together.

Kim I was very hesitant too, with my bass playing. I feel a lot more confident now. So we were probably minor players. But it was a matter of confidence, not a matter of not being allowed to.

Peter I remember having the feeling that we didn't play with each other all that much in those days.

Kim Now we do a lot more.

Danny I think we were working out our own relationships with music and our instruments as well. I certainly felt that - I was spending so much time concentrating on what kinds of things I could do with my instrument.

Kim You certainly have to learn that first, before you start interacting dialoguing with the other people playing.

Peter So maybe it was like four people playing pieces of their own, which may coincide. Probably a lot of music is like that.

Kim It's amazing what things sound like when you stick them together. [laughter]

So how long were this version of Flies together?

Peter Flies Mark 1 probably finished about mid-'94.

Danny I was in France for about four months in the winter of 1994.

Kim And Brian said he didn't want to play with me and Peter.

Danny And I got back and that was Rain.

Peter But I think it was finished before you went away.

I'm confused.

Danny Coming up to 1994 we were doing mixes for the first album, which never got finished. In about the month before I left, we were thinking about what would happen - I wasn't sure how long I would be away, or when I would be coming back. So we were definitely finishing up a period, but we were still interested in keeping on going, perhaps in the future, and then Brian said that he was…

Kim He went through sort of a musical crisis of his own. He was sick of being in other people's bands and wanted to do his own work. He had a problem with Peter and me.

What did you do to Brian, Peter?

Kim Brian decided that he didn't want to play.

Peter There was probably not a lot of communication at the time, and perhaps the perception of Kim and me as a couple, there wasn't the balance.

Kim There were various reasons why he didn't want to play. When Danny came back from France we formed Rain.

Peter And that was the end of Flies, for all intensive purposes. Rain came after Flies, as far as we knew it then. This was around September '94.

You obviously took the name Rain from the Wreck Small Speakers song.

Danny There were quite a few things. Bruce Russell's novel was called Rain before it got its current title. When Peter mentioned it, I immediately thought, man, are they going to associate us with Oasis. This was just before Oasis got big, and I knew they were going to be big [laughter] We talked about a lot of titles, we had a shortlist, and Rain was one of the ones that came up. I really liked it. Boat was one of the other ones - I liked it because it looks really nice in small letters. [laughter]

Kim All the ones that I came up with, Danny and Peter were saying no way, because they were like heavy metal bandnames. [laughter] Crocus, or flower names.

Peter Which is quite a nice name, but they're a Swiss heavy metal band.

Danny Krokus with a k. Two k's. Or maybe three.

Where does the name Flies Inside The Sun come from?

Peter It's a lyric. The last line of the last song on the Dadamah CD.

Kim [to Danny] By that time you and me were more confident about playing our instruments.

Danny Yeah, we felt much more comfortable about playing by ourselves.

Kim We didn't want to do songs any more.

Peter Yeah, and I think my drumming had made that leap by that time. [laughs]

Danny Just to backtrack for a second, I should say that the Flies album title comes from a book by Angela Carter.

Why did you quote Foucault on the record?

Kim It was Foucault quoting a Chinese encyclopedia.

Danny Foucault used it, but he actually pulled it from one of those bloody tortured modernist guys, Robert Musil or someone? We didn't really attribute it properly.

Did you think about the wider social implications of quoting Foucault on your record? [laughter]

Danny [sardonically] It was obviously going to look pretty wanky.

Peter [laughs] There was the odd sniff about us being a bit too clever for our own good.

Danny A bit too arty. And, you know, we don't play proper songs or anything.

Kim The next Flies album was going to be called *So You Think You're A Motel*.

Danny Is it still going to be called that?

Peter No, we're just calling it *Flies Inside The Sun*. I hope you don't object. [laughter] It's our Metallica record.

Kim That came from a discussion on improvised music and structure that I had with Brian.

Do you have a tape of it?

Kim Damn, I don't. He was going off improvisation at the time.

Peter This was at the end of Flies Mark 1.

Kim The Renderers were trying really hard to get their message across, and they were getting more and more precise about what they were saying, because they didn't want any confusion. I was going, "You want to be able to accommodate more people, you want to be more open". I kept using the word "accommodate", and he turned around and said, "So you think you're a motel?" [laughter] Anyway, he's come around again.

Peter But we have to stay chronological, Rain.

Danny Kim and I were just learning to play, really.

Kim And Peter was starting to play

24

synth and radio, branching out. And then I started up Doramaar about this time.

Danny That might be another interview. [laughter]

Kim But Doramaar comes into it because when they started up I ended up playing twice a week. And I started burning out, it was getting a bit too much.

And what happened?

Kim I was just hysterical. [laughs] For months on end. Blaming everything else. Being burned by your own pleasures is just terrible. [laughter] So I extracted myself, first of all from Rain.

Danny You started playing with us every second week.

How did Kim not being there change things in Rain?

Peter It took quite a while for Kim not to be there, it was a gradual thing.

Danny And we started bringing in other people, and that just made it different. We did a couple of duo things, a few with Greg Cairns, two drummers. And at least on with Susan Ballard on violin.

Kim And then Brian came back.

Peter He heard Rain, and he really liked it. I remember we were in the car, we went to Christchurch for a Terminals show - we played a Rain tape in the car and he really liked it.

Kim He decided improvisational music wasn't so bad after all, and that he could be a motel too. [laughter]

Danny He's really good at it. Brian's an *amazing* player.

Kim But there's weird problem with a lot of those people. They seem to be split down the middle - at one time they despise improvisation, and other times they despise structured songs, and they don't seem to be able to reconcile the two.

Peter I've had that over the years, too. It's thinking in dualities.

Danny And that's another duality, Kim. On the one hand you're saying that all structured music is evil, and the root of patriarchy…

Peter Conveniently forgetting the abstract expressionists. [laughter]

Danny "We won't worry about them. They weren't really abstract."

(**Kim** Excuse me, it's not I that talks in dualities. I merely speak of consequence.)

Peter And that's what's happened with The Terminals - virtually everybody apart from Stephen [laughter] is playing freely. But I think Brian is much more at ease now.

Danny You can still do both. It's not like you have to be indoctrinated into the club [laughter] and renounce all your fealty to structured music.

Peter Have it stamped on your forehead.

Danny "Free Musician". [laughter]

So the material on Sediment *was all trio stuff?*

Peter Honorlea played drums on 'Lost Angel Memory'. I play synth. That's Janine from Dadamah, she changed her name to Honorlea. She stayed here a week when she came back from overseas and did a couple of sessions with us, mainly keyboards.

Danny I was really scared they were going to try and make me play like Roy. [laughter]

Peter No, we were thinking of making you sing like Roy.

You mentioned a second Rain album?

Peter There's lots of stuff, easily enough trio stuff. As with Flies Mark 2, Kim's done vocals.

Danny I should make special mention of the first trio practices which Brian and Peter and I did. They were really wild - that was when I was first starting to listen to Iannis Xenakis stuff, and it sounded a lot like that, very biological, really close-miked insect swarms.

25

91

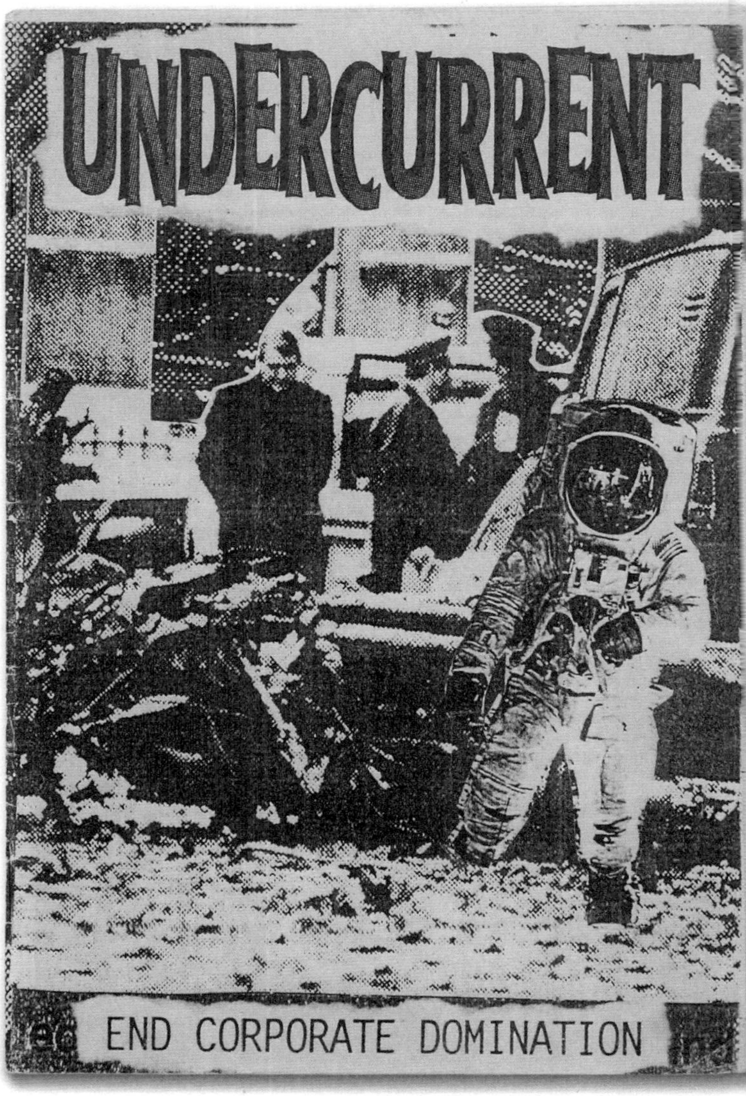

Dave White I bought my own photocopier. It was just one of those one-page-at-a-time things, and I bought an old typewriter. My first wife was a typing teacher and she taught me how to touch-type, which is awesome because I can *clackety-clack* really fast. Those old typewriter keys are a strain to push down. Lucky I'm also a piano player so I have strong fingers. I started off with all these double-page spreads from like 20 or 25 bands. That's the good thing about CDs: I think you can squash about 29 tracks onto a CD. So that was half the magazine. Then there were people I wanted to interview. I did crazy things, like when Jello Biafra performed spoken word in Wellington, I had a Walkman and I recorded his whole show. It was like three hours long or something! I typed it all out word-for-word. It must've taken me fucking days.

Andrew Schmidt I didn't have much confidence right up until the point I got accepted into journalism school, which I did on the back of one of those *Ha Ha Ha* zines. I was lucky because Jim Tully at University of Canterbury was a sixties person, a counterculture person — that's what he told me pretty much straight away: 'I'm a sixties person' — and he was used to the countercultural media. So having somebody producing their own media from a community outside the mainstream wasn't alien to him. That was a little bit of luck because he was not typical, but he was also right, and he was validated not just by my success as a writer but by a guy called Andrew Heal, who created a fanzine called *Whole Weird World* out of Nelson. That was a Flying Nun fanzine. Andrew went on to be the deputy editor of *Metro* in later years. So we sort of developed this pathway from fanzines through into the mainstream media that wasn't there before. Richard Langston, of course, also did the same thing, and we were aware of Richard, but Richard started as a journalist, then became a fanzine writer.

Features were generally things you wrote on your own time. That's what we were told when we entered the profession: 'You write this on your own time. This is not what they want. They want the news. That's what people buy the newspapers for.' That changed over time, pretty quickly actually. Originally the *New Zealand Herald* in Auckland said, 'You have to work as a reporter for *nine* years before you become a feature writer', and I thought 'Fuck that'. I said 'I'm *gonna* be a feature writer.' Nine years doing reportage doesn't make you a feature writer. Writing features makes you a feature writer. Reading lots, experiencing lots, being honest enough to be subjective and saying 'I am actually here, I am influencing what's going on, it's running through my mind, so I'm part of it . . .' It took a while to get to that point, but they did get there. That was all the influence of New Journalism coming through New Zealand media. It took a little bit of time to filter through, I think.

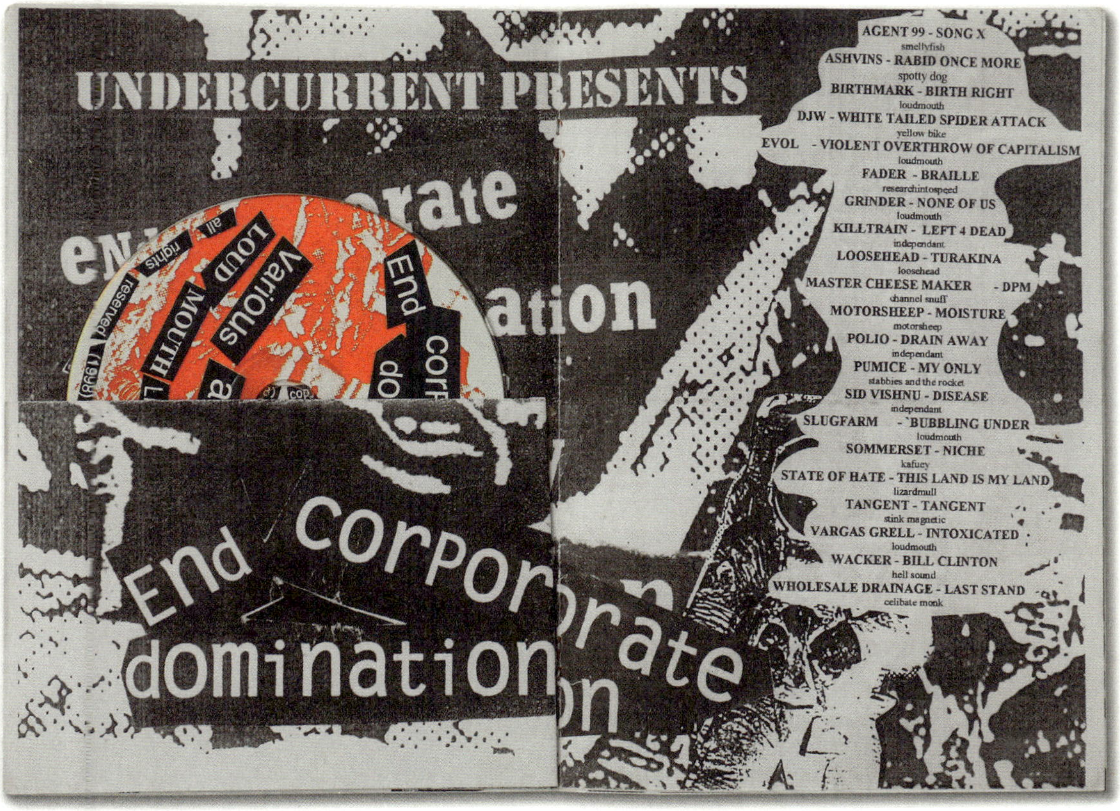

92

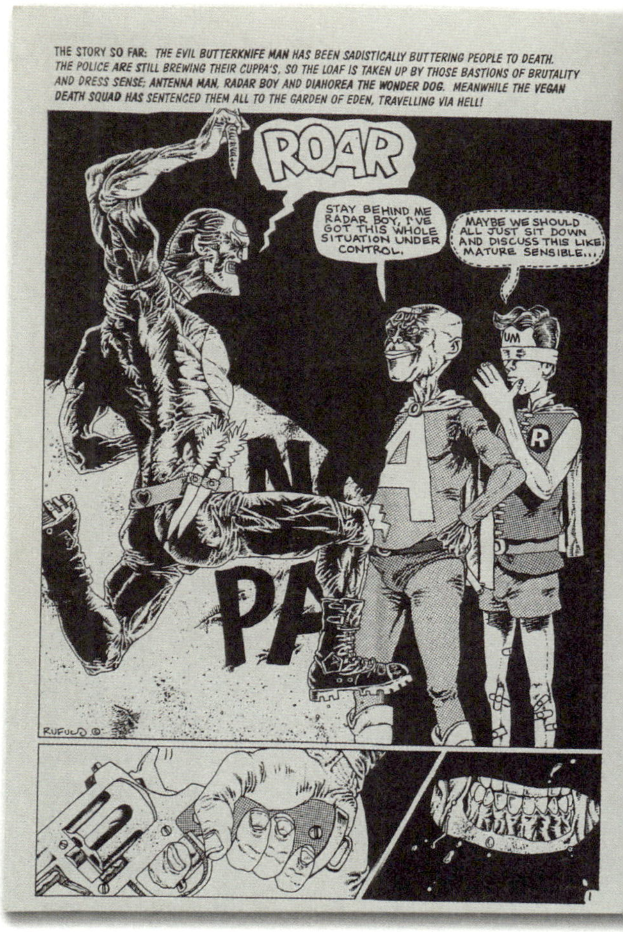

91. *Undercurrent* cover and spread (with CD), edited by Jarrod Love, A5, 1998. Te Papaioea Palmerston North.

92. *Pistake* #11, page by Rufus Dayglo, edited by David Tulloch, A5, 1994. Te Whanganui-a-Tara Wellington.

Andrew Stephens The spelling and grammar in other zines did always shock me. Didn't you read that after you'd written it, for god's sake?

Ross Gardiner Yeah yeah, I remember Rufus Dayglo was a massive *Tank Girl* fan, and then he was making his own comics, which not many people were doing back then in the early nineties. Now he draws for *Tank Girl*. Sort of living the dream.

93

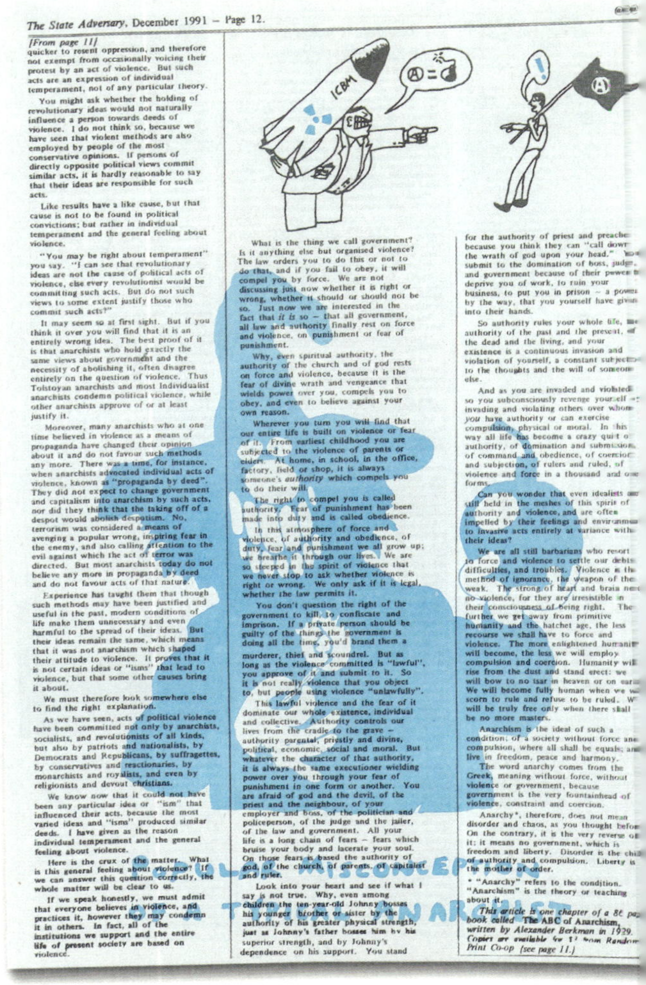

The State Adversary, December 1991 – Page 12.

[From page 11]
quicker to resent oppression, and therefore not exempt from occasionally voicing their protest by an act of violence. But such acts are an expression of individual temperament, not of any particular theory.

You might ask whether the holding of revolutionary ideas would not naturally influence a person towards deeds of violence. I do not think so, because we have seen that violent methods are also employed by people of the most conservative opinions. If persons of directly opposite political views commit similar acts, it is hardly reasonable to say that their ideas are responsible for such acts.

Like results have a like cause, but that cause is not to be found in political convictions; but rather in individual temperament and the general feeling about violence.

"You may be right about temperament" you say. "I can see that revolutionary ideas are not the cause of political acts of violence, else every revolutionist would be committing such acts. But do not such views to some extent justify those who commit such acts?"

It may seem so at first sight. But if you think it over you will find that it is an entirely wrong idea. The best proof of it is that anarchists who hold exactly the same views about government and the necessity of abolishing it, often disagree entirely on the question of violence. Thus Tolstoyan anarchists and most Individualist anarchists condemn political violence, while other anarchists approve of or at least justify it.

Moreover, many anarchists who at one time believed in violence as a means of propaganda have changed their opinion about it and do not favour such methods any more. There was a time, for instance, when anarchists advocated individual acts of violence, known as "propaganda by deed". They did not expect to change government and capitalism into anarchism by such acts, nor did they think that the taking off of a despot would abolish despotism. No, terrorism was considered a means of avenging a popular wrong, inspiring fear in the enemy, and also calling attention to the evil against which the act of terror was directed. But most anarchists today do not believe any more in propaganda by deed and do not favour acts of that nature.

Experience has taught them that though such methods may have been justified and useful in the past, modern conditions of life make them unnecessary and even harmful to the spread of their ideas. But their ideas remain the same, which means that it was not anarchism which shaped their attitude to violence. It proves that it is not certain ideas or "isms" that lead to violence, but that some other causes bring it about.

We must therefore look somewhere else to find the right explanation.

As we have seen, acts of political violence have been committed not only by anarchists, socialists, and revolutionists of all kinds, but also by patriots and nationalists, by Democrats and Republicans, by suffragettes, by conservatives and reactionaries, by monarchists and royalists, and even by religionists and devout christians.

We know now that it could not have been any particular idea or "ism" that influenced their acts, because the most varied ideas and "isms" produced similar deeds. I have given as the reason individual temperament and the general feeling about violence.

Here is the crux of the matter. What is this general feeling about violence? If we can answer this question correctly, the whole matter will be clear to us.

If we speak honestly, we must admit that everyone believes in violence, and practices it, however they may condemn it in others. In fact, all of the institutions we support and the entire life of present society are based on violence.

What is the thing we call government? Is it anything else but organised violence? The law orders you to do this or not to do that, and if you fail to obey, it will compel you by force. We are not discussing just now whether it is right or wrong, whether it should or should not be so. Just now we are interested in the fact that *it is* so – that all government, all law and authority finally rest on force and violence, on punishment or fear of punishment.

Why, even spiritual authority, the authority of the church and of god rests on force and violence, because it is the fear of divine wrath and vengeance that wields power over you, compels you to obey, and even to believe against your own reason.

Wherever you turn you will find that our entire life is built on violence or fear of it. From earliest childhood you are subjected to the violence of parents or elders. At home, in school, in the office, factory, field or shop, it is always someone's *authority* which compels you to do their will.

The right to compel you is called authority. Fear of punishment has been made into duty and is called obedience.

In this atmosphere of force and violence, of authority and obedience, of duty, fear and punishment we all grow up; we breathe it through our lives. We are so steeped in the spirit of violence that we never stop to ask whether violence is right or wrong. We only ask if it is legal, whether the law permits it.

You don't question the right of the government to kill, to confiscate and imprison. If a private person should be guilty of the things the government is doing all the time, you'd brand them a murderer, thief and scoundrel. But as long as the violence committed is "lawful", you approve of it and submit to it. So it is not really violence that you object to, but people using violence "unlawfully".

This lawful violence and the fear of it dominate our whole existence, individual and collective. Authority controls our lives from the cradle to the grave – authority parental, priestly and divine, political, economic, social and moral. But whatever the character of that authority, it is always the same executioner wielding power over you through your fear of punishment in one form or another. You are afraid of god and the devil, of the priest and the neighbour, of your employer and boss, of the politician and policeperson, of the judge and the jailer, of the law and government. All your life is a long chain of fears – fears which bruise your body and lacerate your soul. On those fears is based the authority of god, of the church, of parents, of capitalist and ruler.

Look into your heart and see if what I say is not true. Why, even among children the ten-year-old Johnny bosses his younger brother or sister by the authority of his greater physical strength, just as Johnny's father bosses him by his superior strength, and by Johnny's dependence on his support. You stand for the authority of priest and preacher because you think they can "call down the wrath of god upon your head." You submit to the domination of boss, judge, and government because of their power to deprive you of work, to ruin your business, to put you in prison – a power by the way, that you yourself have given into their hands.

So authority rules your whole life, the authority of the past and the present, of the dead and the living, and your existence is a continuous invasion and violation of yourself, a constant subjection to the thoughts and the will of someone else.

And as you are invaded and violated, so you subconsciously revenge yourself by invading and violating others over whom *you* have authority or can exercise compulsion, physical or moral. In this way all life has become a crazy quilt of authority, of domination and submission, of command and obedience, of coercion and subjection, of rulers and ruled, of violence and force in a thousand and one forms.

Can you wonder that even idealists are still held in the meshes of this spirit of authority and violence, and are often impelled by their feelings and environment to invasive acts entirely at variance with their ideas?

We are all still barbarians who resort to force and violence to settle our debts, difficulties, and troubles. Violence is the method of ignorance, the weapon of the weak. The strong of heart and brain need no violence, for they are irresistible in their consciousness of being right. The further we get away from primitive humanity and the hatchet age, the less recourse we shall have to force and violence. The more enlightened humanity will become, the less we will employ compulsion and coercion. Humanity will rise from the dust and stand erect: we will bow to no tsar in heaven or on earth. We will become fully human when we will scorn to rule and refuse to be ruled. We will be truly free only when there shall be no more masters.

Anarchism is the ideal of such a condition; of a society without force and compulsion, where all shall be equals, and live in freedom, peace and harmony.

The word anarchy comes from the Greek, meaning without force, without violence or government, because government is the very fountainhead of violence, constraint and coercion.

Anarchy*, therefore, does not mean disorder and chaos, as you thought before. On the contrary, it is the very reverse of it; it means no government, which is freedom and liberty. Disorder is the child of authority and compulsion. Liberty is the mother of order.

* "Anarchy" refers to the condition. "Anarchism" is the theory or teaching about it.

This article is one chapter of a 86 page book called **The ABC of Anarchism**, *written by Alexander Berkman in 1929. Copies are available for $1 from Random Print Co-op (see page 11.)*

Indira Neville You don't get good at it unless you train yourself, so it's a skill that can be developed. I believed with all my heart that if I really wanted to apply myself, I could learn to draw like the 'competent boy comics'. In fact, I kind of can if I really feel like it. I don't believe that any one of them could learn how to draw like me. I don't believe it. Even if they let themselves, I don't think they could. Actually, it was really funny, we used to make these little Oats catalogues, which had pictures of all the comics, and I remember Glen making one and trying to replicate my style for one of the ads. Just couldn't do it. Just *couldn't* do it. Whereas I went straight in and replicated everyone else's style relatively easily.

Ross Gardiner Having a typewriter and learning to keep the keys clean, so that when you type the 'o', for example, it wasn't just a black dot; making sure all the raised type didn't get clogged up with ink. Learning how wide to type so you could make some sort of rough column on the page . . . Finding interesting little graphics to put in the background that you could cut-and-paste texts over. Not doing it right up to the edge of the page, so that when you photocopied, it didn't fade out on the edges. All those sorts of things.

Tony Renouf I already knew about layout and stuff. Working on *Treacle* tightened up my use of crop-marks and other bits and pieces. What else did I learn? A little bit about organising people and hassling the fuck out of them to meet deadlines.

Bruce Grenville I wasn't self-taught. My high-school teacher taught me on the weekends. He had an Adana as well. He was a fan of printing, but also did it for money. He'd do things like wedding invitations, elegant gold embossing and all that sort of thing. So I learnt all the cool stuff.

David Tulloch SMUT had really good lyrics. I actually typeset their lyrics for a cassette release because I was working at a desktop-publishing company at the time. They were trying to make me wear a tie, so I'm sure SMUT was a bit of a culture clash. But the company actually liked it because a cassette sleeve was something they'd never done before, so I got permission and the company let us run it cheap.

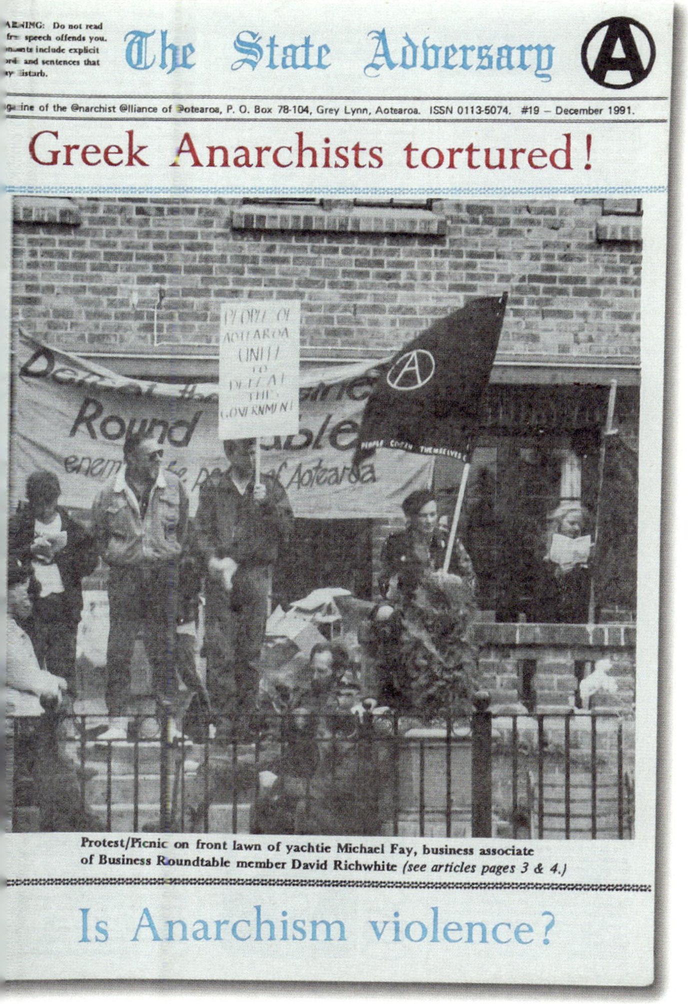

NING: Do not read
speech offends you.
include explicit
and sentences that
istarb.

The State Adversary

ine of the @narchist @lliance of otearoa, P. O. Box 78-104, Grey Lynn, Aotearoa. ISSN 0113-5074. #19 – December 1991.

Greek Anarchists tortured!

Protest/Picnic on front lawn of yachtie Michael Fay, business associate of Business Roundtable member David Richwhite *(see articles pages 3 & 4.)*

Is Anarchism violence?

Liz Mathews When I was younger I just didn't have a computer. It also didn't occur to me to use a computer. My brother was a computer guy. I was like 'Oh, that's geeky stuff.' Now I wish I had some computer skills. Whenever I got on a computer and tried to do anything I would get stressed out and my back would just get really sore from the posture and the stress; not having any control over it, like anything could happen at any time. You never know what that computer might do. **Beth Dawson** You know what the scissors are gonna do.

David Merritt I lucked into it very early. I saw the first issue of *Wired* magazine at the Otago University Book Shop in 1993 and I thought 'Fucking hell, look at this: it's quite big, thick, glossy, full of ads, full of real interesting stories.' I thought 'This is the future, I can tell this is the future', and by then I had an email address, and I was using Usenet. There was no web, that was a few years away yet, but you could tell that the whole cultural imperative of America was behind this thing called the internet and boy oh boy was it gonna blossom. I had no cynicism to start with, the cynicism came later.

Moira Clunie I was working for an internet service provider and was friends with all the network engineers who were keeping an eye on the Y2K stuff. I don't remember them particularly freaking out, but I remember that fear of a global computing collapse being a general concern.

Moira Clunie 1996 was my last year at high school. Towards the end of my time there the school got the internet, but that was like a new thing and you had to book time on a computer in the library to go on the internet, and then you may or may not be able to find anything about your topic. You were still also looking at Microsoft Encarta CD-ROMs to find out information, and books of course; old technology. It was all becoming more popular, but when I first started making webpages I definitely didn't have the sense that anybody in the world could read them, just other people as nerdy as me about the potential of this technology.

David Merritt I was worse than that: I became a cultural theorist. My master's at AUT was about the cultural theory of open-source operating systems and the geeks that wrote it. I went right back to valve radios and Marconi, and I followed that progression all the way through to transistors, the military industrial complex, World War II, DARPA, APRONET, all those geeks that wrote all that hardware and software. The Apollo moon landings, for example: fucking amazing.

93. *The State Adversary* #19 front and back covers, edited and typeset by Bruce Grenville and Ross Gardiner, A4, 1991. Tāmaki Makaurau Auckland.

Moira Clunie Both zines and websites appeal as forms of quick publishing, under your own control; no publisher or gatekeeper, not too much costly additional stuff that you have to pay for. At least that was the promise of the internet before the billionaires. You can still publish online away from the noise of advertising, but that's a pretty nerdy pursuit that still requires some technical know-how. I never saw zines as less relevant because the internet started to take over. I learned about zines and got involved in organising around zines in parallel with being online. In terms of learning what a zine was, that was through message boards, mailing lists and websites, looking at other zine distros overseas who had their own webpages. Learning about zines and getting the word out about zines was also happening online. It wasn't ever a completely manual process for me.

Kerry Ann Lee You'd be writing some stuff on a typewriter or early desktop-publishing program and get it printed out on a home printer. Cutting it up and laying it out with some photocopies from some shitty magazines that you'd got from the library, or some junk mail that arrived in the mailbox and photos that you collect in a shoebox that you've saved for a time. You're doing your layout and you're like 'Oh, that looks nice, it looks pretty', and then, 'Okay, that's a page; next page . . .'

Then it comes time to paginate, so you do that weird pagination game where you make a little paper dummy — I still do that.

David Tulloch There were no struggles with pagination as I worked at a desktop-publishing company at the time, so that was my job. We would gather together at the flat Rufus [Dayglo] and Simon [Morse] had above the comics shop — VMS — and we'd sit there and fold them all, put them all together, staple them in a sort of production line, each one passing them down the line. And then we did stupid things, like on one cover Simon had drawn we had to individually cut and adhere this reflective sticky stuff to Straitjacket Ninja's visor.

David Merritt You could liken Xpressway to zine production in a way, or at least Bruce Russell's methodology. When I met him, he was just down the road in Port Chalmers and he had a hallway . . . He and Alastair Galbraith and Peter Jefferies had bought 10 duplicating cassette machines, and he had them lined up down the hall. He'd worked out [that if] he put a blank cassette in here and pressed 'copy', by the time he'd got to the tenth one and put a cassette in and pressed 'copy' the first one was ready to turn over. Around the clock.

David Tulloch We'd get together and compile about 50 copies of the comic in a sitting. We did reprint some of them, but I honestly have no recollection of how many we ended up printing of each issue. I haven't got it written down anywhere.

I was receiving photocopies of original comic art in the mail. If Simon and Rufus didn't think it was good enough it would end up either not being used or becoming a mini-comic. We put an A6 mini-comic inside some of the issues because we ended up getting too much stuff. We were churning them out, but we still got more stuff than we could print.

Marty [Martin Emond] got a bit pissed off with me for misspelling his name in issue 10. I don't blame him, but we were putting them out so fast, it was ridiculous. We were trying to churn them out, we really were.

94. *Pistake #12*, cover by Rufus Dayglo, edited by David Tulloch, A5, 1994. Te Whanganui-a-Tara Wellington.

95. *Treacle #2*, edited and cover by Tony Renouf, A4, 1993. Ōtepoti Dunedin.

94

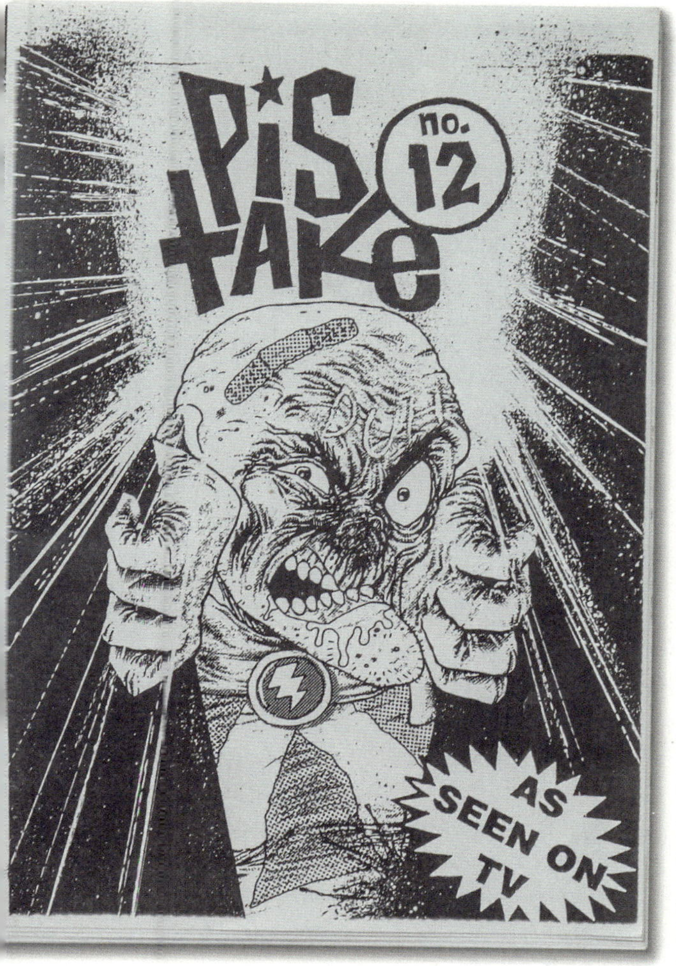

95

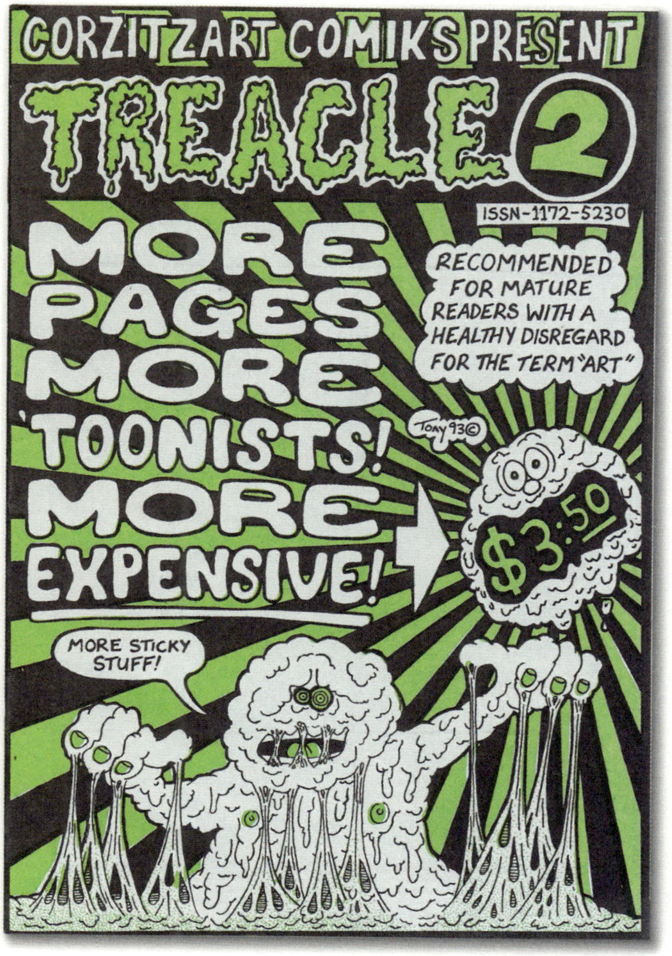

Tony Renouf By the time I got to *Treacle* I'd been involved in some small-press stuff and I used to work in the bindery, so I'd done hand collation. The guys in the art department showed me what to do. If you fold the pieces of paper up, then write the page numbers across the top, when it's unfolded you know which are the facing pages. Your even pages are your leading pages (apart from the cover, which is number one). I don't think I got it 100 per cent right all the time, but I had the knowledge. There were guys who'd done typography as their trade. So I'd go 'Does this look right to you?' I'd be making bromides because I'd already done bromide work at Budget Print. I worked with a guy who was a journeyman typesetter. Have you ever watched guys setting type? They'll chat to you while they're doing it, and they'll glance at the copy and then they'll go back to chatting to you as their hands are darting at a tray of lead letters. I was really lucky: without actually being a tradesman I got to work in lots of different parts of the printing industry. I did operate a small Heidelberg Platen, but that was set up for me so it was just stop/start. It wasn't anything about applying ink or anything like that. I was really lucky that I got down here and had the knowledge within arm's reach. I'd ask, 'How do I do this?' and somebody would show me, or I'd say, 'Here's a dozen of piss, can I have 500 copies?'

Bruce Grenville This is a typecase. There's the map of it. You see all the capitals are all here, the rest of it's all there, and like a QWERTY keyboard, every printer is totally familiar with that. The 'e's are always there and 'a's are always there, so we can actually typeset quite quickly because we know where they all are. Hold that letter in your hand. Now, notice it's got a little nick on one end of it? That's to show you that's the bottom because if you get a letter like a capital 'O' it could be the same either way, so it's important to know which is the bottom, otherwise your line's going along and then suddenly — wobble. Everything is the same height. It's .918 of an inch, which might seem an odd size but it's the size they standardised everything to. Once you've set it all up and printed, then you've got to clean it and put everything back.

96

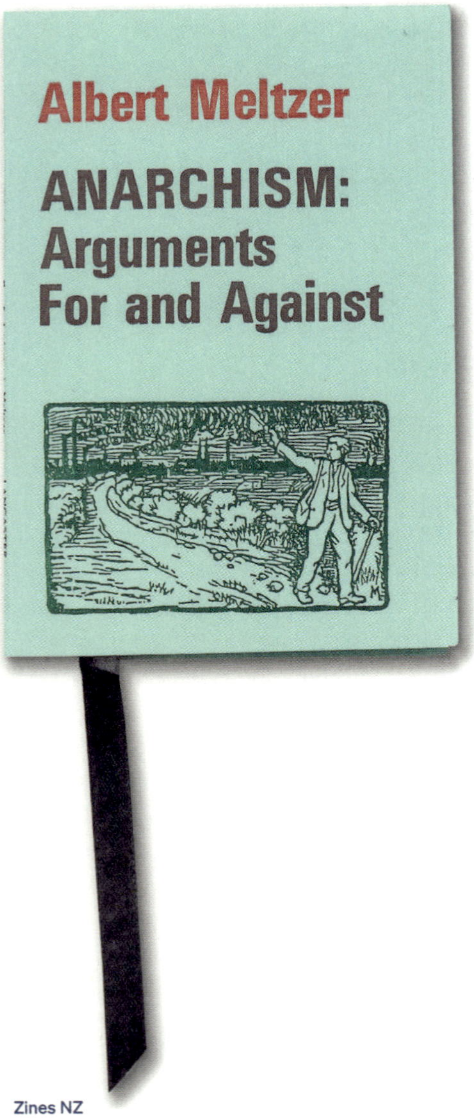

David Merritt The older economics of scale have gone. If I'm printing on web offset, sure, I may as well print 1000 copies as print 10, because the [major, fixed] cost is in setting up the fucking job, but if I've got a photocopier, it's just the cost of paper and toner for each copy. There's no economy of scale. The paper costs the same, the toner costs the same.

Bruce Grenville I ended up having lots of these typecases. In fact, that cabinet we were looking at there came from that same studio at Auckland University. As did quite a few of my chairs and things as well. I also got heavily into offset, which is much easier than letterpress printing because you just provide your copy and then photograph it and a relief is made of the photographic image. It's much easier to print.

Lyn Spencer And you could get little pictures made up — what were those called again? **Ross Gardiner** Polymer blocks. **Lyn Spencer** Polymer blocks, yeah. So, you'd get a picture and put it on the press, if you wanted a logo for your zine or something then you could just use that to make pictures as well. **Ross Gardiner** Print it in colour. Yeah, it was basically like woodcut-style printing.[2] You'd just take a picture into some [graphic reproduction] company, and they'd duplicate it onto a sort of plastic resin-type stuff [and mount the resin image on a piece of wood]. So, you could make any graphic into a raised block, and then you'd print it on a letterpress machine. It could be a photograph or just a line drawing or whatever.

96. *Anarchism: Arguments For and Against*, by Albert Meltzer, reprinted by Bruce Grenville, A6, 1991. Tāmaki Makaurau Auckland.

97. *A day mournful and overcast*, anonymous, reprinted by Ross Gardiner at Bruce Grenville's Tāmaki Makaurau print studio for The Freedom Shop in Te Whanganui-a-Tara, A5, mid-1990s.

Bruce Grenville I showed Ross Gardiner and quite a few others how to use the press. Here's [Larry Law's] *Revolutionary Self-theory: A Beginners' Manual.* I didn't see Ross print this one, he just set up and did it without me. What he's done here is print a front and back cover on nice card, then all the complicated inside pages are just photocopied from the existing book. He's sewn it, because in the printing industry we consider staples a very bad idea because they [rust away and damage the paper, and] are not archival. Here, on the other hand, this linen thread will last forever.

Here's another Ross-ism. This is *A day mournful and overcast* [1937],[3] which, once again, he printed without asking me, because if he had I would have said, 'Well, red-on-red is not gonna show up well.'

This is *The Heretic's Guide to the Bible* [edited by Chaz Bufe , 1992].[4] It's all photocopied, but Ross has done a bit of letterpress at the bottom in green to make it look nice. A very good book, but it's all bootlegged, just photocopied from an overseas product because he was doing [it for] the anarchist bookshop in Wellington, The Freedom Shop; they wanted copies to sell.

This one here is the *Cycle of Starvation: The Third World War,* which is one that Ross actually wrote and researched. Originally it was an article for *The State Adversary*, but then he thought he'd better do it as a stand-alone zine. It's all done on my IBM [Selectric] Composer so it's all quite nicely typeset. The IBM Composer is that golf-ball typewriter. It has interchangeable 'golf-balls' with different fonts so you can go from 6-point to 12-point [and change typefaces]. If we wanted bigger stuff, we used the photocopy machines that enlarged things. Originally, photo-copy machines wouldn't do enlarging, they'd just do the same size you started with. And early days, everything from a typewriter was basically one size, 10-point or whatever it was.

97

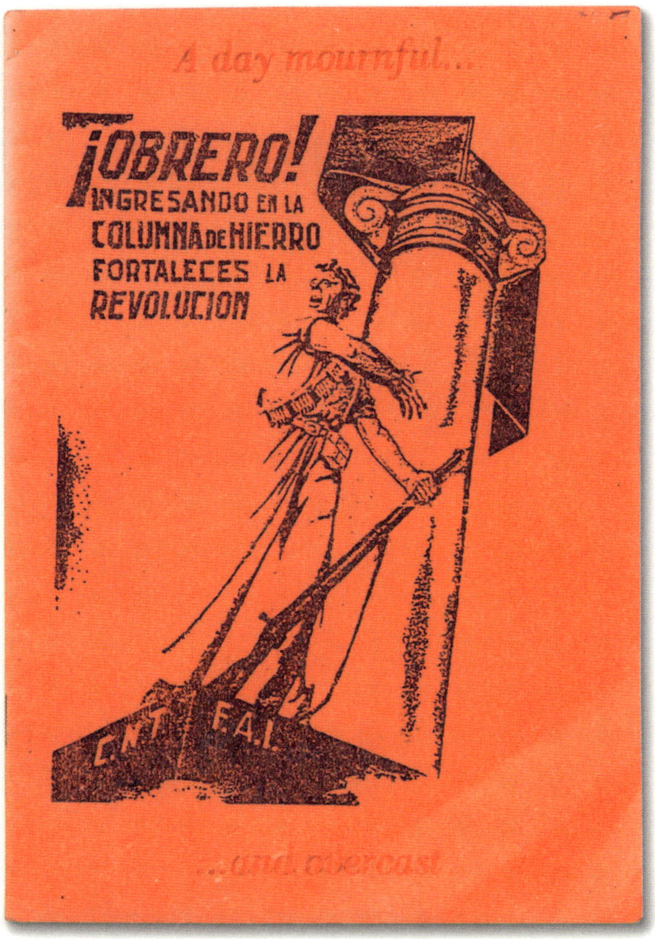

Kerry Ann Lee Thank goodness for kindly parents who let you use their work photocopier after hours! Sometimes you get money from zine sales; all those $2 zines might add up to a hundred bucks if you've got a few titles and you've been saving. Then you could lay down some serious change at a photocopy shop like Datastream, and they'd help you out because they've done it more than once. Kay and Tony at Datastream would help. 'Do you want this?' 'Is it like this?' 'Is it good like that?' and you'd work with them.

`'Okay, what can I do?'`

`'You be useful and you fold these things.'`

You'd co-create with them. You'd learn how a photocopy shop works. Know what to do with paper jams: especially if it's not your photocopier, you don't want to get your friend's parent in trouble. They gave you the key and they trusted you and you don't want to fuck up their work machine.

Andrew Stephens I printed some at my library job for a while, and then it just wasn't cool anymore so I got them done at the print shop. I'd stopped paying for any of it at the library. I considered it a work privilege, but after a while they thought I was taking the piss. In the end I bought a little flatbed single-sheet printer and started doing it myself, very slowly and painstakingly.

Jarrod Love's a guy in Palmy who used to write zines. He had all the gears so I used to talk to Jarrod about zines and borrow stuff like his long-reach stapler so I could staple in the middle of an A4 page. Jarrod wrote a damn good zine, eh. He was really funny. I remember he wrote an article about his addiction to sliced cheese. **Trish Stephens** He spent a month or something living off white bread and processed cheese slices.

98. *Undercurrent* #5 cover and spreads, edited by Jarrod Love, A5, 1997. Te Papaioea Palmerston North.

98

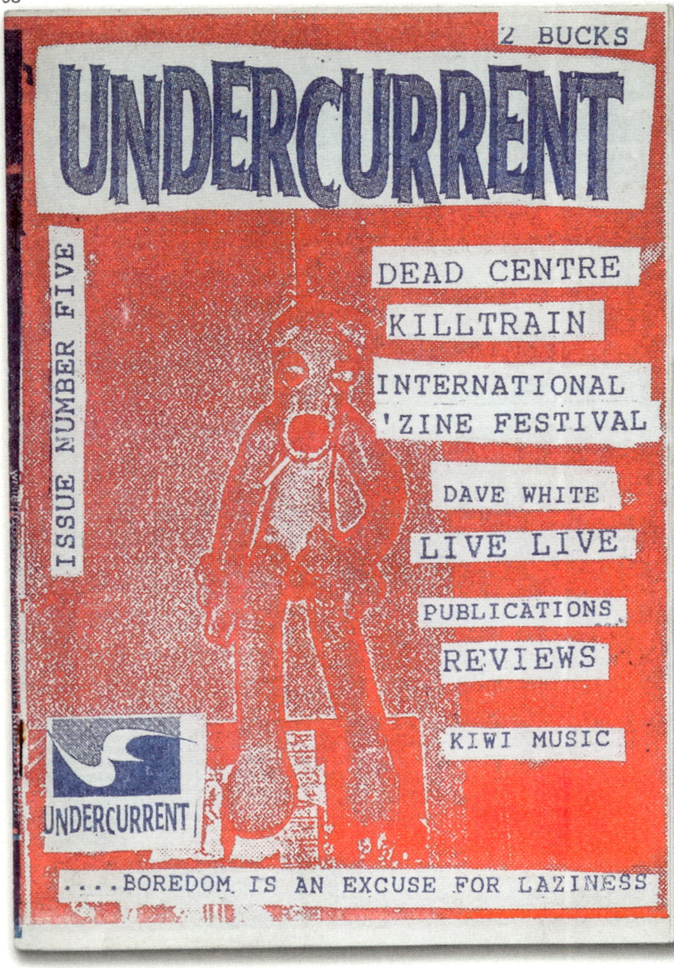

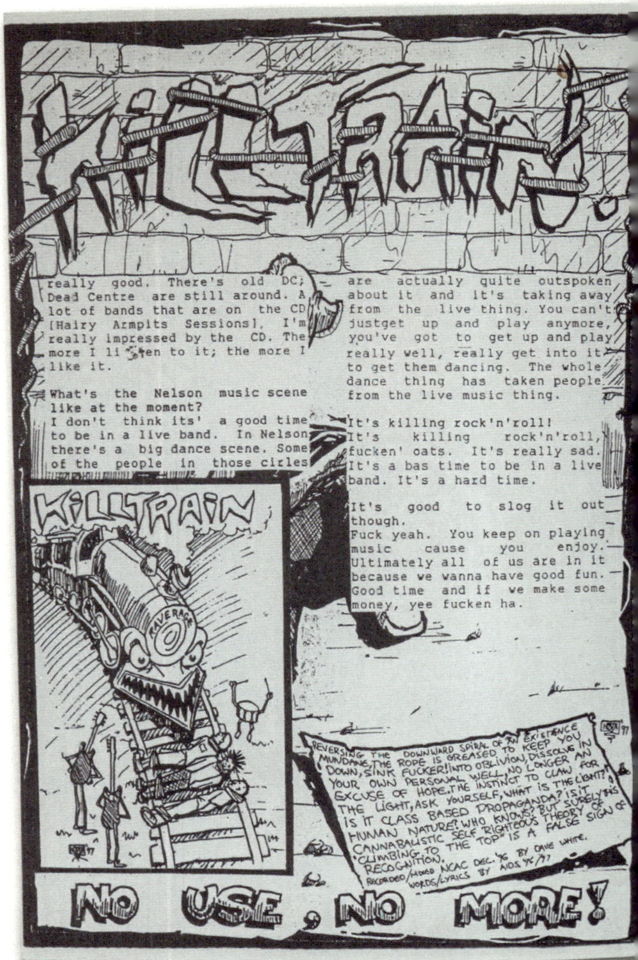

99

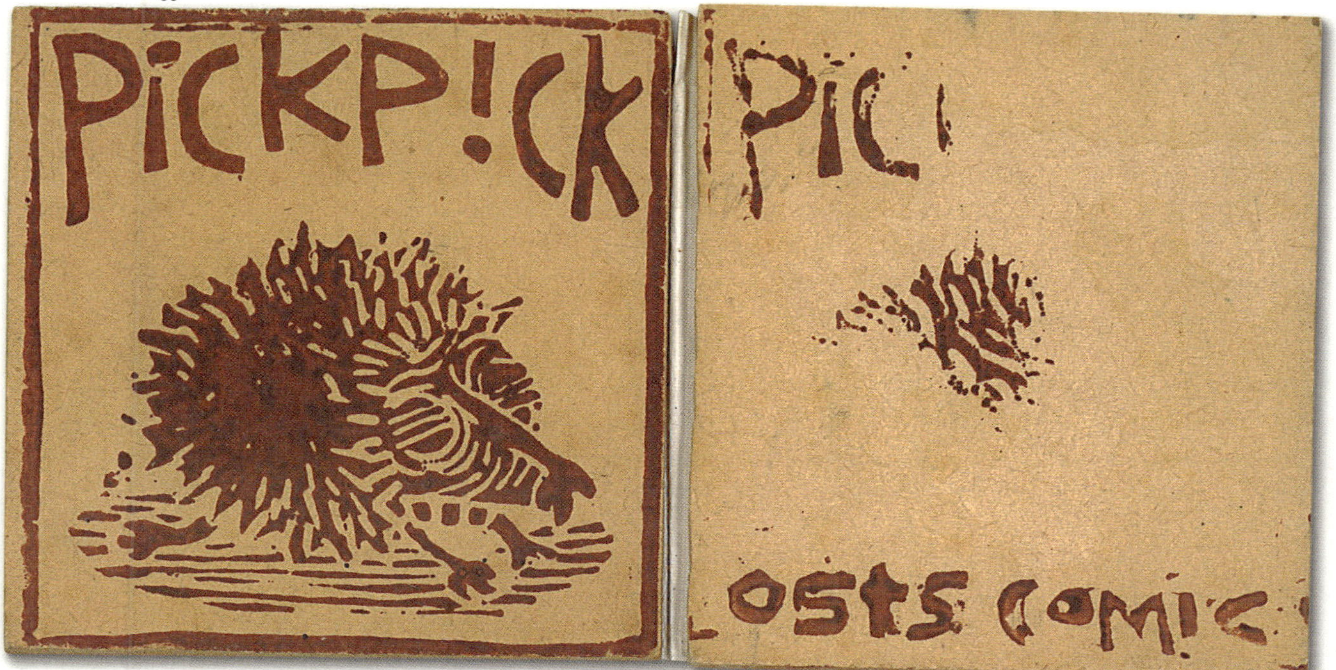

99. *Pick Pick* front and back covers, words by Indira Neville, pictures by Stefan Neville, Oats Comics, 105 × 105mm. Whāingaroa Raglan.

Indira Neville We just photocopied everything in Hamilton at the Centreplace copy centre, and it was great because the people there got to know us. You get the photocopying the wrong way round, or cut off or something, and you'd just secretly chuck them all away and do it again and again. I don't know what they thought of us, 'There they are again, photocopying weird things, not CVs or anything', and it just got to the point where they'd overlook the number of wrong copies and not charge us for the 15 crap ones that ended up in the bin.

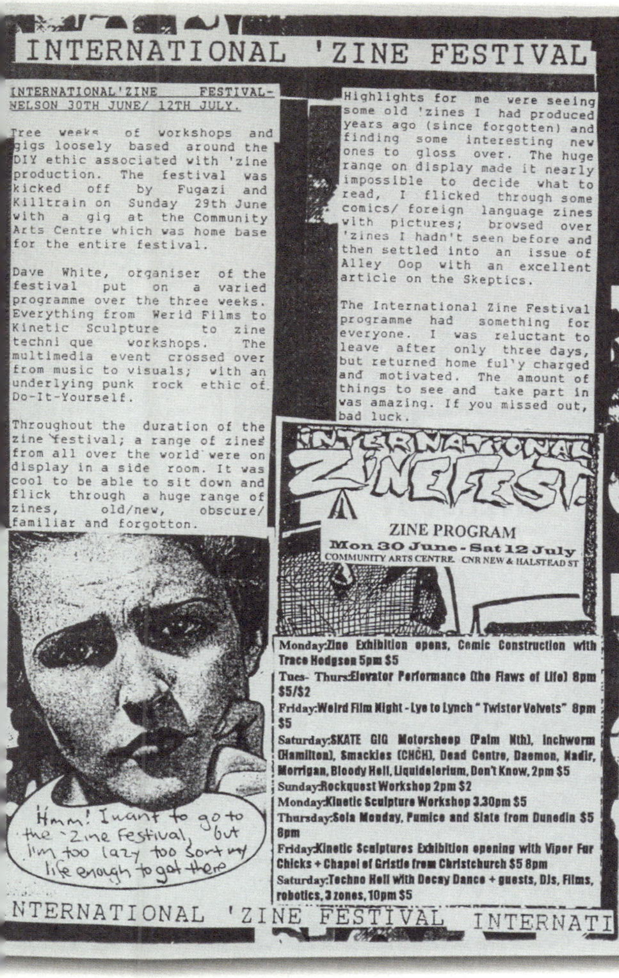

INTERNATIONAL 'ZINE FESTIVAL

INTERNATIONAL'ZINE FESTIVAL-NELSON 30TH JUNE/ 12TH JULY.

Tree weeks of workshops and gigs loosely based around the DIY ethic associated with 'zine production. The festival was kicked off by Fugazi and Killtrain on Sunday 29th June with a gig at the Community Arts Centre which was home base for the entire festival.

Dave White, organiser of the festival put on a varied programme over the three weeks. Everything from Werid Films to Kinetic Sculpture to zine techni que workshops. The multimedia event crossed over from music to visuals; with an underlying punk rock ethic of Do-It-Yourself.

Throughout the duration of the zine festival; a range of zines from all over the world were on display in a side room. It was cool to be able to sit down and flick through a huge range of zines, old/new, obscure/ familiar and forgotton.

Highlights for me were seeing some old 'zines I had produced years ago (since forgotten) and finding some interesting new ones to gloss over. The huge range on display made it nearly impossible to decide what to read, I flicked through some comics/ foreign language zines with pictures; browsed over 'zines I hadn't seen before and then settled into an issue of Alley Oop with an excellent article on the Skeptics.

The International Zine Festival programme had something for everyone. I was reluctant to leave after only three days, but returned home ful'y charged and motivated. The amount of things to see and take part in was amazing. If you missed out, bad luck.

INTERNATIONAL ZINEFEST

ZINE PROGRAM

Mon 30 June - Sat 12 July

COMMUNITY ARTS CENTRE. CNR NEW & HALSTEAD ST

Monday: Zine Exhibition opens, Comic Construction with Trace Hodgson 5pm $5

Tues- Thurs: Elevator Performance (the Flaws of Life) 8pm $5/$2

Friday: Weird Film Night - Lye to Lynch " Twister Velvets" 8pm $5

Saturday: SKATE GIG Motorsheep (Palm Nth), Inchworm (Hamilton), Smackles (CHCH), Dead Centre, Daemon, Nadir, Morrigan, Bloody Hell, Liquidelerium, Don't Know, 2pm $5

Sunday: Rockquest Workshop 2pm $2

Monday: Kinetic Sculpture Workshop 3.30pm $5

Thursday: Sola Monday, Pumice and Slate from Dunedin $5 8pm

Friday: Kinetic Sculptures Exhibition opening with Viper Fur Chicks + Chapel of Gristle from Christchurch $5 8pm

Saturday: Techno Hell with Decay Dance + guests, DJs, Films, robotics, 3 zones, 10pm $5

Hmm! I want to go to the 'Zine Festival, but I'm too lazy too sort my life enough to get there

NTERNATIONAL 'ZINE FESTIVAL INTERNATI

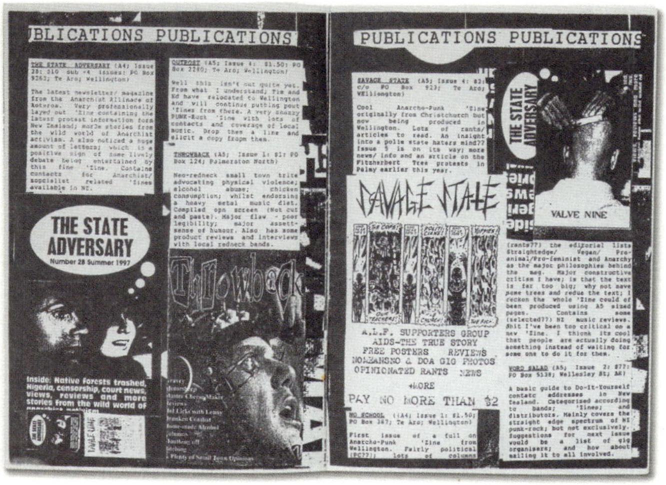

BLICATIONS PUBLICATIONS

THE STATE ADVERSARY (A4; Issue 28: $10 sub 4 issues: PO Box 9263; Te Aro; Wellington)

The latest newsletter/ magazine from the Anarchist Alliance of Aotearoa. Very professionally layed out 'Zine containing the latest protest information form New Zealand; more stories from the wild world of Anarchist activism. A also noticed a huge amount of letters; which is a positive sign of some lively debate being entertained by this fine 'Zine. Contains contacts for Anarchist/ socialist related 'Zines available in NZ.

THE STATE ADVERSARY

Number 28 Summer 1997

Inside: Native forests trashed, Nigeria, censorship, court news, views, reviews and more stories from the wild world of

OUTPOST (A5; Issue 4: $1.50; PO Box 2280; Te Aro; Wellington)

Well this isn't out quite yet. From what I understand; Tim and Ed have relocated to Wellington and will continue putting pout 'Zines from there. A very snazzy PUNK-Rock 'Zine with lots of contacts and coverage of local music. Drop them a line and elicit a copy fropm them.

THROWBACK (A5; Issue 1: $1; PO Box 124; Palmerston North)

Neo-redneck small town trite advocating physical violence; alcohol abuse; chicken consumption; whilst endorsing a heavy metal music diet. Compiled opn screen (Not cut and paste). Major flaw - poor legibility; major asset- sense of humour. Also has some product reviews and interviews with local redneck bands.

Throwback

PUBLICATIONS PUBLICATIONS

SAVAGE STATE (A5; Issue 4: $2; c/o PO Box 923; Te Aro; Wellington)

Cool Anarcho-Punk 'Zine originally from Christchurch but now being produced in Wellington. Lots of rants/ articles to read. An insight into a polie state haters mind?? Issue 5 is on its way; more news/ info and an article on the Fitzherbert Tree protests in Palmy earlier this year.

SAVAGE STATE

A.L.F. SUPPORTERS GROUP

AIDS-THE TRUE STORY

FREE POSTERS REVIEWS

NOMEANSNO & DOA GIG PHOTOS

OPINIONATED RANTS NEWS

+MORE

PAY NO MORE THAN $2

NO SCHOOL ((A4; Issue 1: $1.50; PO Box 387; Te Aro; Wellington)

First issue of a full on Anarcho-Punk 'Zine from Wellington. Fairly political (PC??); lots of columns

THE STATE ADVERSARY

VALVE NINE

(rants??) the editorial lists Straightedge/ Vegan/ Pro-animal/Pro-feminist and Anarchy as the major philosophies behind the mag. Major constructive critism I have; is that the text is far too big; why not save some trees and redue the text; I reckon the whole 'Zine could of been produced using A5 sized pages. Contains some (selected??) NZ music reviews. Shit I've been too critical on a new 'Zine. I think its cool that people are actually doing something instead of waiting for some one to do it for them.

WORD SALAD (A5; Issue 2: $??; PO Box 5138; Wellesley St; AK)

A basic guide to Do-It-Yourself contatc addresses in New Zealand. Categorised according to bands; 'Zines; and distributors. Mainly covers the straight edge spectrum of NZ punk-rock; but not exclusively. Suggestions for next issue would be a list of gig organisers; and how about mailing it to all involved.

Beth Dawson When we moved to Dunedin I started to recognise the aesthetic of certain band posters. I'd be thinking 'Oh, those drawings are cool, probably the music will be, too.' I was aware of Space Dust in that way. Then I met the people involved in Oats: Tokerau Brown, Stefan Neville and Clayton Noone.

Stefan was this person that I'd see carrying stuff everywhere. I soon realised that he and the Oats people had this whole comics scene going on. I'd been drawing comics so I figured I could add to that. I didn't make any distinction between comics and zines and the artwork for my band. That's all the same world to me, and the same aesthetic.

David Tulloch Back in the nineties, zines and comics operated in *slightly* different orbits but there was also a lot of crossover; hanging around with Simon Morse and Rufus Dayglo, they were heavily into the local punk scene so there was a lot of crossover there. Simon Morse and Martin Emond were more into heavy metal than punk, but Rufus had been a punk from about the age of 12.

100

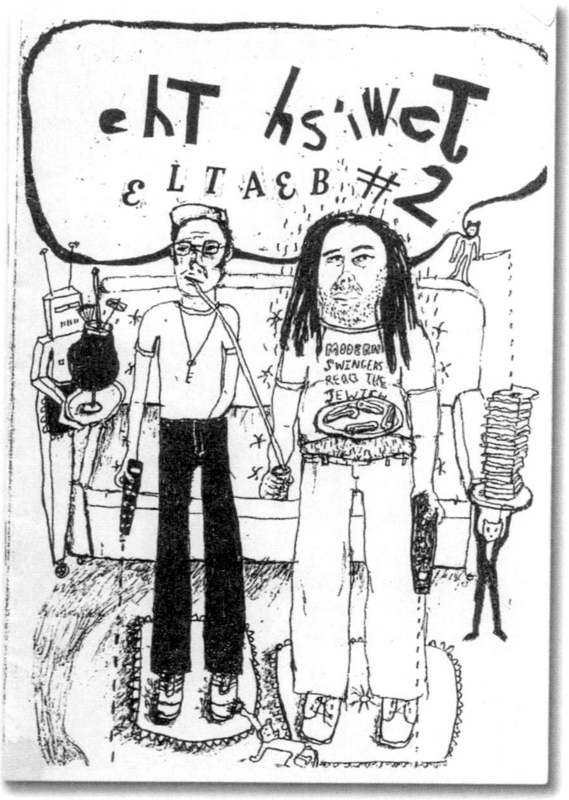

Pritika Lal The very first stuff that I saw was when I was at high school in the mid-nineties, when I was hanging out in and around K Road. Andy Conlan had this A5 zine or comic called *Strumming Teeth*. It was pretty amazing. He used to leave them in Real Groovy Records and different cafés along K Road. It was fully printed with really beautiful illustrations, sort of like *Black Hole* Charles Burns-style illustrations. Certain themes and characters repeated each time it came out. It was quite amazing to find this thing for free, considering its quality and how substantial it was. It had little studies of different people, like 'Let's take a moment to look at this character, what is up with this guy?', and they might be people that you'd see in the street. It was like finding the grotesque in everyday life, it was quite extraordinary.

These were left for free in places. I'd find one, and then a month later it would be 'There's another one!', until I realised there was a series. My whole friend group got really into it. I kept them for ages. I eventually donated them to a zine library because I just found it really hard to keep hold of things.

David Tulloch I was always impressed with Doug Ford's art, and Andy Laughlin's, and a whole bunch of people who could just sit there and out it came. It just seemed like it flowed naturally. It didn't, they worked at it, but that's what it seemed like to me

Andrew Schmidt *The Jewish Beatle* — which is Duane Zarakov's fanzine — was really good and had some great writing in it, and there's another one called *Sunburn* by a guy called Grant McDonagh. Grant's an old anarchist friend of Bill Direen's. Yeah, Brian Epstein, the 'fifth Beatle', who's Jewish. I'm guessing that's where the name of Duane's zine came from.

100. *The Jewish Beatle* #2, edited by Duane Zarakov and Bruder Liebe, A5, 2000. Ōtautahi Christchurch.

101

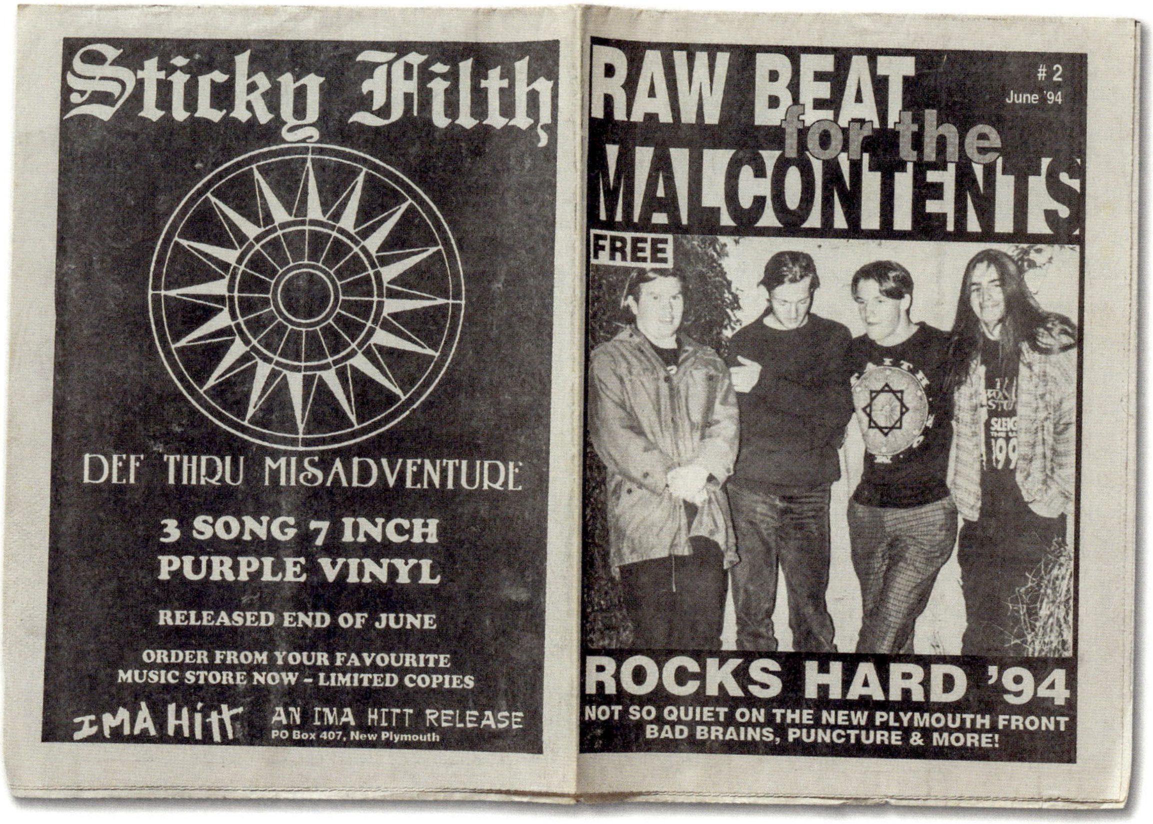

Bruce Grenville I met Ross Gardiner through *The State Adversary* because Ross spotted a *State Adversary* self-adhesive sticker that I had printed and stuck on the back of a bus seat. Back in those days the backs of the bus seats in Auckland were Formica, very nice and shiny. I had to go from my home in New Lynn into Auckland University every day by bus, a 45-minute ride, and I always made it a goal to have a big supply of self-adhesive stickers in my bag to put around the place. The best place to put them was on the back of the seat in front for the next passenger to find. I'm sure many passengers would be looking at this thing going 'Grrr, angry, angry', scratch, scratch, scratch, and waste their fingernails scratching it off, or, in the case of Ross, go 'Oh, that looks interesting . . .' Ross wrote down the post box number for Anarchist Alliance and wrote in. That's how we met. He ended up getting quite involved, and then he ended up being co-editor and eventually I said, 'Well, why don't you just be editor?'

Andrew Schmidt *Raw Beat for the Malcontents* came out of New Plymouth in the early nineties, when Brian Wafer and all those punk bands were really active down there. Ima Hitt. Sticky Filth were hitting their stride. Yeah, and the Mushroom Ball, and a big local punk scene. I think they went to about four issues.

Bruce Grenville Ross got into it through seeing a sticker on the bus, which you probably can't do these days. I think buses have carpet on the back of their seats now. They probably put carpet on the back of the seats because of me, but it also makes the bus warmer and less echoey and stuff — but no more stickers. Trains could be an option. I haven't considered trains.

101. *Raw Beat for the Malcontents* #2 front and back covers, Brian Wafer and Ima Hitt Records, A4, 1994. Ngāmotu New Plymouth.

Andrew Stephens Dave White and I met at a church group, hard to believe, but there you go. Well, we had a glancing acquaintance with the church, but were both on our way out at that point. Dave was a musician even then. In those days he had this terrible long red hair down to his waist and fairly hippyish clothes. He looked like Prince Valiant on acid. He looked very strange, and he played this almost proggy stuff in a band called Thin Red Line. Then he disappeared off to Auckland to do something. I don't know how long he was away for, but when he came back he'd shaved all his hair off and he was wearing bovver boots up to his knees and black tights. He'd just changed totally. He'd turned into Johnny Rotten on the spot.

You could get around Palmy looking like that without being hassled by farming students. They had their own bars, their own life. You never ran across them really. If you went to Harvesters or The Stomach or places like that where the gigs were, you never came across those clowns.

David Merritt *Spec* was the Radio One magazine in Dunedin. It was like *@Punnet*, but A3 landscape. *@Punnet* was a big A2, like a newspaper. We were printing on web offset out of Whanganui, I think, and that was cheap. Danny Butt and Caroline McCaw got funding for *@Punnet*. They applied for a couple of grand to run a Fringe Festival publication, and so we just picked up the whole of the Radio One infrastructure that we'd been using to do *Spec* and shifted it to Wellington for the summer. I was on my way out of Dunedin by that point because my marriage had failed. I'd lost the custody battle for the kids, and I knew I had to move north to be near them.

David Tulloch Rod Mills and Leo Hupert ran VMS. They were both sub-editors at *The Evening Post*, and they would bring in telex of any comic-related stuff that had just come in for the comics shop staff to read. That was nice.

Moira Clunie Before Moon Rocket I had a personal website where I'd have pages about my own zines. I was also sending them to distros overseas and trading with people through the mail. It was quite a thriving scene. One of the big platforms around that time would've been a mailing list on, I don't know, Yahoo! groups or its predecessor, one of those discussion groups. I think it was just called Zinesters, and people would raise various topics, get into online debate about things, but also just share about whatever they were publishing and offer to do trades. I was more often trading with people rather than getting them to post me money at that point.

Tony Renouf Bag End Books had started by the time I was working on *Treacle*, so there was more of a comics hub closer to the university. I didn't have to stand over anybody to get their contributions on time. [Laughs.] Certainly, I was able to tap into the focus at Bag End Books. More people were leaving their details with Bag End's owner Derek about the possibility of contributing or at least making contact. That was nice. I was starting to learn about distribution, setting up a comics stand at Bag End Books. I just said, 'There's a space right there, can I set something up?' I reached out to Cornelius Stone, and I reached out to Peter Johnston. Where was he based? Tapanui? It was one of those weird little places where you could buy a house for a buck. I just reached out to all those people. A lot of Ant Sang's[5] stuff came through. By the fifth issue I decided we should be part of the Fringe Festival, that we could have a day where we tried to accumulate as many cartoonists as possible, sit in a room for a day and draw and collaborate on something. If you didn't finish your work on the day, that was cool, you could take it away and get it back to me, and then we'd compile everything and put it out as a post-Fringe Festival publication.

The Christchurch guys from Funtime heard about it and came down. They must've read about it in some promotional stuff, and that led to the Funtime Comics thing where they actively get together on a monthly basis for a 'comics jam' — or they used to, I don't know if they're still kicking.

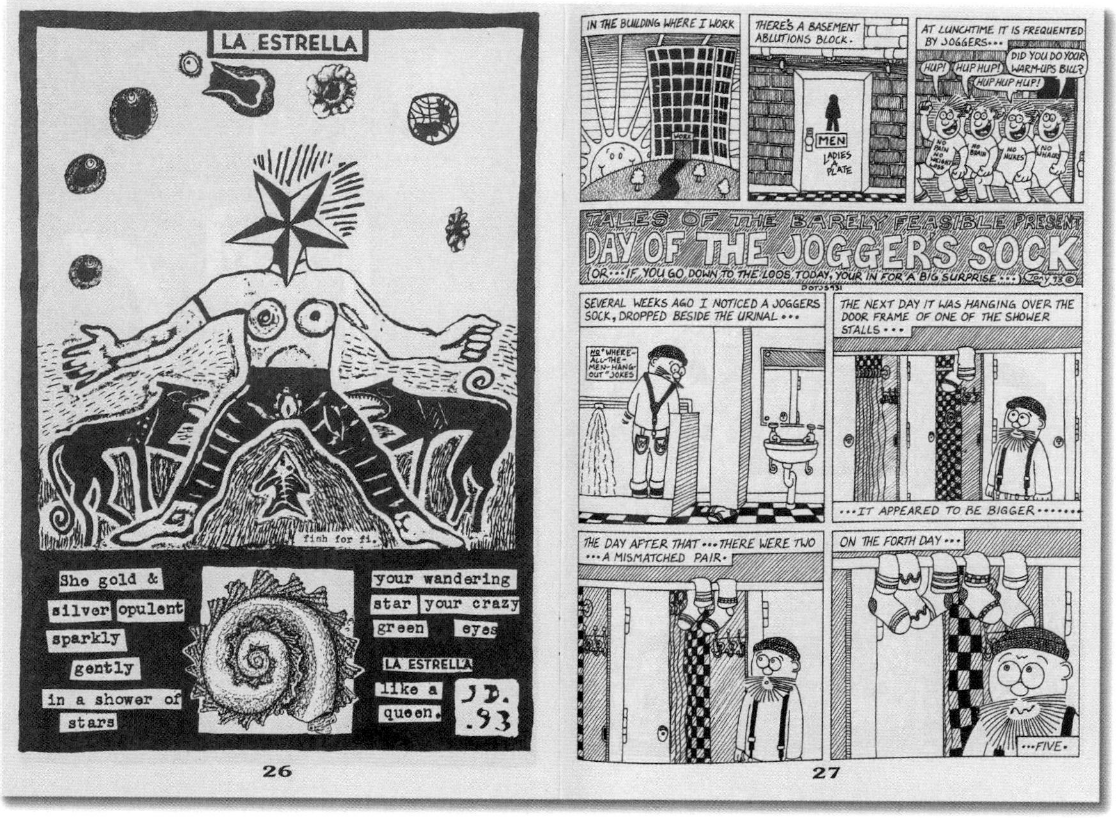

Ross Gardiner In central Auckland in the early nineties landlords were desperate for tenants. Some friends found this shitty warehouse that used to be a panel beater's, then a gay and lesbian nightclub, and then the landlord couldn't find anyone who was interested in renting it, so he said 'You can live there, and I'll give you two months' rent free if you tidy the place up', and so we moved in and put on a few music events among other things, and then we thought 'Oh, we could build a bookshop out the front', because I'd been to Black Rose Books in Sydney and was quite inspired by that. So, we opened Books from the Black Lagoon.

It wasn't very successful because there wasn't a lot of foot traffic. It was kind of a weird location, so we never really sold much stuff. Then Lyn and I went overseas, then to Wellington, and the shop folded, sometime in '94.

Bruce Grenville I had an Adana. I trained up Ross and numerous others on how to use it, and then an Adana came up for sale. One of the old ladies at the Association of Handcraft Printers was retiring and wanted to get rid of her Adana, and so we dreamed up this scheme. Four of us went shares in it: me, Ross, and two others. This new Adana moved into Ross and Lyn's place at Books from the Black Lagoon, and because I was a shareholder I'd quite frequently go over there and print things on it just to get my usage.

102. *Treacle* #2 spread, Jane Dodd (page 26) and Tony Renouf (page 27), edited by Tony Renouf, A4, 1993. Ōtepoti Dunedin.

David Tulloch We tried our best to send *Pistake* places, but it was really hard to get people to accept it. They'd often ask for one copy or three copies. We did send them around, but we'd often never get any money back:

> 'You got your three copies, did you sell them?'
>
> 'We don't know.'

It felt like you were just sending them off into the void. Nothing came back.

Tony Renouf *Treacle* went to Mark One in Auckland. They were also at this alternative shop in Christchurch called 'Weird' or 'Wired', depending on how you pronounce the spelling of 'Wyrd'. I had them in the local record and comics shops. I can't remember if there was a comics shop in Hamilton at that stage. It was pre-internet, connections involved having to find a postal address, write a letter and then wait for a response, maybe even a follow-up letter. It wasn't as immediate as it is now, and once I'd got the damn things printed, the motivation to get out and do the distribution stuff was not great. I could do a little bit locally. I just wanted it to exist.

Lyn Spencer When we first went overseas, we noticed that people were having zine stalls at gigs, which wasn't happening in New Zealand before we left. I remember going to pub gigs in the UK and someone would be walking around trying to sell their zine; sometimes from a table. So when we got back, we started selling zines at shows.

Ross Gardiner By the nineties people started doing zine tables at punk gigs. It was just a way of coming across zines; you'd go and see some bands and buy some zines while you were there.

Tony Renouf It was exciting to make my own comics. Exciting because it was a way of sharing that I could actually put into somebody's hands so that I knew that they'd seen it, as opposed to contributing to something like *Critic* or *Jesus on a Stick*; then you've got no idea, unless you see a copy floating around somebody's house, you don't know if somebody's picked it up.

Dave Hegan Even though I was cleaning up back then, I had quite an itinerant lifestyle. I was always moving around, which is a great way of avoiding your problems. Some of my zines were in record shops in Christchurch; Al Park who worked at Echo Records was quite encouraging. I think I thank him in the editorial. I was hitch-hiking everywhere, and wherever I went I'd ask people 'You wanna buy a zine?' sort of thing. Not at gigs, but more just going around to people's places, catching up with people, because everyone knew everyone and it was a pretty tight punk scene. They all sold. With the second one I think I even reissued it. I never advertised it or anything, it was just organic, word-of-mouth. Within a matter of weeks I could be in Christchurch, Wellington, New Plymouth and Auckland.

David Tulloch There was no feedback, and you had no quick way of communicating. I didn't have the phone numbers of the shops we were supplying. And I couldn't afford to make a lot of toll calls[6] at the time anyway, especially once I stopped working, but even when I was working I wasn't getting paid that much. It just felt like we were sending stuff out into the void. Even the shop in Christchurch, which was owned by the Wellington shop where I worked, wouldn't take that many of them. But we did manage to get them out there, and people would turn up from out of town and buy several copies so they could take them back to their friends.

Indira Neville There were all of these mail networks, and there were all these distribution opportunities, too. Somehow I got hooked up with the feminist distribution world. Australia offered a few opportunities, and we had these weird catalogues that we'd send through the mail and leave in places, and then word-of-mouth was quite a big thing. Contact FM giveaways, if people were into the music-into the comics, into the comics-into the music. Again, it wasn't really a conscious kind of thing. Later, everyone knew you could just take your comics to Mark One, it was no big deal.

Lyn Spencer We had an anarchist office at the top of Cuba Street, right next door to where The Freedom Shop was later started. There was the anarchist office, there was the Vegetarian Society, the Peace Movement. Who else was in there? **Ross Gardiner** Campaign for a Better City. **Lyn Spencer** There was a little shop run by NORML [National Organisation for the Reform of Marijuana Laws] next door. I think it was only open one day a week. A friend and I were walking up the street and we thought it'd be really cool if we could join in with them and run a shop there, and we could staff it for the rest of the week as a kind of deal with NORML. We were able to staff the rest of the week just among the punk and anarchist scene. We'd get a lot of records in as well, and there'd be a lot of people screen-printing patches and things, and we'd sell those. **Ross Gardiner** Sam Buchanan had been doing a bit of booklet publishing using the name 'Committee for the Establishment of Civilization', and this guy George was keen on opening a bookshop, and I was like 'Oh, God, we could never afford it in Wellington', but then, as Lyn said, we ended up splitting the shop with NORML.

103

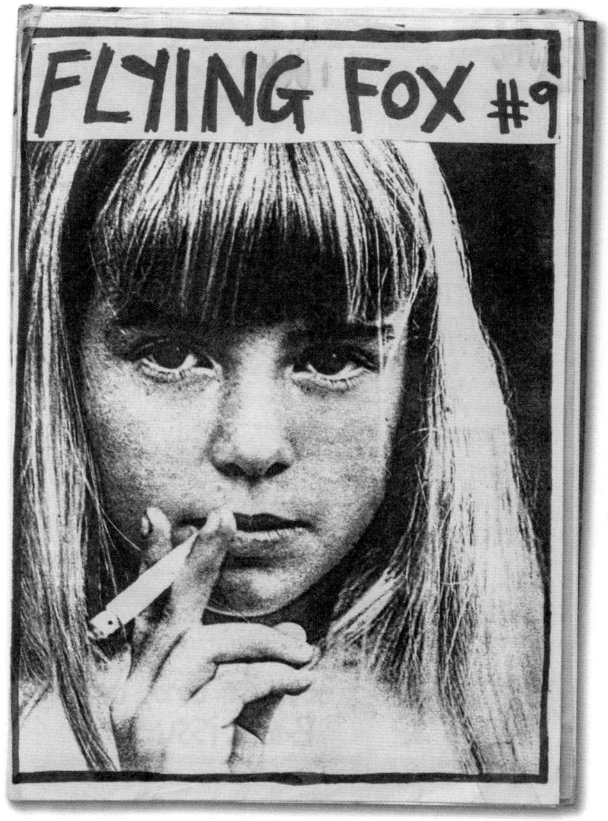

Liz Mathews I had my *Flying Fox* zine in Crawlspace Records, and then right next door to Crawlspace was Bunny Boutique run by Stella Corkery who was in the band Fake Purr and into making space for women in rock. She was interested in the zine so I had it in two shops in Auckland, but the two shops were right next-door to each other. [Laughs.] Then I had them in The Freedom Shop in Wellington, and some small bookshop in Christchurch. Ross and Lyn at The Freedom Shop befriended us, and encouraged our band Goldifox to head south and play Punk Fest. I was 17. Mainly I was giving my zine to friends and sending it to pen pals.

Moira Clunie I guess I was making zines before I knew what zines were, and then I connected up with the concept of zines through online message boards and found a distro in Canada. I decided to make a zine for them, and got connected up with different scenes overseas, mostly Canada, the US and Australia.

103. *Flying Fox* #9 (analogue master for photocopying), Liz Mathews, A4, 1999. Tāmaki Makaurau Auckland.

Beth Dawson When I was at high school a friend and I made a zine that we were too unsure about to put in Crawlspace Records. Growing up in Auckland we were a bit more self-conscious and uptight about putting it out there. I was like 'Oh my gosh, Liz Mathews is amazing, being like "Here's my zine, here's my life in Kerikeri."' **Liz Mathews** That could've been a bit of naïvety on my part. I never really thought, 'Oh, all these people are reading about my personal life.'

David Tulloch My drawings were awful. One of the people who contributed to the first *Pistake* was Michele Perry[-Madsen]. She was doing this thing where she would go into schools and get the kids interested in drawing comics. Once she asked Simon and me to go along with her, and we talked about our comics and scarred the kids for life. At the end of our presentation they got everyone in the class to draw a comic, and mine was voted the least well-drawn of them all. They weren't kidding. The kids were way better than me. When I was 14 my art teacher at high school told me that I should never draw again. When I got back into comics I was looking for a way to do them without drawing, that's where the photos of the Playmobil narratives come in.

Beth Dawson I remember when Liz and I were teenagers, our mutual friends being annoyed or having a little teenage drama about turning up in one of Liz's zines, but now they're this great diary of that time.

Andrew Stephens I think I'm probably like a lot of zinesters. It's a self-indulgence really. I don't know how many zinesters think about their audience. Do I have an audience? I liked making it. That was the thing. I liked making the artefact and holding it in my hand and reading it myself, and if other people liked it too, sweet as, that's great. But it was really for me. **Trish Stephens** Remember when you gave one of your zines to your father to read and he was horrified. He thought Massey would disown you and that [our son] Sam (here) would be sacked, and all sorts of things. Sam had done a doodle cartoon about how boring it was being in this meeting at work, and Andrew's father was really worried that Sam would lose his job, and Andrew was going 'They're not gonna read this.'

David Tulloch I honestly don't know if it had much of a reputation or not. I did hear from some of the Auckland crowd that when they first saw *Pistake* they felt like they had to raise their game, but I don't know if that's just them being nice or not.

104

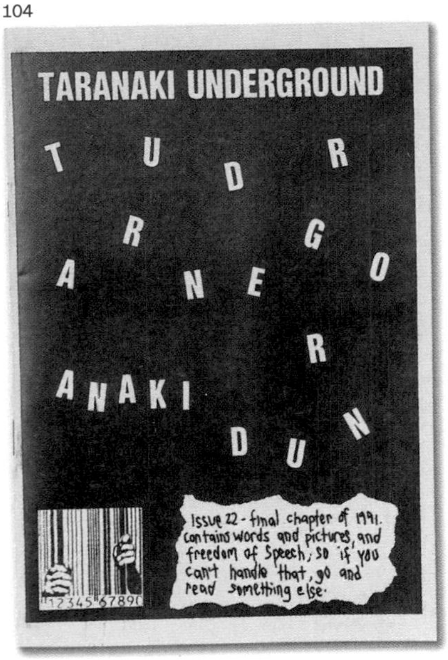

105

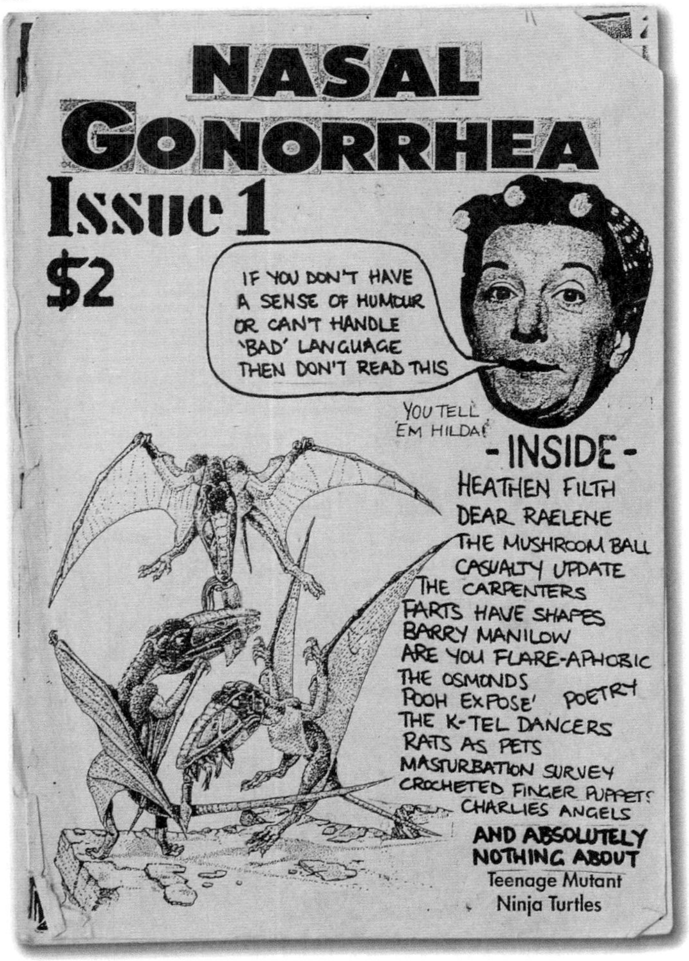

104. *Taranaki Underground* #22, Brett Taylor, A5, 1991. Taranaki.
105. *Nasal Gonorrhoea* #1, Brenda Crooks, A4, 1990. Ngāmotu New Plymouth.

Dave White Nelson was nothing like Palmerston North in terms of the scene. I did that last issue of *Valve* there and then that was it. I thought 'It's finished now', because, even though I was starting to include bands from all around New Zealand and overseas, the scene in Nelson wasn't enough to kick my ass into being bothered. Plus I had a full-time job, which was one of those jobs that never ends because I was recording bands all weekend and at nights . . . and basically I didn't have the time.

Richard Davies We spent a lot of time going to Palmy. Palmy was another scene that was doing what we were doing in Taranaki, doing the home ethos, do-it-yourself.

Christchurch had a bit of the positive DIY culture, but I think there were four different groups of skinheads at war with each other down there. So, like, how can you do anything when you're looking over your shoulder and living in fear?

The United Skins were white power and they were also a prison gang. They were all from Paparua Prison, then you had The Firm, you had the Christchurch Skins who were traditional, and Hammerskins.

106

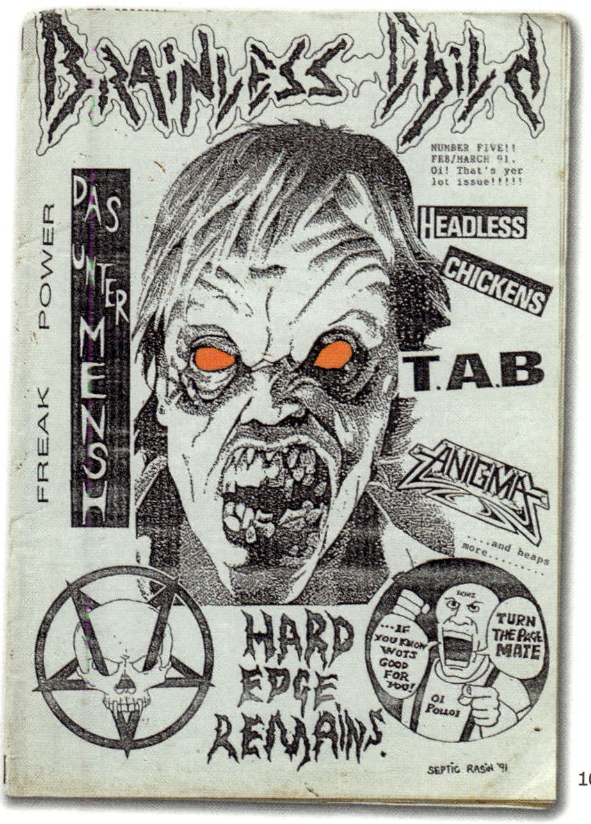

106. *Brainless Child* #5, by Kelvin, A4, 1991. Taitoko Levin.

Dave White Palmerston North was famous for being the most uncool town in New Zealand, after Hamilton. Meltdown Records recently had a reunion and panel discussion at The Stomach. There was Jeremy Corbett, because he was in Dosage B, a dude from Fat Freddy's Drop, and some reasonably famous people. We were all just sitting around and had an hour-long discussion that got turned into a podcast. We talked about the mechanics of what actually happened in Palmerston North, and people were going 'Is there a Palmy sound?' People try to go 'Yeah, there is', and I'd say 'Nah, bullshit'. There's a Palmy attitude, and that's something that we fought really hard for because we felt left out of the rest of the country. Auckland had its thing, Dunedin had its thing, Christchurch had its thing, Flying Nun ruled the whole country, and we just thought 'Fuck it, we're just gonna do whatever we want.' Then a few lucky things happened to us, like we found that EMI record-mastering machine at Foxton Beach that had been saved from being dumped in Wellington harbour, so we started making our own records, and that just gave us crazy credibility. Jello Biafra bought, I don't know, 20 copies of everything we put out.[7]

Liz Mathews People were also making their own tapes at that stage, tapes with artwork.
Beth Dawson And the covers for 7-inch singles. We were making lathe-cut records as well. I had a band with two friends at high school, and we decided that the thing to do would be to move to Dunedin. This was 1997. In retrospect I think I went from a scene in Auckland that was so great in terms of being feminists and Riot Grrrl-led to being on the outside down there. When Liz came to stay with us it was so exciting, like we were in our own little bubble of a world, making music together and collaborating on zines.

David Tulloch *Pistake* was big in Wellington. We ended up getting invited to be on some TV show that ran on Sunday mornings, some show looking at the arts. They didn't usually cover comics, but we got on there somehow. It really felt like something big was happening, and then it didn't.

Tony Renouf I stopped drawing. We were gonna do the family and the career thing, and so I stopped drawing. It'd been quite a while since I'd attempted to draw or publish anything, it just felt like a dead-end. So I packed up all my original artwork and my entire collection, apart from a few bits and pieces, and it all went down to the Hocken Library.

David Tulloch We were quite well organised in some ways. For a tatty black-and-white comic, we were quite serious about it. We wanted to try and keep it going, get another issue out. Every time we did an issue, we just forgot about it and moved onto the next one. Intense in some respects, but we were having fun.

Lyn Spencer I was involved in *The State Adversary* as well, and moved up to Auckland for the period of time I was involved. And then we did this anarchist-feminist magazine too — *Sekhmet* — and we'd pass that around. There were a few collectives around the country, and we'd take turns doing it so no one got worn out.

107. *Sekhmet* #3, Anarchist-Feminist Federation of Aotearoa, A4, 1992. Printed in Tāmaki Makaurau Auckland.

108. *The State Adversary* #18, edited and typeset by Bruce Grenville and Ross Gardiner, A4, 1991. Tāmaki Makaurau Auckland.

David Tulloch We didn't put out everything, but we tried to put out most things that people submitted because that was our philosophy: you submitted something, 'Great, thank you!' But I was terrible at communicating with people. I'm the worst letter-writer and -replier, and I feel embarrassed about that when I think back on how many times I didn't get back to people. When it all fell apart we still had enough stuff for the next two issues. We wanted each issue to include a story by either Rufus or Simon, preferably both, but it was getting harder and harder for them to do stuff in a timely manner. They had other commitments. And we'd all stopped working at VMS, so I was worried the sales would dry up. I didn't get back into comics for a good 10 years after *Pistake*.

107

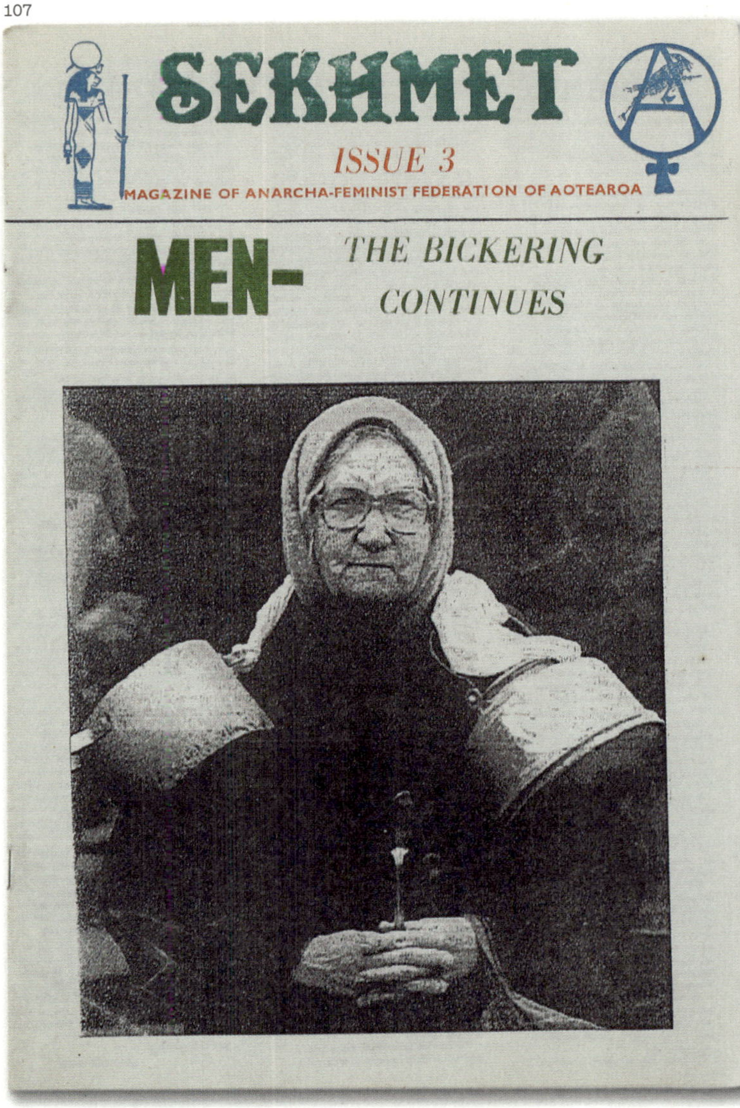

108

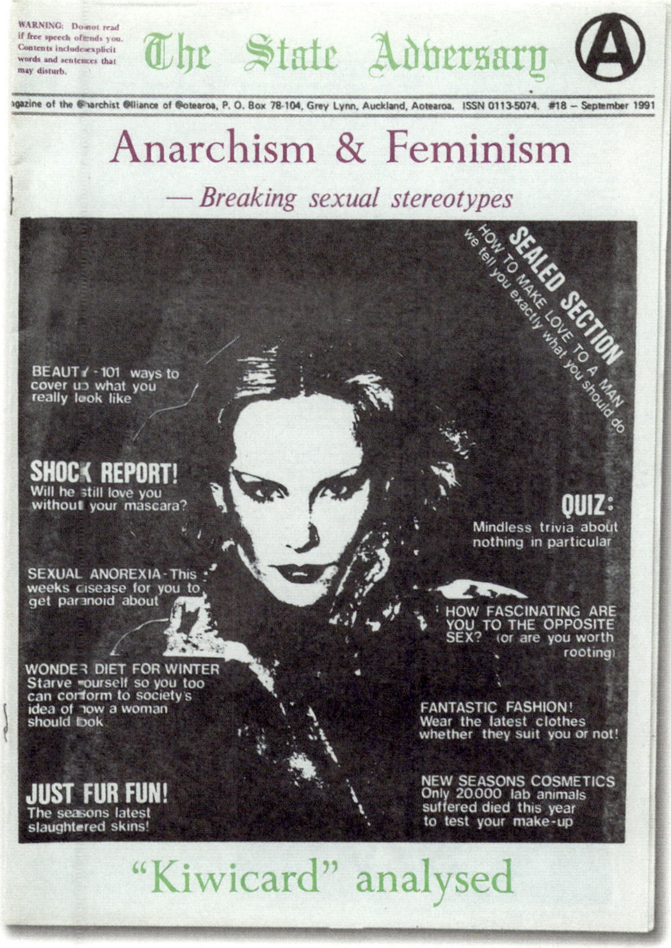
WARNING: Do not read if free speech offends you. Contents include explicit words and sentences that may disturb.

The State Adversary

agazine of the Anarchist Alliance of Aotearoa, P. O. Box 78-104, Grey Lynn, Auckland, Aotearoa. ISSN 0113-5074. #18 – September 1991

Anarchism & Feminism

— Breaking sexual stereotypes

SEALED SECTION
HOW TO MAKE LOVE TO A MAN
we tell you exactly what you should do

BEAUTY - 101 ways to cover up what you really look like

SHOCK REPORT!
Will he still love you without your mascara?

QUIZ:
Mindless trivia about nothing in particular

SEXUAL ANOREXIA - This weeks disease for you to get paranoid about

HOW FASCINATING ARE YOU TO THE OPPOSITE SEX? (or are you worth rooting)

WONDER DIET FOR WINTER
Starve yourself so you too can conform to society's idea of how a woman should look

FANTASTIC FASHION!
Wear the latest clothes whether they suit you or not!

JUST FUR FUN!
The seasons latest slaughtered skins!

NEW SEASONS COSMETICS
Only 20,000 lab animals suffered died this year to test your make-up

"Kiwicard" analysed

Lyn Spencer The Freedom Shop was a collective, and because it was in the central city and there were lots of people living in the central city, it was easier for people to just wander in or do a shift. A lot of high-school kids came past, too. Kerry Ann Lee was one of those . . . They'd come through, check out The Freedom Shop in their lunch breaks or after school.

Bruce Grenville The reason we didn't have ads was because: (a) we didn't think what we were making would appeal to an advertiser because advertisers like looking at circulation and stat figures and stuff like that, and we didn't really have circulation figures, we'd just print a couple of hundred or 50 or whatever and send them to friends; and (b) we were so busy doing the fanzine. Who's got time to go and hunt for advertisers?

Dave Hegan This one here's $2.50. I have no idea how I came up with the price. I wasn't interested in making money out of it. It wasn't my reason for doing it. I probably just made it up as I went along. I didn't look at how much I'd spent, or whatever, and try and figure out how I'd get my money back. It wasn't like that. I just put a price on it and that was that. I imagine the pricing of other people's zines would have given me some idea what was acceptable.

Simon Cottle Biggest frustration? Entitled people that think they should get it [for free], when postage costs money and paper costs money. So even if you take nothing for your own artistic input, it's like 'I can't afford to just divvy them out.' I guess some of that was frustrations with the scene as well. I mean, you had real down-to-earth working-class kids and you could relate to their homes and family life and everything else, but then you had people from more privileged backgrounds, rebelling and dallying in the scene, and good on them, but it's that sense of entitlement . . . I guess the other frustration is it's an artistic endeavour and life gets in the way, and artistic endeavours take time. You can only juggle so many balls.

Andrew Schmidt I pretty quickly moved outside of mainstream journalism because the opportunities were rarely there to partner up with people who would enable me to take control of the tone of the writing and the magazine . . . Which meant paying for ourselves, living on very little, establishing distribution networks, taking the knocks, all that sort of thing, but it wasn't actually that negative an environment. We found an audience out there quite quickly. It was already there, so, we were connected.

Dave Hegan Punk encouraged not being worried about what people think of you, not trying to fit through conforming to anything in particular, just trying to be yourself, which I'd hope everyone would do, not just punk-rockers. It definitely set up how I see the world. And the communist stuff actually, that's in there, too. You just evolve, you never stay exactly the same. You learn something new and then you learn something else, and you just keep on moving. Punk's definitely the basis, but I'm also into lots of other stuff as well. Now my main passion's climbing mountains.

Moira Clunie I was doing all the coding for Moon Rocket myself. It wasn't just HTML webpages, there was a database behind it. I taught myself through tutorials on message boards and webpages; there was no such thing as YouTube back then. I would've learned how to make webpages around the same time that I was figuring things out about zines, so it came from a similar impulse around self-expression, making information more accessible, sharing things about niche topics that I was interested in.

109

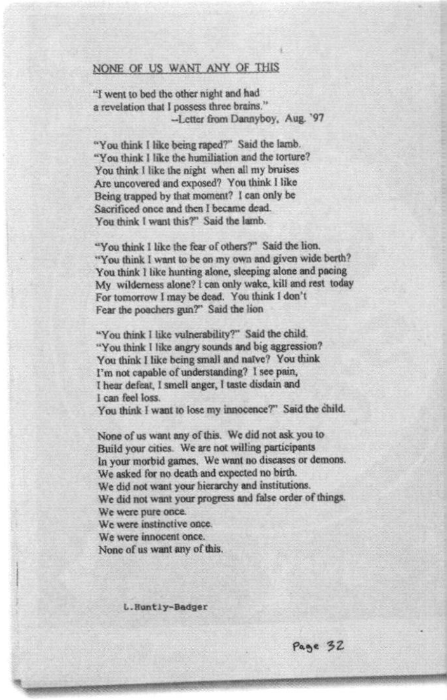

NONE OF US WANT ANY OF THIS

"I went to bed the other night and had
a revelation that I possess three brains."
--Letter from Dannyboy, Aug. '97

"You think I like being raped?" Said the lamb.
"You think I like the humiliation and the torture?
You think I like the night when all my bruises
Are uncovered and exposed? You think I like
Being trapped by that moment? I can only be
Sacrificed once and then I became dead.
You think I want this?" Said the lamb.

"You think I like the fear of others?" Said the lion.
"You think I want to be on my own and given wide berth?
You think I like hunting alone, sleeping alone and pacing
My wilderness alone? I can only wake, kill and rest today
For tomorrow I may be dead. You think I don't
Fear the poachers gun?" Said the lion

"You think I like vulnerability?" Said the child.
"You think I like angry sounds and big aggression?
You think I like being small and naïve? You think
I'm not capable of understanding? I see pain,
I hear defeat, I smell anger, I taste disdain and
I can feel loss.
You think I want to lose my innocence?" Said the child.

None of us want any of this. We did not ask you to
Build your cities. We are not willing participants
In your morbid games. We want no diseases or demons.
We asked for no death and expected no birth.
We did not want your hierarchy and institutions.
We did not want your progress and false order of things.
We were pure once.
We were instinctive once.
We were innocent once.
None of us want any of this.

L.Huntly-Badger

Page 32

109. *Plastic Green Trees* spread and cover, edited by Daniel Powell and Traicy-Lee Cranston, A4, 1999. Ōtautahi Christchurch.

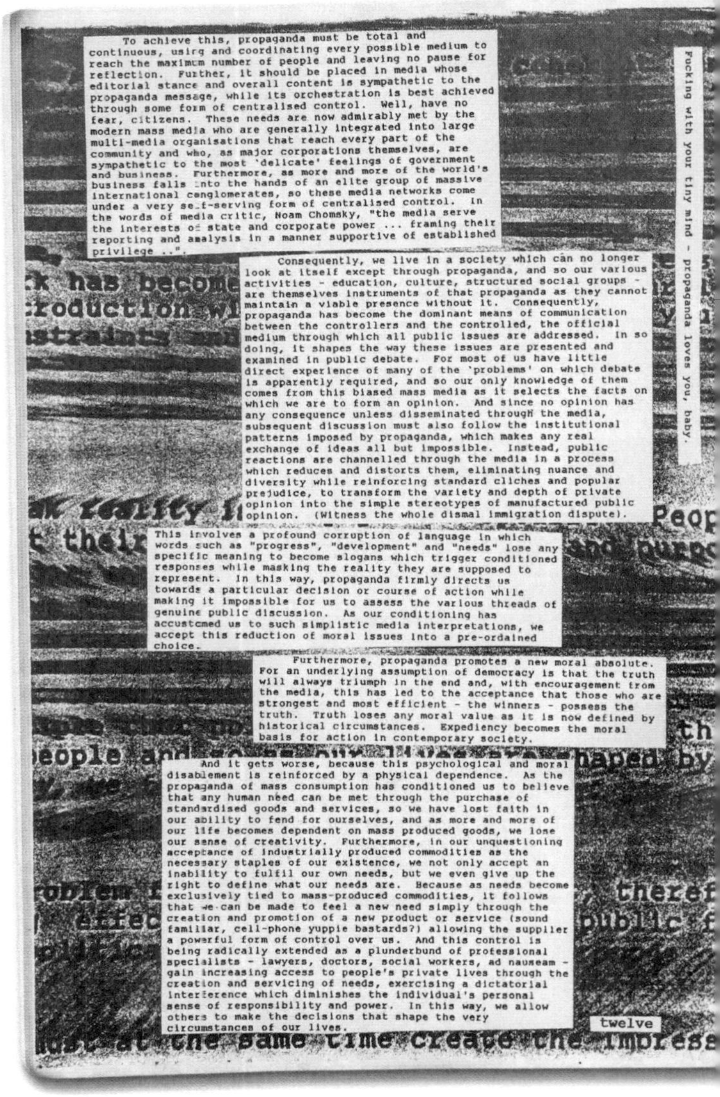

To achieve this, propaganda must be total and continuous, using and coordinating every possible medium to reach the maximum number of people and leaving no pause for reflection. Further, it should be placed in media whose editorial stance and overall content is sympathetic to the propaganda message, while its orchestration is best achieved through some form of centralised control. Well, have no fear, citizens. These needs are now admirably met by the modern mass media who are generally integrated into large multi-media organisations that reach every part of the community and who, as major corporations themselves, are sympathetic to the most 'delicate' feelings of government and business. Furthermore, as more and more of the world's business falls into the hands of an elite group of massive international conglomerates, so these media networks come under a very self-serving form of centralised control. In the words of media critic, Noam Chomsky, "the media serve the interests of state and corporate power ... framing their reporting and analysis in a manner supportive of established privilege ..".

Consequently, we live in a society which can no longer look at itself except through propaganda, and so our various activities - education, culture, structured social groups - are themselves instruments of that propaganda as they cannot maintain a viable presence without it. Consequently, propaganda has become the dominant means of communication between the controllers and the controlled, the official medium through which all public issues are addressed. In so doing, it shapes the way these issues are presented and examined in public debate. For most of us have little direct experience of many of the 'problems' on which debate is apparently required, and so our only knowledge of them comes from this biased mass media as it selects the facts on which we are to form an opinion. And since no opinion has any consequence unless disseminated through the media, subsequent discussion must also follow the institutional patterns imposed by propaganda, which makes any real exchange of ideas all but impossible. Instead, public reactions are channelled through the media in a process which reduces and distorts them, eliminating nuance and diversity while reinforcing standard cliches and popular prejudice, to transform the variety and depth of private opinion into the simple stereotypes of manufactured public opinion. (Witness the whole dismal immigration dispute).

This involves a profound corruption of language in which words such as "progress", "development" and "needs" lose any specific meaning to become slogans which trigger conditioned responses while masking the reality they are supposed to represent. In this way, propaganda firmly directs us towards a particular decision or course of action while making it impossible for us to assess the various threads of genuine public discussion. As our conditioning has accustomed us to such simplistic media interpretations, we accept this reduction of moral issues into a pre-ordained choice.

Furthermore, propaganda promotes a new moral absolute. For an underlying assumption of democracy is that the truth will always triumph in the end and, with encouragement from the media, this has led to the acceptance that those who are strongest and most efficient - the winners - possess the truth. Truth loses any moral value as it is now defined by historical circumstances. Expediency becomes the moral basis for action in contemporary society.

And it gets worse, because this psychological and moral disablement is reinforced by a physical dependence. As the propaganda of mass consumption has conditioned us to believe that any human need can be met through the purchase of standardised goods and services, so we have lost faith in our ability to fend for ourselves, and as more and more of our life becomes dependent on mass produced goods, we lose our sense of creativity. Furthermore, in our unquestioning acceptance of industrially produced commodities as the necessary staples of our existence, we not only accept an inability to fulfil our own needs, but we even give up the right to define what our needs are. Because as needs become exclusively tied to mass-produced commodities, it follows that we can be made to feel a new need simply through the creation and promotion of a new product or service (sound familiar, cell-phone yuppie bastards?) allowing the supplier a powerful form of control over us. And this control is being radically extended as a plunderbund of professional specialists - lawyers, doctors, social workers, ad nauseam - gain increasing access to people's private lives through the creation and servicing of needs, exercising a dictatorial interference which diminishes the individual's personal sense of responsibility and power. In this way, we allow others to make the decisions that shape the very circumstances of our lives.

twelve

110

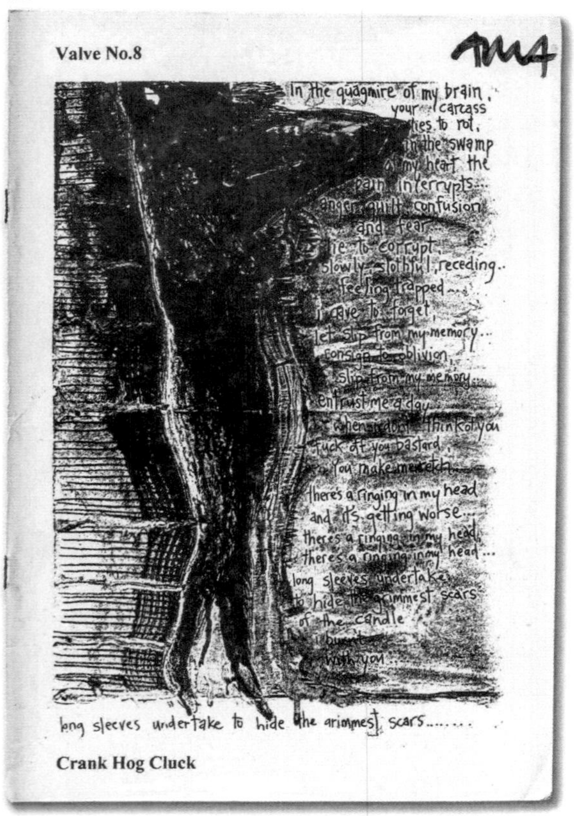

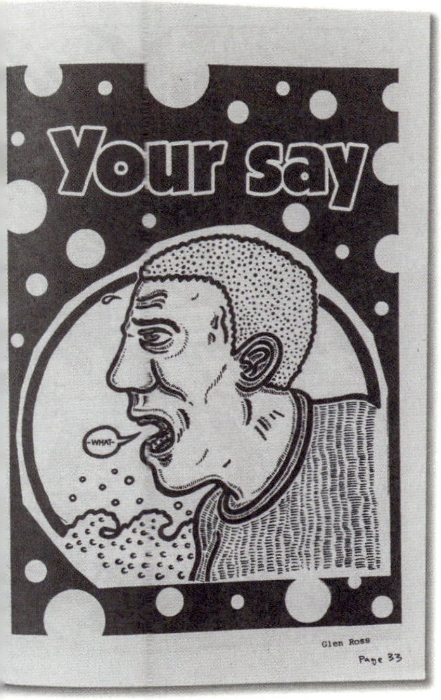

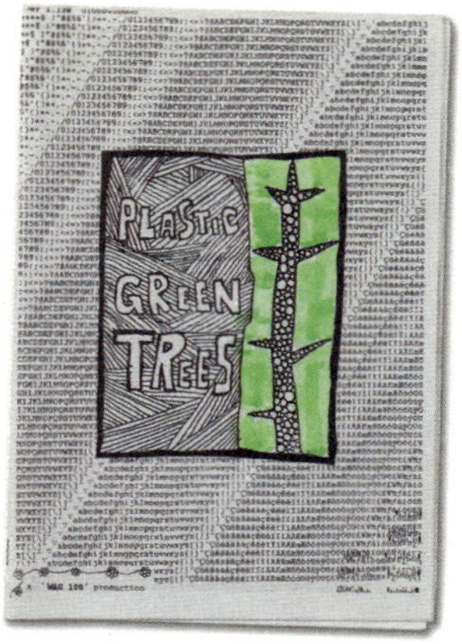

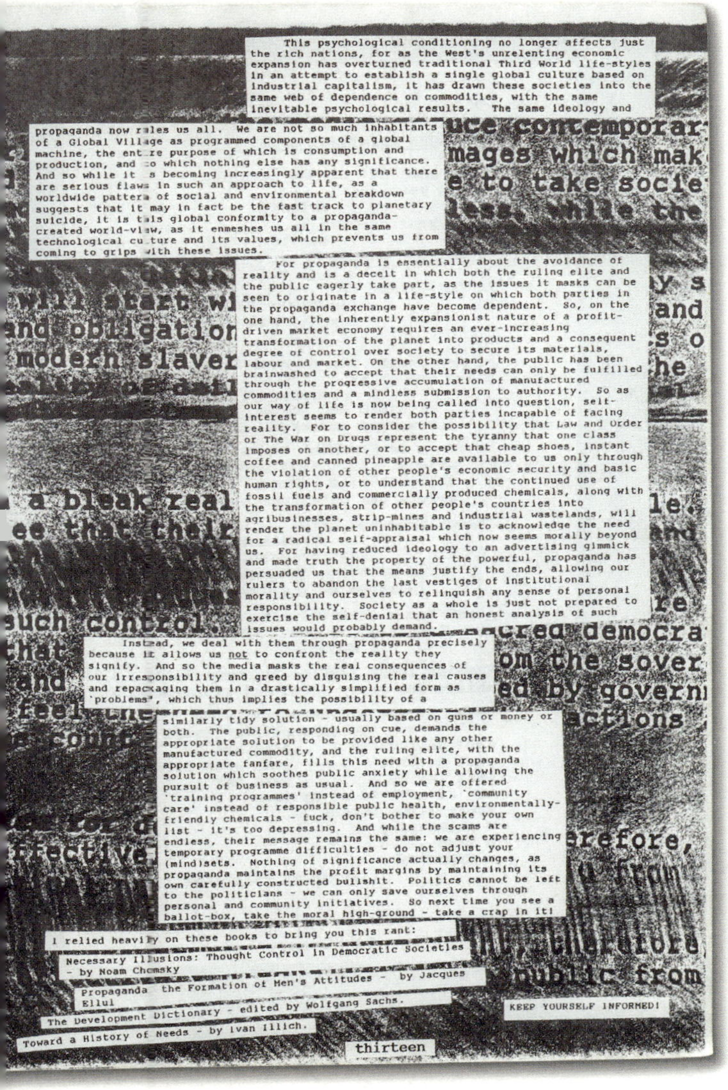

This psychological conditioning no longer affects just the rich nations, for as the West's unrelenting economic expansion has overturned traditional Third World life-styles in an attempt to establish a single global culture based on industrial capitalism, it has drawn these societies into the same web of dependence on commodities, with the same inevitable psychological results. The same ideology and propaganda now rules us all. We are not so much inhabitants of a Global Village as programmed components of a global machine, the entire purpose of which is consumption and production, and to which nothing else has any significance. And so while it is becoming increasingly apparent that there are serious flaws in such an approach to life, as a worldwide pattern of social and environmental breakdown suggests that it may in fact be the fast track to planetary suicide, it is this global conformity to a propaganda-created world-view, as it enmeshes us all in the same technological culture and its values, which prevents us from coming to grips with these issues.

For propaganda is essentially about the avoidance of reality and is a deceit in which both the ruling elite and the public eagerly take part, as the issues it masks can be seen to originate in a life-style on which both parties in the propaganda exchange have become dependent. So, on the one hand, the inherently expansionist nature of a profit-driven market economy requires an ever-increasing transformation of the planet into products and a consequent degree of control over society to secure its materials, labour and market. On the other hand, the public has been brainwashed to accept that their needs can only be fulfilled through the progressive accumulation of manufactured commodities and a mindless submission to authority. So as our way of life is now being called into question, self-interest seems to render both parties incapable of facing reality. For to consider the possibility that Law and Order or The War on Drugs represent the tyranny that one class imposes on another, or to accept that cheap shoes, instant coffee and canned pineapple are available to us only through the violation of other people's economic security and basic human rights, or to understand that the continued use of fossil fuels and commercially produced chemicals, along with the transformation of other people's countries into agribusinesses, strip-mines and industrial wastelands, will render the planet uninhabitable is to acknowledge the need for a radical self-appraisal which now seems morally beyond us. For having reduced ideology to an advertising gimmick and made truth the property of the powerful, propaganda has persuaded us that the means justify the ends, allowing our rulers to abandon the last vestiges of institutional morality and ourselves to relinquish any sense of personal responsibility. Society as a whole is just not prepared to exercise the self-denial that an honest analysis of such issues would probably demand.

Instead, we deal with them through propaganda precisely because it allows us not to confront the reality they signify. And so the media masks the real consequences of our irresponsibility and greed by disguising the real causes and repackaging them in a drastically simplified form as 'problems', which thus implies the possibility of a similarly tidy solution – usually based on guns or money or both. The public, responding on cue, demands the appropriate solution to be provided like any other manufactured commodity, and the ruling elite, with the appropriate fanfare, fills this need with a propaganda solution which soothes public anxiety while allowing the pursuit of business as usual. And so we are offered 'training programmes' instead of employment, 'community care' instead of responsible public health, environmentally-friendly chemicals – fuck, don't bother to make your own list – it's too depressing. And while the scams are endless, their message remains the same: we are experiencing temporary programme difficulties – do not adjust your (mind)sets. Nothing of significance actually changes, as propaganda maintains the profit margins by maintaining its own carefully constructed bullshit. Politics cannot be left to the politicians – we can only save ourselves through personal and community initiatives. So next time you see a ballot-box, take the moral high-ground – take a crap in it!

I relied heavily on these books to bring you this rant:

Necessary Illusions: Thought Control in Democratic Societies – by Noam Chomsky

Propaganda the Formation of Men's Attitudes – by Jacques Ellul

The Development Dictionary – edited by Wolfgang Sachs.

Toward a History of Needs – by Ivan Illich.

KEEP YOURSELF INFORMED!

thirteen

Dave White I ran a zinefest at Nelson Community Arts Centre in 1997 to celebrate that last issue of *Valve*. I've always been quite good at building a collective; like, the reason I did Yellow Bike Records and got all the bands in Palmy involved and helped them do shit was because it also helped *my* band. Instead of me being in one band coming from Palmy, all of a sudden Palmy had a scene with like 40 bands and we were part of a collective. It meant more people came to gigs, more people bought records.

I thought the same thing when I did the last issue of *Valve*. I had no idea how it was gonna go in Nelson, after the shift from Palmy. I'd just moved there, there were only four punks in the Nelson scene, one of whom was my assistant at the Arts Centre job. I didn't know how I was gonna sell one copy, locally. The only Nelson punk band had supported my band Lung when we'd played there a couple years earlier. It was a really bad night. We blew up the PA and there was a fire in the toilet. The Nelson guys were banned from ever playing the venue again, and that was the only venue *in* Nelson. We'd fucked it for them. So there was a lot of hate coming at me when I first arrived in Nelson, even though the punks would usually be my allies.

The previous coordinator was a really staunch lesbian. The community she'd established was really worried about this guy taking over. It was an actual community centre, with courses for IHC, art classes, all kinds of cultural groups using the space. It wasn't just a punk-rock hangout. So, anyway, I thought I've got hundreds of zines at home, we'll have a zinefest. We'll lay them all out and people can read them. I had a *huge* collection, because people would write about my band and then send me a copy. And everywhere we toured, we picked them up. Some of them got used as toilet paper in the van. [Laughs.]

Cartoonist Trace Hodgson was really supportive and did a lot to help, including running a comics workshop. New Zealand bands played throughout the fest, and Fugazi played opening night. Zinefest became the model for the fringe festival that we started running alongside the World of Wearable Art when it was based in Nelson.

110. *Valve* #8 cover and spread, edited by Dave White, 270 × 202mm, date unknown. Te Papaioea Palmerston North.

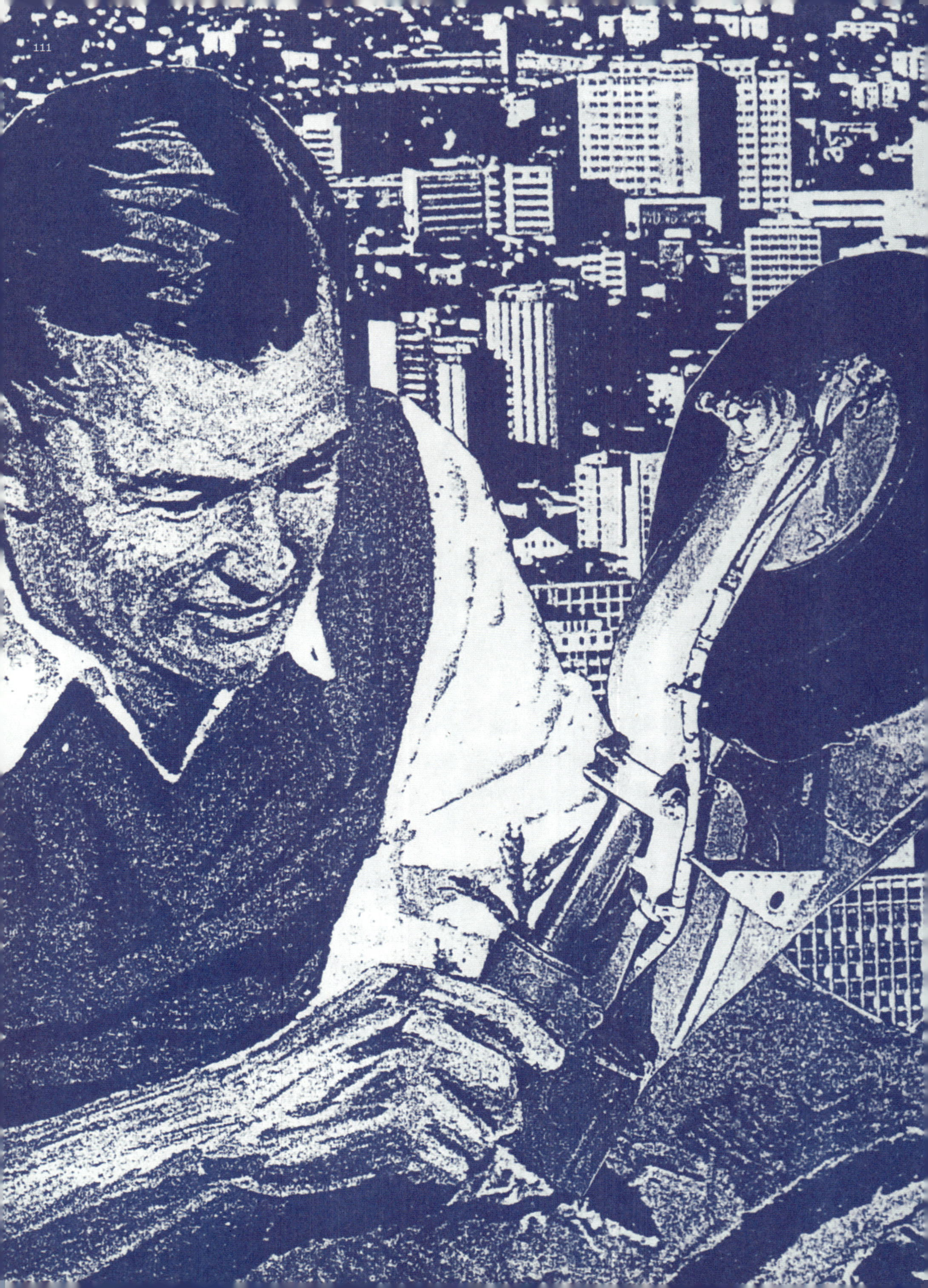

Two-thousands Aotearoa

Beyond the music, eighties punk zines responded to incidents of police brutality, irrelevant royals, the bullishness of Prime Minister Robert Muldoon (who was ousted in the 1984 election), nuclear testing in the Pacific . . . all manner of contemporary issues. But such real-time reaction waned through the nineties, and by the two-thousands had all but disappeared as identity came to the fore. At the level of content, the politics of zines in the two-thousands might be feminist and personal, reacting to the age-old violence of patriarchy rather than zeroing in on a specific governmental issue. Riot Grrrl influenced zines in Aotearoa long after its mid-nineties heyday in the US. Other two-thousands zines were completely apolitical in their content, but mounted a challenge at the level of aesthetics and mode-of-exchange.

111. *looking for a fish-drying plant?* #1 page detail, Stephen Clover, A5, 2001. Te Whanganui-a-Tara Wellington.

Those running Aotearoa zine distros in the two-thousands were motivated by the gift economy of zines rather than capitalist notions of profit. Zine production continued to tax the business model as zinesters used their workplace photocopiers to make their art on the sly, or got hold of someone else's work copier through the friend of a friend. These savings were passed on to the audience; the $2 zine of the mid-eighties was still only $2 in the two-thousands!

A photocopier. *iStock*

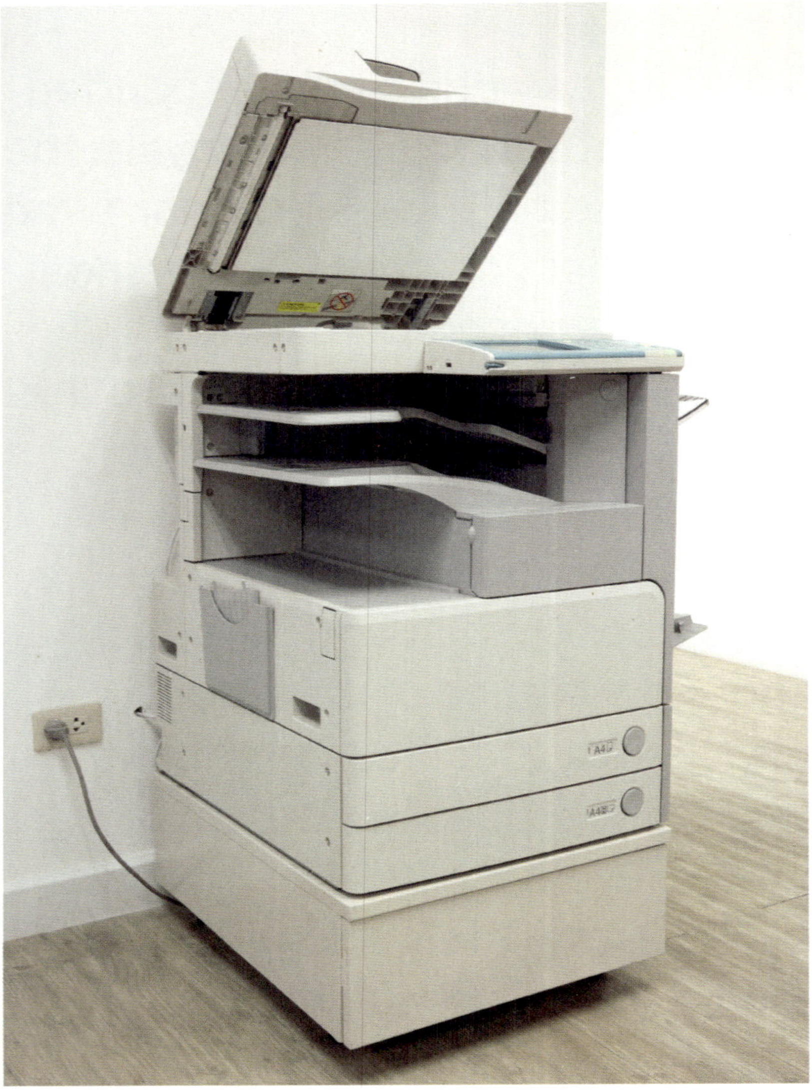

So what political changes were most (but not all) zinesters ignoring at the level of content? In 2001, United States interference in the Middle East led to terror attacks on New York's World Trade Center. In response the US launched its 'war on terror', targeting al-Qaeda, the Taliban, and later, Islamic State, articulating an arch nemesis lacking since the collapse of the Soviet Union. New Zealand, as a compliant Five Eyes partner,[1] introduced the Terrorism Suppression Act 2002, and offered up its own 'terrorists' in 2007 when police raided so-called training camps in Te Urewera and made 18 arrests. The most famous of those arrested was the longtime Tūhoe activist Tāme Iti, who was sent to prison on firearms charges.

Much closer to the zine scene, the community centre at 128 Abel Smith Street in Wellington was also raided by police as part of the Tūhoe raids operation. The centre was home to the Revolting Books zine library, who were regular stallholders at Wellington Zinefest. Zinester Valerie Morse, one of 18 arrested, later produced *The Day the Raids Came* through 'radical left' imprint Rebel Press.

11 September 2001 terrorist attack on the World Trade Center, New York. *Wikipedia*

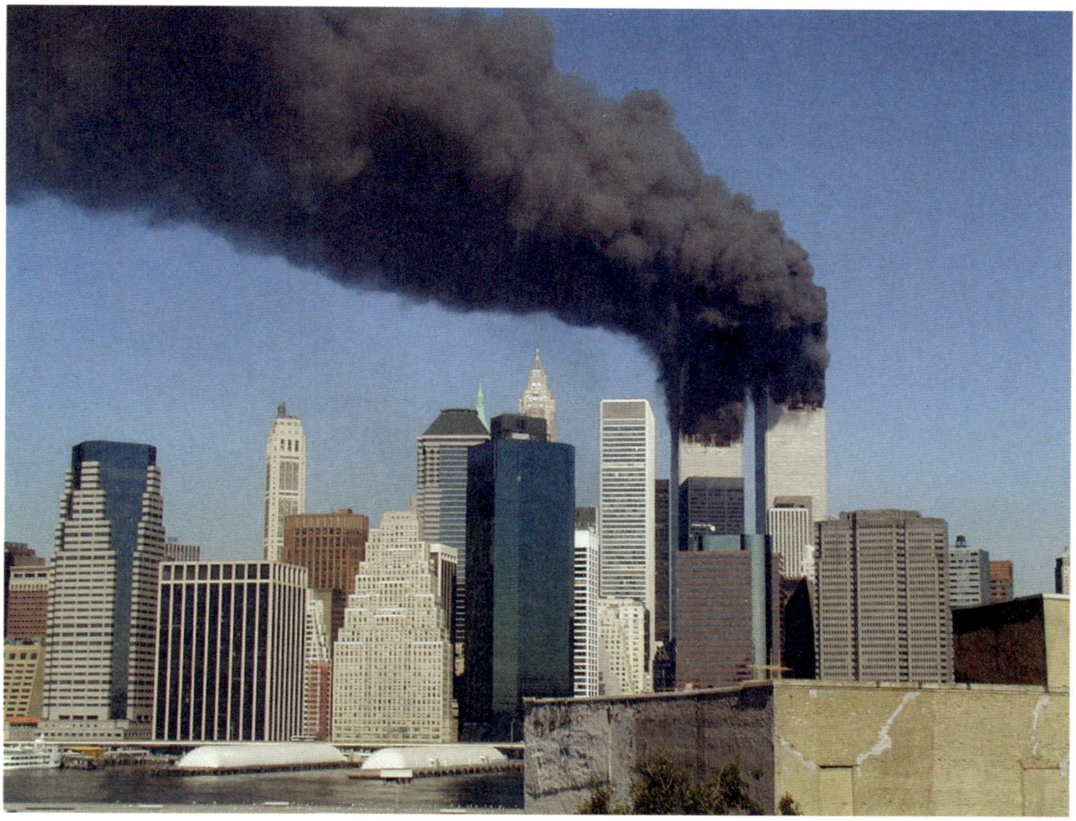

An increase in racism against Islamic New Zealanders was noted after 9/11, culminating in the tragic Christchurch mosque attacks of the next decade.

Helen Clark's Labour government eroded traditional Māori rights to the foreshore and seabed when it enacted the Foreshore and Seabed Act of 2004, putting ownership in the hands of the Crown. In 2009 John Key's National government reviewed the Act as part of a 'confidence-and-supply' agreement with the Māori Party. The Māori Party had been established after Clark removed Labour MP Tariana Turia's ministerial roles when Turia opposed the Act. Turia resigned, triggering a by-election.

The collapse of US banks as the result of risky speculative practices in late 2007 led to a global financial crisis the following year.

After the existential challenge of climate change was taken up by the United Nations' Intergovermental Panel on Climate Change, awareness of global warming took hold in the popular consciousness, even if governments did little in response.

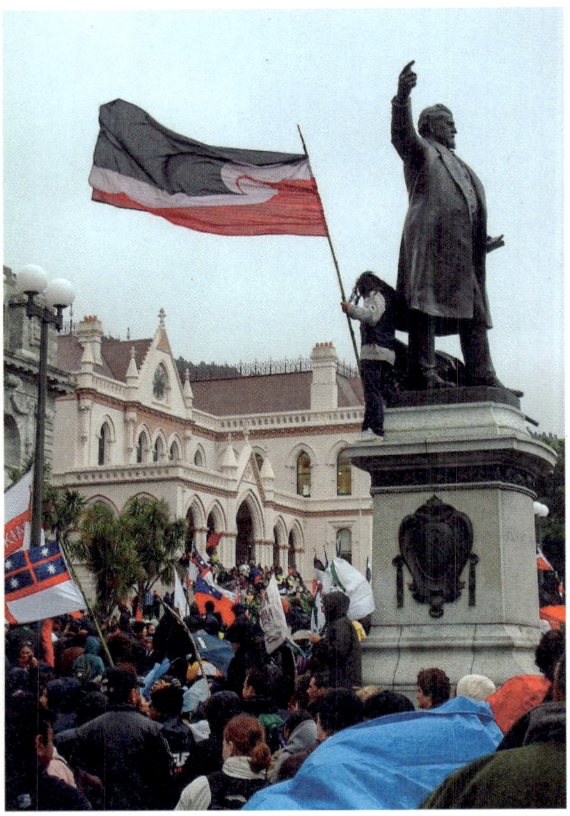

The hīkoi to protest against proposed legislation to vest ownership of New Zealand's foreshore and seabed in the Crown arrives at Parliament, 5 May 2004. *Wikipedia*

WikiLeaks was founded in 2006. Internet platforms were rapidly taking over as the place to publish and communicate, especially at the social level through providers like Myspace, which remained the most popular social networking site until 2009.

Everyday authors moved online to such an extent that by 2006 around 42 million bloggers made up the 'blogosphere'. This zinester fielded repeated enquiries from a friend wondering 'Are you still making that paper blog?' Zines were left with a pronounced sense of 'objectness', even if that was understood on an intuitive rather than an analytical level. Some radical left and anarchist tracts stuck with zines, a surprisingly sentimental turn, but most narrative and informational texts moved online. E-commerce became more and more popular; both of Aotearoa's online zine distros retired when the exchange started to lack any sense of intimacy, connection and community.

***

Enter the 'zinefest'. As we have heard, the first zinefest by name was held at the Nelson Community Arts Centre in 1997, although Dave White's event was more of an exhibition of amassed zines than any sort of market-day exchange. Small Print 2003 and 2005 brought zinesters and their audience together at the Grey Lynn Library hall in Auckland for a zine market, workshops and related activities. Two young women in attendance — Kylie Buck and Tessa Stubbing — would be inspired to start, respectively, Wellington Zinefest in 2007 and Auckland Zinefest in 2009. Both have run annually ever since.

Zine distros and zinefests both made space for zines in and of themselves. Zines were no longer defined as an extension of the music available at record shops, an extension of anarchist politics available from The Freedom Shop, or an aside to the superhero comics found in comics shops. Subsequently, zine genres splintered and blossomed until many defied genre altogether.

Meanwhile, in popular culture the singles charts at the start of the two-thousands were dominated by the phenomenon of manufactured girl bands and boy bands, alongside divas like Britney Spears, Kylie Minogue, Jennifer Lopez, Shakira and the enduring Madonna. By the mid-two-thousands hip hop was back in charge, the most staggering run reserved for Scribe's 'Stand Up/Not Many', which spent 12 weeks at number one.

J.K. Rowling regularly topped book sales as the Harry Potter series continued. Michael King's *History of New Zealand* was a weightier bestseller at the national level.

In film, Miramar became Wellywood through Peter Jackson's *Lord of the Rings* trilogy. Wellington and Weta Digital also played a big part in the highest-grossing film of the decade — *Avatar*. On a comparatively infinitesimal budget, Taika Waititi wrote and directed his first quirky feature — *Eagle vs Shark*. The film's $1.8 million budget is still more money than a hundred volunteer-run zinefests would know what to do with.

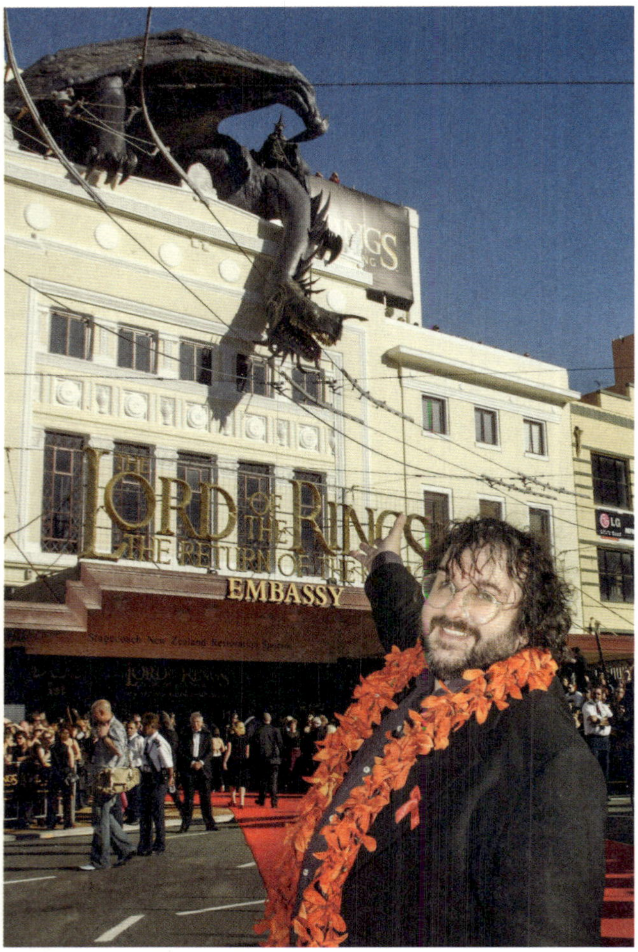

Peter Jackson at the premier of *The Lord of the Rings: The Return of the King* in Te Whanganui-a-Tara Wellington, 1 December 2003. *Waikato Times*

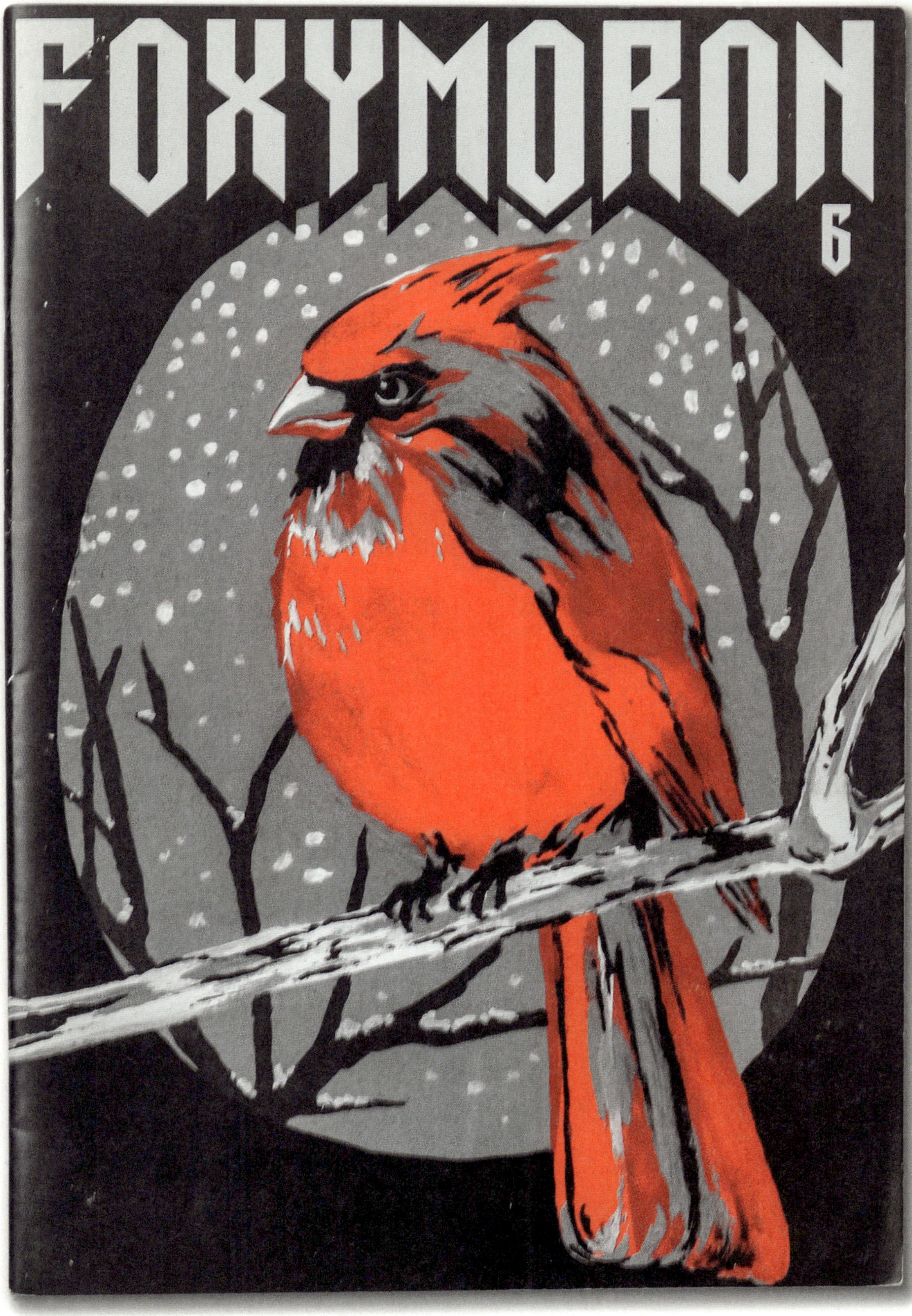

112. *Foxy Moron* #6, edited by Georgie Hill and Melanie Baldwin, A5, 2005. Tāmaki Makaurau Auckland.

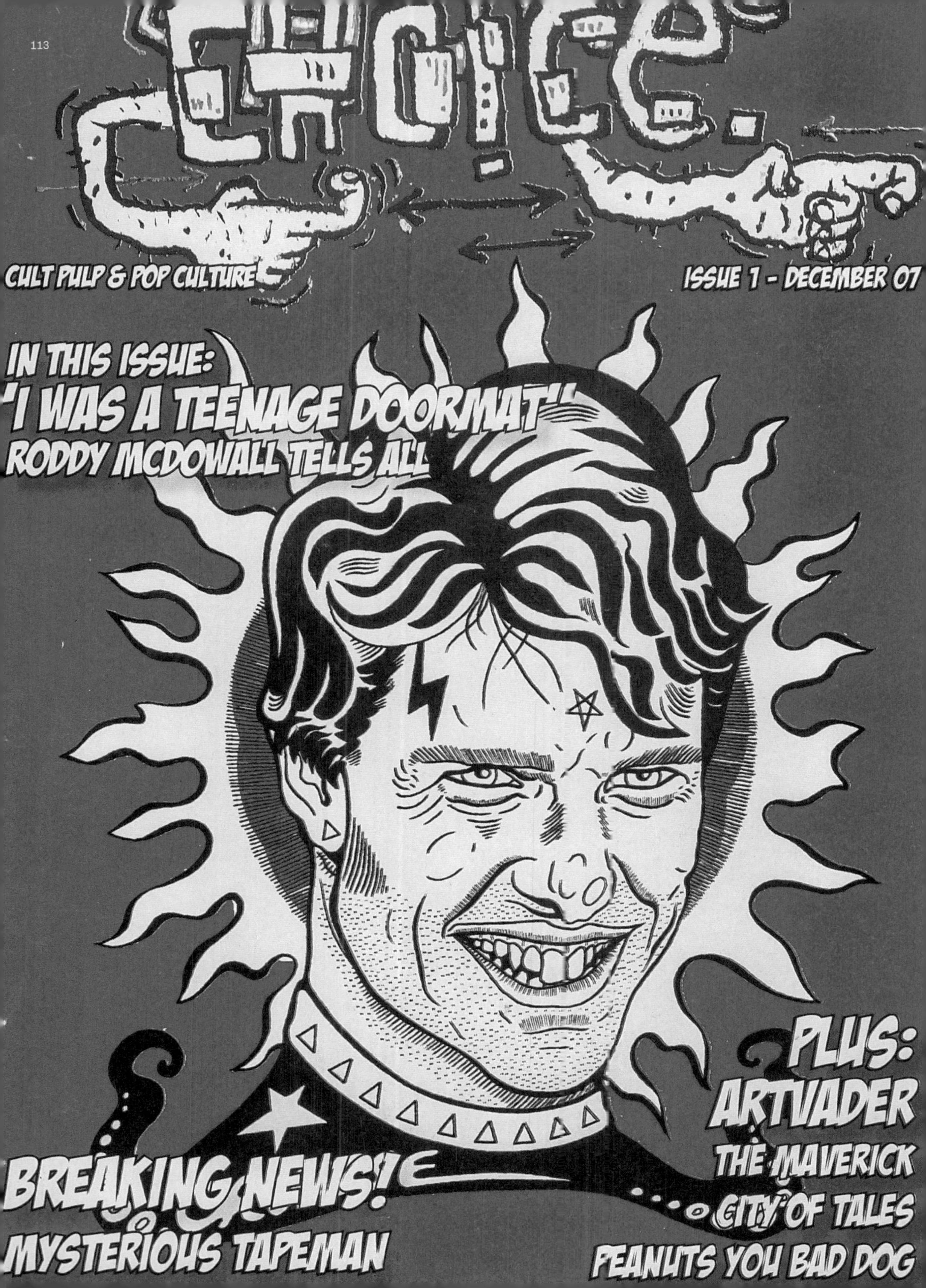
CULT PULP & POP CULTURE
ISSUE 1 - DECEMBER 07
IN THIS ISSUE:
"I WAS A TEENAGE DOORMAT"
RODDY MCDOWALL TELLS ALL
PLUS:
ARTVADER
THE MAVERICK
CITY OF TALES
PEANUTS YOU BAD DOG
BREAKING NEWS!
MYSTERIOUS TAPEMAN

Two-thousands Zines

Pritika Lal You could walk past a café or a music store and pick up a really significant piece of work that someone had just left in the doorway.

That's how I found out about zines, from just picking stuff up out of doorways and then thinking 'What? This is a whole thing — this is not like a flyer. Maybe we could do something like this?'

Tessa Stubbing The first zine I ever came across was something called *Punk Brazil*, which I found in Real Groovy Records when it was on Queen Street. Maybe it was dropped off by a tourist or a traveller or someone who'd immigrated here. Real Groovy had a little rack in the doorway where you'd have all the flyers and stuff. Someone had dropped *Punk Brazil* in there. I don't know if there were more zines there at the time, I just remember that one because I grabbed it and I was like 'This is cool, oh my gosh.' The printing wasn't even double-sided, each page of content sat next to a blank page. It was pretty low-budget, and that was cool.

Did I know it was called a zine? No, I don't think so. We'd just got internet at home with a 14.8K modem — so, so slow. I looked up punkas.com, and from there I found out that this thing was called a zine, and then I found Moon Rocket zine distro. That's where I used to order all my zines from.

Kylie Buck I'm pretty sure that *Incredibly Hot Sex with Hideous People* was the first zine I ever came across, either in Olive café or Midnight Espresso on Cuba Street. I would have just picked one up and been like 'What the hell is this?!'

Pritika Lal A bunch of us K Road people were working at this shitty call-centre in the evenings. Everyone would doodle on the backs of the customer-service info sheets we were supposed to be filling out during calls. Stefan Neville was also working there, and I gave him this info-sheet doodle I'd done. One day he came into work and presented me with a little book of info-sheet doodle art that included my drawing. He'd made this beautiful little book with a hand-printed cover. They'd been photocopied at A4 and then cut into slivers. That was the first time anyone published anything of mine, and I was like 'Wow, this is amazing. This is now a book? This was just a bunch of conversations.'

113. *Choice #1* detail, edited by Mitch Marks, 260 × 170mm, 2007. Te Whanganui-a-Tara Wellington.

114

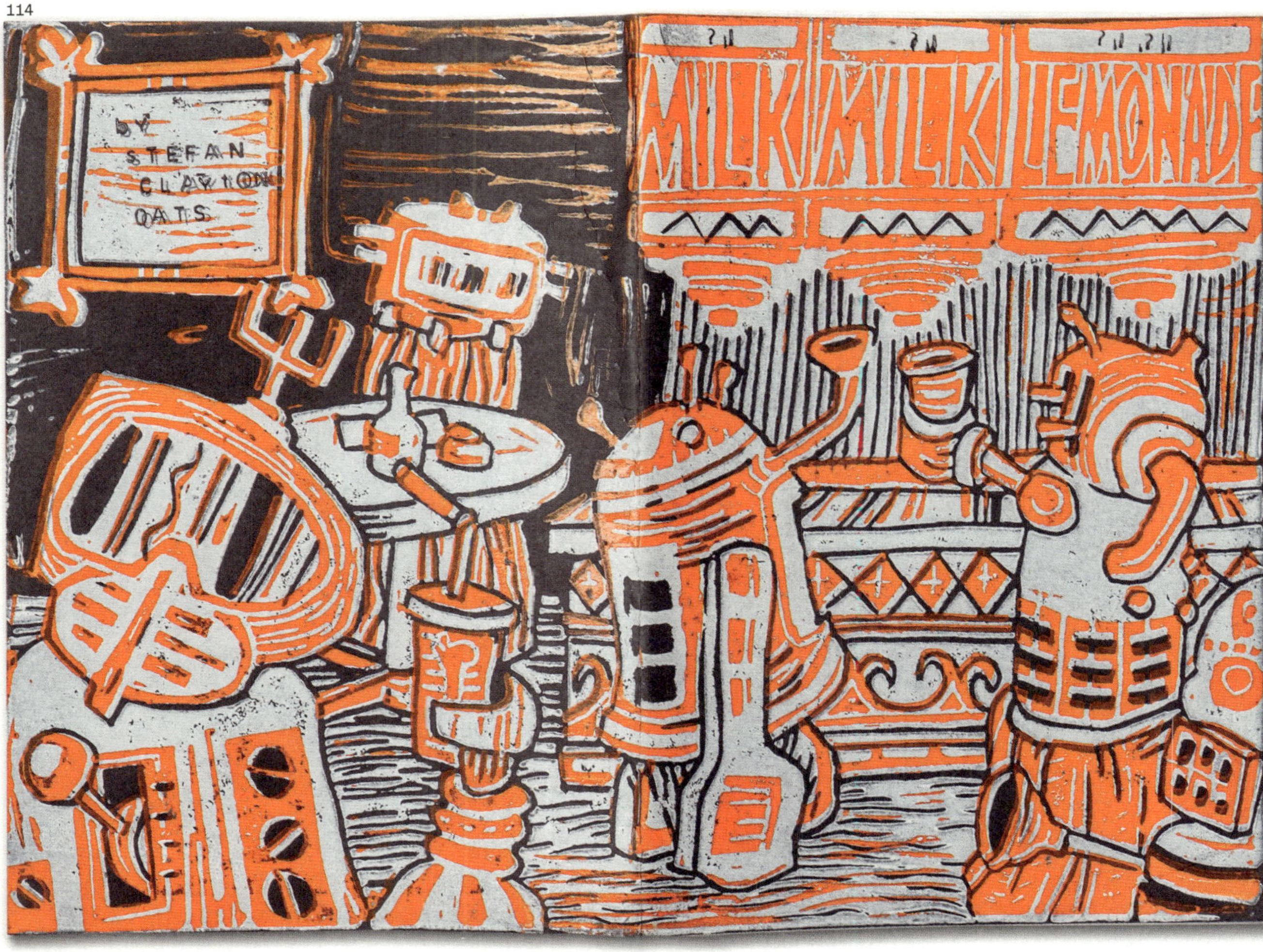

Tui Gordon I left Rotorua and came to Auckland, where I discovered that there were all kinds of people who weren't like the people I grew up with, including people like Ant Sang, who lived in warehouses. I got to see punk zines and comics. It even got me into drawing comics. When I moved to the UK, I used to draw some of Ant's stuff on the walls of my squat. It was really nice being able to do that. I'd been to university and studied literature and stuff. I even remember making a zine before I knew what zines were. I called it a magazine, but it was just a stapled piece of A4, an anti-capitalist thing. I never really understood the whole glossy magazine thing and all of that pop culture, because I was raised by hippie Buddhists, gentle reggae-listening hippies, lentil-eaters, y'know? I definitely had grounding in the animal rights stuff, but the fierceness of punk was pretty alien. I kind of got into punk via ska, because reggae goes to ska goes to punk, and then I got to Riot Grrrl after that, once I realised how cool it was seeing women being tough and making music, which I hadn't really seen before.

114. *Milk Milk Lemonade* front and back covers and spread, Clayton Noone and Stefan Neville, Oats Comics, A5, 2000s. Ōtepoti Dunedin.

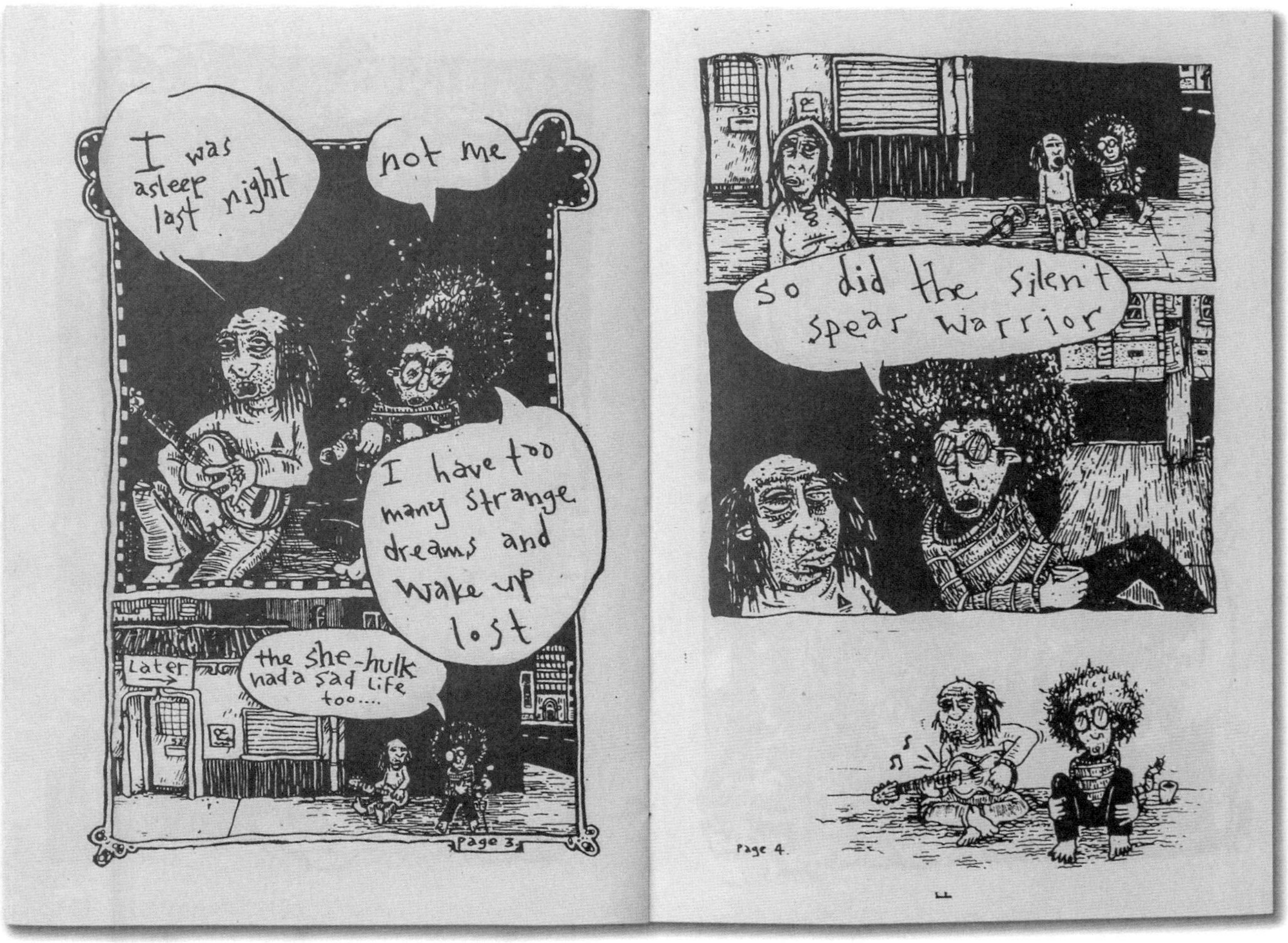

115

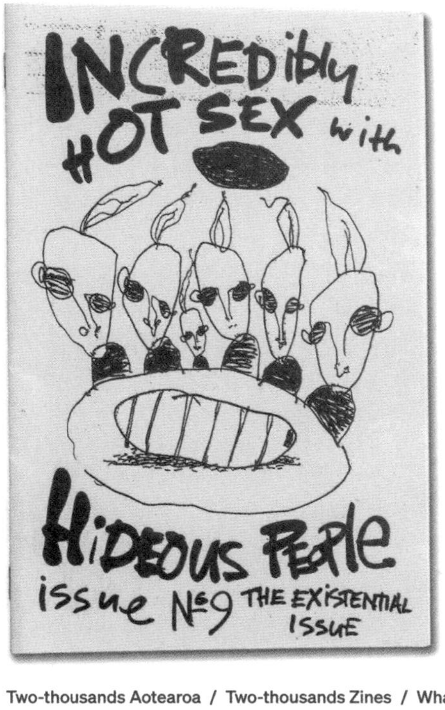

Kylie Buck I just thought it was awesome because *Incredibly Hot Sex with Hideous People* is a perzine. I don't know if people call them that anymore . . . Who wouldn't wanna read some rando talking about their life, that's totally my jam. I was at art school, and you were writing about art and teaching and all sorts. I would've just been like 'Yes, this is my scene . . .' I wouldn't have thought of it as art. I would've just been like 'Oh, sweet, someone wrote a little book about their life.'

115. *Incredibly Hot Sex with Hideous People* #9, Bryce Galloway, A5, 2002. Te Whanganui-a-Tara Wellington.

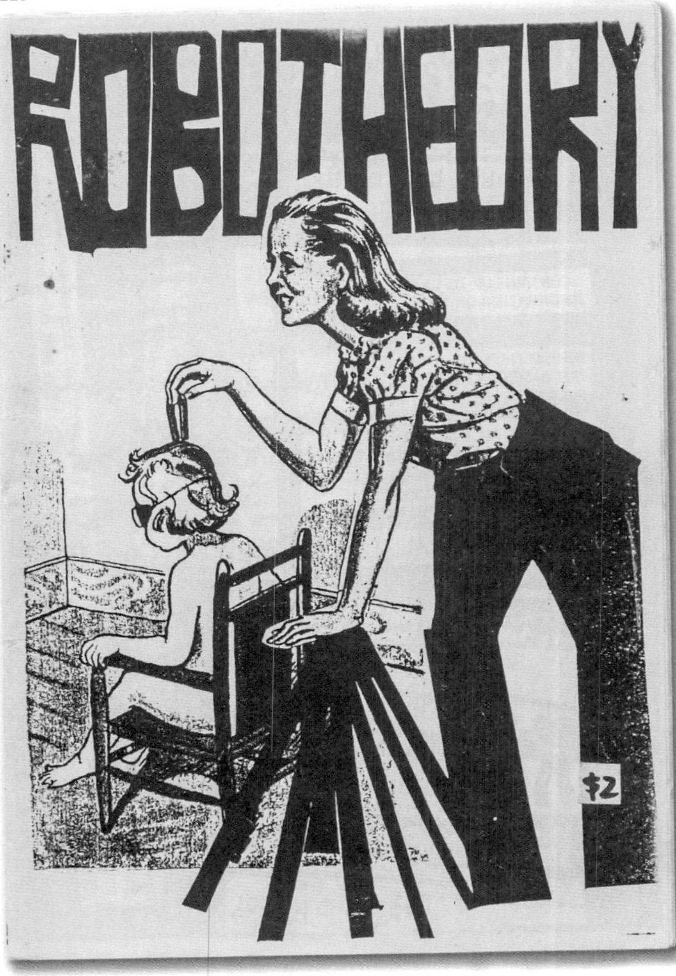

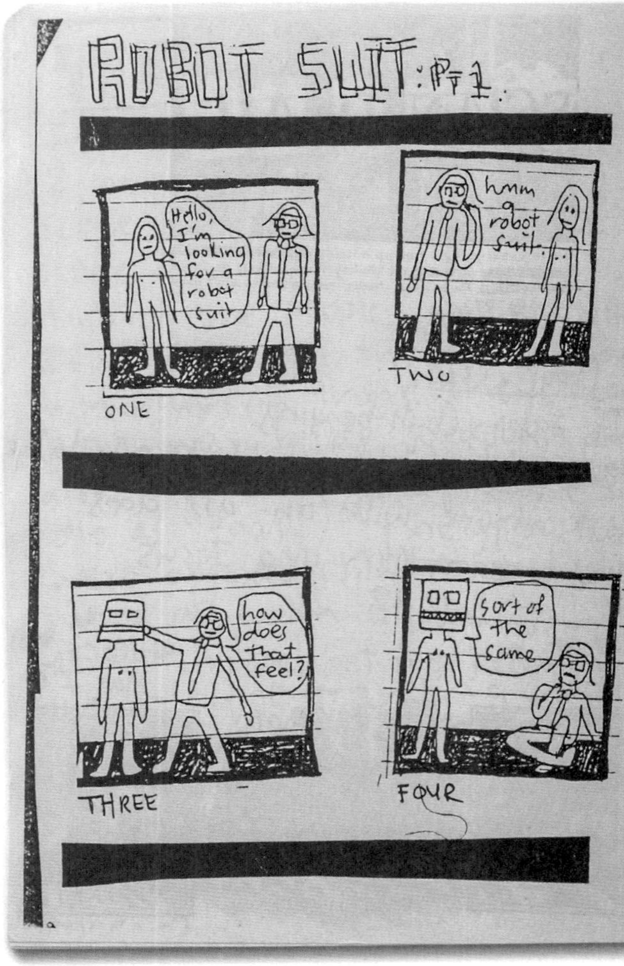

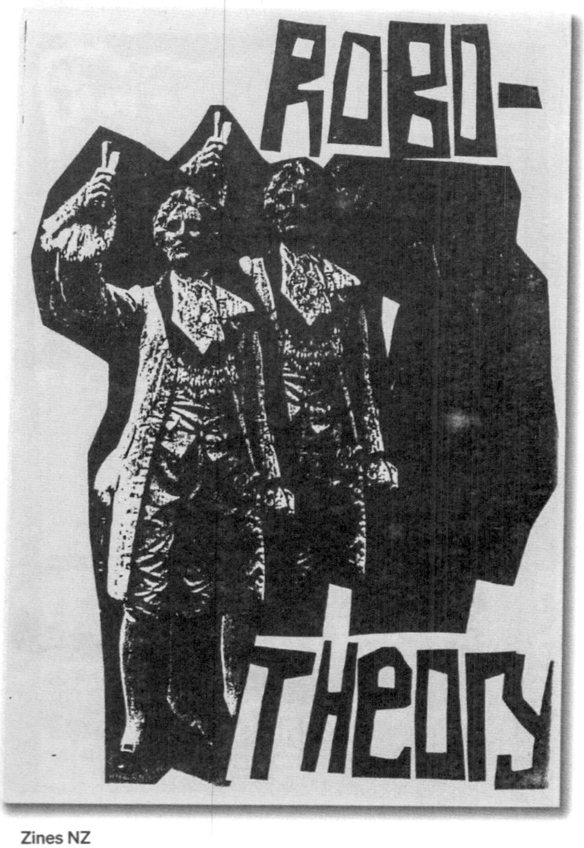

Liz Mathews I express myself by myself, but even though what I'm expressing is really, really personal and a dump from my little brain, I don't mind sharing it once it's done. I can't connect with people in the same way in person. I find it easier to connect with people through something that I make when I'm by myself. I love spending time by myself. I like connecting through the mail and stuff like that.

Years after making friends with Bek Coogan,[2] she said, 'I remember the first time you met me, it was at a Cortina gig.' I'd come up to her because I thought she was so cool, and said [puts on awkward, deferential voice] 'Ugh, this is a zine I made', and then I just ran out. And she was like 'It was this amazing zine that was so funny and so silly and so great, but you wouldn't even talk to me?' Yes, that's right. *Now* I'm able to be friends; a zine is a quicker and easier introduction.

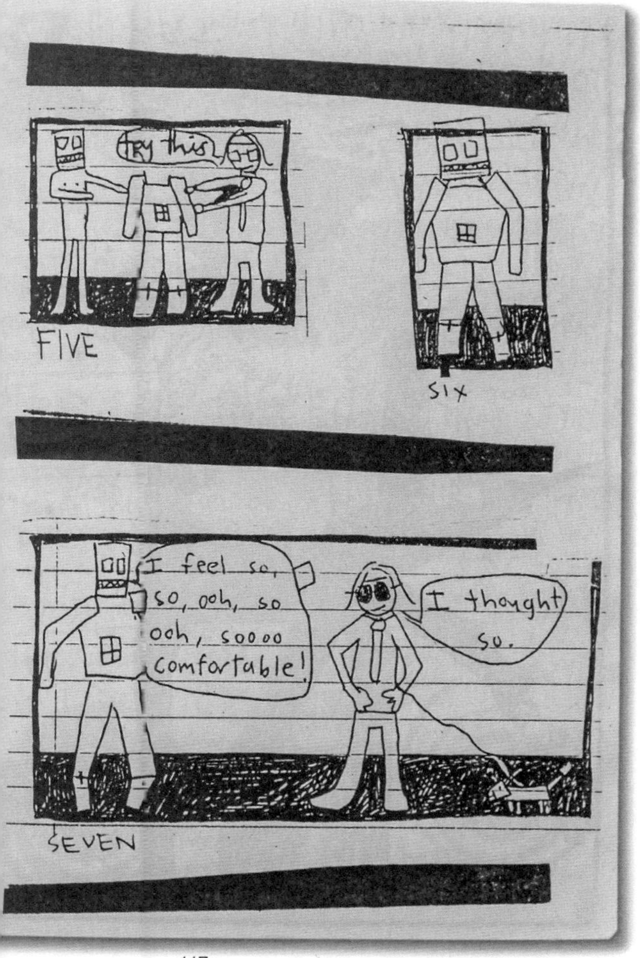

117

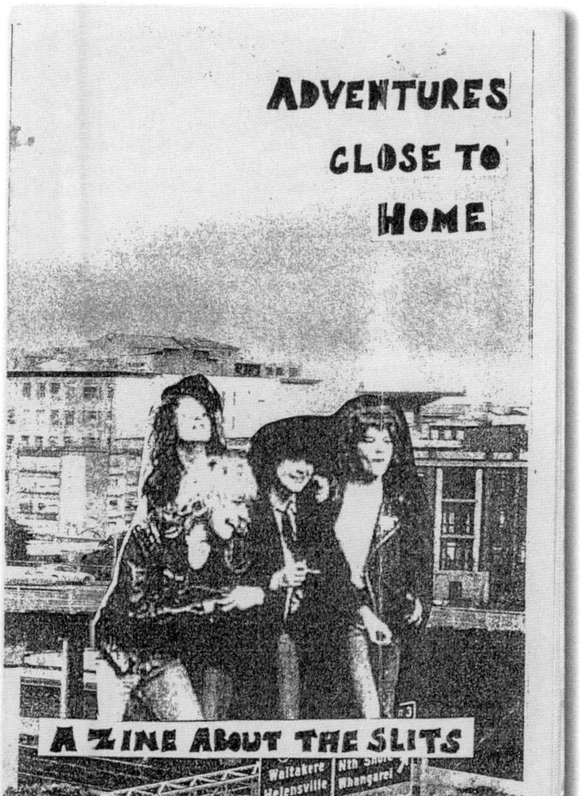

Kerry Ann Lee I saw Liz Mathews the other night at the Bikini Kill gig at the Powerstation and it was so special and actually quite emotional. All of the friends we made through the mixtapes and zines that we traded when we were teenagers . . . we're now in our forties, and some of us have kids who are the age we were when we first met. I remember meeting Liz at one Punk Fest. We had been pen pals for so long, and she used to send me these hilarious, sarcastic, funny-as letters. In my young kid brain I'm thinking 'You must be the funniest person in real life. I can't wait to meet you.' Then I met her. She came down for one of the early Punk Fests in the late nineties and I was like 'I think it's you. You look like your drawing, your cartoon drawing with the glasses and the short hair and the clothes . . .' So I said, 'I think you're my pen pal', and she's like 'Yeah, I'm Liz.' She was really quiet and so shy: '*Are* you my pen pal?' This was on the dancefloor at Thistle Hall at an all-ages gig. She said, 'Yeah, I'm your pen pal, hi.' I was like 'Holy smoke'. I have other long-time friends who I've known half my life through making zines, I haven't met them in person, I only know them through their letters.

Indira Neville I was making these comics and I was interested in Riot Grrrl because it was in the world, but I would never dare call myself a Riot Grrrl. I liked the politics and I liked the bands. I'd go and see Fake Purr at The Kings Arms and I really wanted to make friends with them, so I deliberately made this comic called *I Have Control of My Hair,* which is comic versions of girl-group song lyrics. I did this just so I could take one to them and befriend them, and it totally worked. [Laughs.]

116. *Robo-Theory* #1 and #2 covers and spread, Liz Mathews, A5, 2000/01. Tāmaki Makaurau Auckland.

117. *Adventures Close To Home*, Melissa Steiner, A5, 2000s. Tāmaki Makaurau Auckland.

118

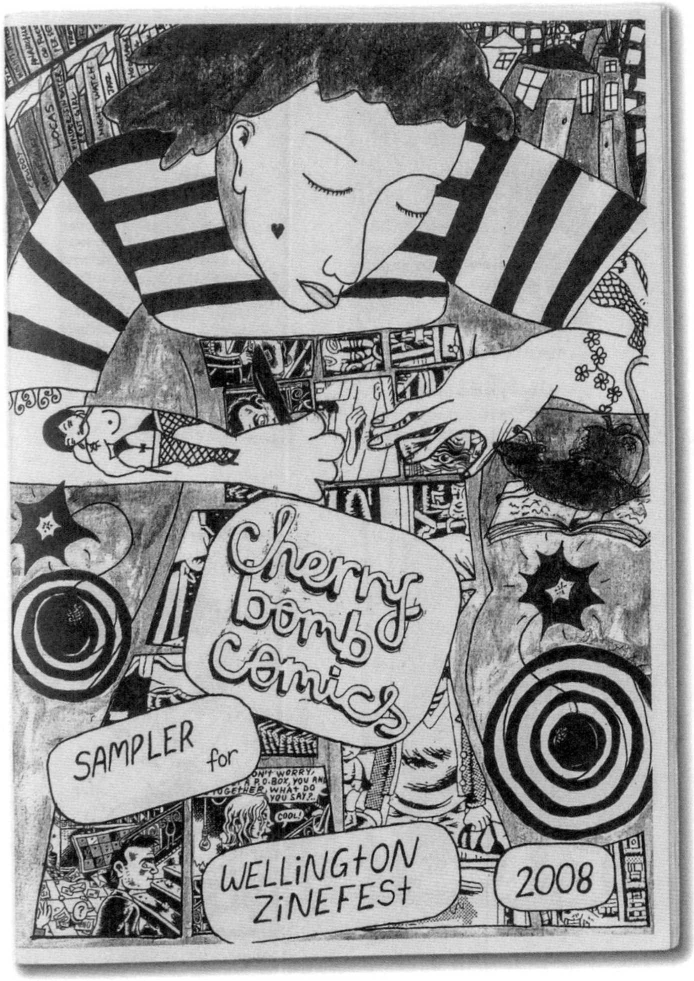

Sam Orchard I started making comics as a film student. I was questioning my gender — well, at that time, probably just my sexuality, because that's all I knew. I was like 'Urgh, I can't find anything in film where there's women who are into other women and where the protagonist doesn't die or kill someone else.' So I went online to try and find those stories. Mostly what I found was comics by lesbian creatives, so that's the kind of stuff that I was drawn to. I'd been drawing since I was little. I did an assignment when I was at primary school in which I said I wanted to be a cartoonist when I grew up.

Drawing pictures was a way for me to express myself and work through stuff. I wasn't great at figuring out what my feelings were or articulating them, but I knew I had a lot of feelings and if I had a piece of paper and a pen in front of me then it would just pour out, and I'd be like 'Oh, okay, that's what I'm feeling.' So comics became a way of expressing that. Usually that was a pretty private undertaking; I didn't share any of that stuff with people until I was at university. I think the first comics that I drew and showed other people were ones that I gave to my friends as a way of coming out.

I just didn't know how to have that conversation with people. I didn't know what their response would be. It felt easiest to just give them a little gift and run the fuck away.

118. *Cherry Bomb Comics Sampler for Wellington Zinefest 2008*, cover by Tui Gordon and spread by Jess Johnson, edited by Melissa Steiner and Tui Gordon, A5, 2008. Tāmaki Makaurau Auckland.

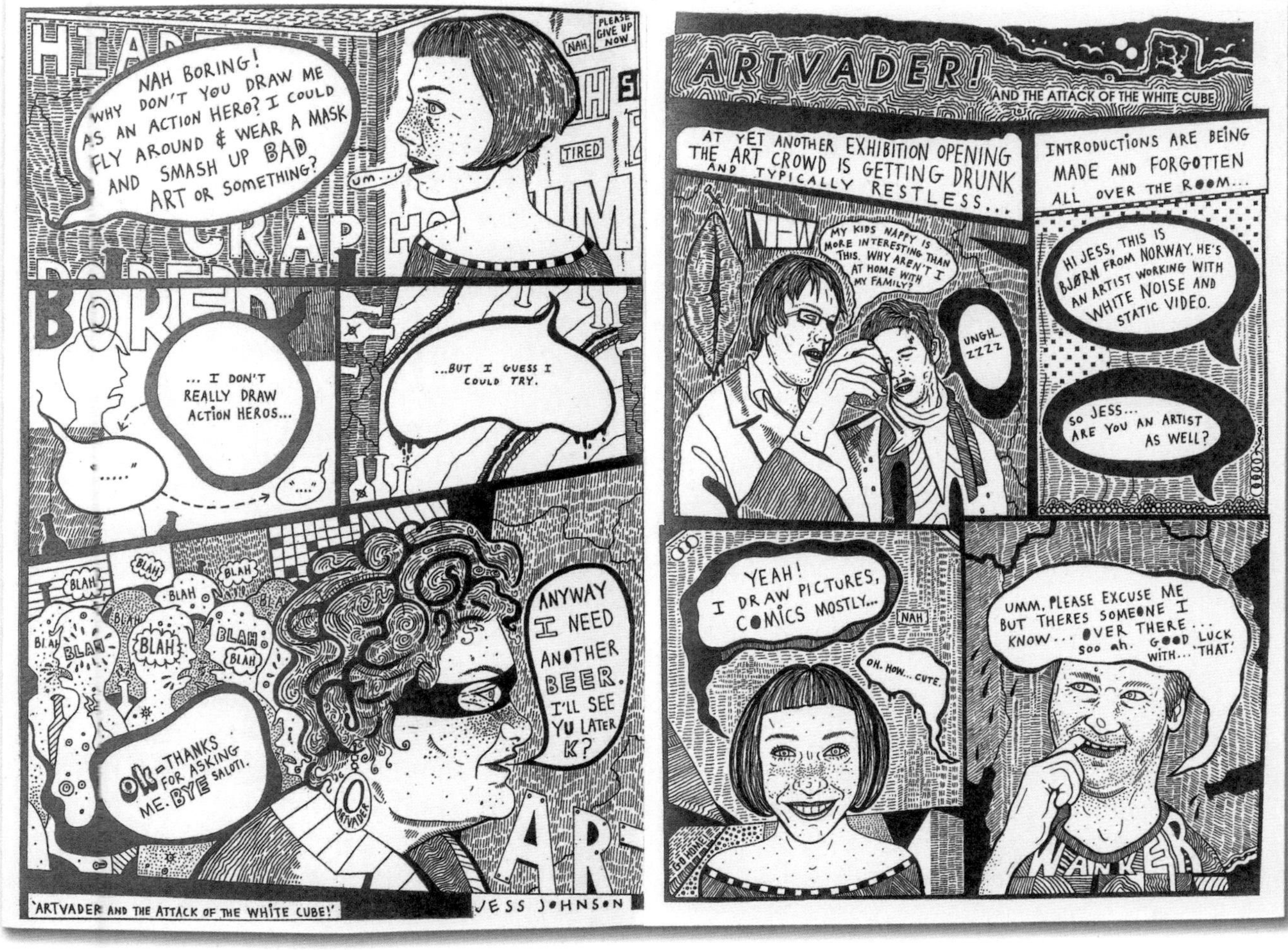

Tui Gordon I'd finished my degree and had my overseas experience, and I was like 'Okay, what do I do now?' Melissa Steiner and I had been discussing what we would do if we could do anything and we'd both become interested in comic books after reading *The Sandman* and stuff like that. Neil Gaiman's feminism's a bit murky these days, but back then we got these strong, interesting, punky women characters. Heaps of the comics that I'd read as a kid hadn't really hit me, but with *The Sandman* I was like 'This is such an amazing way of communicating a narrative, it can be so much more than superheroes and funnies.' Melissa and I both asked: 'Are women making these? Where are the comics that appeal to women?' When you went to Heroes for Sale or whatever, it was all pretty boysie really.

The same day I got offered a job teaching English in Japan we got offered the shop [in Auckland] that became Cherry Bomb. I had to decide which to do, and we decided to do the shop. It was really fun, it was a really good choice.

Moira Clunie The Moon Rocket online zine distro launched on 1 January 2000. I figured that went with this whole futuristic thing.

Kylie Buck We ordered some zines from Alex Wrekk's distro in Portland, and some from Cherry Bomb Comics and Moira Clunie's Moon Rocket distro in Auckland.

Moira Clunie I had a part-time job working for ihug, the internet service provider in the late nineties–early 2000s, and I remember going and getting coffee from a café and the people on the table next to me were talking about email and how interesting it was that their work had decided to get an email address. That would've been around the turn of the millennium, so, y'know, it was still seen as a bit of a business-y thing or a nerdy thing, and certainly in terms of putting content on the internet, that was a bit more technical and involved. It wasn't like you could just sign up for Instagram or get on Facebook and have a presence for yourself online. You had to make your own webpage, figure out where to host it, that kind of thing. There were GeoCities and some of those early web hosts but it was probably quite a niche thing.

Kylie Buck We sent away to Alex Wrekk's distro in Portland for some zines, and I was like 'These are fucking amazing!' In one of my favourites they'd gone dumpster-diving out the back of the university and found all these old submissions for entry into the doctorate programme, and the submissions had all these margin notes from staff about the applicants, like 'Oh, she looks like she'll be pregnant soon, so we won't let her in.' I can't remember what it was called but I loved that one. Yes, it may have been a work of fiction.

Kerry Ann Lee Red Letter Zine Distro was born after I finished design school and I realised that I had accumulated a whole bunch of really wonderful friendships and pen pals through zine-making and I was bringing stuff into New Zealand. I was swapping records for zines and zines for records and things from here in New Zealand for overseas, getting all these packages and letters and circulating them, I'm thinking 'Shit, it's more than just my friends who'd be interested in this stuff. I'm gonna try this out . . .' Do a wee distro inspired by international distros overseas that would stock their favourite records and zines and do a really faithful job of promoting them. So that's what the distro was about. It was gonna be a mail-order distro, and that was why I loved the idea of the catalogue, the idea that you actually go through and — like the school book clubs when you're a kid — tick the books/zines you want.

I was also having the occasional table at the back of a show. At the time Wellington was really open for stuff like that. I'd get my distro catalogues into cafés and independent bookstores that were

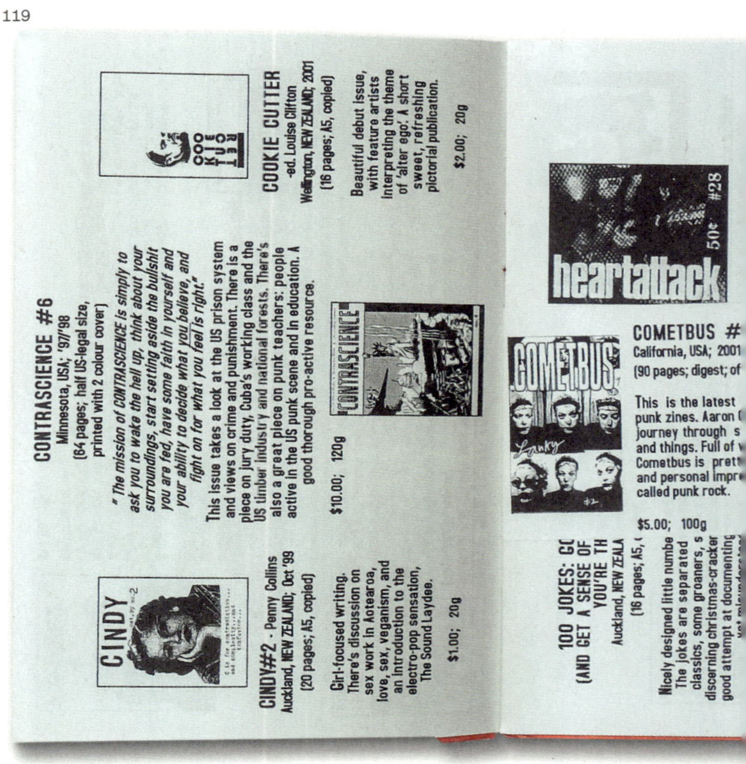

up for trying out zines. Good as Gold used to stock some early Red Letter stuff. Dandelion — which was Rebecca Taekema and Lorene Harris's shop — used to stock zines. There was The Family, which was Jason Lingard and Arlo Edward's store. There were just all these cute little boutique initiatives by folks who were my age and who were like 'Cool, just bring it in and we'll see how it goes.' That was the first time we were getting zines out on the street in Wellington, outside of the anarchist info store, different styles, not completely political, some of them comics. Things like some of Toby Morris's early comics, and zines by the Cookie Cutter Collective that Louise Clifton and Dane Taylor were part of, Ant Sang (he was a friend after I became a fan of his early comic-zine *Filth*, and then he did *Dharma Punks*).

I was distributing *Dharma Punks*, early Disasteradio CD-R releases and *Incredibly Hot Sex with Hideous People*. I got to write to my favourite zines and ask to distribute them, like *Cometbus, Heart Attack, Chunklet and Girlyhead*. They're so beloved, these zines. I mentioned these zines to new friends who grew up in the United States and who also read these same zines, and they're like 'Wow, you carried that in New Zealand of all places?!'

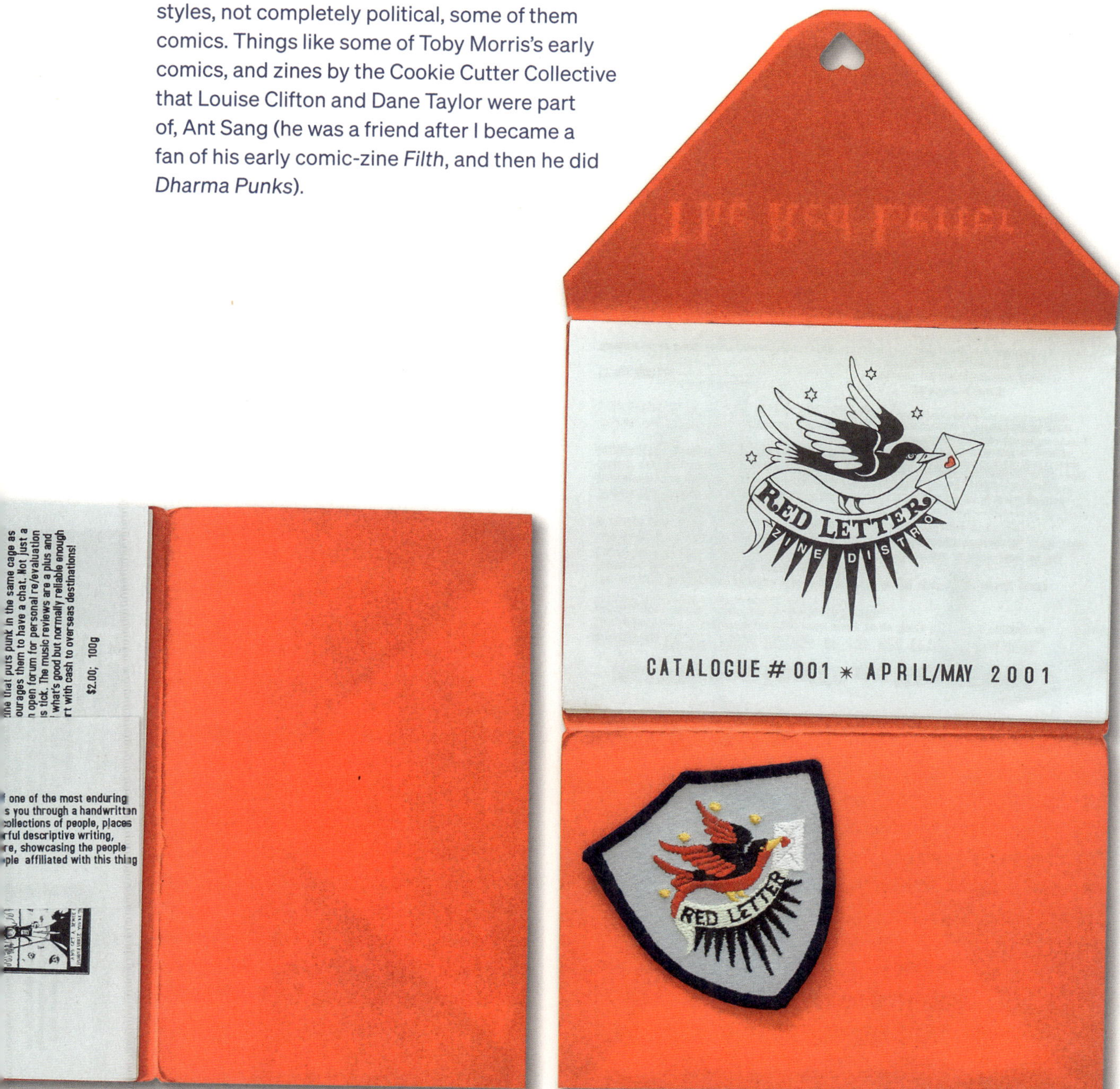

119. Red Letter Zine Distro catalogue and sew-on patch, Kerry Ann Lee, A6, 2001. Te Whanganui-a-Tara Wellington.

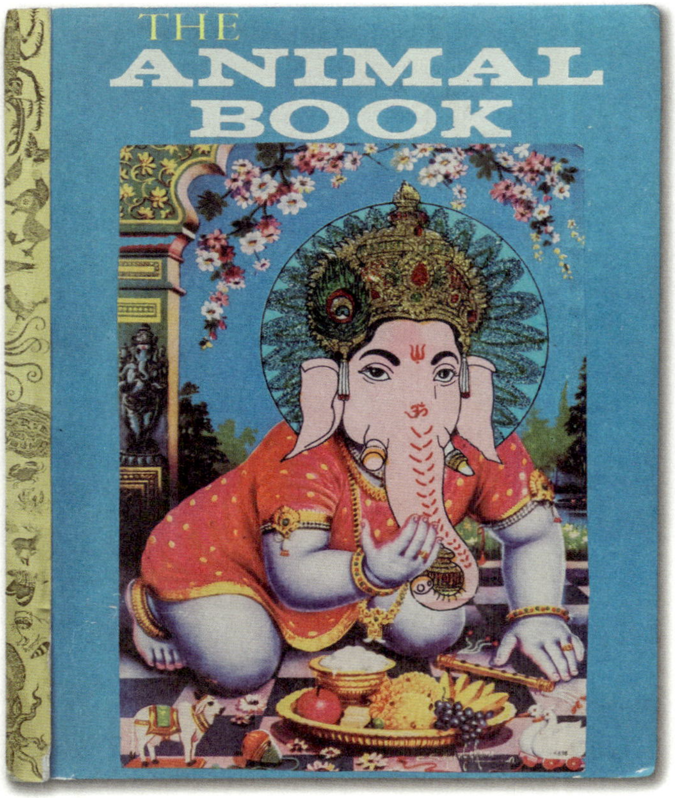

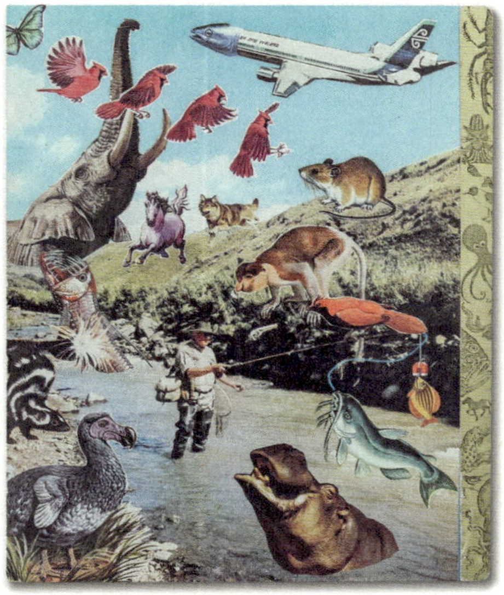

120. *The Animal Book* front and back covers, Dane Taylor and Louise Clifton, 200 × 170mm, 2002. Te Whanganui-a-Tara Wellington.

Tui Gordon I definitely think that part of the excitement of zines was bringing some in from overseas, because there wasn't much on the internet at that stage.

Kerry Ann Lee We all stocked different stuff. Encountering Moon Rocket, I was like 'What is this? This is amazing.' So, we started writing and swapping zines and became friends, and it was like 'Wow, we come from very different places.' Moira's interest and entry point to zine-making was through early internet Web 1.0, LiveJournal, Friendster or some such, communities that were quite different from the underground punk scene that I was a part of. In terms of Cherry Bomb, they came not too long after. They were really localised because they had a shop, an actual venue, in Tāmaki [Makaurau]. Mine was kind of weird international music and comics.

Moira Clunie I had a catalogue online. People would send me things to look at, copies of their zines, comics, self-published books, music as well, and if I wanted to put them in the catalogue I'd organise with that person to send me copies and figure out if I was going to pay them with cash or trades. In terms of the catalogue, I'd scan copies of the covers of things and write little reviews or descriptions and put them into the database that I'd made. I had a post office box in town where people would send things. I'd ask for five copies of some things,and 20 copies of the ones that I knew were going to be more popular or move faster.

Sometimes people would ask me to stock their work and I wasn't interested because the politics was a bit off, but more often it was because I didn't think the work was particularly strong, or it just didn't interest me. The distros I was connecting with overseas were often run by an individual, with zine selection based on personal interests and politics. It's tricky — you're always at risk of seeming elitist. I remember somebody accusing me of being homophobic because I didn't want to stock her and her girlfriend's zine. I was like 'No, I just don't like your zine actually. Sorry.' I remember writing back and explaining, and that was fine, we resolved it.

Tui Gordon I've forgotten how we came up with the Cherry Bomb manifesto. Having a statement of intent like that, might've come from Melissa more than me, because she was very influenced by Riot Grrrl. She was a real Riot Grrrl fangirl. I'd never really been a fangirl, so I didn't really understand that world, but it was really fun to find out about. Some of her heroes, like Tobi Vail from Bikini Kill, made really strong statements about what they were up to and why it mattered and what was fucked in the world.

Kerry Ann Lee I made about seven Red Letter Zine catalogues. I wanna say it ran from 2001 to 2005. It was ridiculous. Every week I'd go to the post office box I shared with my mum, who had her own wedding business enterprise going on . . . She'd be getting all these bridal catalogues and stuff from wineries and estates, and I'd be getting all these punk records and zines . . . crazy packages.

Tui Gordon People would pop in after hours. I didn't mind opening up the shop, I quite liked it. We'd inherited the zine collection from Misfit Theatre. They were prior to us. They had a cute space in Grey Lynn, and occasionally they had bands play out the back. It was more of a punk anarchist shop and more about music than zines, but they had a zine library. There was a library element to Cherry Bomb as well: couches and library shelves in one area and the 'for sale' stuff in another part of the shop. When Misfit Theatre were getting rid of all their stuff, their zines came to us, and when *we* closed we handed them on to this other anarchist group that had just started up. Unfortunately, they folded quite fast. They were all really young, and they hadn't done the maths on how much a shop was gonna cost.

Moira Clunie Misfit Theatre wasn't a theatre, it was like a punk flat and shop space. The same model as Cherry Bomb Comics but a little earlier, people living in the back and then a shop space in the front where they could do different things. They had a shop and a zine library. I went to at least one show in their backyard. I think This Night Creeps played.

Kerry Ann Lee Clearing the post office box was amazing. You never knew who'd be writing to you at any given time. I got amazing mail from teenage girls who were into skateboarding, from big Riot Grrrl punk bands, from cross-cultural kids of all different backgrounds, zines from kids in Eastern Europe . . . I'd post them Red Letter catalogues and the zines that I was making. I'd send copies of my own zine — *Help, My Snowman's Burning* — to bigger publications like *Maximum Rocknroll* or *Book Your Own Fuckin' Life*, and they'd review it and list my post office box. You'd get letters from earnest strangers who would send copies of their zines or records and want to make friends and learn more about this weird place called New Zealand. I made friends in Cuba. I have a goddaughter in Manila due to friends who wrote and connected and swapped zines and records. It's been a really cool portal into the world, and something that I still value a lot . . . It looks different now.

Tui Gordon The shopfront was the biggest room in the building. There was a second shopfront on the other side that we used as a bedroom because it was smaller, more pokey. It had been an office in the past. At first we lived with our landlords, the artists Yuk King Tan and Tobias Berger. They were so excited about us starting a comics shop. They were living upstairs, and out back there was this beautiful little patch of wilderness. We had a little cat, that was pretty cute. We'd sit up on the roof and you could look over the city because it was on a bit of a ridge. That was pretty nice. We'd have little dinners and parties out the back where the kitchen went through. In the past it had been where Aunt Daisy[3] did her radio shows. The shop itself was just one room. We painted pictures all over the walls with help from friends.

It was a mission painting the walls out at the end because we'd used lots of dark colours and even Vivid markers and stuff, and that's really hard to paint over.

Kerry Ann Lee Oh my god: there were envelopes stuffed with money, with cheques. It was super random. It was usually swaps or cheques or cash money. [Laughs.] I don't know what I would net, if I was to really crunch the numbers. It was really more of a 'hobby project' or whatever. I was always budgeting for postage, but postage was *affordable*, so that could work. Now I run the distro and I'm always apologising about the embarrassingly expensive shipping. Also, Red Letter happened during the early Punk Fests, and you'd get a whole lot of people coming from all around the country with money to buy zines. It was just the busiest time.

Tui Gordon The shop was super colourful. Heaps of young people would hang out at Cherry Bomb, and we started to feel quite old in our mid-twenties. Mengzhu Fu [*Mellow Yellow* zine] started coming to the shop when she was like 14. It was so great to have this really passionate teenager around who was really excited about anarchism and animal rights and stuff. We got this weird award from *Metro* magazine saying we were 'the best anarcho feminist comic book-store in New Zealand' or something. Fuck you! Because our manifesto was quite a bold statement as to what we were about, people would come for that. We used to have stitch-and-bitch sessions, sit around and drink beer and sew on patches. A feminist action group met there as well. They'd plan their nights out defacing offensive billboards and stuff.

Kerry Ann Lee The fact that the Red Letter Zine catalogues were paper rather than online was just natural. There was no 'One day I'll make it into a website.' Fuck no. It had to be slow media. Things that are in people's lives, like clutter, junk, things that can be passed around. The fact that these things travelled to places they might not have [otherwise], to people who I might never meet, was part of the thrill of it. I know that people go 'Oh, the internet, it's open to the world, it's the world wide web.' I'm just like, yeah, that doesn't reassure me, that feels very empty to me.

121

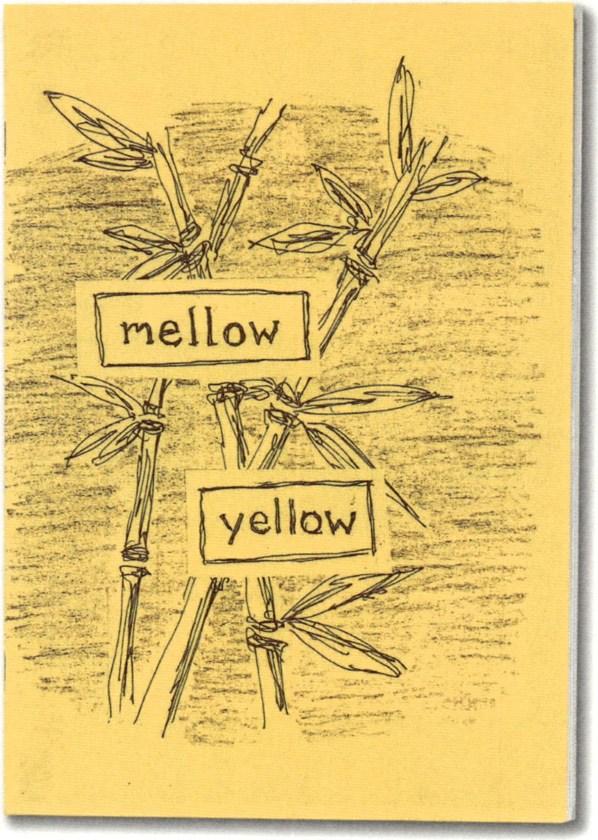

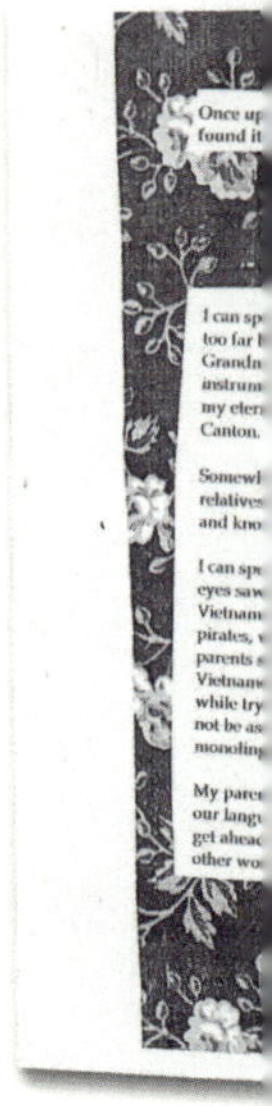

Tui Gordon I didn't really enjoy Cherry Bomb once we closed the shop and took it online. It was a lot more work. When you have a little shop, people come in. You had to be there, but it was a social space, it was nice to be in, even when it was quiet during the week. You could get on with whatever activities you might be up to. Having it online, with people sending in orders, and figuring out all the packaging and posting . . . all of that stuff felt like a total faff.

Kerry Ann Lee Punk Fest was really cool because I'd get to meet some of my pen pals, or people would be like 'Hi, I'm one of your regular customers'. I got to know a few people, repeat orders, a customer base. It was funny to cosplay 'the merchandiser', that retail aspect. Growing up with a healthy cynicism towards capitalism and its limitations can actually be quite useful.

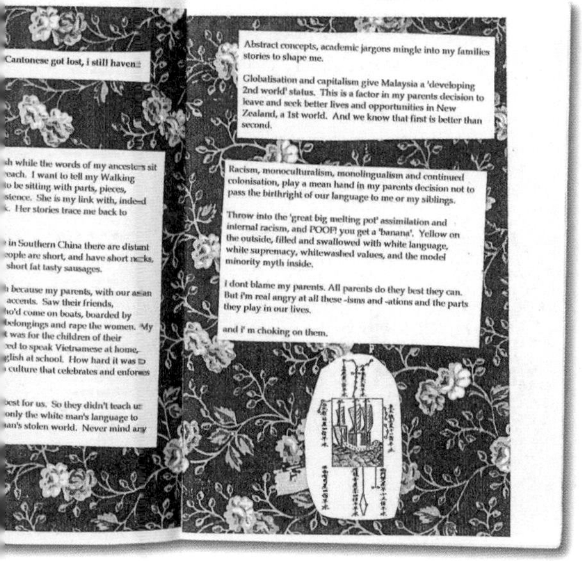

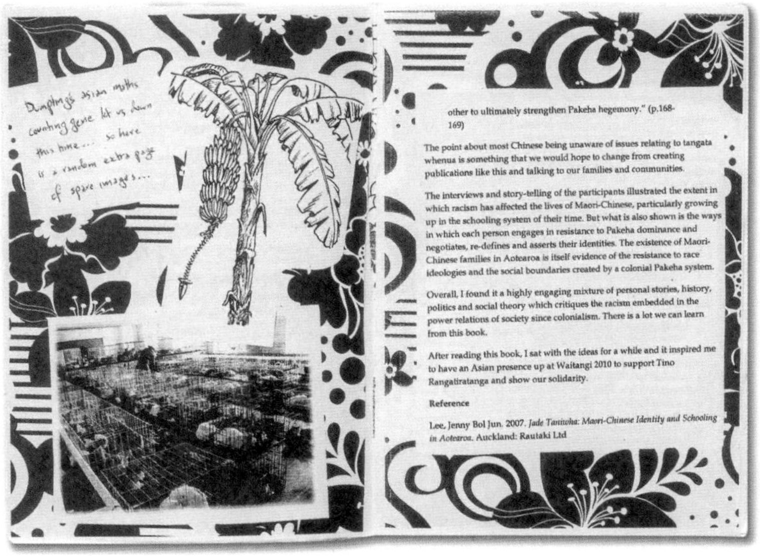

121. *Mellow Yellow* cover and spreads, various contributors, A5, date unknown. Tāmaki Makaurau Auckland.

Tui Gordon Melissa and I divvied up all the jobs pretty evenly. She learnt how to make a website. My brother was doing computer programming and I got him to make us an online catalogue, which was quite cute. We ran Linux. We both painted shit on the walls. I think we had similar skillsets. We each put two grand into the project to start it up. We just happened to have two grand each in our accounts, and we thought, yeah, let's spend that on getting in some stock and buying some paint. All the furniture came for free. Melissa had an eftpos uncle so we even had eftpos, which we wouldn't have got if we had to pay for it. We had heaps of supporters. We both worked half-weeks in libraries, and we did the shop the rest of the time.

Pritika Lal We sent *This Is Not a Comic* to various distros in New Zealand and Australia, mostly Melbourne. I also sent them to libraries, like Auckland Library, and the Auckland University library. One day I found one in a display cabinet at the Auckland Art Gallery library. They'd just pop up, lodged in different places. They found their way to Misfit Theatre and Cherry Bomb Comics. When those kinds of places close down they often donate their zines to a library or the next zine store, and so things just keep on moving around, which is interesting.

Beth Dawson I opened an artist-run space called Space Thing on Adelaide Road in Wellington. At that point I was quite interested in artist-run spaces, so I started a zine called *Space Surveillance Network* or *SSN* and asked for contributions from the people living at None Gallery in Dunedin (a big, shared warehouse space) and from people involved in the High Street Project in Christchurch. I don't know if I had an Auckland connect at that point. It was like a surveillance of our spaces and our scene. I had the idea that *SSN* was the publication that went alongside the physical space that was Space Thing.

Pritika Lal We made enough copies of *This Is Not a Comic* that we could leave them in shop doorways around K Road. I was inspired by the experience of stumbling across those issues of *Strumming Teeth* years earlier.

122. (Following pages) '*Something for nothing*', Kerry Ann Lee, A7–A3 fold-out, 2003. Te Whanganui-a-Tara Wellington.

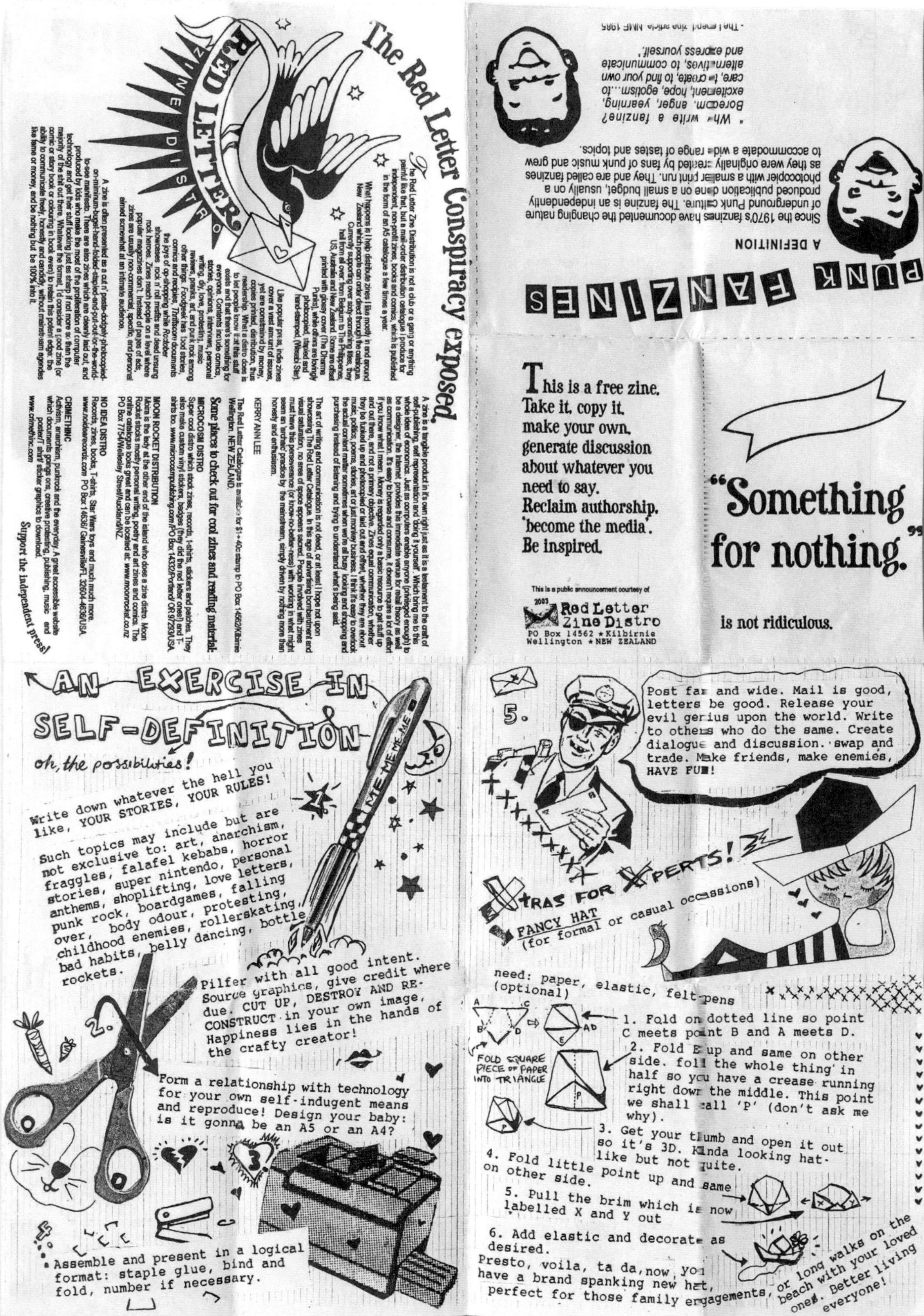

The Red Letter Conspiracy exposed.
Red Letter
Zine Distro
Support the independent press!
PUNK FANZINES
A DEFINITION
Since the 1970's fanzines have documented the changing nature of underground Punk culture. The fanzine is an independently produced publication done on a small budget, usually on a photocopier with a smaller print run. They and are called fanzines as they were originally created by fans of punk music and grew to accommodate a wide range of tastes and topics.
" Why write a fanzine? Boredom, anger, yearning, excitement, hope, egotism...to care, to create, to find your own alternatives, to communicate and express yourself."
- The Legend zine article NME 1985
This is a free zine.
Take it, copy it,
make your own,
generate discussion
about whatever you
need to say.
Reclaim authorship,
'become the media'.
Be inspired.
This is a public announcement courtesy of
2003 Red Letter Zine Distro
PO Box 14562 ★Kilbirnie
Wellington ★NEW ZEALAND
"Something for nothing."
is not ridiculous.
AN EXERCISE IN SELF-DEFINITION
oh, the possibilities!
1.
Write down whatever the hell you like, YOUR STORIES, YOUR RULES!
Such topics may include but are not exclusive to: art, anarchism, fraggles, falafel kebabs, horror stories, super nintendo, personal anthems, shoplifting, love letters, punk rock, boardgames, falling over, body odour, protesting, childhood enemies, rollerskating, bad habits, belly dancing, bottle rockets.
ME ME ME ME ME
2.
Pilfer with all good intent. Source graphics, give credit where due. CUT UP, DESTROY AND RE-CONSTRUCT in your own image, Happiness lies in the hands of the crafty creator!
3.
Form a relationship with technology for your own self-indugent means and reproduce! Design your baby: is it gonna be an A5 or an A4?
4.
Assemble and present in a logical format: staple glue, bind and fold, number if necessary.
5.
Post far and wide. Mail is good, letters be good. Release your evil genius upon the world. Write to others who do the same. Create dialogue and discussion. swap and trade. Make friends, make enemies, HAVE FUN!
XTRAS FOR XPERTS!
FANCY HAT (for formal or casual occassions)
need: paper, elastic, felt-pens (optional)
FOLD SQUARE PIECE OF PAPER INTO TRIANGLE
1. Fold on dotted line so point C meets point B and A meets D.
2. Fold E up and same on other side. fold the whole thing in half so you have a crease running right down the middle. This point we shall call 'P' (don't ask me why).
3. Get your thumb and open it out so it's 3D. Kinda looking hat-like but not quite.
4. Fold little point up and same on other side.
5. Pull the brim which is now labelled X and Y out
6. Add elastic and decorate as desired.
Presto, voila, ta da, now you have a brand spanking new hat, perfect for those family engagements, or long walks on the beach with your loved ones. Better living everyone!

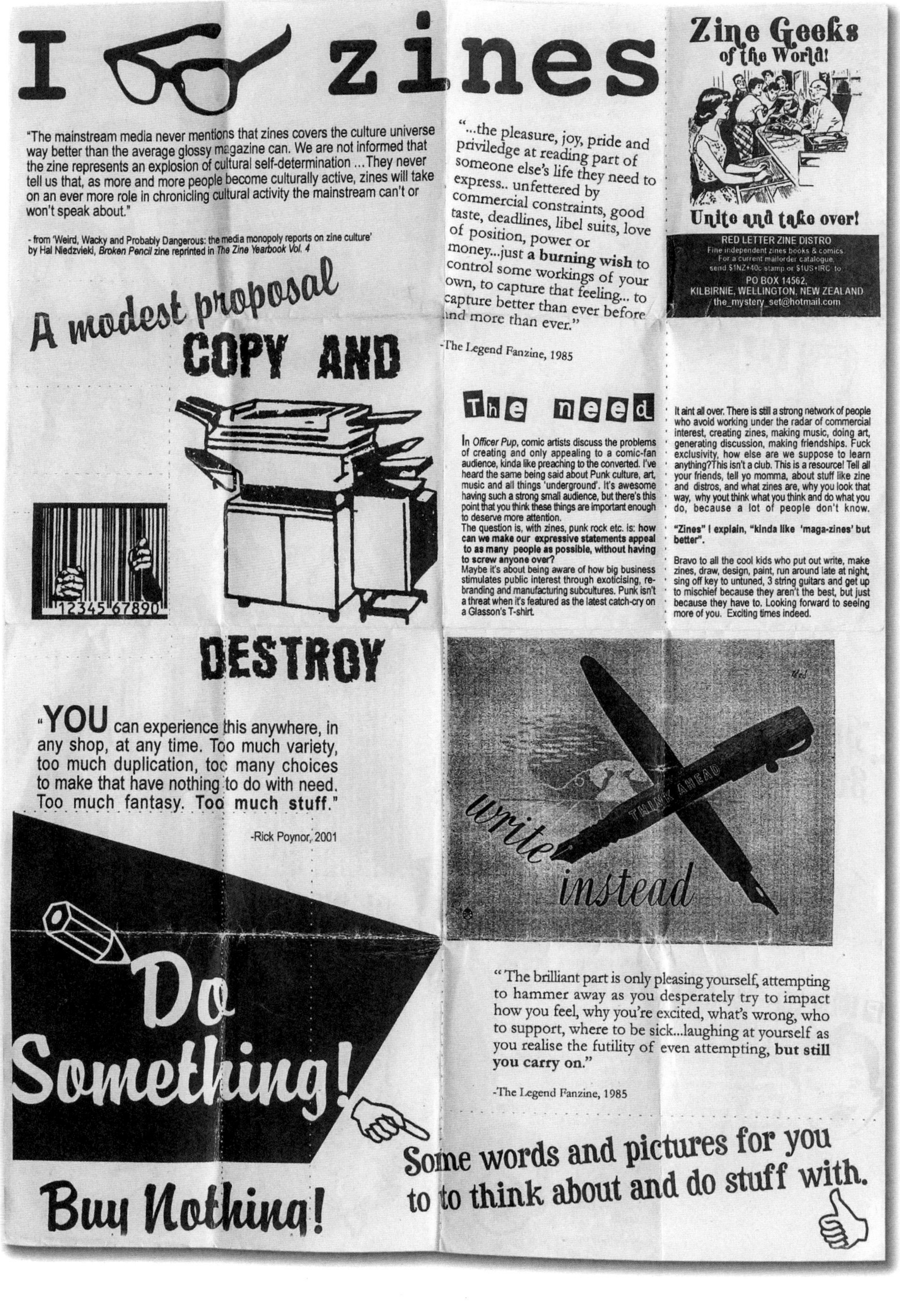

I [glasses] zines

"The mainstream media never mentions that zines covers the culture universe way better than the average glossy magazine can. We are not informed that the zine represents an explosion of cultural self-determination ...They never tell us that, as more and more people become culturally active, zines will take on an ever more role in chronicling cultural activity the mainstream can't or won't speak about."

- from 'Weird, Wacky and Probably Dangerous: the media monopoly reports on zine culture' by Hal Niedzviecki, *Broken Pencil* zine reprinted in *The Zine Yearbook Vol. 4*

"...the pleasure, joy, pride and priviledge at reading part of someone else's life they need to express.. unfettered by commercial constraints, good taste, deadlines, libel suits, love of position, power or money...just **a burning wish** to control some workings of your own, to capture that feeling... to capture better than ever before and more than ever."

-The Legend Fanzine, 1985

Zine Geeks of the World!

Unite and take over!

RED LETTER ZINE DISTRO
Fine independent zines books & comics.
For a current mailorder catalogue,
send $1NZ+40c stamp or $1US+IRC to
PO BOX 14562,
KILBIRNIE, WELLINGTON, NEW ZEALAND
the_mystery_set@hotmail.com

A modest proposal

COPY AND DESTROY

12345 67890

The need

In *Officer Pup*, comic artists discuss the problems of creating and only appealing to a comic-fan audience, kinda like preaching to the converted. I've heard the same being said about Punk culture, art, music and all things 'underground'. It's awesome having such a strong small audience, but there's this point that you think these things are important enough to deserve more attention.
The question is, with zines, punk rock etc. is: **how can we make our expressive statements appeal to as many people as possible, without having to screw anyone over?**
Maybe it's about being aware of how big business stimulates public interest through exoticising, re-branding and manufacturing subcultures. Punk isn't a threat when it's featured as the latest catch-cry on a Glasson's T-shirt.

It aint all over. There is still a strong network of people who avoid working under the radar of commercial interest, creating zines, making music, doing art, generating discussion, making friendships. Fuck exclusivity, how else are we suppose to learn anything?This isn't a club. This is a resource! Tell all your friends, tell yo momma, about stuff like zine and distros, and what zines are, why you look that way, why yout think what you think and do what you do, because a lot of people don't know.

"Zines" I explain, "kinda like 'maga-zines' but better".

Bravo to all the cool kids who put out write, make zines, draw, design, paint, run around late at night, sing off key to untuned, 3 string guitars and get up to mischief because they aren't the best, but just because they have to. Looking forward to seeing more of you. Exciting times indeed.

"**YOU** can experience this anywhere, in any shop, at any time. Too much variety, too much duplication, too many choices to make that have nothing to do with need. Too much fantasy. **Too much stuff.**"

-Rick Poynor, 2001

THINK AHEAD

write instead

Do Something!

"The brilliant part is only pleasing yourself, attempting to hammer away as you desperately try to impact how you feel, why you're excited, what's wrong, who to support, where to be sick...laughing at yourself as you realise the futility of even attempting, **but still you carry on.**"

-The Legend Fanzine, 1985

Buy Nothing!

Some words and pictures for you to to think about and do stuff with.

Beth Dawson A big part of being able to make stuff during the period that I was in Dunedin — whether it was music or comics or zines — was that because rent was so cheap we could afford really nice big studio spaces to produce work in. Rather than getting the bus to town to go to this one particular shop, I think it turned into this thing of just going to each other's flats. Zines were more part of the music for me, popping up on the merch table at gigs. When I had a show coming up, I'd be like 'Right, gotta make something to put on the merch table', a zine with a quick deadline.

I remember doing that for a show at The Crown. I thought, 'The band is going to be live in 3D!' and, again, went really labour-intensive and cut out all of these 3D glasses to go with a little 3D comic. I imagined the whole crowd wearing these 3D glasses, but they were so time intensive to make that I only ended up making about 10 pairs. [Laughs.] At gigs like that, and with things like Liz's Get Set Go Festival, there was always a zine table. We didn't want to have the music separate to the tangible visual culture of it. They had to be together.

Kenneth Merrick In the early to mid-2000s I was living on Karangahape Road with a whole bunch of people in a big warehouse-y flat. At that time there was a lot going on. Disrupt Gallery was next door, and there was quite a healthy graffiti scene in Auckland. There were three or four local comic shops running. There just seemed to be lots going on. I'd sort of wound up my music and audio engineering studies and started getting back into drawing, started making a few things. Fast-forward a few years: I enrolled in the visual arts programme at Unitec and started to develop my interest in image-making and art and trying to learn about these things. A lot of the time was taken up with painting and working large-scale on canvas. Then, having moved through that, I realised 'Wow, you actually have to have the space to store this stuff.' [Laughs.] It became a problem.

123

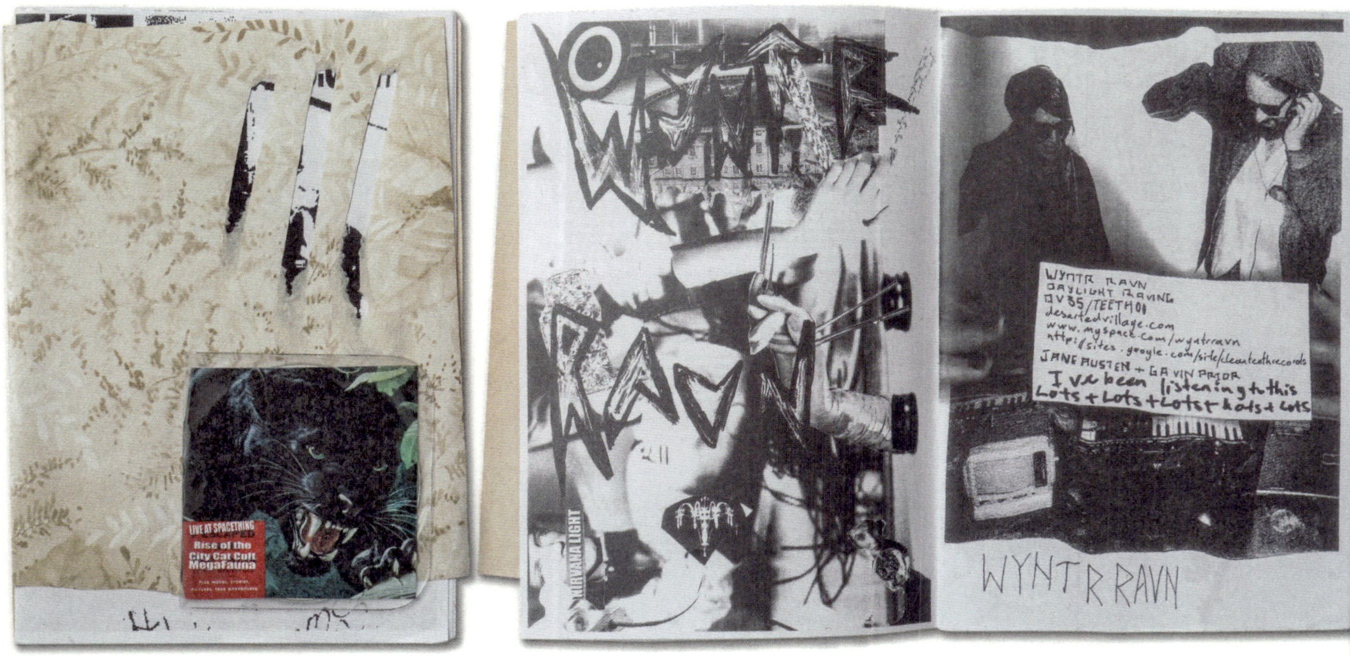

123. *SSN* (*Space Surveillance Network*) cover and spread, Beth Dawson, A5, 2008. Te Whanganui-a-Tara Wellington.

124

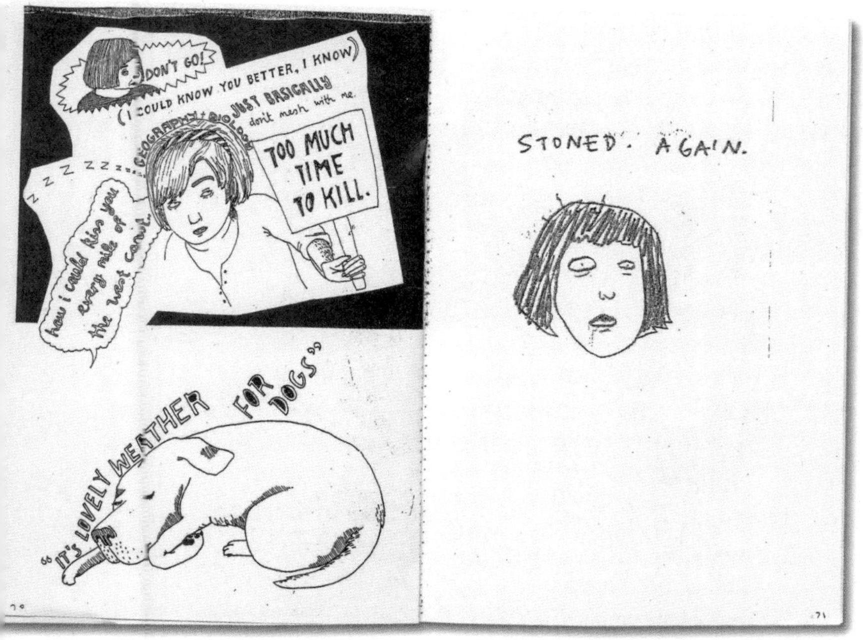

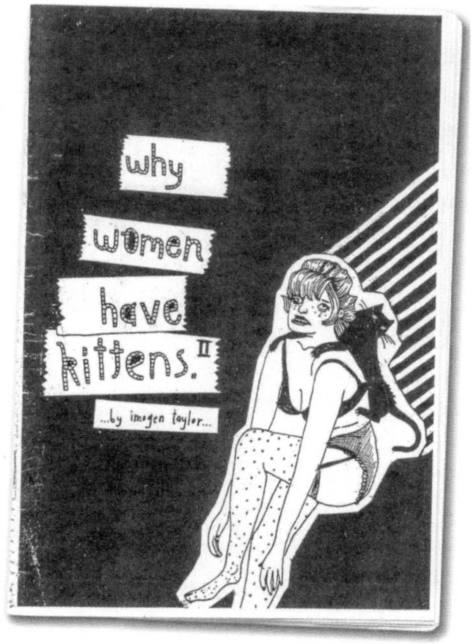

124. *Why Women Have Kittens II* spread and cover, Imogen Taylor, A5, 2007. Tāmaki Makaurau Auckland.

Sam Orchard It made more sense to me to publish online. Being someone who likes a lot of attention but who is also an introvert, putting things online was much easier. I got lots of attention but I didn't have to talk to anyone. [Laughs.] And it was cheaper to just get a free WordPress website and put my comics up each week.

Three years into it I was probably telling myself that the narratives were too important to exist as an exclusive print thing, but in reality it was just because I like a lot of attention. And I had no one else feeding me those stories. I really wanted to be a film-maker and I was studying film and media at university, but it was cheaper to draw a comic than it was to convince my friends to act in a very low-grade crappy film.

Part of it was that the trans community that I was aware of in New Zealand at that time was pretty small. So you reach more people online. Most of the comics that I was reading by queer people were coming out of the States, so it was a way of communicating with them. It just made sense; that's where I found them, so that's where they belonged.

Moira Clunie I got involved through the zines that were connecting with Riot Grrrl, feminist punk, queer and trans movements. I don't know what the connection might've been around music zines, I wasn't so connected to that, and I wasn't really being approached by those people. A lot of the US Riot Grrrl zines were about providing spaces to open up about experiences of discrimination or marginalisation or abuse, generating a lot of that really intense personal zine content.

Pritika Lal We headed to Wellington for the Eric Awards. I guess there's a difference between comics and zines, but I'm not too worried about the categorisation. I think I liked the zine communities way more than the comics communities, but then again it really depends on the individuals you meet. When I was working at Auckland Central Library there were a lot of comic-book makers and zine-makers on staff. I also worked at the Academy Cinema, and for a period of time they had me putting up posters around the city, which was kind of like what I did anyway, making band posters. There was a really big crossover between posters, zines, comics . . . I don't know if I could claim to have created a book in that time period, but the rest just bleed into each other. It was always more about the community and less about the artefacts themselves.

Sam Orchard We were always encouraged to draw, and I was always drawing as a little kid — that was my happy place. I had three brothers, and they were all pretty sporty and I was not, so my safe place was books and drawing and I just loved it. I've always loved it. I'm pretty shy, and being able to draw allows you to converse with people, or it opens up a topic of conversation. I like making funny things.

I had a job at the supermarket all through university. I had to do those horrible 13-hour Saturday-night shifts until closing; that was awful. So I'd just draw comics on the back of the receipts, either different ways that I could die, or that I could kill the customers with implements from the supermarket. [Laughs.]

I never printed them but I think I put a few on Myspace, I can't really remember. The nihilism of a 20-something-year-old who was like 'I'm depressed, I hate life, I don't really know why but I'm just gonna draw about death and destruction.'

Tessa Stubbing I'm a twin. I've grown up my whole life with somebody else always there, right? So to do something without my twin was quite scary. I'm over it now, but at the time, making my first zine [*Plectrum*] with someone other than my twin was scary. I had a friend who was also into punk. I don't even know if she made a page in the end, she might've made *one* page, but she was there in support.

I was only 15 years old, so it was your generic punk zine with a vegan recipe, a gig review, a DIY thing etc., etc. But how many 15-year-olds are super-critical thinkers and prepared to be different?

Fuck, why was I thinking about that first zine just the other day? Cringe. I remembered one of the pages was a picture of Davey Havok from AFI next to a picture of Michael Jackson, just because they both had similar long dark hair, and I was like 'Oh my god, they could be twins.' Like, what even is that?! *I'm being edgy, taking the piss out of someone . . .*

David Merritt I was on tour with musicians, and I had to work out a way to earn money to stay alive on tour. They would feed me, but I didn't have enough money to buy cigarettes or coffee. I had that rubber-stamp-pad set, and I had one of those really old G3 Clamshell Macs [first iBook]. It didn't even run InDesign. I was doing it in TextEditor, but it had the font, and once I had the font that matched the stamp set I was away. I could make the PDFs using a compatible font. I'd make 10 books a day and I'd sell them and make $50, and that was the level I operated at for a long, long time.

Beth Dawson The first zines that went beyond my friend group were the ones that went with music releases; little publications that were inserted into 7-inch singles or cassette covers or CD-Rs. Then I formed a band called The Futurians with my friends, and we had a really strong band identity and a real focus on sci-fi. We made little zines in response to song titles and from our identity as a band.

Sam Orchard By about 2007 I was doing comics for [Otago University's student magazine] *Critic*. (I did a series that I'm not gonna name because I don't want anyone to ever find it and attribute it to me, because it was real edgelord shit. I thought I was being funny but it's actually gross.) I met a whole bunch of people through creating comics for *Critic* and that was real cool, and I felt like I'd found a drawing community. Daniel Alexander was one of the lead people, and there were a couple of others. We started going to Arc Café and drinking beer and drawing, and that was real nice. I was like 'Oh, I feel like one of the boys here, this is lovely', and around that same time I first discovered that trans men existed. I'd just blanked on that. I thought it only went one way, that there were trans women, but nothing in the other direction. It sounds stupid but that was the reality portrayed by the media that I was consuming, but probably also [indicated] a readiness in me to know about it.

I realised that when I was drawing with those guys, but it was also about what I was drawing. I felt like I had access to and could express some sort of masculinity. That started to make sense when I met my first trans guy, who casually said 'I'm trans'. I was just like 'Fuck, what?! It can be like that?! Oh, okay, this makes sense now. I'm not a lesbian. I'm trans.' And all of the stuff around the complexity of my sexuality was suddenly like 'Oh, this is why it hasn't been feeling right, because it's not a sexuality thing, it's a gender thing.' I feel like I came to it through access to comics, which is not to say that only boys draw comics, it was just that the people who I was hanging out with at the time, who were drawing comics, were boys, and there was something about the expression of me drawing myself . . .

125

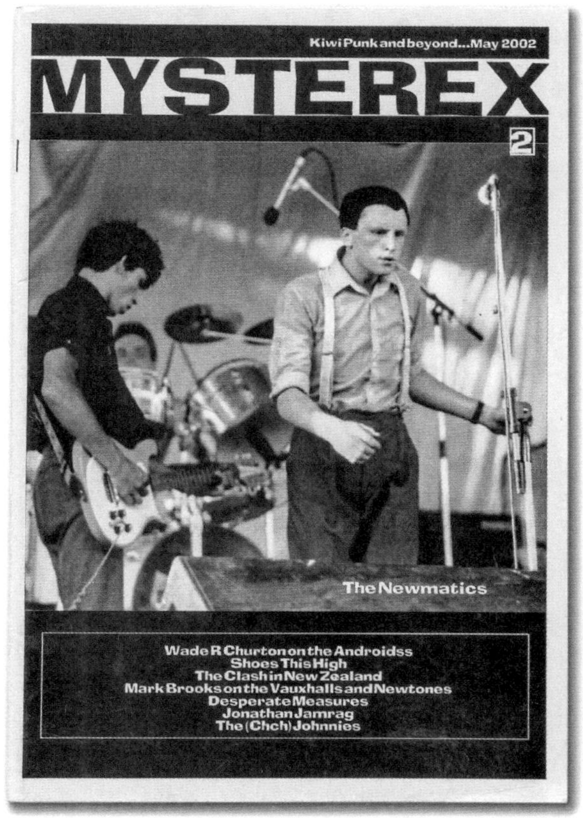

125. *Mysterex #2*, edited by Andrew Schmidt and Simon Kay, A4, 2002. Tāmaki Makaurau Auckland.

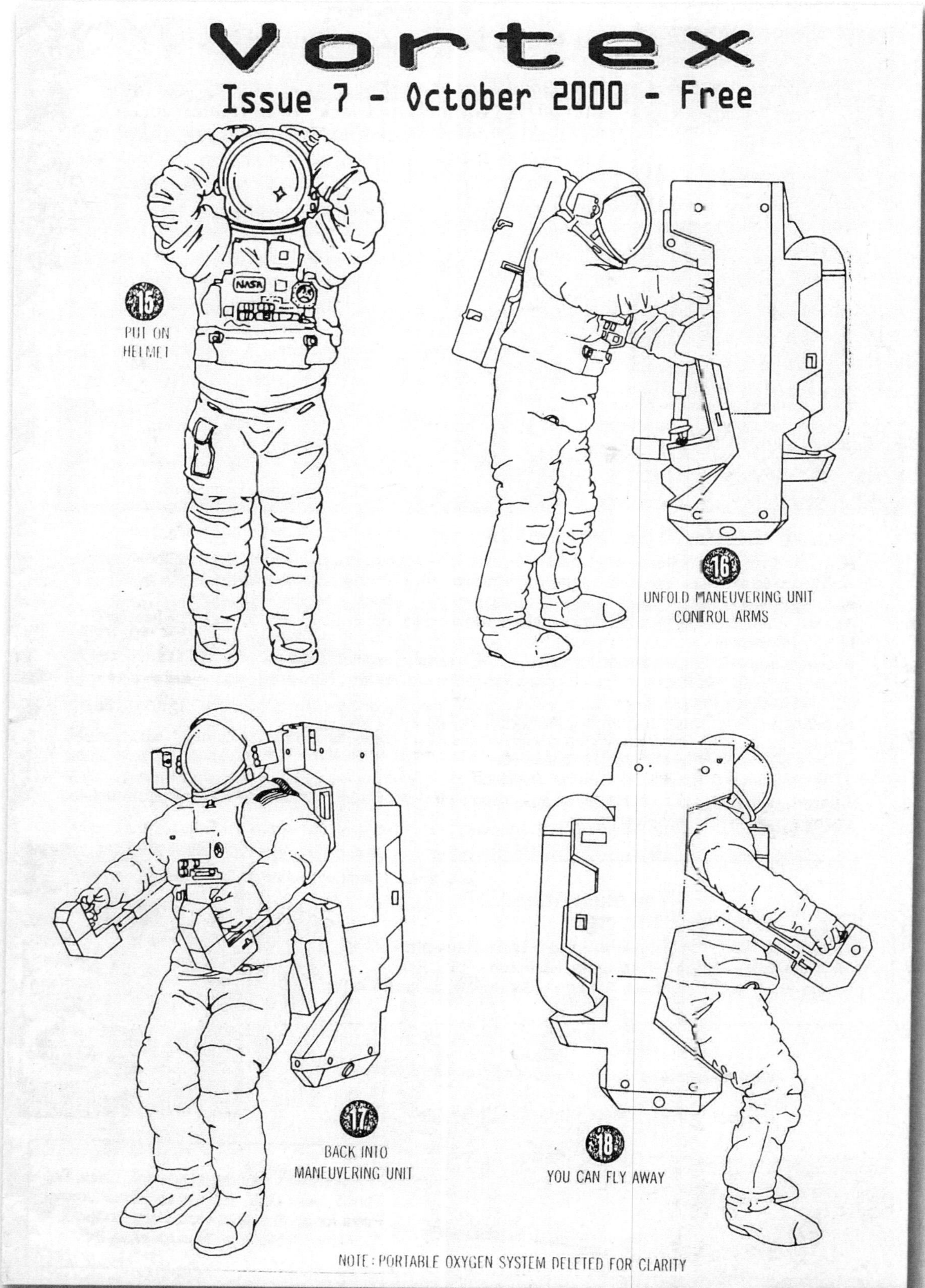

126. *Vortex* #7, anonymous, A5, 2000. Kirikiriroa Hamilton.

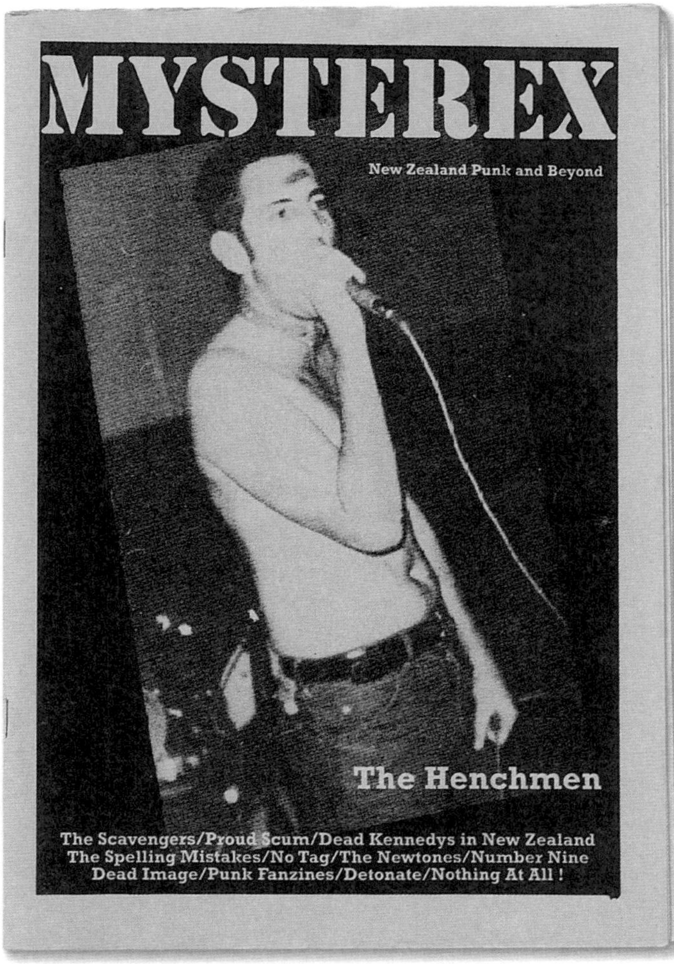

127. *Mysterex* #1 cover and spread, edited by Andrew Schmidt and Simon Kay, A4, 2000. Tāmaki Makaurau Auckland.

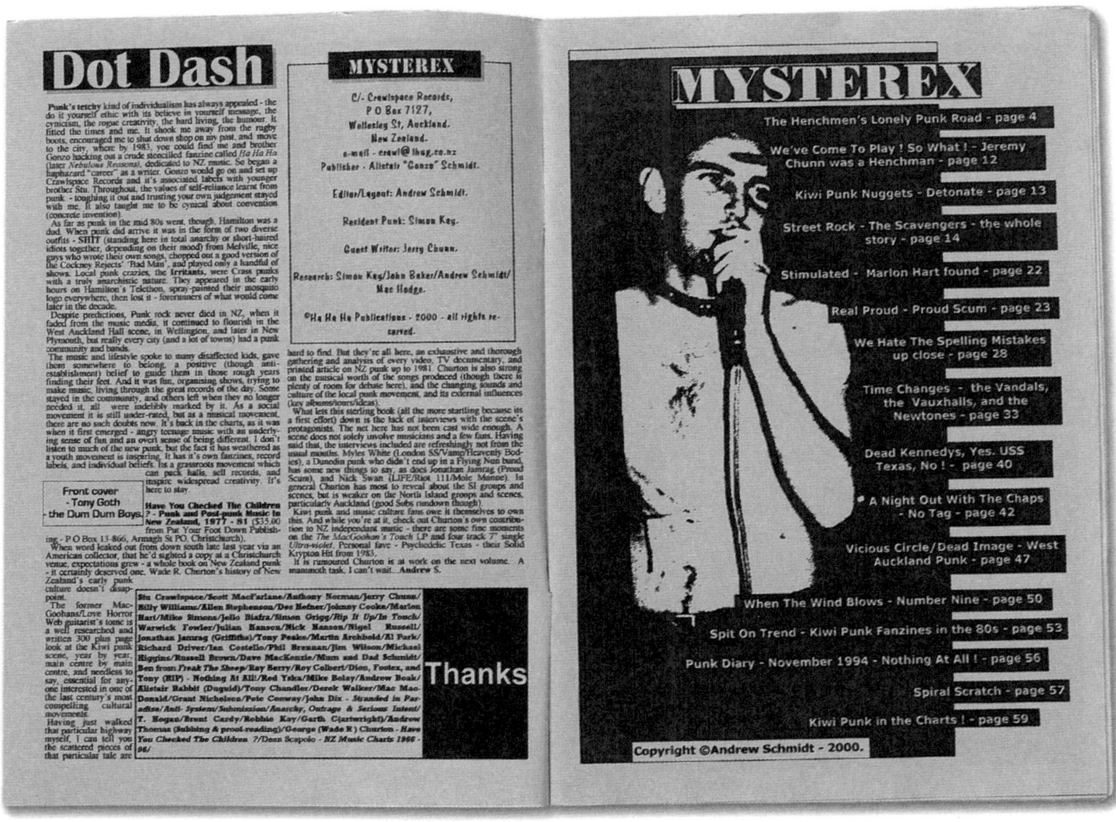

128

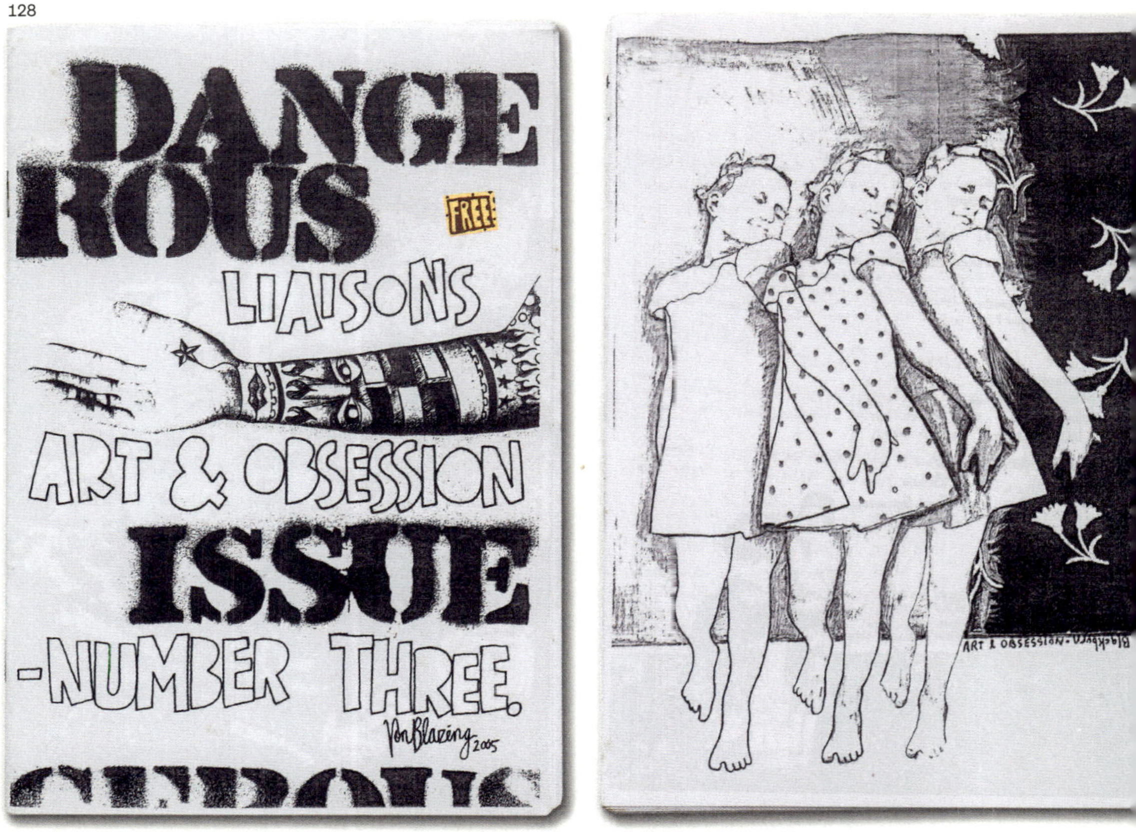

Kylie Buck I started making collaborative art at art school, discovered zines and decided that'd be the perfect medium.

We made this zine called *Dangerous Liaisons*, and people could submit their stuff. We had a different theme each issue . . . One of them was 'art and the beret'. I can't remember what the other themes were. I think we made about five issues. The very last issue got into an exhibition. We ended on a high, got into an emerging Wellington artists exhibition at [Michael] Hirschfeld Gallery at City Gallery. Our zine was chained to the wall and there were copies that people could take for free. Mark Amery reviewed the show, and my collaborator Chantelle Gribbon — who was way more into the academic side of things — was over-the-moon. She read his arts column every week and she was a real big fan. So we ended *Dangerous Liaisons* on a high.

David Merritt Those particular publications of mine started in 2008. The *Reader's Digest*, the rubber-stamp set, I got that in 2008. I felt like I was medieval. Between 1986 and 1995 I'd put out six collections of poems, but then I got the internet bug and I became a high-end geek. I didn't write any poetry for about 10 years. When I got the rubber-stamp set that was a critical part . . . I wasn't reliant on having to lug around 1000 copies of my latest poetry book. I could kind of make them as I went, and that was a big breakthrough.

I met Sonic Youth, and the American indie bands taught me that everything was about merchandise, so I took what I learnt from them about merchandise and just applied it to literature.

The only reason some American bands do shows is so they can have a merch table.

128. *Dangerous Liaisons* #3 cover and spread, edited by Kylie Buck and Chantelle Gribbon, A5, 2005. Te Whanganui-a-Tara Wellington.

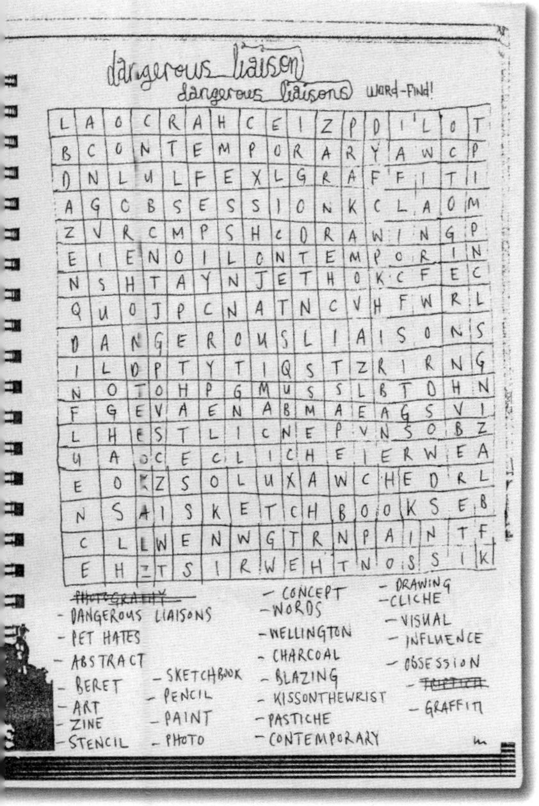

Kylie Buck Grant Corbishley was our tutor when we made *Dangerous Liaisons*. Anything that students were super excited about, he was like 'Yeah! Go for it!' If you've got students who are into something and invigorated, then you mostly just try to get out of their way. He was into it.

Sam Orchard I realised I was trans in 2008, which would've been around the same time that *DUD* [*The Dunedin Comic Revue*] started. A couple of us were like 'It'd be so cool to do an anthology comic.' We applied for Dunedin City Council funding, got the grant and had to set up a bank account for the funds. None of us really knew what the fuck we were doing and we got pretty burnt out. We didn't really know how to make it happen. It wasn't until 2010 when Spencer Hall said, 'Hey, you have this money, you have this website. Can we just print it already?' Spencer was very helpful, just kicking us along and doing the work to make it happen.

Spencer Hall I think the other big inspiration for *DUD* and engaging with the wider comics-zine community was going down to the Hocken Library and going through all their old local publications, mostly music- and comic-related. I'm talking about things like: Tony Renouf's *Treacle*; *Razor,* which was Dylan Horrocks and Cornelius Stone and that crowd; and the earlier generation before that who were doing anthologies. *Jesus on a Stick*, Chris Knox's one, as well, and the earlier guys like Joe Wylie and Barry Linton and their one, which was called *Strips*. That ran for a long time. Then also things like Funtime Comics out of Christchurch, who have been publishing stuff for a long time.

Just seeing all this stuff and seeing that it was local, and seeing that there was so much local talent and being like 'What's this guy Glenn Ross up to? I've seen his stickers around. He does these amazing comics. What would it take to see something else that he's done?' It's like 'Well, wouldn't it be great if we had him and the younger comics crowd together in something?'

So I guess it was just somewhat selfishly wanting to see more art by these people because I feel like a lot of people — especially in Dunedin — are exceptionally talented but they're not going to go out of their way to put their work out, or they'll make a whole bunch of artworks but then just keep them around the house.

Another one of the publications that I saw at the Hocken, and that I loved, was *Spec*, which was like a student newspaper for Radio One in Dunedin. It had work like Chris Stapp's early comics and all this other amazing artwork.

David Tulloch I never felt like I was a particularly good drawer, so when I got back into comics I didn't draw. Instead I ended up using photos of Playmobil to make narratives. That was fun. I posted them on a webcomic site called DrunkDuck, which I still belong to today, and that got a lot of feedback. People all over the world read what I put up there. Because it was a Dungeons and Dragons-related thing, it got mentioned in other people's forums as a comic to seek out. I did a page a day for two and a half years or something, maybe longer, roughly 1000 pages.

Tessa Stubbing I made the first version of *10-22-38 Astoria* while I was at uni doing the zine course. I'd done all this research into Chester Carlson and the first photocopier. What I made was more magazine-style, with articles and all that sort of stuff: 'Here's all the information I can find out about photocopiers', as opposed to any sort of art zine. But I wasn't very happy with it, and it didn't really look the way I wanted it to look, not the right aesthetic. So then I went to the public library, and I looked up old photocopier manuals. They got them out of the basement for me, and because they were more than 50 years old I didn't have to worry about copyright. I just made hundreds of fucked-up pages on the photocopier and laid them all out on the floor. I played with all the copier settings, or if a page got stuck I'd just pull it out and recopy it to capture the cool texture. That zine was made entirely on the photocopier, no computer. Even the compiling of all the pages was all photocopier. That was a key part of the process.

129

129. *10 22 38 Astoria* spread and cover, Tessa Stubbing, A5, date unknown. Tāmaki Makaurau Auckland.

Tony Renouf Mrs Axelgrinder's neighbours are loosely based on me and my cousin. They're bored brothers who live by themselves and are very, very naïve. They get licences to do stuff out of cereal boxes.

I started writing the story in another nightshift situation. I was working at a metal cabinet-making place, and I was given a notebook to write down settings for my machines. Because I was doing repetitive mindless shit I ended up writing over 190 pages of ideas in these notebooks. I think I've still got another 50 or 60 ideas to complete. The nocturnal working seems to be quite productive. The nightshift at AHI Plastics in the eighties started me on sequential art.

Moira Clunie *Child That Mind #3* is photocopied, black-and-white, it's one-sixth of an A4 size, so it's almost square, a little bit wider than it is tall, and it's hand-bound. It's got a sewn binding, just a basic pamphlet stitch. The cover title has been typed out on a typewriter, accompanied by a lino print image of a typewriter, photocopied black-and-white. Most of the internal text is printed from a computer, then cut-and-pasted onto flats. Some of the texts have backgrounds: maps, photos I've taken, graph paper or music scores. I've pretty much always put zines together as an analogue cut-and-paste. During the COVID lockdown I produced a zine entirely using a computer. It just wasn't as satisfying, partly because I felt like I didn't have as much control over the process as when I was physically cutting-and-pasting. Then, you are directly controlling exactly what it looks like. I just don't have that level of proficiency with digital tools.

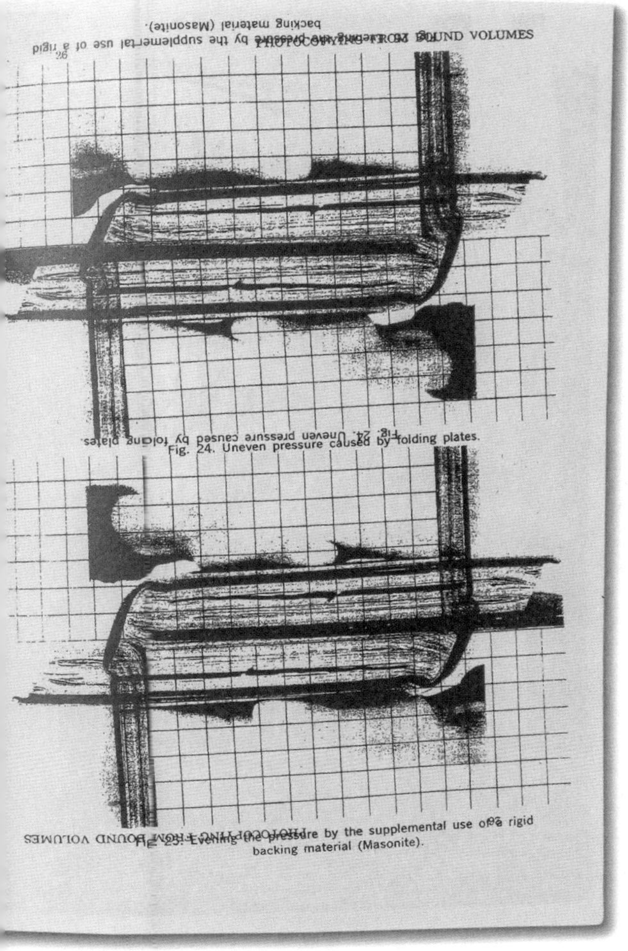

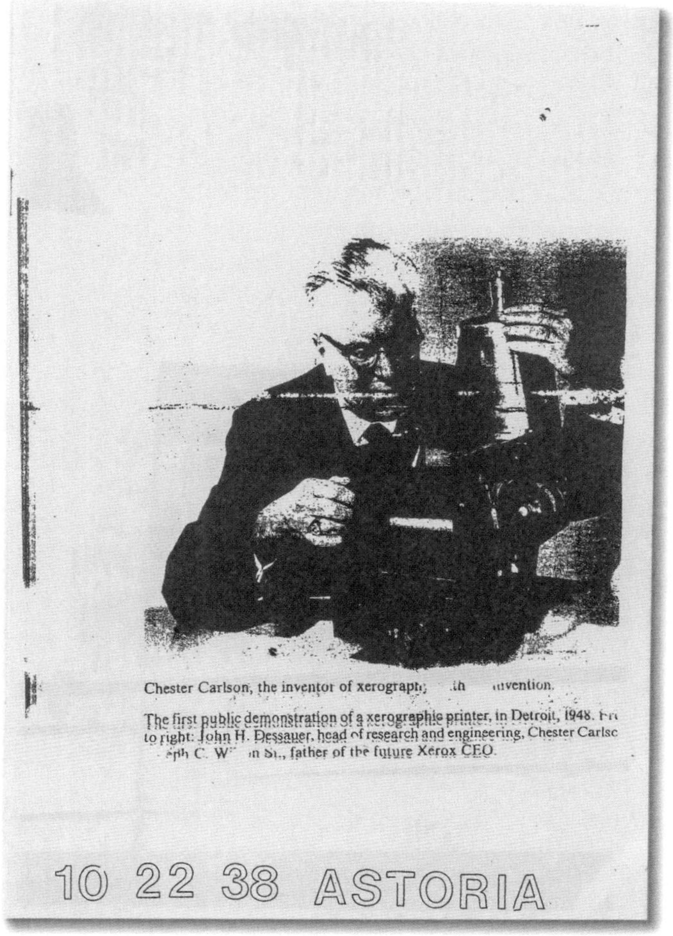

Tessa Stubbing Computer stuff's easy for me as someone who has a design background, but most of my zines aren't made using a computer. I used to do that for a job, so I make zines by hand. I usually work bigger and then scale down, so if it's going to be for an A5 zine, I work at A4. When you do an illustration, if you do it larger then when you scale it down your strokes are tighter. Working big, you've also got more room to play around, but you've also got to think about what's going to happen to the margins when you scale down, the 5mm situation. You've got to account for that, so you don't get stuff cut off at the page edge.

I've made heaps of textures on the photocopier, ready for doing the old-school textured background with cut-and-paste type on top. I've got a whole library of handmade textures to pull from. If I'm making a collage zine, I'll go through all of the resources I've collected and then pull out pages until I've got a stack of interesting stuff. Then I'll cut pieces out with a scalpel and see what works together. Sometimes you've cut out a weird image of a fish fillet or chicken or whatever, something random, but then the page that you've cut it from looks cooler than the thing you've cut out. Or you turn the piece over and on the other side you've got this random thing, that's cool, so a bit of that. It's not really planning anything out, just kind of getting in the zone like an ADHD hyper-focus or something. You just get in there and see what happens. I do the final layout and get it ready for print using InDesign.

Pritika Lal Everything was drawn and written by hand. There was a lot of pencilling, then inking, though sometimes just straight in with the ink if you were into the flow of things. At some point we went to a studio upstairs from Illicit, which was a clothing store and tattoo shop that was really big in the nineties. Upstairs from there was a bunch of comic-book artists like Karl Wills and Martin Emond (maybe Martin had already moved overseas). Anyway, they had a studio upstairs from Illicit and there was a bunch of people in there, I didn't know who all of them were. We were working on *This Is Not a Comic* and I saw a mess of ink pens and card with someone's drawing on it. They'd used [the correcting fluid] Twink! I was like 'Oh, shit, people are using Twink on their drawings?!' I hadn't realised that Twink wouldn't necessarily show up on the photocopier, so that was quite a breakthrough [for me].

I also saw that they were just drawing by hand with pencils and pens and it wasn't some secret magic trick. These experienced cartoonists still made mistakes, and I was really blown away by that. When I went back to working on *This Is Not a Comic*, I felt like things didn't have to be so perfect.

Moira Clunie Early on I was involved in a little mailing-list network called Lo-Fi Artists' Books. The whole purpose was producing artists' books that were cheap and cheerful, possibly using recycled materials, and not being too stuffy about it. I've always seen the connection, and considered the spectrum that covers poorly made urgent tracts to beautifully crafted objects. There's always been people making zines with hand-stitched bindings (I often do that), or that feature individual handmade, hand-stamped covers and other bespoke book production techniques.

Often the beautifully crafted object isn't being produced to make money, once you consider the time spent. There are different motivations for people who are making complicated hand-made things, but it often has nothing to do with commercial viability, it's a love of the object or the artistic process.

130

131

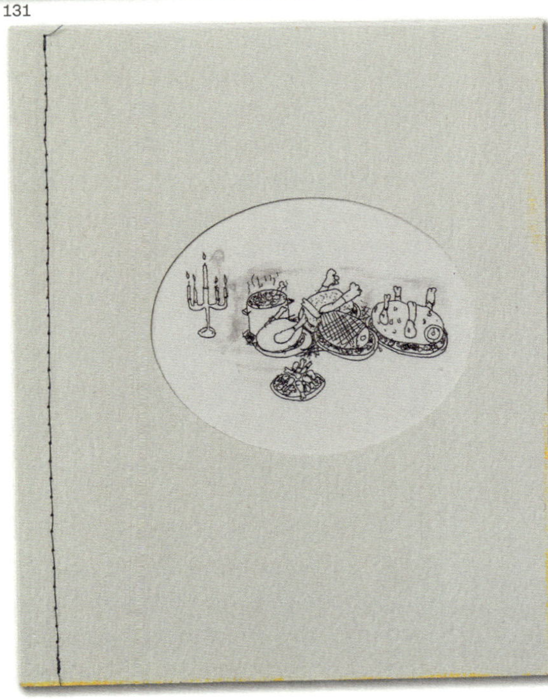

130. *This Is Not a Comic #3*, Pritika Lal and Coco Solid, A5, 2005. Tāmaki Makaurau Auckland.

131. *Menagerie*, poems by Hannah May De Cuba, drawings by Vincent Lum, 182 × 152mm, date and location unknown.

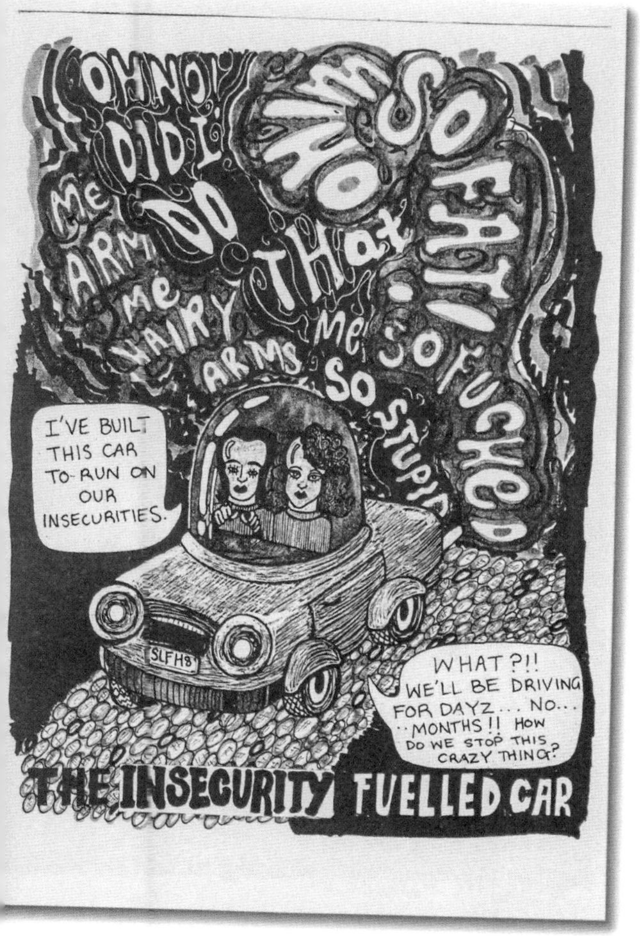

Pritika Lal I saw that people not only used Twink, but also cut things out to stick together on a page. That was pretty freeing: to not have to make everything perfect all at the same time, to just be able to get the good bit and cut it out and stick it on or get out the Twink. I'd often write something and accidentally skip a whole letter. If I missed a letter out of the word I thought I was fucked, so it was pretty cool finding out about these liberating processes.

Tessa Stubbing When I was getting into zines as a teenager I discovered a website — maybe through Moira's Moon Rocket zine distro — with instructions on you how to set up your spreads for photocopying at Kinkos [printing centres] or something. But [eye roll] of course US paper sizes are different to the international 'A'-scale formats used everywhere else. What, you didn't know that?!

132. *This Is Not a Comic* #3 page, Pritika Lal and Coco Solid, A5, 2005. Tāmaki Makaurau Auckland.

133. *Child That Mind* #2 cover and spread, Moira Clunie, A6, 2002. Tāmaki Makaurau Auckland.

133

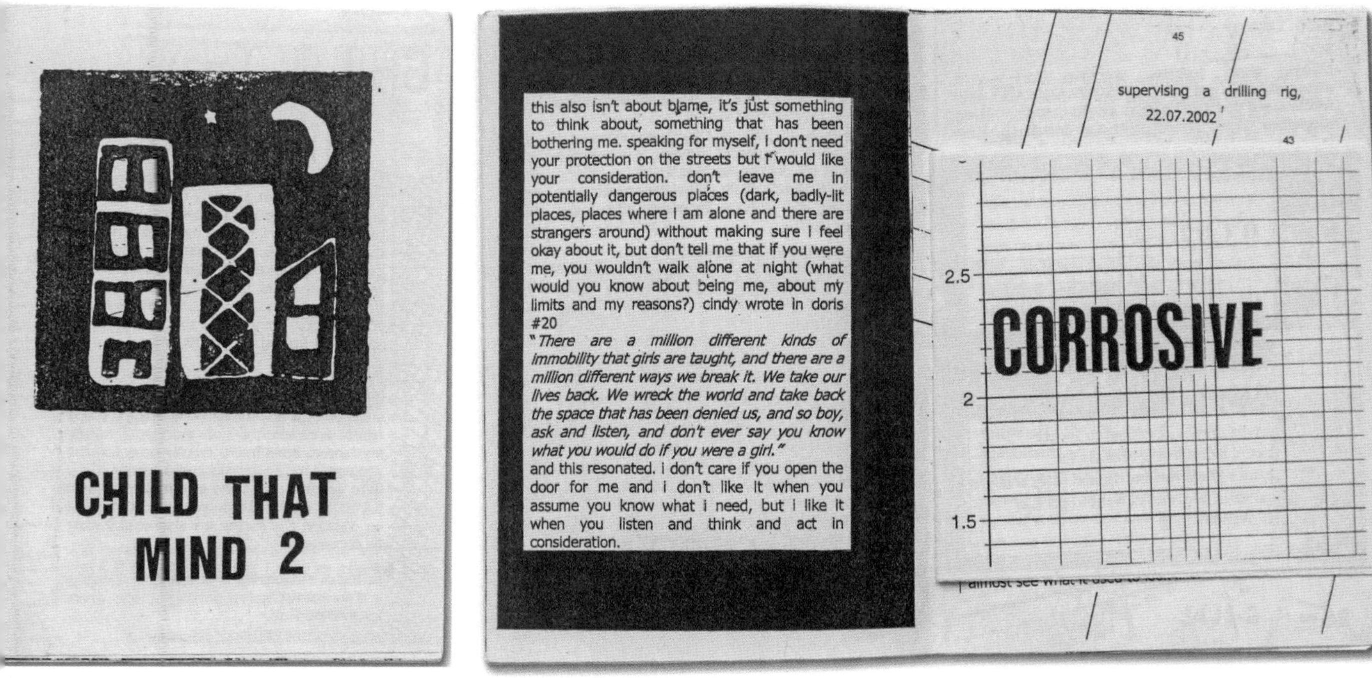

Tony Renouf I was born in Jersey. [Many years later] I was hanging out there with my cousin when he said 'Why don't you draw comics anymore? You should give it another go.' So I returned to drawing, not worrying about whether the stories joined up. I was back working nights and it all started coming back to me, these loose storylines started coming out. I bought some coloured pencils and started drawing full-colour cartoons in my journal. They were all at A5.

When I got back here, I opened a record shop and I started doing the A4 again. I'd bought my first computer and scanner while I was in the UK. To be able to get my artwork out there on my own blog, and be doing it in full-colour and not have to worry about the reproduction costs was just like — *kabluey!* — mind explodes.

Andrew Schmidt That black-and-white layout in *Garage* was a big influence on *Mysterex*. That was probably our primary fanzine influence; we couldn't do colour, it was prohibitively expensive.

Sam Orchard This is the second version of that very first coming-out comic. I have no idea where the first version has gone or if it still exists. It's so bad. Everything about it. The writing's bad, I'm trying to work a metaphor . . . It's awful. The drawing's also terrible, and to think this is the *second* version of it! The font choices!? Oh, man. But yeah, it was basically a little comic to say 'I'm really scared of telling you something; I'm still trying to figure it out. I don't know how you're going to react, but I just want you to know that I think I'm queer.'

Then there was the fear of printing it out and having to run to the printer to make sure no one else saw it, because it's visual. I felt like I had this giant neon sign above my head that said, 'I'm printing gay shit at the university.' *Everyone will know*. I was only ready to tell my closest friends. I was like, I need to tell my friends but I don't know if I'm going to physically be able to let the words leave my mouth or if I'm just going to vomit. So I gave them a comic because that was somehow easier and likely to be more comprehensible. After all that, I still had a friend who read it and said, 'I don't know what you're trying to say.'

Tessa Stubbing Kylie and I would have little clashes. I'd be like 'I want the art zines', and she'd be like 'I don't! I want the personal zines.' Eventually we made some personal zines together.

Liz Mathews *Dirty Pictures by Dirty Girls* was a collaboration with my friend Jana Te Nahu Owen. It started at Punk Fest. We were drawing dirty pictures and then thought 'Let's get some other people to draw some.' Then 'Let's get everybody to draw some . . . but we're only asking girls.' So we had this big pile of really funny pictures to compile into a zine.

Indira Neville I really like it when you know that something has been made by someone. I always did these really fancy frames with my own comics, because I wanted to remind people that they were reading a comic and if the frames were

134

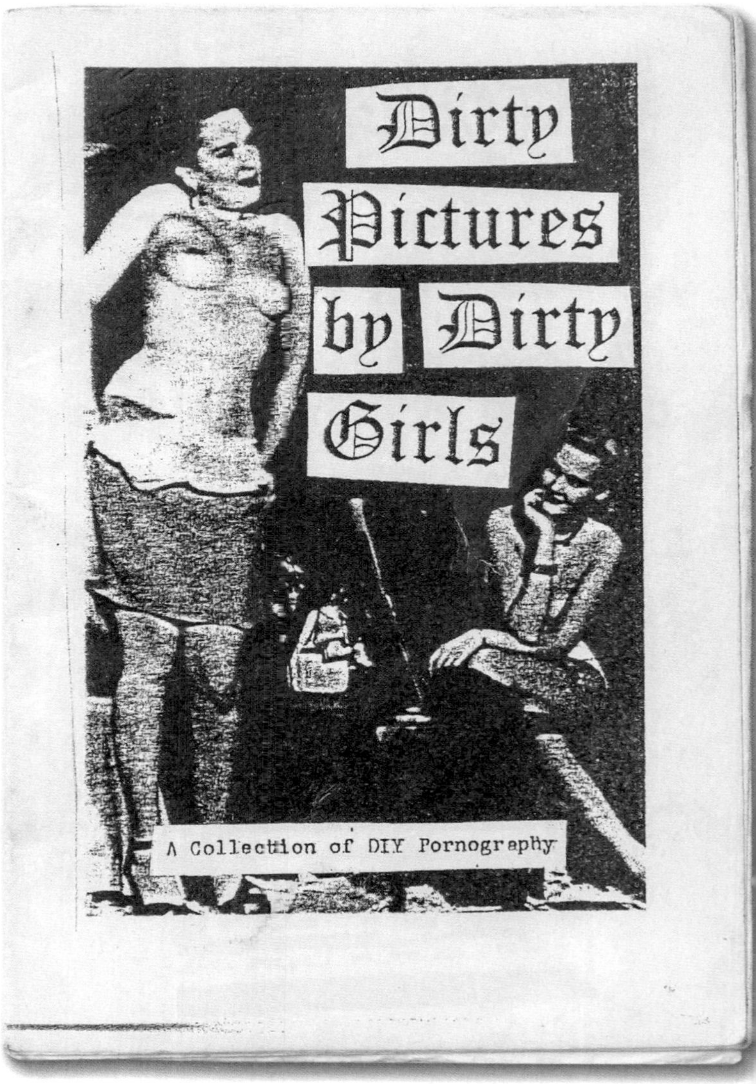

nice and fancy then you couldn't forget it. I don't like the idea of frames as a kind of narrative tool; I like the idea of frames as their own important bit of the comic. I really like things that are *made*, which is another reason why my cartoon characters often talk to the reader, whereas 'competent' comics just like this seamless world-building. I like it when my characters don't look the same in every frame. I think that's quite important. I like it when random things happen because that's cool, y'know?

In one frame something's going on, and then suddenly in the next frame a gigantic bat can appear. I don't like the kind of cause-and-effect thing: 'This will only happen if there'd been some kind of lead-up.' It's a big thing for me, seeing that something has been *made*, that's radical in and of itself. And jokes are really important to me as well.

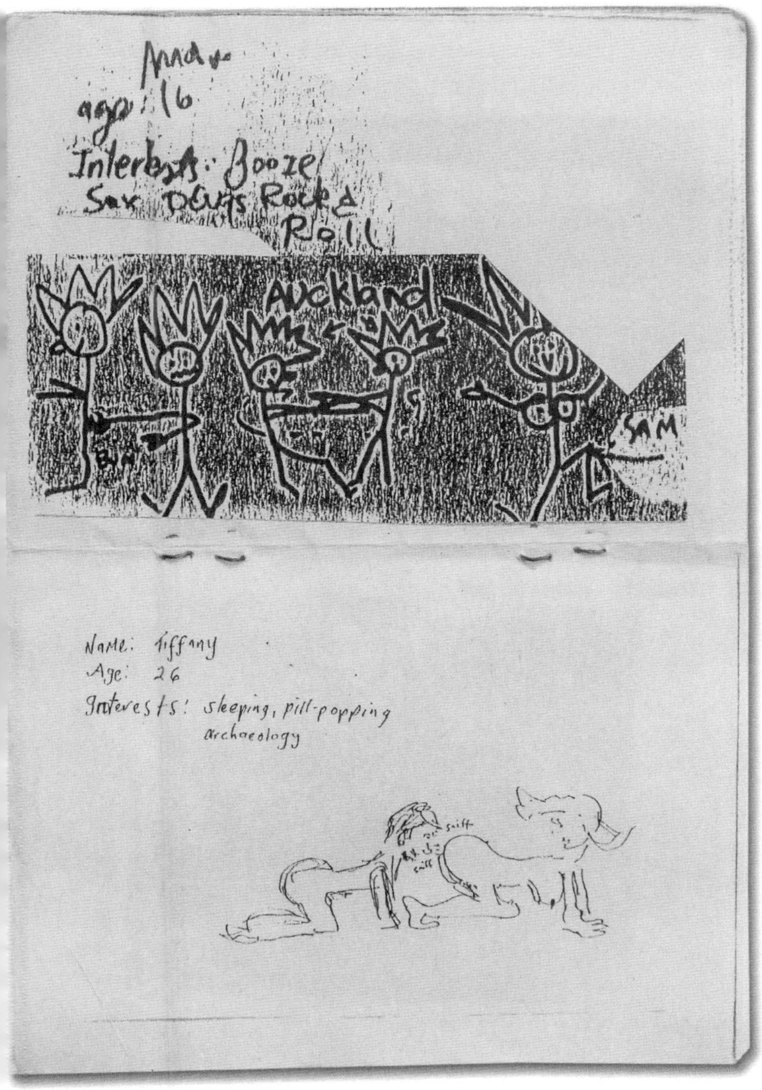

134. *Dirty Pictures by Dirty Girls* cover and spread, Liz Mathews and Jana Te Nahu Owen, A7, 2003. Tāmaki Makaurau Auckland.

Another 'competent' comic thing is the idea that comics aren't just for kids anymore because they tackle depression and they tackle this and that, like Alison Bechdel going on about her relationship with her father blah blah blah. I don't care about that. I think making someone laugh is the heaviest thing in the world, so I really care about the jokes, and the word 'comic' means funny. So that's another thing. The 'amazing' contemporary comics are quite disparaging of funny comics.

Tui Gordon The first zine I ever made was called *Scratch and Sniff*. It was a real mix of different stuff, but with an anti-capitalist theme. The second one was *Sphagnum Girl*, a superhero comic about a girl from the West Coast whose superpower was ultra-absorbency. She was on an eco-crusade. She also had power armpit hair which she could use to swing on vines and grab stuff. Then came *Para ser de la Tierra*. It was a whole bunch of pictures and drawings and writings about stuff I'd discovered during a trip to South America. After that I got onto the *Revolutionary Women Stencil-Book*, which got picked up by a distro in Canada.

Liz Mathews In the early 2000s I moved to Wellington for a year, and I was making a zine called *Golden Opportunity*, which was dirty queer-sex-focused, lots of hand-drawn dirty pictures and stuff.

Beth Dawson I started making a whole lot of little zines that were related to solo musical projects and their themes: lyrics were written out; song ideas that were drawings . . . To me those zines feel like little music scores as much as anything else. I can look at them and know them as a song.

Tessa Stubbing There was a zine I got from Moira's distro called something like *Mama Zine*, it was all about women giving other women abortions when abortion was illegal in America. I remember reading that and thinking 'I'd like to think that I could be that person if needed.' But I could never, I'm too squeamish. Isn't it crazy, the things that you read about in zines?

Beth Dawson I know he's problematic, but I like what Billy Childish said about the amateur: that he'd rather see amateur work because it's something the author/creator is just *really* interested in outside of it having a profit motive. As a consumer of them, zines are like that for me. That's what I like at the new zinefests that are so much bigger. 'Wow, that person's chosen to make a zine about Octavia Butler', or the one I picked up today about food their mum made.

Indira Neville I didn't really need an introduction to zines with my dad doing drawings for the school newsletter. Later in life, when I became a school principal, I did the same thing. I don't know if you've seen that comic *100 School Demons* that I made. That was originally in the school newsletter, and it was awesome. I had this captive audience.

The first bit of DIY publishing I saw was probably my dad's school newsletters, which were printed on the Banda Machine with that smelly purple stuff.[4] You stood there and rotated this big purple drum by hand. Imagine if you had one of those today. Imagine how cool and retro you'd be.

Tessa Stubbing I called the zine *10-22-38 Astoria* in reference to the first-ever photocopier. Astoria New York was the place that Chester Carlson invented the very first photocopier on 22 October 1938.

I'm not sure when photocopiers actually became common, but Chester Carlson used to get a royalty on every copy that was made, which is why he became a millionaire. He had grown up dirt-poor — literally, like, on a dirt floor dirt-poor — and he was uncomfortable with all this wealth and gave most of his money away. He was a white American who gave his money away to black causes. Apparently, there are a lot of buildings in America with little plaques that read 'Funded by Chester Carlson'. He was also very low-key with his philanthropy. What a cool guy.

David Merritt Have you read Steve Albini's treatise on independent music? Dig it out, it's up on the net. He said: this is how it works. Every year 1000 new bands come knocking on the doors of the indie record labels around America, and it's like picking up big wads of pasta and chucking it against the wall . . . By the end of the year only 5 per cent of that pasta has stuck and the rest is just in a pile on the floor. That 5 per cent get the second album deal, and then there's a whole new year's worth of pasta being thrown at the same wall . . . And this doesn't stop. This is always going on.

We've got to the critical point now where that pasta-throwing phase has hit literature. We've got so many creative-writing schools churning out creative writers, we've got so many music schools churning out musicians . . . When I was a young poet there was no creative-writing school, you just had a fucking life and that was it and you could make a poetical journey out of it if you wanted. But that all changed once IIML [International Institute of Modern Letters, Victoria University's creative-writing programme] started, and once they commodified the creativeness of writing like they have with music and with painting and everything else.

135

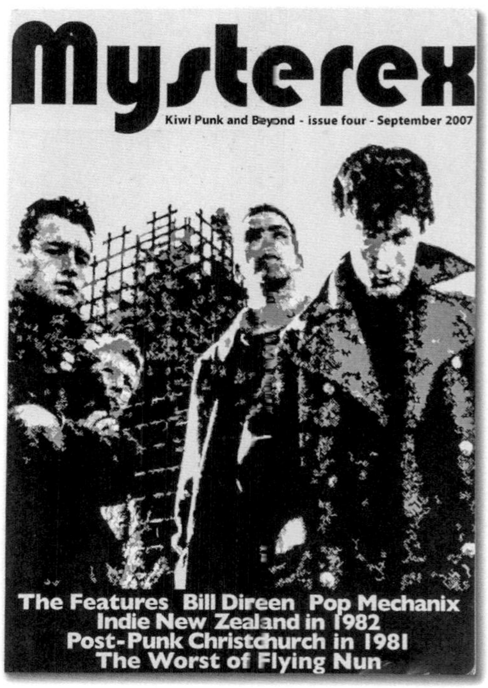

135. *Mysterex* #4, edited by Andrew Schmidt, A4, 2007. Paeroa.

136

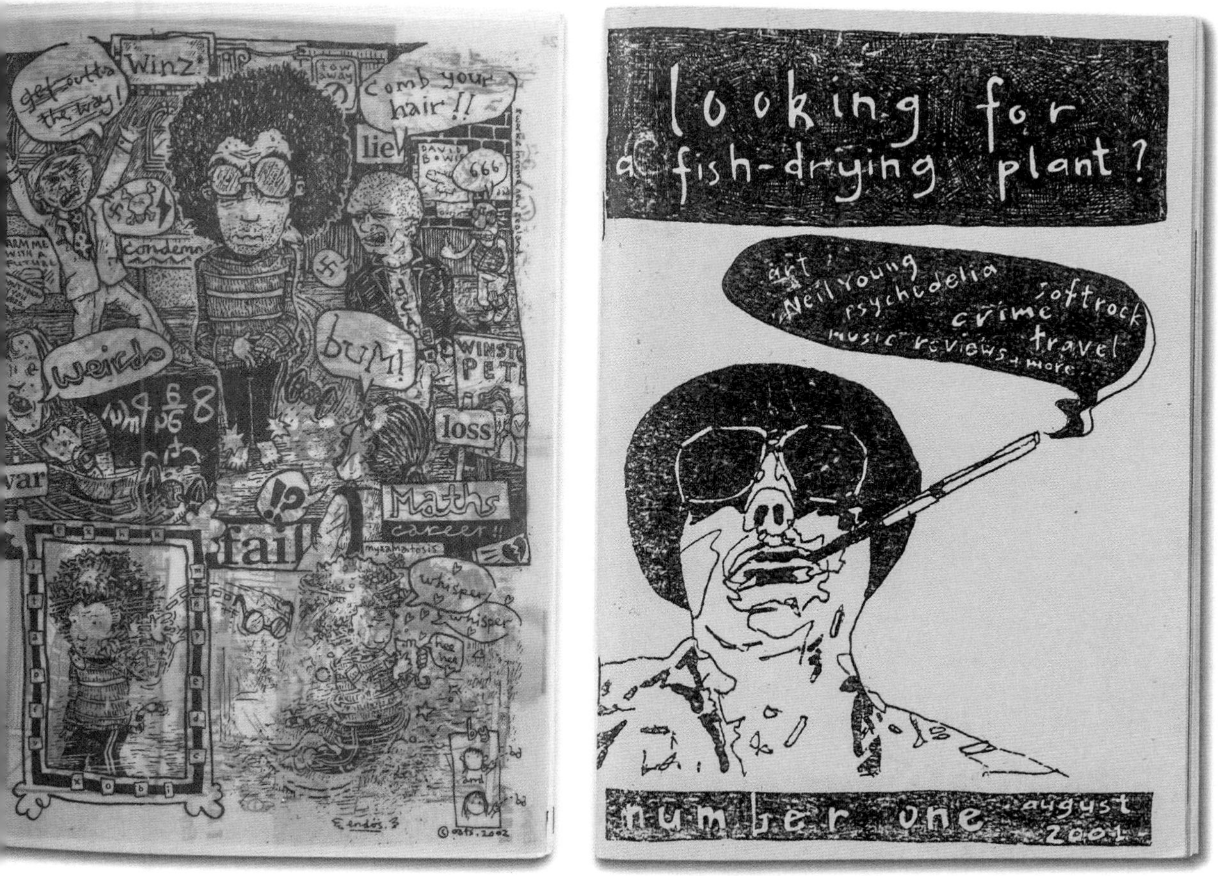

136. *looking for a fish-drying plant?* #1 page and cover, Stephen Clover, A5, 2001. Te Whanganui-a-Tara Wellington.

Tessa Stubbing When I was at uni, Jonty Valentine was one of my lecturers. In third year, a new lecturer came in who was really young and hip and cool. She used to work for *Pavement* magazine, which used to feature all these semi-naked young girls. She talked about having to navigate that world. She created a zine course for design students who wanted to be magazine designers. It was a really popular class. Everyone wanted to take it.

So Jonty, who wanted to introduce students to typeface design, ended up having to teach zine class. Nobody wanted to study typeface. To be honest I should've done typeface, because I already knew zines, right? For him it was like, 'We're going to create a self-published magazine, not so much "a zine".' I remember thinking 'What the fuck?! This is a zine class and you're not showing anyone a zine. Why?'

Now I'm a teacher, I think maybe he didn't give us zines because he didn't want us mimicking the material. Maybe he was giving us more latitude. But at the time I was like 'What the fuck?!' So, I went home and I got a whole bunch of zines, and I brought them in and showed the class. I think Jonty was a little bit upset about that. But I was just like 'Hey, guys, here are some zines, check them out', and they were like 'Oh, oh, I get it now.'

In retrospect, I have a problem with the idea of a zine course in a design school. Kids were at AUT wanting to learn magazine design. You had kids who were going to go on to design corporate manuals, and they were making zines. There's absolutely nothing wrong with being at design school to learn the tools of the trade. I was there for that, too. To me, a zine is a very different thing.

Sam Orchard I haven't thought about those comics until you sent me an email yesterday, and I went rummaging through my stuff and I thought, 'Oh, yeah, I guess that's technically published. I gave it to a number of friends.'

When I was looking through them, I was like 'Oh, shit, I have literally glued two pieces of paper back-to-back because I didn't know how to print a booklet.' I had flashbacks to drawing something, trying to scan it, putting it in Word, trying to angle it, trying to work out what order you have to lay things out, printing it using the uni computers, knowing that it's 10 cents a page, which was so much money for me as a student.

Pritika Lal I made a lot of stuff in that time. I did community murals and mechanical installations, a lot of stuff, but creating anything that I would call a zine wouldn't have been until *This Is Not a Comic* with Coco Solid around 2002–2003. We bought a second-hand photocopier online. Was that on Trade Me? Did that exist back then? Anyway, we had to raise money to buy this really shitty $50 photocopier, so we held a raffle. I drew a big tiger face and stuck it to polystyrene. I cut out the mouth and put a clock inside. We called it the Tiger Clock, and we put it in the window of Stella Corkery and Alan Holt's shop, Bunny [Boutique], in St Kevin's Arcade off K Road. We sold raffle tickets up and down K Road to anyone who was interested, and we raised the $50 we needed and got to buy the photocopier.

The photocopier ended up being so shit that we couldn't use it and we had to find another way to print *This Is Not a Comic.*

We found a guy who did really cheap printing and we started trying to get funding through Creative Communities. That first zine was a big messy experiment. I didn't really know what it was, but you just make stuff and go next step, next step, 'Oh, we've gotta get a photocopier', 'Oh, that doesn't work' . . . y'know, just like next step, next step.

Liz Mathews I left Wellington after a year and moved to London to escape a bad relationship. I made the zine *The Wishbone Your Majesty?*, which was kind of about London. But then I stopped making zines. There was just so much going on, I didn't have the time. And when I lived in London we were squatting in abandoned buildings. I did have a typewriter, but that was a heavy thing to carry around when you also had to carry your mattress, all your clothes, your books . . . You just had to really strip it down. We were getting evicted about every three months, so it wasn't the best set-up for making zines.

137

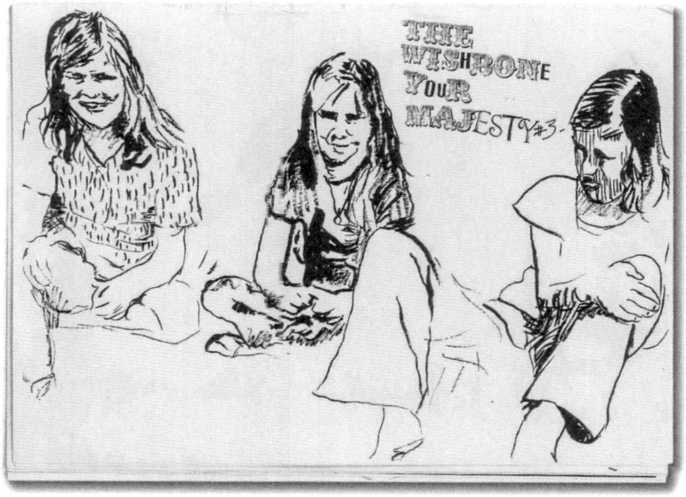

Pritika Lal This guy in some printing place out the back of K Road would print them pretty cheaply, and they were pretty good quality. They were black-and-white photocopies and we used coloured paper stock for the cover. Stapling them was really time-consuming. We made 1000 each time. They were available for free. At some point we needed to run ads so we could pay for it.

Later on I came across that 'no ads' definition of zines and various other rules. I feel like that's what was really good about coming from our *own* place of trying to do something. We were like 'This is what we're trying to do', and people are saying 'It's not a zine because of these reasons' and 'It's not a comic because of these reasons.' But you only encounter that once you start making things.

138

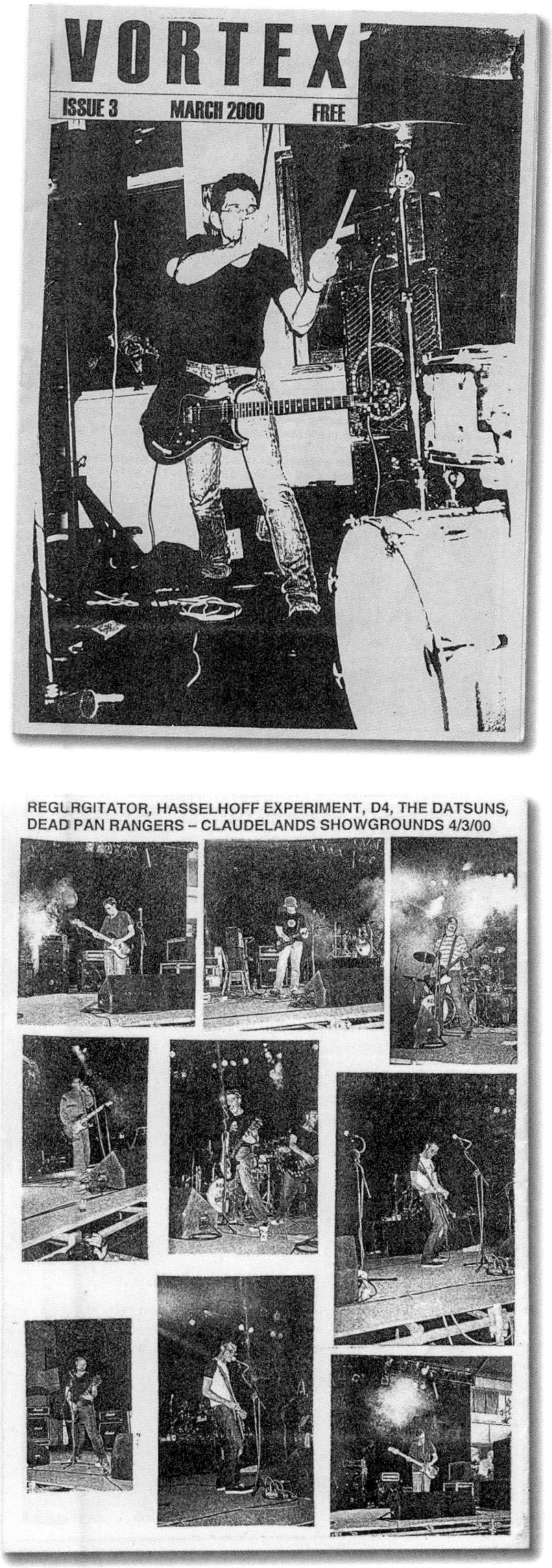

Indira Neville As I got older I got jobs. When I was a teacher I'd use the school photocopier, when I worked at the National Library I'd use the work photocopier. I'd come in early so I wasn't getting in the way, but no one really seemed to mind. I thought that's the best use of taxpayer money ever — photocopying comics. I would go to a copy shop if I needed to. I'm not precious; whatever's around.

Kerry Ann Lee A really kindly local pharmacist had a photocopier, and I got friendly with them because I used to get my postage stamps from them when I was doing my distro. They gave me free rein on the photocopier to do some of the catalogues if I was running out — small runs.

Kylie Buck Chantelle was printing them at her uncle's work. And then we started using the photocopier in the polytech staffroom. We just finessed someone into letting us print stuff without having to pay for it.

David Merritt I started off with a little book called *Geek Prayers*. I could make two of those out of one kids' book cover; I'd cut the book in half. Then I'd get the scalpel out and I'd cut eight pages which, once folded, front and back, gives you 32 pages for the inside. I could fold those pages in half and staple them inside the cover. Those were the first ones I made. Then in about 2009 there was this one poem I started to fold up and put inside a book cover. Eventually, they were all made like that.

Moira Clunie I punch through the thick pages of the spine with an awl and then hand-stitch my zines, punching through into an old phonebook or a piece of foam.

137. *The Wishbone Your Majesty* #3, Liz Mathews, A5, 2009. Tāmaki Makaurau Auckland.

138. *Vortex* #3 front and back covers, anonymous, A5, 2000. Kirikiriroa Hamilton.

139

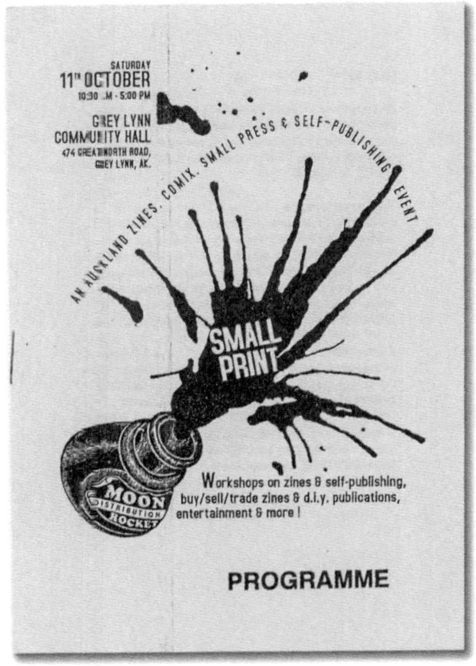

Liz Mathews The main way I distributed the zines I made was by posting them to people. A few went out through Kerry Ann's distro Red Letter and Moira's Moon Rocket, and Penny Collins was doing something, but mostly it was my network. I did lots and lots of trades. By the time the zinefests arrived I'd pretty much stopped making zines, so I never had to deal with the awkwardness of engaging with the public.

Indira Neville I did Armageddon [pop-culture convention] a couple of times, but I was never fully into it. I never really liked zinefests that much either. I just want to make stuff. My favourite, favourite way of distributing comics was just to leave them around the place. I used to love leaving them in the inorganic rubbish collection to see what would happen, or just give them to people who asked me for them. Fronting up with your comics can be ghastly. And that's really why computers are kind of awesome, because they're the means of distribution as well as production if you want them to be. You don't have to go anywhere, and you can share your work with hundreds of people.

Kerry Ann Lee At one of the early zinefests that Moira Clunie organised, Small Print 2003 or 2005, Duncan Greive, who's now with The Spinoff, was writing for some pop-culture magazine and he asked, 'Are you worried about this whole arcane zine-making practice being usurped because of blogs?' I replied, 'No way!' This was just as Myspace was happening, and punkas.com — the New Zealand forum for punk — was having a moment. I was like 'Is this just another form of communication? Nah, this is a whole different thing.' That was my art-design side coming out.

Moira Clunie Most of the organisers are named in that first 2003 *Small Print Programme*, and then for the 2005 one it was mostly the same people, some additional crew. [Reading:] 'A huge thanks to the other organisers, Laura C . . .' (my sister Laura), 'Laura A' (Laura Alp), her friend Nate (Laura's partner), and Annette. My friend Angela also helped at the 2005 one. It was a little crew, various other people contributed different things.

Kerry Ann Lee designed the logo for the 2005 Small Print. We all met at my house. I've still got copies of some of the minutes of our meetings. [Laughs.] It wouldn't have been possible as a solo effort, I'm sure.

I was aware of zinefests overseas through those mailing lists and message boards that I was on. I remember seeing an online video of a New York feminist zinefest. This was before YouTube. It was a real low-res clip of one of the panel discussions, but I found it so inspiring and interesting. I was thinking 'Gosh, it'd be cool if we had something here.' I was connected to a few locals who were making zines, so I knew there'd be enough people interested in a thing like that. Also, there'd been related markets and things; there was a punk market called Chump Change that happened a couple of times in a punk house

139. *Small Print Programme* cover, various contributors, A6, 2003. Tāmaki Makaurau Auckland.

at the top of Symonds Street. I had a blanket on the floor and I was selling zines and things, people had different handicrafts for sale. Ladyfest Auckland also happened in 2003, I think maybe a little bit after Small Print, but there was that organising happening as well. Ladyfest sort of came through Riot Grrrl.

Kylie Buck We went up to Auckland and had a stall at Small Print. We had a couple of issues of *Dangerous Liaisons* at that stage. Nobody would take them, it was something about them being free. We were like 'Why don't people want these?' We didn't have any zine stuff happening in Wellington and we just thought 'Everyone will want these!'

One guy took one, and then he came back and said 'Oh, I don't want this after all,' and we asked him 'Why?', and he said, 'Because it's got non-vegan food in it'. We said 'Okay.' We were like 19 or something. I just thought 'What a dick.'

Moira Clunie I'm pretty sure I found out about Kerry Ann Lee's Red Letter Zine Distro through Crawlspace Records. I picked up a flyer about Red Letter from there and then wrote to her. Kerry Ann was at both Small Print events. I've got a photograph of her taking a graphic design workshop.

140

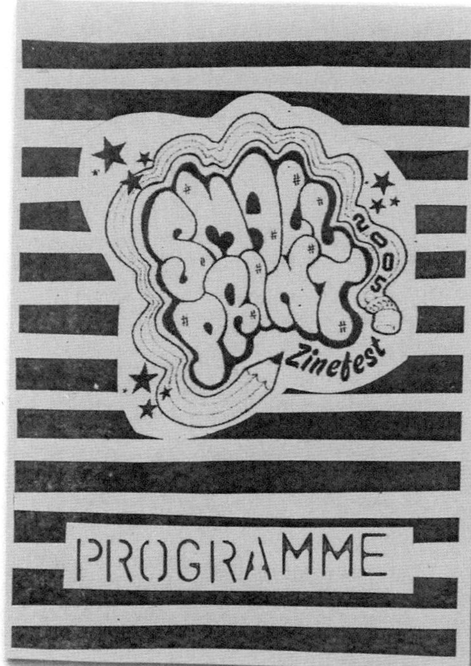

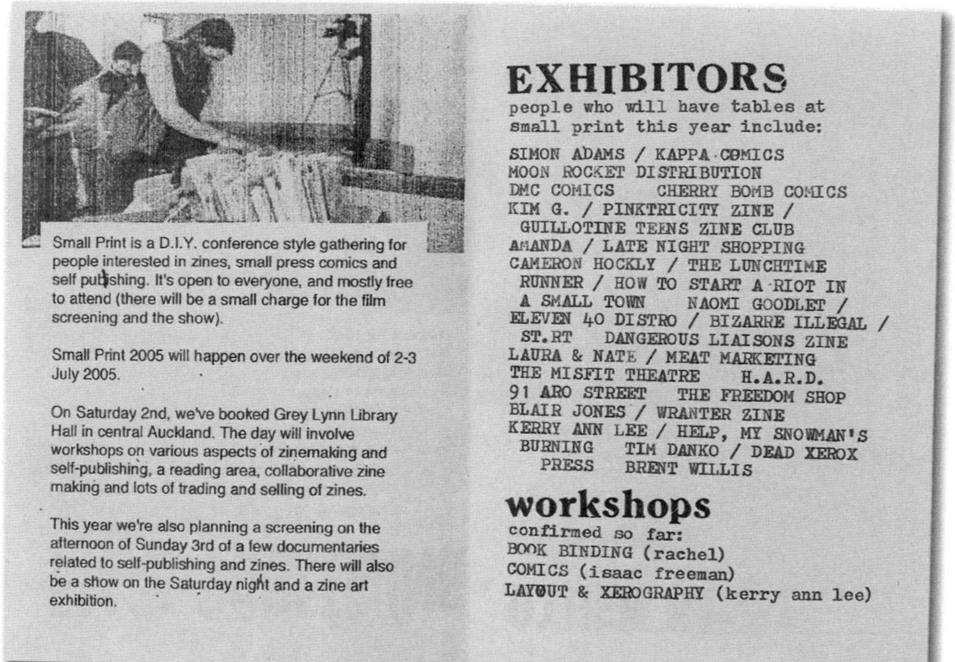

Small Print is a D.I.Y. conference style gathering for people interested in zines, small press comics and self publishing. It's open to everyone, and mostly free to attend (there will be a small charge for the film screening and the show).

Small Print 2005 will happen over the weekend of 2-3 July 2005.

On Saturday 2nd, we've booked Grey Lynn Library Hall in central Auckland. The day will involve workshops on various aspects of zinemaking and self-publishing, a reading area, collaborative zine making and lots of trading and selling of zines.

This year we're also planning a screening on the afternoon of Sunday 3rd of a few documentaries related to self-publishing and zines. There will also be a show on the Saturday night and a zine art exhibition.

EXHIBITORS
people who will have tables at small print this year include:
SIMON ADAMS / KAPPA COMICS
MOON ROCKET DISTRIBUTION
DMC COMICS CHERRY BOMB COMICS
KIM G. / PINKTRICITY ZINE / GUILLOTINE TEENS ZINE CLUB
AMANDA / LATE NIGHT SHOPPING
CAMERON HOCKLY / THE LUNCHTIME RUNNER / HOW TO START A RIOT IN A SMALL TOWN NAOMI GOODLET /
ELEVEN 40 DISTRO / BIZARRE ILLEGAL / ST.RT DANGEROUS LIAISONS ZINE
LAURA & NATE / MEAT MARKETING
THE MISFIT THEATRE H.A.R.D.
91 ARO STREET THE FREEDOM SHOP
BLAIR JONES / WRANTER ZINE
KERRY ANN LEE / HELP, MY SNOWMAN'S BURNING TIM DANKO / DEAD XEROX PRESS BRENT WILLIS

workshops
confirmed so far:
BOOK BINDING (rachel)
COMICS (isaac freeman)
LAYOUT & XEROGRAPHY (kerry ann lee)

140. *Small Print Programme* spread and cover logotype, Kerry Ann Lee, A6 foldout, 2005. Tāmaki Makaurau Auckland.

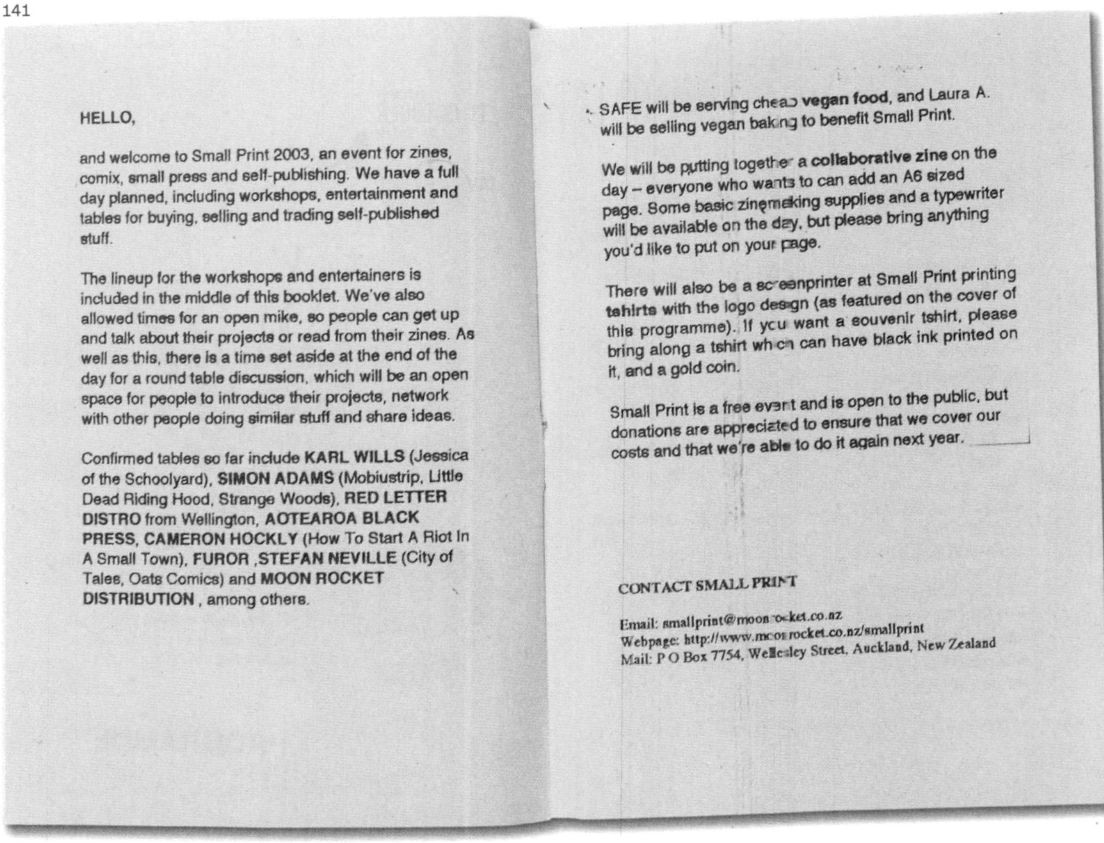

HELLO,

and welcome to Small Print 2003, an event for zines, comix, small press and self-publishing. We have a full day planned, including workshops, entertainment and tables for buying, selling and trading self-published stuff.

The lineup for the workshops and entertainers is included in the middle of this booklet. We've also allowed times for an open mike, so people can get up and talk about their projects or read from their zines. As well as this, there is a time set aside at the end of the day for a round table discussion, which will be an open space for people to introduce their projects, network with other people doing similar stuff and share ideas.

Confirmed tables so far include **KARL WILLS** (Jessica of the Schoolyard), **SIMON ADAMS** (Mobiustrip, Little Dead Riding Hood, Strange Woods), **RED LETTER DISTRO** from Wellington, **AOTEAROA BLACK PRESS, CAMERON HOCKLY** (How To Start A Riot In A Small Town), **FUROR ,STEFAN NEVILLE** (City of Tales, Oats Comics) and **MOON ROCKET DISTRIBUTION** , among others.

SAFE will be serving cheap **vegan food**, and Laura A. will be selling vegan baking to benefit Small Print.

We will be putting together **a collaborative zine** on the day – everyone who wants to can add an A6 sized page. Some basic zinemaking supplies and a typewriter will be available on the day, but please bring anything you'd like to put on your page.

There will also be a screenprinter at Small Print printing **tshirts** with the logo design (as featured on the cover of this programme). If you want a souvenir tshirt, please bring along a tshirt which can have black ink printed on it, and a gold coin.

Small Print is a free event and is open to the public, but donations are appreciated to ensure that we cover our costs and that we're able to do it again next year.

CONTACT SMALL PRINT

Email: smallprint@moonrocket.co.nz
Webpage: http://www.moonrocket.co.nz/smallprint
Mail: P O Box 7754, Wellesley Street, Auckland, New Zealand

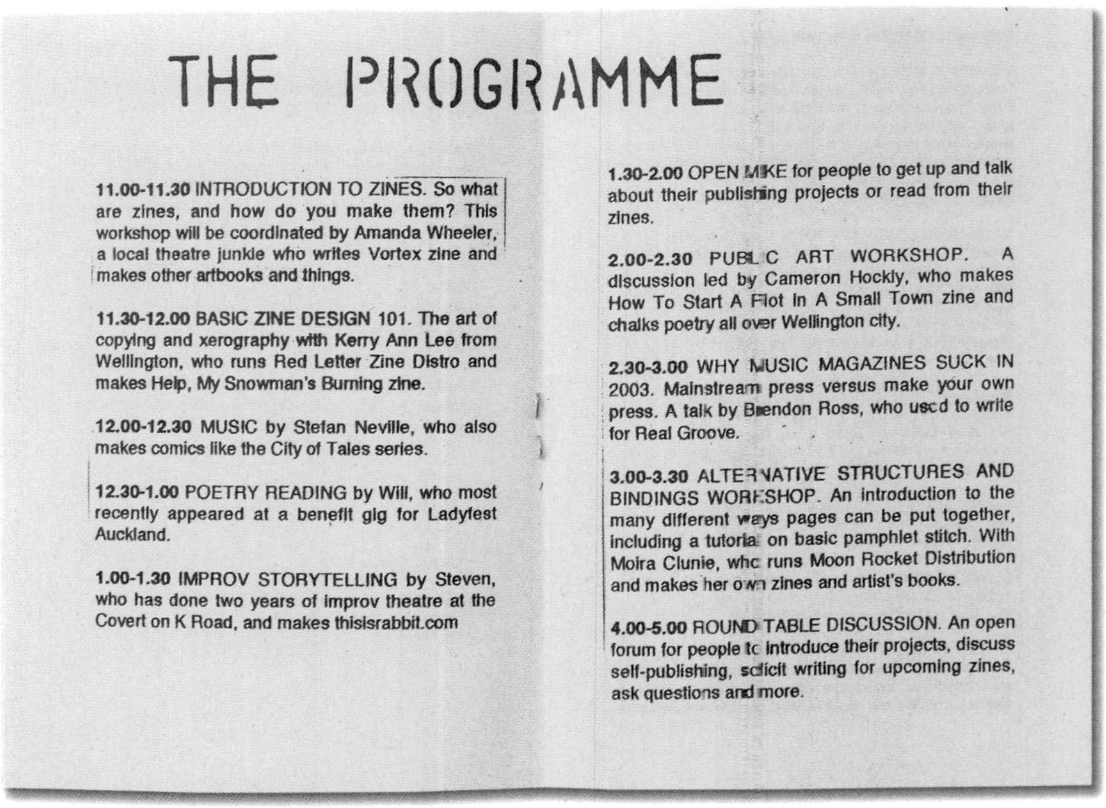

THE PROGRAMME

11.00-11.30 INTRODUCTION TO ZINES. So what are zines, and how do you make them? This workshop will be coordinated by Amanda Wheeler, a local theatre junkie who writes Vortex zine and makes other artbooks and things.

11.30-12.00 BASIC ZINE DESIGN 101. The art of copying and xerography with Kerry Ann Lee from Wellington, who runs Red Letter Zine Distro and makes Help, My Snowman's Burning zine.

12.00-12.30 MUSIC by Stefan Neville, who also makes comics like the City of Tales series.

12.30-1.00 POETRY READING by Will, who most recently appeared at a benefit gig for Ladyfest Auckland.

1.00-1.30 IMPROV STORYTELLING by Steven, who has done two years of improv theatre at the Covert on K Road, and makes thisisrabbit.com

1.30-2.00 OPEN MIKE for people to get up and talk about their publishing projects or read from their zines.

2.00-2.30 PUBLIC ART WORKSHOP. A discussion led by Cameron Hockly, who makes How To Start A Riot In A Small Town zine and chalks poetry all over Wellington city.

2.30-3.00 WHY MUSIC MAGAZINES SUCK IN 2003. Mainstream press versus make your own press. A talk by Brendon Ross, who used to write for Real Groove.

3.00-3.30 ALTERNATIVE STRUCTURES AND BINDINGS WORKSHOP. An introduction to the many different ways pages can be put together, including a tutorial on basic pamphlet stitch. With Moira Clunie, who runs Moon Rocket Distribution and makes her own zines and artist's books.

4.00-5.00 ROUND TABLE DISCUSSION. An open forum for people to introduce their projects, discuss self-publishing, solicit writing for upcoming zines, ask questions and more.

141. *Small Print Programme* spreads, various contributors, A6, 2003. Tāmaki Makaurau Auckland.

Kylie Buck But otherwise Small Print was a good time. Kerry Ann Lee was there, and we were like 'Wow', and we went and bought her stuff. I believe she was selling a zine about touring America — *Help, My Snowman's Burning.*

There was a comics' jam and there were workshops and I loved it.

Moira Clunie We had poetry, music, workshops, presentations, vegan food, a fundraiser, market stalls . . . Some of my ideas for the shape of a zinefest, or Small Print in this case, would have come from that early online research. But a couple of the friends involved in the first Small Print had put on shows before, they knew how to organise benefit shows and they had those skills just through punk existence. I probably picked up ideas from zinefests overseas and just thought about what might appeal here.

Kylie Buck A funny thing about Small Print was that when we were there someone swapped a tiny zine with us that I still have. The author of that zine was a very baby Tessa Stubbing. So we met before we met; we had an incidental meeting. It wasn't until years later — once we'd established a friendship — and she said, 'Here's all of my zines' that I was like 'OMG!', and we worked out that she had come to our stall. She was like 16 or something at the time.

Moira Clunie Small Print was a weekend gathering of people interested in zines and self-publishing — I guess 'zines' broadly defined, including comics and artist books and individual home-made publications, that kind of thing. We had a zine market at the Grey Lynn Library hall, a community hall space with tables around the edge and people selling their own wares. I had a table for Moon Rocket distro both times, with a big selection of different things. There were people selling their anarchist political diatribes, and there were personal zines and designed objects and comics and all sorts. The space also included a 'screen-print your own Small Print t-shirt' setup. Somebody bought a badge-maker so you could make your own badges. We had crafty spaces, and a collaborative zine space where people could make-a-page that would be compiled into a zine. The first issue of that was published in 2003, but the second issue wasn't published until August 2023.

Kylie Buck We were mostly wide-eyed, y'know. We'd just started making zines, had only just met you, and that was the extent of our zine experience when we drove to Auckland for Small Print. That was pretty crazy. We bought lots of zines and read them all once we got to the backpackers. We had an argument over one of them. I was like '*I* bought that one', and Chantelle was like 'No, *I* bought that one!'

This guy Mike Marsh came up with us. He'd made zines before, and he showed us how to physically lay the pages out. We had a bit of his art on the stall. He was like our third musketeer.

142

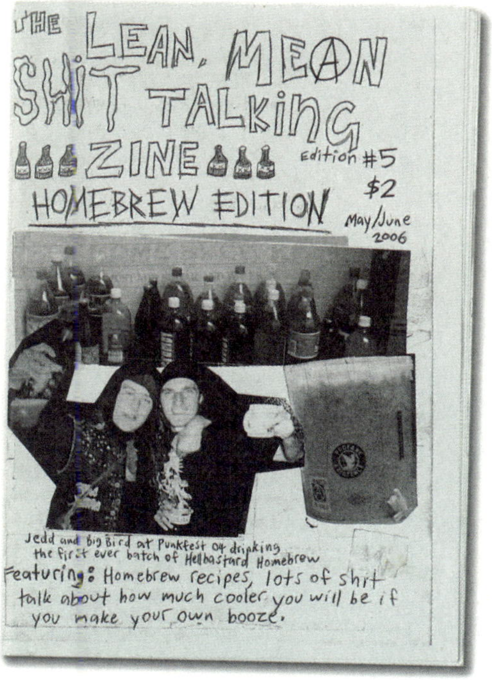

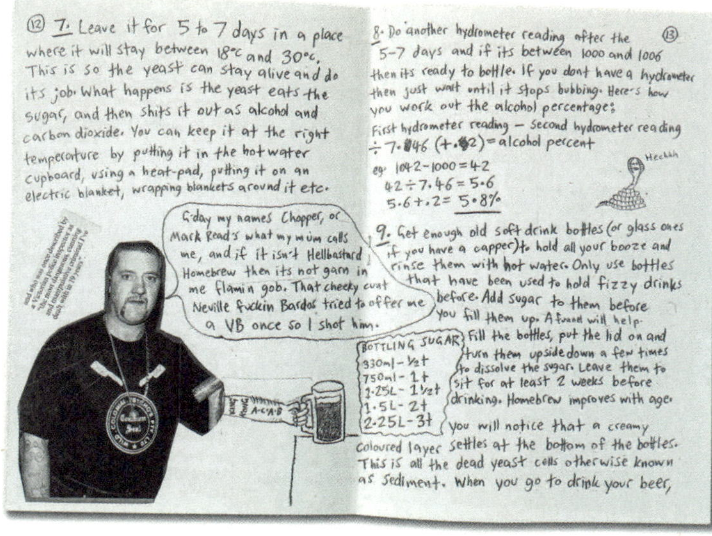

142. *The Lean Mean Shit Talking Zine* #5 cover and spread, Bosun and Big Bird, A5, 2006. Te Whanganui-a-Tara Wellington.

Moira Clunie Small Print was buzzing with interested people, a bustling market space, different crowds coming through. On the day of one of the Small Prints there'd been an anarchist anti-capitalist protest in town and some of that crowd came along afterwards with some of their banners. I remember somebody looking at the Moon Rocket table and asking if I had any political zines and I was pointing out all the Riot Grrrl, feminist, vegan recipe stuff, and he goes 'No, I mean like anarchist. Not girl politics.' We had workshops where people were learning about design, layout, binding techniques, different things . . .

Kylie Buck Small Print was pretty busy. They had workshops and there were lots of people at them, whereas later when we tried to run workshops in Wellington we didn't really get anyone. But I don't know if maybe it's just the much larger population in Auckland.

Moira Clunie With both Small Print 2003 and 2005 we ran satellite events to the market: a benefit show to help pay for everything, and an after-party. Chris Knox played the benefit show and a bunch of people turned up just for that. With Small Print 2005 we had a film screening at The Wine Cellar on K Road where we showed some zine documentaries. We also had a zine exhibition displaying zines from my collection at a gallery space on K Road. It had a window box where we exhibited for a couple of weeks.

Kylie Buck It can't have been that long after starting the Wellington Libraries collection, probably less than a year. I was like 'Now we need to have a zinefest.' Because I'd been to Small Print in Auckland, and I thought 'This is fucking awesome, we need to do one in Wellington.' Then we were like 'If we're gonna do a zinefest, how're we gonna pay for it?'

I had lots of . . . lofty ideals about how everything should be free: you shouldn't have to pay for a stall, you shouldn't have to pay for zines, we should just be trying to share our work. At the time the average cost of a zine was about two bucks, so I was thinking 'If you don't sell any zines, how are you going to afford a stall?' I just wanted to make it cheap. So we pitched the idea that the library would have a stall, and, as an institution, would pay $2000 for their stall, and that's what we ran the first Wellington Zinefest on.

Moira Clunie The Small Print organisers were friends and family. We put the call out through our networks. We made paper flyers and had those around town in Crawlspace Records and other places. I connected with some of the comics people and zinesters who we were stocking through Moon Rocket, so I had connections locally with people who might be interested in having a table. We put posters up in the street ourselves — this was pre the Phantom Billstickers monopoly.

Kylie Buck Stephanie Poulopoulos and Kim Gruschow helped organise the first Wellington Zinefest. Kim designed the t-shirt. We had soup and curries, and there was Foxton Fizz and K Bars (I was eating unsold K Bars for two years afterwards). I basically just made the event that I wanted to attend. That's what you do, right? Like, this is my idea of what it should be. I knew somebody who was really into food, and he wanted to start his own restaurant, so I said, 'Do you want to come do this? I'll give you two hundred bucks; I'll pay for the ingredients if you'll run a kitchen for a day and make all the food.' So, that's what he did. My boyfriend's mum made a big thing of pumpkin soup. Some people didn't want to eat it because it was reheated in a microwave. Lots of people helped out with that first one. Kim had a friend who screen-printed the t-shirts for a case of beer.

Moira Clunie In Tessa Stubbing's final year of high school she had to do a design assignment and she chose Small Print as the client. She developed designs for a future Small Print. I think she'd been hoping that there'd be more. Tessa would've been quite young. It would take a bit of extra thinking to feel like you were ready to step into the role of running an Auckland zinefest, I guess.

Tessa Stubbing I did the branding for a third Small Print while I was still at high school. It wasn't a commission; I just designed new Small Print branding and sent it off to Moira Clunie. Oh my gosh, such a little fangirl.

My designs looked very David Carson, I know that. Love me some David Carson. My other artist model was et al. That's the style I like. That's the aesthetic. I'm still into it; that whole grungy, cut-and-paste texture. I know that zine-makers don't do that anymore, but that's what I like. Well, maybe they do, but it's in colour and it's very crisp and clean and there's none of that texture from an old black-and-white photocopier, the distress. I like it dirty.

I can't remember what the high-school brief was. I did a thing for Misfit Theatre as well: I got one of their little flyers and reworked it.

Kylie Buck When I was trying to set up the very first Wellington Zinefest, I just didn't know who was out there. Kim Gruschow would've been way more hooked into the whole scene than I was. She knew Kerry Ann Lee, she probably had ties with the anarchist bookshop, and she was running her own distro-y thing. A lot of the stallholders came through Kim. I would've been cold-calling, emailing people from the backs of the zines that were in the library.

I emailed this guy I knew who made poetry zines, and said 'Can you do Wellington Zinefest in three months?', and he said 'Oh, I'm busy that day', and I remember thinking 'In three months?! You're busy in three months?!' The fuck. I was really worried that we wouldn't get enough stallholders. I made a few people come. Blink from *A Low Hum* zine came after I convinced his partner Sally that he had to do it. I knew Sally, and I knew Heather [Barnes] from *Neighbourhood Cats* zine because of these craft fairs that I used to attend.

Then there was *Fluro Mag*!? They had a Mac setup, and we were like "What the heck is this?' And *White Fungus* was also a zine at that stage. They were also kind of distro-y, and they brought along a few other things. They just came along with their stand, set it up and pissed off. [Laughs.] They just left their stuff set up.

Kerry Ann Lee arrived very late, and I remember being very, very irritated. [In Lee's defence, this was due to printing issues.] A few people just didn't turn up at all, and I was just like 'What is happening?' It was probably because it was free. I remember emailing someone afterwards and saying, 'I can't believe you just didn't turn up', and they said 'Oh, I've just had a mental breakdown.' I felt terrible for doing that.

Wellington City Libraries had a whole setup. You could borrow stuff from their new zine collection, so that was pretty cool.

143

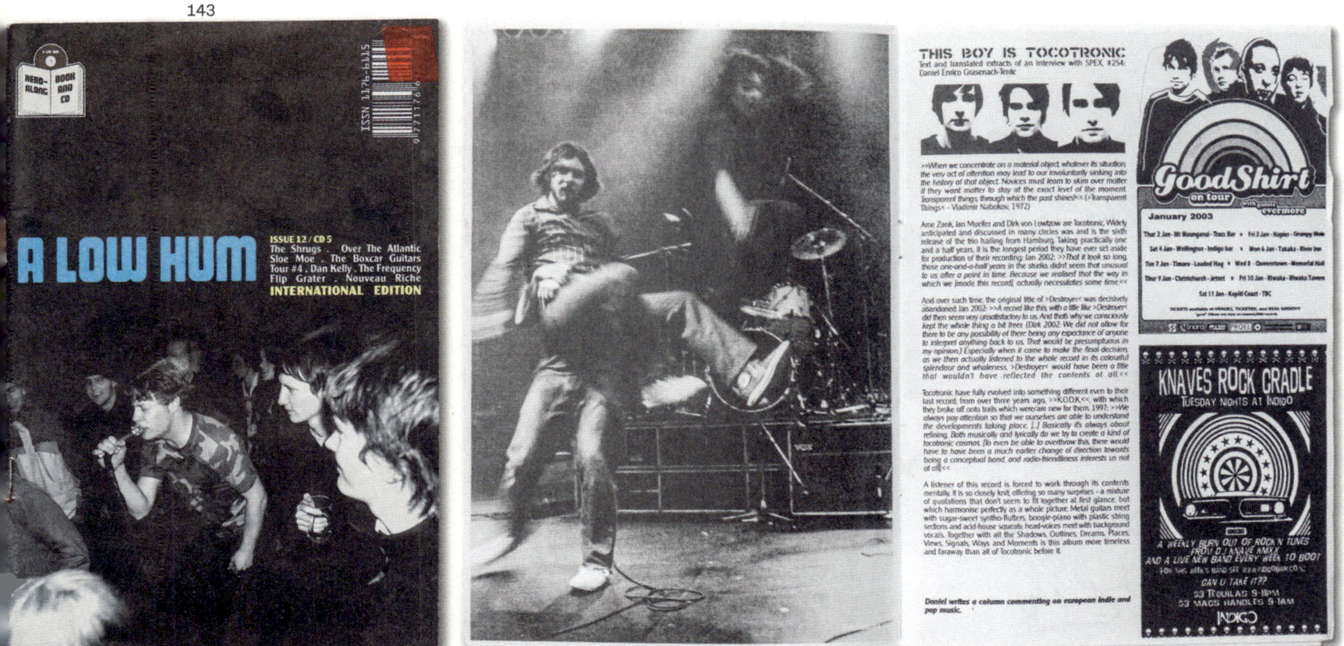

143. *A Low Hum* #12 cover and spread, Blink, A5, 2002. Te Whanganui-a-Tara Wellington.

Tessa Stubbing I'd heard about the Wellington Libraries zine collection. The website listed the staff email addresses and I just picked one at random, which happened to be Kylie Buck's email address. I sent off my zine and then I emailed Kylie: 'Hey, have you got it?' She said 'Yeah, and as an aside, do you want to be pen pals?', and I was like 'Sweet, yeah, I want a pen pal.' So we became pen pals and then she started organising the first Wellington Zinefest. When I went down for that she invited me to stay with her. In Auckland I had just moved into Cross Street Studios, which was an art space with a gallery and studios. Wellington Zinefest was so cool, and I wanted something like that in Auckland.

I was just freshly into Cross Street Studios, freshly into having this space. If you've got the space you can do whatever you want, right? Cherry Bomb Comics was closing so there was really nowhere else in Auckland for zines. I figured that if someone does it with me it won't be as scary. So Cross Street ended up hosting it, and I organised it with Nick Boyd, who also lived at Cross Street. I was freelancing as a designer so I had time, and then I quit my job, so I had even more time and just did it.

Kylie Buck When Tessa Stubbing came down from Auckland for the second Wellington Zinefest it was the first time she'd ever been on a plane.

Small Print didn't happen again and Tessa said 'I'm gonna do something', and I was like 'Great!' I went up for Tessa's Auckland Zinefest quite a few times. I'd never been like 'Oh, I'm gonna start a revolution, gonna have zinefests all over the country.' When they first started popping up I was like I'm gonna go to all of these, and then I was like 'Nah, I've got a kid now. I can't go to *any* of them!'

The second Wellington Zinefest was a largely positive experience, but I had to pull together a lot of disparate groups and I must admit that sometimes I felt a bit used. Well, not used exactly, but the comics people would say 'Oh, you're putting this thing on? Great. We have demands: we want to be grouped together and we want this and that . . .' They really saw themselves as a group within. I always found that confusing. Some people would say 'Oh, it's too far from the centre of town.' It was on fucking Taranaki Street, one block from Cuba Street, but that was a common complaint.

The anarchists also wanted to sit together, but eventually we decided 'Nah, it's random, you're getting mixed up', because otherwise it meant that there would be three or four stalls together that all looked the same and a lot of the content would be the same. The anarchists also had their own thing going on already. There was the anarchist bookshop — The Freedom Shop. If we'd just had the zine individuals we'd have been shit out of luck. We needed the established comics and anarchist groups to get enough stalls and bring in the people. It was good that they came along and got involved, because at the end of the day the more the better, right?

144. Wellington Zinefest 2008 poster by Bryce Galloway and David Buck. Te Whanganui-a-Tara Wellington.

144

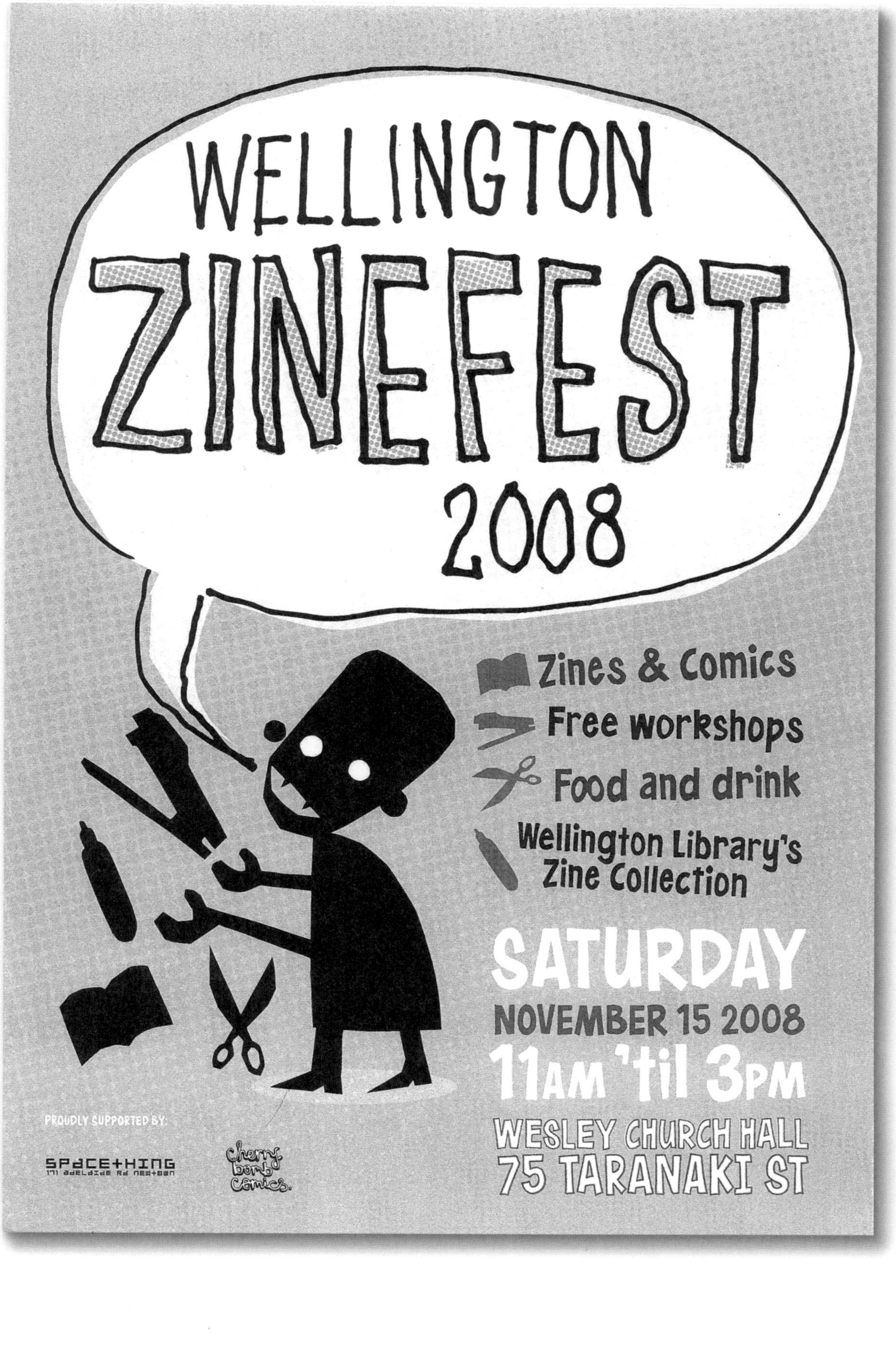
WELLINGTON
ZINEFEST
2008
Zines & Comics
Free workshops
Food and drink
Wellington Library's
Zine Collection
SATURDAY
NOVEMBER 15 2008
11AM 'til 3PM
WESLEY CHURCH HALL
75 TARANAKI ST
PROUDLY SUPPORTED BY:
cherry bomb comics

Tessa Stubbing We just picked a random day in August for that first Auckland Zinefest, but it happened to be the same day as Semi Permanent, which David Carson was giving a talk at. David Carson! The inspiration for my whole aesthetic, right!? I was like 'Do I cancel Zinefest to go and see David Carson — the person who I love — or do I keep doing Zinefest? Keep doing Zinefest.' Didn't go see the David Carson talk. I'm sure I would've been disappointed. Never meet your idols, eh?

Kenneth Merrick I was sort of shocked to see the number of people turning up at Auckland Zinefest. I was a bit overwhelmed. I was just looking around at the number of people making stuff, and the number of people wanting to buy or participate or understand what was going on. That was really interesting.

Kylie Buck I think workshops at zinefest are a great idea, especially if they're around introducing people to making zines, because they're a super lo-fi way of expressing your ideas. It's great to target young people and teenagers because they're the people who are wanting to express themselves and get their ideas out into the world.

Tessa Stubbing Auckland Zinefest started the Best-of-Fest awards tradition to encourage a bit of healthy competition. *Neighbourhood Cats* won that first Best-of-Fest.

I've always wanted to win Best-of-Fest, but I never have. I managed to win Best Art Zine for *HWAH* in 2014. I've still got my certificate somewhere. Nah, actually, I think I threw it out.

Kylie Buck By the time I was done I was like: 'There's no point trying to run workshops. There's no point running talks. Nobody comes.' And then new blood comes in and they go: 'We're running workshops, we're doing talks', and they do it in a different way.

Kerry Ann Lee I was quite happy for my zines to be 'sporadicals', I didn't invent that term, but I've used it quite often. The sporadical — not adhering to quarterly publishing deadlines or monthly deadlines like the magazine industry. Same with the Red Letter distro catalogues, I was like, I just don't want it to be a small business enterprise, fuck that.' It's an occasional distro, and it was — up until the [COVID-19] pandemic. Suddenly it would pop up, on invitation, share a table or do something somewhere.

Pritika Lal I never tabled *This Is Not a Comic* at a zinefest. Instead, we had our own exhibitions in community halls. Maybe we were represented through some distro and community tables, but we never ran our own stall.

145

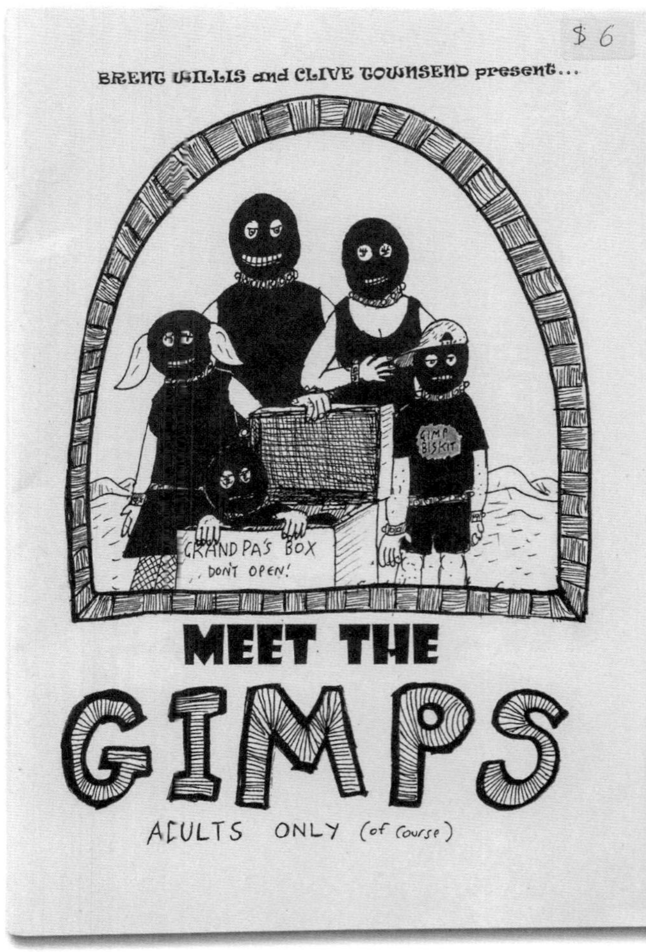

Kylie Buck I never thought about zinefests killing off the distro scene, though [it was] not really [likely] eh, because a lot of distros were real old-school anyway. You send in your paper money and your stamps, and they send your zines. It was before most had a website, and the digital innovation of buying things online. I just thought 'Oh, it's so bloody hard to get anything.' With Zinefest I just thought: 'I want a bunch of zines, and here's a bunch of people I can buy a bunch of zines from.'

Tim Danko I got out of art school, had a studio, was doing paintings, had a few exhibitions, but y'know, thought 'Why am I trying to push stuff through a relatively unreceptive art community? Why don't I just make comics?'

I started making my own comics, did *Dead Xerox Press*, then *Silent Army*, and we started doing events. We comics people were closely affiliated with the stencil-art/street-art scene in Melbourne. We had lots of connections there. Part of the worldwide push for *Silent Army* was coming over to New Zealand for Armageddon. Michael Fikaris and I came over around 2004/2005. It was just a little trial run, taking stuff overseas, not too full-on.

I met Indira Neville and we started a long-distance relationship, then I moved to New Zealand. We lived on Great Barrier Island for five years. I was still making stuff, screen-printing on Great Barrier Island. I still had connections with Melbourne. My comics were published in France through a few different groups, one publisher in particular. So even though I was living on an island I was doing all that.

145. *Meet The Gimps* cover and spread, Brent Willis and Clive Townsend, A4, date unknown. Te Whanganui-a-Tara Wellington.

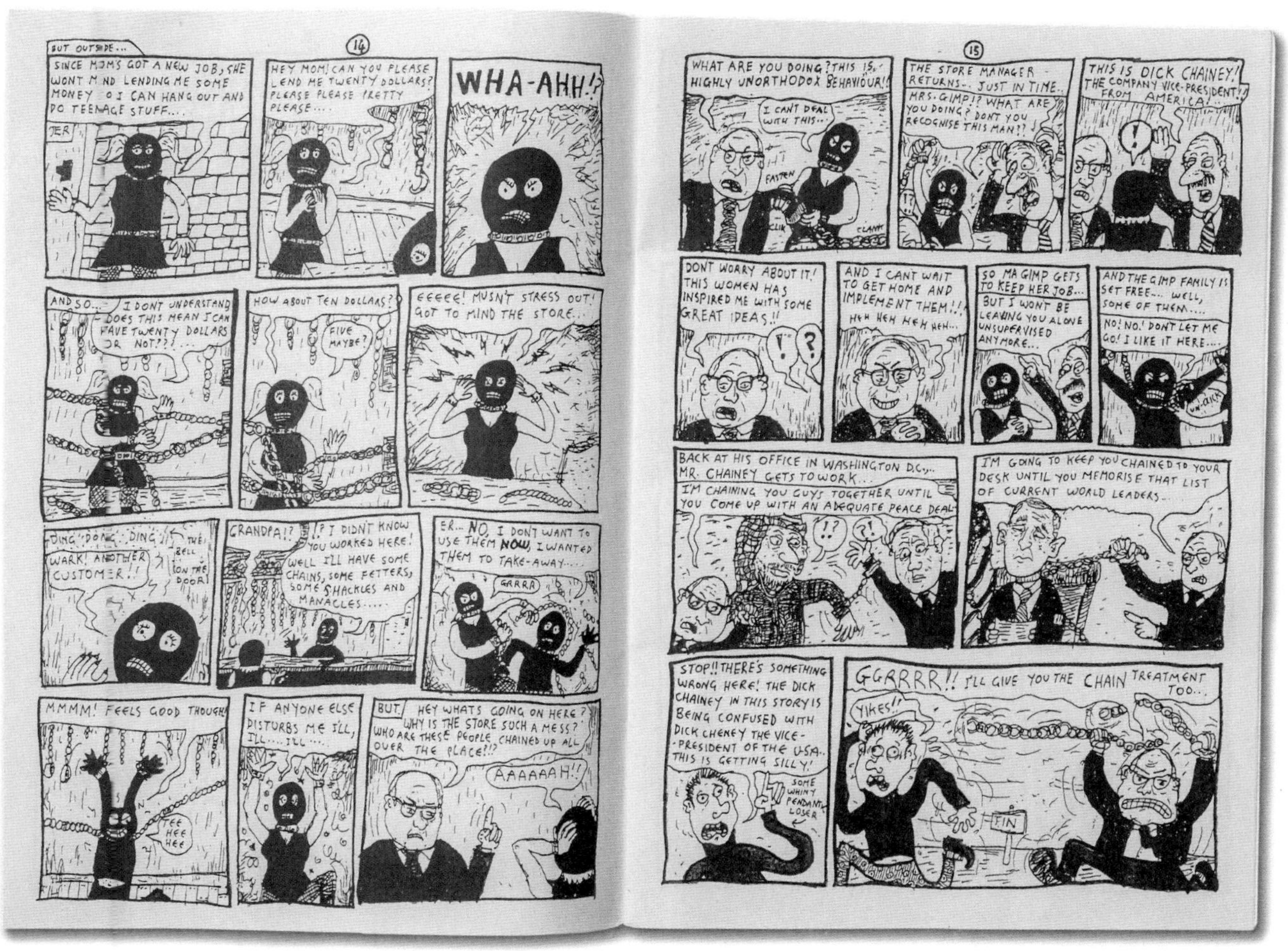

Kylie Buck I worked in the 'fiction' area at Wellington Libraries. They had this amazing staffroom, and they would leave out all these librarian magazines that you could read while you were on your lunch break. One of the magazines covered Salt Lake City Library's massive zine collection. I'm pretty sure it was the first library collecting zines. I remember reading about it and thinking 'This is awesome, man, like, we should do this!' I went round the library just telling everyone about it. A librarian who I didn't know — Stephanie Poulopoulos — overheard me talking about it to someone and said 'Hey, I heard you talking about this zine thing. I'd really like to help you with that.'

She worked in collections, which are the people who buy the books, and so she was perfectly set to do all the things that I couldn't do, like write a business case and all the technical things that you need to do to get a library to agree to something like that. Basically it's because of her that we have the Wellington Libraries zine collection. She did all the necessary writing and the library agreed.

But there was still no budget for the thing, and we were thinking 'How can we get some zines for our collection?' So we got some post-cards made. We put the call out: 'We want some zinesters to design some postcards for free, and you'll get a bunch of postcards in return.' We left the postcards in cafés. On the back of the cards it said, 'Donate a zine', and through that we just started receiving donations.

At first the Wellington Libraries zine collection was reference-only. [That is, you could only read them on-site, not borrow them.] It was easy enough to get the zines rolling in, but to catalogue all of them takes a long time and we just couldn't convince the cataloguers to do it. So, initially, individual zine titles weren't searchable through the library [cataloguing system] and you couldn't loan them out. But those things changed once it proved popular enough — a bit of pushing the boat out, I guess.

Moira Clunie I'm sure snobby attitudes around zines existed, but Moon Rocket and Small Print tended to use the language that people used about their *own* publications. I wouldn't want to assign somebody the label of 'zinester' or call something a 'zine' if it wasn't what they were calling it themselves, and my interest was not just zines, it was across self-publishing. Trying to find inclusive language about that was always a bit of a puzzle. We called Small Print in Auckland a 'zines, comix, small press, and self-publishing event', so that's an attempt to be inclusive.

Tui Gordon We probably alienated some people by being too strident, but then again, after Misfit Theatre, which was way more punk than Cherry Bomb, to some people we might've seemed a bit too nice.

Indira Neville Comics is cut-throat, y'know? None of this faffy zine community . . . I was one of the few Oats people — apart from Stefan — who would participate in anything outside of the Oats universe. I was forever getting kicked off the Black River Digital comics platform, but if you're a woman you have to be a pain in the ass. Even now, except I'm bored and tired of it.

Pritika Lal I feel like there were haters along the way, but I don't know if I remember anyone specifically. There were questions around what is or isn't a comic, or can you or can't you do this stuff? I certainly haven't held onto it. I vaguely remember having some annoying conversations with comics nerds who were super particular about 'This is the episode where this happened, and this is that exact moment that's pictured in this comic, and this is the name of this artist, and this is the name of this comic' — this fact-remembering nerdery — but I don't recall anything in particular. It's all rolled in together with the other artistic tensions in the same period. For example, there was a big thing between Elam artists and graffiti artists during this mural event I was involved in. Or with making music: 'Are you a conceptual band? Because now you're really playing instruments and warming up for the headline acts, but is your band even *real*?'

In those early days there would have been lots of people who had tensions with each other, but invariably, years later, you work on something together and discover that maybe that person wasn't as much of a jerk-off as you thought, or maybe they did say something about you but now they know you better. A lot of it was just fronting or something like that. Maybe there was tension in those creative circles and I just moved towards people who I could work with.

Indira Neville I'm a shit-stirrer, y'know? Back, back, back in the day was Black River Digital. Before social media you had a list server or a chat room or something, and that was for New Zealand comics. I was forever getting kicked off for hassling Karl Wills and starting a flame war with Andy Conlan or whatever. I think, again, I was just a bit of a ratbag, and a woman who was in this space, a feminist. It wasn't just me taking a position: I just didn't like them, didn't like their comics. It was fucking brutal, that arena. Young comic-makers today have no idea. You ask anyone from back in the day and they'll go 'Woah, Black River Digital!?' It was weird because we were all sort of a community, but we all hated each other. I don't know why, that's just what it was like.

Tui Gordon Cherry Bomb did get some funny feedback, but we never actually got really hassled. We refused to stock certain titles if there was some content we found a bit iffy. Looking at it now, I would have quite a different sense of what was okay, but in my early twenties things were still quite black-and-white for me: what was cool and what was racist or sexist or fucked-up.

I do remember being called 'feminazis' once. The artist in question had done a show at a strip club and Melissa had taken exception to it. We got told we were feminazis for that. I doubt we'd take such exception to a strip-club thing now.

Moira Clunie Moon Rocket was curated. People would send me their zines and I'd choose which ones to showcase and which ones not to. It felt fair enough, because quite a bit of work went into scanning each cover and writing a profile, figuring it all out and interacting with the zine-maker. I only wanted to represent things I could stand behind. There was a bit of push-back around that sometimes.

Tim Danko I understand that people have no frame of reference. At the start of my master's people came up to me after a crit session talking about comics as journalism and Joe Sacco and all this other stuff, and I'm like 'Man, that is not what I'm doing at all.' [Laughs.] I showed in 2000 at West Space, which is a high-end artist-run space in Melbourne. This was a big group anthology project, and the director of West Space was like 'Oh, can you get Art Spiegelman? We would like you to do the comic stuff, but none of that juvenile stuff, eh?' Unfortunately, that attitude is no surprise, but it's still disappointing.

Tui Gordon There was an anarchist distro for zines and self-published books in Canada called Kersplebedeb. We used to send them stuff, and I sent them a copy of my *Revolutionary Women Stencil-Book*. They were so happy with it that they sent it on to friends who'd started a publishing company: PM Press, an offshoot of AK Press. They wanted to make it into a book, so I got a bunch of friends together and we made it into a book, which took heaps of time and energy. I tried to do a second edition and it just sort of failed. I haven't really felt the urge since.

There was this lovely book about making zines that had something about surrendering to that incredibly strange urge to make a zine. It is quite a weird urge in a way. Why do we want to make these little books?

Moira Clunie It's tricky. This work is often just voluntary: if you're not happy with the platforms that exist then you do the work yourself, but sometimes the people who are complaining aren't prepared to do that.

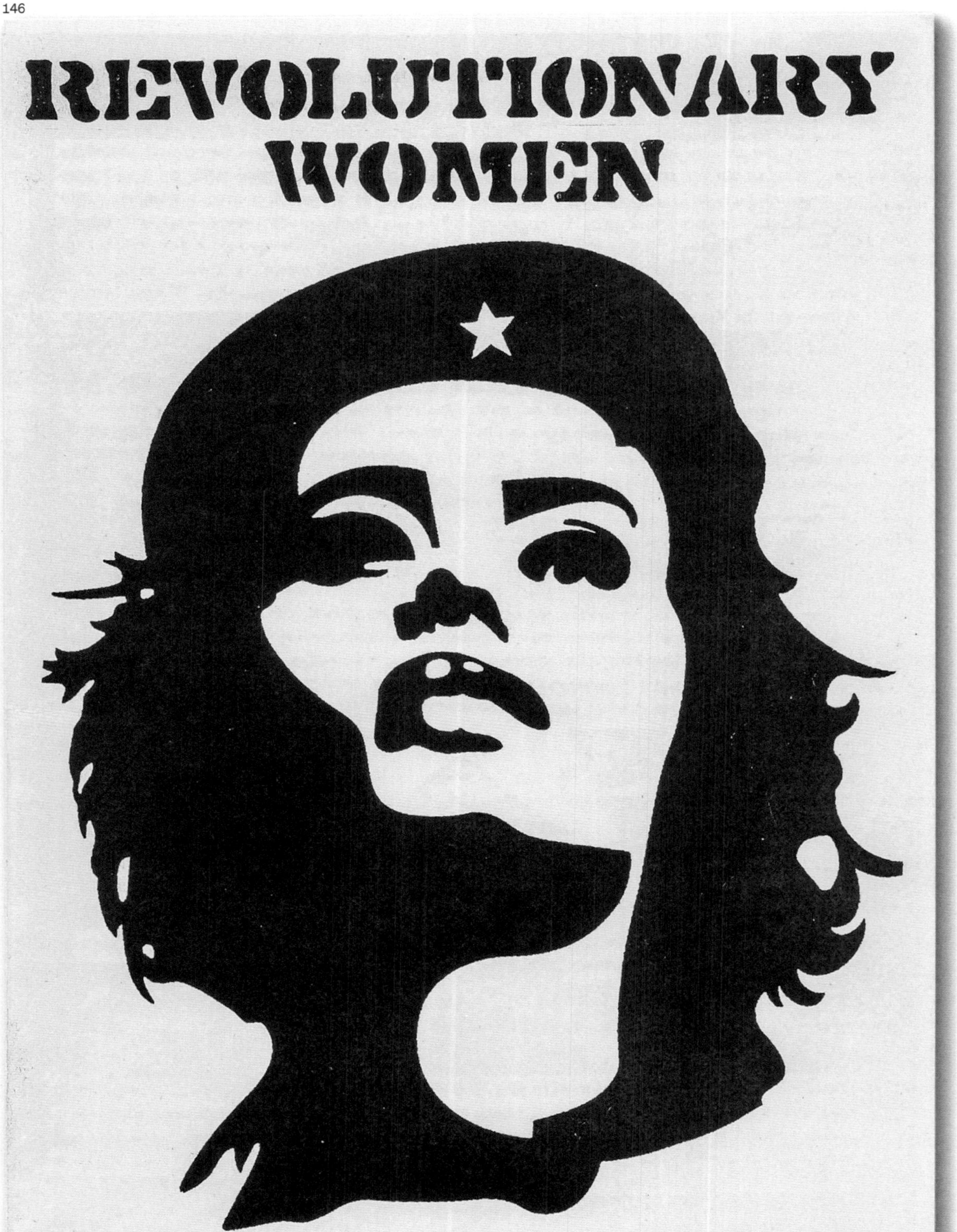
REVOLUTIONARY
WOMEN
STENCIL-BOOK

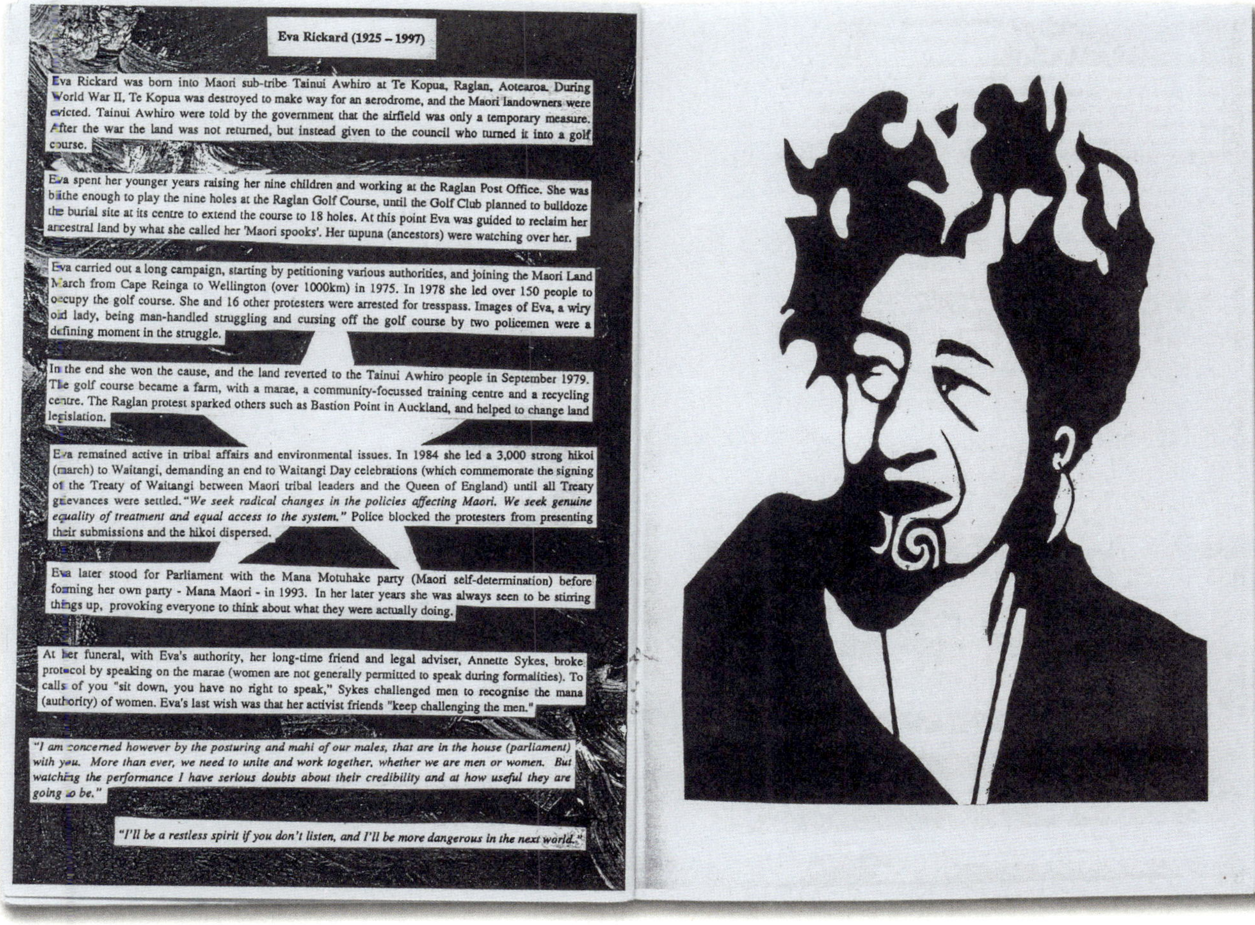

Eva Rickard (1925 – 1997)

Eva Rickard was born into Maori sub-tribe Tainui Awhiro at Te Kopua, Raglan, Aotearoa. During World War II, Te Kopua was destroyed to make way for an aerodrome, and the Maori landowners were evicted. Tainui Awhiro were told by the government that the airfield was only a temporary measure. After the war the land was not returned, but instead given to the council who turned it into a golf course.

Eva spent her younger years raising her nine children and working at the Raglan Post Office. She was blithe enough to play the nine holes at the Raglan Golf Course, until the Golf Club planned to bulldoze the burial site at its centre to extend the course to 18 holes. At this point Eva was guided to reclaim her ancestral land by what she called her 'Maori spooks'. Her tupuna (ancestors) were watching over her.

Eva carried out a long campaign, starting by petitioning various authorities, and joining the Maori Land March from Cape Reinga to Wellington (over 1000km) in 1975. In 1978 she led over 150 people to occupy the golf course. She and 16 other protesters were arrested for tresspass. Images of Eva, a wiry old lady, being man-handled struggling and cursing off the golf course by two policemen were a defining moment in the struggle.

In the end she won the cause, and the land reverted to the Tainui Awhiro people in September 1979. The golf course became a farm, with a marae, a community-focussed training centre and a recycling centre. The Raglan protest sparked others such as Bastion Point in Auckland, and helped to change land legislation.

Eva remained active in tribal affairs and environmental issues. In 1984 she led a 3,000 strong hikoi (march) to Waitangi, demanding an end to Waitangi Day celebrations (which commemorate the signing of the Treaty of Waitangi between Maori tribal leaders and the Queen of England) until all Treaty grievances were settled. *"We seek radical changes in the policies affecting Maori. We seek genuine equality of treatment and equal access to the system."* Police blocked the protesters from presenting their submissions and the hikoi dispersed.

Eva later stood for Parliament with the Mana Motuhake party (Maori self-determination) before forming her own party - Mana Maori - in 1993. In her later years she was always seen to be stirring things up, provoking everyone to think about what they were actually doing.

At her funeral, with Eva's authority, her long-time friend and legal adviser, Annette Sykes, broke protocol by speaking on the marae (women are not generally permitted to speak during formalities). To calls of you "sit down, you have no right to speak," Sykes challenged men to recognise the mana (authority) of women. Eva's last wish was that her activist friends "keep challenging the men."

"I am concerned however by the posturing and mahi of our males, that are in the house (parliament) with you. More than ever, we need to unite and work together, whether we are men or women. But watching the performance I have serious doubts about their credibility and at how useful they are going to be."

"I'll be a restless spirit if you don't listen, and I'll be more dangerous in the next world."

147

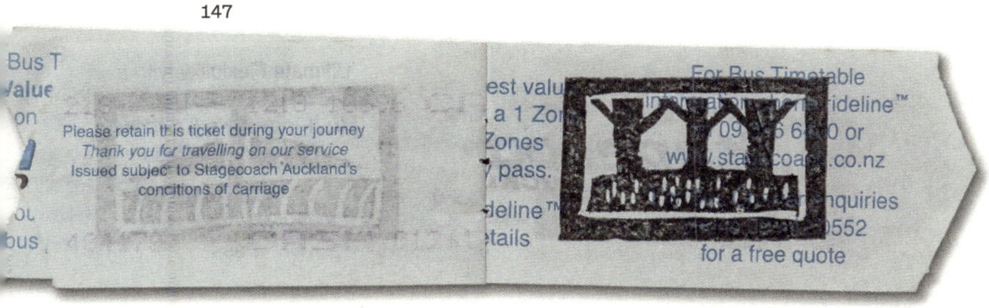

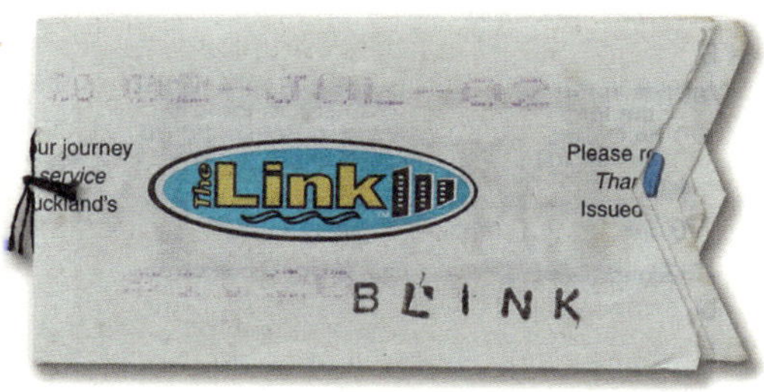

148

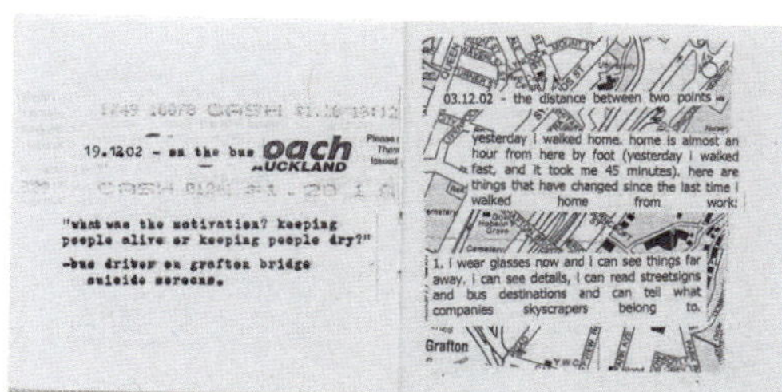

146. *Revolutionary Women Stencil-Book* cover and spread, Tui Gordon, A5, 2005. Tāmaki Makaurau Auckland.

147. *Blink* spread and cover, Moira Clunie, 75 × 37mm, 2004. *Tāmaki Makaurau Auckland.*

148. *Child That Mind* #3 cover and spread, Moira Clunie, 105 × 100mm, 2004. Tāmaki Makaurau Auckland.

Tui Gordon We had volunteers, but it was mostly just me and Melissa Steiner. We opened the shop four days a week. Mad Merryn [Mcaulay] worked on Tuesdays. She was really diligent. We all had other part-time jobs as well. That was part of the ethos with the shop — less about working for the man and more about doing something that you actually wanted to do, because it was never a shop for making profit. I don't think we could've made a profit even if we'd tried. Anyway, it doubled as a place to live. We lived above the shop, and out back, and the shop was basically our living room. We had curtains we could hang up there in the evenings.

Pritika Lal It felt like quite a crossover to start having ads, but then we *drew* all our own ads, and we just did the same thing that we did with the Tiger Clock raffle. We went around everybody we knew who had a business or a shop — a lot of it on K Road — and just peddled: 'Hey, you want to put an ad in this? It's like really cool, y'know. We can draw it for you.' I think people were just like 'Here's a charity ad'; well, not charity, but they wanted to support what we were doing. Bunny Boutique put an ad in, Illicit put an ad in, and maybe we ran an ad for the printing guy. But yeah, we had to pay for the printing and also the postage.

We wanted *This Is Not a Comic* to be free. We got so much out of the freeness of them. We wanted to put them in a lot of different places. I remember posting heaps of them away, putting them in envelopes to Real Groovy in Wellington so they could leave them in the doorway with all the flyers.

Sam Orchard Price point's an interesting one. There's differing levels of access. When I was a student I could only print off a few, and I needed to make my money back in order to eat. The student allowance certainly wouldn't cover photocopying comics. Other times in my life I've made comics that I can afford to just give away. I don't care about the money, I just want them out in the world. So the charging thing can be about privilege. I'm privileged enough to be able to print my comics beautifully. Or they're printed beautifully and I really need that money back. When you're living in poverty, sneak into Rainbow YOUTH [LGBTQI+ support services charity] and use their stuff.

Y'know, sometimes it relies on the DIY of sneaking into your dad's work and using the photocopy machine. I guess that's harder to do now, because all of those office copy machines have swipe-card access and your printing gets monitored. Back in the early 2000s and pre-that, there'd just be a photocopier in the corner of the office and endless paper.

I remember doing some tutoring at Vic [Victoria University of Wellington] and people would be drawing their comics for assessment, and when they had to print them out they'd say 'That's *how* much per page?! No one has the money for that!' It's a tricky thing.

Spencer Hall Like those other things that we talked about — community radio, people busking on the street, but also other things like graffiti, say — I like the accessibility of zines. Generally, they're so cheap; you can just get one for $2 or trade. It's accessible on the other side of the equation, too. You don't have to have too many resources to make the thing. That's what I like the most. If you want to make a movie you have to have equipment and probably a budget and people who are willing to give you their time, but what's the cost of a pen and a piece of paper and some staples and a friend's photocopier?

Sam Orchard One of the hard things about the New Zealand comics community is that most people are just making stuff because they have something inside of them that needs to get out and comics is their way of doing that, but if you want to also use that to make money, it's got to go international. Lots of New Zealanders have managed to do that, eke out a career.

Moira Clunie When I stopped Moon Rocket I was worn out. Life got in the way. There was also an aspect of feeling like things were shifting in terms of online shopping and online commerce. It *had* felt like more of an exchange: people were writing to you and writing down all the zines that they wanted, there was often a bit more interaction. The more things shifted online, the more people were paying through PayPal with their credit cards with the expectation that you were just a shop that would respond to things immediately and post things out straight away. It felt a bit more like a capitalist model of exchange than I was going for. It was not giving as much back in terms of connection and positive feelings, and I was tired.

Tui Gordon I quit on zines partly because I got sick of doing stalls. It's really exhausting. Some people can get quite energised by it, talking to people all day, but I just remember finding it pretty exhausting. I'm definitely not an extrovert, but then I don't know many zine-makers who *would* be considered extroverts.

Tony Renouf I made my last physical comic in 1998. It would have been 8 to 10 years before I got back to drawing again. I bought a scanner and said to somebody 'How does blogging work?' And they said, 'Check out WordPress'. So I started putting stuff up on WordPress. Also, I'd given up smoking cigarettes and figured I'd better do something with my hands. Y'know, it just made me fucking manic, insane, manic . . . with large nicotine patches on my arms.

Tui Gordon I still like a zine as an object, but I look back to what we were doing with them before, in the early-2000s. When I made *Revolutionary Women Stencil-Book* there was really very little information around, but now if you look up any of these women everything you need to know is on the internet. You just don't need this kind of zine anymore. I spent a long time working on a second edition, with new art. I did better research, but it all got very hard. I got stuck; I couldn't finish it. It also stopped being relevant in quite the same way because of the way the dissemination of information had changed. Zines were a way of sharing stories, but now, because people just share stuff on the internet, it feels like it's more about the handmade object.

David Tulloch The other thing that was useful with the web comic site DrunkDuck that I went to was that they had started a little anthology comic, and they were looking for scripts for other people to draw. That was something I could do, so I started writing a whole bunch of short stories for other people to draw. That went really well. I've met some great people online.

Moira Clunie Zines aren't the most effective medium for the more immediate or time-sensitive calls to action. Zines can provide a space to kind of dig into and learn about a topic in more detail, learn about the issue. I was just thinking back to a compilation zine my sister put together about genetic modification/genetic engineering — *(Com) modified: Genetic engineering & New Zealand*. That's a longer zine with essays by various contributors. It wasn't designed for immediately organising around the issue, but more the raising of the topic and sharing some thoughts about it. That's definitely a thing that zines can be great for, particularly . . . producing whatever you want to produce and not having an editor or anybody deciding to modify your words or toning them down.

149

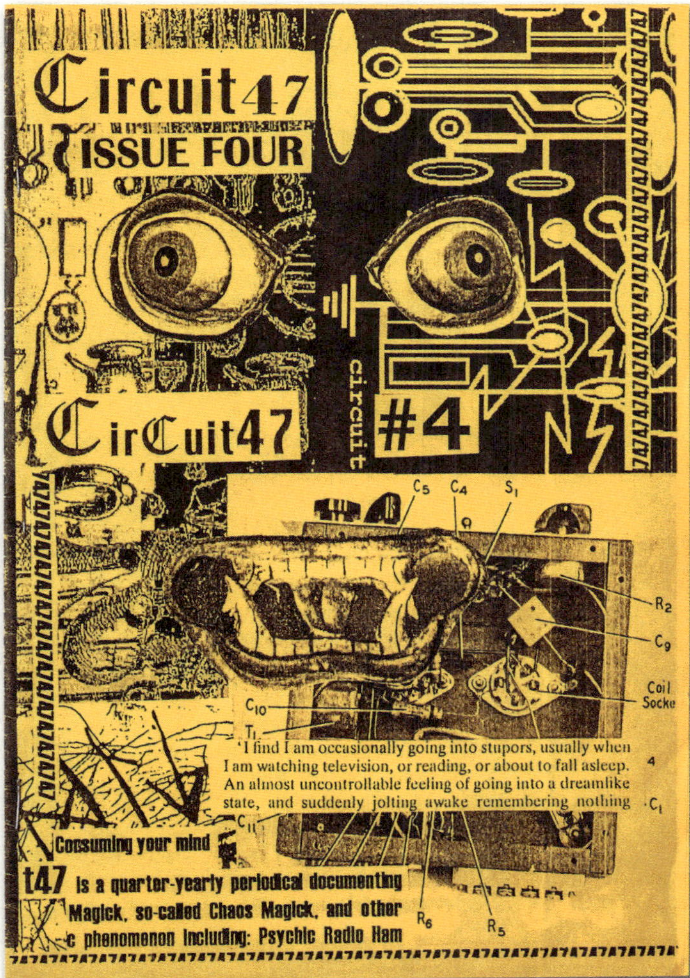

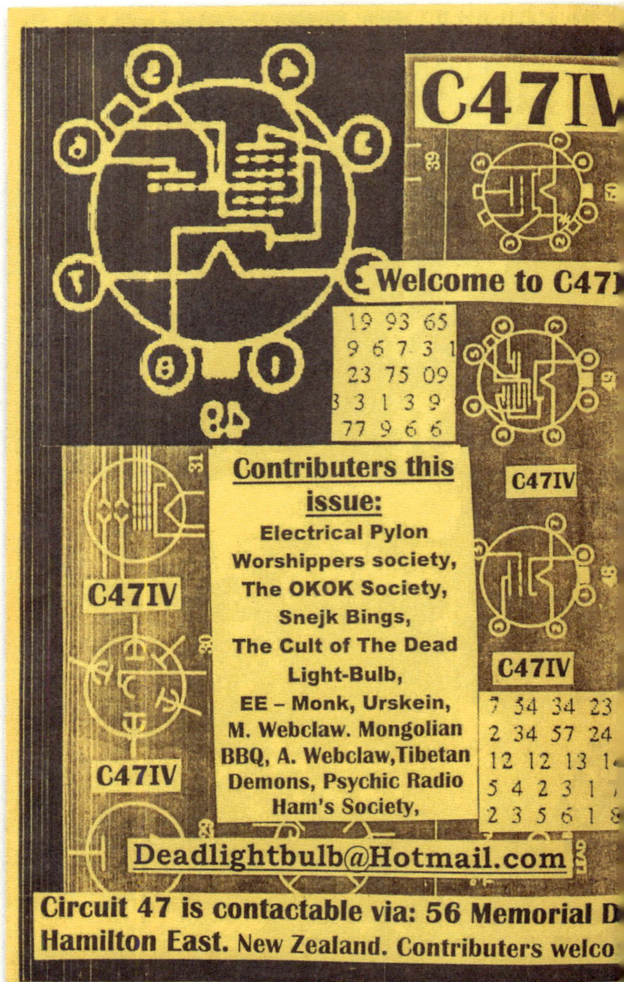

Pritika Lal I had an awesome zine collection that I loved so hard. I had heaps of *Strumming Teeth*, I had quite a lot of Stefan Neville's work, I obviously had all of our *This Is Not a Comic* issues and the *Foxy Moron* issues that Melanie Baldwin worked on with Georgie Hill. I gave them all to a zine library, which I kind of regret. I had a lot of beautiful things from that time which I no longer have; it was just too hard to carry stuff around. I only have things that I need right now. It gets so expensive here in Auckland, and having the space to put things is actually pretty difficult, I've found. I move often, and things just have to go.

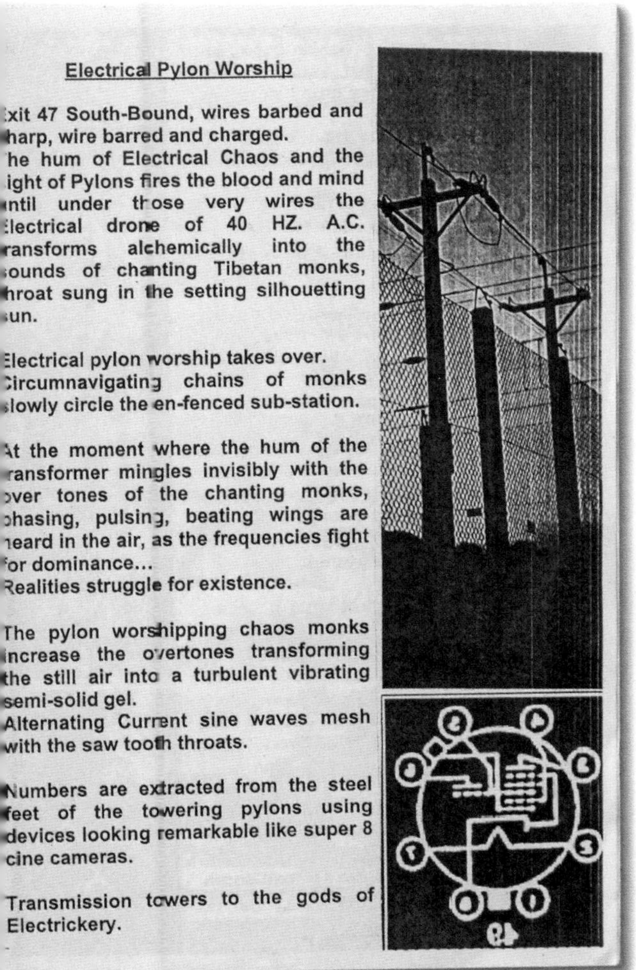

149. *Circuit 47* #4 cover and spread, edited by Emit Snake-Beings, A5, 2000. Kirikiriroa Hamilton.

David Merritt I had no cynicism about the internet to start with. The cynicism came later, when I started to see that my Google search results were dominated by conventional media sources. CNN, ABC, stuff like that would be prioritised. It's like 'Hang on, you've got no more standing than this xyz anonymous blogger in Pakistan: why are you up here and an anonymous blogger is now buried way down there?'

Dave White I guess I've always just grabbed whatever tool's available, whether it's a bit of paper and some glue or some way of communicating on the internet. I mean, our tours of America would've been so much easier with the internet.

But you see bands that buy followers. I got offered a thing a few weeks ago: for $3, we can sell you 1000 followers. You see bands and on their Facebook page they've got 2 million followers, and people use that as a clue to whether they're gonna book them for their festival. When I got Lung going again, I applied to play a couple of festivals and all the information they wanted I didn't have. How many Facebook followers have you got? Oh, three. How many likes have you got on your band page? Ah, seven. And they were only interested in the millions, which is why people spend the money and buy followers, but it's just bullshit. It's not even real.

Andrew Schmidt It's about the object as well. You have a tactile object that you can hold, and you can put in a bookshelf, and you can pull out, you can look at, you can flick the pages. It's a really physical experience. It's a whole pile of things that the internet doesn't have.

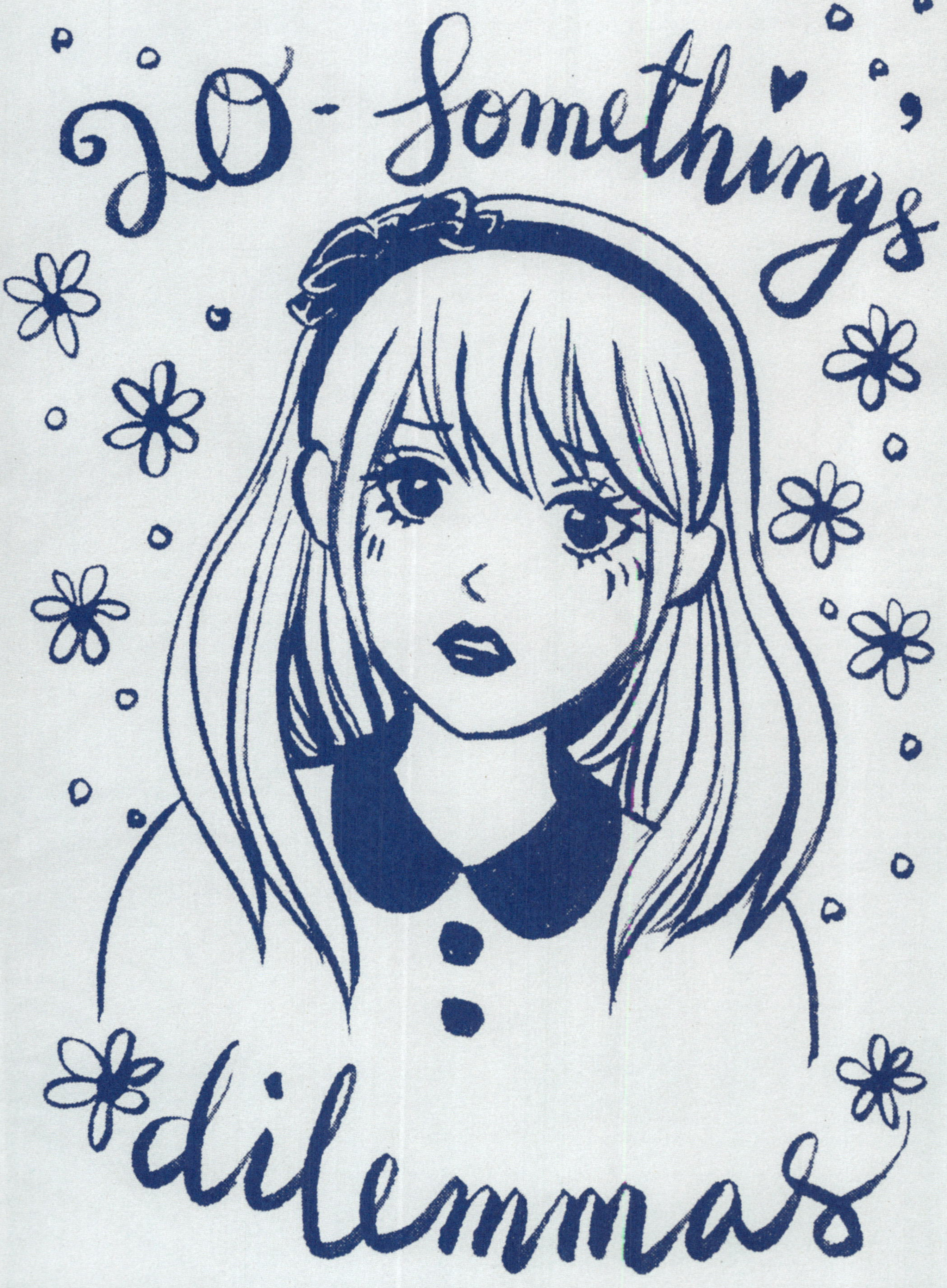
20-Somethings'
dilemmas

Twenty-tens to -twenties Aotearoa

The zinefest model exploded through the 2010s and 2020s. By 2010, there were two annual zinefests: one in Tāmaki Makaurau Auckland and one in Te Whanganui-a-Tara Wellington. Over the next 15 years they were joined by the annual or sporadic Ōtepoti Zinefest (from 2011), Ōtautahi Zinefest (2011), Kirikiriroa Hamilton Zinefest (2014), Tauranga Zinefest (2016), Palmy Zine Fest (2020), Whanganui Zinefest (2020), Kāpiti Zinefest (2022), Whau Zine Fest (2023), Taranaki Zinefest (2023) and Zine Fest Nelson (2024).

150. *20-Something's Dilemmas*, Chloe Or, A7, 2017. Tāmaki Makaurau Auckland.

One zinefest informed the next, establishing a model. A zine market is always at the heart of any zinefest, with many zinesters wearing 'open to swaps' stickers. Relevant talks and workshops are likely, as are 'best-of-fest' awards and merch featuring the year's artist-branding. Some mount after-parties where local bands and DJs entertain; others include craft zones that are overrun by the children of adult visitors; or are preceded by a series of workshops or a 24-hour zine-making challenge.

The roughly 20 stalls at the first Auckland and Wellington zinefests became 40 stalls, then 60, encouraging both zinefests to find bigger and bigger venues, and then to run two-day markets with different stallholders on each day. The Auckland and Wellington zinefests each currently present at least 120 stallholders over two days, with more zinesters dropping off one or two titles for sale from the fest's community table. Rather than the simple ambition to get bigger, the move to larger venues and two-day events has been driven by the politics of zines as an all-comers medium that eschews exclusivity. Despite trying to accommodate the inclusive politics of zines, both the Auckland and Wellington zinefests have to turn stallholders away, such is the demand.

This growth in popularity is also partly responsible for zinefests being invited into institutional settings, moving from community halls, pubs and cafés into Te Herenga Waka Victoria University, Auckland Art Gallery Toi o Tāmaki, Christchurch Art Gallery Te Puna o Waiwhetū, Hamilton Central Library, Tauranga Art Gallery, Te Manawa Museum and the Govett-Brewster Art Gallery, places that would have once asked security to monitor any punk zinesters who dared sully their hallowed halls. If some interviewees consider these institutional environs as evidence that zines have lost their countercultural edge, more celebrate the shift as the legitimisation of a once-marginalised media. Meanwhile, Ōtepoti Zinefest is run out of the 'post-capitalist' café Yours, which charges customers whatever they want to pay for food and coffee.

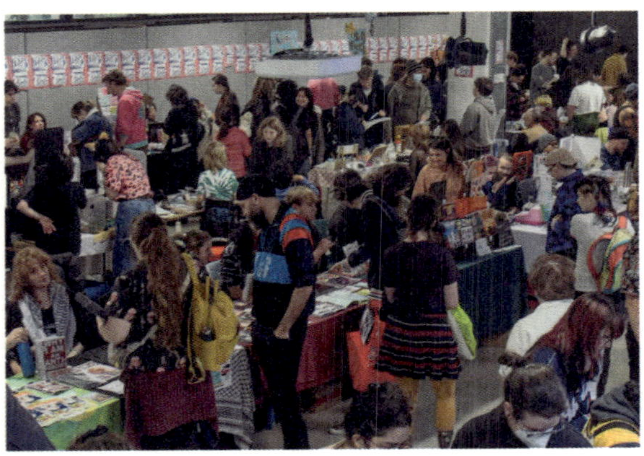

Wellington Zinefest mid-winter Trade Wars market, where the public were encouraged to trade items other than money for zines, 2025. *Charlotte Page*

The kaupapa of accessibility sees zinefests charging between just $5 and $10 for a stall. This, alongside swelling audience numbers and an increase in artisanal zines, has proven to be a magnet for artisans of a different kind: those who make single-page art prints, or jewellery, patches or soft toys. Zinefest organisers have found themselves in the difficult position of having to police who's applying to table. Some awkward conversations have been had, and there's a little resentment on both sides of the conversation.

There's less anarchist politics (except for Sam Buchanan and the ever-touring Freedom Shop) and almost no punk-rock journalism, but personal politics has continued to flourish. The personal-political narratives that existed in the 2000s in the wake of Riot Grrrl laid the groundwork for queer and trans narratives in more recent years. Many zinefests publicise a code of conduct, insisting that stall-holders and their zines are free from discrimination, and this has also built a zinefest culture that is now visibly queer, and perhaps even the safest celebratory queer space open to the general public.

There has also been an increase in the number of neurodiverse and autism-spectrum zinesters. At a glance, this might seem surprising, as zinefest markets are usually a veritable mosh pit of activity that could be described as overstimulating. An 'accessibility hour' at the start of Auckland and Wellington zinefests goes some way to bridging this divide as far as visitors are concerned. In that hour there are fewer visitors, and stallholders know to soft-sell rather than act like hawkers and barrow boys. Still, this doesn't explain the growth in stallholders who would rather draw obsessively than chat with customers.

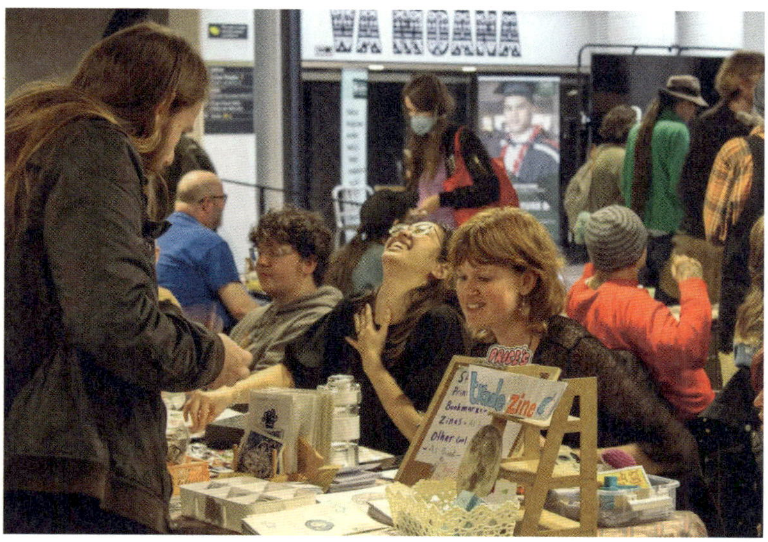

Zine-makers at Wellington Zinefest Trade Wars market, 2025. *Charlotte Page*

The 2010s became the decade of smartphone adoption. No longer are phones just for calling or texting, they're also for gaming, music, news, movies and social media. Nevertheless, smartphone adoption has not dented the interest in the papery world of zines; in fact, zines seem to exist as an extolled alternative to screen time, fostering embodied, localised audiences as opposed to a faceless, global one, and promising sensorial materiality and tactility not limited to the ocular (and tapping thumbs).

What pop-culture icons or pop-cultural shifts will help us understand the recent 2010s and 2020s? The boy bands and girl bands of the 2000s all but disappeared from the upper reaches of the charts; in fact, bands of any description were few and far between as solo artists continued to take over: Katy Perry, Rihanna, Ed Sheeran, Bruno Mars, Justin Bieber and, of course, Taylor Swift with her army of obsessed Swifties. And from these shores, Tāmaki Makaurau's Lorde (aka Ella Yelich-O'Connor). Te Whanganui-a-Tara's Flight of the Conchords moved from performances at the 85-seat Bats Theatre on Kent Terrace to securing two seasons of their own HBO television series. Their mate Taika Waititi continued to command bigger and bigger budgets, until he was in Hollywood directing *Thor: Love and Thunder*. We got to giggle at the humble Kiwi cadence ushering from Korg the towering Stone Man when Waititi decided to not only direct, but also take on that role.

Hamilton Zinefest, 2015.
Kirikiriroa Hamilton Zinefest

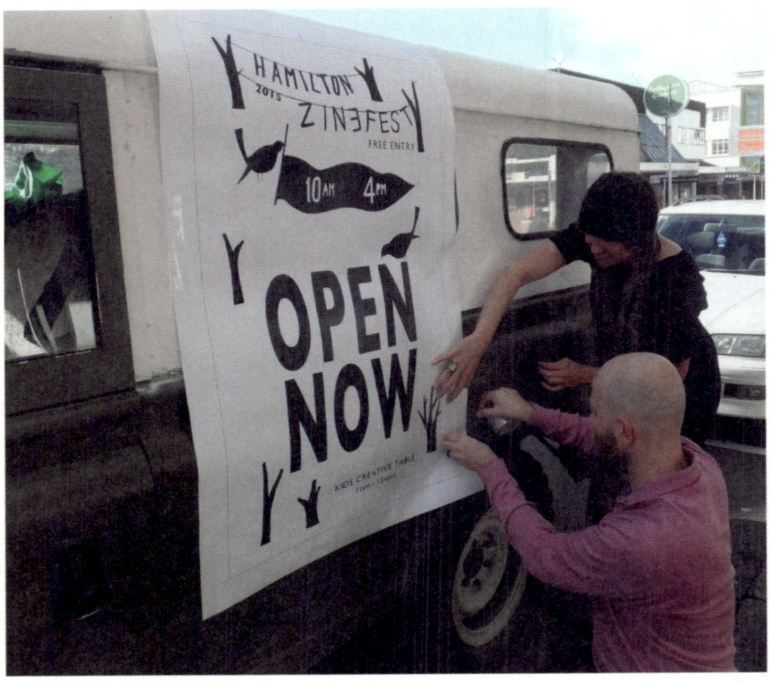

Hamilton Zinefest Committee, 2017.
Bryce Galloway

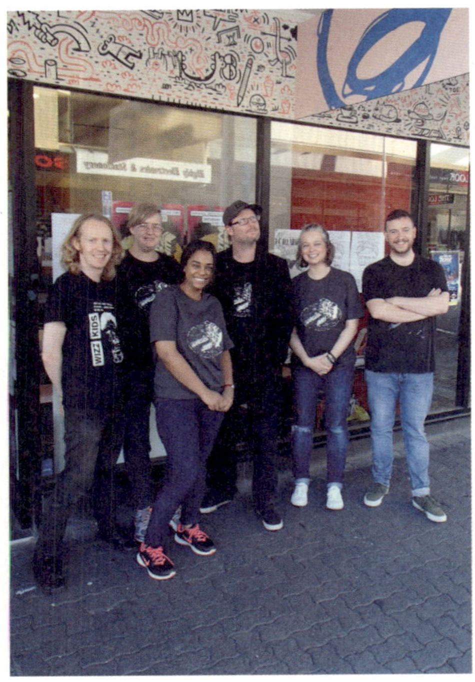

* * *

Eleanor Catton's *The Luminaries*, a novel set in the Hokitika goldfields of 1866, took out the 2013 Booker Prize. Renowned writers such as Sarah Laing, Dylan Horrocks, Rose Lu, David Merritt, essa may ranapiri, Always Becominging, Nadine Anne Hura and Cassandra Barnett could also be found tabling at zinefests. Some started out at zinefests and then found mainstream publishing deals. Others started in mainstream publishing but recognised in zinefests what writer Pip Adam would call 'community outside the capitalist, colonial project'[1], evidence that zines and zinefests continue to mount a political challenge to more conventional publishing. Visual artists Kerry Ann Lee and Andrew McLeod also grew out of or into the zine scene.

These luminaries (pun intended) are mentioned only to illustrate the growth in zines as a considered alternative to mainstream publishing, rather than to diminish the value or the experience of the zinester who makes 20 copies of a single title and drops them off at the community table. That remains a meaningful exchange that's pertinent to the politics of zines.

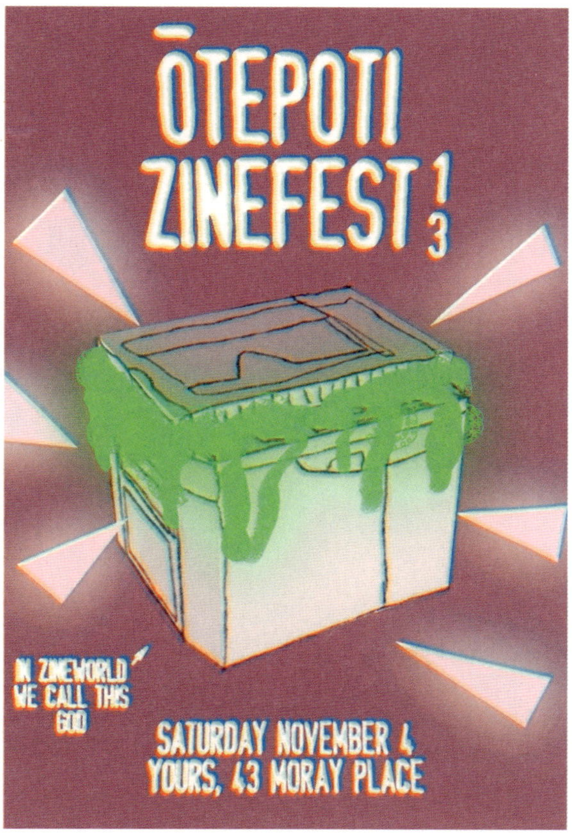

Poster for the 2023 Ōtepoti Zinefest, by Spencer Hall.

What defined the 2010s and 2020s beyond the cultural exchange? A series of anti-government protests and rebellions rocked the Arab world. The so-named Arab Spring began in early 2010, and by the close of 2012 had toppled leaders in Tunisia, Libya, Egypt and Yemen. The Western commentators who coined the expression 'Arab Spring' could not have anticipated the Syrian civil war or the rise of ISIS (also known as Islamic State, a transnational jihadist group designated as terrorists by the United Nations and many countries) that also followed.

The Christchurch earthquake of 22 February 2011 killed 185 people and collapsed buildings leaving a hollowed-out CBD. A staggering 21,000 people left Christchurch over the course of the following year.[2]

Earthquake damage on Hanafins corner, Colombo Street, Christchurch, 22 February 2011. *The Press*

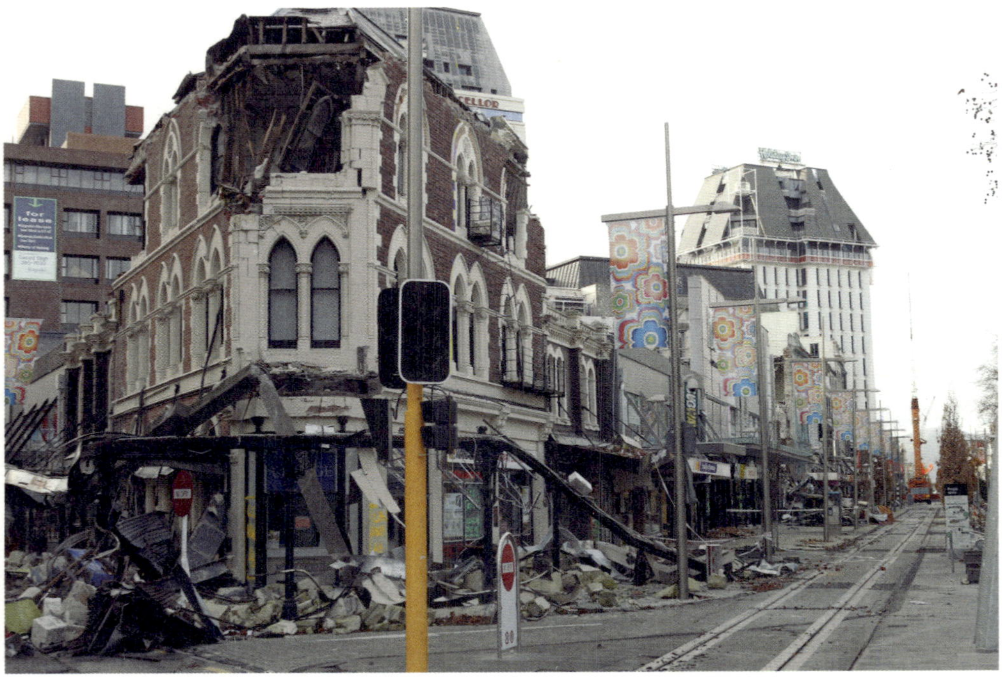

Occupy Wall Street kicked off in October 2011 when protestors occupied Zuccotti Park, two blocks from the New York Stock Exchange. The event spawned an international movement as groups occupied other sites around the world (there were seven in Aotearoa), protesting corporatisation, inequality and a lack of real grassroots democracy. 'We are the 99 per cent' was the rallying cry, which advocated people power rather than the economic influence of a tiny elite. As the divide between the influential super-rich like Elon Musk, Jeff Bezos and Mark Zuckerberg and the rest of us has grown ever-wider, the 0.1 per cent has started to seem more apt.

As the number of refugees displaced by war, persecution and climate change has increased, so have the number of populist right-wing governments promising to close the borders. Donald Trump was voted in as the forty-fifth president of the United States in part because of promises to deport refugees and build a wall between the United States and Mexico. Another catchphrase of Trump's first term as president was 'fake news', returned from the podium whenever Trump's agenda was not served by the facts being presented. Trump's war against the mainstream media (MSM) bolstered conspiracist claims against all manner of received knowledge, and when the world faced a global COVID pandemic and pushed for the rapid development of vaccines, their rollout was marked by claims that we were shooting up nanobots in an elaborate control experiment masterminded by Bill Gates.

Donald Trump supporters storm the Capitol building in Washington DC, 6 January 2021, to protest the US election results. *Wikipedia*

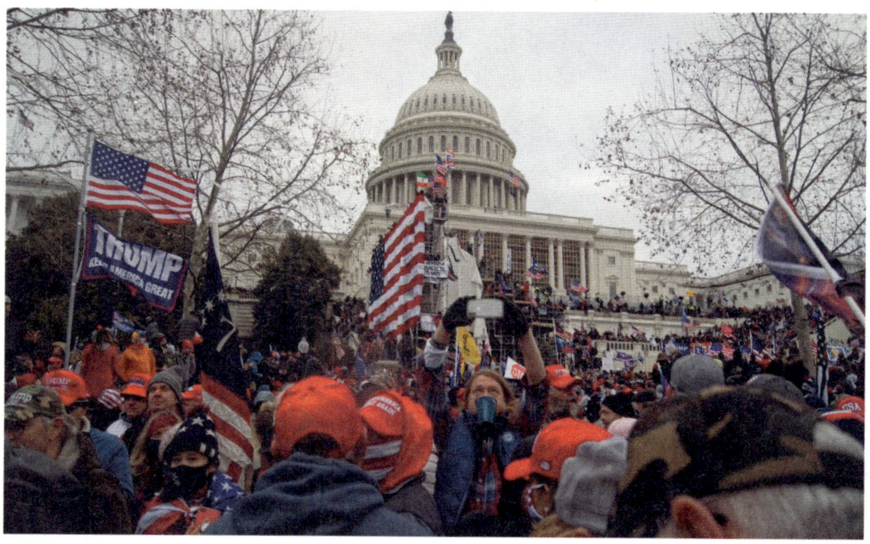

In 2020, the Labour Party became the first political party in the era of MMP (mixed member proportional; a proportional voting system) able to govern alone. The popularity of its leader, Jacinda Ardern, skyrocketed when, during her government's first term in office, tough COVID restrictions minimised related deaths in Aotearoa. Just 16 months later, anti-mandate protestors had built a tent city across Parliament's lawns. Some were nanobot crazies, while others had more grounded concerns. Ardern received a tsunami of hate mail and death threats from anti-mandate protestors and conspiracy theorists, but has never confirmed whether this had any bearing on her standing down as prime minister at the start of 2023.

Closer to the zine scene, titles were more likely to represent the immuno-compromised than the conspiratorial margins. The disability community zine *Anti-vaxxers want me to stay home* comes to mind. The vast majority of zines are less overt, considering the politics of process, aesthetics and context with a sense of whimsy rather than making such bold proclamations. But either way, zines are now wide open for whatever aesthetics and non-discriminatory content (well, punching up's OK) the maker wants to explore. If it's short-run and self-published, it's a zine. Where to from here?

Protestors on the lawn in front of Parliament, Wellington, January 2022. The occupation lasted just over three weeks and ended with violent clashes with the police after they attempted to move the protestors on. *The Post*

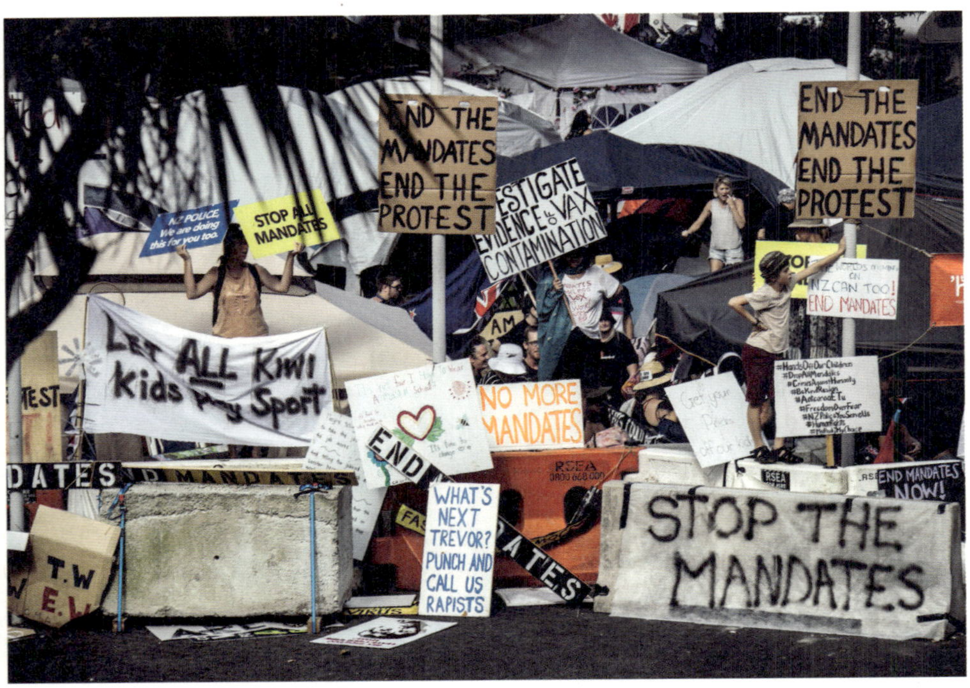

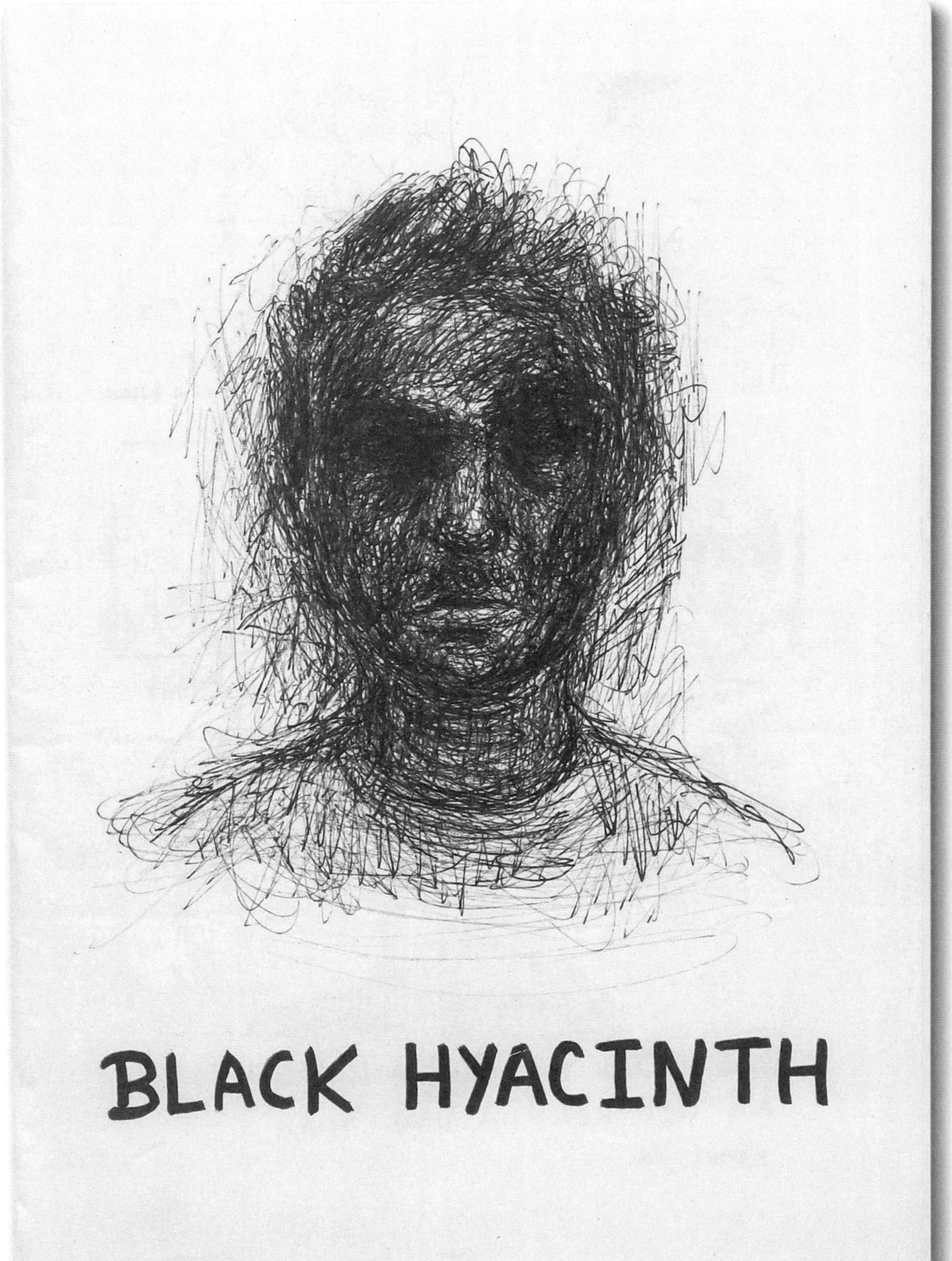

151. *Black Hyacinth*, Darcy Woods, A5, date unknown.
Te Whanganui-a-Tara Wellington.

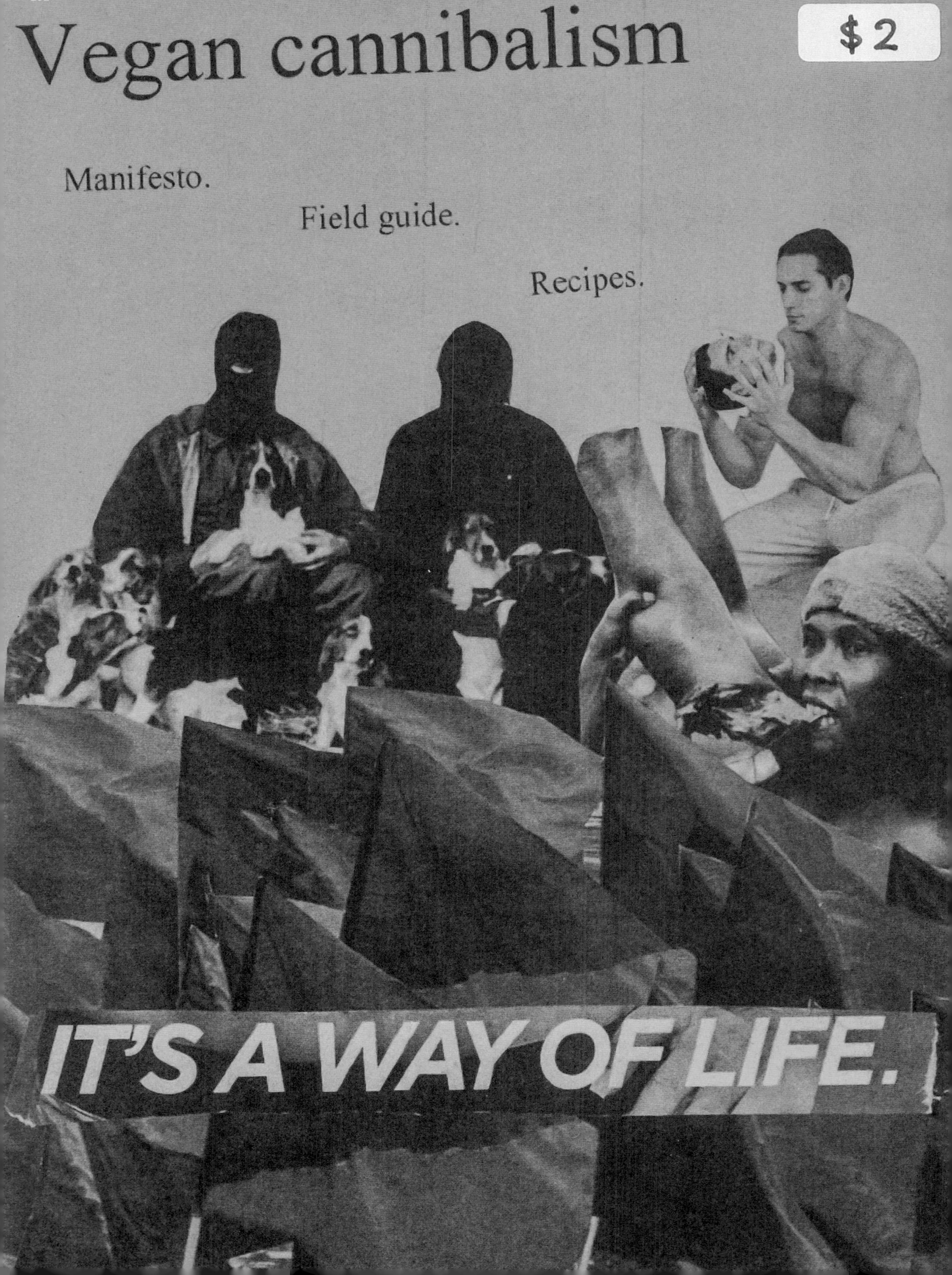
Vegan cannibalism
$2
Manifesto.
Field guide.
Recipes.
IT'S A WAY OF LIFE.

Twenty-tens to -twenties Zines

Mieke Montagne I like to mispronounce the word 'zine' for fun.

Liam Goulter When I was 15 I volunteered at The Freedom Shop, back when it was on Left Bank off Cuba Street. I didn't really care about politics at the time, but my friend was really into animal rights and there was animal rights stuff happening there. So I tagged along with her when she volunteered. They had a whole bunch of zines about stuff that I didn't really know about. One of them was about polyamory, and I bought it because I thought it would be cool to leave it at my house to piss off my mum.

Murtle Chickpea There were about 20 of us in the 91 Aro Street collective. We each paid 10 bucks a week to do whatever we wanted with the space; people would have exhibitions out front or sell their stuff from the shop out back. I remember looking at the zines and not quite getting them. One girl had written a zine about being unattractive and how she wore leather jackets and red lipstick to compensate. It made her feel powerful. I remember thinking 'That's weird.' And someone else had made a photo comic about bike riding or something. I was like 'Oh yeah, okay, is that what people do . . .?' I still didn't get it.

Years later I went to the mid-winter zine market and just went 'Oh my god', bought heaps of zines and then started making my own. I just lost my mind at that mid-winter zine market. Suddenly I just thought 'Oh my god — zines are amazing.' I didn't know that before. I'd also seen quite a few zines in the anarchist book shops in Melbourne, but they were all political, not my thing. I remember looking around at the people at the market and thinking 'Oh my god, my crowd: everyone's just a little bit wonky', and I really liked that. I talked to a guy who had this zine about being awkward, we just talked and talked. I would do a lot of talking and buying zines and then I'd go to the next stall and talk and buy zines. My friend and I went out for beer afterwards at the Southern Cross. We were reading all our new zines and it was like something had just gone . . . *click!* 'This is what we should all be doing.'

Liam Goulter The Freedom Shop seemed like the waiting room at the GP's; all of those flyers like 'Want to Stop Snoring?', but in this case geared toward anarchist thought. The publications were really cheap-looking, in a way that I found very cool. They appeared to be made by people rather than institutions, but people I was probably a bit afraid of.

152. *Vegan Cannibalism*, Callum McDougal, A5, date unknown. Kirikiriroa Hamilton.

Catalina Paz Nuñez Elevancini The first zine I came across was probably my sister's. She was showing me what she was making and telling me she was going to be participating in this thing called Zinefest. I didn't know that what she was working on was called a zine, but I feel like I understood it pretty quickly as I was already interested in graphic novels and things like that. So I understood it as 'You make your own graphic novel.'

Mieke Montagne I was already doing a lot of drawing and crafting and making little birthday cards and things for my friends, but I had no idea what zines were until my sister brought me along to the 2018 Christchurch Zinefest (before the name change to Ōtautahi Zinefest). I was like 'This is crazy, I didn't know this existed.' And then, yeah, I fell in love with them.

Hannah Wynn Lynette Fisher was the year below me when I was in my last year of the Bachelor of Creative Industries at Toi Ohomai in Tauranga. She just said 'Hey, do you want to run a zinefest with me?' And I went 'What's a zine?' I was a graphic design major and was interning for an events company at the time, and she told me that I could do all of the things she didn't want to do. I was like 'What's a zine? It sounds interesting?'

essa may ranapiri I must've known someone who was selling work at Kirikiriroa Hamilton Zinefest, and I just went along and thought 'Wow, this is so cool', there's so much variety and everyone's so lovely. It's a really nice community vibe. I can't remember the first time I had a stall, I don't know what year that would have been. I remember loving the swaps at the end of Zinefest where stall-holders trade zines with each other.

There aren't a lot of events in Hamilton where you can share your writing or stories. There's also a large presence of queer artists and writers at Zinefest, which was exciting to see because sometimes I felt very isolated, especially in my early twenties in Hamilton. Getting to meet people outside my circle who were also queer and producing art was a really cool thing about Zinefest.

153

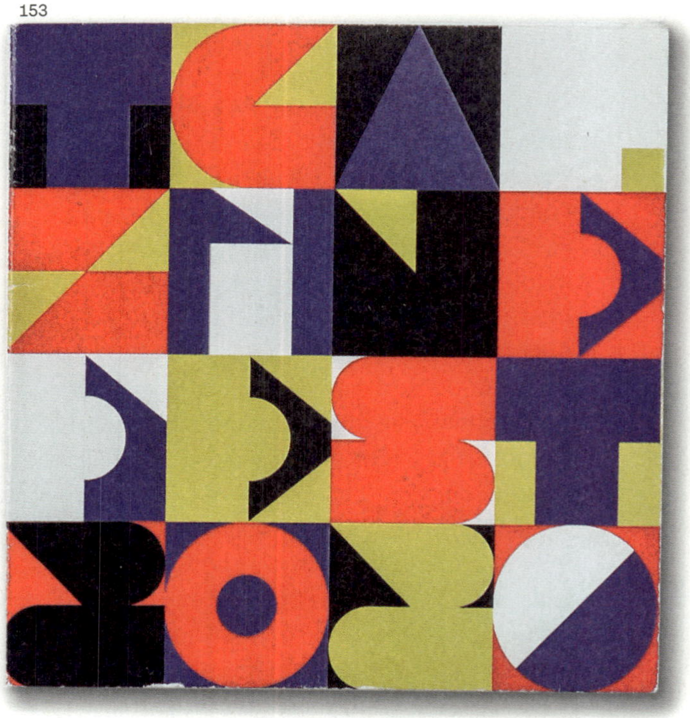

153. Tauranga Zinefest 2020, Hannah Wynn, 70 × 70mm concertina format. Annual stallholder freebee of selected kupu.

154

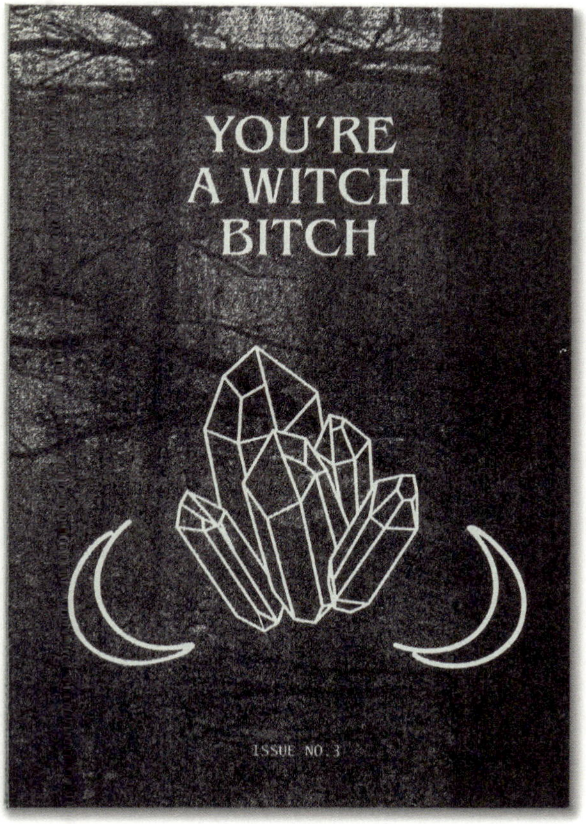

Liam Goulter The zines at The Freedom Shop were lo-fi, with heavy political content. A lot of it was completely inaccessible to me. Learning about political theory at 15 was just too much, and I didn't care. But some of the countercultural content available at the market events was a bit more accessible. I love subcultural stuff but I also have a real love of pop culture, so seeing zines like Claire Harris's Lindsay Lohan zine — which is like pop culture but through a sub-cultural lens — really spoke to me.

Regan Kupu Stokes T'Nealle Worsley of Bang! Bang! Eche! and I flatted together for a month in Lyttelton, 10 years ago. She started The Darkroom in 2011. This is post-earthquake, the entire centre of town [Christchurch] was red-zoned and cordoned off, and for a long time you just couldn't even get in, so it was activity around the fringes. People talked about a doughnut city. The Darkroom was on St Asaph Street, but kind of towards Fitzgerald Avenue, so just within CBD but on the fringes. We'd go there to see live music and stuff. In the foyer was a cupboard labelled 'Zine Library'. You'd open it up and there'd be a bunch of zines. You could even borrow them. There was just a pen and pad for writing 'I'm borrowing this', or whatever. The Darkroom really supported zines, and they really struck a chord with me.

Marijke van Schaardenburg The first proper zine I ever encountered was issue three of *You're a Witch Bitch*. My partner was friends with the editor, Alice Bush, who was studying graphic design. (I was studying film.) Alice had seen me doing these Elder Futhark Viking doodles. They suggested Alice talk to me. It was a very shy situation where I left some doodles on her desk and later received the finished product. I hadn't really seen anything like it before, and when I opened it up it was this lightbulb moment of 'You can just tell this never could've been a magazine or a book and if Alice hadn't made this, this content would not exist on the page.'

Gini Jory I'm in the publishing team at the Hocken Collections, which is the historical archival library part of the University of Otago. It's a collection that was gifted by Dr Hocken to the people of New Zealand. My introduction to zines was going through a donation of zines from Ōtepoti Zinefest a couple years ago. I thought 'This is cool, I feel a new craft and a new interest coming on.' [Laughs.]

I had been vaguely aware of the existence of zines. Every now and again you'd see a poster for Zinefest or a post on social media, but I don't think I'd really looked into them before.

154. *You're A Witch Bitch* #3, edited by Alice Bush, A5, 2016. Ōtautahi Christchurch.

155

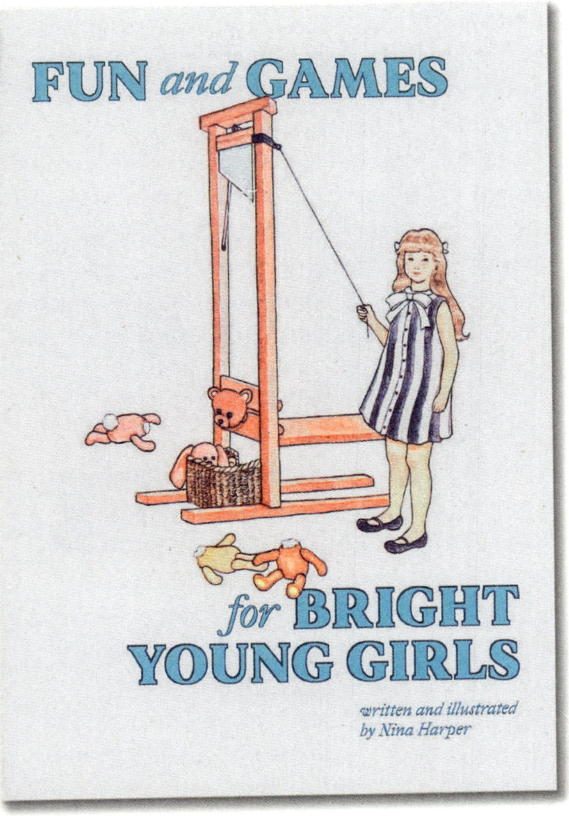

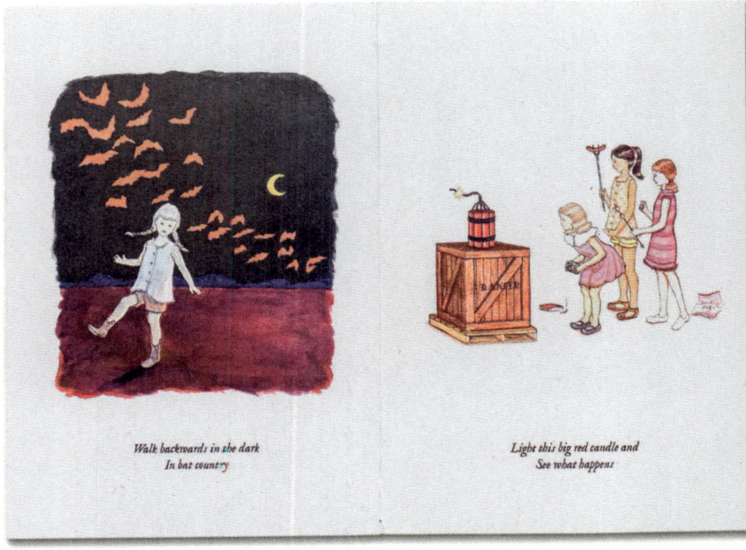

155. *Fun and Games for Bright Young Girls* cover and spread, Nina Harper, A5, 2023. Kirikiriroa Hamilton.

Arwen Miriama Sommer When I was about 13 I read *The Dharma Punks* in its original zine format and I thought 'This is the coolest thing I've ever seen.' It was given to me by a family friend, and he told me the story of how he bought it from Ant Sang off the side of the road in Auckland. Ant was just sitting there, selling them: 'Do you want this for like two bucks?' I just thought 'Cool, I want to sell stuff like that.' Then a couple of years later there was the first-ever Christchurch Zinefest. I found out about it the day before it happened and thought 'I want to do that.' I went into my Google Docs, grabbed a bunch of poems I'd written, printed them out, stapled them together and turned up the next day. The event was so small back then you didn't even have to book, you just turned up and asked, 'Have you got a table for me?', and they'd say 'Sure, there's like 10 people here, go ahead.' I've been every year since.

Nina Harper I made my first zine in 2018, the year after I dropped out of AUT. I had been to one or two of the Hamilton Zinefests before that and really liked it, then in 2018 I saw a post for Zinefest on Instagram and thought 'Oh, I could do this, like this is a totally accessible thing for me to try out', a way to get back into a more illustrative style and get back into self-directed work. I felt a little bit disillusioned with art after that year at AUT. It was a worthwhile experience, and I learnt some good things on the courses, but I was looking for something I wasn't going to get from a fine arts degree. I was trying to turn it into an illustration degree, which is not really something you can get in New Zealand.

Kenneth Merrick Zines probably clicked around 2011, when I was at Unitec doing painting. The artist Andrew McLeod came to do a talk about his fine arts practice and some big oil painting. I'd gone to a couple of shows at his dealer gallery, Ivan Anthony, and had thought 'Woah, these are incredible!' A couple of years later I decided 'Okay, I'll do a Zinefest', and I ran into Andrew there, selling black-and-white photocopied sketchbooks from his summer drawings. I couldn't quite figure out the disjunction between him selling expensive stuff in a gallery and then almost giving stuff away at Zinefest. He also had these huge prints . . . He was super gracious. He traded me a whole bunch of stuff, just took a couple of the ones I had and said 'Enjoy. Hope to see you again next year' sort of thing. That was really cool. I sort of figured out 'Okay, you can actually do both things.'

Hannah Wynn Our second-year tutor [at Toi Ohomai], Dale Sattler, had touched on zines a little. He'd made zines in the past and he'd come to the Tauranga Zinefest as a maker, but prior to Dale's intro, honestly I knew nothing about them. Before moving into the degree I thought art was like stuff that you found in Briscoes. Terrible canvas prints of pōhutukawa.

I grew up in the UK and there was a cereal called Golden Grahams. It was a treat, and there were tokens in the box that you could collect and send away for badges. One year they did tiny little comics. I got tiny copies of *The Dandy* and *Beano* that I've still got. I was probably about five. I was obsessed with those comics. They were readable, maybe not for an older eye but for kids who were into it. I have a thing for anything miniature. So zines definitely fit the bill. I've never been a reader, but I love books. I've got so many books, but I don't read them, I just flick through them. The amount of unread books that I've got is ridiculous. So I guess there were signs that I'd like zines, or that this all makes sense. It probably didn't click until a couple of years of doing Tauranga Zinefest, then I thought 'Oh, yeah that's right, this is definitely my jam.'

Catalina Paz Nuñez Elevancini It was exciting to hear that my sister was going to have a stall with her comic. It was like 'Oh my god, you can just show your own work at this place and people are interested in it?!' It was really exciting. My brother and I were 14 and 13, and we offered to help her out on the stall.

Spencer Hall In an interview, [underground comics artist] Robert Crumb said that they just did it themselves because no one else was going to publish it. That you'd get the covers printed one place, and then get the inside printed at another place, and then staple them together and sell them out of a baby's pram. I thought 'Oh, of course, you don't need to actually get someone else to make the thing for you.' That was sort of the big thing in my mind that clicked.

Maya Templer My dad had some zines by Tim Bollinger, the Wellington cartoonist. I remember finding them and reading them and stealing them and never giving them back. I still have them now. They're just black-and-white and photocopied, but super intricate, detailed. Political? I couldn't even tell you what they're about. I wasn't old enough to understand them, but I still gravitated toward them. I also found some comics by [Jhonen Vasquez], the guy who did the animation *Invader Zim*. He's done some comics called *Johnny the Homicidal Maniac* and they're quite freaky. The author's American but the copies I found were all in French. I also stole them and never gave them back.

Helen Yeung I discovered zines through Tumblr when I was still in high school. I was very much into blogging, like women's fashion blogs, alternative fashion subcultures, punk . . . I discovered all of that on Tumblr and through WordPress blogs mostly. That's also where I started learning more about the Riot Grrrl movement. I was already really into subcultures, Japanese street fashion . . . All of that became a catalyst for me learning about digital feminisms and connecting with other feminists on Tumblr. A lot of people who were into those things offered free mixtape downloads and free zines that they'd scanned. I really enjoyed that kind of aesthetic growing up. I also think that because I went to a predominantly white school, I found it really hard to find my voice and speak about certain things. Being able to go on the computer after school and discover all of these voices that were resisting the status quo was what really got me into zines.

I would imagine that older zinesters discovered zines through communal means like going to zine shows, but I grew up in a migrant family and my parents weren't always supportive of me doing art or going to those sorts of events.

156

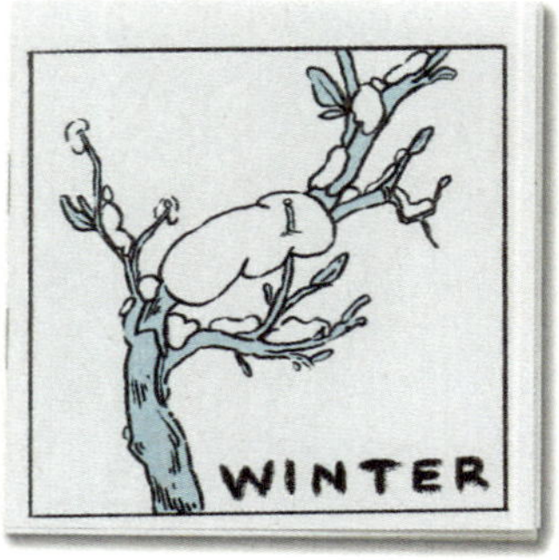

156. *Winter* cover and spread, Maya Templer, 105 × 105mm, 2022. Ōtautahi Christchurch.

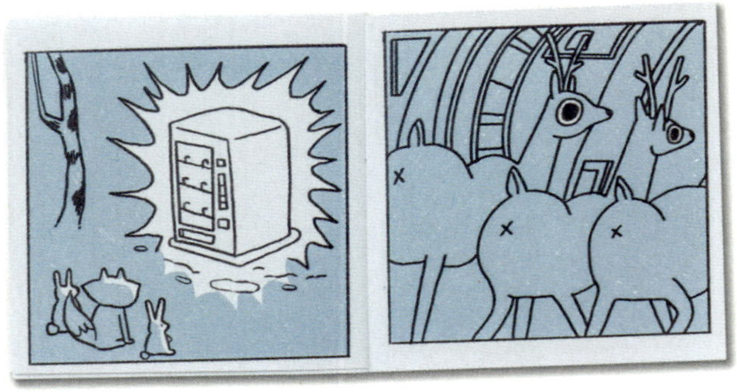

Maya Templer Yes, my dad's an illustrator, and I definitely credit his influence. We would watch heaps of cartoons together, especially Cartoon Network stuff, and he'd show me the cartoons he liked when he was a kid. They'd be on YouTube. I'd stay at his house every weekend or every second weekend, and we'd just hang out and watch cartoons and do art. In the British show *The Mighty Boosh*, one of the main characters, Vince, makes comics about Charlie the bubblegum monster, so we started making comics about Charlie the bubblegum monster. In the show they would say 'Oh, we put them in Weetabix packets in the supermarket', so my dad said 'Yeah, we can put them in the Weet-Bix packets.' I don't think we ever did, but when I was a teenager I'd print comics and leave them for people to find. That was probably inspired by that.

Helen Yeung There's an early Riot Grrrl zine for feminists of colour called *Slant* and it really resonated with me, even though I could only see some of its pages on Tumblr. There was a lot of cool punk imagery and comic-book imagery. The person who started *Slant* is Mimi Thi Nguyen. She's Vietnamese and is based in the States, where she's a professor. Her writing about zines and girls of colour is really good.

Jewelia Howard I found out about zines through the emo pop-punk scene on Tumblr. I made a lot of friends in that scene. You talk about your other interests, so zines come up because it's that kind of scene. It wasn't like sitting down and having a conversation about zines, it was seeing it mentioned and being like 'Okay, what is this?' Bookmark it in my brain to come back to later. I followed up by getting some books about zines out of the library. I remember thinking 'What the fuck are these things?

I didn't find out about Auckland Zinefest in time, but I was moving to Wellington and remember being really, really excited that I was going to get to go to my first zinefest and see zines for real. By then I'd already bought my first art zine off Etsy. Well, maybe it's not a zine but more a small art book. I still have it.

157

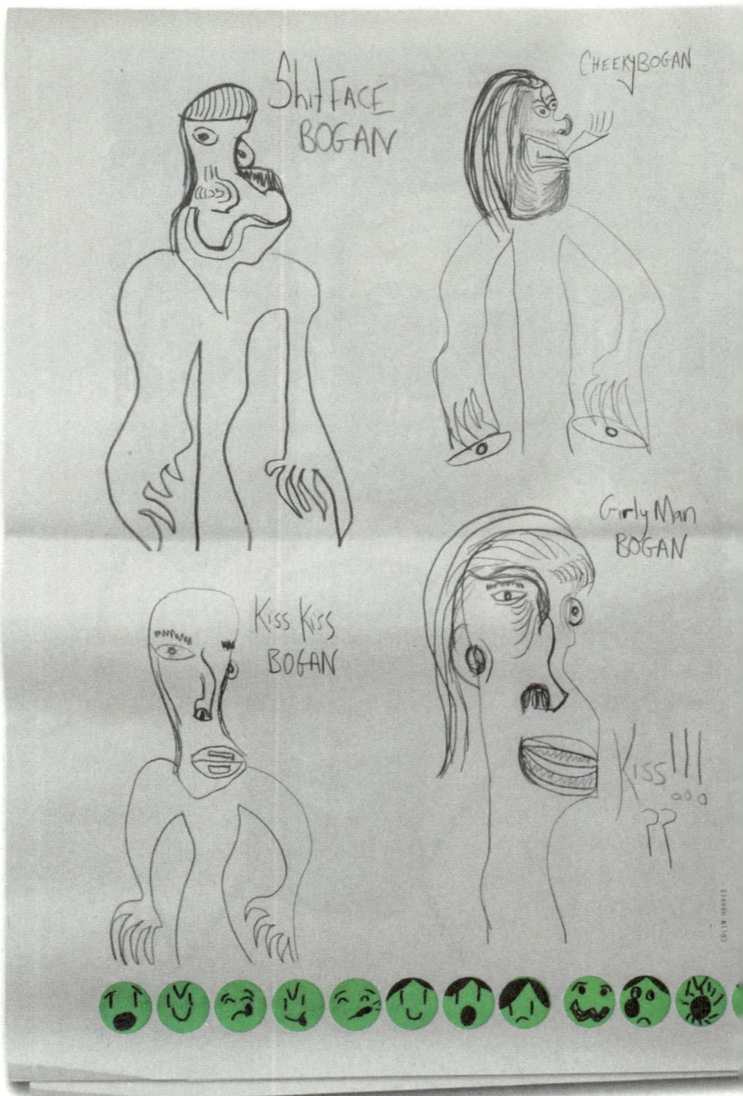

157. *The Dawn of Comic Planet*, page by Colin Harris, Māpura Studios comic group TV Competition: FutureFutureFuture, A2, 2019. Tāmaki Makaurau Auckland.

158

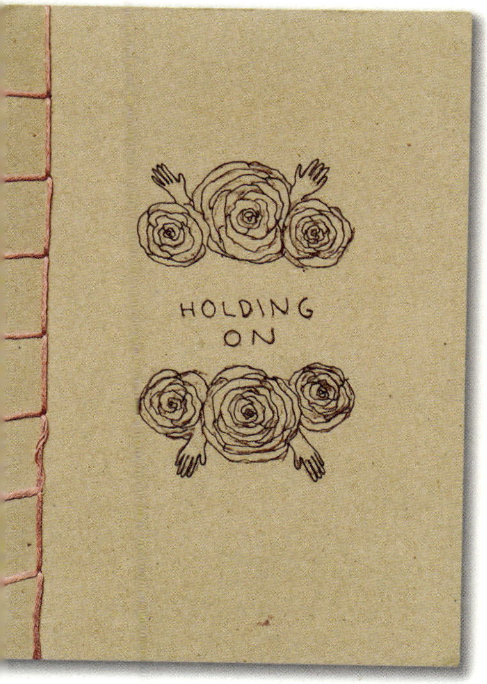

159

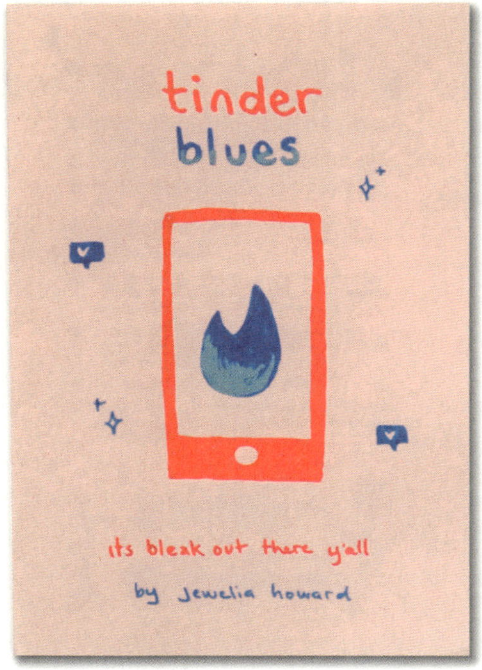

158. *Holding On*, Jewelia Howard, A6, 2015. Te Whanganui-a-Tara Wellington.

159. *Tinder Blues* #1, Jewelia Howard, A5, 2023. Te Whanganui-a-Tara Wellington.

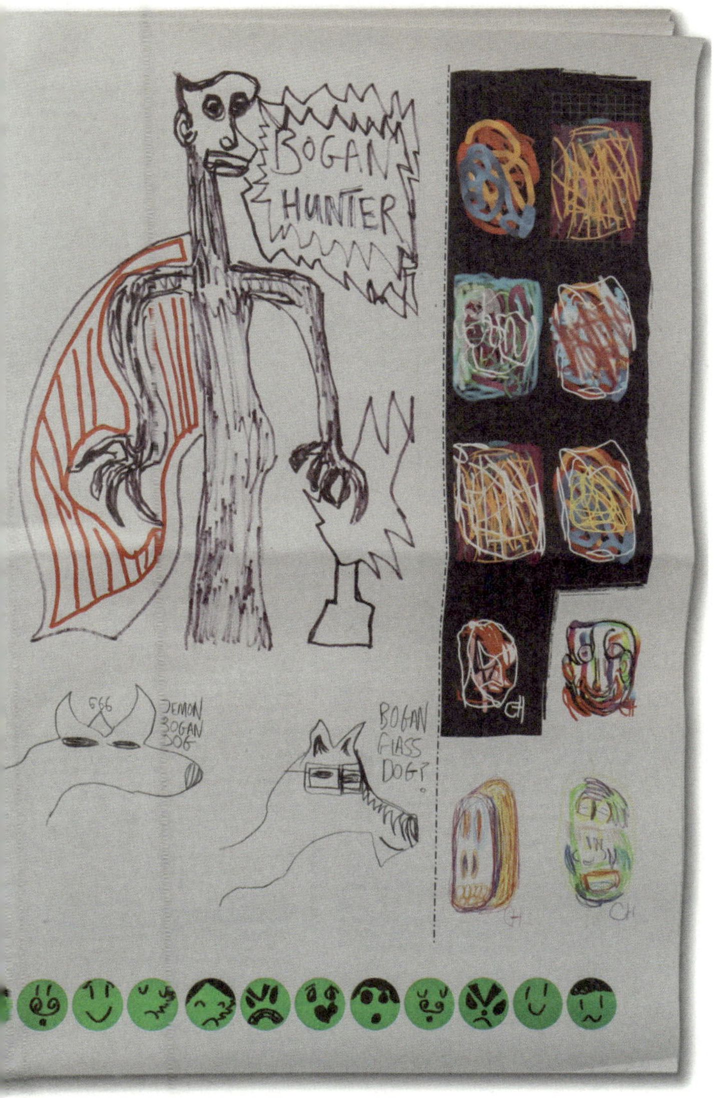

Tim Danko We moved back to Auckland from Great Barrier Island around 2010. I did my master's, and toward the end of the degree I started volunteering at Māpura, because Stefan Neville was working there. I went to an open day, was seeing the work that was being done in the studio and was just like 'Oooooh'. I had an inkling that this was going to be the kind of artwork that I was interested in. After about a year of volunteering I started working in open studio sessions, and there were people doing comic work and comic-related work that ticked all the boxes. This was the stuff that I'd been reading about since my bachelor's. When I did my master's, there was even more engagement with the critical theory. That was really cool. At Māpura I thought 'Man, these guys are *being* what the theory is talking about.' Eventually, after a couple of years, the director of Māpura said, 'We've got all these guys doing comic work. Do you want to start a comic group?' So Stefan Neville and I started the comic group TV Competition: FutureFutureFuture. You're actually meant to say the 'future' repeatedly until it collapses in on itself. Futurefuturefuturefuturefuturefuture . . .

Jewelia Howard Making a bread-pun zine is a bit of a detour from the emo pop-punk, but, to be fair, it was about four years after I first found out what a zine was. It took me a while to actually make one. I was only 15 and at the peak of my emo-band obsession. I was deeply unhappy at school. I sketched band members during class because I didn't want to do any work and I had no friends. My whole support system was the emo punks I knew on Tumblr. It was like all-consuming for me at the time. It was my autistic special interest before I knew I had autism. I just felt 'This is the only thing I have because my life is shit.'

Tim Danko I now realise my entire life has been spent around autistic people. The comics community was totally autistic, y'know? Now I'm working with non-verbal guys, all sorts; I mean it's not like I don't see it, but my definition of autism has been so broadened out . . . It's not like *Rain Man* kind of shit, not that stereotype, it's a community of people.

Helen Yeung I went to very white schools because I grew up on the North Shore [of Auckland]. That was the place my parents were offered by the migration office in Hong Kong. The people that I went to school with had difficulty understanding who I was. There was a lot of identity crises growing up, rejecting my culture to fit in with my peers, and then embracing it at the risk of being bullied. Those experiences informed my starting of Migrant Zine Collective and wanting to express myself through art.

Billy Douglas My mum wants to be supportive, but also 'When are you going to get a job?' It's not supportive. It's words coming from her mouth. I love my mother dearly, but, yeah, I don't think we, especially Victoria, get the support we deserve from our parents. **Victoria Armstrong** I just try to do what I enjoy now. Because I grew up with such a focus on what other people thought. I've now gone the complete opposite way, just trying to fulfil myself.

Marijke van Schaardenburg This year at Auckland Zinfest I picked up a zine from The Charlotte Museum called *Lesbians in Print*. It was published in the eighties and there's a section about the Homosexual Law Reform Act [1986] going through. I treasured this when I found it. I think it harks back to a more connected time within our community, where in some ways, because of that struggle, people really had to band together. I was reading it and thinking 'We don't have any of this. Where are my gay softball teams?!' The advertisements in the back say things like 'Flatmate wanted for large luxurious lesbian household.' There are all these 'come join us' things in there.

Liam Goulter This is *Homocore* #7. It's a zine by and for queer punks. I'm showing you this because it reminds me of the relationship between punks and queers. The thing that really struck me reading this — and it's long, there's a lot of words in here — is that it's mainly people's letters. It's mainly a vessel for people to communicate with one another.

I always felt this really strong pull towards seventies punk, but when it moved into more hardcore vibes it just felt inaccessibly macho to me. Maybe if I'd known about homocore [the movement] or I was in a bigger city, there would have been a space where I could be shy and gay but also into punk rock, but in Wellington it didn't feel like the two things coexisted.

160

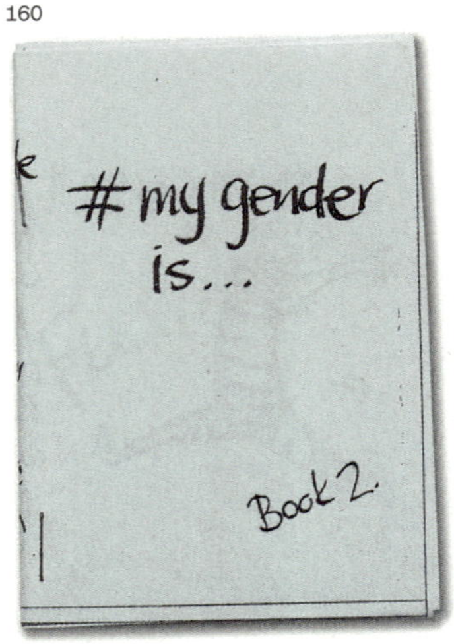

160. *My gender is...* cover and spread, Sam Orchard, A7, 2012. Tāmaki Makaurau Auckland.

161

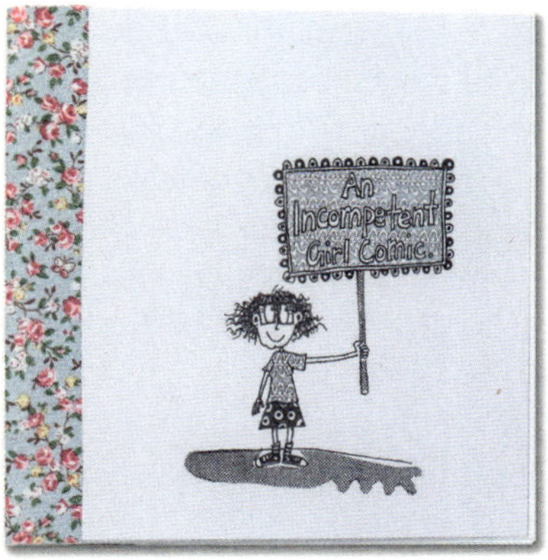

161. *An Incompetent Girl Comic* cover and page, Indira Neville, 146 x 146mm, 2016. Tāmaki Makaurau Auckland.

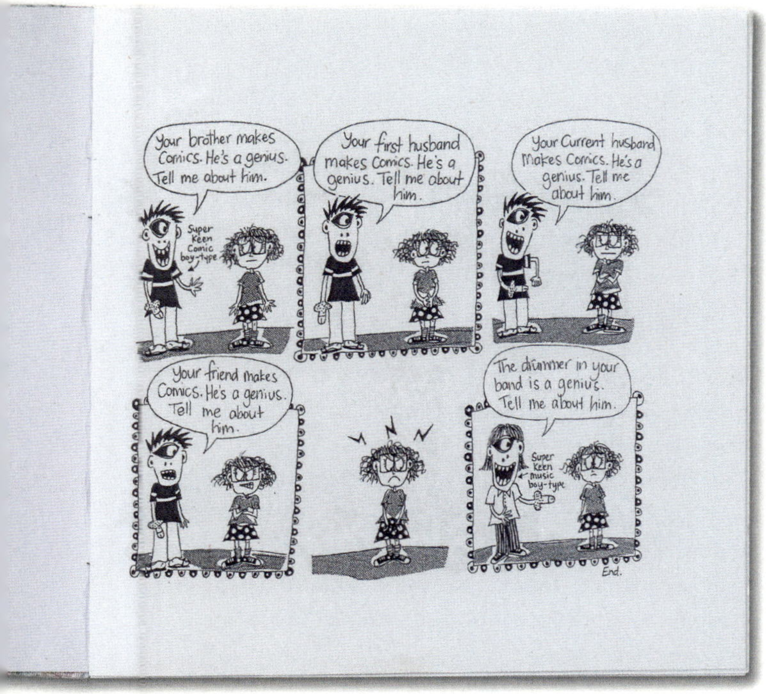

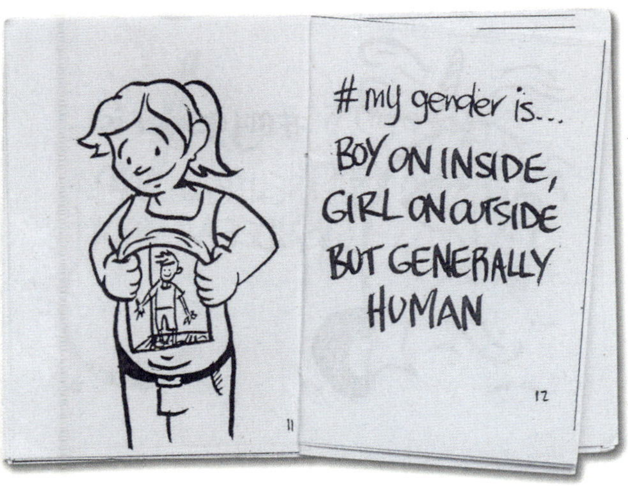

Sam Orchard I feel like the intentional work that essa may ranapiri and a bunch of other people have done to build up and make space for trans and queer storytelling and takatāpui storytelling in this country is phenomenal. Comics is a somewhat different area in that there's a tendency for people to see them as being a youth thing, and the idea of youth and trans being together has become very political in recent years. It's got quite scary.

Maya Templer I like to think that transphobia is similar to homophobia. The people who are really upset about it die and then everyone else is kind of chill.

Sam Orchard Comics as a 'boys' club?' I only entered into those conversations in the 2010s. They were complicated feelings after the affirming experience of hanging out with boys and drawing comics and feeling like my gender was acceptable in a way that it hadn't been before, then recognising that it was a fucking 'boys' club' that was awful and patriarchal and exclusionary . . . Because my ultimate experience with comics was that it wasn't until I was drawing as Sam and doing comics as a boy that other boys were like 'Your comics are legit'. So I agreed with the stuff that Tony Kenealy and Indira Neville were saying about the 'boys' club' because it's very true. Apart from that first core group of guys down in Dunedin, where we were all just super nerds, and I don't think they cared what gender I was, we had women in the group as well. It was just whoever wanted to turn up at the time.

Indira Neville There were three or four women in the whole of Adrian Kinnaird's [*From Earth's End: The*] *Best of New Zealand Comics*, and that really fucked me off because I knew heaps of women who made comics, so that and my misgivings about 'competent boy comics' overlapped. Lots of women made comics that weren't in that 'competent boy' style, so that inspired Sarah Laing, Rae Joyce and I to do the *Three Words* anthology about the work of New Zealand women in comics.

Murtle Chickpea As a kid you're just drawing because that's what you do, and then, for me anyway, I started to realise that 'Oh, that doesn't look like a . . .' I find adults are a lot harder to get going when I do zine-making workshops at the community centre. Adults are a lot harder to crack, especially on the spot. It's like 'Hey, this is what we're going to do today, got a story?' And they'll just respond, 'I haven't got a story'. But with kids . . .

When I did a prompt zine for Featherston Booktown I handed out a blank zine with silly prompts to get people thinking. Things like 'God exists. True or false? Elaborate . . .' 'Describe your first sexual experience in three words'. 'Draw your soul.' Just silly stuff that only adults would get. A lot of adults were having fun with that, especially with the sex-experience one — they were pissing themselves.

162

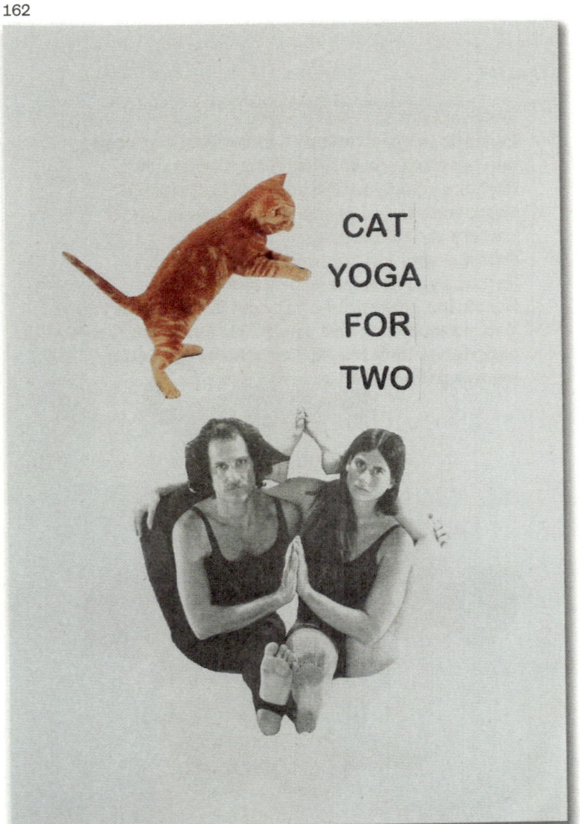

Maia-Jeanne Woolkirk We allow children to be creative, and then we indulge their anxiety and perfectionism, so as 20-somethings we don't usually follow creative pursuits. People have kids and then offload all of that joy and responsibility onto the children; they'll enjoy kids crafts *with* their kids, but they don't translate that into their *own* joy in adult creativity. I think they lose that. The people who haven't lost that joy in adulthood, that's who comes to zinefests.

Everyone loves to tell stories, but they don't necessarily have the level of security or commitment to put them down on paper. Once you're outside of the zinefest bubble, this professionalism thing comes in, it's like 'Oh, it's not very good.' You're no longer doing it for the fun of it. I just think convincing adults to have fun in a way that doesn't involve alcohol and involves a level of effort and vulnerability is quite difficult.

Maya Templer I need to reach out to more primary schools. We've done some workshops with high schools and the Ara polytech in Christchurch, but it would be cool to do one with younger kids. Lots of kids draw comics, but showing them how to fold an eight-page mini-zine is like [makes explosion sound]. I'm a big believer in the eight-page mini-zine fold. It's powerful!

I was shown that technique when I was 14; I made a zine every week for more than a year after that. There are over 60 zines in my mum's shipping container. None of them are very good, but they were really fun to make. I would draw one on a Thursday, and then on Friday I'd photocopy it, maybe like 10 copies, and then I'd walk into science class halfway through and distract my friends and get them to help me fold them, and then I'd leave and go and distribute them before the break in places around the school. I might put one on a table in the library or leave one on a seat outside. They were attributed to 'M.K.', so no one knew it was me.

162. *Cat Yoga For Two*, Murtle Chickpea, A5, 2020. Paetūmōkai Featherston.

Regan Kupu Stokes I made my first zine around the time that I was involved with Occupy Christchurch. I don't have a copy of it anymore, but I can remember the cover. I was still at uni at that time and I was living at home with my mum, but when Occupy started I moved into Hagley Park and lived there for a few months to support that kaupapa. I was involved with the media and communications side of things, and one of the things we did was create a kind of 'Who Are We?' type zine. I knew of the medium through The Darkroom, and it just felt easy. Through Occupy I met a lot of cool creative people and ended up supporting the Bryndwr community.[3] I went flatting after Occupy, and then the year after that I started flatting in the Bryndwr community with a lot of people who were also interested in zines.

Bryndwr's a suburb of Christchurch that's kind of near the university but kind of lower-socioeconomic. It was one of those 1960s state-housing projects, but they got young architects to design all of the streets and houses. So all of the streets are kind of curved, there's lots of very cool walkways between them, all centred around a park, where some of our friends started a community garden.

Mieke Montagne My first zines didn't really have titles; they were purely visual. 'Untitled.' Thinking about it now, that was so bold of me. No, it was more just me drawing stuff on a bit of paper and then folding it up. I'd fold a piece of paper and then draw through so that it worked as a single motif when it was opened up or as a broken motif across the individual pages.

Hannah Wynn When I was running Tauranga Zinefest I thought 'Shit, I should really make a zine.' I made a phobias zine, little illustrations of obscure, possibly fake, phobias. One's the phobia of having peanut butter stuck to the roof of your mouth. My favourite was the fear that at any given moment a duck could be watching you somewhere — apparently that one's a real phobia. Well, it is according to the internet, so who knows? The zine's simply called *Phobias*.

163

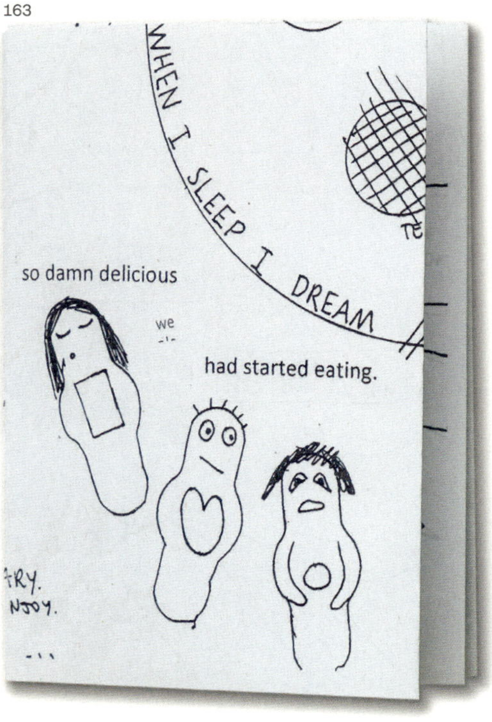

164

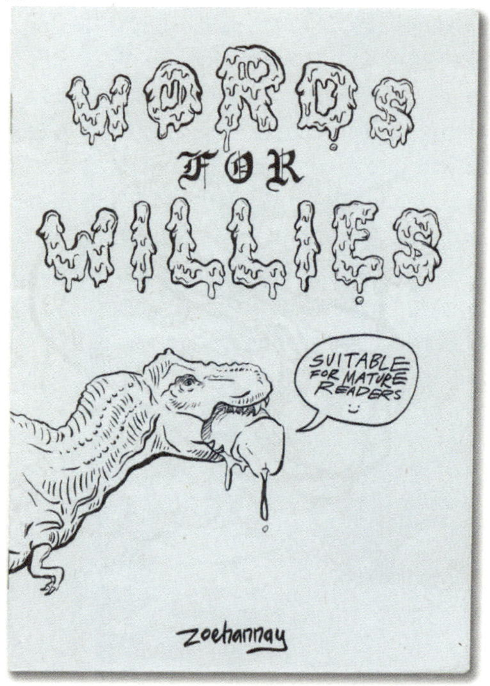

163. *When I Sleep I Dream*, Regan Kupu Stokes, A7, 2013. Ōtautahi Christchurch.
164. *Words for Willies*, Zoe Hanney, A5, 2018. Te Whanganui-a-Tara Wellington.

Billy Douglas Victoria coerced me into doing some writing for the *Screaming Monkeys* zine. I used to do creative writing in school but it never got marked, I always got sent to the with-draw room or the counsellor because I used to try and write the most obscure things I could possibly think of, things you wouldn't expect some 14-year-old kid to turn out. Everyone was really worried. Every year the counsellor got involved, and then my parents, obviously. One story was about a boy my age. He did things that I did, had the same hobbies I had, and all of a sudden he kills his brother and his parents split up. Everyone was like 'What the fuck's wrong with this kid?' I was just sitting there with a smile on my face, going 'This is getting some attention, this is pretty cool.' It stopped once I left school.

So, when Victoria asked if I'd like to write for the zine I said 'Fuck, yes, I would love to.' But it's been so hard to pin me down, especially during the first six months of my apprenticeship, when it was 12-hour days, six days a week. Finding the time to sit down and write was very difficult.
Victoria Armstrong I was trying to get you in on it because I knew that you'd enjoy writing zines. And I knew that people would enjoy your writing, even if it wasn't as horrible as what you were turning out as a teenager. **Billy Douglas** I don't think the teachers realised that I was just going for shock value. I truly believe they thought something was very wrong with me. I played on that as a teenager. I don't have those stories now. I wasn't allowed to keep them. I remember asking the counsellor for my stories back and she just refused.

165

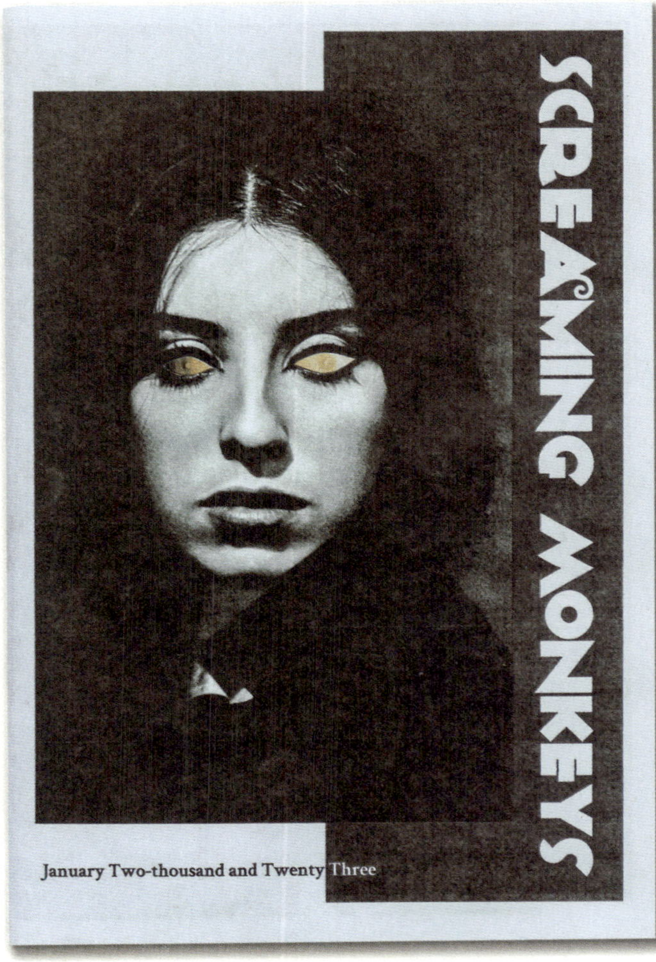

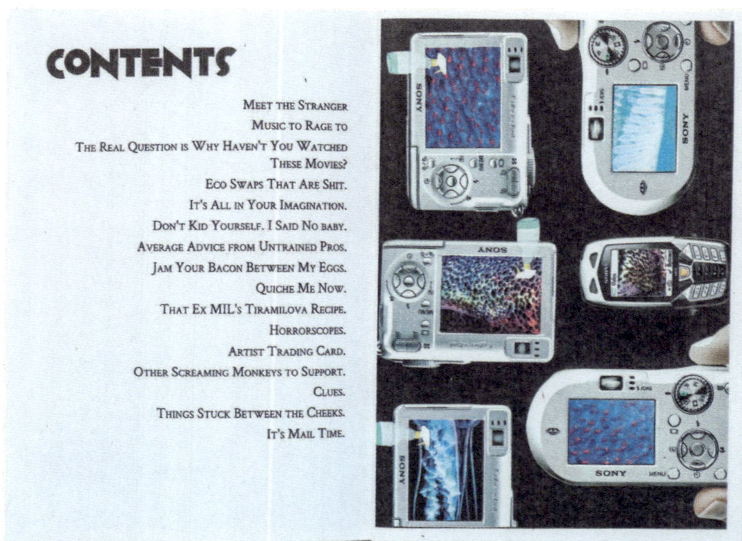

165. *Screaming Monkeys* cover and spread, Victoria Armstrong and Billy Douglas, A5, 2023. Te Papaioea Palmerston North.

Gini Jory I don't know that I would have started making zines if I'd only come across the punky ones. I don't feel like I'm part of that scene. I'm definitely a feminist but I don't know that I would've made feminist zines either, because I don't feel like I've got anything new to add.

Some of the zines I was selling at Ōtepoti Zinefest yesterday were by one of my workmates — Kari Wilson-Allan. *Discount Witches* is sort of a feminist zine that she made using stuff from Papers Past [the digitised archive of New Zealand publications]; I think it's quite possible to do that in an artistic way. I really like the zines that she made. We started making zines around the same time: when I told her I was going to start making zines, she told me she'd been collecting material and wanting to make zines for a while. 'We should do this,' she said. So we started making them and bringing them into work. Kari gave hers out to our colleagues. I didn't photocopy mine until a bit later, but I would show people pictures of what I was working on, what I wanted to include.

166

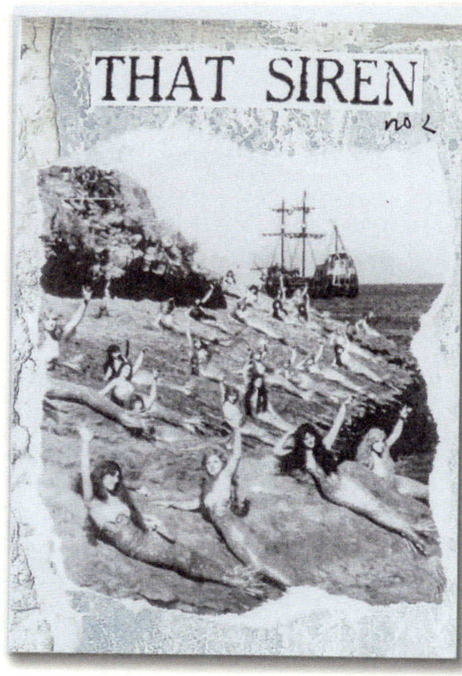

Kenneth Merrick I was teaching English in Japan, then art and design as well. I was fortunate. Some of the students who were making a lot of stuff at the school said, 'Hey, you should go check out Comitia [a convention of original, self-published works] if you like people making their own stuff. Go check out [the other self-publishing convention] Comiket also, but be careful. It's just huge, you can get lost. Don't go to the wrong stalls — there's some extreme stuff.' It got me thinking 'Yeah, this is something I actually used to like doing and I think I want to get back into making', and then we came back to New Zealand and there were two weeks of MIQ [quarantine under the COVID-19 pandemic regulations] and I thought 'Okay, I'm just going to start making more stuff, doing more drawings again.'

Nina Harper The first zine that I made was a simple series of illustrations of archetypal horror characters, but all female. My drawing style was very influenced by some classical illustrators. Before that I'd just been doing one-off prints and illustrations that weren't really connected in any way, so I just thought I'll have a loose horror theme so they hold together as a zine.

166. *That Siren* #2, Gini Jory, A7, 2023, Ōtepoti Dunedin.

Kenneth Merrick When I'm making the sketchbooks, I'm just sort of working daily. It gets to the point where I've got enough material that I can scan them, and then it's at that point [when] I start looking for combinations, like 'Would this work well next to this because of the colour?' or 'Maybe Bela Lugosi or Christopher Lee next to this picture of a bat.' The drawings might have been completed three or four months apart. I'm creating a very *loose* narrative without being too on the nose, just trying to keep it flowing, with some kind of dynamic between facing pages and what's overleaf.

167

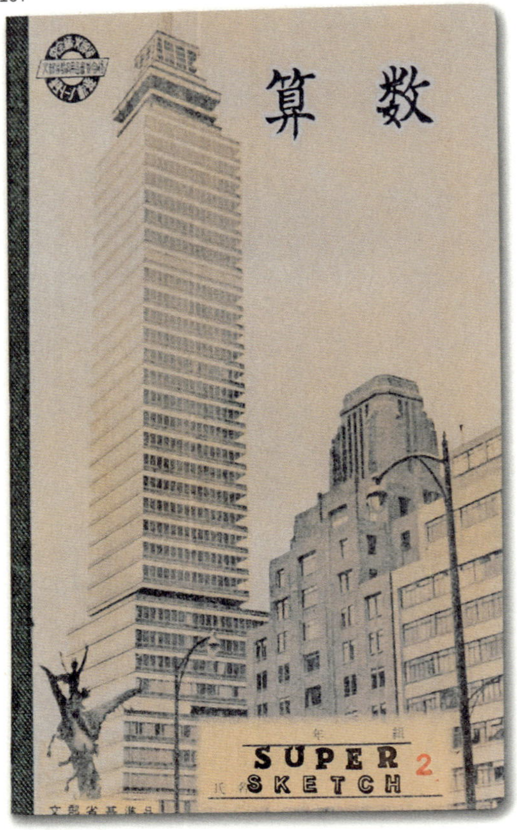

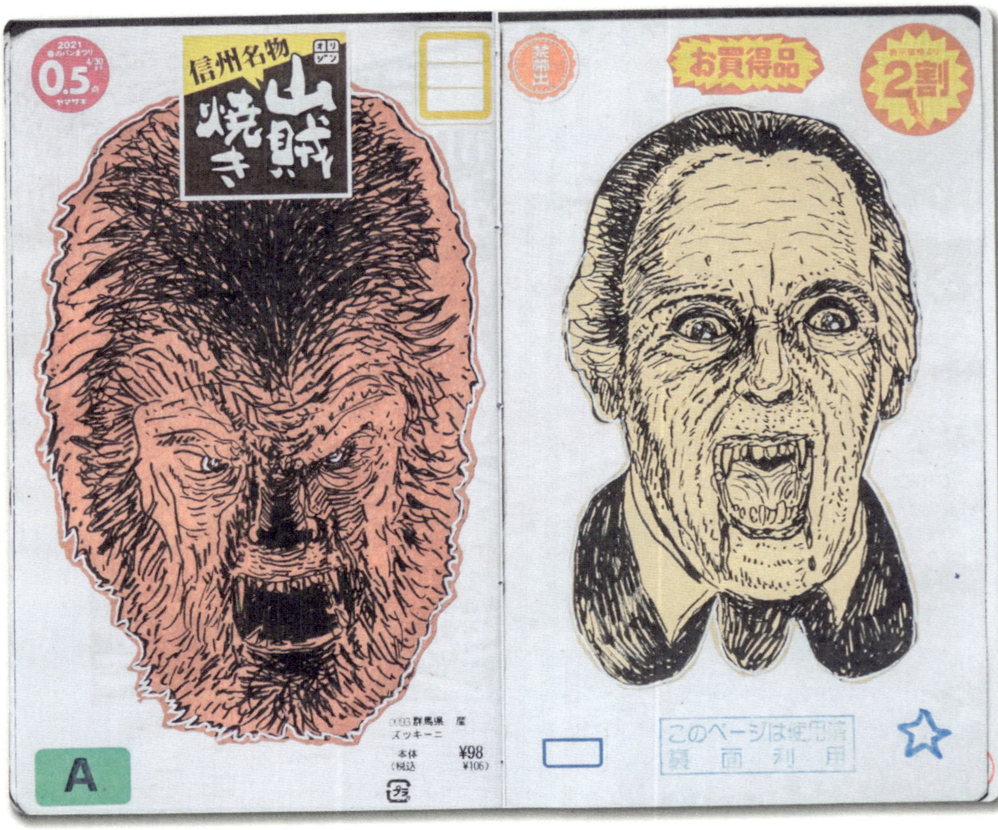

167. *Super Sketch* #2 cover and spread, superhyperpaper aka Kenneth Merrick, 125 × 202mm, 2023. Tāmaki Makaurau Auckland.

Panty Baggers PB1 The very first book happened before COVID. It was a little early reader. One person would collage into it and then put it in another Panty Baggers' letterbox, then that person did a bit more and passed it on. That's how we got together, it was just determined by who the book was passed on to. We didn't plan the Panty Baggers grouping. So the early reader went to us four, and then it went around again. **PB2** It was totally driven out of friendship and us all being creative and looking for a bit of fun. It wasn't formal, it wasn't organised, it was random. Then we started getting excited because we could see what was evolving with the more 'finished' works, and thought 'Yeah, we really like this process, and we really like what's actually coming out of this process.' **PB1** We did a wee book for the Brooklyn Art Library[4] in the US. We just sent it off and it went into their library. We were like 'Wow, we can actually do something with these!' It gave us the idea that we could do something more than just enjoy the process. The submissions to the Brooklyn Art Library could respond to a theme, or not. I think they had themes for contributors who found it tricky to think of something. We made ours fit a theme in the end — 'Secret Women's Business'. That project formalised what we were doing. **PB2** Like most of our work, the book doesn't construct a particularly coherent narrative. Each page talked about different aspects of the 'Secret Women's Business', whatever that might be. That first project was the spark.

168. *Panty Baggers Go Exploring in an Unmanned Spacecraft to Investigate Earth's Dessert on Mars*, Panty Baggers collective, 145 × 190mm, 2022. Ōtepoti Dunedin.

169. *Our Animal Instinks*, Panty Baggers collective, 148 × 200mm, 2020. Ōtepoti Dunedin.

168

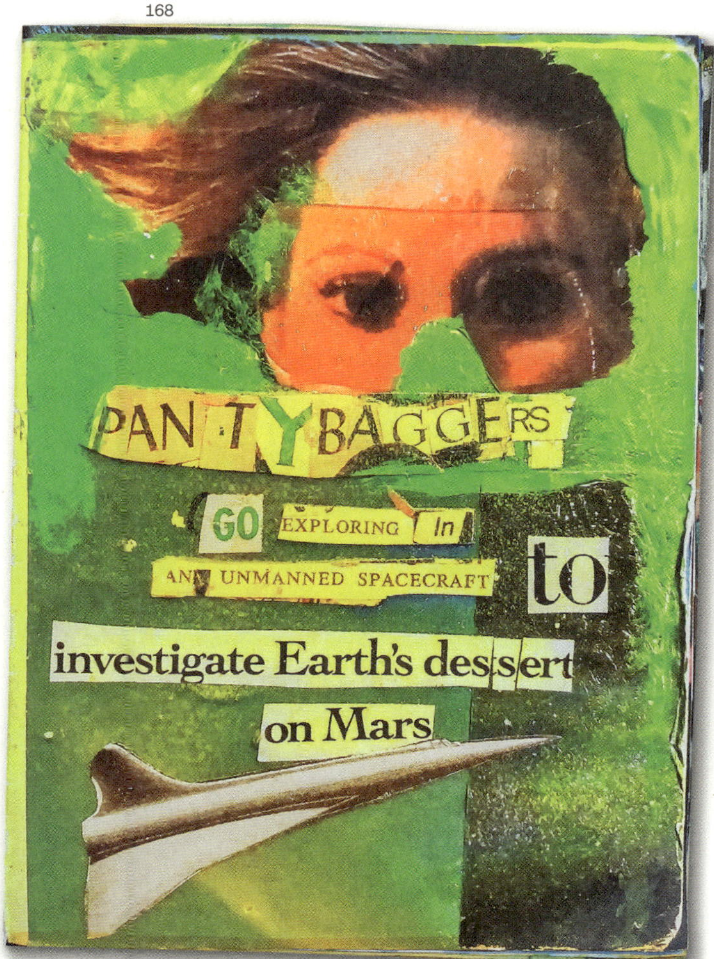

169

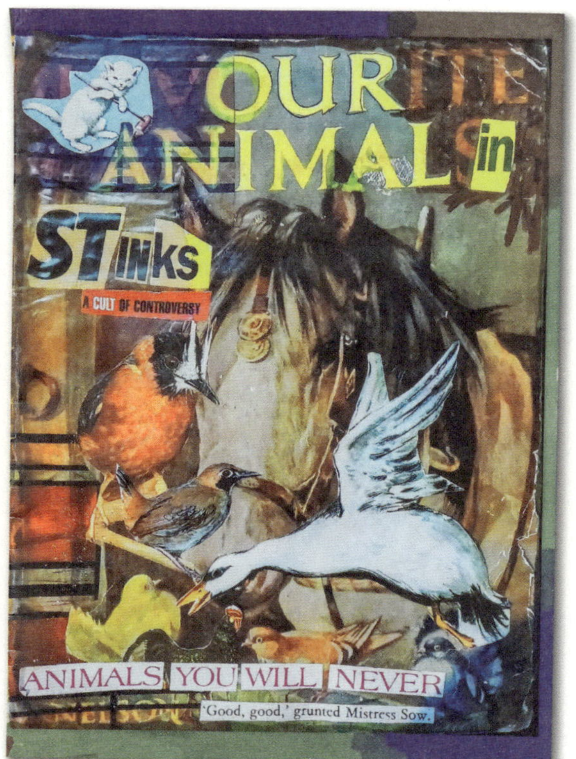

Nina Harper I did one year at AUT and found out that illustration is very much *not* the focus of a lot of fine arts degrees anymore. It's a lot more conceptual, a lot more abstract — not that there's anything wrong with that, but after a year of it I realised it was not at all what I was wanting from art school. I pulled back from that completely and used zinefest as a motivation to return to more illustrative stuff. I started experimenting with little illustrative zines and things, and then once I started working in a fine arts supply store I could experiment more with the materials and with my style.

Jewelia Howard I'm prolific but I've got no idea how to organise my creative time. This is my problem. I sit in choice-paralysis until I have a deadline. That's kind of my thing.

Tim Danko Each Māpura group has its own dynamic and the cartooning dynamic is quite intense. One of the great things — and one of the things that clicked into my critical theory mind-set — was the idea that boundaries are really fluid. We have guys who are intensely focused on their own process, so we've tried to make quiet areas within the studio, but space is such a privilege and we don't have a lot of it. Then we have the guys who are broadened out. When Allegra was there, if something was going really well she would get up and run outside and jump up and down. So there's that kind of physical moving around the space. We have Edward, who is a system-engagement queen; at the moment they're doing a big timeline of the comic group and all the publications we've produced, so sometimes there'll be a big, long roll of paper with this long timeline and people are invited to add to it. Edward also makes comics or zines called *The Atom in Fiction*.

We provide headphones for the guys who require it. My work is to try to balance the room. In the disability community people are behaviourally managed so much in their interactions with the outside world, so we try to keep the space as free as possible, within certain limits.

Jewelia Howard I just talk out my ass a lot without filtering, and then I'll say a thing and someone will say 'God, that's good'. So, I definitely keep lists in my phone of things I should make into stickers and zines. I try to write things down as much as possible because my memory's not great.

essa may ranapiri I've done some zines which are *responses* to the published books [of my poetry], but otherwise there's not much crossover between the poems for zines and poems for books. The books are very intentional projects: I know when I'm writing for a zine versus when I'm writing for a collection. The zines are usually to get something out that I don't think will fit in the book.

Panty Baggers PB1 At the moment we've got quite a few books on the go. So you'll be like 'Oh, I haven't seen that one for a while' or 'Have you done any in this one yet? Yeah?' We need to finish some. How many have we got on the go at the moment? Like, eight?

Gini Jory The first zines I made are called *Story of the Sword*. They're made using Papers Past. I basically just put the word 'sword' into the search field to see what came up.

essa may ranapiri There are two zines which are responses to the [poetry collection] books: one that's a response to *Ransack* and one that's a response to *Echidna*. It felt like a nice thing to do a year after each book had come out. They might not make much sense without the books. With the other zines, I might find a bunch of poems I've written in a Word document and go 'How do these fit together?', because I like having a theme regardless. You can publish a lot more zines in the same amount of time as publishing two books. So the zines have a lot more of a range and I'm less strict about whether something fits or not.

Gini Jory When my friend Britney [Sleight] was at the Ōtepoti Zinefest, she said 'I can't believe how many zines you made.' She really gets in her head about every little detail, whereas I'm just like 'This is funny' or 'These work together'. I'm not a perfectionist; I'm just putting things together and seeing what works. I guess I'm not making elaborate comics like some of the things I saw at Ōtepoti Zinefest. Britney's zines included a lot of her original artwork. I'm not really an artist in terms of drawing or painting or anything like that. I guess if you're doing that kind of work for a zine it might take a while, whereas I'm just mashing pre-existing resources together and seeing what works.

Helen Yeung The Migrant Zine Collective workshops are collage. We built the collective on a DIY cut-and-paste ethos. I always enjoyed magazines because they showcase the status quo and pop culture, and that gives people the chance to reflect on their own experiences and offer critique. What they're seeing acts as a prompt. In a sense it's a remixing of ideas that already exist and making that your own. For example, we had a workshop in the early days called 'Goodbye Turmeric Latte', which was designed to critique Western adaptations of non-Western food culture. Auckland Libraries supplied us with lots of food magazines. From these magazines, participants were able to take a lot of images of recipes that white people had 'stolen' and write about how angry they were that the foods they'd grown up eating had been turned into this awful Western commodity.

170

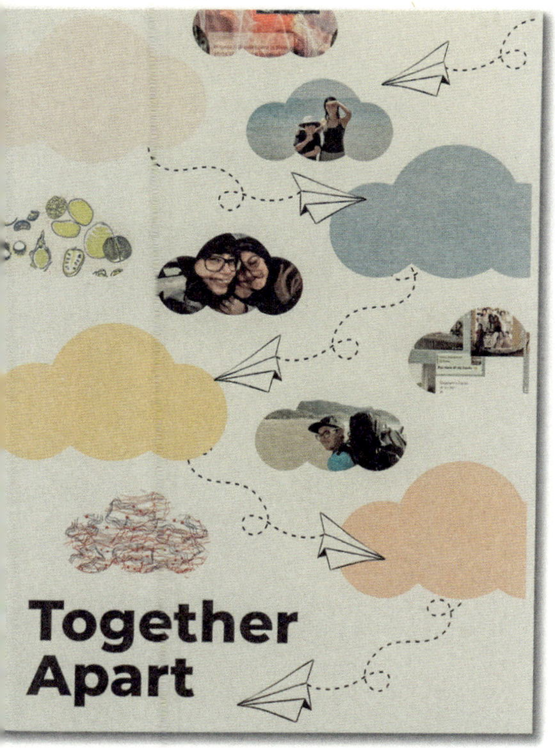

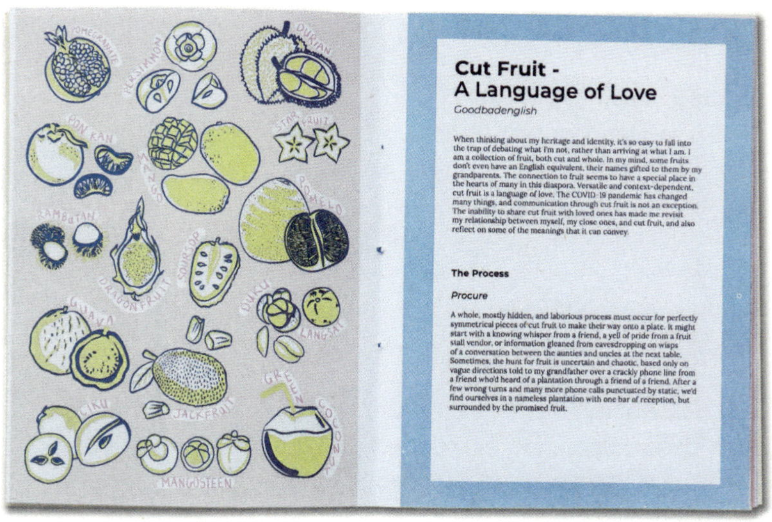

Victoria Armstrong Collage is accessible to everyone. You don't need to be a good drawer or have traditional art skills. Anyone can cut up a magazine and rearrange other people's images and make it their own. It's so accessible, and you can do more with it than people think. You can add your own drawing or text or other elements.

170. *Together Apart* cover and spread, Migrant Zine Collective and Wellington Zinefest, 182 × 140mm, 2021. Te Whanganui-a-Tara Wellington.

Murtle Chickpea I just always liked collage because you don't have to be able to draw. There's good collage and shit collage though, and I think after a while I realised how to do it well.

Maia-Jeanne Woolkirk Mostly I cut up *National Geographic*. Love them. Found in second-hand shops. I also have some UFO magazines. They have captions like 'Is this badger psychic?' There are places where you can find absurd sentences and you're like 'Let's use that!'

Marijke van Schaardenburg I spilt a glass of red wine over this stack of my friend Matt Joils's zine *Hot Queer Summer* which were waiting to be folded. At first I was like 'Shit', but then Matt and I just laughed about it and said, 'The wine spills really embody being in the park, drinking in the sun, just me and some other queers.' All those subtle pink marks are the spilt red wine.

Hannah Wynn One of my favourite zines a couple of years ago was by local artist Paul Darragh who made a Karen zine. It's hilarious, and that was obviously very topical at the time. There was definitely some dark COVID stuff coming out during the pandemic. I've had enough of that, but zines are fast enough to be topical.

Maya Templer I usually go to bed at 10.30 p.m. and I wake up around 7 a.m. I'm not a big night person. I used to be — as a teenager, I'd sleep in 'til 1 p.m. — but I find I think better in the morning. The best time for me to come up with weird ideas is during meetings. When I'm supposed to be listening to what someone else is saying, I'll just be drawing in my sketchbook. Recently I made a zine about my favourite recipe, which is for mac and cheese with pumpkin. I planned out that whole zine during a meeting at work, all of it. Then I drew it in a day at the University of Canterbury library.

Spencer Hall I had all of these half-finished projects, and that was the impetus for that first issue of *Scraps*, harvesting half-finished projects for parts. Also I was living in Canada, far away from many friends and not wanting to have to write individual letters to each person. That zine was meant to be a newsletter of my life, but a most lavish, well-constructed and artistic newsletter.

It also had to work for people beyond my friend group. On the back it says, 'I also think of it as a kind of beacon that's been lovingly crafted in the hope that my favourite people will be ignited with kinship and zest', and that includes people I don't know. In one Montreal comic shop in particular I saw some self-published comics and I thought 'These are amazing.' Bought them. Went to a comics festival, met the people who'd made them and then became friends. There's something to be said for making something and putting it out in the world like a beacon, connecting with people that way.

171

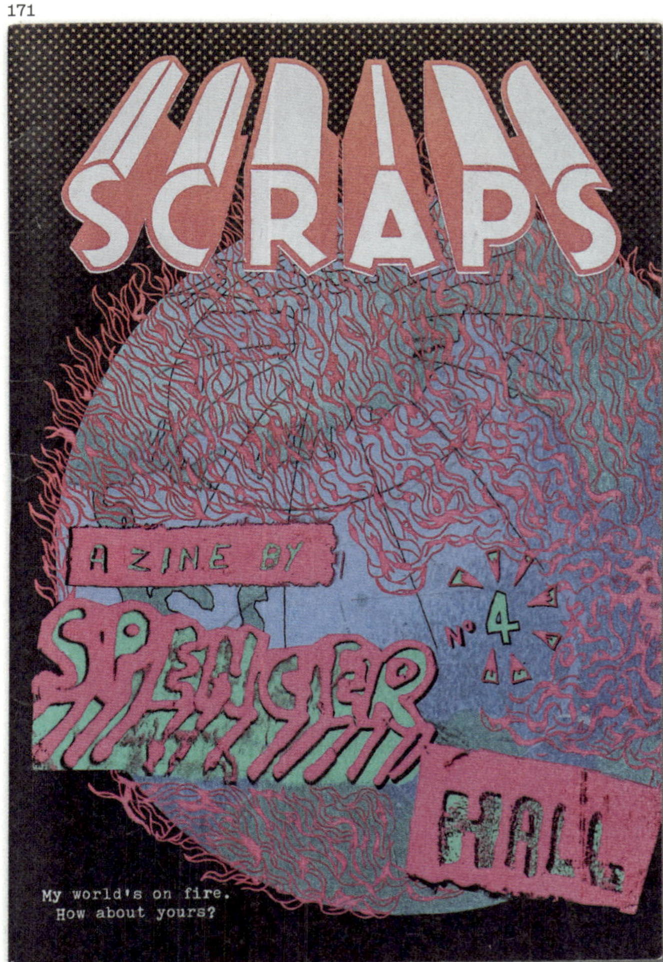

171. *Scraps* #4 cover and spread, Spencer Hall, A5 (includes sub-zine at A6), 2022. Montreal, Ontario, and Ōtepoti Dunedin.

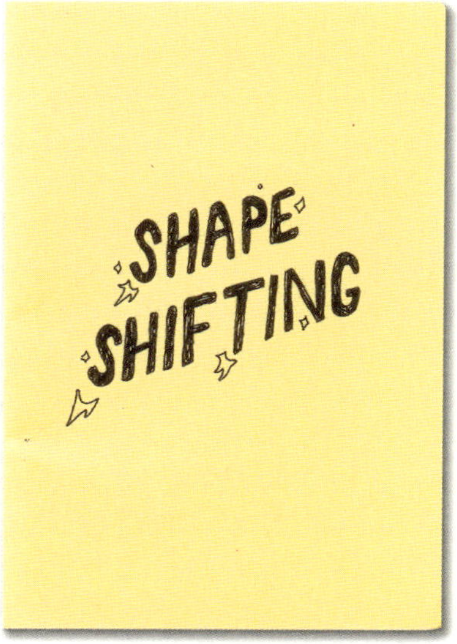

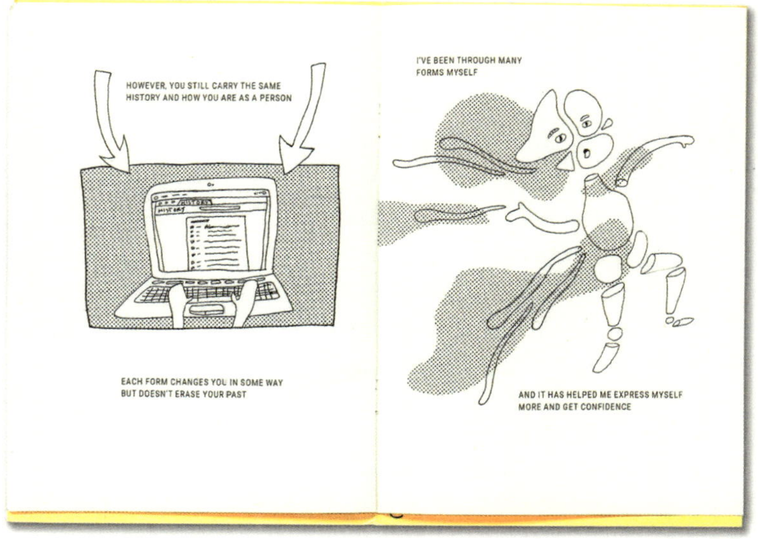

172. *Shape Shifting* cover and spread, Catalina Paz Nuñez Elevancini, A5, 2018. Tāmaki Makaurau Auckland.

Catalina Paz Nuñez Elevancini I'm in the process of making a zine about being a dog, it's called *In Another Life I Was a Dog*. It's my dog habits. Once I publish it people are gonna call me a furry or something, but it'll be fine. Anyway, screw them. It'll be fine. You think what you think, y'know? But yeah, I'm using a similar process to my other zines *Shouts Out to Nature* and *Shape Shifting*: plan the concept for the zine on my phone in my Notes app. I kind of go 'Oh, what's the gist of the zine?' I come up with a working title, which might change. Very similar to a professional design brief: set yourself a brief on your Notes app. Then I start sketching, drawing — not digitally, on paper. I just grab any kind of sketchbook and start sketching and thinking about what kind of style I want to employ . . .

Murtle Chickpea You might just have one silly little story, but you can actually turn it into quite a hilarious little zine. I really like that. Just one thing that happened — it doesn't have to be a novel or a massive blog post — it can be teamed up with some little pictures or silly drawings, and then someone will just read it and go 'Oh my god, I feel exactly the same', and it's just different than a book and it's different than TV and it's different than blogs.

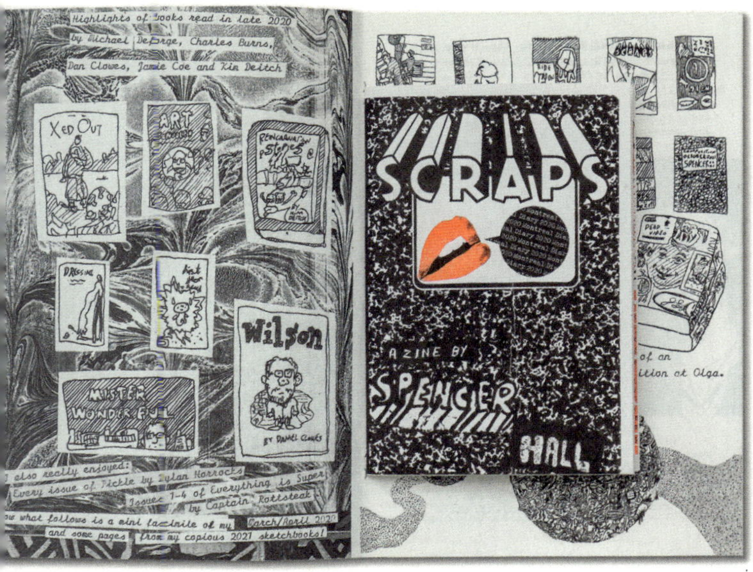

173. *Scraps* #5 cover and spread, Spencer Hall, 180 × 50mm, 2023. Narrm Melbourne.

173

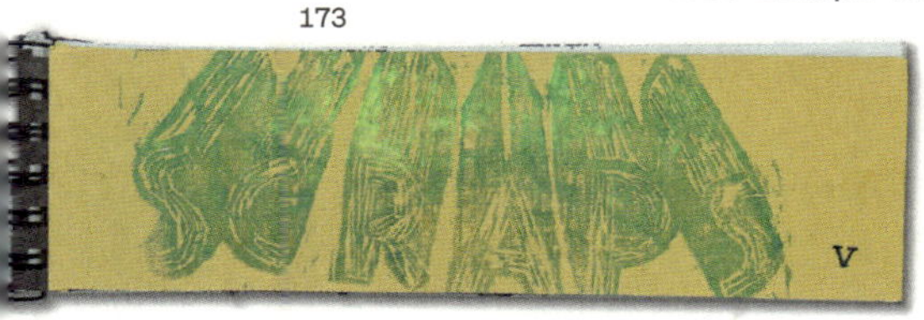

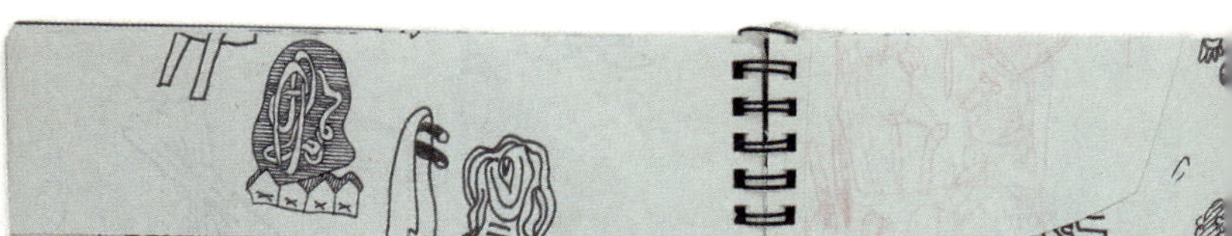

Mieke Montagne I just need to sit down and do it. I made one zine because I just had a spare moment. I was like 'Well, this needs to be a zine because I think it's funny and I have this big hatred for Sandra Bullock and I don't really know why', so, I made a zine unpacking why I hated Sandra Bullock so much. That idea came organically. This one had a title: *I Don't Know Why I Hate Sandra Bullock*. I don't know where ideas come from. I always have ideas for zines that I want to make. I just don't always have the time and energy, but the urge is always there.

Maia-Jeanne Woolkirk I have two strong motivations for organising Whanganui Zinefest: to support people creatively and help bolster this loving community, but also to strongly encourage people not to make cat zines anymore. My first experience of zines was seeing something like *Always Never Fun* and thinking 'This is amazing', and I don't even like punk rock, but I love the aesthetic of that zine. I read every single article. I loved the passion that went into it and the detail and the dedication. I came to that zine quite late, like issue five or six. This was at the Greek Community Centre in Wellington, my first zinefest, and it was so crowded and sweaty, and I was just so impressed by the amazing amount of effort people had put into making these beautiful products.

Liam Goulter I don't fuck with poetry. I don't really like anything that's too cute. Anything that's a fan culture I don't know about, I'm not interested in learning about. I don't care. We made this collaborative cat zine because Lucy Black and I would always joke about the people who made cat zines. I wasn't a cat-zine buyer. I think I'm only ever drawn to things that are weird and horny . . . and lo-fi . . . without feeling contrived . . . and cheap. I'm a cheapskate.

Murtle Chickpea I looked through my collection and thought 'Oh my god, I do a lot of cat zines.' It's really weird because I work with dogs, and I love dogs. I'm a dog person, but you can't do dog stuff in the same way. I've never done a dog zine, just lots of cat zines.

One is called *Good Kitty, Bad Kitty*, and it's just cat collages: the good cats have eyes and I black the bad cats' eyes out with pen, and that's all it is. I remember a woman at zinefest saying 'Oh my god! This is my humour right here!' It's just completely ridiculous. There's nothing deep going on.

174

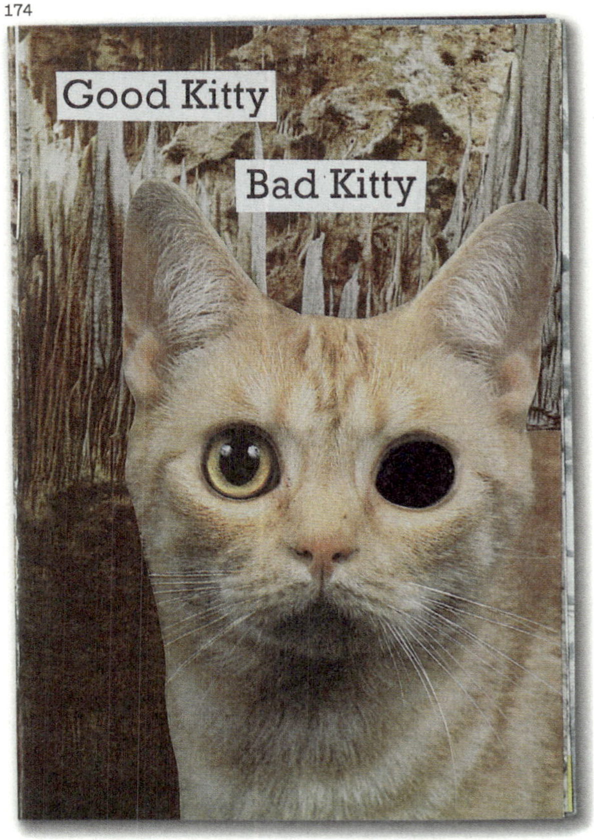

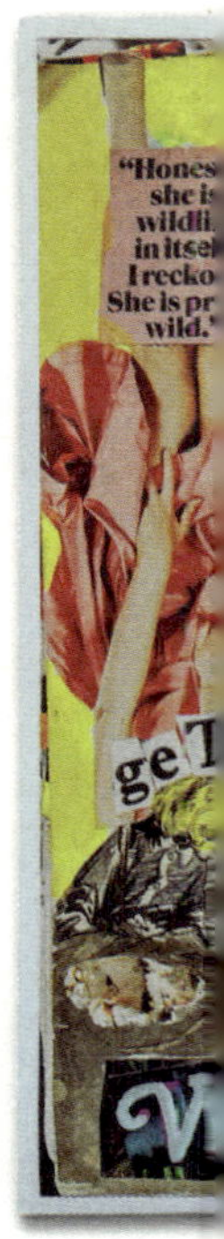

174. *Good Kitty, Bad Kitty*, Murtle Chickpea, A6, 2020. Paetūmōkai Featherston.

Billy Douglas We noticed yesterday one of our favourite things was watching people pick up the *Lickin Wildlife* zine that Victoria had done. You'd just watch their facial expressions change. There were a lot of smiles, but there were also a fair few . . . **Victoria Armstrong** uncomfortable responses as well. **Billy Douglas** Close it, put it back down. **Victoria Armstrong** I love making people uncomfortable, but I also want to sell the work.

Jewelia Howard A lot of my zines are quite silly because I like making people happy and making people laugh. And I like spewing about my special interests. A lot of my zines are like that.

Catalina Paz Nuñez Elevancini I try to work black-and-white if possible, especially if it's just a personal zine — a perzine, a silly zine. I shouldn't run down perzines, but if I'm next to this huge political zine I'm like 'Urgh, imposter syndrome!'

Panty Baggers PB2 It's cathartic, it's utterly cathartic. I love cutting into those high-end glossy magazines of long-legged beauties and fucking them up. But while I'm doing that my jaw drops open . . . even in recent magazines there'll be objectifying images of women and offensive text and I think 'How can you be publishing this shit, still?!' It's so dangerous. I mean, sometimes I look at things and I think 'Fuck. Okay, it's the 1970s; okay, I can forgive you.' Then it's the eighties: 'Ouch, I can forgive you.' And then I'm looking at something and I go 'Jesus Christ, when was that published? 2019?!' and I'm like 'How the fuck are you getting away with that shit?!' **PB1** We actually see it a bit, don't we? **PB3** Sometimes we use the vintage-y retro stuff to point at the more contemporary stuff, because not everybody is seeing how bad it is. But using that vintage stuff and putting it together with the other stuff really does help to clarify that there are still so many problems. **PB1** Today, online, I saw an image of Adele from 2018 next to an image of Adele now, and the caption was 'Look what a bit of self-love does'. I was like 'Ew, what the fuck?' That's today!

A lot of stuff we do is really thoughtless, but some of it is thoughtful. The *Beauty Bible* is more deliberately aimed at these things. We'll rumple up the page and paste this beautiful model and add some giant eyelashes and . . .

175. *Panty Baggers Go Exploring in an Unmanned Spacecraft to Investigate Earth's Dessert on Mars* spread, Panty Baggers collective, 145 × 190mm, 2022. Ōtepoti Dunedin.

176. *Sister Sister O Brother*, Panty Baggers collective, A4, 2022. Ōtepoti Dunedin.

175

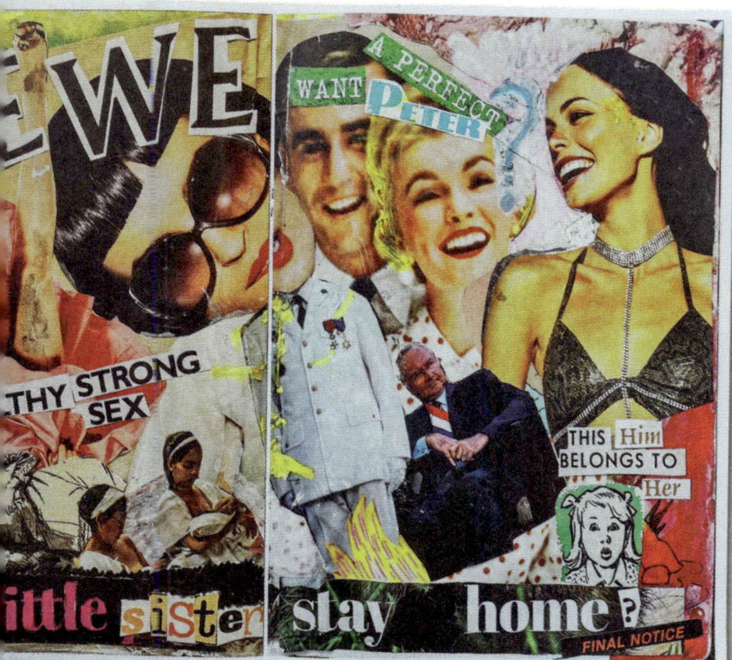

176

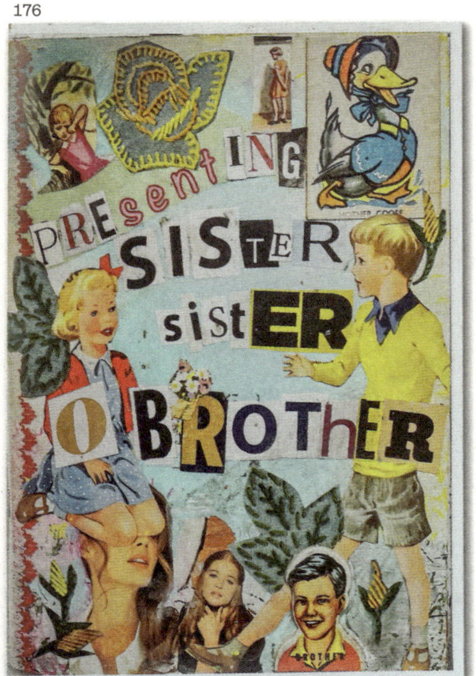

Spencer Hall *DUD: The Dunedin Comic Revue* (Dunedin Comic Collective) were the first comics I put out. It's an anthology. Both issues capitalised on the strong ties between the music and comics communities in Dunedin. The first issue came out with a CD, the second issue with a download. With the first issue we made connections between particular songs and particular comics.

David Tulloch These days there are fewer differences between comics and zines, mainly because comics are having a bit of a bad time, so anywhere you can get in is a good place, like zinefests. Back in the day they were considered very different things, although a lot of the people I knew who contributed to our *Pistake* comic were also contributing to zines and stuff.

177

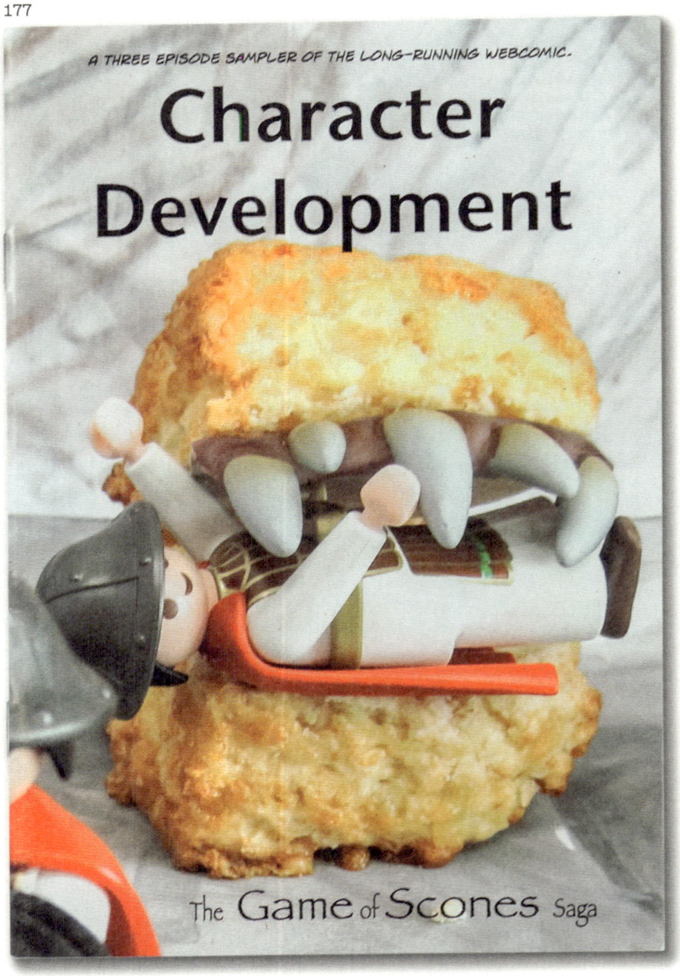

177. *Character Development: The Game of Scones Saga*, David Tulloch, A5, 2016. Te Whanganui-a-Tara Wellington.

178. *Feral Wench* cover and spread, Gini Jory, A6, 2023. Ōtepoti Dunedin.

178

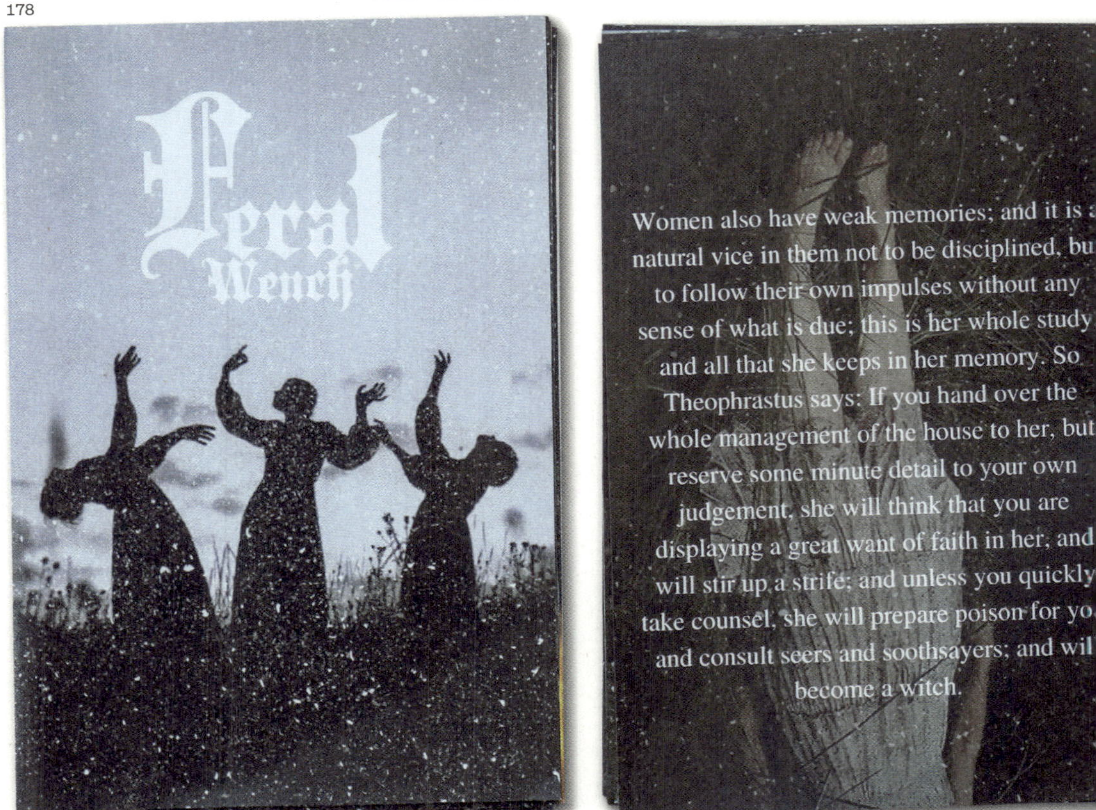

179

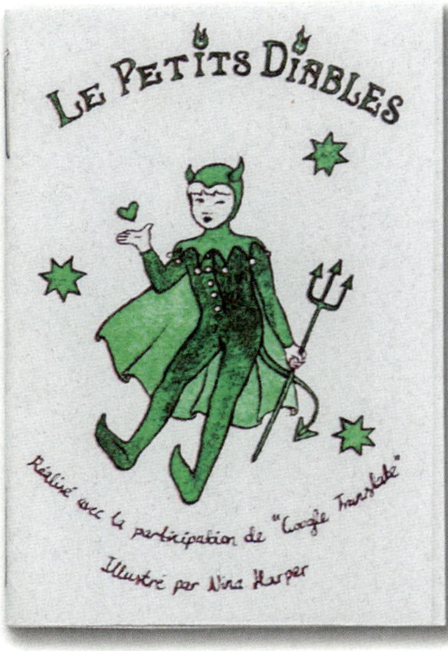

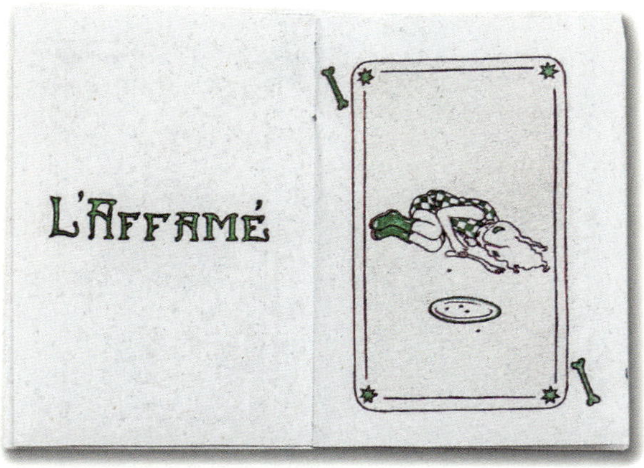

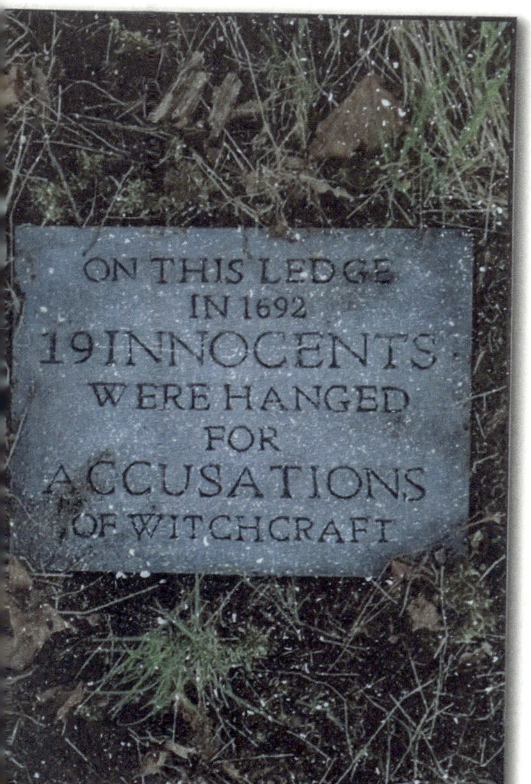

Marijke van Schaardenburg When I'm making my zines I really push myself to be unapologetic, unequivocally queer.

Gini Jory In general, mine are fantasy zines, mostly done in a collage style, with queer undertones. That vaguely covers it. A lot of that *Feral Wench* zine came from the *Malleus Maleficarum*, which was a witch-hunting text from the 1400s, basically an instruction manual on how to identify and legally persecute witches. Quite a bit of that 'They're in league with the devil' stuff came from that book. Witches are really just women with skills in healthcare or women who don't need men, and men didn't like that.

Nina Harper I have always really liked the concept of the weird little girl. I look back on how I was as a kid: people think of little girls as being a certain way, but little girls are actually a lot more morbidly curious and more into witchy stuff and horror stuff, and have the same kind of curiosities that boys are thought to have. My zines are still very stereotypically girly-looking, but with a twist, finding ways to make it a little bit icky and a little bit weird. I like the juxtaposition.

Sam Orchard From what I've seen, comics at zinefests have changed dramatically in the past 10 years. When I started doing them, there was a dip in the very queer stuff and most of *my* comics at that time were like 'I'm trans! I have a little trans flag on my stall, and this is some queer shit right here.' At that time, people would come past and think 'Woah! Don't go near that unless you're gay.' Now you turn up to a zinefest and if you don't have queer shit on your stall it's almost like you're out of step. It's present in a way that it wasn't when I first started doing stuff.

Arwen Miriama Sommer One of my all-time favourites is *We Need More Epsom.* It's satire, obviously. I love it. This is zine-making to me. Just badly Photoshopped pictures of David Seymour saying stupid things. I think it cost me 20 cents.

179. *Le Petits Diables* cover and spread, Nina Harper, A8, 2025. Kirikiriroa Hamilton.

Regan Kupu Stokes For me it's just tika, if you're releasing something on vinyl you have to have a lyrics sheet or something . . . Many bands just do the double-sided: lyrics on one side, band photo on the other, and kei te pai tēnei, that's totally fine by me. In terms of my design experience, I can use Microsoft Paint, that's it. I would much rather just get out a pen and an A4 piece of paper and write the lyrics down and say, 'There you go.' It's just natural to me. I've done a lot of the posters for HOIHOI and stuff. They're posters, but zine-like in terms of being a Vivid marker drawing. It was quite nice to maintain that aesthetic for the lyric zine while also having a more professional-looking record cover. The cover painting is by my son, Tāwhiri. He did a painting at kindy and gave us permission to use it as the cover artwork. I paid $10 for that.

Tim Danko When we first started the group, and to get funding, we had a programme based on my previous teaching experience. I worked at Natcoll[5] teaching digital media stuff, and I had experience running comics workshops with Silent Army back in Melbourne. So I had a set group of skills-based workshops and we tried that at the start. It wasn't a complete disaster, but it just didn't work. We quickly moved to 'We figure out what your process is, and we support your process.' With a lot of autistic guys demand avoidance is a really big feature.

Kenneth Merrick I like a low-pressure approach rather than 'Shit, man, this pen cost 40 bucks, every line's gotta count.' I mean, there's some expensive stuff I've bought where I'm like 'One day I'm gonna use that thing', but I'll never use it, it'll just sit there. I also love paper or surfaces with a bit of a history or some prior marks. It's like 'Okay, I'm not the first person to fuck this up.' I guess it's a weird collaboration with some off-printing or somebody's scribble from workplace notes or whatever.

Spencer Hall I always kept sketchbooks. I kind of wish someone had said 'Why don't you just photocopy these and put them out in the world?'

180

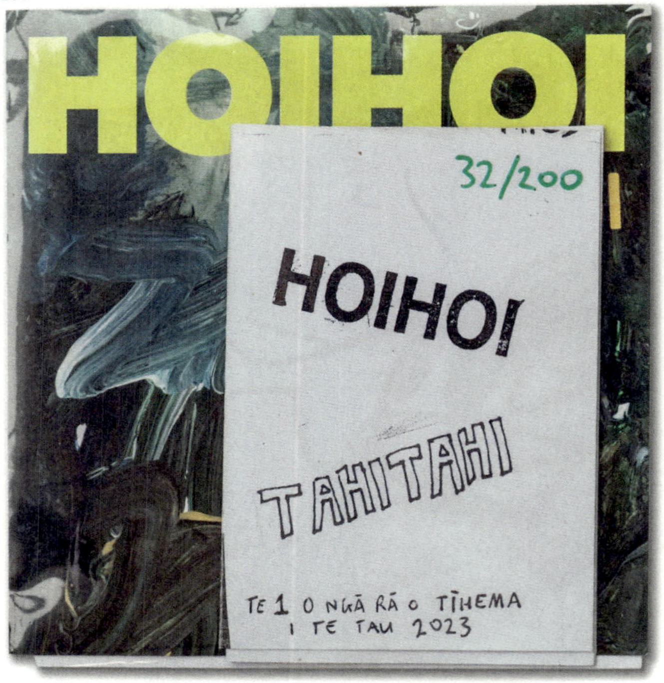

181

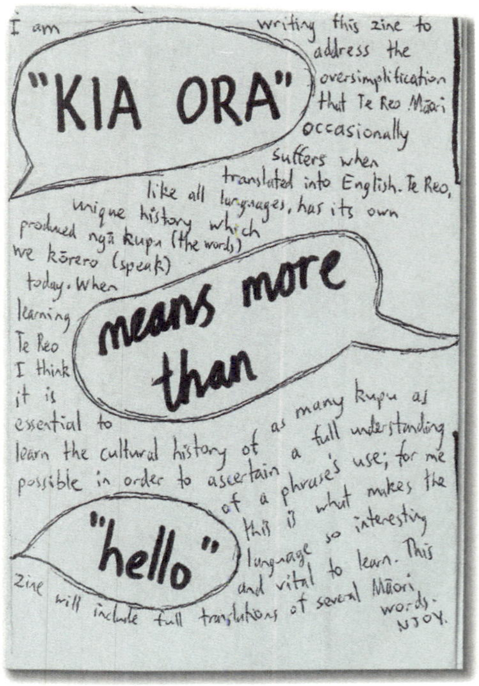

180. *Tahitahi* 7" record and A6 lyric zine *HOIHOI*, Regan Kupu Stokes, 2023. Ōtautahi Christchurch.

181. *'Kia ora' means more than 'hello'*, Regan Kupu Stokes, A7, 2013. Ōtautahi Christchurch.

182. Untitled (*'Sometimes your teenage dreams become your adult nightmares'*) cover and spread, Arwen Miriama Sommer, A5, date unknown. Ōtautahi Christchurch.

Jewelia Howard I made a series of zines about my Tinder dating experiences called *Fuck Boi Diaries* for a while. I painted screenshots of the messages that people would send me. They were pretty feral. I ended up doing three volumes of that before I met and started dating Jonny, my ex. It was A6. Black-and-white. I wrote it out with Micron fineliner and then did a grey water-colour wash over the text boxes and photocopied it. Very lo-fi.

Nina Harper I definitely have to clean up my watercolour illustrations digitally. I eventually want to get a better set-up with a high-quality camera so that I can capture the colours a lot better. That's important to me. If it was something that was going to be more widely published, for example, I'd want them to look how they look in person. That was something I had to figure out when I switched from black-and-white. Scanning black-and-white was a lot easier, and that was one of the motivations for sticking with black-and-white early on. It was easier to scan and compile on the computer, and cheaper to print as well. All of that is stuff that I've had to consider, but it's just so much more interesting to me to have it all in colour and to be able to fully flesh out those scenes and not just have them as outlines. Trying to figure these things out is worth it to me. Moving to the water-colours has completely changed my style.

Arwen Miriama Sommer Bar a couple of titles, my zines have always started their life as digital. I was kind of a techy kid. I know, a Steiner kid who was techy! It was a secret. It was *such* a secret. Everything was hidden under my bed. It's like the more you're not allowed something, the more you want to have it, which is why I now own every single gaming console because I was not allowed computer games. Now I'm like 'It's gaming time!'

So, anyway, I started out printing from Google Docs. I loved formatting the text and then figuring out how to print as a booklet, doing that duplex printing. I still print all my stuff at home rather than going into Warehouse Stationery or some-thing because I just hate printing. It's so frustrating, but I also love it. It's like that battle of a million test prints that don't work, but once you get it right it's so satisfying. It's also really expensive.

Panty Baggers PB2 I come from a sculpture-ceramics background but got made to teach graphic design. I'm from Christchurch and I moved down to Dunedin and did my teacher training here. The second school I got posted at was King's [in Dunedin] — the school I teach at now — and at the end of the posting the HoD said 'Hey, there's a job teaching design', and I said 'I can't even turn a computer on. I'm not teaching design.' Then, during the summer holidays, he came around to my flat, lugged this huge desktop computer up the stairs and said, 'Learn how to use Photoshop.' **PB1** Now look at you.

182

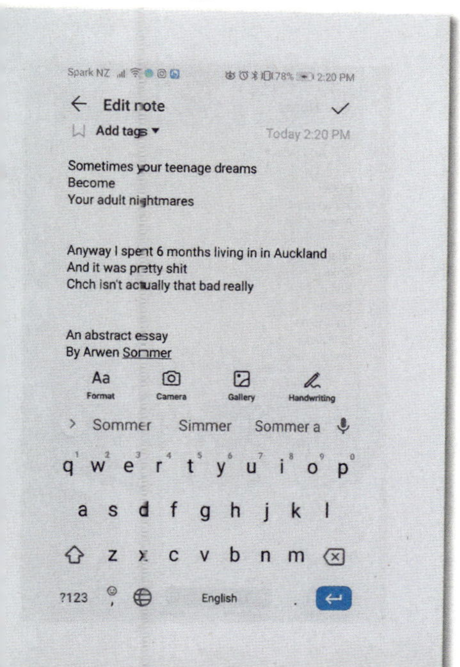

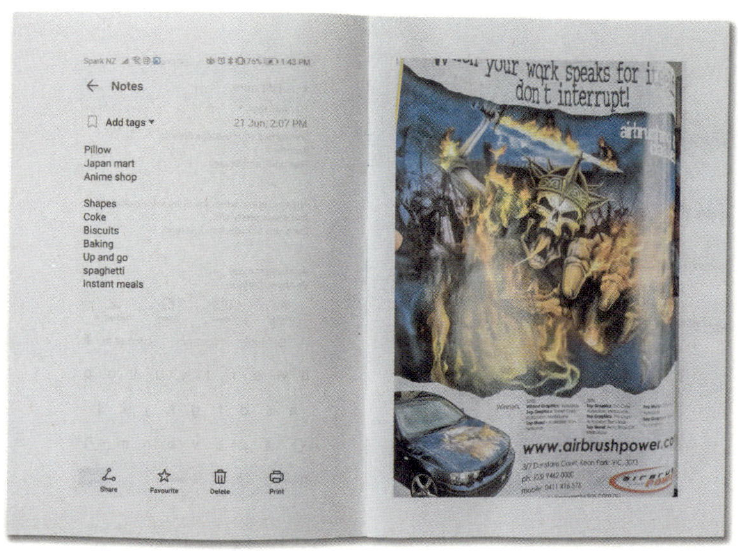

183

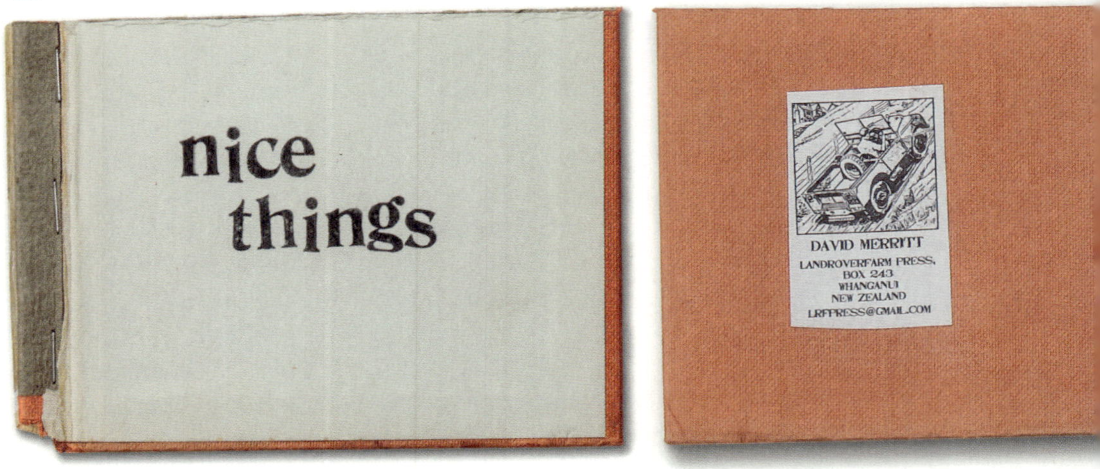

Helen Yeung I've released one zine since arriving in Guåhan. It's called *Agu'ot*, a Chamorro word that means 'to hold each other'. It's basically a queer zine, working with different community members, the kind of thing I've done in Auckland already. It came together really beautifully, but sadly it would cost me about $500–$600 just to print about 40 copies over here, so I'm planning to put it online instead at some point. People submitted their colourful paintings and collages, and I just didn't have it in me to print cheaper black-and-white.

We migrated our website to Squarespace recently and I wanted to upload the zine there as a free download, but it wouldn't support the file size so I'm just trying to find another way to make it accessible for people.

Maia-Jeanne Woolkirk Well, the only hard-and-fast rule is that you've got to photocopy it at work. Do not pay for photocopying.

David Merritt I thought foolishly that I could make big visual art prints of my work on A1 pieces of paper and sell them in galleries for thousands of dollars. That's what I thought. That's how stupid I was when I started, because clearly that's just a bad business model. It's wrong. By the time you've laboriously printed out your big A1 copy of a poem and assembled 23 of them to put into a gallery and you've priced them at $1200 each or whatever, you're not making any money. You've spent weeks of your life laboriously hand-stamping out something, and the dealer gallery's gonna take 45 per cent of the income off the ticket price anyway.

It didn't sour me, it just made me rethink: don't make expensive one-offs, make them cheap, lots of them, and that's what happened. I just started to make $5 objects rather than a $5000 object. I thought: this is bullshit, I'm not a visual artist, I'm a writer and a poet and a publisher and that's it. My job is to make things, and to make them as efficiently and as cheaply as I can. I mean, fuck, I was only copying the ideas of Colin McCahon and Ralph Hōtere once they started to put the words of poets into their paintings — and this is in the fifties and sixties — so, nothing new there. I would've just been aping what was going on before.

183. *nice things*, David Merritt, 100 × 145mm (A3 when unfolded), date unknown. Ōtepoti Dunedin.

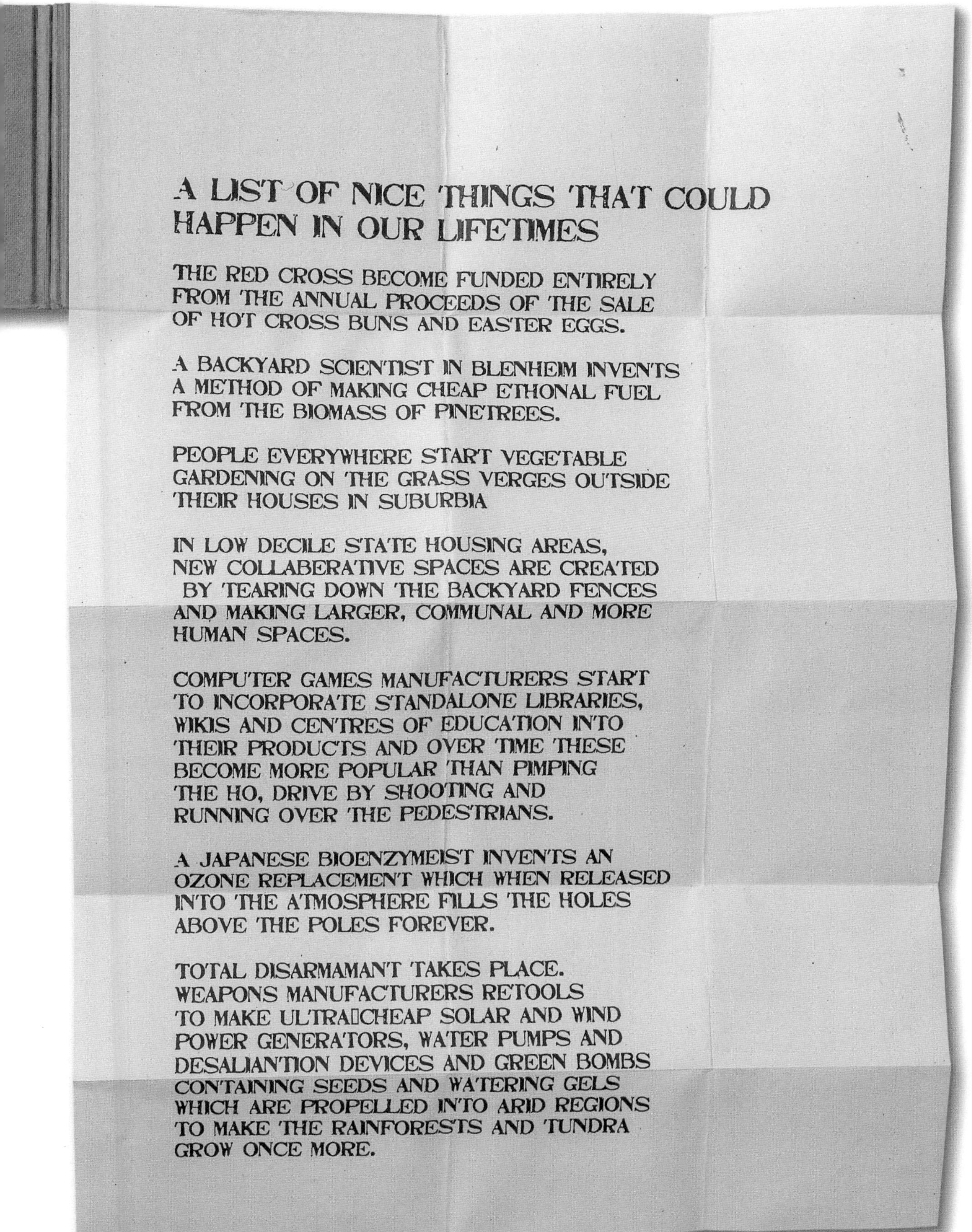

A LIST OF NICE THINGS THAT COULD HAPPEN IN OUR LIFETIMES

THE RED CROSS BECOME FUNDED ENTIRELY FROM THE ANNUAL PROCEEDS OF THE SALE OF HOT CROSS BUNS AND EASTER EGGS.

A BACKYARD SCIENTIST IN BLENHEIM INVENTS A METHOD OF MAKING CHEAP ETHONAL FUEL FROM THE BIOMASS OF PINETREES.

PEOPLE EVERYWHERE START VEGETABLE GARDENING ON THE GRASS VERGES OUTSIDE THEIR HOUSES IN SUBURBIA

IN LOW DECILE STATE HOUSING AREAS, NEW COLLABERATIVE SPACES ARE CREATED BY TEARING DOWN THE BACKYARD FENCES AND MAKING LARGER, COMMUNAL AND MORE HUMAN SPACES.

COMPUTER GAMES MANUFACTURERS START TO INCORPORATE STANDALONE LIBRARIES, WIKIS AND CENTRES OF EDUCATION INTO THEIR PRODUCTS AND OVER TIME THESE BECOME MORE POPULAR THAN PIMPING THE HO, DRIVE BY SHOOTING AND RUNNING OVER THE PEDESTRIANS.

A JAPANESE BIOENZYMEIST INVENTS AN OZONE REPLACEMENT WHICH WHEN RELEASED INTO THE ATMOSPHERE FILLS THE HOLES ABOVE THE POLES FOREVER.

TOTAL DISARMAMANT TAKES PLACE. WEAPONS MANUFACTURERS RETOOLS TO MAKE ULTRA□CHEAP SOLAR AND WIND POWER GENERATORS, WATER PUMPS AND DESALIANTION DEVICES AND GREEN BOMBS CONTAINING SEEDS AND WATERING GELS WHICH ARE PROPELLED INTO ARID REGIONS TO MAKE THE RAINFORESTS AND TUNDRA GROW ONCE MORE.

184

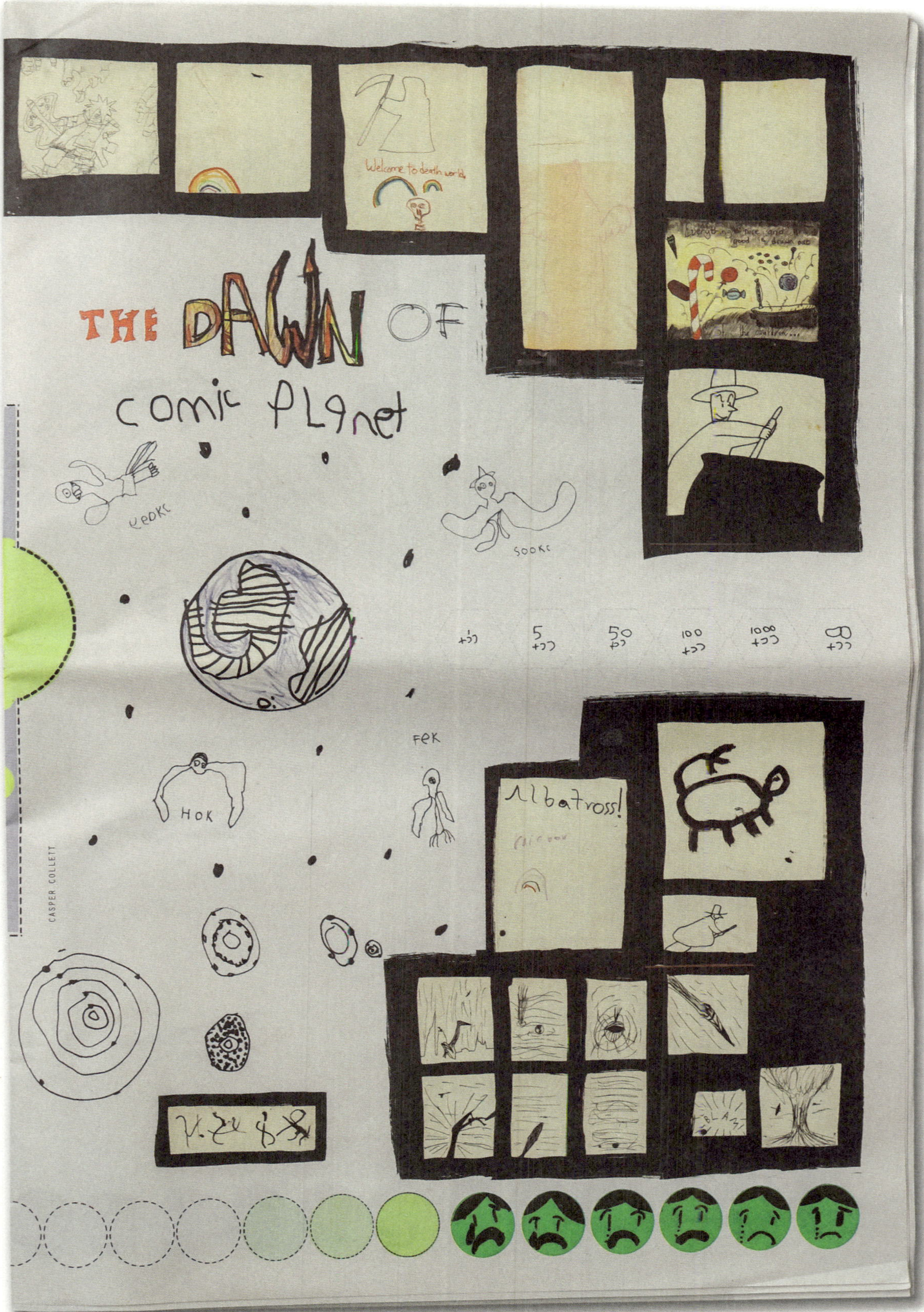

184. *The Dawn of Comic Planet*, Māpura Studios comic group TV Competition: FutureFutureFuture, A2, 2019. Tāmaki Makaurau Auckland.

Tim Danko The printing is my passion project. I really want to put this out, and I get a lot of pleasure out of it. Some of the people I work with have very specific ideas about what they want and others aren't so engaged. For example, Heidi came into the South Auckland group for about five years. Came in, used the session to sit and draw a page for her comic. Made this comic that's like however many pages long. After about three years, completes the final drawing and announces, 'I've finished the comic', and I said 'Okay'. I'm all emotional and she's like [assumes casual tone] 'Okay, I'll see you next week.' We printed it with her input about scale, paper, et cetera.

Wherever possible I try to engage the artists in those formal printing and production decisions. But for some of the artists it's a fluid process; I'll make a test version, give it to the artist, see how they react, what they react to.

Matthew, who's essentially non-verbal, and just a great artist in general, has these sketchbooks that are just . . . All I do is reproduce the sketchbook page-for-page. When he attended a comic group at the start, he'd do this outline of a drawing and then totally black it in, which was awesome. Stefan Neville asked him 'Did you not like the drawing?' and he'd say 'Oh, no. It's too noisy.' So there are all these different relationships to material.

Matthew would draw, and then the drawing would bleed through the page to the second drawing. Similarly, when he's painting, it's all layered up. When he came to the comic group, the work went horizontal, the layers just spread out across the table. I presented him with a draft print of his work and he just started drawing on top of that. So, that's like 'Wow.' That's an editorial interaction. Just use it as another form of engagement to keep going.

Arwen Miriama Sommer It kind of came out of laziness, but I feel like that's where a lot of good things come from. With that Auckland one, I had always gone into my Google Docs or my Notes app, typed things up painstakingly, done all that formatting that I thought looked really nice, always taking quite a long time. Then I had my battle with the printer. I just had no time, and I thought, just screenshot it — and it looked so good!

My favourite thing about that is you've got all the metadata. You could see some had been written at like 2 a.m., and others at some random time in the afternoon. Some you could see my phone had almost no battery . . . I feel like that's all really telling information. There's something about a four-line poem on its own that's a bit weird, but there's something *so* different when you can tell that that same poem was written at 3 a.m. with my phone on 6 per cent battery. It makes it a totally different poem. You can see my wifi desperately hanging on in the corner because I'm so far away from the router. I just find that really fun.

Panty Baggers PB1 Pagination fucks me off. That's the trickiest thing, especially as we have bits that fold out and we add pages and we have all these— **PB2** I end up doing most of it. **PB1** Because she can do computer work. **PB3** We've worked out a system now, but we have to have the right amount of pages in a book or it won't zine. **PB1** So sometimes we leave pages of the book out of the zine. We might look through and go, well, we can drop that page. **PB3** We've only just got to that point since the last zinefest, figuring out that we have to drop pages to make them easy enough to print and construct. Sarah can then set it up. Sarah's our digital design guru if you didn't get that already. **PB2** Yes, after the lugging of the desktop computer, I accosted the boy up the road who was disgusting but knew how to use Photoshop. I used my womanly ways to get him to teach me. Then he turned up one night with his shirt unbuttoned down to here [gestures] and a bottle of wine. 'Hi.' I just said, 'I'm about to go out, sorry. Can't do Photoshop lessons tonight.'

Arwen Miriama Sommer At the libraries we have a resource that is a zine showing you how to make a zine. One of my friends Alisha made it a couple of years ago. It's fantastic. It's a mini-zine, one of the ones where you fold, fold, fold, do the little cut, and as long as you fold it back the right way, you're good to go. You unfold it and print it out as a flat A4, then practise *on* the sheet of instructions. Then you take it home and you have a zine about how to make a zine. It's a genius way of doing it. Half my work's already done as soon as I have that resource.

Then I bring out a bunch of collage things, like withdrawn books and magazines to cut up. One thing I've found is that you've got to de-spine the books *before* people turn up to the workshop. As a library assistant, I'm very immune to just chopping books up. Members of the general public do not like to see that. It's sacrilege. I can just rip a book out of its spine without thinking about it. I was running late to a workshop once and did that in front of a bunch of teenagers and they were not happy about it. They were like [mimics distressed voice], 'Can I take it home and glue it back together?' I'm like 'No, we're chopping this up for collage'.

185

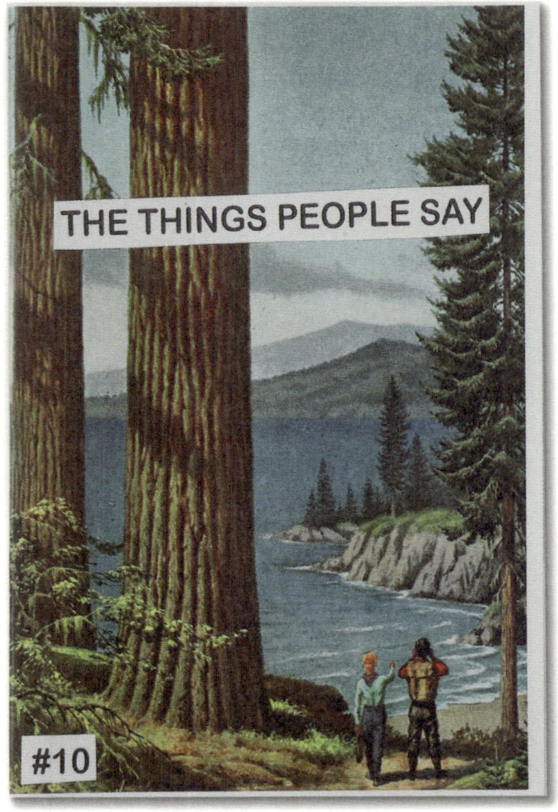

185. *The Things People Say* #10 cover and spread, Murtle Chickpea, A5, 2023. Paetūmōkai Featherston.

186

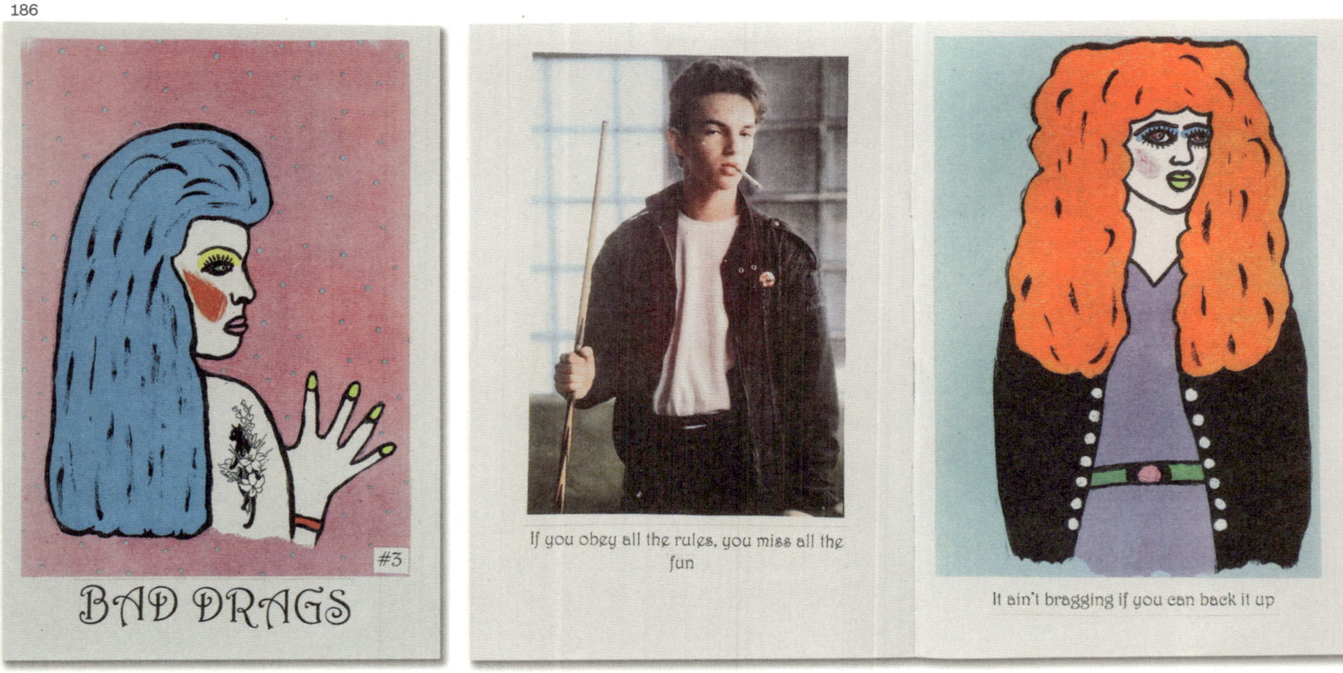

186. *Bad Drags* cover and spread, Murtle Chickpea, A5, 2022. Paetūmōkai Featherston.

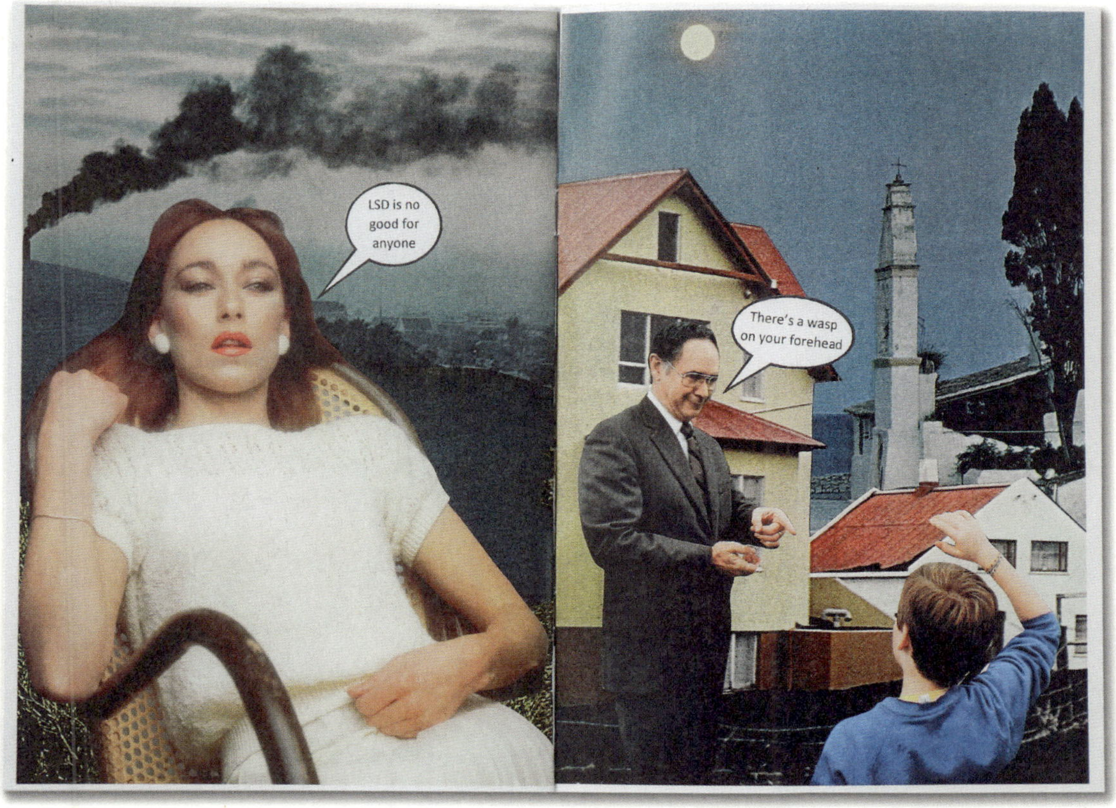

Murtle Chickpea I did a tour from Featherston to Gisborne through Penny Griffin, the librarian in Featherston. She organised a zine workshop tour for the school holidays. That was a massive learning curve in terms of what people think zines are, how libraries respond to them, and how kids respond to them depending on how the libraries set up a space for you to work in. Sometimes there was a tarp on a floor, and I'd think 'Well, that's fucked. Kids aren't gonna respond. They're just gonna be messy and crazy on the floor', but other libraries set up a proper space with scissors and glue, with chairs for everyone, and they'd introduce you and they'd do it properly.

Tim Danko I get the occasional neurotypical person coming along to do comics. Generally, the Friday group at Papakura is a bit quiet and introverted. It's not totally autistic, in that we have participants from [disability support service] Real World Living who have various other conditions. It's inclusive but we cater to the neurodiverse first, so I say that at the start; the programme's set up for that. I'm happy to work with others, but this is our primary focus because there's not that many spaces out there supporting autistic and neurodiverse artists, so that comes first. But I really admire the neurotypical guys — the allistic guys who stick it out. A couple do that, but some sessions, like the Wednesday afternoon main comic group, are quite intense. They challenge people's ideas about behaviour and boundaries. I might have made it sound difficult, but it is a really joyful environment. When it clicks it's amazing.

Catalina Paz Nuñez Elevancini I believe a lot of first-time Zinefest stallholders come from the local universities like AUT and Elam at Auckland University. They want to make these nicely crafted pieces of ephemera, they know how to bind, and they love their paper, y'know? It's just a way for them to experiment with the craft and with high-quality print art. There's also a lot more digital artists these days, so things are really looking quite polished. I feel like the rougher zines still exist, it's just really hard to find them in the sea of crafters and small print presses.

David Merritt Perhaps Auckland is more polished with more graduates who have come out of graphic design schools, etc. Their work is very polished and stuff but, nah, it's the same people up and down the country . . . various people in various stages of career development.

David Tulloch There's so many people at Armageddon. There's so many people going past, and so many will come up to you and look at what you're selling and then immediately walk away. You feel like you don't belong. The comics artists have discussed this over the years. Part of the problem is it's New Zealand comics and most of the people are there for the overseas content. In some ways we almost don't belong, but William [Geradts] the organiser wants us there because that's how it all started. As the New Zealand comics group, we don't have to pay for our booth.

Beth Dawson Nowadays 'zines' is the umbrella term that indie comics find themselves under. Even 10 years ago, I would've been surprised that that was gonna happen. Comics has an entire industry attached, so maybe it's nicer that they're zines now. It's nicer to put your comics in with zines and in with zine culture than in with the whole mainstream publishing world.

David Tulloch Armageddon feels more like plastic swords and Funko dolls now. It is a bit more corporate than it used to be, and the booths are so expensive. A lot of the artists I know no longer have individual booths there because they can't afford to. They just don't make enough money to cover it.

187. *Masks* cover and spread, Ash Spittal, A5, 2014. Tāmaki Makaurau Auckland.

188. *gender: a work in progress*, Jewelia Howard, A6, 2023. Te Whanganui-a-Tara Wellington.

189. *FAG/FREAKS/REBELS/GEEKS* front and back covers and spread, with complimentary glitter, Ash Spittal, 150 x 150mm, 2015. Tāmaki Makaurau Auckland.

187

188

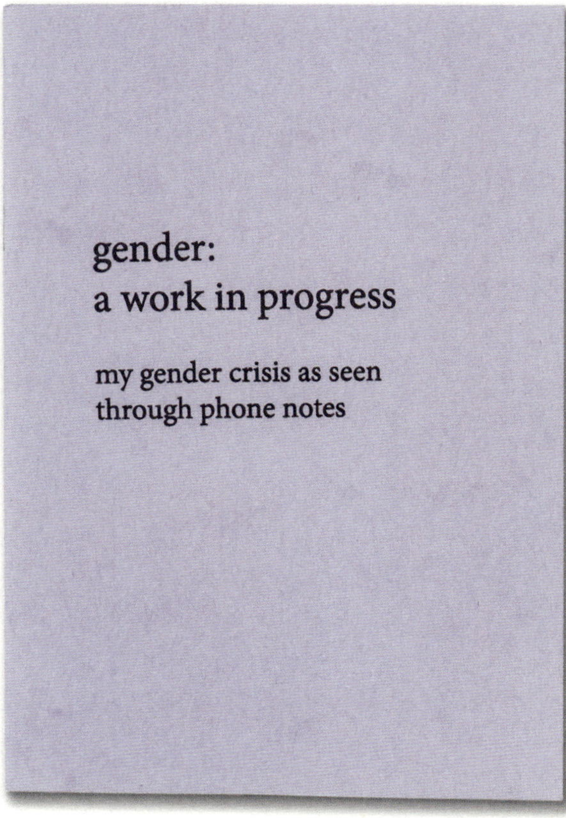

Jewelia Howard I made a zine out of the 3 a.m. phone notes from when I was having a gender crisis. I'd just lie there. I couldn't sleep, just feeling like I wasn't the person I should be and writing from that. It feels like my skin is being torn off every time someone reads that zine in front of me, but people will buy it and they'll say 'This is so real. I understand this feeling.' That's the most affirming thing.

Sometimes people pick it up and I'll think 'Don't make eye contact with me after reading that, please. I'll throw up.' At the market I did last weekend, a mum bought it for her trans kid who was there with her. That makes me feel a lot better about being so vulnerable with that one. In the past year or so I've gotten a lot better at being really vulnerable in my zines, just opening up and being 'Hey, this is all my messy bullshit.'

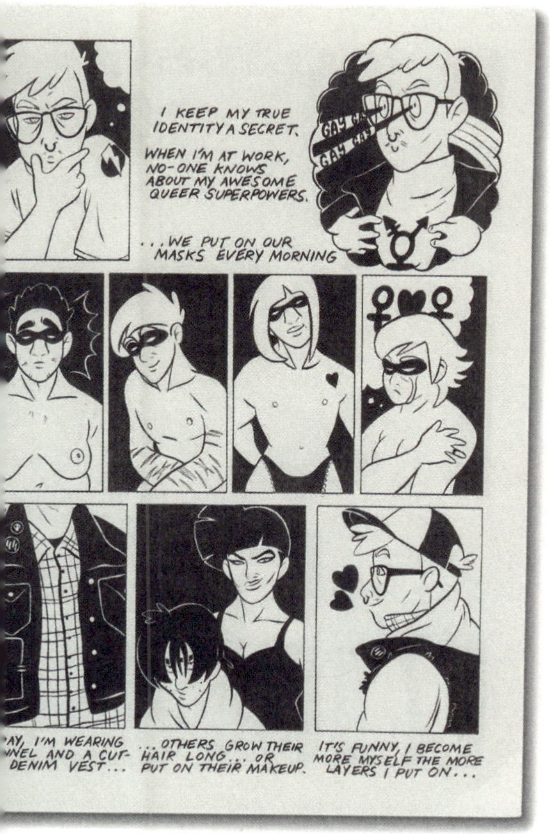

189

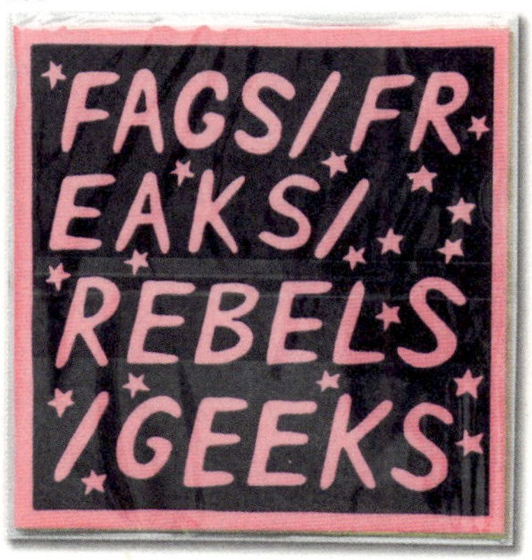

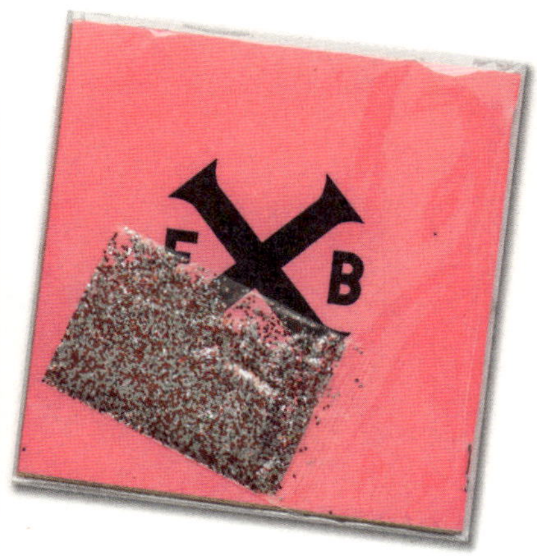

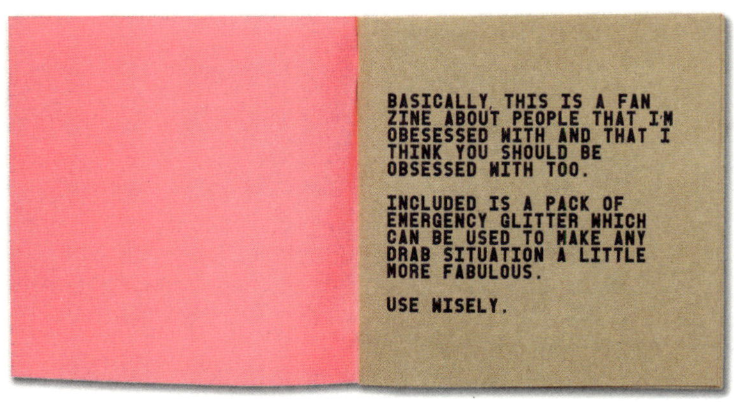

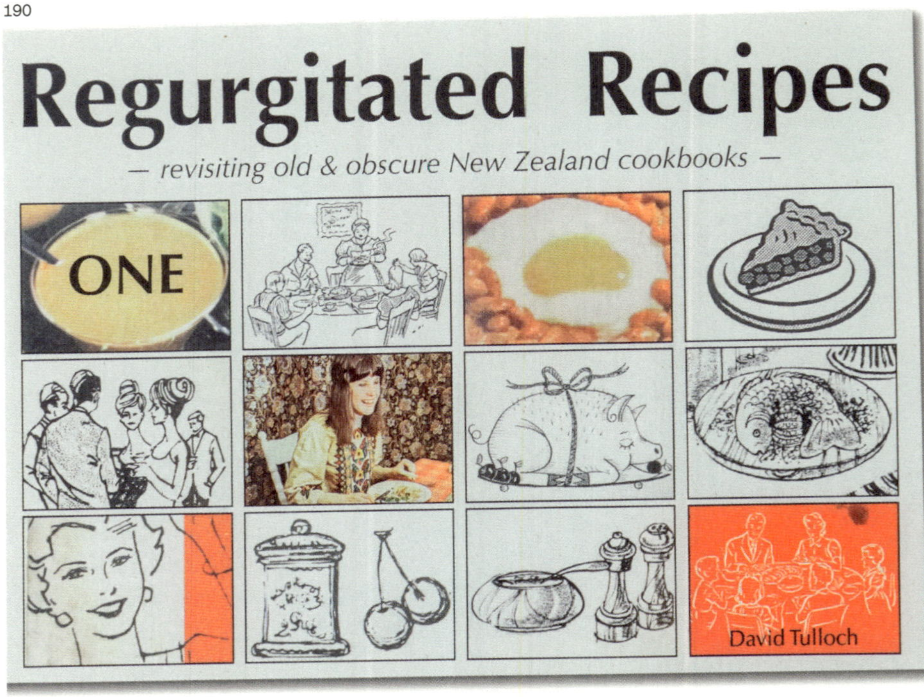

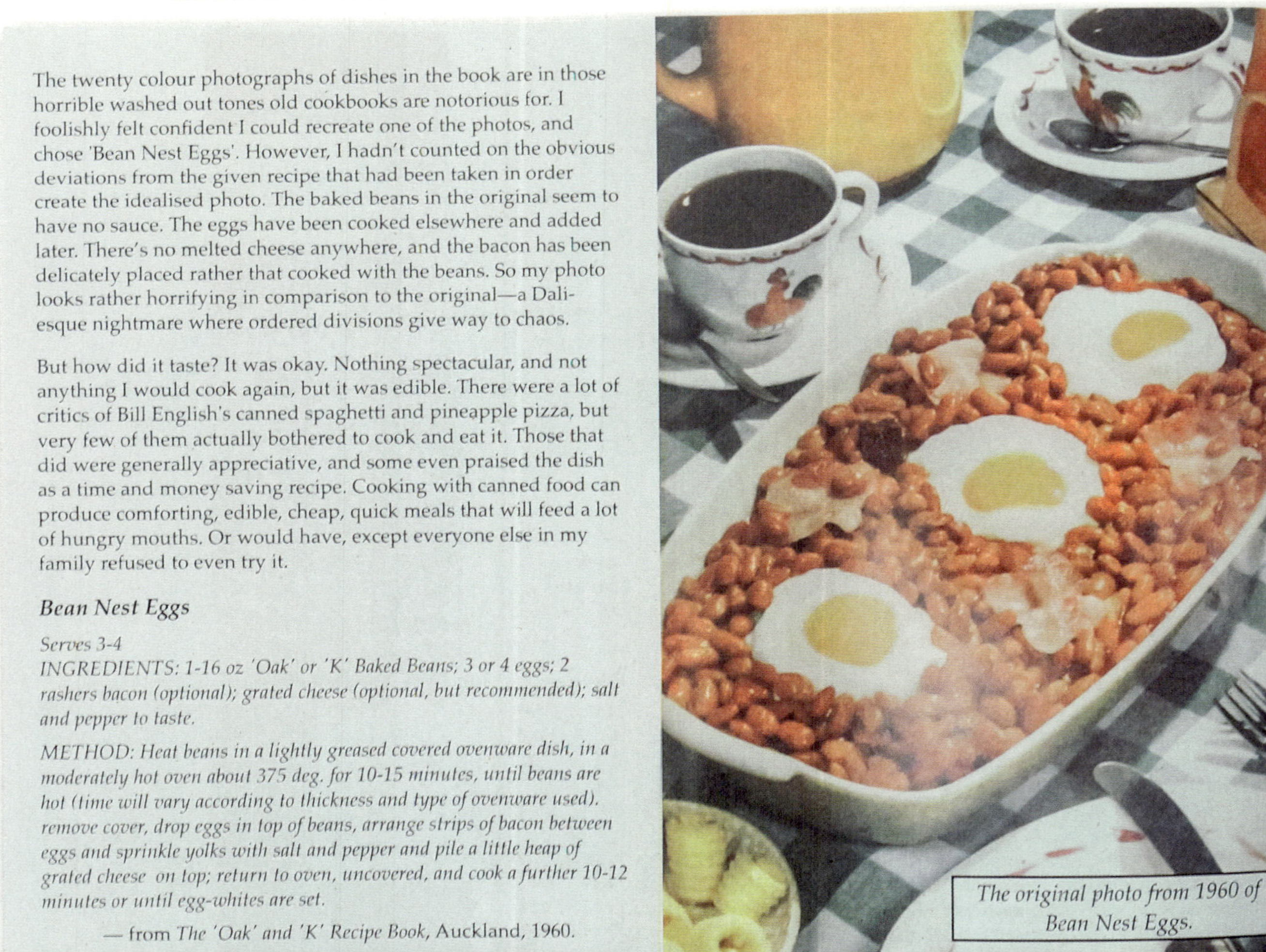

The twenty colour photographs of dishes in the book are in those horrible washed out tones old cookbooks are notorious for. I foolishly felt confident I could recreate one of the photos, and chose 'Bean Nest Eggs'. However, I hadn't counted on the obvious deviations from the given recipe that had been taken in order create the idealised photo. The baked beans in the original seem to have no sauce. The eggs have been cooked elsewhere and added later. There's no melted cheese anywhere, and the bacon has been delicately placed rather that cooked with the beans. So my photo looks rather horrifying in comparison to the original—a Dali-esque nightmare where ordered divisions give way to chaos.

But how did it taste? It was okay. Nothing spectacular, and not anything I would cook again, but it was edible. There were a lot of critics of Bill English's canned spaghetti and pineapple pizza, but very few of them actually bothered to cook and eat it. Those that did were generally appreciative, and some even praised the dish as a time and money saving recipe. Cooking with canned food can produce comforting, edible, cheap, quick meals that will feed a lot of hungry mouths. Or would have, except everyone else in my family refused to even try it.

Bean Nest Eggs

Serves 3-4
INGREDIENTS: 1-16 oz 'Oak' or 'K' Baked Beans; 3 or 4 eggs; 2 rashers bacon (optional); grated cheese (optional, but recommended); salt and pepper to taste.

METHOD: Heat beans in a lightly greased covered ovenware dish, in a moderately hot oven about 375 deg. for 10-15 minutes, until beans are hot (time will vary according to thickness and type of ovenware used). remove cover, drop eggs in top of beans, arrange strips of bacon between eggs and sprinkle yolks with salt and pepper and pile a little heap of grated cheese on top; return to oven, uncovered, and cook a further 10-12 minutes or until egg-whites are set.

— from *The 'Oak' and 'K' Recipe Book*, Auckland, 1960.

The original photo from 1960 of Bean Nest Eggs.

190. *Regurgitated Recipes* cover and spread, David Tulloch, 210 × 150mm, 2021. Te Whanganui-a-Tara Wellington.

191

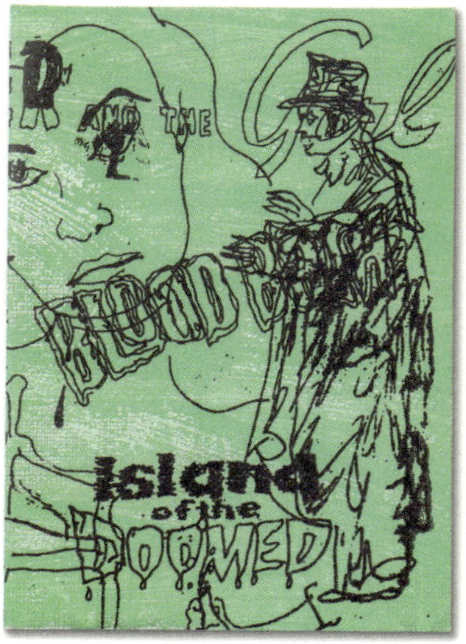

192

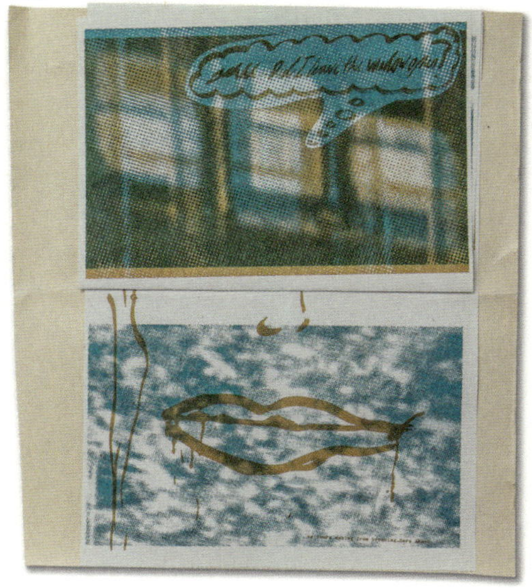

191. *The Girl & the Monster*, Ducklingmonster aka Beth Dawson, 175 x 250mm, 2022. Tāmaki Makaurau Auckland.
192. *City Rose, City Rise*, Ducklingmonster aka Beth Dawson, 270 × 150mm, 2021. Tāmaki Makaurau Auckland.

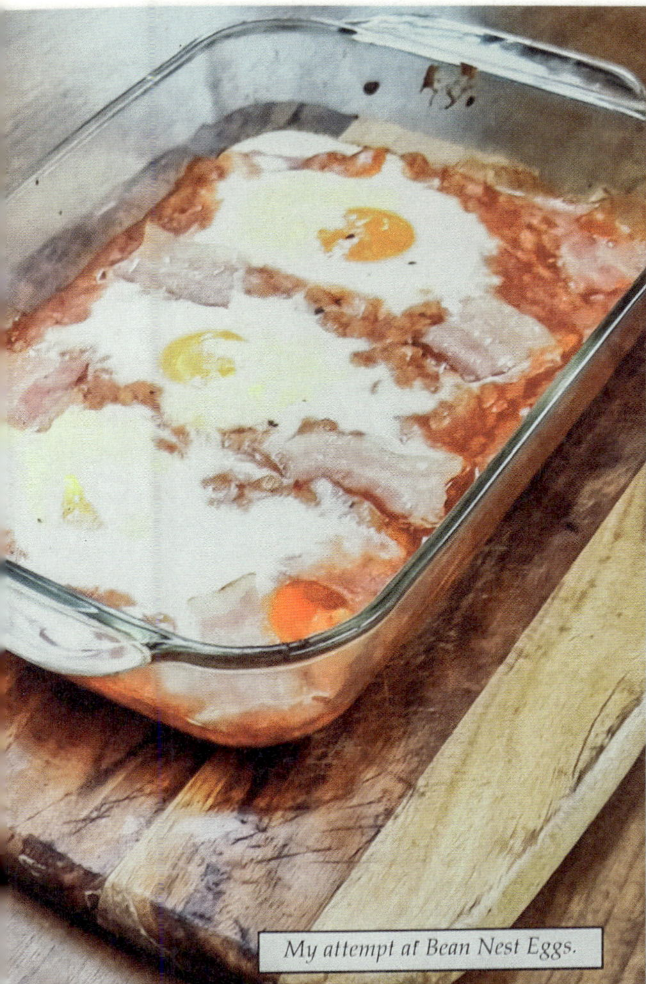

My attempt at Bean Nest Eggs.

"Greys Are Great" Recipes, Volume 2

Grey Power, Christchurch, NZ, unknown date and price

The scariest thing about this Grey Power recipe booklet is that there must be a Volume 1 out there as well. It's a recipe book that knows its audience, of that there is no doubt. It contains recipes by women over fifty, to be cooked by women over fifty, and eaten by those woman and their over-50s husbands, most likely in front of the TV One News.

All-in-all it's not a terrible recipe book. There's several nice, healthy dishes in the first few pages alone. The "Healthy Eating" section has a tasty looking *Carrot and Orange Soup* that uses actual oranges, and a *Stir Fry Fish and Vegetables* recipe that even suggests adding a pinch of "5 spice powder (optional)". You could question just how heathy the next recipe in the section is, *Spiced Meat Balls*, since it's basically just mince served on rice, but at least they're trying. Oddly enough, the exact **same** *Spiced Meat Balls* recipe turns up again just a couple of pages on. They really want you to make those meat balls.

The soup section is a little daring. It contains a *Cream of Kumara and Coconut Soup* for those who enjoy "a very tropical touch". *Watercress or Sorrel Soup* is certainly not your standard out of a can fare. There's also a *Vichyssoise*, to be served chilled, of course, and *Soupe a l'Oigmon*, which is French Onion Soup to most of us. The French-ness continues with *Pistou*, or pesto soup, and something calling itself *Potage Creme d'Onge*, which is a pearl barley based soup with chicken stock, celery and cream, but no onion (*d'onge*) is involved. It does not resemble any specific French cuisine dish I'm aware of, but still seems like a hearty meal in a peasant-style.

essa may ranapiri A friend's grandmother — a very conservative Christian woman — read one of my saucier poems about Adam and Eve. It was just real awkward, it was like her trying to be generous, but you could tell that she was a bit troubled by it. That was mostly harmless, but it can be 'This is revealing a lot about who I am and what I believe about the world', and not always in ways that are accessible or friendly. So you're left thinking 'What is this person thinking?' as they're going through the zine. That's why I like it when people laugh. It's like 'Oh, okay, there's something there that's resonated.'

Kenneth Merrick That barrier to entry into galleries, that sort of façade, can be quite intimidating to some people. I really enjoy the zero-barrier to entry to zines and that community, and the kind of face-to-face interaction you get through tabling at a zinefest. I really enjoy that sort of thing. Whenever possible I try to squash the costs. Galleries can be quite expensive, though I guess there's lots of types of galleries now. Then there's the perception of the function of the gallery and who's allowed in, who's not allowed in. Ultimately, anybody could just walk into a gallery if they wanted to.

193

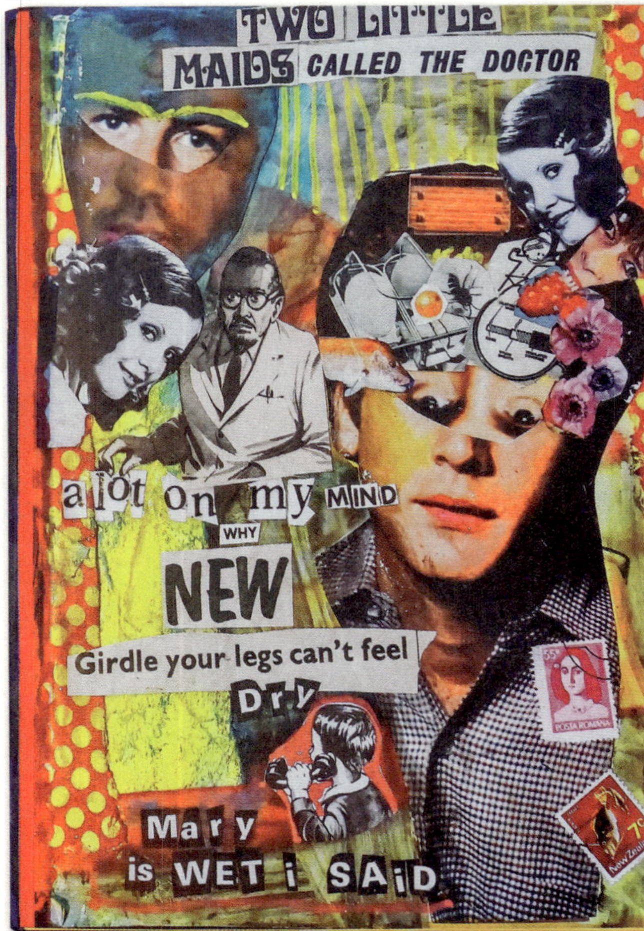

194

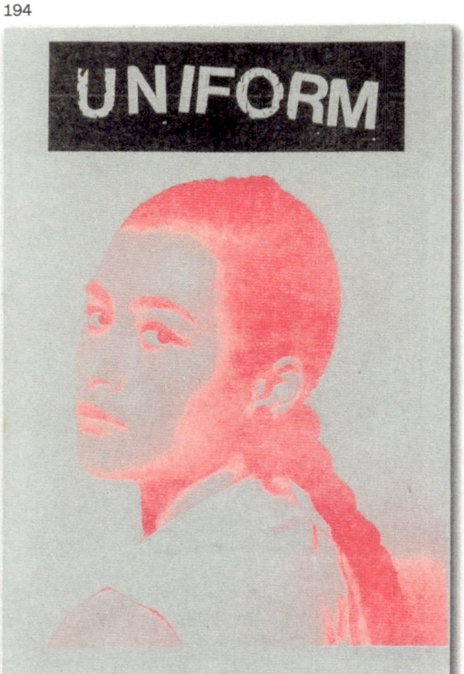

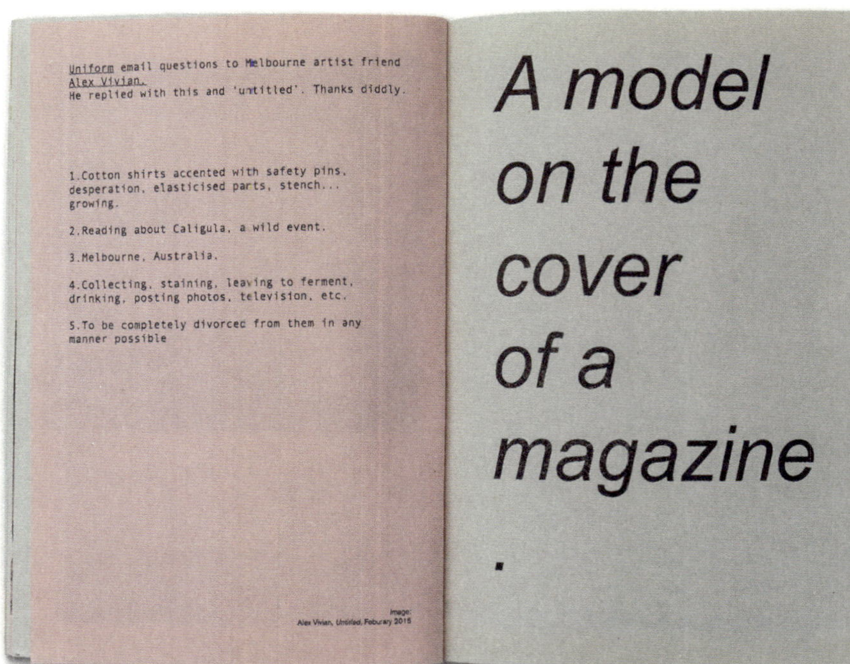

Uniform email questions to Melbourne artist friend Alex Vivian.
He replied with this and 'untitled'. Thanks diddly.

1.Cotton shirts accented with safety pins, desperation, elasticised parts, stench... growing.

2.Reading about Caligula, a wild event.

3.Melbourne, Australia.

4.Collecting, staining, leaving to ferment, drinking, posting photos, television, etc.

5.To be completely divorced from them in any manner possible

Image:
Alex Vivian, Untitled, Feburary 2015

A model on the cover of a magazine .

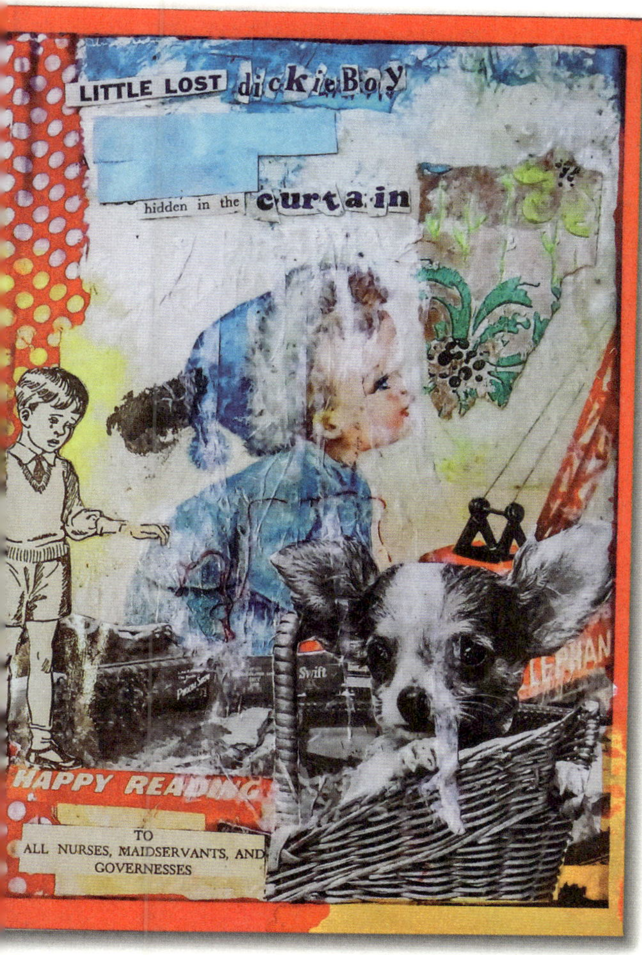

Panty Baggers PB1 We really enjoyed Ōtautahi Zinefest. It was so friendly and well organised. **PB2** We really liked the energy. We felt pumped-up about getting there in terms of being outsiders, driving all that way, and then it was just a really cool vibe. We felt very included, which is great because we almost feel like outsiders within the Dunedin scene sometimes because of our age. I'm not talking for you, Sapph, but that's how I feel, and I know that's how Pru often feels — there's that 'judging a book by its cover'. Last year we did this little experiment. We weren't selling very many zines, and so Anna and I took off and went and sat in the park, and said to my daughter Emi: 'Hey, why don't you just look after the stall for a while?' We weren't getting many sales, but in the half-hour she was there she sold more zines than we did the rest of the day. It's bullshit to me. It's bullshit. It's like okay, you're a punk: you were doing these things in the eighties and you still want to do these things when you're 50 . . . **PB1** I mean, if we don't do it, that internalised ageism becomes for real, doesn't it? It's good to be present. **PB2** I agree. It's good to be present and to continue to challenge the stereotypes. Just being there is almost part of the politics of it. **PB1** There's also this thing that women in their fifties shouldn't be immature and talk about dicks, so that in itself is a bit punk, and we quite like that liberating feeling. We don't think about it amidst the creative process — everything's allowed.

195

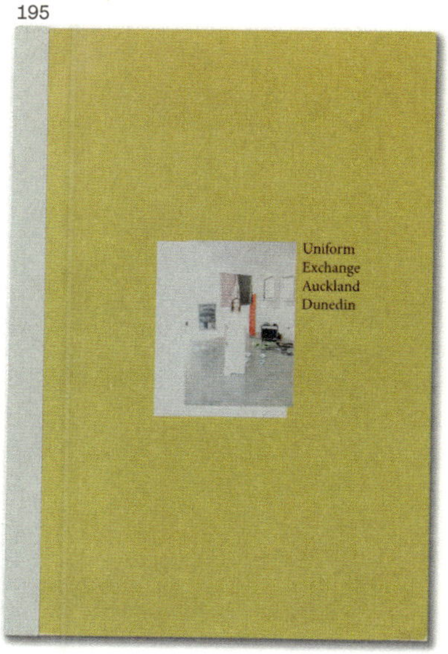

196

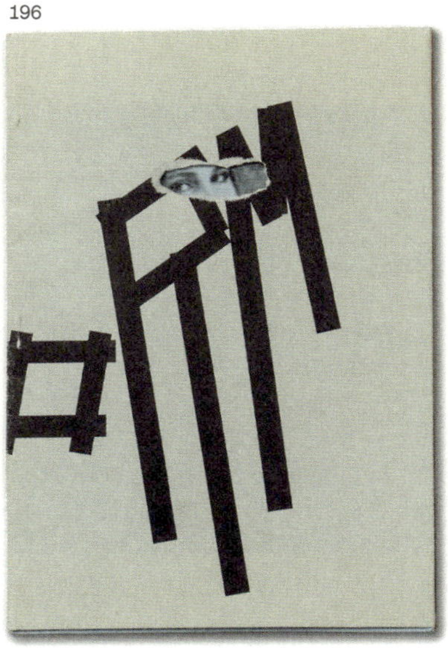

193. *Our Animal Instinks*, Panty Baggers collective, 148 × 200mm, 2020. Ōtepoti Dunedin.

194. *Uniform* #1 cover and spread, edited by Beth Dawson, Kiran Dass, Hanna Lacey, Tina Pihema and Maryann Savage, 170 x 240mm, 2015. Tāmaki Makaurau Auckland.

195. *Uniform (Exchange, Auckland Dunedin)*, editors Beth Dawson, Kiran Dass, Hanna Lacey, Tina Pihema, Bonni Tamati and Sjonel Timu, 175 × 250mm, 2016. Tāmaki Makaurau Auckland and Ōtepoti Dunedin.

196. *Uniform #4*, edited by Beth Dawson, Kiran Dass, Hanna Lacey and Tina Pihema, 170 × 240mm, 2017. Tāmaki Makaurau Auckland.

Hannah Wynn The zines are always super-responsive to what's going on. The first year Trump was elected, there were so many Trump zines which were hilarious. But I would say there has been a swing to really fancy production of zines rather than the cutting it up, collaging it, photocopying it kind of style . . . Maybe that's actually swinging back a little bit. Do you know Ezra Whittaker-Powley? He makes beautiful zines, he's probably one of my favourite zine-makers but I like the real rough-and-ready ones as well, because that's where zines came from.

For a while there seemed to be a swing toward really beautifully made, perfectly printed, perfectly bound zines. I don't know if that was just a Tauranga thing, but there was quite a feminine feel, a lighter feel. Not a bad thing, just what was happening.

essa may ranapiri All the poets I know and have talked to about Kirikiriroa Zinefest are really into it and it's just another kind of creative outlet for them. My friend Aimee-Jane Anderson-O'Connor has made zines that include a lot of collage as opposed to her usual poetry work. I haven't come across the snobby poet who doesn't like doing zines. Everyone I can think of has either done a zine or gets excited about Zinefest whenever it comes around, because there's a lot of writing you won't see anywhere else, and there's all sorts of different genres and forms.

197

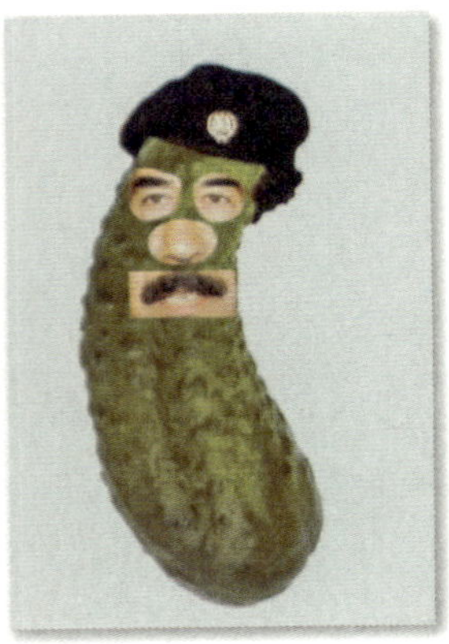

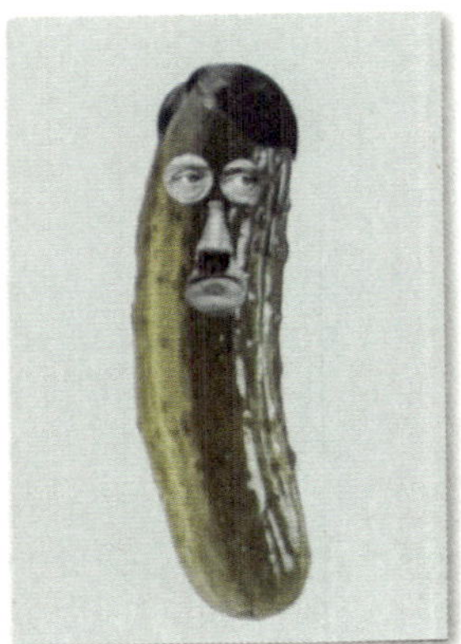

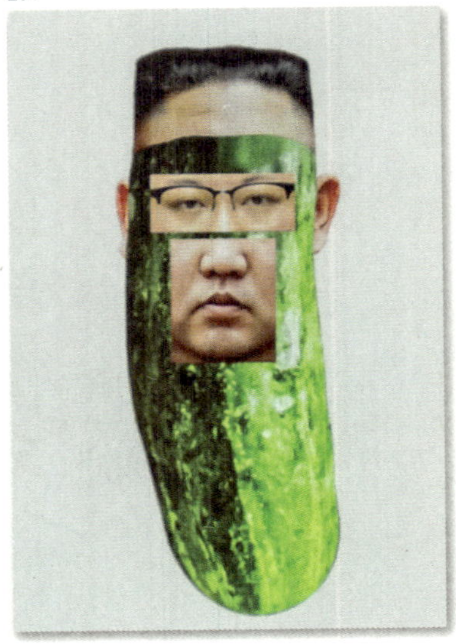

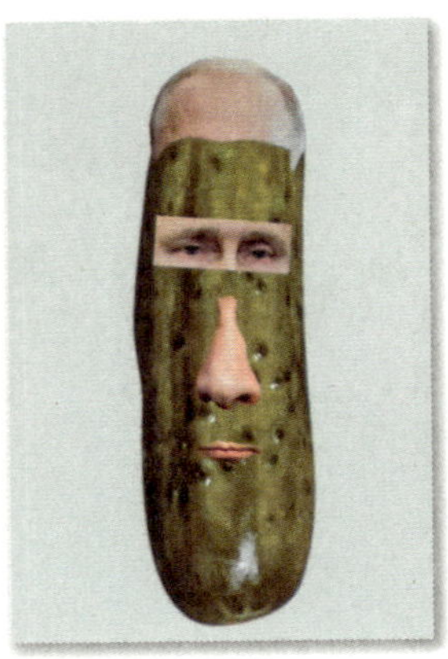

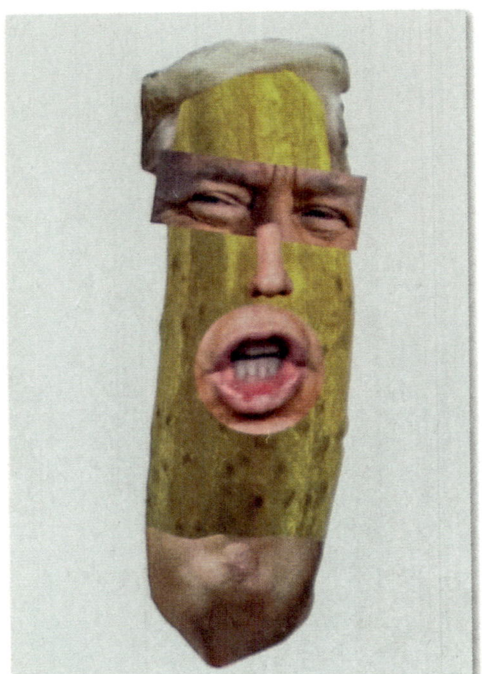

197. *Dic(tator) Pic(kles)*, Hannah Wynn, 74 x 52mm, 2021. Tauranga.

198. *Coping With Time* cover and spread, Single Dad aka Camila Araos Elevancini, A6, 2016. Tāmaki Makaurau Auckland.

David Merritt If a person has elected to go down the zine avenue rather than the established publishing avenue they're already punk rock, they've made that decision for any number of reasons. The thing that drew me was that I quickly worked out that the publisher was taking 45 per cent and the bookshop was taking 45 per cent of anything that I was making under that traditional business model that they still keep trying to shove down our throats. If you're at a zinefest, well, you've probably rejected that business model already, although, increasingly . . .

Four or five years ago at Wellington Zinefest I saw a couple of big-name poets selling their own little handmade books as zines. They had publishing careers dating back 20 years with Victoria University Press, Auckland University Press or whatever, but they'd elected to go to Zinefest to sell their wares directly to the public. I thought 'Woah. I never expected to see you here, and here you are.'

198

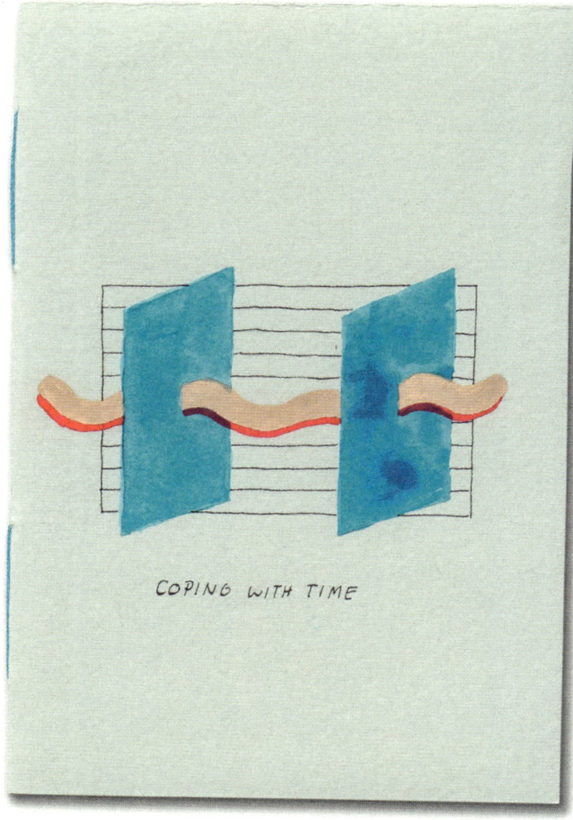

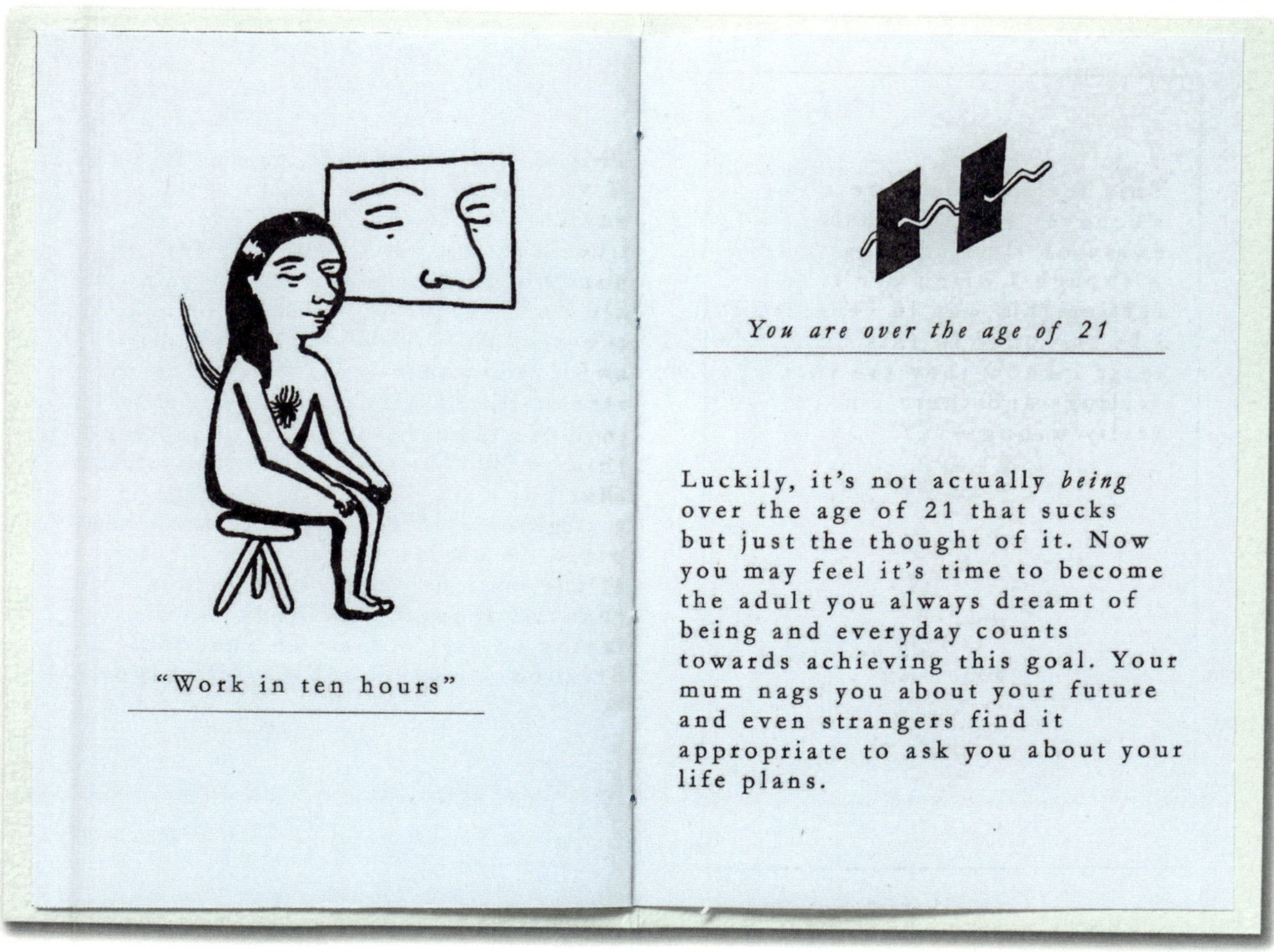

Hannah Wynn How does Zinefest complement the cultural goings-on of Tauranga? Does it complement it, or does it sit outside of it? I don't think it does complement it, it's so blue here. I mean, there's a great art community here, but even the art community is full of money . . . There's so much money here, and so many people have moved here in retirement and bought up large in Papamoa on the beach, and it's old money. I think as soon as the old money arrives things turn very blue. The beauty of Zinefest being in the gallery is that you do get those people coming in and going 'What the hell have I stumbled upon?', and some of those people make the best event-goers because they're like 'Oh, okay, sweet', and then you'll lure them onto the craft table and they can make their own zine and carry on.

But I don't think it does complement the goings on here. I think it fights it, in a good way, in a gentle way, in a nonconfrontational way, and again the beauty to me of zines is that they're so accessible for the makers and the readers. It doesn't need to be this big heavy novel or this big statement. It can be funny, it can be whatever, and people can afford them, too. They can go 'Oh, yeah, sweet, I can buy 10 zines. Oh, look at that.'

199

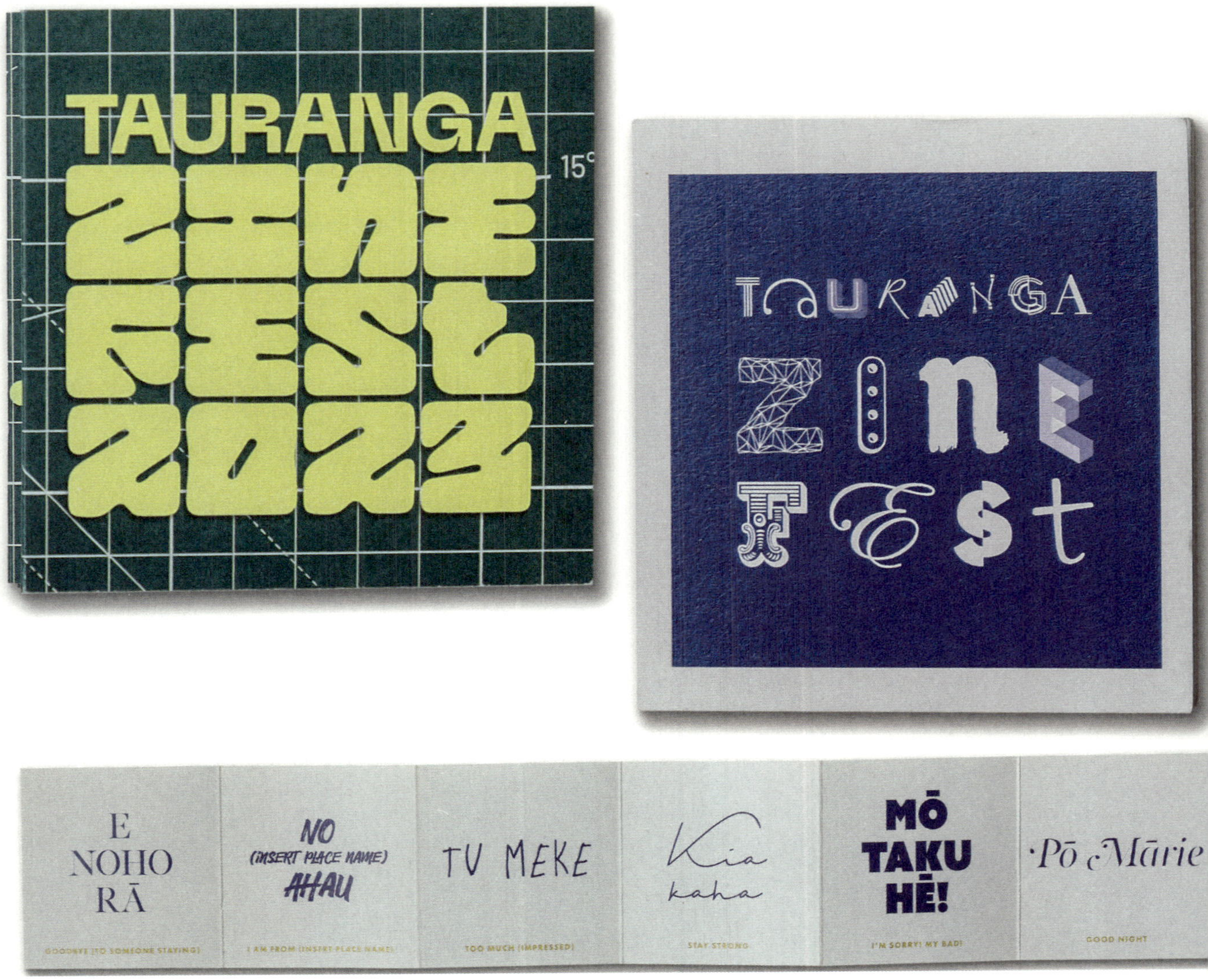

199. Tauranga Zinefest 2023 and 2019, annual stallholder freebees of selected kupu, Hannah Wynn, 70 × 70mm concertina format.

essa may ranapiri I feel like things have *started* to improve a little bit. There seemed to be more Māori creatives at the last Kirikiriroa Zinefest. I think having people be part of the organising — this is something I talk about a lot in regard to publishing. We need more Māori editors, because it's not just about encouraging more publications by Māori, it makes our work better if we're being edited by people who get what we're doing. I feel like having more people of colour or tangata whenua or tauiwi in positions where they get to make decisions is really important for the changing of these spaces. I think there's some positive stuff happening, but, yeah, I do remember a friend in Wellington saying to me 'I don't go to Zinefest, it's too white.' So, yeah, there's definitely issues.

Just put the right people in the right positions. Again, I think a lot of that comes from a lot of our community experiencing intense degradation, right? The more we can stop that, the more we can be spending time making zines or making art or being in communities in other ways that aren't just about trying to make ends meet. That's a broad problem. Will this government do anything about it? Probably not.

Tessa Stubbing How do you form a zinefest committee that has ethnic diversity? How do you do it in a meaningful way so you're not box-ticking, you're not quota-filling? I'm Māori and Pākehā, not that you could tell that from looking at me. Is quota-filling always wrong? I think it has to be done with the right intentions.

Spencer Hall I mean, you can have whatever zines you want at Ōtepoti Zinefest as long as they're not gonna incite a riot or whatever. Though I guess that could be cool, too.

Jewelia Howard The Wellington Zinefest accessibility hour is definitely important for people like me. A lot of my friends say, 'I would love to go to Zinefest, but it's too overwhelming for me.' I say to them 'Accessibility hour's a thing.' I know people who will come through specifically during that hour because the rest of the time it's so intense.

Maya Templer A few of the stallholders had asked *heaps* of questions leading up to Ōtautahi Zinefest. I was like 'Hmmm, I wonder what you're like', and then I met them and could tell they were neurodivergent. It left me thinking: 'It's cool that you discovered enough about Zinefest to feel comfortable about having a stall, even though it's like a big, bustling market.'

Mieke Montagne Ōtautahi Zinefest was great, especially compared to last year when it was just me and Maya [Templer]. Usually we'd have Alice Bush and Jane Maloney from M/K Press, but people get older, they have kids. Alice went travelling, moved to Auckland. The 2022 Zinefest wasn't much fun. We just pulled it out of our ass and made it happen because we wanted it to happen after lockdown, and we needed it. 2022 felt very rushed. This year, it was so nice to see it fully formed with proper funding and proper marketing. We took a lot of inspo from Wellington and Auckland, how they do their marketing and stuff. There were four of us organising it this year, so it was much easier to share jobs. We really pushed to make it better this year, and it totally was, it was beautiful, much better attended. We just shoved it in a bar last year, which cut off half our audience. It was a free venue, so we took it.

Regan Kupu Stokes We announced the 2013 Christchurch Zinefest at a PechaKucha. I'm not sure how effective it was in terms of getting the word out. We also ran a few zine-making workshops beforehand. It was pretty small-scale. Not a huge venue or anything. It wasn't a huge community back then, whereas now it's at the art gallery or at Tūranga [Christchurch public library] and it's like 'Woah, this is awesome.' Back in 2013 it wasn't hugely professional or super organised. It was pretty slapdash, much like a zine I guess. In recent years it's become bigger and more legit, and that's great.

Tessa Stubbing One person can't support a community, and if one person is trying to hold a community together it's not a community. So I was like 'Okay, I'm not doing Auckland Zinefest by myself again, and if it stops then it stops, and that sucks.' I didn't want it to stop, it'd been my life for four years. It was all I talked about.

I put out a call 'Who wants to join the committee?', and a bunch of people responded and that was the start of the Auckland Zinefest committee. I said, 'I'm gonna help set it up, let you know everything that I used to do — not that it has to be done that way — but here's what I learnt through trial and error. I'll take a step back and you guys take over.'

Spencer Hall I'm organising the next Ōtepoti Zinefest from my current home in Melbourne. I tried to get other people involved, but, I don't know, they find it too daunting or something. So it's me. I'd like other people to take over.

Liam Goulter I went to my first Wellington Zinefest committee meeting and was just really impressed and amazed by Rachel Lynch, Milly Hampton and Caitlin Lynch. They were the ones left from the old Zinefest crew. They were like 'Yeah, we do this, this, this . . .' I had just come from my day job at the theatre company, where we would have these infinitely long meetings where nothing would really get done and everything was very vague. Rachel, Milly and Caitlin were just really smart, onto-it people, and they were like 'Yeah, we need to do this, this and this.' I just found that really impressive.

Mieke Montagne We were a good team, we shared tasks. Personal capacities can be an issue. I was quite sick and quite sad for a while, so I stepped back a little just before the event. I was at my capacity with mental health and things like that, my other three jobs, burning out . . . I just needed a couple of weeks off. The others had to pick up my work during that period. Maya Templer did so much work. Her drive is just insane, I don't know how she does it. I'm just happy to be beside Maya and say 'You need anything? You need a tissue?' I'm a bit worried about how we'll cope when Maya moves to Australia.

Liam Goulter The Wellington Zinefest committee never had assigned positions. It was just, if you've got the energy and the interest, then you take on whatever aspect.

Jewelia Howard The best thing about being on the Wellington ZInefest committee is getting to hang out. I really like going to the meetings and catching up with everyone and feeling like I'm part of something, part of the community. We just end up rambling.

The worst thing is that I have a lot of imposter syndrome about being on the committee. I'm like 'I have no idea how to write a grant proposal', and I often can't commit to some of the tasks that need doing. I feel like I just show up for comic relief . . . which is important in its own way.

Catalina Paz Nuñez Elevancini At this point Auckland Zinefest is run by a group of people. We're in the middle of incorporating as a society. It's all volunteer-based. We get our funding from Creative Communities;[6] they're pretty much our only funder.

Liam Goulter Wellington's two-day zinefest only came about because we couldn't fit everyone in, and we couldn't find a venue that was big enough. Even with the two days, there's still been a wait-list of people we can't fit in.

Catalina Paz Nuñez Elevancini I guess the annoying part is people seeing your association with an institution like Auckland Art Gallery and assuming that you're being paid for what you do. We have talked about posting more about being volunteer-run, kind of showing our faces more to get that through to people. Adding an 'Our Values' tab to the website feels so corporate, but we just might have to.

Spencer Hall Often at zinefests, if you've got a table, you don't get a chance to get around and see everyone else's stuff. At the 2015 Wellington Zinefest, Suus Agnes and I thought we'd bypass the table altogether, chop up cardboard boxes and make them into wearable stalls. We walked around wearing those.

Catalina Paz Nuñez Elevancini Yes, you're not imagining it: the branding for Auckland Zinefest has become consistent. That was the main change of my reign, I guess. I come from a design background, and my sister Camilla works in marketing. We're not branded in the way most businesses would understand it. Mainly, we just insist on a particular colour palette. Every year we commission a different poster artist. We just say to them: 'This is the colour palette. Feel free to use different hues or shades.' We do pick artists with a particular style — playful, attractive to a younger audience, not particularly gritty, cartoony for sure, keeping with the influence of comics.

Jewelia Howard The Wellington Zinefest branding changes every year. It'd be weird to commit to one thing because zines aren't one thing. It's nice to experiment. There's no one good way to encapsulate Zinefest as a singular thing.

Catalina Paz Nuñez Elevancini It's a paradox. We've got Auckland Art Gallery hosting and we've got some funding, but we're really trying to make sure we're not too corporate-looking . . . To make sure people understand we're by the people for the people.

Liam Goulter When Lucy [Black] and I were working together on Wellington Zinefest we tried to communicate with the old committee members, but everyone had kind of tapped out. I remember Rachel Lynch telling me that at one point she was left holding everything. I suspected that that could happen again. It just didn't feel correct to me. When Rachel was doing everything, it was not only unfair on her but also meant Zinefest wasn't an event representative of a community. So when Lucy said, 'I'm not gonna do this anymore' and it was just me, I thought 'Fuck. No, no. I have to rope in some other people!'

It felt hard to ask people to come back and do a whole bunch of unpaid labour, especially when I was about to get paid. I didn't know how long that would last or if I wanted it to last, but it felt like a hard ask trying to get a committee back together. Everyone else had burnt out. I felt that old organisational model wasn't gonna work, but having people who only had to meet occasionally in an advisory capacity might be an easier sell. That's where the Wellington Zinefest board and incorporation came from. It also meant we could apply to a bigger pool of funders.

Mieke Montagne Christchurch Art Gallery was really good to work with. Nick Priddy, who is the events person, was amazing. He's younger than a lot of the others so was able to level with us. It was nice being able to talk logistics with someone who felt like a cool friend rather than . . . [assumes grumpy voice] 'What-do-you-need-from-me?' or someone who says, 'You can have it here, but there's a list of conditions.' Nick was just 'Don't stick stuff on the windows and we're all good.' The Art Gallery's great. They wanted to have us, and it was really awesome.

Jewelia Howard I've done zinefests in Christchurch, Hamilton, Auckland and Wellington. Oh, yeah, and Kapiti, Whanganui and Palmy. Regional difference? People outside of the larger cities definitely don't know what zines are. In Wellington especially, the people coming through are they're there for Zinefest. They know what Zinefest is. At zinefests that are held in public spaces like the Palmy one at a library or at Auckland Art Gallery, a lot of people are there to borrow a book or to look at painting, so they're like 'What the fuck is this? What's with all the freaks?' They wander through and they're thinking 'What are we looking at?' I don't actually find it frustrating, it's just different.

Catalina Paz Nuñez Elevancini Auckland Zinefest has been around since 2009, and we've been doing the market at Auckland Art Gallery for quite a few years. Auckland Art Gallery's a major institution, but they let us use the space for free. It's goes toward their fulfilling their duties, being more of a community institution.

Maia-Jeanne Woolkirk At our first Whanganui Zinefest we had a rule: you had to be selling at least two zine titles. I don't wanna be a craft fair. I don't want your badges and your cushions to take over. You lose something when you move away from that DIY, paper-based, language-based thing.

200. *What is a Zine?* cover and spread, Jewelia Howard, A7, 2024. Te Whanganui-a-Tara Wellington.
201. *Soul Coughing* cover and spread, Maia-Jeanne Woolkirk, A5, 2022. Whanganui.
202. *i called you home* cover and spread, Jewelia Howard, A6, 2023. Te Whanganui-a-Tara Wellington.

200

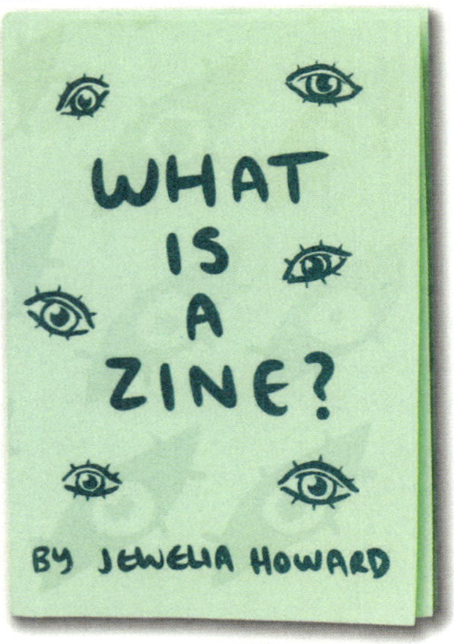

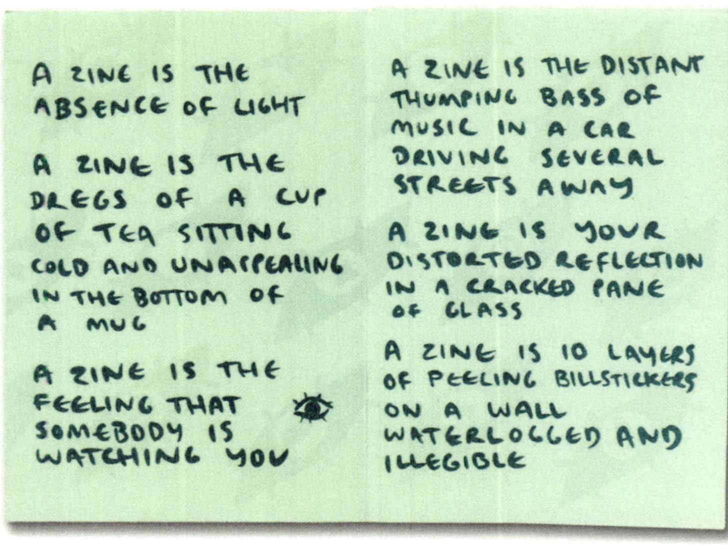

201

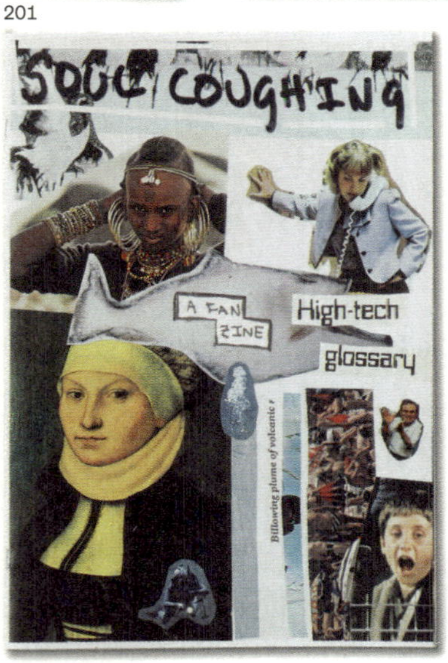

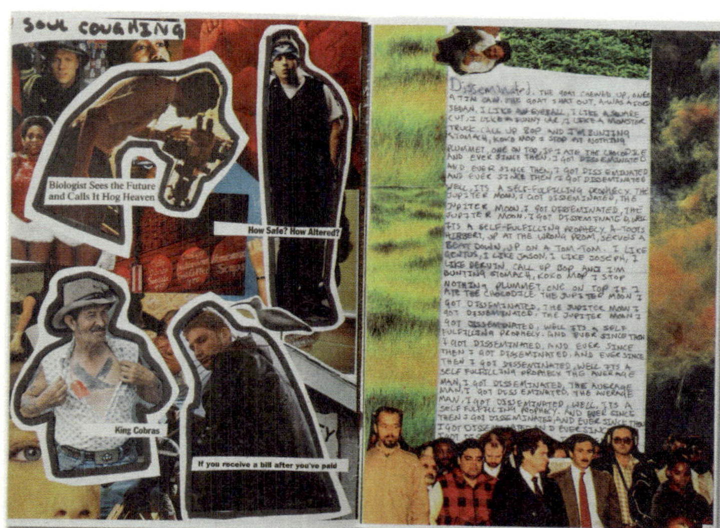

Catalina Paz Nuñez Elevancini We leave the stallholders applications open to make sure everyone gets a chance to apply. The application form is pretty detailed. We ask for links and evidence and that. We've become bigger and bigger, and we're having trouble telling crafters — who don't have zines — not to apply. The reason we run a curated zinefest rather than a first-come-first-served model is because we only have a certain amount of spots and we want to make sure those are going to zine-makers.

Maya Templer There was someone who asked if they could have a stall, and I looked on their Instagram and they just sold flowers. I was like 'Do you have zines?', and they were like 'No, but I have pressed flowers which is sort of like zines.' I had to say 'The only requirement for Zinefest is having a zine: this market runs once a year, like, that's the bare minimum. I'm sorry, you can't have a stall, but next year if you have zines . . .'

Jewelia Howard People travel for zinefest because the vibe is so good. I do *a lot* of markets, and I would choose a zinefest over any of them other markets any day, just for vibes alone. The people who seek out zines are the freaks, and the freaks are fun. The freaks are cool. People aren't there to make money. People are just out there trying to share things they love and that's the best kind of space.

202

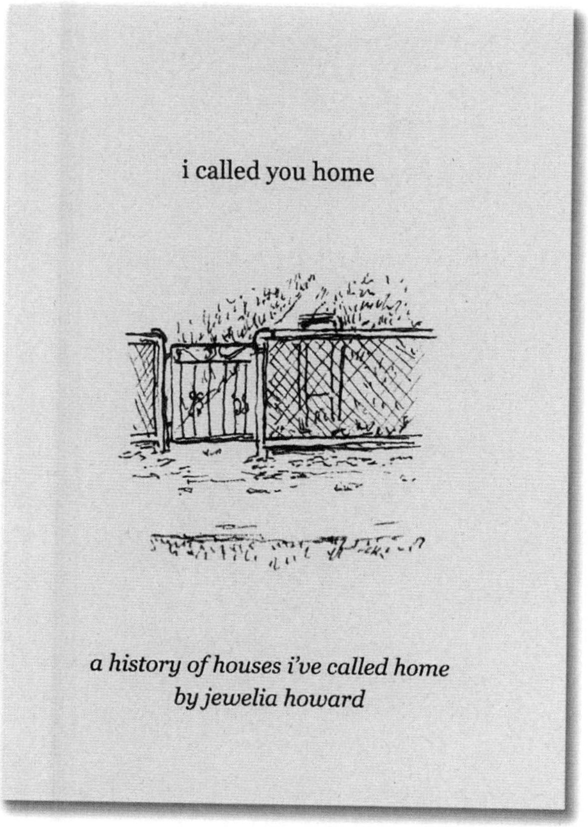

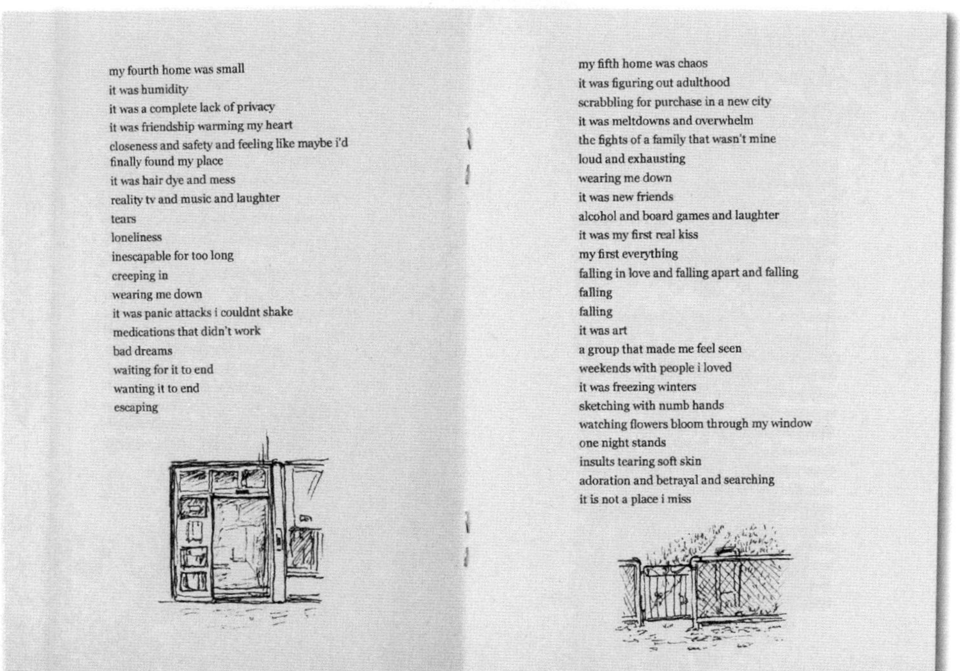

my fourth home was small
it was humidity
it was a complete lack of privacy
it was friendship warming my heart
closeness and safety and feeling like maybe i'd finally found my place
it was hair dye and mess
reality tv and music and laughter
tears
loneliness
inescapable for too long
creeping in
wearing me down
it was panic attacks i couldnt shake
medications that didn't work
bad dreams
waiting for it to end
wanting it to end
escaping

my fifth home was chaos
it was figuring out adulthood
scrabbling for purchase in a new city
it was meltdowns and overwhelm
the fights of a family that wasn't mine
loud and exhausting
wearing me down
it was new friends
alcohol and board games and laughter
it was my first real kiss
my first everything
falling in love and falling apart and falling
falling
falling
it was art
a group that made me feel seen
weekends with people i loved
it was freezing winters
sketching with numb hands
watching flowers bloom through my window
one night stands
insults tearing soft skin
adoration and betrayal and searching
it is not a place i miss

Mieke Montagne What's a Ride On Super Sound customer like? We get a lot of record introverts. In general I'd say our customers give the same kind of vibe as you get at Ōtautahi Zinefest. They're mostly introverts, but they're also freaks. I love them. The freaks come in.

Ride On Super Sound started with conversations at The Darkroom. Nick White and I worked in the bar at The Darkroom, and our friends would come and hang out, including Johnny Electric, the crazy genius lathe-cut music guy. Nick and Johnny were quite good friends. They were young and there was a cheap space, so over beers and chats the boys just started entertaining the possibility.

Galaxy Records was there prior, and when it closed they said: 'We could do a better record store. Let's add the comics and zines and make something less stagnant. Let's make it cool, let's have the weird shit.'

I have this fond childhood memory of walking into a comic shop and thinking 'This is fucking awesome', and I want that for *other* people. Just to be like 'There is this cool shop that you can go to to find the weird shit.' I think the boys kind of made that, they were just like 'Fuck it, let's just try it — if it doesn't work, it doesn't work.'

They put a lot of money into it, but collectively made the decision that it would just sell on behalf, so we take a small 25 per cent commission rather than the usual markup, just to pay the rent. It kind of worked, but the rent was very cheap.

Alice Bush was involved at the start, but after a while she wasn't feeling it, didn't wanna do it. So Nick said to me 'You like zines, you like comics, come work for us', and I said 'Fuck, yeah, happy to be there for the cause. Give the little baby Mieke inside the fulfilment of being the person that sells the cool shit.'

Marijke van Schaardenburg There aren't many distros in New Zealand. There used to be Strange Goods up here in Auckland. I stocked some with them. Ride on Super Sound in Christchurch is an amazing distro. I hit them up and was like 'Do you want some zines?', and they were like 'Fuck yeah.' Then there's the occasional pop-up.

203

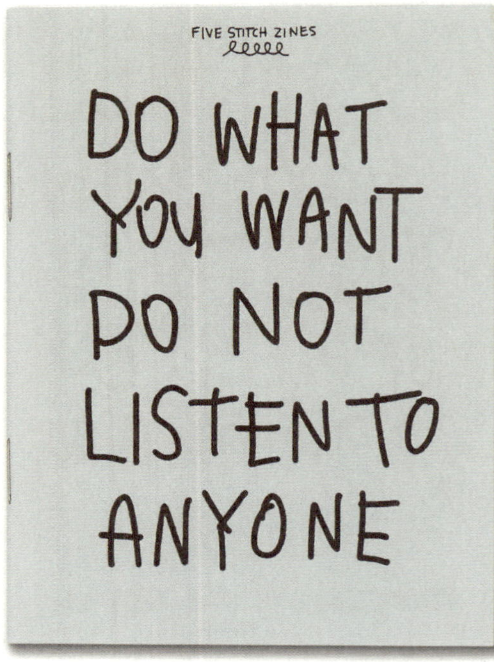

204

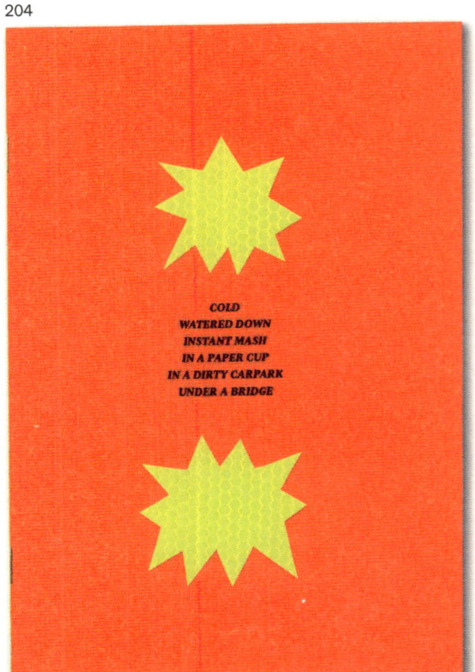

205

Tessa Stubbing The website was called New Zealand Zine Review, but it wasn't really about reviewing zines, it was more about having a record of what's out there, a platform for promotion, a way to connect zinesters and their audience. When you go to a zinefest, there's so many stalls, right? And you don't get to see everyone's stuff, especially if there are crowds of people. We wanted to offer a way of seeing what zines were coming out. You might read a review or whatever and think 'That sounds interesting, I'd like to buy it'; we'd also post the contact details and how much it cost. You could message the author and get a copy, that was the idea. All the zines that got reviewed were donated. We didn't buy them, we didn't have any money. Once we had reviewed them, they would be donated to the respective public libraries: Kylie in Wellington and me up here in Auckland.

We also printed zine review annuals, which got slayed in an online review in Australia.

Kylie Buck That was always my dream: 'I'm gonna make a review zine.' There was one called *Zine World* that I got from a distro in America. It was printed on newsprint. I'd pour over these tiny little reviews of zines and would think 'This is the best.' So, then I started writing reviews, but it was really hard. New Zealand's too small. My reviews were definitely way nicer than they might have been, but I was scared that someone would say 'Hey, I can't believe that you gave my zine a bad review!?' Conflict-averse. I'm quite empathetic as well. I just didn't like the idea of someone getting put off zine-making because of a bad review. Other reviewers were probably the same. Why would you slate something that someone put so much energy into? Although quite often I'd write something like 'Priced at $10, it's too expensive.' They're probably all $10 now.

203. *Do What You Want, Do Not Listen To Anyone*, Marijke van Schaardenburg, A6, 2021. Tāmaki Makaurau Auckland.

204. *Cold Watered Down Instant Mash in a Paper Cup in a Dirty Carpark Under a Bridge*, Marijke van Schaardenburg, A5, 2023. Tāmaki Makaurau Auckland.

205. *A Bundle of Sticks*, Marijke van Schaardenburg, A5, 2022. Tāmaki Makaurau Auckland.

206. *New Zealand Zine Review*, edited by Kylie Buck and Tessa Stubbing, A5, 2013. Te Whanganui-a-Tara Wellington and Tāmaki Makaurau Auckland.

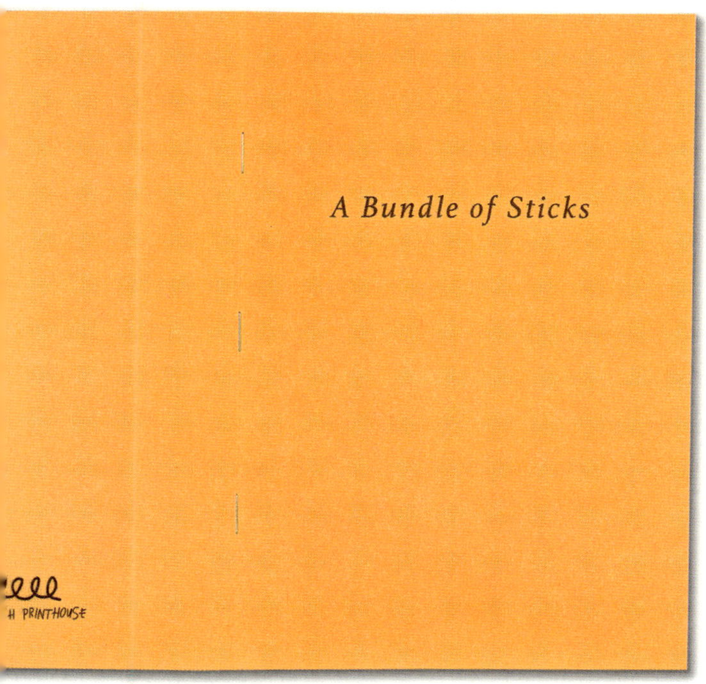

206

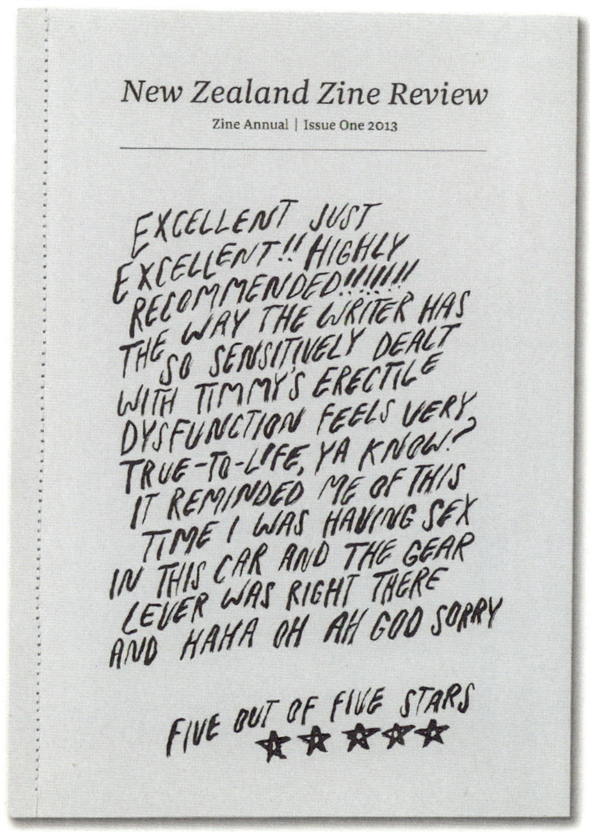

Murtle Chickpea The thing with Etsy is that hardcore fancy illustrators are making zines, beautifully printed, beautiful paper, $25 each. And even though I rejected those anarchist zines back in Melbourne, with these Etsy ones even *I'm* thinking, That's not a zine! A zine's made on a photocopier. They'll use beautiful see-through paper stock. It is still a zine, but I think there's a lot to be said for that really basic photocopied zine you can sell for just three to four bucks.

Gini Jory Zinefest has been my only way of getting the work out at this stage. I will probably donate some to the Hocken Library, and I'll donate some of the ones I purchased to the Hocken as well. Outside of Zinefest, I'm just not sure of the right avenues for distribution. Etsy kind of sucks. They take a lot of your money. I'd rather set up my own website, but that's a lot of effort and management. I might just give them to people. Chuck a couple of zines in everyone's Christmas stocking this year.

Nina Harper I have seen people upload their zines digitally, even supplying printing templates for people so that they can print them out and construct them with the page order intact.

207

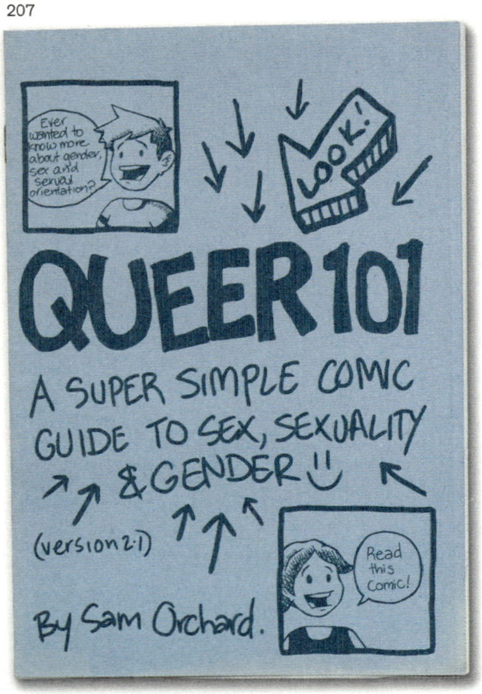

Murtle Chickpea When I started that initiative, I called it a 'Zine Museum'. It was really a travelling zine library, but I called it a museum because I just wanted something different. One zine-maker wrote back to me saying that zines are meant to be seen and read and touched, and so she didn't think a museum was a good idea for her zines. I was like 'Oh no, no, no. It's a library. I called it the Zine Museum for something different'. After that she was like 'Oh, okay, sweet', and she donated something.

I was really impressed with how many people donated zines, and that was just from Etsy. I put the call out on Etsy and on my blog. I particularly wanted to get international zines because they weren't really available here.

After the Zine Museum had travelled to the Massey University library in Wellington, I thought 'Y'know what, when they're not on display they're just in boxes under my bed.' I felt that they needed to be seen more than I was giving them time to be seen, and so I asked Lauren Deacon at the library 'How about I donate this to you guys?' She said, 'Oh my god, yes!' So, I put a thing up on the blog to all the zine-donors: 'Thank you so much for everything. This is where the zines are now, in a library being looked at more often than I was able to make happen.'

Gini Jory I've been saying we should get more zines at the Hocken. I think they cover a lot of the gaps in our collection . . . a lot of queer culture, different ethnicities, different religious views, a lot of minority group activity.

My team and my manager at the Hocken have been very supportive. Kirstie Ross has asked me if I want to run a workshop and said she will support me. 'Oh, yup, you wanna order zines for the collection? Yup, I'll let you do that . . . You wanna do all this zine stuff? Do it.' It's been cool to have support in the workplace.

Indira Neville It's hilarious. I'm like, why the fuck does the Alexander Turnbull Library want my tat? I just think that's hilarious: that a bunch of drunken people, sitting around making outrageous shitty things are now part of the nation's memory. It's weird.

Sam Orchard This is the pitch that I give to people around why they should deposit their zines at the National Library. In 2016 we ended up with Indira Neville, Sarah Laing and Rae Joyce doing the *Three Words* anthology, which was pretty much a reaction to the idea that there were no women creating comics in New Zealand. *Three Words* was challenging a particular book, but it was also challenging a series of events that happened over time, where every New Zealand comics history just focused on the same straight white boys. When the propagators of that were questioned on the gender disparity, they'd be like 'Well, these are the people who've been creating comics', and it's like 'Hang on!'

It's really easy to leave people out and pretend that they don't exist, but that's much harder if you put them into national institutions and Crown institutions. It makes it harder for researchers to deny our existence. That's part of the reason why in the past I have donated to the library, because I want to make it really hard for people to say that trans people don't exist or trans people haven't been creating their own stories and that we haven't been speaking for ourselves. And the other reason is that *this stuff is cool*. One of the reasons people self-publish material is because they're denied by the mainstream, so you get voices that are telling different stories. Self-publishers get more opportunity to experiment and do things in a different way, but these things do get lost.

Indira Neville I would hate to think of that book [the *Three Words* anthology] as only a response to *From Earth's End*. It's its own amazing, wonderful thing. Since *Three Words* I've had a whole lot of women ask me 'Are you gonna do another one?! Are you gonna do another one?!'

The rhetoric of the 'competent boys' club was 'But there are no New Zealand women comic artists'; the classic thing. They only let one token woman be in the comic scene at a time.

207. *Queer 101*, Sam Orchard, A5, 2011. Tāmaki Makaurau Auckland.

208. *Under the Rainbow* cover and spread, compiled by Sam Orchard, A5, 2019. Tāmaki Makaurau Auckland.

208

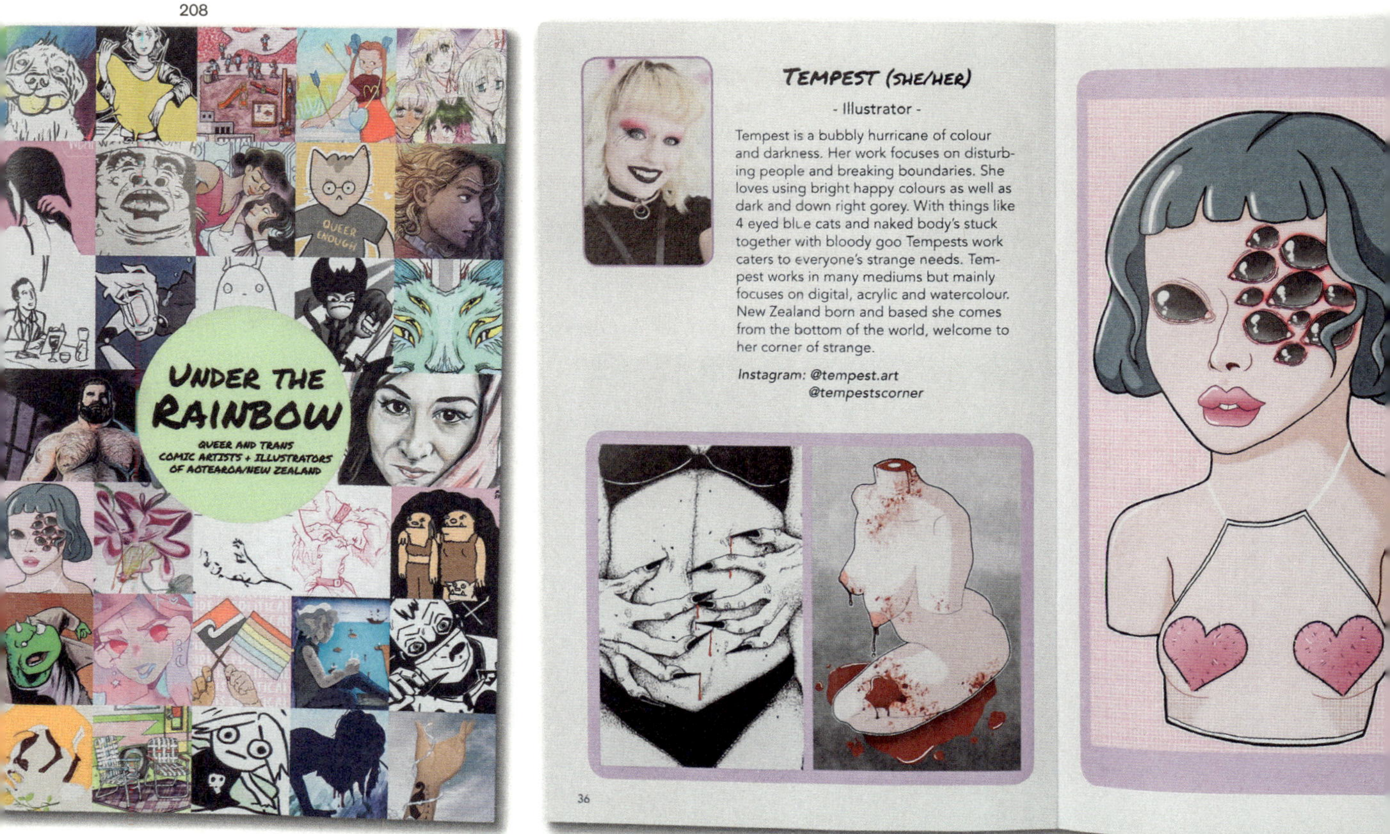

essa may ranapiri My way into zines was definitely through poetry. I wasn't being published when I started making zines. One of the cool things about making zines is that you can just do it yourself. There's none of the gatekeeping or barriers that exist within the publishing industry. A lot of it was doing collaborations with friends, like the early zine I made with Wairehu Grant, and another one with Tyla Armstrong; my words with someone else's illustrations, in conversation with each other. Collaborations are hard to get published in New Zealand. I remember sending off a collaborative manuscript and waiting a year and a half just to be rejected. So, yeah, the zine is important to me in that there is less time between the writing and it being in the world, and being able to collaborate more freely.

209

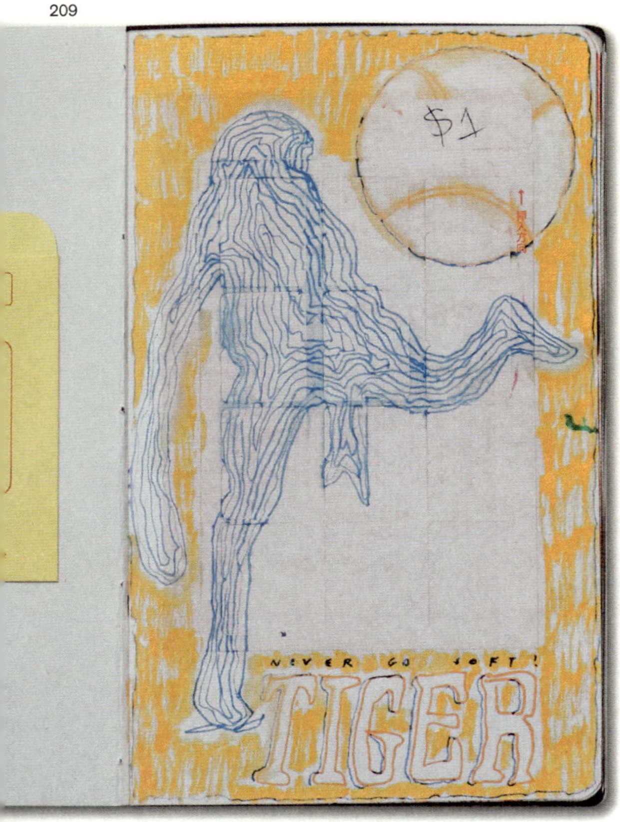

Kenneth Merrick My brother and his family came down to Auckland Art Gallery for Auckland Zinefest last year. It's not a place they would normally hang out. They were really taken aback by how many people were there and what it was. They said, 'Wow, we just thought it was gonna be a lecture theatre with 10 people selling stuff.' I'm hoping to get other family members to come down, niece and nephews who already have slightly book-ish interests, just to show them that this is a whole thing they can get involved in. I don't think my family currently have an understanding of how you go about doing it, that basically you can just make these things at home.

Sometimes I'll give zines to family members. They'll say 'Wow, what is this?', and I'll just tell them that it's basically a drawing diary. I'll give stickers to the kids. They'll turn them upside down and ask, 'What is this?' It's still quite perplexing to my family in some ways: 'You make what?! And people buy it?! Are you for real?!'

Panty Baggers PB3 One day I was at the Auckland airport wearing an Ōtepoti Zinefest t-shirt and a guy comes out of the kitchen and asks 'Are you a publisher? I'll just go get you my zine.' He was working in a kitchen and he gave me this great little zine that he had made about the war on drugs in Mexico and the cartels and how fucked up the whole situation is, how corrupt the government is . . . It's just amazing that when there's these little signals put out you really meet some great people and get to share some fabulous bits of self-publishing. He just ran out of the kitchen with his zine when the boss wasn't looking and gave it to me. **PB1** Pru, you put yourself out there. Pru panty-bags in airports, buses, boats . . . **PB3** I do, I've got no shame. I do lots of travelling and don't have much spare time and so I've always got a glue stick and scissors. I pick up in-flight magazines, newspapers, whatever, and if I've got time to kill at an airport I'm just there cutting up.

209. *Super Sketch #2*, superhyperpaper aka Kenneth Merrick, 202 × 125mm, 2023. Tāmaki Makaurau Auckland.

210. *Hero to One*, Marijke van Schaardenburg, A5, 2021. Tāmaki Makaurau Auckland.

Maia-Jeanne Woolkirk The best reaction to a zine was when I was printing *Soul Coughing: A fan zine* out — at work, naturally — and one of my co-workers came in who's a big muso, and I said 'Oh, Zinefest is coming up. Do you wanna look at my zine?' He was like 'I love Soul Coughing!' And I was like 'I love Soul Coughing!' And then we spent 20 minutes screaming at each other, and then he went and played Soul Coughing albums in the work shed for the rest of the day. We now have this thing in common. It was so delightful.

He even had a track of theirs that I didn't have and so he emailed it to me. There was a trading of artefacts from this band. It was so cool.

Marijke van Schaardenburg I won the art category in Best-in-Fest the year I did *Hero to One*. Moira Clunie was one of the judges and I remember when they announced it, they made a point of saying it felt 'radical and necessary'. It's taken time for me to start owning that statement, but I recognise the sentiment now, of this being work that needs to happen and hasn't been, or if people are making it, it's scary to put it out there.

I was really chuffed that I got the award. After that it was very much like 'Okay, I've got to keep doing this, this is a lifeline for expressing myself creatively, this is what I can do while also working as a corporate brat.' I'd been so lost as to how to express myself creatively and how to express myself as a queer person, and so to get these reactions . . .

Hannah Wynn One person said 'Yeah, but what do you do with them once you've bought them?' and I said 'Read them. Smell them. Touch them. Lick them. Do whatever you want with them.' They didn't get it.

Billy Douglas That Tauranga Zinefest was my first. I didn't really know what to expect. It was so inviting. I made so many friends. To be around so many talented people all at once who are so humble about their work . . . I don't think a single person there had a bloody chip on their shoulder, going 'This is the shit, I am the shit.' Everyone was just 'Hey, this is what I do, really trying my best.' I was absolutely amazed at some of the stuff there and the people being so nice. Such a cool community. I was just fizzing on it when we got back home.

Hannah Wynn There's a lot of blue. Absolutely. Tim Danko came for a couple of years, and then he stopped registering for a stall. I was like 'Bro, what?' I saw him at Kirikiriroa Hamilton Zinefest or at Auckland Zinefest, and said 'Why have you not been?', and he said 'Urgh, Tauranga. Just full of pretentious people, and you don't take care of the homeless that are right outside the art gallery.' And I was like 'Yeah, because we need people like you . . .' He was just like 'Tauranga's gross', and I'm like, 'I hear you, but we need people like you to be in those pretentious people's faces', not overtly but . . . And he was like 'Oh, yeah', and he's been back ever since.

210

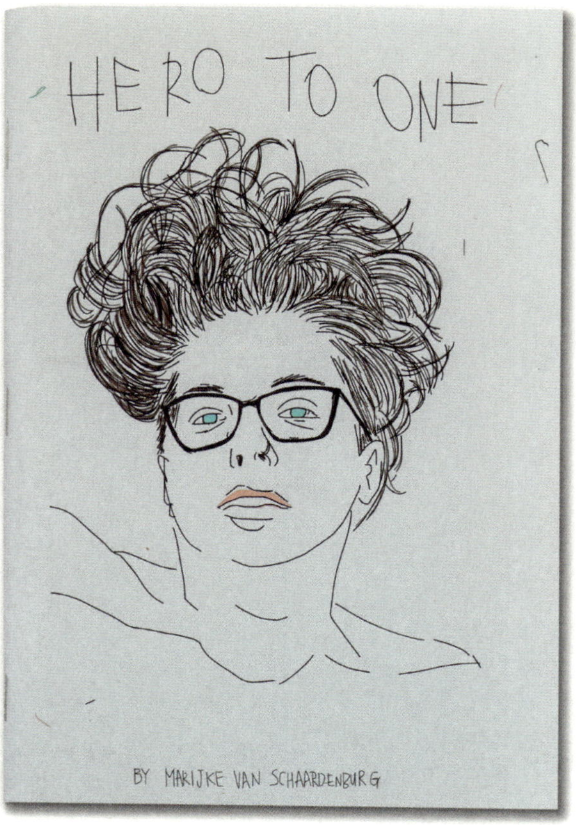

Marijke van Schaardenburg I see zines, specifically in that sense, as a way for individuals to reclaim themselves, their community, their art, culture and history, filling the void that has been left by marginalisation, by discrimination.

I really found a sense of community in zines. I was coming from an arts background and I'd moved to Auckland, and the art scene here — and probably in a lot of places — is very cliquey and exclusive. I remember my first exhibition opening and everyone looking at me and my partner like 'Who are these people? We don't know them. What are they doing here?' And, y'know, no one really talking to you.

When I entered Zinefest and the zine community I found the total opposite. It's very welcoming, very loving, open to anyone and anything, all thoughts and ideas, obviously within reason. You can just come along and bring your whole self and people will be like 'Cool'.

Victoria Armstrong Finding my own voice has been great for my mental health. I think it's what turned everything around. My entire life there's been this depression in the background, but then it was like: Okay, well, if I have this outlet and I can make artwork for myself and it's what I enjoy, then everything else seems much easier. When I stop making, I feel myself spiralling. Creativity keeps you grounded. You've got to make yourself laugh, you've got to have fun.

Nina Harper Hamilton is definitely a very agricultural kind of place. I mean, Zinefest is the first thing that I've found that's seemed like a really exciting creative opportunity for people. It's like there's Zinefest or there's ArtsPost—the Waikato Society of Arts gallery — which is available to local artists. But even ArtsPost feels a bit inaccessible for younger people, especially up-and-coming artists. So up until I started doing Zinefest it didn't feel like there were a lot of creative opportunities here.

David Tulloch Locally produced comics, indie comics, have in a sense been sidelined as zines by the market. There's a lot of work that goes into one page of a comic, but it doesn't pay. Simon Morse, for example, got into tattooing because it was a way of doing a single drawing and getting paid a lot of money for it. I mean, there were other reasons, but . . . That was a very smart move on his part because he was a bit burnt out, especially after Martin Emond died.[7] When you look at the level of detail in one of his pages, it takes a long time and then you get nothing for it.

211

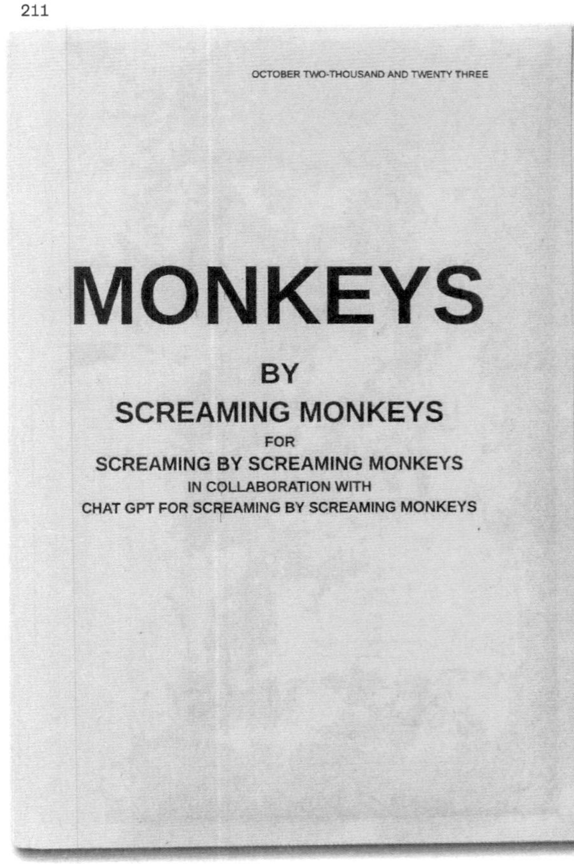

Marijke van Schaardenburg I finished art school at the end of 2016, and the following year I'm in a corporate job trying to pay the rent, but I also needed a creative outlet. I was a bit lost, like 'How do I express myself creatively? I don't have the same resources or time I had before', and that's when I created my first zine, which is called *Bus*. *Bus* #1 and #2 are these zines that I created on my commute to and from work. I'm on the bus and I'm drawing on my tablet, observing things on the bus. So they're shaky. I printed them in secret on the office printer at work and then gave them to friends. I didn't really put them out beyond that, I wasn't quite at that point. But those are the first zines I made myself.

Regan Kupu Stokes There were six or seven flats in Bryndwr that all knew each other. Lots of creative stuff happened over several years because of the connections, everyone working part-time or studying. It was kind of the last foray before we sank into full-time jobs.

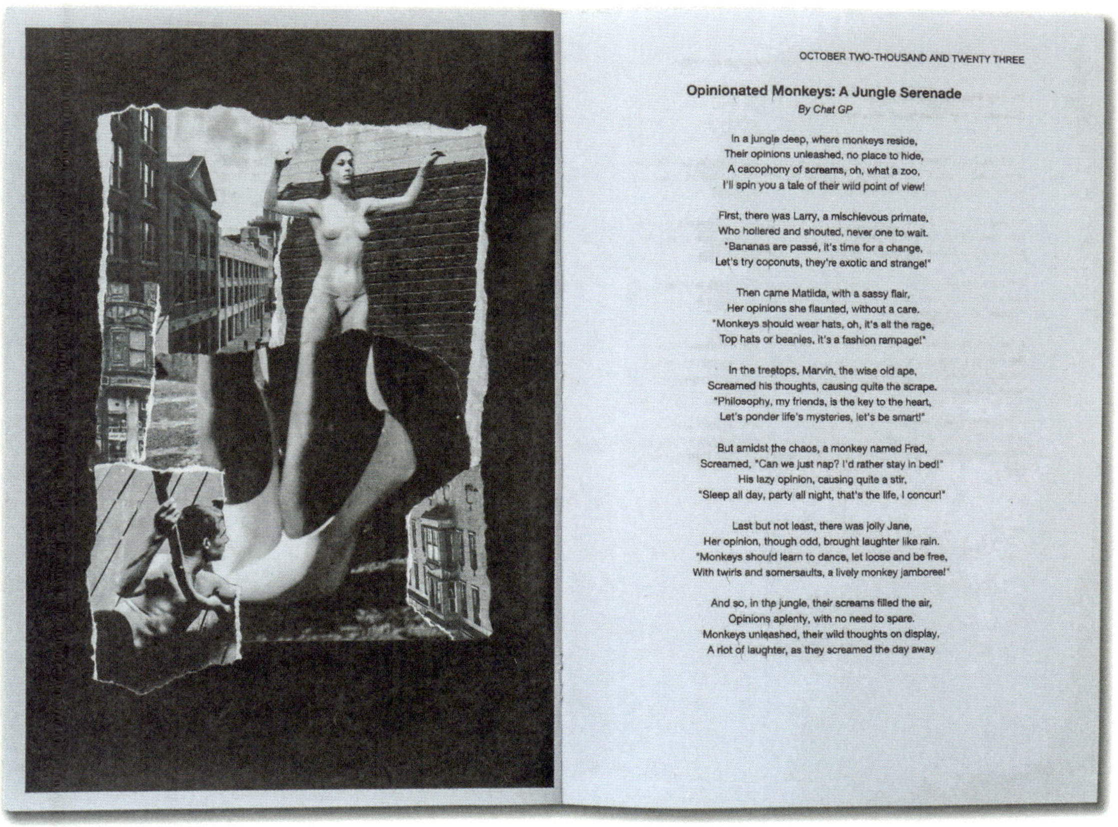

OCTOBER TWO-THOUSAND AND TWENTY THREE

Opinionated Monkeys: A Jungle Serenade
By Chat GP

In a jungle deep, where monkeys reside,
Their opinions unleashed, no place to hide,
A cacophony of screams, oh, what a zoo,
I'll spin you a tale of their wild point of view!

First, there was Larry, a mischievous primate,
Who hollered and shouted, never one to wait.
"Bananas are passé, it's time for a change,
Let's try coconuts, they're exotic and strange!"

Then came Matilda, with a sassy flair,
Her opinions she flaunted, without a care.
"Monkeys should wear hats, oh, it's all the rage,
Top hats or beanies, it's a fashion rampage!"

In the treetops, Marvin, the wise old ape,
Screamed his thoughts, causing quite the scrape.
"Philosophy, my friends, is the key to the heart,
Let's ponder life's mysteries, let's be smart!"

But amidst the chaos, a monkey named Fred,
Screamed, "Can we just nap? I'd rather stay in bed!"
His lazy opinion, causing quite a stir,
"Sleep all day, party all night, that's the life, I concur!"

Last but not least, there was jolly Jane,
Her opinion, though odd, brought laughter like rain.
"Monkeys should learn to dance, let loose and be free,
With twirls and somersaults, a lively monkey jamboree!"

And so, in the jungle, their screams filled the air,
Opinions aplenty, with no need to spare.
Monkeys unleashed, their wild thoughts on display,
A riot of laughter, as they screamed the day away

211. *Monkeys* cover and spread, Screaming Monkeys aka Victoria Armstrong, Billy Douglas and ChatGPT, A5, 2023. Te Papaioea Palmerston North.

Kenneth Merrick I haven't made any big works in a while; I really enjoy the physicality of it. At the moment I'm working from home, so there are space constraints. I *kind of* miss it, but not so much. It's nice being able to work with materials like old paper or receipts. I quite like the portability of being able to carry work around.

I'm living with my partner, I'm not in a studio, I'm not in a room by myself making something. I could be on the couch, or outside, and just be present and accessible, like 'Hey, could you actually take the rubbish out or do the dishes?' And then just drop what I'm doing: 'Oh, yeah, sure, I can do that.' Which I think is quite an important thing if you're not a completely selfish bastard, to not lock yourself away. Being able to do it anywhere, I guess.

212

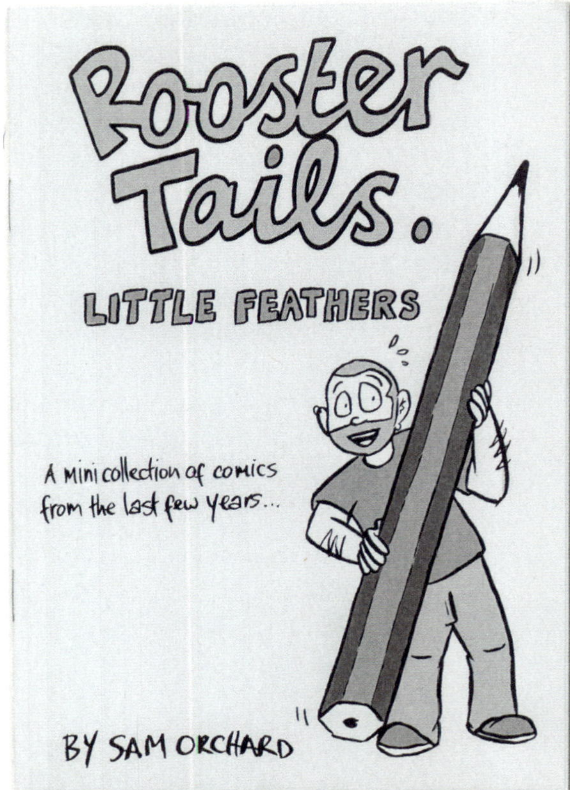

213

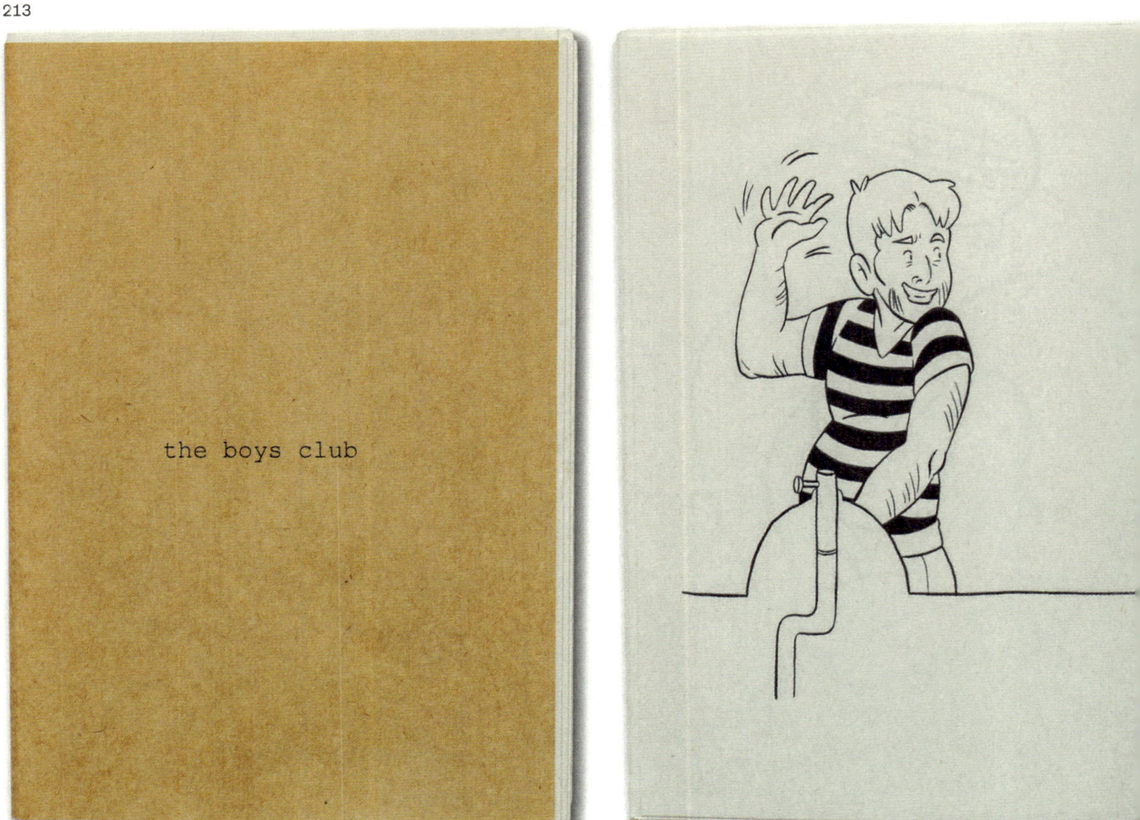

212. *Rooster Tails (Little Feathers)*, Sam Orchard, A5, 2019. Tāmaki Makaurau Auckland.

213. *The Boys Club* cover and spread, Ash Spittal, A5, 2013. Tāmaki Makaurau Auckland.

214. *Four Quotes on the Queer History of Zines*, Arwen Miriama Sommer, A7, date unknown. Ōtautahi Christchurch.

214

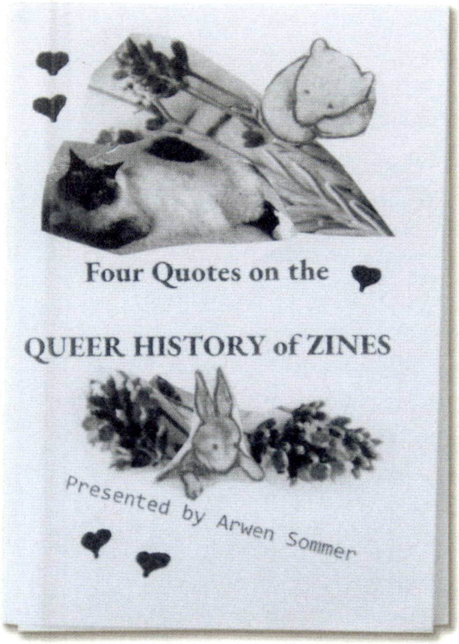

Nina Harper Family and friends have all been really supportive. For my parents especially, it's a more tangible art experience. They've always been very supportive of me in everything I do, but when you're purely an artsy creative person, and that's all you want to do with your life, you do feel the pressure to have something to show for it. There has to be stuff that I'm making that people are engaging with; I'm not just like sitting in my room endlessly doing little projects for my own amusement.

Maya Templer I definitely abuse the printer at work. All the Zinefest stuff was printed on the work printer, and all my comics.

Arwen Miriama Sommer I generally leave things really late, too late to get to a proper printing place, but I'm blessed in having a home printer. It's a really old one, it's a good old one. I bought it specifically because it does not have the proprietary chip in it so I can just use any ink cartridge. I just go get them refilled.

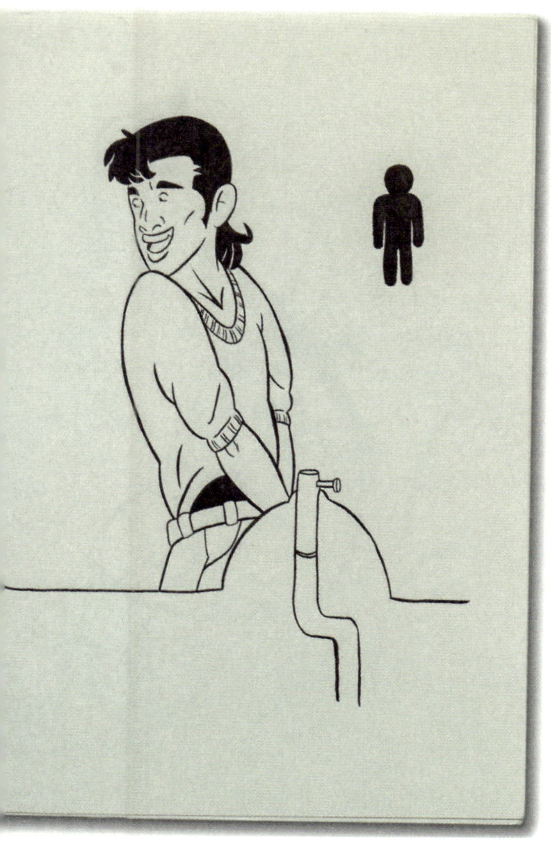

Hannah Wynn Zinefest sits under Tauranga Arts Festival's umbrella now. So it will be part of the wider festival promo. I worry that the stallholders comms and documentation might drop a bit, but other than that I think they'll do an incredible job. It was always my plan that they would eventually take it on. That's where I wanted it to go. I mean, not my plan since year one, but I had begun to think that I couldn't keep doing this and then I moved to Cambridge. I was like 'It's mad to keep doing this, and honestly, I was so over trying to get money because the Creative Communities Scheme kept saying, 'This might be the last year we can give you money because we have to spread it around.'

Mieke Montagne The attendance was amazing. We've never got those numbers in the past, and doubling the number of stallholders . . . It was all I could have hoped for. Where did all of those stallholders come from!? I don't know that many creatives in this fucking city.

Kenneth Merrick It's hard to say where zines will go. It might get to the point where it's like syndicated distribution through Phantom or somebody, with little boxes installed on shop counters: 'Hey, we've got this new thing — everybody's got their own zine.' I don't know, maybe it'll be a *Coffee News*[8] apocalypse where you walk in and are like 'Oh my god!' Yeah, hard to say. I hope it keeps growing, but if it gets too big, I don't know.

Hannah Wynn *Coffee News* is not a zine.

Victoria Armstrong When my grandfather was alive he would write a newsletter for family and friends and send that out every year. I didn't know that other people did that, I just thought it was him. **Billy Douglas** The [Baby] Boomer zine. **Victoria Armstrong** I remember everyone getting cut about what got written about them that year.

Maya Templer I like to think that people will still be making zines in 10 years, but who knows? There might not be time, or maybe we'll all just be plugged into the machine. I really hope that I get to look back on this and think 'I was really wrong — the future is beautiful.'

Richard Davies I've tried to describe what we were doing with zines to my son, but he just didn't get it. 'What would you want to do that for? I just get out the computer and diddlee-da-da-da-eek, does it for ya!' I've tried to tell him: 'But we didn't have computers. It was a creative process and enjoyment and therapy and the Zen of it all and passing time . . .' He kind of heard it, but he does things his own way.

Panty Baggers PB3 Everybody I work with can't wait to get away from their computers at the end of the day. **PB1** Offline is a better way to share and make a connection. **PB3** But [sigh] my students, they love screens.

Dave White The good and bad of the internet; the sheer wealth of information makes it hard for anything to stand out, whereas if you make a zine and you give it to someone, they've got it. They can choose to read it or not, but . . . I mean, there's billions of posts on the internet, some of which I might be interested in, but I just can't be bothered. I seriously can't be bothered.

Pritika Lal I think that people really love books in the same way they love records, and so zines? People who want to make something physical are interested in slowing down to make a zine, a handmade book, do a drawing. That's wanting a different kind of creative experience. In the world in which people are overrun mentally by the sheer pace of things, slowing down to read a book, slowing down to make a book, I think there will always be people who want to do that, and that there will always be a new generation of people who have a deep passion and commitment to it. It's just that their set of references and their reasons will be different from what went before. There'll always be a place for paper-based storytelling.

Bruce Grenville Auckland Zinefest is great. It's great that they're actually happening. I was very impressed. Usually I go along and take a pile of mine and trade. That's how we used to do it back in the eighties: you send the person one of your zines and they send you one of theirs.

David Merritt My big hope is that at some point I'll be able to put out a succession of ebooks that get downloaded half a million times and make $100,000. These models are everyday now. There's a couple of New Zealand writers earning millions of dollars a year just down to ebook sales of bodice-ripping bullshit.

Kylie Buck The whole *fan*zine thing hasn't had a resurgence, right? I don't know the last time that I saw a zine that was based on someone's fandom, which used to be a huge part of the whole impetus. I'd love to see some more change, y'know? Like, I don't know, is anyone even making climate-change zines?

Maya Templer I'm surprised about that lack of eco zines, too, but I guess I'm a bit of a hypocrite. I don't make any eco zines myself.

Indira Neville After *Three Words* I got really quite full-up and quite yucky about comics. I went deep, deep into it and it was brutal, the great comic gender wars of 2016, I call it. I was really at the vanguard, and now that I'm not there I was hoping someone else would take it up.

Catalina Paz Nuñez Elevancini I think zines will become a bit genre-less. I'm picking up more and more zines that are a mishmash of writing and illustrations. They feel kind of overwhelming and they don't really have a story or anything, but they're nice to have. As the reader, you're trying to pull together a storyline, but they're just a collage of content overall, stapled together and printed at Warehouse Stationery or the library, and you're like 'Damn!' I think that's the new punk zine — not even considering if it makes conventional narrative sense.

Maya Templer I think contemporary zines are often quite subject-less, or they don't necessarily have a message. They might be 'cute drawings that I did today' or 'pictures of my cat'. People aren't making zines for the same reasons they used to. They're not making zines because they can't reach an audience through mainstream publishers. They're not making zines because they want to get an idea out and this is their only means of doing it. I think people are making zines because they wanna make a little book and sell it at the market. As to why that is, I'm not 100 per cent sure, because there's still lots of things to fight for.

Helen Yeung I would like to think that more collectives or more zine-makers of colour will come through. Auckland Zinefest has the ability to expand and continue doing what they're doing. But I also wonder will zines die out at some point and be replaced by something more digital? I'm not sure. I've definitely had my own struggles thinking that zines are no longer activist or political, and it makes me sad; but then I also appreciate a silly zine about frogs or a zine of recipes and stuff.

There's definitely a lack of conversation about 'Hey, zines used to be a bit more political and activist.' That's something I struggle with, too, but . . . you don't want to end up trying to play some gatekeeper role.

Mieke Montagne Just love it all, eh? I think zines are so important, for culture, and for people who want to figure shit out, and for getting to read someone else's thoughts. It's nice. I like it.

Maya Templer Panty Baggers. I love them so much. I'm so happy they came up for Ōtautahi Zinefest. I want to be like them in my fifties.

Marijke van Schaardenburg They're not just something silly you did on your photocopier. Okay, yes, they are, but they're also part of something bigger.

Tessa Stubbing How have zines changed? Heaps. I think this comes from technology. It's the technology available. Everyone's got a computer and [graphic-design platform] Canva. Everyone can make things look nice, right? But beauty is in the imperfection or the happy mistakes. You don't get a lot of that on the computer, you get that by hand.

Mieke Montagne Zines are sort of no one's but everyone's, right? So . . . what is the politics of that? What defines a zine? Who's to say what a zine is? There are no rules with zines, that's the one thing I know about zines.

Tim Danko The other day Heidi in my Friday group brought in a *frankie* magazine that featured Australian zinesters. I can bring shit in, but when that happens and they're finding that themselves, that's gold. It's showing that what they're doing is valued. Even if it's not them personally being represented they'll see that the medium and the format is being celebrated. Didn't it start with fanzines in the forties? I've got a guy who's tracing images from screens, like *General Hospital* and *Harry Potter*. I feel like this is going back to the roots of fanzines, taking something you really like and making it your own, pulling out certain bits. I feel like that is just a continuing thing, it's not specific to the zine format. People doing mods to games, fuck, that's a zine, man. That's the next level, for me.

Any accelerated niche personal interaction and using that matter and taking it away from a closed system and creating an open system with your own input. I mean, that will always be there, and the zine is a representation of that, but it's not the only representation. It's kind of the thing that keeps me hopeful and alive really. Seeing that, we all win. It's like hacking or pirating, you're not going to be able to stop it. There's too many of us, not enough of them.

Every time you create a closed system, someone's going to break it open. For me, part of the Mickeys [Mouse] is that, because Disney is such a fucking intensely closed aggressive system, to see people doing their own versions or degrading their own versions of it opens that up, and that's what comics and zines are for me, too.

215. Untitled, Eden J. Short, 190 × 142mm, 2015. Tāmaki Makaurau Auckland.
216. Untitled, Fynn Salm, White Room Publication, A6, 2023. Ōtautahi Christchurch.
217. *Wandering Wolves*, Prabha Mallya, A6, 2017. Ōtautahi Christchurch.
218. *Gross Girls*, Laura Gigi Allin, A7, date unknown. Tāmaki Makaurau Auckland.
219. *Deep Breaths*, Zoë Colling, A5, 2017. Tāmaki Makaurau Auckland.

215

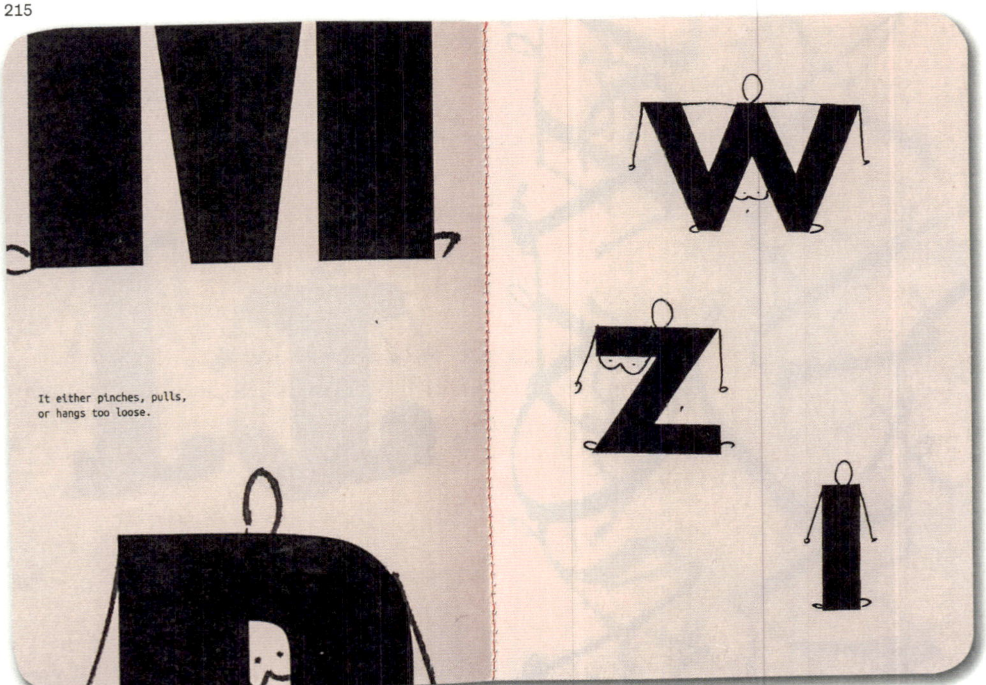

216

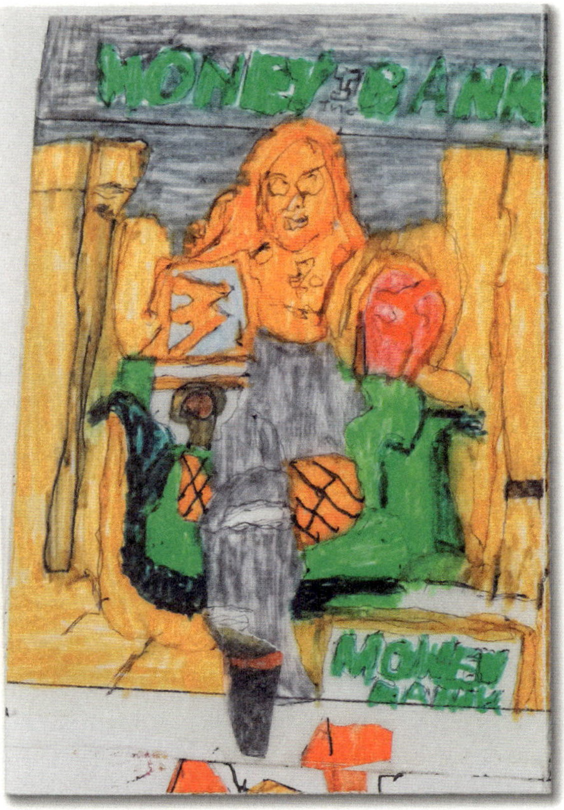

217

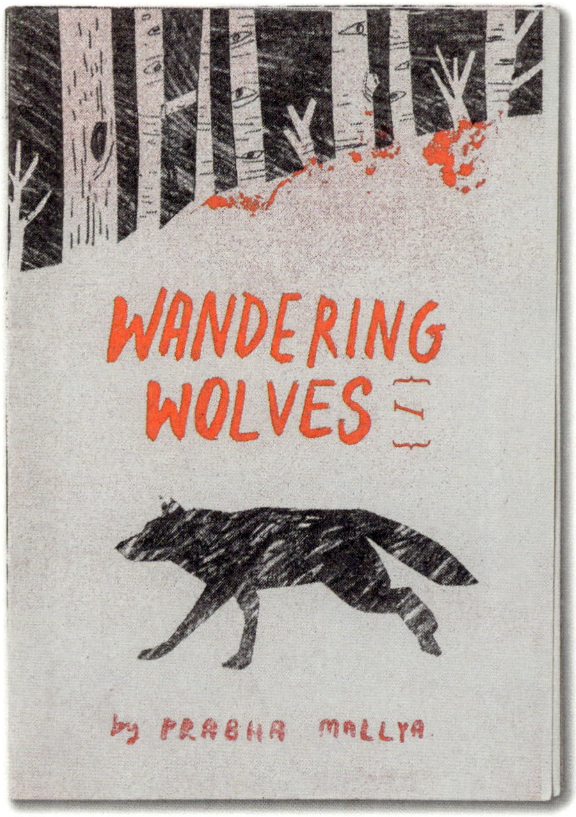

218

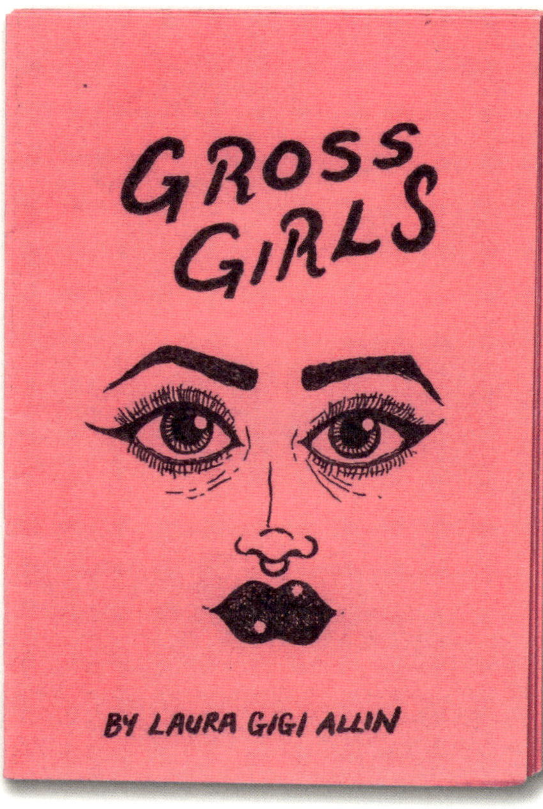

219

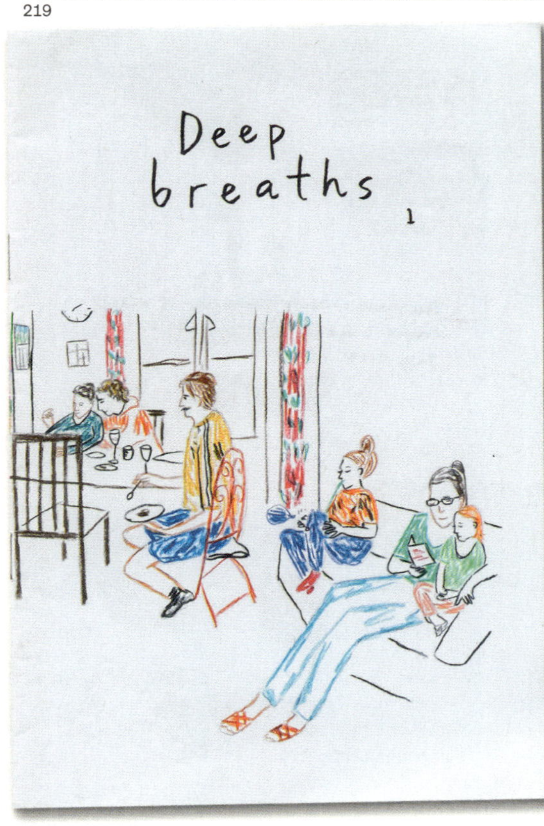

Notes

Intro

1 The Gestetner is named after its inventor, Hungarian-born David Gestetner, who manufactured from London throughout the twentieth century. The Gestetner operated in competition with Thomas Edison's mimeograph machine, although the competing companies would eventually strike a deal over territories. The machine functioned using a stencil made of waxy paper through which ink was squeezed. Ricoh of Japan brought the Gestetner Company in 1995, using the technology to develop the modern-day Risograph machine so popular with zinesters.

2 Originally a 1960s UK subculture associated with working-class pride and Jamaican ska, the skinheads of the 1980s were recruited by far-right groups (e.g. National Front, British Movement) to become violently anti-immigration and racist. These sentiments made even less sense in Aotearoa where whites were the recent immigrants, but that didn't stop the subculture from being imported.

3 Riot Grrrl is an underground feminist punk movement that started in Olympia, Washington, in 1991 before going global. It is often associated with third-wave feminism. Riot Grrrl was a reaction to the sexism of the male-dominated punk scene. The name is an inversion of the 'girl riot' credited to Bratmobile's Jen Smith.

The Eighties

1 Nambassa was a hippie music and alternative lifestyle festival that took place between 1976 and 1981 at various Waikato and Hauraki locations.

2 *Rip It Up* was a free monthly music magazine that reached a circulation of 30,000 copies by the mid-eighties. *Rip It Up* was initially printed tabloid-style, later taking on a magazine format. The magazine ceased publication in 2015.

3 The *New Musical Express* (*NME*) started life as a British entertainment magazine in 1952. The *NME* was produced tabloid-style. During the late 1970s and early 1980s the tabloid became closely associated with the music of punk and post-punk through the writing of Caroline Coon, Tony Parsons, Julie Burchill and others.

4 British music magazine *Melody Maker* launched in 1926, became something of a jazz magazine, then a rock magazine, and eventually followed the influence of *NME* to cover punk and post-punk. *Melody Maker* was also a tabloid-format weekly. In 2001 it merged with its old rival *NME*.

5 *Creem* magazine was started by Barry Kramer in Detroit, USA, in 1969. Some credit the magazine with coining the terms 'punk rock' and 'heavy metal'. In 1971, influential rock journalist Lester Bangs took over as editor, leaving *Creem* in 1976.

6 *Sounds* magazine was yet another weekly British music tabloid. It ran from 1970 to 1991. Through the writing of Garry Bushell, the magazine became more closely aligned with Oi! or skinhead music than the other weekly tabloids.

7 British music magazine *Record Mirror* ran from 1954 to 1991. *Record Mirror* had a greater focus on sales charts than some of its rivals. It was the first magazine to feature The Beatles, The Rolling Stones, The Who and The Kinks.

8 The Letraset company produced sheets of dry transfer lettering from 1961. These were in popular usage until desktop publishing took over in the mid- to late 1980s.

9 Hamish Kilgour (1957–2022) co-founded indie rock band The Clean with his brother David Kilgour in 1978. The Clean was one of the most influential bands on the Flying Nun record label and is associated with what came to be known as the 'Dunedin sound'.

10 Peter Jefferies (vocals) and Graeme Jefferies (guitar) formed Statford punk band Nocturnal Projections at the start of the 1980s with Brett Jones (bass) and Gordon Rutherford (drums). The brothers later formed This Kind of Punishment before Graeme launched The Cakekitchen and Peter went solo.

11 Heidelberg's GTO (Grosser Tiegel Offset) is a very popular and versatile offset printing machine for producing smaller-format labels, leaflets and posters.

12 'Photolitho' is an abbreviation of 'photolithography'. Not to be confused with the manufacture of semiconductors, the photolithographic printing process involves the production of an image surface treated to repel ink except where it is required for printing.

13 Albert Meltzer (1920–1996) was an English anarcho-communist, activist and writer.

The Nineties

1 Te Whanganui-a-Tara comics shop Visual Media Services (VMS) was started by Rod Mills and Leo Hupert in 1982. The shop later changed its name to Comics Compulsion, then Graphic. The shop has existed at eight different locations in and around Cuba Street and is still going to this day.

2 With woodcut printing, an image is drawn onto a planar wooden surface, and then the negative image is carved out to leave the positive image in relief (raised) for printing.

3 *A day mournful and overcast* was written by an anonymous member of the Iron Column, a Valencian anarchist militia fighting during the Spanish Civil War. It was written in response to the impending militarisation of the militias by the Republican government.

4 *The Heretic's Guide to the Bible* is an edition of the King James Bible, edited by Chaz Bufe and published in 1987, which focuses on the Bible's most hateful, misogynistic and sadistic passages.

5 Ant Sang is a celebrated comics artist from Aotearoa. Sang self-published his own titles *Filth* and *The Dharma Punks* in the 1990s and early 2000s, before picking up funded and/or commercial work, including character design for the animated TV show *bro'Town*.

6 Before deregulation and competition entered the telecommunications market, a toll was charged on any telephone calls made outside one's region.

7 Jello Biafra was the lead singer of seminal US punk band Dead Kennedys. Biafra is also a spoken-word artist and the director of Alternative Tentacles record label.

The Two-thousands

1 Five Eyes is a Western intelligence alliance between New Zealand, Australia, Canada, the United States and the United Kingdom. It was formed immediately after the Second World War at the beginning of the Cold War era, shifting its focus to the 'war on terror' after the 9/11 attacks on the World Trade Center in New York. In New Zealand, the Waihopai Station data-collection radome has become a countercultural emblem for Five Eyes spying.

2 Musician and performance artist Bek Coogan has performed in numerous bands, including Cortina, New Zealand, Full Fucking Moon and Fantasing. Her performance personae include a Nicola Willis take-off (largely prior to Willis becoming minister of finance in the 2023 National-led coalition government).

3 Aunt Daisy (Maud Ruby Basham, 1879–1963) was a New Zealand radio broadcaster and personality from 1930 to 1963. Very popular, she was known for her fast-flowing patter. She received an MBE in 1956.

4 A common school experience until the photocopier took over in the mid-eighties was receiving a Banda-machine printout from the teacher. The Banda machine — aka the ditto machine (USA) or the rolio machine (Australia) — was a spirit-duplicator; the ink was likely to be purple and mixed with methanol or ethanol. Students invariably took a big sniff of the paper (a scene portrayed in the movie *Fast Times at Ridgemont High*).

The Twenty-tens to -twenties

1 Sapeer Mayron, 'What I'm Reading: Pip Adam', *Sunday Star-Times*, 3 November 2024, www.waikatotimes.co.nz/culture/360471997/what-im-reading-pip-adam?mc_cid=2dc375e0ba

2 Sally Murphy, 'Christchurch city fringe suburbs see huge growth 10 years since earthquake', RNZ, 19 February 2021, www.rnz.co.nz/news/national/436735/christchurch-city-fringe-suburbs-see-huge-growth-10-years-since-earthquake

3 Bryndwr community is a revolving group of young people in Bryndwr, Ōtautahi Christchurch, from the early 2010s to the present day, with its members often connected through environmentalism and Christianity.

4 The Brooklyn Art Library sketchbook project was an uncurated archive of original artists' sketchbooks by artists from around the world. The project was started in 2006 by Steven Peterman and Shane Zucker. In February 2022, the moving trailer transporting the sketch-books to be exhibited in St Petersburg, Florida, caught fire. This saw 25,000 of the sketchbooks destroyed. The remainder have now been relocated to various museums and libraries across the United States and Canada.

5 Natcoll Design Technology changed its name to YOOBEE School of Design in 2012 after being purchased by Renaissance Corporation Ltd.

6 Creative Communities is a form of contestable government funding available from Creative NZ (Arts Council of New Zealand Toi Aotearoa). This tranche of Creative NZ funding is redistributed at a regional level through local government (city or regional councils).

7 Martin Emond was a celebrated comics artist from Aoteraoa. Unpaid independent creations for local *Pistake* comics was followed by paid work for international comics like *White Trash* and *Toxic!* The success took Emond to Los Angeles. Tragically, he took his own life in 2004. Many of his illustrations were also produced extensively as screenprints on clothing for the popular Aotearoa streetwear label Illicit, then franchised through California-based clothier Cinder Block.

8 *Coffee News* is a newsletter available free from cafés, and is part of an international franchise with approximately 1000 licensees (25 of whom are in Aotearoa). Licensees fill the newsletter with local advertising in exchange for the *Coffee News* brand, template and weekly content: 'unusual news stories, jokes, trivia, horoscopes, amazing facts, and more'.

Acknowledgements

Thanks to the many interviewees who were so generous with their time and memories, and who let me borrow the rarest of zines for photographing. Thanks to interviewee Andrew Schmidt, whose entry *Spit on Trend* for audioculture.com proved a great starting point for this project. Thanks to Toi Rauwhārangi College of Creative Arts at Massey University for research funding, and to technical staff Jane Wilcox and Harry Culy for supporting the photographic documentation of zines.

Thanks to my wife, Jakki Galloway, and my daughters, Sadie and Esther (former zinesters). Thanks to Sadie Galloway for transcribing the fifty 90-minute interviews and suffering her dad's same opinions and anecdotes over and over again. A big thank you to book designer and friend Greg Simpson, who may have regretted asking to design this book once I sent him folder after folder of zine images indexed in a way that made no sense at all (apologies).

Thanks to Nicola Legat and Massey University Press for backing the project and not getting too antsy as I failed those initial deadlines. And to MUP's Anna Jackson-Scott, Anna Bowbyes and editor Kate Stone.

Finally, thanks to zinesters everywhere for creating a small utopia amidst the cracks.

Index

Entries in **bold** refer to illustrations.

MASSEY UNIVERSITY PRESS

First published in 2026 by Massey University Press
Private Bag 102904, North Shore Mail Centre
Auckland 0745, New Zealand
www.masseypress.ac.nz

Design by Greg Simpson

A catalogue record for this book is available from the National Library of New Zealand

Printed and bound in China by Everbest Investment Ltd

ISBN: 978-1-991309-04-4

The assistance of Creative New Zealand is gratefully acknowledged by the publisher

creative nz
ARTS COUNCIL OF NEW ZEALAND TOI AOTEAROA